H.D. & Bryher

H.D. & Bryher

An Untold Love Story of Modernism

Susan McCabe

UNIVERSITY PRESS

OXFORD
UNIVERSITY PRESS

Oxford University Press is a department of the University of Oxford. It furthers
the University's objective of excellence in research, scholarship, and education
by publishing worldwide. Oxford is a registered trade mark of Oxford University
Press in the UK and certain other countries.

Published in the United States of America by Oxford University Press
198 Madison Avenue, New York, NY 10016, United States of America.

© Oxford University Press 2021

All rights reserved. No part of this publication may be reproduced, stored in
a retrieval system, or transmitted, in any form or by any means, without the
prior permission in writing of Oxford University Press, or as expressly permitted
by law, by license, or under terms agreed with the appropriate reproduction
rights organization. Inquiries concerning reproduction outside the scope of the
above should be sent to the Rights Department, Oxford University Press, at the
address above.

You must not circulate this work in any other form
and you must impose this same condition on any acquirer.

Library of Congress Cataloging-in-Publication Data
Names: McCabe, Susan, 1960– author.
Title: H.D. and Bryher : an untold love story of modernism / Susan McCabe.
Description: New York, NY : Oxford University Press, 2021. |
Includes bibliographical references and index.
Identifiers: LCCN 2021022647 | ISBN 9780190621223 (hardback) |
ISBN 9780190621247 (epub)
Subjects: LCSH: H. D. (Hilda Doolittle), 1886–1961. | Bryher, 1894–1983. |
H. D. (Hilda Doolittle), 1886–1961—Relations with women. |
Bryher, 1894–1983—Relations with women. | Poets, American—20th century—Biography. |
Novelists, English—20th century—Biography. | Lesbian authors—Biography. |
LCGFT: Biographies.
Classification: LCC PS3507.O726 Z776 2021 | DDC 811/.52 [B]—dc23
LC record available at https://lccn.loc.gov/2021022647

DOI: 10.1093/oso/9780190621223.001.0001

1 3 5 7 9 8 6 4 2

Printed by Sheridan Books, Inc., United States of America

For Kate

Contents

List of Figures — ix
Acknowledgments — xi
Abbreviations and a Note on the Archives — xiii
Dramatis Personae — xvii

THE VOYAGE OUT 1886–1915

1. The Meeting: "We Two" and Modernism — 3
2. H.D.'s Ancestors Circle — 16
3. Bryher's Family Closet — 29

LINE 1 *FLORIDE* 1909–1919

4. Sentimental Educations — 43
5. Love & Art: Being Phantoms Together — 56
6. Romance of Rescue & "the Jellyfish Experience" — 71

LINE 2 *BORODINO* 1920–1928

7. Parting of the Veil: Greece, 1920 … — 89
8. Questing America & Marianne Moore — 101
9. Inconvenient Marriages & Wanderlust — 114
10. Cinematics: We Three — 130

LINE 3 PSYCHOANALYSIS 1929–1939

11. Film Morphing into *Borderline* — 145
12. Enter Freud: Dreaming through the Houses — 160
13. Death Drive & "the Perfect-Bi" — 173
14. "Group Consciousness" & *Ion* — 184
15. Abdication, Aggression, Anschluss — 196

LINE 4 BLITZ 1939–1945

16. Twilight Zone & "the Combined UNK"	211
17. Walls Falling & the Drive Inward	223
18. Séance Nights	232
19. The Writing on the Wall	246

LINE 5 VIKING 1946–1961

20. Losing One's Mind to Find It	259
21. Tidying Up Modernism	270
22. Cold War Romances	281
23. Recovery & Illuminations (1953–)	296

Notes	313
Bibliography	363
Index	375

Figures

2.1	Helen Wolle Doolittle and her father, 188?	21
2.2	Gilbert, Harold, and Hilda Doolittle, c. 1890	22
2.3	Charles Leander Doolittle at his telescope, undated	24
3.1	Sir John Ellerman and Bryher, undated	30
3.2	Bryher and her father, c. 1897	34
3.3	Bryher in Paris for the World Exhibition, 1900	36
3.4	Bryher in Egypt, 1903.	37
3.5	Bryher and her mother on a ship, c. 1905	39
4.1	H.D.'s high school graduation photo, 1904	44
4.2	H.D. in 1909 or 1910	47
4.3	Bryher on a ship, with notebook, 1912	54
5.1	Scrapbook with clippings of D. H. Lawrence and Richard Aldington	64
5.2	Bryher and John Jr., undated	65
6.1	H. D. and Perdita, c. 1919	76
6.2	Scrapbook images of Bryher and H.D., 1919 or 1920?	81
6.3	H. D. at Mullion, Cornwall, c. 1919	84
6.4	Bryher seated on rocks, c. 1919	85
7.1	Passport photograph of Bryher, c. 1920	90
7.2	H.D., 1920(?)	95
8.1	Bryher in Cornwall, c. 1921	104
8.2	Marianne Moore, 1932?	105
8.3	Bryher, H.D., and Perdita, 1920	106
8.4	H.D. on wooded path, 1920	108
9.1	Helen Wolle and Perdita, 1921 or 1922	115
10.1	Kenneth Macpherson and Bryher, 1927	131
10.2	Scrapbook photomontage of H.D. and Bryher, undated	141
10.3	Photomontage of Bryher with Athena haircut, undated	141
11.1	Bryher, Kenneth MacPherson, and Robert Herring in Norway, 1929	146
11.2	*Borderline* still of Bryher, 1930	147
11.3	*Borderline* still of Paul Robeson, 1930	149

11.4	*Borderline* still of Paul and Eslanda Robeson, 1930	150
11.5	*Borderline* still of H.D., 1930	151
11.6	*Borderline* still of Eslanda Robeson, 1930	151
11.7	Program for *Borderline*, 1930	156
15.1	Photograph of Bryher by Gisele Freund, 1938	206
22.1	Swiss stamps, 1951	288
23.1	H.D., Norman H. Pearson, and Bryher, 1956	305
23.2	Sylvia Beach and Bryher with a photo of H.D., undated	311

Acknowledgments

There were many angels along the way.

Much gratitude goes to the Schaffner Family. Val Schaffner generously hosted me for lunch in 2009 for an interview in early days to discuss his grandmother and Bryher, and very recently, provided several family photos. I thank Timothy Schaffner for permission to quote from *Bryher's unpublished and published works, granted courtesy of the Schaffner family*. Further thanks goes to Declan Spring, agent of H.D.'s estate for *permission to quote from the published and unpublished works of H.D. granted by New Directions Publishing Corporation, and The Schaffner Family Foundation* to quote from *previously unpublished letters by Hilda Doolittle*: © (*Untold Love Story*, 2021). Permission to quote excerpts from *Notes on Thought & the Wise Sappho* © 1982 by the Estate of Hilda Doolittle. Reprinted with the permission of The Permissions Company, LLC on behalf of City Lights Books, citylight.com.

Richard Deveson's brother, James Alt, alerted me of Klara's letters to her sister, Alice Modern, who escaped Vienna with her husband to New York, with Bryher's aid before World War II began. I thank Richard for permission to quote from *My Dearest Family: An Austrian Refugee's Letters from London* © (Richard Deveson, 2017). I am more than grateful to Susan Stanford Friedman's *Analyzing Freud @* (Friedman, 2002), and for her permission to quote from private correspondence she provided: first, Perdita Schaffner who spoke of her "two mothers," and next, H.D.'s close friend, Silvia Dobson, along with interviews with Norman Holmes Pearson, the professor who befriended H.D. and Bryher.

I thank my editor, Norman Hirschy, for his incredible patience. I am grateful to the University of Southern California, Dornsife College, for its belief in this project: it awarded me an Advancing Humanities Fellowship, and other travel and research funds necessary for this decade long project. In the ancient days of 2009, I met Virginia Smyers, librarian at Harvard, who handed on an interview she had with Bryher.

Making annual trips to the mecca of modernist papers, the Beinecke Library at Yale University, holding the bulk of H.D. and Bryher's writing, receiving two fellowships, I thank Nancy Kuhl, Curator of Poetry in the Yale Collection of American Literature, for her warm assistance, and thanks as well to emeritus curator, Patricia Willis, whose wisdom radiated through early H.D. scholars. Gisèle Freund's photo of Bryher in 1938, used by permission from the *Institute of Contemporary Publishing Archives* in Paris. I thank Valentine Schaffner for providing family shots from the Schaffner album. The remaining shots are all Courtesy of the Beinecke Rare Book and Manuscript Room.

This book would not have been possible without the Modernist Studies Society and the H.D. Society, with support at various stages from Julie Vandivere, Cynthia Hogue,

Annette Debo, Jane Augustine, and Demetres P. Tryphonopoulos. Sawnie Morris published a much earlier version of Chapter 6 in *Taos Journal of Poetry* © (McCabe 2014). I owe special thanks to Marjorie Perloff, for her translation of letters from Dr. Theodore Brunner. Gratitude also goes to Linda Leavell, Langdon Hammer, and in the final stages, Judith Sensibar, key biographers who lit my way.

I thank the American Academy in Berlin, where I researched fascist Europe, reading Bryher's letters to Walter Benjamin at Akademie der Kunst, "Archiv 33." Pamela Rosenberg directed me to the music scholar, Ivan Nagel, the lover of H.D.'s last analyst, Erich Heydt. He knew both women. The Center for the Humanities at Stanford granted me the Marta Suttons Weeks fellowship in 2016. While there, Elaine Pagels delivered an influential lecture on Gnosticism. Writing this dual biography felt like déjà vu, with all its echoes with the present—the desire for tenderness and the desperate need for social justice. Gratitude as well goes to the poets, Brenda Hillman and Bob Hass, who invited me and my wife to Inverness to tune in to Code Pink. An inspiring friend, the poet 'Annah Sobelman, dead from breast cancer in July 2017, had buoyed *my* stamina when I hiked the Santa Clara mountains.

I owe much to friends, Brian Lizotte, Maja Liliqviust, Marianne Thormählen, and students, among others, Amaranth Borsuk, Brandon Som, Doug Manuel, Elise Martin, Marcie Vogel, Diana Arterian, Catherine Pond, Austen Leah Rosenfield, and Christopher Adamson. Steven Aaron Minas stepped in as miracle during my drafting of the manuscript draft in 2018. Catherine Theis, poet and H.D. scholar, has been an inspiring interlocuter. I thank Janalynn Bliss for her fortitude and kindness. I thank the Chair of English at USC, poet David St. John, for his generous faith. I thank Dolly at Patton's Pharmacy, and Ray-man at Votre Sante, born in Bethlehem, P.A.

I thank my sister, Marilyn McCabe Seeman, for her belief in me, and for finding *The Conquest of Illusion* at a used bookstore when we were teenagers; this esoteric work was written by a major figure in H.D.'s world, J.J. van der Leuww, another patient in the waiting room on her way to see Freud. My gratitude extends infinitely to my beloved wife, Kate M. Chandler, who endured reiterations of this tale, essentially its midwife.

Be bold, dear reader, as this curious story unfolds—in writing it, I entered and exited tunnels, feeling like H.D.'s grandmother, who always carried matches and a candle. May this story of an *untold love* under the surface allow other such stories to arise.

Deo Volente.

Abbreviations and a Note on the Archives

H.D

"Advent"	In *Tribute to Freud* (New York: New Directions, 1974)
"AN"	"Autobiographical Notes"
Angels	"Tribute to the Angels" in *Trilogy* with *Walls. Trilogy*. New York: New Directions, 1973.
BID	H.D, *Bid Me To Live*, Gainesville: University Press of Florida, 2011.
CP	H.D., *Collected Poems, 1912–1944*, edited by Louis Martz (New York: New Directions, 1982)
Compassionate	in H.D. *Magic Mirror, Compassionate Friendship, Thorn Ticket: A Tribute to Erich Heydt*. Edited by Nephie J. Christodoulides. Victoria: ELS Editions, 2012
"Euripides"	"Notes on Euripides, Pausanias, and Greek Lyric Poets" (1920), H.D. Papers, Beinecke Library, Yale University
Flowering	"Flowering of the Rod," in *Trilogy* with *Walls. Trilogy*. New York: New Directions, 1973.
Gift & "Notes to *Gift*."	*The Gift*. Edited by Jane Augustine. Gainesville: University Press of Florida, 1998.
"H.D."	"'H.D.,' by Delia Alton," *Iowa Review* 16:3 (1986): 180–221
Helen	*Helen in Egypt* (New York: New Directions, 1961)
Her	*HERmione* (New York: New Directions, 1981)
	Kora and Ka (New York: New Directions, 1996)
Majic	*Majic Ring*, edited by Demetres P. Tryphonopoulos (Gainesville: University Press of Florida, 2009)
Compassionate	in H.D. *Magic Mirror, Compassionate Friendship, Thorn Ticket: A Tribute to Erich Heydt*. Edited by Nephie J. Christodoulides. Victoria: ELS Editions, 2012
"Meleager"	In "Notes on Euripides, Pausanius and Greek Lyric Poets" (1920), H.D. Papers, Beinecke Library, Yale University
Notes	*Notes on Thought and Vision* (San Francisco: City Lights, 1982)
Paint It	*Paint It To*-Day, edited by Cassandra Laity (New York: New York University Press, 1992)
"Pausanius"	In "Notes on Euripides, Pausanius and Greek Lyric Poets" (1920), H.D. Papers, Beinecke Library, Yale University: University Press of Florida, 2009)
Sappho	"The Wise Sappho," collected with *Notes on Thought and Vision* (San Francisco: City lights, 1982)
Sword	*The Sword Went Out to Sea (Synthesis of a Dream)*. Edited by Cynthia Hogue and Julie Vandivere. Gainesville: University Press of Florida, 2007.

Thorn	in H.D. *Magic Mirror, Compassionate Friendship, Thorn Ticket: A Tribute to Erich Heydt*. Edited by Nephie J. Christodoulides. Victoria: ELS Editions, 2012
Tribute	*Tribute to Freud* (New York: New Directions, 1974)
Walls	*The Walls Do Not Fall* (Oxford: Oxford University Press, 1944)
Within	*Within the Walls*, edited by Annette Debo (Gainesville: University Press of Florida, 2014)

Bryher

Days	*The Days of Mars: A Memoir, 1940–1946* (New York: Harcourt Brace, 1971)
Development	*In Two Novels*, introduction by Joanne Winning (Madison: University of Wisconsin Press, 2000)
Fourteenth	*The Fourteenth of October* (New York: Pantheon, 1952)
HA	*The Heart to Artemis: A Writer's Memoirs* (New York: Harcourt Brace, 1962)
Two	*Two Selves*, in *Two Novels*

Collaborations

Cinema and Modernism	A selection from *Close Up*, edited by James Donald, Anne Friedberg, and Laura Marcus (Princeton, NJ: Princeton University Press, 1998)
CU	*Close Up*, a monthly literary magazine devoted to film published between 1927 and 1933, edited by Kenneth Macpherson with Bryher as assistant editor
L&L	*Life and Literature To-Day: An International Monthly of Living Literature*, a journal dedicated to literature and the arts that ran from 1935 to 1950, with Robert Herring as editor in chief

Additional Abbreviations and Abbreviations Used in References to Secondary Works

AF	Susan Stanford Friedman, *Analyzing Freud: Letters of H.D., Bryher and Their Circle* (New York: New Directions, 2002)
BGT	Robert McAlmon, *Being Geniuses Together, 1920–1930* (Baltimore, MD: Johns Hopkins University Press, 1968)
BHP	Donna Krolik Hollenberg, *Between History and Poetry: The Letters of H.D. and Norman Pearson Holmes* (Iowa City: University of Iowa Press, 1997)
Dearest Family	Klara Modern, *My Dearest Family: An Austrian Refugee's Letters from London to America, 1938–1945*, ed. Richard Deveson (privately printed, 2017)
"Friendship"	Carol Tinker, ed., "A Friendship Traced: H.D. Letters to Silvia Dobson," *Conjunctions*, no. 2 (Spring 1982): 112–157
"Mirror"	Silvia Dobson, "Mirror to a Star," unpublished autobiography, Dobson Papers, Beinecke Rare Book and Manuscript Library, Yale University

ML	Frances Gregg, *The Mystic Leeway*, ed. Oliver Marlow Wilkinson (Ottawa: Carleton University Press, 1995)
MMSL	Marianne Moore, *The Selected Letters of Marianne Moore*, ed. Bonnie Costello, Celeste Goodridge, and Cristanne Miller (New York: Penguin Books, 1997)
RAHDEY	Caroline Zilboorg, *Richard Aldington and H.D.: The Early Years in Letters* (Bloomington: Indiana University Press, 1992)
RAHDLY	Caroline Zilboorg, *Richard Aldington and H.D.: The Later Years in Letters* (Manchester: Manchester University Press, 1995)
Silverstein	Louis Silverstein's H.D. Chronology, Introduction and Parts 1–6 (1905–1986), http://www.imagists.org/hd/hdchron.html
SSF	Susan Stanford Friedman Correspondence
"UA"	Perdita Schaffner, "Unpublished Autobiography," Beinecke Rare Book and Manuscript Library, Yale University

Archives

Although this book draws from individual works by H.D., Bryher, and others, it significantly depends on archives. The Beinecke Library at Yale University houses most of the papers I rely upon: unpublished works, letters, photographs, and other material. All references to letters not indicated by a source are from the unpublished works at Beinecke. Other archives (e.g., Houghton at Harvard) are noted after citation.

Amy Lowell Papers	Amy Lowell Papers, Houghton Library, Harvard University
Bryher Papers	Bryher Papers, Beinecke Rare Book and Manuscript Library, Yale University
Dobson Papers	Silvia Dobson Papers, Beinecke Rare Book and Manuscript Library, Yale University
H.D. Papers	H.D. Papers, Beinecke Rare Book and Manuscript Library, Yale University
HDPBM	H.D. Papers, Bryn Mawr Library Special Collections, Bryn Mawr College
Jordan Papers	Jordan Papers, Beinecke Rare Book and Manuscript Library, Yale University
Moore Papers	Rosenbach Museum and Library, Philadelphia, Pennsylvania
Pearson Papers	Pearson Papers, Beinecke Rare Book and Manuscript Library, Yale University
Pound Papers	Pound Papers, Beinecke Rare Book and Manuscript Library, Yale University
RLM	Rosenbach Library and Museum, Philadelphia
WBA 33	Akademie der Künste, Berlin, Walter Benjamin, Archiv

Dramatis Personae
(in order of appearance)

Bryher (Annie Winifred Ellerman; aka "Dolly," "Fido," "Sir F," "Gareth," "Bay," "Small Dog," "Fitho," "Fiend," "exo"), 1894–1983

H.D. (Hilda Doolittle; aka "Dooley," "Astarte," "Horse," "Unicorn," "Cat," "Kat," "Dryad," "Hyacinth," "Lynnix," "Mog," "Helga Doorn," "Moggles," "Delia Alton," "eso"), 1886–1961

Sir John Ellerman (Bryher's father), 1862–1933

Lady Ellerman (Hannah Glover; Bryher's mother; "Lady E," "Goat"), 1867–1939

Charles Leander Doolittle (H.D.'s father), 1843–1919

Eugenia Doolittle (Helen Eugenia Wolle; H.D.'s mother; "Beaver"), 1853–1927

Elizabeth Weiss Seidel Wolle (H.D.'s maternal grandmother; "Mamalie"),1824–1906

Francis Wolle (H.D.'s maternal grandfather; "Papalie"), 1817–1893

Frances Josepha Gregg, 1884–1941

Ezra Pound, 1885–1972

Brigit Patmore ("Mimosa"), 1882–1965

May Sinclair, 1863–1946

Violet Hunt, 1862–1942

Richard Aldington (H.D.'s husband, father of stillborn; "Cuthbert," "R.A.," "Faun"), 1892–1962

Frances Perdita Macpherson Schaffner ("Pup," "Puss," "Lizard"), 1919–2001

Amy Lowell ("Armory"), 1874–1925

D. H. Lawrence, 1885–1930

Cecil Gray (biological father of Perdita; "Hare," "Vanio," "Cissie"), 1895–1951

Havelock Ellis ("Chiron," "Centaur"), 1859–1939

Marianne Moore ("Rat," "Dactyl"), 1887–1972

Mary Warner Moore (Marianne Moore's mother; "Mole"), 1862–1947

Peter Rodeck ("Piotor"), 1876–?

George Plank (illustrator), 1883–1965

Dorothy Richardson ("Rat"), 1873–1957

Robert McAlmon (Bryher's first husband of convenience; "Piggy"), 1896–1956

Norman Douglas ("Oncle"), 1868–1952

Blanch Lewin ("Mouse")

Kenneth Macpherson (Bryher's second husband of convenience; "Dog," "Dawg," "Rover," "Kex," "K," "Kay," "Big Dog"), 1902–1971

Paul Robeson, 1898–1976

Eslanda Robeson, 1895–1965 (anthropologist, civil rights activist)

Robert Herring ("Bud," "Buddy"), 1903–1975

Hanns Sachs ("Turtle"), 1881–1947

Elizabeth Bergner ("Die B"), 1900–1986

Dramatis Personae

Sigmund Freud ("Papa," "Professor," "Maestro"), 1856–1939

J. J. van der Leeuw ("Flying Dutchman"), 1893–1934

Alice Modern, 1908–1968

Klara Modern Deveson, 1913–1998

Walter Schmideberg ("Bear"), 1890–1953

Melitta Schmideberg ("Bearess"), 1904–1983

Silvia Dobson ("Sylvio," "Dragon"), 1909–1993

Mary Chadwick (British psychoanalyst, "Chaddie"), ?–1943

Dorothy Cole Henderson ?–1961

Gerald Henderson (St. Paul's Cathedral's librarian)

Norman Holmes Pearson ("Chevalier," "Puritan"), 1909–1975

Walter Benjamin 1892–1940

Elizabeth Bowen 1899–1973

Osbert Sitwell, 1892–1969

Edith Sitwell 1887–1964

Hermann Hesse ("Maestro"), 1877–1962

Elizabeth Siddal ("Sid," "Lizzy"), 1829–1862

Elizabeth Ashby ("Herrison")

Erich Heydt ("Chevalier"), 1920–1977

Ivan Nagel (theater and music critic), 1934–2012.

THE VOYAGE OUT 1886–1915

1
The Meeting

"We Two" and Modernism

> We two remain: / yet by what miracle
> —H.D., *Heliodora and Other Poems* (1924)

Cryptic enough to be a man's initials, H.D., born Hilda Doolittle (1886–1961) in Bethlehem, Pennsylvania, while Bryher, born Winifred Ellerman (1894–1983), in London, felt like a young man, enduring a yet unnamed condition. Their "union" disappears from most appraisals. They hid in plain sight. The illegitimate daughter of Sir John Ellerman when he died in 1933,[1] Bryher's greatest pleasure during adolescence was venturing to Cornwall with her school chum, Doris Banfield, to satisfy her invisible inner "boy." Spurning her father's surname, she took the moniker Bryher after the wildest island in the Scilly archipelago. At twenty-three, she learned she could not come out as a man and take the reins of her beloved father's empire, nor could she come out as a debutante or be forced into "womanhood," its customs and binding limits.

With Doris hosting Bryher in Zennor, she arranged to meet the poet H.D., then staying at Bosigran Castle at St. Ives, only five miles away. H.D.'s *Sea Garden*, published in 1916, transported Bryher, who memorized its stark, broken lines. Struggling to make literary ties, Bryher succeeded in befriending the lesbian poet Amy Lowell, her first transatlantic pen pal. Lowell also corresponded regularly with H.D. and her husband Richard Aldington. Receiving Bryher's recent pamphlet *An Appreciation of Amy Lowell* as a calling card, H.D. invited her to "chat over tea," directing her to "a square house standing by itself just below the ruins (with two tall red chimneys) that stand close to the road."[2]

Bryher wound her long brown plaits up into two chignons. Her heart racing, she pulled on a flared skirt under a middy blouse hanging from her shoulder to below the waist, tied with a loose belt, a style adapted by Coco Chanel from the kit of French seamen. If she could not be a sailor, at least she could dress like one. As she set off for H.D.'s cottage, a storm approached.

Cornwall, at its widest, forty-five miles, narrowed to five miles at Land's End. It hypnotized Bryher with its rugged trails, an intoxicating braid of smells: heather, chamomile, gorse, comfrey, repeating H.D.'s lines, guided by their instruction "to find a new beauty / in some terrible / wind-tortured place," escape from "dead grass,"³ savoring the "stunted" sea rose, with "marred" and "meager petals,"⁴ feeling personally addressed by "The Shrine": "Are your rocks shelter for ships?"⁵ When the breeze turned to strong gusts, Bryher regretted not donning doublet and hose like the Elizabethan "girl-pages" she was then writing about.

H.D. paced in her cottage on a promontory about two hundred feet above the sea. Torn whether to write to her husband in the trenches, the difficulties she faced felt overwhelming. During a leave, he started an affair with another woman. The composer Cecil Gray asked H.D. to his cottage in 1918, and she too had an affair. It was the modern way. Their succinct intimacy left her with child. H.D.'s pregnancy aggravated flashbacks to the traumatic stillbirth of her baby conceived with Aldington, coinciding with the sinking of the *Lusitania*, a Cunard liner, on May 7, 1915, by a German U-boat. Paired with the loss of 1,198 lives and the consequent entry of America into World War I, their lost baby doubled with global loss. H.D.'s brother, Gilbert, her elder by two years, was fighting in France, the rest of her family in America, her intimates missing in action, among them, her former fiancé, Ezra Pound, and her first real love, with whom she shared clairvoyant adventures, Frances Josepha Gregg, now married. Self-identified "witches," H.D. knew their love was considered "unnatural," and both "she and Josepha should be cast out of the mass of the living ... as useless as natural wastage, excrementitious."⁶

H.D. asked the gods to have mercy upon her in birthing this second baby. She tucked her terror away under a blanket of absurdity—she would write Aldington. He might be amused at an island coming to tea. Bryher easily found the solitary stone shelter, spying a shadow bent over pages, and then memorialized "[a] tall figure opened the door. Young. A spear flower if a spear could bloom." Then she heard "[a] voice all wind and gull notes" saying, "'I was waiting for you to come.'"⁷ Towering over Bryher, only five foot two, H.D., this "spear flower," at six foot, with angular determination and magnetic eyes, at home in this landscape, bordering the wild Celtic sea. If H.D.'s poems awed Bryher, meeting her thrilled like an illumination.

Scattered sunlight passing through storm clouds presented an opening. Bryher's glazed eyes took in the half-furnished rooms, a shelf with a painted Osiris, an egg-shaped mummy owl, and a bronze Isis at the end. With the pouring of tea, Bryher numbered her enthusiasms for Egyptology, Shakespeare, and Ruskin. H.D. spoke of translating, falling in love with Euripides' *Ion*. Self-startled, Bryher spoke of escaping clinging fog to America to meet writers. H.D. noted her guest's slight slouch, energetic timidity, a characteristic clenching of fists, and wide stare. "Are you the island, or the person?" H.D. might have teased. Bryher tried explaining her self-renaming at fifteen in favor of an island, with its delicate flowers, like the dwarf pansy, found nowhere else in England. Producing a map to locate "Bryher," H.D. took the visitor's small hand to put a finger to *place* her, as if intuiting Bryher's sense of predominantly "'geographical emotions.'"⁸

Bryher resisted "Ellerman" as her passport into the world. Her mother, she explained, expected her to behave as "Dolly," her childhood nickname. Why was her brother allowed to be *the* boy, she fumed, despising the ambience of the "straitlaced ... footmen on the stairs, stately expeditions in a Rolls Royce; hats and white gloves."[9] Sensing H.D.'s approval, Bryher spoke of her childhood fantasy of stowing away as a cabin boy.[10] With her dizzying ability to absorb and respond, an ability that could overwhelm her, H.D. took in Bryher, who, on this first encounter, nearly asked the poet to rescue her, claiming herself prisoner at 1 South Audley, the family's Mayfair mansion. That summer, Bryher and Doris slept on a roof open to the stars. For herself, H.D. enjoyed the secrecy and freedom of her two initials, manifested when Ezra Pound crowned her an *imagiste* six years earlier in the British Museum's tearoom.

Stepping outside, they spotted a blue swallow. Bryher wooed H.D. through her own poems, reciting bits from memory. Bryher's awkward boyishness and stated longing to wear men's clothes intrigued and frightened. Armed with promises to reconnect, H.D. assigned Bryher the task of translating the names of Greek flowers. The meeting produced an electric charge, a set of recognitions. H.D. saw the possibility—they might be "crystallized out, orient pearls," wondering how this compact tense person, little more than one hundred pounds, might alter her confused straits.[11] Erotically drawn to both sexes, H.D. relished reading Swinburne with Frances Gregg in the days before Aldington. Akin to Frances, Bryher more thoroughly rejected gender conformity—and H.D. was fascinated.

Before combining their fates, each had to remedy their situations: Bryher, walled up by her family, and H.D., confronting her shell-shocked husband and the tangible fact of impending motherhood. Thirty-one years later, H.D. wrote Bryher, "Remember that it all began with the bluuue swalllllow and in Bosigran."[12] Over the next forty-two odd years, the couple annually celebrated their meeting—July 17, 1918.

* * *

A love story of modernism began with the anguish of the so-called Great War (1914–1918). H.D. nearly died in childbirth. With desecrated lands and obliterated lives, what was true before now rang false. At the same time, the zeitgeist opened for those sexually unsure, offering provisional hope. After meeting Bryher, H.D. rearranged pieces of a Latin tag throughout *Paint It Today*: "Let those love now, who have never loved before / let those who always loved, now love the more."[13] As moderns, H.D. and Bryher desired more than aesthetic innovation—but also to tap into newly embodied identities, awaiting expression. Forerunners, they helped transform invisible, even persecuted lives into more livable ones. Contemporary global right-wing homo- and transphobia have risen, thwarting queer lives. This untold story reclaims the pair as unseen activists.[14]

They lived as lovers during a period that condemned and punished sexual outsiders. Oscar Wilde, born before our pair, set minds trembling over deviance. Heather Love describes "the pervasiveness of non-normative desires in the making of the modern" and "queer" more "permissive" than gay or lesbian. Quite literally in this case, Bryher's meeting H.D., "*[q]ueer*" itself is "the uninvited guest, unexpected but not totally unwelcome, that shows up without visible relations or ties."[15] Bryher's extrasensory intelligence, her liminal gender status, and awakening to a world that "den[ied] sex and work for women," leaving unsatisfying "innumerable tiny sublimations."[16] This dissatisfaction compelled H.D., while Bryher saw in H.D.'s flint-like determination and porous sensitivity a path toward freedom.

Bicenturians, they straddled several epochs, the Victorian and the Edwardian, their adult lives spanning the modern through the inception of the postmodern. As Victorians, they were laced up, restricted in the Edwardian era, and then the modern woman stepped forth, but not without limits. Homophobia, peaking during 1930s Fascism, the Cold War of the 1950s obscured same-sex ties. Without a frame to hold them, the couple's atypical identities led them to forgo full "welcome." Then in the atomic age, rampant suspicion muted free expression, though words akin to *let them love now* slowly re-emerged with the likes of John Lennon.[17] Bryher collected sex-change articles, one in 1936 of the athlete, the Czech Zdeněk Koubokva (1913–1986), who as a woman in the 1934 Women's World Games won two jumping championships; Koubokva underwent surgery for gender reassignment, only to leave sports altogether.[18] Sex-change surgery in the thirties was dangerous, with unknown outcomes. Prescient with today's framing of "genderqueer," which the Oxford Dictionary denotes as "a person who does not subscribe to conventional gender distinctions but identifies with neither, both, or a combination of male and female genders," Bryher gathered homosexual men as part of the couple's circle, supporting her enactment of a masculinity without labels. Both sought a nonbinary view of their bodies, history, and the cosmos, and in fact, "genderqueer" accurately applies to H.D., who identified as male and female and had male and female lovers.

In our period, even with updated vocabulary, "to understand and accept that they were neither a man nor a woman, that they were nonbinary, gender fluid, gender expansive" is challenging. H.D. would probably be happily startled that nonbinary gender, one of her critical discoveries about herself, is finally being fleshed out; Bryher might grumble over the time taken to find more liberating nomenclature. The pronoun "they" denotes the intermediate state they navigated. Nonbinary types "yearn not to go from one category to the other but to escape altogether."[19]

Connected on an almost neuronal level, the pair's new postwar freedoms did not mean they could flaunt their intimacies. Both were frightened of the social stigma still attached to any queer identity. They developed a nautilus perspective of history that "repeats itself or life advances in a spiral."[20] Their time had not quite come. They lived a half-century before Stonewall, before Gay Pride parades, and before two women could legally marry; "their devotion to each other was a revolutionary act," their union without legal footing.[21] And now, a full century later, with gay marriage and trans and nonbinary identities emerging, the spiral reveals new repressions, new liberties. Nonbinary types continue to experience gargantuan doses of shame, and when they view their bodies, some still find the mirror foggy.

* * *

In 1972, writing Norman Holmes Pearson at Yale, Susan Stanford Friedman feared "[H.D.] will undeservedly slip into the oblivion of imagist magazines."[22] Although Pearson ensured transmission, compiling their papers on his "H.D.-Bryher redoubtable shelf,"[23] he feared the neglect of H.D.'s post-Imagist work, pursued after meeting Bryher, stemmed from a "general dislike of anything bordering on hermetic."[24] By "hermetic," he meant the unpublished works, the pair's "wisdom search," and H.D.'s bisexual quest with Bryher as co-visionary. The couple embodied the basic gnostic tenet of "yearning for experiential knowledge" of unseen truths.[25]

By 1977, Friedman's early digging and groundbreaking article, "Who Buried H.D.?" catapulted H.D. out of her crypt and into the literary canon. Louis Martz's hefty 1986 *Collected Poems* (1912–1944), her World War II *Trilogy*, *Tribute to Freud*, and *Helen in Egypt*, each republished by New Directions, constitutes a substantial opus itself, though much remains unappreciated. "H.D. studies" now abound. The International H.D. Society boasts The H.D. Biography Wiki, tracing her life and works.[26] The release of H.D.'s previously unpublished manuscripts, the republishing of several of Bryher's lost works, along with the availability of their collaborative film, *Borderline*, now on a film disc of its star, Paul Robeson, all herald documentation of the pair's shared lives and works.[27]

H.D.'s life story was more enmeshed with Bryher's than the only extant viable biography, Barbara Guest's *Herself Defined* (1984), lets on.[28] Freidman wrote H.D.'s daughter that she believed "Barbara's biography" was "really the story of two women, almost entitled We Two."[29] Yet while Guest reinforced H.D.'s reputation as a feminist poet, she simplified Bryher as "a permanent child," split between "the good fairy's gift of common sense" and "the bad fairy."[30] H.D. and Bryher's love story could not yet be told. The current gratifying resurgence of H.D. in modernist studies with Bryher's near absence in narratives of H.D. invite the need to study *the pair together*. Never attempted before, guided by over a decade-long hunch, substantiated by their archives, a picture emerges of an unusually creative couple.

This dual biography answers Friedman's initiating question by recognizing Bryher's "resurrections" of H.D. as well as H.D.'s bids for Bryher to expand her own gifts. Each can be read alone, but without exposing their entangled lives, their stories remain incomplete. From 1918 forward, they were the central figures in each other's lives. "A word opens a door," H.D. repeated, as they sought language both to hide and to express their love.[31] Their lives, precursor-like, braved the elements. Both recognized that they could not exist "alone," as their male counterparts had and did, and who, when married, usually segregated their wives from their art. They pursued an uncharted voyage to seal their togetherness. Thriving on not being *pegged*, they formed an odd couple: one already married and pregnant, the other, a virgin. Born eight years and eight days apart, H.D. had a compatibility chart cast with Bryher, also a Virgo, verifying deep kinship, not a small matter to H.D., who regarded astrology as a respectable science, dating from Ptolemy.[32]

Almost Bryher's entire adolescence was trance practice, directing her gaze beyond the improbability of her material existence, suiting H.D., who wrestled with the invisible. Both suffered war neurosis, the result of surviving two global conflagrations, and their frustration with pathologizing nomenclature to describe themselves individually, let alone as a couple. Like H.D., Bryher, no stranger to preternatural experiences, thought the Elizabethan period more tangible and "saw" and heard bodies dropping contemporary dress and speech during World War I. Cultivating visions to express their queerness as well as the reverse, both thinned divisions between temporal and eternal, visible and invisible, and, by extension, masculine and feminine, black and white. The "combining of two worlds" made "another world," H.D. thought, finding unseen geologic signs of how they might fit into a war-damaged world.[33] When they set sail for the Scillies in 1919 and Greece in 1920, there were still undetonated explosives under the sea's surface, yet submerged mythical islands, sunk matriarchies, unseen spaces beckoned—experiences they could have only with each other.

In the literary world, the exceptional male poet could establish visionary lineage through Dante to Blake to Yeats, while *two women together* had little precedent besides Sappho and her girls. In spite of their joint quest, H.D. studies has focused on the poet's so-called male initiators. Rachel Blau DuPlessis traced the poet's chronic attachment to overpowering men as "erotic thralldom."[34] Bryher's support enabled H.D. to grapple with these flawed "heroes," who temporarily derailed her—such as H.D. refuting Pound's freeze-framing her as an Imagist. "I have the flowers of myself, and my thoughts, no god / can take that," articulates a Eurydice who outwits Orpheus.[35] Michael Schmidt asserts in *Lives of the Poets* that Freud "helped [H.D.] make connections" that stood "apart from the anchored and anchoring love between herself and Bryher"; though uniquely recognizing their love's "anchoring," he overlooks H.D.'s challenging Freud: "The Professor was not always right."[36] The list of taunting men include Lord Dowding, who during World War II acted the heroic air marshal; learning he believed in psychic matters, H.D. tried sharing "their" findings, but he refused welcome to his séance circle. H.D. weathered rejections by toppling expectations, bolstered through intellectual, sensory, sensual exchange with Bryher through what amounted to telepathic connection, refined over years. Bryher brought H.D. into 1920s Paris "circles," the new worlds of cinema and psychoanalysis, and in the 1930s her refugee work paralleled H.D.'s search, as she put it, "to feed the light."[37]

Unlike her chief poetic peers, Eliot, Pound, and Yeats, H.D. took on authorial anonymity, for good reason. Interviewed by Friedman in 1979, the Beat poet Robert Duncan believed London literary circles rejected H.D. after she went to Greece with Bryher.[38] H.D.'s writing, after *Sea Garden*, was occluded. Seizing H.D.'s own oft-used metaphor of a "cocoon" hatching into a butterfly, Lawrence Rainey writes in *Institutions of Modernism* that "[h]er world was a cocoon, and she neither needed nor pursued the give-and-take of exchange with others."[39] Unmoved by the creative aspect of a larval process or H.D.'s persistent *exchange with* Bryher and their circle of friends, he dismisses her as "one whose writings circulated, like bonbons at a dinner party, among a cénacle of friends and hangers-on in wealthy bohemia."[40] The fiercely interior workhorse H.D. would have guffawed at such an estimation.

Neither yet fully recognizable, a second uprising in H.D. studies shows a critical community ready to "catch up" with the couple. H.D.'s initials approximated her desire, with Bryher's, "to wear the cloak of invisibility." The initials marched until they didn't, and then after a hiatus from poetry, H.D. re-embodied them in her translation of *Ion* (1936). Quoting from her own quintessential Imagist poem of 1912, "Oread," H.D. quipped that "you can keep writing 'whirl up pine trees, whirl up tulips' but you can't go on."[41] Hatching from cocoons, key to her creative process, her last long poem, *Hermetic Definition*, pulled no punches: "I am delirious now and mean to be, / the whole earth shudders with my ecstasy."[42] With a kindred sense, Hugh Kenner calls Eliot the ultimate "invisible poet," quoting Moore, who dubbed him "master of the anonymous," "never sure whether his gift was not on the point of exhaustion."[43] This would have reassured H.D., who followed "the lure of the invisible."[44] Likewise, Bryher inhabited necessary invisibility, fantasizing herself as "among anonymous craftsmen who spent a lifetime" devoted to a patch on some cathedral wall.[45] Both turned to autobiographic prose to *discover who they were through writing*, and both felt split, finding consolation in their mediumistic practice. Voices spoke through them. H.D. persisted in a neoplatonic understanding "every concrete object // has abstract value, is timeless / in the dream parallel."[46] Sheltering and transmitting their experiences, they embraced what T. E. Hulme cast as "spilt religion,"[47] impelled by unseen vibrations, to abide in two planes.

* * *

At a time when this step was unthinkable, the unconventional pair coparented H.D.'s daughter, Perdita (1919–2001). Nine months after meeting H.D., Bryher committed to raising her as *their* child. Perdita celebrated her two mothers, writing Friedman of their "legend": "A great admirer of her work appeared on the scene and took over. Winifred Ellerman, daughter of Sir John Ellerman—she writes under the name of Bryher. She adopted us both; still alive, she is my 'other mother.'"[48]

"They were always together, those two; the one tall and dreamy, the other short and purposeful, austere with close-cropped hair and tailored suits," Perdita elaborated, confirming H.D.'s "closest, most lasting relationship was undoubtedly Bryher," entirely implicated in H.D.'s work and peace of heart and mind.[49] One now needs ask, "Who buried H.D. & Bryher?"

Writing from Vienna, H.D. capsulized Bryher as representing "food, help, support, mother, though of course, it mixes over into father too. It is really reversible."[50] This reversibility allowed them to live on and off with each other, to travel in Greece, America, Egypt, Italy, France, Austria; when apart, they kept in almost constant epistolary contact: volumes of letters exist between them about daily life, creative projects, mutual friends, and reiterated assertions of love, and sometimes aggravation. Replete with nicknames for themselves and their circle, they created an alternate universe, where H.D.'s mother was "Beaver," Bryher's "Lady Goat" after her astrological sign; Bryher was "Fido," H.D. "Cat," and Perdita, "Pup." H.D. addressed Bryher as "him" whenever possible. They constructed a private language where "Fish" denoted the psychical, "ps-a" psychoanalysis, and "Unk," the unconscious. Innovating with cerebral eroticism, H.D. referred to a "combined Unk," and asked "your Unk or mine?" More evocative, after a phone call with Bryher, she felt her "unk licked."[51]

Nurturing an extended family of exiles, psychoanalysts, pensioners, writers, and troubled souls, Bryher provided for, among others, Marianne Moore, Dorothy Richardson, Edith Sitwell, Adrienne Monnier, and Sylvia Beach. Bryher surrounded herself with templates for a desired bodily identity, queer men whom she called "boyfriends," key among them Kenneth Macpherson, Robert Herring, Osbert Sitwell, and the analyst Walter Schmideberg, nicknamed "Bear."

Before World War II, guided by an ideal they might together save the world from ruin, both made epic attempts. Bryher faced the diaspora head on, taking great pains to aid European refugees. Obtaining passports and visas, settling exiled psychoanalysts in London, where in a circular "give-and-take" she subsidized analysis for many friends. Moore diagnosed Bryher as suffering from "suicidal generosity";[52] Bryher's own "feeding the light" paralleled H.D.'s poetics in a manner akin to Marcel Mauss's exploration of the gift in archaic cultures, binding receiver to giver, and in this case, widening their duo to a circle of essentially strangers, spreading bounty.[53] Luckily, some refugees Bryher helped kept in contact. Among them were the Austrian Jew Alice Modern, a tutor for Perdita, and her sister Klara, who stayed in London during the Blitz. In July 2017, during a phone conversation, James Alt, Harvard professor emeritus and son of Alice Modern and Franz Alt, simply said, "Bryher saved my family's life." His parents emigrated to New York in 1938 and could not have escaped without Bryher's aid of $5,000.

Inspired by Einstein, H.D. intuited that wisdom lay within the new physics, which was progressing rapidly during the poet's formative years.[54] When World War II broke out, she sensed a new formula was in process and that "only Einstein could make the proper numerical diagram for this 'dimensional state.'"[55] Moreover, H.D. believed that "lost" voices often arose in "aftertimes," that her work might well be for another generation, more like ours, with more nuanced vocabulary for gender struggles. Against the current backdrop of proliferating gender designations, it behooves us *to understand the distress and erasure facing those living before any words, much less legal sanction, for visible expression existed*. When H.D. and Bryher feared walking arm in arm, names had bubbled up in their youth that *almost* fit: "invert," "mannish lesbian," "Uranian," "the third sex." H.D.'s "We Two" courts the present: they were both a him and a her and a "we" and a "they," with a lived sense of nonbinary gender as well as of multiple dimensions, past lives, parallel universes.

This study forgoes ultra-close readings of their texts. Instead, it links their writing to the duo's gender insecurities, tying visionary experience to its messy genesis in real life: thwarted desires, inconvenient marriages, divorces, abortion, breakdowns, and wars. As a countervailing force, H.D. imagined hermetic "boxes" of wisdom "hidden, buried under the rubble of prescribed thinking, of inevitable social pruning and taming of emotion and imagination," but noted that "you just stumble" on treasures.⁵⁶ Together, they germinated and safeguarded acute visceral experiences through writing, meditation upon a "great wide stillness."⁵⁷ Yet far from living in an airtight cocoon, they met multiple obstacles during modernity's intrusive brutality, united by their sense of persecution, real and imagined, and their faith in overcoming it. Their joined quest for a time and space *safe* for their love and ideals tallied with H.D.'s prescription "There are no great artists without great lovers."⁵⁸ "Bryher was my special heritage as I had been hers," H.D. described their ancestral relationship.⁵⁹

* * *

Not a conventional love story, Bryher dynamized H.D.'s already intuited sense of herself as "psychic," here broadly indicating an ability to communicate or to sense the thoughts or feelings of another with or without words as well as an ability to intuit events. In 1918–1919, after H.D.'s rough brushes with male modernists, she began a search for the divine maternal, to reveal with Bryher that patriarchal rationalism, dominant in their immediate cultural backdrop, needed powerful revisions to avert wars and destructive upheavals. H.D. urgently directed, "Try to understand the gods for really they are to be understood; love, love, love beauty and mysterious things."⁶⁰ Was H.D. instructing Bryher, or echoing her? With Bryher, "she saw what [H.D.] did not see," keeping them both in dialogue with the hidden.⁶¹ In H.D.'s view, "Ghosts to speak must have sacrifice."⁶²

Freud intuited H.D. wanted to create a "new religion," which required thinking about time in a nonlinear fashion, while he cast Bryher as a "northern explorer," a travel mania compelling her to locate and relocate. H.D. gave her entire being to the ineffable; Bryher acted as "shield," providing sanctuary for "visions" or trances, but also *seeing*.⁶³ In 1943, H.D. metaphorically retraced their steps to Greece in 1920, reflecting that taking "off a mere 20 years and you get a revenant, a girl who has found God."⁶⁴ After World War II, H.D. suffered a severe breakdown, and Bryher stimulated H.D. to fabricate out of "madness" new poetry and prose, while she launched her own novels.

H.D. very specifically called Bryher an "alter ego," someone so closely resembling her she could be a secondary self. Bryher assisted in "concentrations," while H.D. liberated Bryher from what felt like madness—a paralysis induced by alienation from her birth gender. In short, both suffered from the sense they could easily be erased. With stark disharmony between her body and her psyche, Bryher suffered a near-crippling bodily dysphoria, with Victorian garb a "nightmare."⁶⁵ During World War I, she kept rat poison on hand if suicide became necessary. Similar to the experience of a contemporary trans person, Bryher's inner boy felt hallucinated. Transsexuality is still pathologized, cast "as a mental disturbance" of "a person fantasiz[ing] herself to have the genitals of the sex to which she does not belong," "understood to signal a break from reality," "characterized as a psychosis rather than a neurosis."⁶⁶ Not psychotic but rather an exceptional modernist companion, Bryher's bond with H.D. suitably pivoted upon the ability to "envision" an unprecedented identity, navigate the mist, retracing frayed history.

Both suffered high degrees of shame and self-doubt.[67] Both might be called pathological, but for what they faced, they managed exceptionally. Feeling she "never, never met so tragic a personality,"[68] seven months into their relationship, H.D. urged Bryher to visit Dr. Havelock Ellis, who confirmed Bryher was "a girl only by accident."[69] Still Bryher remained illegible as one who "fought for a place in life, in a social scheme" that didn't yet exist, causing dissociations, selective mutism, and suicidal ideation.

Neither woman was able to conform, and that looked and often felt like pathology. With this in mind, H.D. herself advocated expanding the border between "hysteria" and psychosis. Suffering "slight" or "minor" breakdowns at various turnstiles, H.D. regularly described herself as "shot to bits," "in pieces," "shattered"—applied when inner demands met repressive outer constraints, leading to depressions, often premonitory of creative exhilaration. "Traumatophiles" like Baudelaire, who, at least in Walter Benjamin's estimation, made it his "business to parry the shocks, no matter what their source, with his spiritual and physical self."[70] This couple's very embodiment shocked others. Like Bryher's, H.D.'s body did not conform to stereotypes: taller than most men, her ungainly height and elongated torso made her self-conscious. Similar to widening the distance between the neurotic and the psychotic, H.D. parried with two genders as "an unexplored waste-land, a no-man's land *between them*."[71] As her posthumously published *Pilate's Wife* put it, "woman is not enough" and "man is not sufficient."[72] She "tried to be a man or woman but [she had] to be both."[73] Bryher was trained as a fencer in childhood and learned to cut her way through inertia to embody a highly active persona.

* * *

The modernity of their love stemmed from their queer longings and their high ideals, but also from their spiritual inquiries. The occult, from the Latin *occulere*, meaning "to cover over," doubled with their uncategorized love. Spiritualism of many sorts permeated post–World War I life, providing H.D. with vocabulary to bridge science, art, and religion, an imperative to this astronomer's daughter, capable of naming the most distant stars. By ancestry Moravian, a sect driven underground, she arrived in London with an unusual faith tucked in her back pocket.

In the late nineteenth century, London was a center for seekers, populated by "a swirling mix of freethinkers, Masons, Gnostics, mystics and other experimenters in religion and the divine, blended with writers, travelers and Orientalists fascinated with the so-called Near East."[74] Religious syncretism won followers, propelled by the idea that some new belief system might provide global unity. Other modernists, such as Yeats, Eliot, and Conan Doyle, discovered entries into invisible worlds. Still H.D.'s specific mystical exploration led back to "De-meter" and to chanting, "Mary, Maia, Miriam, Mut, Madre, Mere, Mother pray for us. Pray for us, dark Mary, Mary, mere, mut; this is the nightmare, this the dark horse, this Mary, Maia, Mut, Mutter. This is

Gaia, this is the beginning." "God-the-father" blocked her view, finding "beneath the carved super-structure of every temple to God-the-Father, the dark cave or grotto."[75] Though aspirational, both wearied of absolutes, H.D. reminding, "[W]e must not step right over into the transcendental, we must crouch near the grass and near to the earth that made us."[76] Ultimately, H.D. and Bryher shared gnosis, supplemented by "mystery religions" and belief in an "underground" spiritualism preserving "the original great-mother."[77]

Eminent scientists, among them Pierre and Marie Curie, Cesare Lombroso, Camille Flammarion, and Henri Bergson, explored whether spiritualism might explain the occult aspects of nature.[78] H.D. and Bryher were attracted to antirationalists, harkening back to natural forces discovered in the late eighteenth century, with Franz Anton Mesmer among the first to understand what our pair intuited—that thought transfers were not only possible but extremely probable. Mary Shelley's *Frankenstein* (1818) also loomed in its vision of an electrically charged resurrection of a shunned body.

Growing up with Thomas A. Edison (1847–1931), inventor of the telephone, electric light bulb, portable recording device, motion picture, and power grid, the couple found electricity an opportunity to investigate connective tissue and vibrations. At eighty, Edison seized upon his last great invention: a "spirit phone" or Ghost Machine to open up electronic communication with the dead. Relying upon Einstein's special theory of relativity, Edison's universe consisted of eternal matter, incapable of being created or destroyed. He designed a machine to communicate with this reservoir of shared "eternity," transmitting signals—a flow of electrons—to and from the other side. Edison hypothesized a memory storage area in the brain, with "clusters" independent of physical reality, functioning "like a phonograph, tape recorder or film reel," capable of reviving those in the past.[79] Edison's spirit phone failed, though he set currents flowing.

Like an innovative scientist, H.D. thought deep memory, akin to Edison's "life clusters," could be tapped. She had a palpable sense of having lived elsewhere in time and space, believing she could contact as "an actual psychic entity, that continent, for the most part buried, of the self, which contains cells or seeds which can be affiliated to the selves of people, living or long dead." Boldly she wrote, "[A] little cell of my brain responds to a cell of someone's brain, who died thousands of years ago."[80] This was *not* Eliot's "mythic method," "a way of controlling, of ordering, of giving shape and significance to the immense panorama of futility and anarchy which is contemporary history,"[81] but an *embodied psychic mythopoetic method*, one to contact, for instance, the Egyptian goddess of wisdom, Isis, or the Greek Artemis, the chaste huntress.

H.D. didn't build a spirit phone, but she schematized her relationship to Bryher as a "whole machine," generating creative sparks. They had séances at "a sort of receiving station," modifying that she was "*not the whole machine. Gareth's intense psychic quality is concealed, she is like the inner springs and wheels, or the careful wrapping around live-wire. I have been the live-wire, I receive the live-messages. But not now.*" When H.D. needed a "conductor," she called Bryher "Gareth" or "Garry," referring to Gawain's brother knight. Malory's Gareth was the "fair unknown," arriving armored, on horseback, yet mistaken for a "lowborn." Tasked with cooking, feminized for his beautiful hands, Gareth, despite gender bullying, was sent on a quest by Arthur. Possessing her own "inner springs," Bryher, as Garry, provided "wrapping" for H.D. as "live wire."

> If my being had flowed and quivered and responded to that wind of inspiration, like the branches of a paper-birch or like the strings of a harp, Gareth's [Bryher's] had remained the static lode-stone, the north-star, the steel of the magnetic horseshoe, around which the iron-filings collect in different patterns.[82]

Literally pulling H.D. together, Bryher acted the provocative enigma, steadying H.D., who needed psychic collaboration, admitting "what [Bryher] said was oracular and always had been."[83] It was as if they followed W. H. Auden, who asserted that "[q]ueers, to whom normal marriage and parenthood are forbidden" seek out "tasks which require collaboration and the right person with whom to collaborate."[84]

Called many things, when called anything, Bryher is dubbed H.D.'s partner, friend, companion, or "cousin"; there is reluctance to accept her as H.D.'s lover, her nearest intimate, but she was. To erase Bryher, *the* crucial person in the poet's life, is to blot H.D., a point evading those who would like, for whatever reason, to keep her in heterosexual brackets; no one has appropriately gauged Bryher's intellectual and psychic imprint, with her Cassandra-like predictions of war and economic fallout, along with her near total care of H.D., one of the most perfectionist poets of all time, who could dissolve or blend with the wind, who had the guts to cross a Nazi barbed-wire fence in Vienna to hear a bit of opera. Whatever either said, both were willfully child-like; both suffered lifelong instabilities. H.D. was emotionally intense, both a strength and a weakness, while Bryher, as Gertrude Stein observed, enacted another Napoleon and had a devilish side as "Fiend," another of H.D.'s nicknames for Fido. If the former was demanding, the latter was commanding. Quite simply, H.D. identified as doublesexed, yet Bryher almost embodied an entirely new species.

* * *

This is a story of "we two" on a quest, seeking alternative realities. H.D. provided an implicit charting:

> The first decade of my adventure opened with the Argo, Floride, a small French-line steamer, sailing for Havre. The second of my adventures with the Argo, Borodino, a boat belonging to "one of the lines," Bryher's phrase for her father's shipping. The third decade of my cruise or quest may be said to have begun in London with my decision to undertake a serious course of psychoanalysis.[85]

H.D. correlated psychic experiences as ocean voyages, as "lines," poetic and nautical, a nod to Bryher's father, the shipper. Each voyage in the pilgrimage spawned texts and trials. The first section, "The Voyage Out," explores ancestral inheritance to chart H.D.'s and Bryher's shared obsessions. Line 1, the *Floride*, fills in H.D.'s prior loves, with H.D. inducting Bryher as co-voyager; Line 2 follows the *Borodino*, staging the pair's early romance and shared visions; Line 3 follows psychoanalysis, which H.D. deemed "high explosives," and Bryher "second sight." They lived in London through what I call the "Blitz line," Line 4, for after all, H.D. left ellipses, knowing she might catch another ocean liner or two. Finally, Bryher joined H.D.'s "*Viking* line" after the ship they conjured during their séances between 1943 and 1945. Line 5 tracks H.D.'s retreat to a dissociative paranoia, her recovery, followed by Bryher's escalating fears of another war. In the fifties, Bryher joined queers leaving the United States for jaunts to Capri, and even Pakistan.

In stark contrast to the presumed openness of the twenty-first century, H.D. and Bryher were bound in a clinging web of silence. Yet today's explosion of gender and sexual possibilities as well as an oppressive backlash offers a chance to look anew at this couple seeking an alternative idea of "family" and creative collaboration. This dual biography rescues their lives together as an improbable miracle. The grain of their daily life, responsive to major historical shifts, figures forth their mediumistic poetics. In its broadest sense, the twentieth century marked them, as they marked it. We must catch their measure.

2
H.D.'s Ancestors Circle

> We are all haunted houses.
>
> —H.D., "Advent" (1948)

H.D.'s first nine years, 1886 to 1895, in Bethlehem, Pennsylvania, were magical but also haunted by ritual and loss. By 1890, the city's population was just shy of twenty thousand, mainly newly arrived European immigrants clustered around Bethlehem Steel, its blast furnaces forging modern inventions: I-beams for girder skyscrapers and bridges, armor plate to bolster tanks, airplanes, ships, railroad tracks, and munitions. Approximately one-third of its inhabitants, including H.D.'s family, lived across the Lehigh River in "Old Town," whose spirit of connectedness stemmed from the town's founders, congregants of the Moravian Church. This unusual faith set itself apart by claiming no human mind could comprehend God.

H.D.'s closest link to Bethlehem's distant past came through her maternal grandmother, Elizabeth Caroline Weiss Seidel Wolle (1824–1906), "Mamalie," who in 1842 married Henry Augustus Seidel, called "Christian." He practiced as a minister in a small Moravian church a hundred miles from Bethlehem and died two years later of typhus.[1] Elizabeth returned with their five-year-old daughter and only child, Agnes, born in 1843, and taught in the Young Ladies' Seminary, founded in 1749, dedicated to women's education. She married again, on July 6, 1848; Francis Wolle (1817–1893), "Papalie," also a Moravian minister, was principal of the seminary. In 1853, Elizabeth gave birth to H.D.'s mother, Helen Eugenia.

During Hilda's childhood, handmade beeswax candles lit this quaint late nineteenth-century town. Advancing secularism tempered expansive rituals, such as the Moravian belief that Christ's side wounds were holy openings and that every soul was considered female and equal, with Jesus conceived as vaguely bigendered. Moravians celebrated "love feasts" where Holy Communion "developed through social gathering of friends," "singing praises"; in H.D.'s day, these feasts were celebrated with "coffee with cream and rolls," combined with breathing exercises and music, creating euphoria.[2] Hilda belonged. "Everyone knows our mother so we are never sure who is related and who is not," she wrote, especially joined through their "candle service on Christmas Eve," Freud applauding this ceremony as "the true heart of all religion."[3]

H.D.'s grandfather Papalie was the pastor; her mother's brother, Uncle Fred, led the choir, initiating an annual Bach festival. For Christmas, Papalie crafted with Hilda a small universe of animals to adorn the crèche. Though her household pivoted around her father, Charles Leander Doolittle (1843–1919), he was a misfit in Moravian circles, unhappy on Sundays and at Christmas, never having had a tree as a child.

The Doolittle family occupied 10 East Church Street, a block away from Hilda's kindergarten. At home, everything doubled: "2 fathers and 2 mothers, for we thought Papalie and Mamalie (our mother's parents) were our own 'other' father and mother" with "2 of everybody (except myself) in that first house," including "2 brothers who shared the same room."[4] From home, walking past vestigial dormitories segregated by sex, the "Single Men's House," the "Single Women's House," and the "Widows' House," the child easily reached the seminary, where her mother taught German, art, and singing. In Bethlehem's early years, Moravians divided congregants into same-sex living arrangements, placing them into "choirs," based on divisions of age, marital status, and gender, to advance each group's spiritual development. In her youth, Helen Eugenia, "child of a long line of musicians," could tell by the hymn played if *"someone was born or someone had died."*[5]

Governed by the "General Economy" for a golden pocket of time roughly between 1722 and 1788, there was no great chasm between wealthy and poor. The Church owned everything and collectively cared for its members.[6] Sunday school taught H.D. that "Moravians never acted as isolated individuals but always worked with the concept of group endeavor."[7] Dying was "going home." No one wore black at funerals. A short climb to Nisky Hill Cemetery, children played, lovers met, and Hilda saw where many of her forbearers lay under unadorned stones, spotting unusual names, Native Americans, who had once lived side by side with Moravian settlers.[8] Sensing ghost traces of "old Indian tracks," Hilda feared slipping on a jagged stone through a "trap-door."[9] With fascinated ear, the child heard Mamalie's tales from nearly two centuries earlier, when Moravians fled persecution across the sea from Germany.

During World War II, while bombs rained down, Bryher coached H.D. through childhood memories, tunneling backward in time, and space, from London to Bethlehem. Their research for her autobiographical *The Gift* went into its "Notes," itself "an interesting little pocket of religious persecution and survival."[10] H.D. discovered an earlier Christian Seidel, an important Moravian voyager on the *Catherine* in 1742, part of the "first Sea Congregation." In German, the surname Seidel translates to "chalice" (*der Kelch*) or "calix," derived from Greek, formed by the petals protecting the bud, a motif throughout H.D.'s work, signifying the communion chalice, for her an invitation to creativity and, ultimately, the unknowable.

H.D.'s modernism unexpectedly depended upon her ancestry's radical break from dominant Abrahamic dogmas, which preached that the male gender wielded a monopoly on divinity. Like twentieth-century refugees from Fascism, her Moravian ancestors were hounded out of Europe. Often feeling loosely tethered to the world, H.D. happily rediscovered the initiating John Hus (1370–1415), called the "burning reformer," who fought for liturgical celebration in the vernacular, leading "Papal authorities" to burn Hus at the stake on July 6, 1415, "to intimidate the uprising hosts." This was major, sharing the Communion cup with an entire congregation instead of limiting it to the clergy. It gave his followers a "new lease on life," leading to the founding of the Moravian Church in 1457. After a Bohemian civil war, they flourished, until the Jesuits forced them back underground in 1622, creating a Moravian diaspora. This "almost annihilated" brotherhood H.D. likened to earlier persecuted believers: Gnostics, Templars, Troubadours, St. Francis of Assisi, St. Teresa of Avila, a diverse group in an "Invisible Church," forced into anonymity by the Inquisition and Counter-Reformation, yet H.D. railed that an "underground river, you can never destroy."[11] Scholar Elaine Pagels similarly tracks this river, observing that Eastern and Western religions were not "separate streams" two thousand years ago; in fact, "Oriental religion" and "Hellenistic culture" mingled, making gnosis "an intuitive process of knowing oneself." By "A.D. 200," Christianity was a "three-rank hierarchy of bishops, priests, and deacons," driving spiritual dissidents underground.[12]

The Moravians' eighteenth-century leader, the mystically oriented and charismatic Count Nikolaus Ludwig von Zinzendorf (1700–1760), a religious exile from Austria, feminized Jesus and the soul itself.[13] In Lower Saxony, he offered sanctuary to ten brethren to establish on his estate a community called Herrnhut (the Lord's Watch) in 1722. Until Zinzendorf's death, Moravians experienced an "expansive period."[14] He reignited belief in God as a melding of "male and female elements together constituting the finest production of the Mother."[15]

Some of H.D.'s "brethren" believed that Christ's "side hole" wounds, received at his Crucifixion, unified male and female. Rather baroque for an anti-Papist religion, Moravian iconography portrayed healing fluids gushing from the savior's side, assigning it both erotic and maternal qualities. Eighteenth-century Moravians even created dioramas on colorful little cards, bidding the supplicant drop into the wound to be taken care of by the maternal "great comforter," too fantastical for most other sects to tolerate.[16]

In 1741, persecution motivated a group of Moravians to sail with Zinzendorf and two young leaders, David Zeisberger with David Nitschmann, leaving Europe for another Herrnhut, seeking asylum in Pennsylvania with other nonconformist Protestants, among them the reclusive Quakers and the Amish. They bought land from John Penn on the forks of the Delaware and Lecha (now Lehigh) rivers. These three officially founded Bethlehem on December 24, 1741. On that day, the early settlers, with John Christopher Pyrlaeus, a musician and a scholar of Indian dialects, proficient in Mohican, shared a meal of corncake, washed down with roasted rye. Matching musical notes and tones, he steadily compiled Iroquois and Algonquian dictionaries.[17]

A year after arriving in 1742, Zinzendorf negotiated a peace treaty with the Six Nations of Iroquois. Contemporaneously, the Moravians dispatched missionaries, led by Christian Henry Rauch, to the Mohicans in eastern New York along the Hudson River. Chief Tschoop accepted Rauch, allowing Moravians to live with his tribe. Enraged white settlers, bitter because this "peace" impeded their exploitation of Native Americans through land grabs and alcohol trafficking, spread false rumors about the Moravians, whom authorities arrested and fined in Milford, Connecticut. Retreating to Bethlehem, Native Americans and Moravians built Friedenshuetten, "Habitations of Peace," in 1744, with a "summer house" for religious gatherings behind the seminary, leading across a "rustic foot bridge" to Wunden Eiland, the Island of Wounds, named after Christ's lacerations.[18] This same year, the sheer number of Christianized Native Americans in Bethlehem exceeded whites. Non-Moravian colonists threatened eviction so vociferously that the Indians stopped gathering, which for Mamalie's Henry Christian spelled the loss of what had held their church together. Moravian elders then established Gnadenhuetten (Habitations of Grace) for the persecuted tribes, a day's journey up the Lehigh by canoe.[19] German words like Gnadenhuetten opened for H.D. "like a bee-hive" buzzing with "Count Z."[20]

Zinzendorf's son, Christian Renatus (1722–1752), known as Christel, assumed stewardship in 1748 of Herrnhaag, one of the Count's German estates. Even more explicitly than his father, he preached that Jesus was both male and female, all souls female, and all single brethren were sisters and brides of Christ. "Charged with energy, piety and hormones," Christel led the 1748 Single Brothers' Festival, where he presided as Christ, re-creating the Last Supper, featuring an exchange of kisses with his male apostles that ascended into ecstasy. One brother described the "astonishing feeling [that] we were all accepted and declared as single sisters."[21] These genderbending "performances" provoked the elder count to recall Christel to London to establish a British headquarters on Sir Thomas More's Chelsea estate; in 1749 the British Parliament recognized it as belonging to the Protestant Episcopal church.[22]

Fleeing Europe for Bethlehem, John Christopher Fredrick Cammerhof (1721–1751) and his wife, Anna von Pahlen (1717?–1786), enacted an explicit ceremony to make peace with Paxnous, the Shawnee chief, at Gnadenhuetten. Bishop Levering, H.D. remarked, suggested the couple's arrival was partly responsible for "the craze that broke out," with "a rage for the spectacular," the very aspect of her ancestry that excited her. Cammerhof and von Pahlen performed a peace ritual that Mamalie described to the not yet adolescent Hilda in 1895, who had lived nine years in Bethlehem before learning "the secret," as she called it.

* * *

While H.D.'s Moravian heritage contains much that remains intangible, her ancestry also had a far more concrete existence, which she absorbed subliminally and at school. For instance, during the Revolutionary War, after General George Washington's 1777 defeat at Brandywine, Bethlehem served as an army hospital. Applying native herbal remedies, Moravian women nursed the wounded.

Mamalie's father, Jedediah Weiss (1796–1873), built the grandfather clock that kept time in H.D.'s home. For over four decades he ran a cottage industry crafting such timepieces.[23] Mary Stables Weiss (1796–1872), Mamalie's mother and H.D.'s nearest biological link to Europe, born in Virginia to Scottish immigrants, reputedly possessed "second sight" and was gifted in music, cultivating Mamalie, an "expert musician," who played the spinet.[24] Within the hour of the death of her son, George Augustus Weiss (1821–1853), while he was on a mission in the West Indies, Mary stopped in her garden, hearing a distinct voice; when she turned to greet her son, no one was there. She taught Mamalie the Scottish ballad "The Four Marys":

> Last night there were four Marys;
>   Tonight there'll be but three.
> 'Twas Mary Beaton and Mary Seaton
>   And Mary Carmichael and me.

One of the Marys, a lady-in-waiting, was hanged for seduction and infanticide.[25] As Mamalie's favorite, the song, grim in its original meaning, was "more precious to [H.D.] than the St. Matthew's Passion and the Mass in B Minor," so that it made "a furrow or runnel in [her] emotional or *spiritual* being." It summoned seasons, the compass, the quatrain, the fourth dimension.[26]

Mamalie's second husband, Francis Wolle, "Papalie," started as a clerk in his father's grocery store. Noticing that customers were unable to carry all the goods they'd purchased, by 1852 he had perfected a machine to fabricate paper bags. His patent approved in 1869, he founded the Union Paper Bag Machine Company; he soon ceded its management to his brothers. Papalie became a bishop and principal at the seminary. After the bloody Gettysburg battle, he opened it as a hospital for Union and Rebel soldiers, a particularly humane gesture. H.D. worshiped her grandfather as "the naked eye," "the apple of [her] eye," "the apple of God's eye," and Bethlehem's last curator of a European tradition, soon overshadowed by American industrialism.[27]

This Moravian innovator combed the wooded shores and mountains around Bethlehem, searching out mosses and algae. Carrying home "invisible finds," the fund of arduous labor and curiosity, Papalie allowed Hilda and her siblings to gather around his workbench to observe through his microscope that pressing a specimen "between two glass-slides" shows "we know so little about even a drop of water, how can we know the inner secrets of God?"[28] A respected "pioneer in micro-botany," Papalie published *Desmids of the United States* and *Freshwater Algae of the United States*, two volumes, with colored plates, and *Diatomoceae of North America*.[29]

After the Civil War, H.D.'s mother witnessed "progress," shrinking the bucolic landscapes portrayed in her paintings. "Pitilessly ravaged," Bethlehem mutated from a retreat of "lovely Arcadian simplicity," nestled among hills, into a noisy mill town. H.D.'s elders feared that billowing smoke might kill the trees grown from cuttings their ancestors had brought from Germany. Helen taught music and painting at the seminary she had attended and met her soon-to-be husband, Charles Leander Doolittle, while teaching German in a night class. In 1882, Helen broke with Moravian tradition and married this outsider from Indiana. A photograph shows Francis Wolle overseeing Helen, instructing art pupils at an easel and, beside it, a tripod table (Figure 2.1).

Figure 2.1 Helen Wolle Doolittle standing in front of her father in the seminary, 188? Unsourced family photograph, H.D. Papers.
Courtesy of Beinecke Rare Book and Manuscript Library, Yale University.

Charles Doolittle had two sons from his first marriage, Alfred (1868–1920) and Eric (1870–1920), with Alice, who died in 1876. In this second union, the couple lost their first child, Edith, born in July 1883, alive for only four months, followed by Gilbert (1884–1918), Hilda (the odd girl out), and Harold (1887–1968). When H.D. was born, Charles consulted a name book; closing his eyes, his finger settled first upon the old Testament prophet Hulda, reputed to have heard God directly, then traced his finger back to Hilda.[30] A photo of the siblings catches Hilda's intense gaze (Figure 2.2).

Born in Ontario, Indiana, on November 12, 1843, H.D.'s father was the son of Charles, a lawyer, and his wife, Celia. The Doolittles spent "[s]ix generations weathered and shaped by the rock and flint of New England."[31] She traced the "Doolittle" line to northern England during Elizabeth I's reign. "Their most important kinsman," Thomas (1632–1707), a Cambridge-educated nonconformist, served as pastor of St. Alphege, London Wall, and authored several religious tomes.[32] During the 1660s, Parliament barred dissenting ministers from their pulpits, prohibiting nonconformists from civil or military office or matriculating at Cambridge or Oxford. After the Great London Fire in 1666, Thomas defied the law, preaching on sites where churches lay in rubble. Evading arrest, he founded a dissenters' church.

Part of the great Puritan exodus, Thomas' relative, Abraham, migrated to New Haven, Connecticut, in 1640. H.D. half-joked that her father's line stuck to their English pedigree: stubborn New Englanders refrained from striking first, but once attacked, struck to kill. After controlling state legislatures, these Puritan ancestors,

Figure 2.2 (Right to left) Gilbert, Harold, and Hilda Doolittle, c. 1890. Unsourced family photograph, H.D. Papers.
Courtesy of Beinecke Rare Book and Manuscript Library, Yale University.

targets of the English Crown's campaigns of state violence, themselves launched similar attacks, suffering neither witches nor Native Americans.

H.D.'s paternal grandparents headed toward California in a covered wagon, following a "Viking call" to the ocean; Charles' father, disappointed, stayed in Indiana, where bounty hunters tracked down runaway slaves, and his father dug up a buried Indian skull. H.D.'s father's "far-sighted grey eyes" picked out "the ten stars of the Dipper or the eight of Orion's sword-belt"; "this satisfied him." In 1860, at seventeen, Charles abandoned his studies at the University of Michigan, lied about his age, and along with his nineteen-year-old brother, Alvin, enlisted in the Union Army.[33]

Without killing a single Rebel, Charles fought, only to see Alvin die not in combat but of typhoid. He never told his grieving mother the real cause of his brother's death. Charles' "domed forehead" and irresolute mouth and chin betrayed a melancholy at his mother's evident disappointment that he, rather than Alvin, had survived.[34] Charles married Martha Cloyes Farrand in 1866. After graduating from the University of Michigan with a Civil Engineering degree. In 1874, he worked a summer for the U.S. Boundary Commission, sleeping in a tent during rough weather. The following year, he arrived with Martha and two sons in Bethlehem as professor of mathematics and chair of astronomy at Lehigh University, where students affectionally called him "Poppy Doo."[35] Martha died two years later.

Other scientists did not initially perceive Doolittle's research as entirely empirical, but over time his work gained credence. In his alumni address at Lehigh, delivered on June 17, 1885, a year before H.D.'s birth, he observed the "transits of Venus, only two of which occur in a century," with the sun "surrounded with a gaseous envelope or atmosphere of considerable extent," while "the planet Venus has an atmosphere probably much like our own," producing "a blending or haziness of outline when the two discs are near the point of tangency." (Much like H.D.'s embodied mind, tangent with Bryher's.) The field was "inexhaustible," he admitted, while "our capacities" were "finite."[36] Doolittle authored a textbook, *A Treatise on Practical Astronomy as Applied to Geodesy and Navigation* (1885), reprinted in multiple editions over three decades, with practical applications for shippers, like Bryher's father. A former student stated that there was no rival "contribution to the problem of the latitudinal variation."[37]

By H.D.'s estimate, her father studied "cold and absolute beauty" for thirty years and minimized that the *only* thing she knew "about this variation is that the earth itself floats like a ship in the ocean. The earth does not go around in perfect circles. It sways slightly or 'wobbles.'" The child was frightened by earth's "precarious voyaging,"[38] and by her father, who traced the movement of "the earth round the sun, the variation of latitude," adjusting "a graph on a map started by Ptolemy in Egypt."[39] Doolittle's stealthy tracking of parallel lines circling the earth, locating stars through symbols, numbers, code, this very abstract method of thinking planted itself in H.D., unable to make parallel lines meet, addicted to widening circles.

Like H.D.'s maternal grandfather, who sought invisible specimens, Charles too slipped out at night, but to study galactic entities, privy to what no one else could see. Thomas Hardy's *Two on a Tower* (1882) observes of astronomy that of "all the sciences it alone deserves the character of the terrible," the lonely star-gazer making his "way through a heaven of total darkness, occasionally striking against the black, invisible cinders of those stars."[40] Doolittle slept most days to make up for his nightly vigils. He gave H.D. a gigantic snowy owl, encased in a bell jar perched on his bookshelf; flanking the other end was the Indian skull his father had given him, displaying results of excavation. Charles singled out "his one girl" to inherit his scientific prowess instead of his sons, leading to "a terrible responsibility."[41] A photo catches Charles at his telescope, catapulting him towards distant constellations [Figure 2.3].

Figure 2.3 Charles Leander Doolittle at his telescope, undated. Unsourced family photograph, H.D. Papers.
Courtesy of Beinecke Rare Book and Manuscript Library, Yale University.

Before learning her alphabet or how to read the clock face, tantalized by its roundness, in the nursery, under her half-brother Eric's tutelage, she was "a thing of hunched shoulders and sparrow claws, who with unabated intensity, scratched 7, 7, 7, 7, 7 across the entire length of great sheets of brown wrapping paper ... more portent, more cabalistic than the two marks of equal length joined, tent-wise, and fastened in the middle." Numbers signified with special meaning, Eric providing "over-time," a means of sensing timelessness. Defying the proprieties of her starched cornflower pinafore, H.D. recalled her "colt knees crawling into the rabbit hutch," "[c]rawling, crawling with elbows scraping the rough lathes and end of wire netting," confronted "at last with a vision of eight pink bodies, eight unexpectedly furless and rigid bodies," struck by the rigid newborns, and "the weary old bunny" who "thumps, disconsolate in the corner." Defiantly, she "scaled the tree" and "shook the branches in a frenzy till the multiplying Edwardses were drenched in the soft, too-ripe, purple blackberries." While fantasizing over a "foundling sister of Princess Minnehaha," H.D. saw her child self as boyish, distinctly separate—"an uncanny monster," fated to join other "curious, misshapen things."[42]

* * *

H.D.'s mother was at origin a myth. The poet surmised that "if one could stay near her always, there would be no break in consciousness" and savored her "laughing, not so much at us as with or over us and around us."[43] The child inherited her mother's passion for choral music and elaborate needlework, stitching "petit point canvases—an occupation which both rested her mind and stimulated it."[44] Helen told her children that a fortune teller predicted she would have a gifted child, then claimed her children were not especially so, possibly due to her own mother's obsessional ramblings over the distant past. Herself tempted by a singing or artist's career, Helen stuck to her fate as the proper principal's daughter and likely discouraged her daughter's rich imagination, out of worry, to help her conform, while Mamalie led the child to intangibles such as telling her that a black rose was really "a shadow of a rose," or Hilda's own overactive mind, wanting to lie down, for instance in the snow, "dangerous" because it would make her "too happy."[45] Helen generally discouraged Hilda's visions, for instance when "that thing that happened, that Mama said didn't happen, when the Young Man who at first I thought was the Gardener, cut off a lily with a short stem that I held in my hand like a cup."[46] Nonetheless, H.D. attributed her poetic "second sight" to her "musician-artist mother, through her part-Celtic mother." When visiting Nisky Hill Cemetery, she longed for a twin sister. With Papalie's death in 1893, he was the first "'dead' person" the seven-year-old had "ever known."[47] Grieving, Mamalie succumbed to encephalitis.

* * *

Shortly before the family moved to Upper Darby outside Philadelphia in 1895 with Doolittle's appointment at the University of Pennsylvania, H.D. ministered to her infirm, delirious grandmother, then seventy-two; with her prim lace cap, pinched face, and piercing eyes, she ailed beneath her quilt, "patches of everybody's best dresses."[48] Burning with brain fever, she spoke of Indian retributions and epigenetic trauma. Spellbound, the child brought chipped ice to Mamalie's lips. With difficulty speaking, she guided Hilda back in time to her first husband, Henry, who, while cataloguing Church records, came across a weathered birch-bark case, a deer-skin parchment so thin that he feared it might dissolve; it dated back to Zinzendorf's time, so he copied the original. Its motto, written in French, translated to "the friendship that passes the grave."⁴⁹ The parchment was signed by Cammerhof, Pyrlaeus, and the first Christian Seidel, whom H.D. considered "the shadow or under-study" of Mamalie's husband "Christian" Henry, proficient in Greek, who believed it documented tribal chiefs, medicine men, and priests in "picture writing," combining characters in "Greek, Hebrew, and Indian dialects," alongside "tones and notes of the Indian voices, like annotations."⁵⁰ His proprietary interest in the document was from fear that church elders might destroy it. Devoting himself, he was assured that *if* he could reconstruct its scrambled fragments, he might fulfill "a Promise": a world without war, and spiritual rebirth.

Untrained in music, he enlisted Mamalie, who had "not only a delicate tone-perception" but also a "working knowledge of musical composition." Deciphering "native rhythms" grafted with Moravian music, Pyrlaeus' Shawnee dictionary helped them link Anna von Pahlen's collage of devotionals to musical rhythms. The document reached back before Bethlehem's havens were betrayed by marauders, the non-Moravian white colonists. Mamalie hinted to the child that the collaboration between her and her husband was like walking blind, tucking candles and matches in her handbag for train travel, should they be trapped in a tunnel.⁵¹

After intensive labor, Mamalie and her husband uncovered a special ceremony that in the eighteenth century symbolically joined Native American and Moravian spiritual practices through mutual understanding that the Holy Ghost and the Indian's Great Spirit were indivisible. They forged a precarious peace. Indian names signaled a person's invisible soul. The Shawnee chief Paxnous pledged his wife through one of her "inner names," Morning Star. In exchange, Cammerhof pledged his wife, Anna von Pahlen, with one of her names, Angelica.

From her bed, Mamalie enacted what transpired after the name exchange, not simply with words but through reverberations, "an inner greeting," "strange pledges," and "rhythms."⁵² The Indians gave Cammerhof an ancient belt, woven from silver and gold with alternating patterns of a rose or daisy and a star, a simple cross, inside a circle. Unlike the T-shaped wood indicating Christ's crucifixion, the simple cross, +, with no elongated horizontal line, signified in the second and third centuries among persecuted Gnostics that it was safe to speak of the feminine Holy Ghost. By matching or mixing church music with Indian rhythms, Mamalie teleported Hilda back to the ceremony on Wunden Eiland. "Songs bring things back." Traveling back to the eighteenth-century ritual,⁵³ Mamalie imagined "herself speaking in tongues, hymns of the spirit in the air, of spirit at sun-rise and sun-setting, of the deer and the wild squirrel, the beaver, the otter, the king-fisher and the hawk and eagle." Bit by bit, she conjured up the talking, laughing, and singing, "with no words or words of leaves rustling and rivers flowing and snow swirling in the wind, which is the breath of the Spirit, it seems." Anna's "high pure silver" voice "breathed the hymn" until the "laughter ran over us," "pouring from the sky or from the inner realm of spirit." Speaking of just such a ritual, H.D. wrote in the 1944 *Flowering*, "[A]ll we know is that it was all so very soon over, / the feasting, the laughter."⁵⁴

A powerful influence on H.D., Mamalie felt as criminal as Cammerhof, or Christel, since the church elders labeled the ceremony "witchcraft" for mixing church rituals with Indian magic, a hybridity despised like miscegenation. Following the prevailing edict, "*thou shalt not suffer a witch to live*," Mamalie feared her devotion to the old parchment's secret would eject her from the fold as much as she feared that the spiritual pact with the Native Americans would never be restored. Zinzendorf had believed that God was "mother of the whole church," a fuse setting off nonbelievers into calling it "gross and scandalous ... mysticism." Mamalie's vision of a hallowed peace resonated with H.D., who saw Mohicans, Algonquins, and the Shawanese as "a great religious body" and, like other such bodies, belonging to an "Hidden Church."[55]

After ceremonies such as the one Mamalie uncovered and described to H.D. became known and mocked, Europeans encroached on Indian territories, breached treaties, desecrated burial sites, and assaulted Indians, culminating in the Massacre at Wounded Knee in 1890. Native Americans then faced a choice: assimilation or extermination. Stunned by her grandmother's tale, the child felt "incarcerated, as a nun might be, ... for some sin—which [she] did not then understand."[56] H.D. bore indelible traces from her ancestry, leading her toward winds, stones, torn flowers, animate environments that could be interpreted like her father's night sky or her grandmother's vision of possible peace between whites and Native Americans, brokered through exchange and song.

* * *

At age ten, H.D. endured one major move, a dislocation aggravated by Mamalie's confession. Departure from singing Bethlehem, "the town of Mary," the home of Mamalie, Uncle Fred, Aunt Laura, as well as the dead sisters and her dearest grandfather at Nisky Hill, terrified Hilda. In essence, her father acted Paris, abducting Helen from Bethlehem, forming the blueprint for H.D.'s "Helen of Troy" obsession. She sensed her mother's complicity with the move, as if to sign on for "rationality" in contrast to Mamalie's ramblings about the distant past.

Charles was named the Flower Professor of Astronomy at the University of Pennsylvania. He occupied the Transit House, holding several astronomy clocks, a prism, a meridian circle, and a Zenith telescope with special convex lenses, installed by John Brashear (1840–1920), the most famous lens maker in America, and rivaled only by one in Greenwich, England. The child Hilda joked with Brashear, this "small, dark, vivid" man, who she thought "the magic *humunculus* of the alchemists."[57]

The new house was larger, with a peach orchard, somewhat easing the loss of Bethlehem. By streetcar it was two miles to Cobbs Creek, Philadelphia's city limit. H.D. attended public school for the first time, deeming it "horrible," the hours "torture," and the walk too long to make it home for lunch. The walls "smelled differently." Approaching adolescence, her body was increasingly a problem. Those who watched said, "[I]t's a pity she's so tall" and "it" "did not fit its body."[58]

The most memorable event for H.D. in Darby gnawed at her for over two decades. She spotted her father stumbling home, his coat dusty, his arm hanging like "a scarecrow or a rag-doll." Managing him inside, blood coursed down his face. She ran for a towel and water basin. When Helen finally arrived, Hilda's services were forgotten. Feeling she had "manned" the crisis well, without notice, she was exiled to bed, fearing the worst—would he die? She finally learned, after several days of worry, he had suffered a major concussion caused by falling off a trolley that braked suddenly. His gash retained its nightmarish aura, exacerbating her painfully exquisite ability to see edges, "death" at work in "life." The incident showed her otherworldly father, in charge of the stars, vulnerable, and herself helpless to aid. Mamalie's tale combined with her father's accident almost paralyzed her "inner masculinity," releasing a mind privy to colonial guilt.

Both of the poet's parents and her ancestors bestowed shocks and "gifts," material and symbolic, casting gigantic shadows. H.D. sought to narrow the gap between male and female, science and art, through spiritual lenses, sifting for glowing radium with laser concentration. Her childhood hypnotized her, and like the lens maker she saw "the world through [her] double-lens."[59]

3
Bryher's Family Closet

Bryher held her early childhood as "above criticism or law, a vivid breathing thing, like a book, like apple-blossom sweeping the rain-blue sky."[1] Her 1894 birth certificate, entered at Somerset House, placed her mother, Hannah Glover, as living at 53 Upper Bedford Place, Bloomsbury, London, with no father's name, an abyss.[2] Paradise shattered when in adolescence she learned of her illegitimacy; she could not *be* or *become* her most admired parent, and person, Sir John Ellerman. A photo of her as a young adult with her father, confidently upholstered, arm tucked around Bryher as he guided her along a ship's deck (Figure 3.1). Smiling and gazing downward, Bryher acted a giddy junior apprentice.

Sir John's ultimate fame as a financier did not change his or his child's origins being amorphous, more so than H.D.'s. Yet Bryher's father, as much as H.D.'s, was a pathfinder, descended from common folk. An accounting genius, John Reeves Ellerman was born on May 15, 1862, in Hull, England, a magnet for Jewish immigrants. Guest points to Ellerman's birthplace as confirmation of his Jewish origins.[3] Passing as Lutheran, a common ploy to protect against ever-erupting anti-Semitism in Europe, her father may have dropped the second "n" in Ellerman for this reason. No absolute proof exists, and though her father claimed ignorance, Bryher strongly suspected being Jewish, eventually engaging a private detective in the 1930s, who traced Ellerman's line back to the late seventeenth century in Hitzacker, Lower Saxony, a stone's throw from Count Zinzendorf's estate. Beginning with an ex-cavalry officer marrying a miller's daughter, Bryher's ancestors included cowherds, greengrocers, carpenters, stewards, and a miller who, due to flooding on the Elbe River, lost his business. Church records show the family as citizens of Hamburg by 1835.[4]

Ellerman's father, Johann (1819–1871), a corn merchant from Hamburg, arrived in Hull in approximately 1850. In 1855, he wed Anne Elizabeth Reeves (1823–1909), the daughter of Timothy Reeves (1795–1879), a prosperous solicitor, who left a fulsome £60,000. Anne's marriage to an unconnected foreigner probably confounded her family. Johann suffered numerous strokes, eventually dying of one in 1871, when John was only nine, and feared the same fate. Although Johann managed the Hull Brewery along with prosperous insurance and shipping interests, he left his son only £600. Perhaps overwhelmed with grief, Anne took the children to Dieppe, France, sending John and his two sisters to live at Edgbaston, a posh neighborhood of Birmingham, with their aunt Mary Butlin, Anne's sister, who occupied herself in "managing trust

Figure 3.1 Sir John Ellerman and Bryher, undated. Unsourced photograph provided courtesy of the Schaffner family archives.

funds."[5] In 1876, Ellerman apprenticed to an accountant in Birmingham rather than entering public school or going into his grandfather Reeve's law firm. By 1881 John was living as a boarder in Edgbaston, working as an "account clerk."[6]

Bryher kept her father's alpine journals, cherishing his dangerous 1882 expedition traversing the Seserjoch pass between Zermatt in Switzerland and Alagna in Italy.[7] John's surviving travel diary, also from 1882, marked "Private" and "Rough," reveals a whimsical side to the incipient Midas. He relished whist games with other passengers, chatting with the ship's captain, and dreaming of faraway places—Elba, Pisa, Constantinople, Paris, and glaciers. He sketched in pencil, even improvised:

look at this the beautiful moon
how splendid it is to
be on deck walking with
the girl you love with
nothing but the moon
above you and no one else nearby[8]

After qualifying as a chartered accountant with highest marks in 1886, Ellerman was hired by Sir William Cuthbert Quilter, a stockbroker and Liberal member of Parliament, instrumental in founding the Institute of Accountants, not an easy man to impress. Before joining Quilter's firm, Ellerman insisted on four months' leave per year. After receiving his grandfather Reeves' bequest of £14,000, about £2 million in today's currency, he set off to climb the Himalayas; striving to ascend Everest, he suffered debilitating frostbite. Another hike in the Swiss Alps nearly caused his death in an avalanche.

A mere two years later, Quilter offered Ellerman a partnership, but he rejected it. At age twenty-six, in 1888 he opened his own business, J. Ellerman and Company, at 10 Moorgate Street, London. He began creating new companies by destroying old ones. Like latter-day capitalists, he identified ventures ripe for takeover. His first purchase, the Brewery and Commercial Investment Trust, appreciated 13,000 percent in nine years.[9] Technological advances, especially the conversion to steam propulsion, made commercial sea ventures less risky, and he snapped up his first line in 1891.

Over the next decade, he spent little time in London, yet consolidated most of its shipping companies. In 1901, he seized an international prize from John Pierpont Morgan, who sought a monopoly of the Atlantic routes. Agreeing to cede them for fourteen years, Ellerman, as part of the deal, swooped up five major shipping lines for a lower price paid in cash, while still retaining routes to Montreal and Antwerp.[10] The deal meant that Ellerman controlled the commercial fleets from Europe to and around Africa, the Middle East, and India, more than compensating for the transatlantic routes sacrificed.[11] Consolidating Britain's expansion efforts, Ellerman transported supplies during the Boer Wars, leading to his barony in 1905. Ellerman's coat of arms displayed two anchors and the head of an eagle, recalling his German roots. Bryher incorporated its insigna, "Loyal jusqu' à la mort," loyal until death. By 1917 he controlled one-eighth of all British shipping tonnage, the equivalent of the entire French navy.

A *Times* obituary configured him as "undoubtedly, a financial genius," who "conducted his vast operations" and "worked unobtrusively but pulled many important strings and wielded much power."[12] A seer of economic events, Sir John correctly predicted the Great Depression. Regarded as an entrepreneurial marvel, he despised celebrity, screening himself and his family from paparazzi. The *Daily Mail* described "the son of poor German emigrants" whose wealth at his death "could buy a whole fleet of shipping with his pocket money" as a man who "never overstepped his rule of strict moderation."[13]

Around the time he began purchasing shipping lines in 1891, Ellerman met Hannah Glover. Details of their courtship have not survived. But this fact pales next to the veiling of her familial origins. Hannah was as if lifted out of nowhere. Like his taste for obscurity in business, Sir John kept his lover's past under wraps. Heavily muted, she was reputed to have said, "He keeps me in a glass case but I keep human."[14] Even in her death, her plinth at Putney Vale Cemetery bears no year or place of birth, only the name Lady Hannah Ellerman, widow to Sir John, while a large mound honors John's mother, whose epitaph bears at least her timeline.[15]

Bryher described her mother as "full of temperament together with a sense of art, that, in her case, was translated into love." She suspected Hannah, silent about her past, "must have had a Celt among her ancestors," tying her to one of H.D.'s lines, claiming that her "mother's side" hailed from "Middle English, not actually from Warwickshire." This casting about, "unable to confirm," exposes Bryher's lifetime inability to know her mother's exact birthplace, leading her to fantasize her mother grew up near "Shakespeare's Stratford."[16]

Guest speculates that Hannah was previously married to George Glover, but this is debunked by both Sir John's obituary in the *Times* and Bryher's younger brother's birth certificate, which confirm George Glover was Hannah's father.[17] The census locates a likely Hannah Jane Glover, born in the first quarter of 1867, in Birmingham, Warwickshire.[18] In the combined Bryher and H.D. archive, reference to Hannah's birthday, January 2, 1867, appears on two astrology charts; prediction in the discipline hinges on the precise birth date. Silvia Dobson, H.D.'s admirer and friend, made in the early 1930s a circular chart of the main figures in the couple's life, and other horoscopes, including Lady Ellerman's when alive, making it doubtful H.D. didn't obtain the precise date. Moreover, numerous letters reveal Bryher's angst at being compelled to be in London at the New Year for Lady Ellerman to celebrate her birthday in early January. But the very fact of there being a controversy over Lady Ellerman's origins foregrounds the family's cherished secrecy, tinted with shame. Before she died in 1939, Hannah burned most of her personal correspondence in a bonfire.

It is likely Hannah's father, a bootmaker born in 1820, in Worcester, Warwickshire, wedded Mary Glover, born 1824 in Weobley, Herefordshire. In 1875, Hannah's father died in Birmingham.[19] Her widowed mother returned to Herefordshire in 1881 as a lodger, but it is unclear if her children accompanied her. By 1891 the trail goes cold, though Hannah appears to have worked in millinery. She helped stitch and brocade a wedding gown for Princess Mary on the occasion of her marriage to the prince, later George V, in 1883.[20] The elaborate gown, embroidered with emblems of a rose, shamrock, and thistle, trimmed with orange blossom and true-lovers knots, required a large entourage. Bryher mourned that her mother could have been a famous dressmaker, observing that "she would have enjoyed having such an establishment," but "her whole life was devoted" to Sir John. She embroidered exquisitely, dressing dolls by "copying old pictures in minute detail."[21] She was disappointed that Bryher didn't identify as "Dolly."

Why Bryher's Victorian parents did not marry is unknown. Historical evidence suggests that stigma surrounding such households had been relaxed. Based on Bryher's sense that Hannah potentially could have succeeded as a dressmaker, the couple's crossing of class barriers may be the answer. Other groups who did not marry were bohemians and socialists.[22] As a pioneer of industry, Ellerman forged new methods, and he likely rebelled against social conventions to pursue Hannah. Referring to her mother "as something of 'an anarchist,'" Bryher hinted at Hannah's choice of love over law.[23] Hannah Glover dissolved into Lady Ellerman. With the swift erasure induced by a name change, her past smudged out, emboldened by her suitor's monetary stability, she embarked on a romance, birthed an illegitimate child, without marrying or scandal.

Like her parents, Bryher kept her cards close. Her memoir, *Heart to Artemis*, focuses on her as a historical being, formed by "a second Puritan age," with early memories of "the sound of hooves" from horse-driven carriages on cobblestones, where "[a]n epoch passed away while [she] was learning to speak and walk." As a child, Bryher wanted to be "a cabin boy and run away from the inexplicable taboos of Victorian life" rather than follow the mandates of "thou shalt sit down to lunch every day at the same time, thou shalt not go out without gloves." She refused to romanticize the treatment of children born in the nineteenth century, a period when they "were imprisoned for a variety of minor offense[s]," and "unmarried women without incomes were treated like slaves." Those vulnerable and unattached raised the specter of her mother's mystery and her own gender nonconformity.[24] It was "a myth" as well "to suppose that the 19th century child felt particularly secure." Bryher knew something of her mother's early privations. Dorothy Richardson, her beloved novelist of thirteen volumes titled *Pilgrimage*, featuring the economically strapped Miriam, captured routine horrors, such as "the disruption of a family through the father's failure in business," a reality "essentially religious in character." As a child, Bryher was "never afraid of animals or the dark," but "they always began to tremble" when hearing "that trade was bad."[25] The Ellerman household, driven by ambition and insecurity, followed the booms and busts of the business cycle.

At an early age, Bryher wanted to be free, disliking the material world of heavy, oversize furniture, immovable luggage, all attempts to hide the world's fragility. She viewed her cumbersome long locks, tangling painfully, as part of the burden. From her perspective, she was a boy, a profound feeling that could not be talked away, and deemed layered petticoats, veils, muffs as designed to keep women from the sun, rain, and wind; she longed to be naked and wild.

The child's insular ménage, consisting of her parents and herself, did not stay put, relocating several times, traveling extensively abroad. Bryher had wordless memories of sea sounds and smells. Not yet three, she experienced a "historical" moment, catching from windows the fireworks and Queen Victoria's Jubilee celebration on June 22, 1897. They relocated the next year to another seaside town, Worthing, ten miles west of Brighton. Bryher mostly played alone, bolstering a belief of "never again be[ing] so completely a whole."[26] Her father took her on seaside walks, captured with snaps of the careerist father on an empty road, before his career skyrocketed, his daughter in uncomfortable ruffles a couple yards away (Figure 3.2).

As a child, Bryher ran away over and over, heading toward the sea. When she caught sight of steamers, she longed for stowaway status, gathered from boys' books, like Robert Louis Stevenson's *Kidnapped* and *Treasure Island*. Of course, the secret would be *to not* appear on the ship's manifest. Each time her father dragged the child home from private adventures or escapes, "something died."[27] Reading, she built a bridge to the outside world, books her dearest allies. But when her nanny offered "Little Red Riding Hood," she threw a fit. Teaching herself to read was a "great victory," attributable to her stubbornness, a quality she prized, reading "every scrap" in her father's library, from novels to timetables.[28] An early favorite, Pastor Johann

Figure 3.2 Bryher and her father, c. 1897. Unsourced family photograph, Bryher Papers. Courtesy of Beinecke Rare Book and Manuscript Library, Yale University.

David Wyss' *Swiss Family Robinson* (1812), featured a family leaving their homeland when Napoleon invaded in 1798. On their voyage to Australia, they are shipwrecked on an island and survive on reefs of their own making, through communal efforts.

Bryher began reading G. A. Henty before 1900. While he published 121 books of historical juvenile boys' fiction, quite popular in Bryher's era, the author's imperialistic and embedded racist perspective has tarnished his reputation. Yet his novelistic renderings led Bryher to puzzle over subjugated populations by colonial forces that could result in unexpected hybridities. Obsessed with migration, Bryher learned geography from her father, setting off in an armchair for distant lands.

Based on her promise not to run away again, in 1900 her parents took her, at age five, on the first of many foreign adventures, a trip across the Channel to Paris for the Exhibition.[29] This trip was eye-opening. When they arrived, the British were engaged in the Second Boer War, started in October 1899, to end on May 31, 1902. Sir John profited handsomely while helping her majesty's navy. Although France remained officially neutral, Bryher spotted American flags in the buttonholes of fearful British tourists. Parisians heckled her and her parents. An initial reaction prompted taking up the cudgels for Great Britain, playing the jingo. After her father explained the distinction between British Royalists, who stood for safety and prudence, and the French ideals of "liberty, equality, fraternity," she adopted the latter. "Everything at that time had to curl: there ought to be some special term to describe the horror a blank space evoked in 1900," the child judged the Exhibition.[30]

With pastry in hand, still in Paris, Bryher gave way to "adventures, and the wind in the branches, the open stall, the food that I was actually holding in my hand, all were a reality straight out of one of my books." Thanks to her German governess, she was given her own cart in the Champs-Elysées. "Astride a horse," Bryher was "a warrior at last." Her father lunched with "elderly gentlemen whose black beards came down to the bottom of their waistcoats" at a café frequented by ministers, she listening at his side. Feeling at home with men, she thought politics exciting and heard whisperings of the Dreyfus affair. There is a photo of the young adult at five surveying the Exhibition grounds (Figure 3.3).

Shortly after returning to England in 1901, she watched the queen's funeral procession on February 7. That same year, at age seven, Bryher read and learned by heart *Tales from Shakespeare* by Charles Lamb and his sister, Mary. A few years later, she hallucinated Imogen from *Cymbeline*, her then favorite play. Peering out at Bayswater Square, the railings became "gently moving reeds, there was water flowing over the gravel path and Imogen herself was standing with her back to me among the rushes." Bryher's powerful memory, hitched to sensory experience, ensured that if Imogen was mentioned, she smelled "the turn of the century and the bitter scent of the slowly burning leaves."[31]

Between 1901 and 1907 her family spent part of every winter but one in Italy and from there embarked to the south, twice to Egypt and once to Sicily; in 1905 they traveled to Spain and Algeria, and in 1908 and 1909 to the South of France. They spent summers in Switzerland with "sandwiches of time in France and England."[32] In

Figure 3.3 Bryher in Paris for the World Exhibition, 1900. Unsourced family photograph, Bryher Papers.
Courtesy of Beinecke Rare Book and Manuscript Library, Yale University.

essence, Bryher's childhood consisted of travel with her parents, not regular schooling. When not abroad, she had tutors, and in one diary lists her favorite subjects as geography, grammar, and history, with fencing "best of the lot," hating German, tolerating French, ending her list with "Howling. No words can describe."[33]

When the Ellermans ventured to Cairo in 1903, they confronted rough, dangerous routes, not suited for tourists. Without passports or motorcars, they journeyed by steamers and trains, dusty and unheated, and sometimes rode horses, mules, or camels. Even though they booked the best accommodations possible, they worried over food and potable water. Nobody around them spoke English. Together they followed the footsteps of the Robinsons, facing smallpox, measles, typhoid, malaria, cholera, influenza, and robbers—a realm of adventure. Not yet ten, Bryher met a fellow traveler, Dr. Boyce, strongly in favor of vaccinations. This, with her mother's partial deafness due to childhood scarlet fever, fed an obsession with germs and inoculations.[34]

Bryher's first impression of Egypt matched that of an earlier traveler, Gustave Flaubert, who in 1849 "gulped down a whole bellyful of colors like a donkey filling himself with hay."[35] Although the family hired a guide, Ali, when they went for a picnic and were discovered by Bedouin bandits, he struggled to negotiate their release. Hannah apparently cried out, "They are going to murder us." Ali insisted the family had no alms, promising to send cash upon return to their hotel—which they did. Bryher relished these experiences. Statues and temples required reliance on camels or donkeys (Figure 3.4). "No one ever gets over their first camel," Bryher joked.[36]

In the Cairo marketplace, the child saw opium and hashish smokers on dingy scraps of carpet. She took up Arabic and sketched, practicing hieroglyphs and calligraphy.[37] Local merchants applauded when she managed the right Arabic word. Sitting cross-legged, Bryher learned the "art" of barter: not to really desire what was for sale, for "to desire it was to lose it." This warning haunted her. "They taught me to feel with my mind across to their own," she recalled. With the Egyptian Sufis, Bryher

Figure 3.4 Bryher in Egypt, 1903. Unsourced family photograph, Bryher Papers.
Courtesy of Beinecke Rare Book and Manuscript Library, Yale University.

developed restraint, not to react until "the touch of thought to thought was as actual as the turquoise hilt of the sword she wanted her father to purchase." Practicing to "think across" space through trance-like concentration, she watched dervishes give themselves up to possession, and herself gave in to an uncategorized spiritual experience: "something began to whirl in my own mind, I was not myself any longer, in a moment I might reach a state beyond my senses," feeling "very, very happy" to be "neither where [her] body was standing nor quite in the air."[38]

Her sketches from her family's trip down the Nile have survived: she drew an anteater, several crocodiles, making drawings in "cartoon" form—boxes on a letterhead from the "s.s. Republic" etched in. "This is Cairo" above her first box, then "The Pyramids" above a second. Above another she scrawled, "Mamma and I had a camel ride." Another marked a "petrified forest" and the last, "camels to tombs," and indicated their first day to the Pyramids and the sphinx. See fig. one. The next day we went to the obelisk and ostrich farm where dada bought an ostrich egg. See fig. two. The next day we went across on trolleys and had lunch on the little boat we had come in. See fig. three. The fourth day we went to Old Cairo and some mosques. fig 4. I mean dada Mamma. I mean me.[39]

They were a blended triad. On this trip, Bryher met an Austrian archaeologist who explained rudimentary hieroglyphics he studied on a wall. Following his lead, she sought symbols for owl, pigeon, and house on rocks with her fingers and heard stones singing. In Kom Ombo, a frontier post, she encountered three Black children, who when she asked them in Arabic if they wanted to play, ran away. She woke to the fact that whiteness terrified them.[40]

Upon return to England, Ellerman relocated his family to Eastbourne, 1 Duke Street. There, Bryher walked with her father at Pevensey Bay, where the Normans had landed. Her father treated her as a boy, indulged in some football if she behaved. A swordsman himself, he sponsored fencing lessons, enabling Bryher's growing attachment to the Elizabethans. She also learned to handle a horse.[41] While Sir John warned her that business would never accept women, Hannah's partial deafness pushed Bryher into a receptionist or "medium" role. The child took over the telephone, transmitting messages for or from her idealized father. Not yet ten, she functioned as parent, having to hear and translate what she received and convey it to her mother. Her father was lost in numeric abstractions.

With H.D.'s father in mind, Bryher later considered Sir John "would have been an austere Pythagorean," distinguishing how "[w]ords had wings for [her] but never numbers."[42] Synesthesia coupled with a photographic memory. Bryher saw and heard letters as colors "in several layers" and could even "feel the discord if there is one syllable too many in a sentence." The polylingual child even dreamed in French.[43]

At twelve, Bryher turned to history after having a vision near the ancient wall of Euryalus, fortress at Syracuse, where, according to mythic lore, fates were sealed. "Seized by the throat," barely able to breathe, "Tyre and Carthage to the Pillars of Hercules spun in front of [her]." With "a terrifying sense of ecstasy," she learned from Clio "to see *before* the beginning and *after* the end."[44] She planned to pursue archaeology and drawing, but when the chapter called childhood ended at fifteen, this was forbidden.

An unusual child, Bryher picked up her father's passion for "trade," yet her family's amorphous roots represented an anxiety, a possible trapdoor. Taking after her parents, who kept their past under lock and key, Bryher hid within the very folds of a modernism she helped create. Her globetrotting childhood imparted a lifelong frenetic need to travel and readied her mind for H.D.'s psychic explorations. H.D.'s maternal spiritual inheritance was a cosmic understanding that all souls are equal; Bryher's early travels revealed that national borders are porous, with teachers cropping up unexpectedly. Though ancestrally more anchored than Bryher, H.D. asked

Figure 3.5 Bryher and her mother on a ship, c. 1905. Unsourced family photograph, Bryher Papers.
Courtesy of Beinecke Rare Book and Manuscript Library, Yale University.

years later, "[W]hat is this mother-father / to tear at our entrails?" She reflected, "At the point of integration and reintegration, there is no conflict over rival loyalties."[45] Bryher remembered feeling whole.

Both Victorian mothers, Hannah and Helen, had truncated careers, one as a teacher, singer, painter, the other possibly as a dressmaker. Hannah's was really the "common woman's fate." Risen from it, she could not "change a cheerful and obstinate hippopotamus" into an "Edwardian miss,"[46] while H.D. was Helen's "odd duckling." In a photograph from 1905, Hannah sits, legs crossed, with plucky Bryher, open-legged like a boy, both smiling, evidently at Sir John, whose secrecy reinforced his daughter's daring modifications of family norms (Figure 3.5).

LINE 1

FLORIDE 1909–1919

4
Sentimental Educations

Ezra Pound was H.D.'s first romance, but Frances Josepha Gregg her first love, a precursor to Bryher. In 1901, Hilda's brother, Gilbert, and her friend, Margaret Snively, introduced her to Pound, a day before his sixteenth birthday, at a fancy-dress Halloween ball. From there, she embarked on a literary courtship with the flamboyant Penn student. One year older than H.D., born October 30, 1885, in Boise, Idaho, Pound grew up in a comfortable middle-class household. Early on, drawn to the "wild west," he aggrandized his paternal grandfather, Thaddeus, who had made and lost a fortune in lumber. He rarely acknowledged his maternal New England ties, even his distant relation, Henry Wadsworth Longfellow, the first American to translate Dante's *Inferno*. His family moved to Philadelphia, where his father, Homer, worked at the Mint.

Meeting for furtive kisses in the woods as teenagers, Pound called H.D. his "Dryad," a spirit of the tree. He shouted out poems as they flew down toboggan runs. William Carlos Williams found H.D. too "bony."[1] On an outing to Point Pleasant with her friend Margaret, she nearly drowned before being dragged to shore. This struck a dramatic chord, much like Pound's ecstatic performance in Euripides' *Iphigenia in Aulis*, where he became "the focus of attention" with his "toga-like ensemble topped by a great blonde wig at which he tore as he waved his arms about and heaved his massive breasts in ecstasies of extreme emotion."[2] Not surprisingly, Pound had recommended James G. Frazer's *The Golden Bough* (1890), which corrected the Victorian image of Artemis as "a straight-laced maiden lady with a taste for hunting"; for the ancients, she was the "embodiment of the wild life of nature" with "all its exuberant fertility and profusion," not virgin, then, but "unmarried woman."[3] He performed as Artemis herself.

In 1903, Pound transferred from the University of Pennsylvania to Hamilton College, studying romance languages. Meanwhile, H.D. graduated from Friends' Central School, an achiever on many fronts, including the basketball team, Scientific Committee, and Literary Society, in 1904 (Figure 4.1). Full of zest, she was confused. In 1905, she took the entrance exams for Bryn Mawr, passing all fields except algebra.[4] A month later, she enrolled as a day student, a logical choice with its doctorates in chemistry and mathematics. By September 1907, Pound had secured a lectureship at Wabash College in Crawfordsville, Indiana, and H.D. was a liminal fiancée. Before leaving, Pound introduced H.D. to Viola Baxter Jordan, who would become a lifelong correspondent, who read H.D.'s tarot cards. From early on, H.D. cast herself more as tree than its sprite, Pound's "Dryad."

H.D. & Bryher. Susan McCabe, Oxford University Press. © Oxford University Press 2021.
DOI: 10.1093/oso/9780190621223.003.0004

Figure 4.1 H.D.'s high school graduation photo, 1904. H.D. Papers.
Courtesy of Beinecke Rare Book and Manuscript Library, Yale University.

Pound composed *Hilda's Book*, spurred by Dante's *Vita Nuova*, between 1905 and 1907, while H.D. struggled at Bryn Mawr. Yet his poems generally subordinated women in his imagination. Craving the roles of both poet and muse, H.D. rejected Pound's insistence on their separation. She devoured Algernon Charles Swinburne (1837–1909), whose writing taught her about fluid eroticism. She reveled in the existence of Sappho, the Poet of Lesbos, and graduated high school in full bloom, but at loose ends.[5]

Excited and disturbed by Pound's hectic overtures, H.D. dashed her father's ambition she would be the next Marie Curie, though later called herself a "research worker in another dimension."[6] She knew science was kindred with art but couldn't prove this logically. After only three semesters, she had a "slight" breakdown, dropping out in January 1907. A doctor, recruited by her uncle Fred, advised against "overwork."[7] Throughout her life, she suffered bouts of overwork and of nervous depression.

Still at Wabash College, Pound witnessed provincialism firsthand. The town sported two music halls. The questing dandy, rebelling against narrow bigotry, invited an itinerant performer, a cross-dresser, to spend a night in his lodgings. The transvestite sleepover led to Pound's dismissal from teaching on February 14, 1908. In March,

Pound left for London, eager to meet his hero, W. B. Yeats. To this end, Pound wooed two new muses, Dorothy Shakespear and her mother, Olivia, who provided requisite introductions. That same month H.D. ended their engagement, a relief to her father.

Pound's belief in "gods" and heightened vision emerged, at least in part, from their brief courtship, his "Rendez-vous," a "courtly love" poem, addressed to his "lady," who "hath some tree-born spirit of the wood." His essay "Psychology and Troubadours" grew out of tramping the woods with H.D.:

> Greek myth arose when someone having passed through delightful psychic experience tried to communicate it to others and found it necessary to screen himself from persecution. Speaking aesthetically, the myths are explications of mood: you may stop there, or you may probe deeper. Certain it is that these myths are only intelligible in a vivid and glittering sense to those people to whom they occur. I know, I mean, one man who understands Persephone and Demeter, and one who understands the Laurel, and another who has, I should say, met Artemis. These things are for them *real*.[8]

For Pound, artistic process accorded with "the spell which has worked, to the witch-work or the artwork," making it possible "to say, therefore, that I saw and heard the God Pan."[5] Noticeably, Pound credited no women with mythic encounters. Yet H.D. took "witch-work" to heart, as a way of being and knowing the world.

H.D.'s breakup with Pound in 1908 left her "feeling that someone had tampered with an oracle, had banged on a temple door, had dragged out small curious, sacred ornaments, had not understood their inner meaning," focusing instead on "their outer value, their perfect tint and caring." An "irreverent male youth" had not "stolen" these "but left them, perhaps worse, exposed by the roadside, reft from the shelter and their holy setting."[9] H.D. defied hurt with determination. After "the blundering" Pound, she sought a female-centered creativity and an erotic double.

* * *

Born in New Orleans in 1885, a year shy of H.D., on the same day as Bryher, September 2, Frances Josepha Gregg was christened by Julia, her schoolmistress mother. Claiming Spanish descent, Frances came from a line "of taunted, thwarted, frustrated, passionate women."[10] Her grandmother Gertrude Heartt raised hell in the Temperance and Women's movements of the 1860s. Julia married an adventurer, Oliver Gregg, who went prospecting, never to return. Leaving a trove of letters and a photo of herself in another woman's embrace, Julia was a woman who loved women.

During her southern childhood, Frances witnessed a lynching, which left her with recurring nightmares. At eight, she attended revival meetings, only to reject organized religion, claiming direct contact with divine forces. Her mother "taught [her] all [her] fears," knowing where "each nerve vibrates." Frances thought her trouble was "a miasma in her brain that ha[d] risen from those swamps in the Southern States of

America where she was engendered." In the early 1900s, Grandmother Heartt brought Frances and her mother to Philadelphia, where they settled in a poor neighborhood in West Philadelphia. Frances rescued wounded kittens and starving children. An activist, Julia started the first school for Italian immigrants, rallying for their rights.[11]

Depressed, H.D. struggled to write poetry after dropping out of college. Her uncle Fred encouraged her to take an apartment in Greenwich village for inspiration in 1909, but feeling cut off, she returned home after five months, tired of "phonies."[12] Enrolled at the Philadelphia Art School as a scholarship student, Frances meanwhile "purr[ed] away the jagged corners of social inequality."[13] Early in 1910, H.D.'s lifelong friend Mary Herr, who attended the Bethlehem Seminary, invited her to afternoon tea to meet someone new. Her photo from her New York stint showed a bewildered H.D. in an artist's smock and tie, hair starkly drawn back (Figure 4.2).

After dissociating over ices and macaroons, she saw Frances Josepha Gregg, and "she knew why she had come." A slate-gray raincoat, her "slightly spotted face" and "stiff straw hat wound with a stiff gray veil" lent her, as H.D. framed it, "an old-fashioned appearance, a distinction in this room filled with the daughters of lawyers, doctors, professors, and over-successful wholesale merchants." Not a conventional beauty, with dark excited eyes and claw-like hands, a humbly clad Frances sat across from H.D. They sensed an unheard language as bond. Facing each other, "the present melted away and they were together in the past and in the future." H.D. fixed her gaze upon the "two veins, throbbing, midway between the space joining eye and ear." This new friend had eyes "the color of wet hyacinths."[14] A current of bodily and psychic energy traversed between them.

This meeting revealed H.D. could desire a woman as much as, if not more than, her former fiancé. Fred Wolle glimpsed her and Frances "soul communing" during their shadowy courtship.[15] Creating a bubble around them, they shared a sisterhood and poems, bonding over Swinburne's "Itylus," with its cry, "O sister, my sister, sweet fleet swallow." H.D. discovered—through Frances—an entry into being co-creative *through love*: "Love was a creature of the senses. Love was not the touching of hands, the meeting of lips."[16] Literal touch, though desired, was forbidden, and infrequently practiced.

Frances recorded H.D.'s unusual appeal "with a face that was daemonic, sexless as death, and as sub-human as a plant," brooding on it "like a thrilling, endless book," sensing in her "a constant ethereal drumming, like the communications beyond the bounds of the meager senses of humans, sight, hearing, that insects have as part of their sexual equipment."[17] They both would have delighted to learn that some insects orient direction by starlight.[18] They practiced reading each other's gestural thoughts. H.D. latched on to the image of a butterfly's antennae, suggestive of their thought transference at high velocity, finding confirmation in their beloved Keats, who wrote that poetry should so "strike the reader as a wording of his own highest thought, and appear almost as a remembrance."[19] Such ideas encouraged their affair, with its minimal "reality," unknown outside themselves. Frances became an Artemis follower, "lov[ing] green things, the sound of water, the chaste, untouched, the gold

Figure 4.2 H.D. in 1909 or 1910. H.D. Papers.
Courtesy of Beinecke Rare Book and Manuscript Library, Yale University.

and frozen daffodils too much. She was undoubtedly unwholesome. She knew no Latin."[20] Embracing the unwholesome and wild, H.D. mocked the smug set who condescended to this stranger.

On a bright spring walk in the woods on April 10 or 11, the same year reporters visited her father to discuss the arrival of Halley's comet, H.D. and Frances came to a patch of hyacinths, signaling the symbolic death of a glorious homoerotic union. The beautiful Hyacinthus ran to catch a discus but was slain by its falling weight; Apollo transformed the beloved fallen boy's blood into a flower through his tears. H.D. recited her "Wild Hyacinths," "O hyacinth of the swamp-lands, / Blue lily of the marshes."[21] Frances thought H.D., though casting herself as "the foolish shepherd," mocked her lack of expertise in classical mythology and astronomy. H.D. fled the brewing conflict, joining her family for dinner. As she ate, a vision of Frances in peril overwhelmed her, and she rushed from the table. Her family, accustomed to her whims, resumed eating. Frances had waded into a shallow dark river, ready to end it all. H.D. found her shivering on the muddy bank. Frances reported, "Hilda always declared that she saw me stars, stream, boughs and all." They glided "so closely entwined," Frances joined "the rhythm of Hilda's long, loping step," a memory that was "the nearest thing to the supernatural that [she had] ever experienced."[22] They communicated, beyond empirical reasoning. With H.D., Frances thought her "migratory soul" followed "the migrations of [her] body," fantasizing their souls met through "emanations."[23]

A doctor was summoned. H.D. undressed Frances, warming Frances' hands against her breasts. The next morning, Frances propped up with a breakfast tray, H.D. asked, picking up her undergarments, "*These???*" Frances' painful response: they were for the "needy," noting H.D.'s face "as wild and fleeting as a maenad's," and accepting the woolen combinations "bred in [Frances] a fealty to [them]," as she was "sure, has never been between woman and nether garment before or since."[24]

* * *

Pound wrote his mother January 1, 1910, "IF THE ARTIST MUST MARRY let him find someone more interested in art, or his art, or the artist part of him, than in him." Otherwise, they could "take tea together three times a week."[25] The "artist part" was expanding. In late June 1910, the returning twenty-three-year-old Pound flirted with Frances Gregg, who daguerreotyped him as "lithe and tall," with "eyes blue but small, fattish cheeks, slightly blobbish nose, a beautiful mouth with lips of dark unfolded sorrow."[26] A love triangle ensued, as they did throughout H.D.'s life—Frances fell for Pound in a brief encounter, amounting to a fleeting, diabolical kiss, understood as a holy bond until he cavalierly rejected her. She blamed her mother for calling sex either a "ludicrous anti-climax" or a "terror," making her laughable to Pound.[27] As the trio broke into a pair, Frances and H.D. shared a "wayside" passion but felt trapped by convention, the former a realist. "But there you have us, two girls in love with each other, in love with the same man," intent upon "the snaring of nice, safe husbands in due course. We got them," Frances modified bitterly, "Nice husbands, they were, but safe they were not."[28]

Pound sailed back to England in February 1911. No doubt his passion for Europe shaped a desire in Hilda and Frances to explore it. H.D.'s parents feared a reunion with Pound. Her father, she knew, was disappointed she did not pursue science. Julia Gregg, as chaperone, promised Mrs. Doolittle that she would bring her daughter back. The trio sailed on July 23, 1911, on a small French boat, *La Floride*, launching

H.D.'s inauguration to ocean liners and to her first "psychic" decade. H.D. was already twenty-five on this first voyage, the same age as Bryher when, with H.D., they independently went to the Scillies.

At odds with the formidable Julia, H.D. was propelled into yet another triangle. Julia promoted the romance, then interfered with it. Needing privacy to woo, the couple crawled to paradise "on hands and knees, over ropes and stanchions, then, grasping books and candy boxes under our arms, we held on to the edge of the lifeboat," finding "a place between boats large enough to spread a rug." They "sat happily for hours," cultivating clairvoyance between kisses.[29] "Kissing in a lifeboat under the tarpaulin" has cinematic possibilities.[30] The space between rail and lifeboats was so narrow H.D. once almost fell overboard. Julia, caught spying, rescued her. Outraged by Julia's intrusions, H.D. kept to poems the remainder of the voyage after a storm sent the Greggs to their cabin.

When the ship docked in Le Havre, H.D., intoxicated by Breton bonnets, the air's salty taste, and "magenta begonias," felt they "were wandering in the pages of a book." On their first stop, Rouen, she and Frances, drawn to the misunderstood "witch," feared Joan of Arc's pull, "strong and small." Visiting the saint's prison tower, the cobblestones warming their soles, they drifted toward her place of incineration. H.D. understood that "[t]hey had trapped her, a girl who was a boy, and they would always do that." By the time she wrote *Asphodel* in 1920, H.D. was addressing St. Joan through both Frances and Bryher, who liked pugilism: "They dragged your armour from you. You died defenceless," and herself not wanting "to be burnt, to be crucified just because I 'see' things sometimes."[31] Self-named "wee witches" in Philadelphia, Frances and H.D. in 1911 envisioned the terrible burning.

To save money, the trio spent the night in a hotel infested with bedbugs. Trying to convince her mother to change their lodgings, Frances spotted a bug that "walked as fast as a horse."[32] Before setting forth for Paris, they visited St. Ouen, founded in the seventh century, with stained-glass windows from the fourteenth to sixteenth centuries; one overlooked the cemetery, where the church sentenced Joan to burn on May 23, 1431. The threesome lit candles and prayed.

* * *

Frances memorialized being with H.D. on a train speeding across France: "We were beautiful, and we were doomed." Staring at their reflections, she saw "Hilda's head, like a second medallion, intaglio, beyond it, my own," set against "the mysterious excitement of being borne on and on through space while the eyes of those phantom girls met, out there." This doubling and merging fated their unnamed love to be "borne on and on through space."[33] Queer women were insubstantial in the world.

They museum-hopped in Paris. The bookstalls, the silver rain on the Seine, Notre Dame jutting into the sky, all intoxicated. At the Louvre, the Venus de Milo excited H.D., who felt she "caught something. That was the answer to prayer. Prayer was asking." After the gallery emptied of tourists, the statues opened up to H.D., who saw "something in their shapes people didn't see, couldn't see or they would go mad with it." She plotted with Frances to come after nightfall to investigate, from multiple angles, the statue of Winged Victory. Her "idea of Paris" was "a sort of holy, holy pilgrimage to the Louvre," finding reality "as if seen thorough a clear slightly magnifying bit of crystal."[34] Wearied by statuary, Frances nonetheless triggered H.D.'s "crystal" gaze, the former wanting to refine their concentration "to the point of clairvoyance," though the Greggs flinched at art as religion. Disappointed in *The Virgin on the Rocks*, Frances called it "a pouter pigeon of a woman with affixed simper." H.D. told Frances that "sex did matter" and "should be treated, and developed, as an Art." Responsibilities must give way so "that we should be artists." Hilda enthused, "The Louvre and the British Museum hold one together, keep one from going to bits."[35] Unlike Pound, she did not elevate art over all else, but art was spiritual to her, for the Greggs, an elitist pursuit.

* * *

While in Paris, H.D. and Frances visited Walter Morse Rummel (1882–1918), part of Debussy's circle. His middle name came from his maternal grandfather, Samuel Finley Breese Morse (1791–1872), a painter and the inventor of the telegraph. In *Asphodel*, H.D. explains to Fayne (Gregg), "His grandfather invented the morse code. Telepahtic. I mean telegraphic or something."[36] In August 1911, they attended a performance in his Passy studio. H.D. cast Frances as "the daughter of a Grecian slave and Roman Emperor."[37] Julia took offense. Rummel's playing enlivened H.D. through loving Frances, who was jealous, sitting between them, feeling like "a specimen insect," with nothing to offer.[38] Listening, Frances sobbed, while H.D. intently followed his notes, that would "[break] off a little crystal bead and fell down, down, down and broke with an infinitude of sound," making "the whole world vibrate." H.D. feared even moving, lest she "get out of key with something and the message wouldn't get through. Morse code. I am a wire simply." Before meeting Bryher, H.D. was already a "live wire" in a period thriving on the telepath and the telegraph, with "things, notes, voices in the air about them. X rays, Morse code." H.D. was convinced "[w]e are only just beginning,"[39] with science, art, and spirituality eventually revealed as intertwined.

* * *

By traveling with the Greggs, economy prevailed. H.D. stashed away her allowance in order to claim independence. She aimed to disentangle Frances from Julia and remain with her in London, yet the former was dissatisfied with Europe's treasures. Though drawn to May Sinclair (1863–1946), recognizing her as "her first English spinster," her manners garlanding her like "an aroma," Frances rejected most of the literati.[40] At one point, Julia and Frances tried dissuading H.D. from meeting Pound for tea as inappropriate. Such disagreements peppered their tour.

Pound counseled H.D. to ditch Frances; H.D. urged Frances to cut the umbilical cord. Extremely bold for the time, she proposed sharing a flat with her co-phantom in Chelsea and argued her case with Julia, who, according to Frances, "wept, wailed, and gnashed her teeth across two continents, accusing Hilda of robbing the widow of her orphan, destroying its morals, besmirching its innocence, leading *it* to betray the sainted duties of daughterhood." Likewise, H.D. railed against Julia, who understood homoerotic affections, for denying her daughter's independence.[41]

Near the end of their sojourn, in the hot summer of 1911, Julia was inspired to go to Birmingham and Manchester, both housing large Pre-Raphaelite collections. To save on a hotel, Julia, a woman who salvaged every piece of string, ate every speck of egg, recycled fabrics, proposed they return to London the same day. Although a pro at deciphering the ABC train timetables, H.D. canceled close to departure. Venturing into the industrial cities, housing the discordant lushness of the Pre-Raphaelites, the Greggs toured Birmingham Museums and Art Gallery, opened in 1885, holding tapestries, sketchbooks, and watercolors of John Everett Millais, Rossetti, and William Holman Hunt. Moved, Frances "loathed Rossetti with a deep and vindictive hatred," judging his works to be "painted in treacle" and "his emotions saccharine."[42] She recoiled from "high art," divorced from common troubles—like battling bed bugs.

Not as enriched as Birmingham's collection, the Manchester Gallery held over one hundred paintings, including the 1882 Holman Hunt portrait of Rossetti with Svengali eyes, boring into Frances. Rossetti's lush portrait of William Morris' wife in *Astarte Syriaca*, a hypnotic goddess whose painted hands flirted with her breasts, bewildered Frances as unfair aesthetic, purveying women for worship while treating them as lesser beings. As if fulfilling Frances' own wish to rid the world of Rossetti's work, three suffragettes in 1913 attacked and damaged artworks, among them this one. Parliament had defeated at least eighteen bills to give women the vote; this was one of their militant acts.

Frances, bred to be a feminist, thought her co-phantom, like Pound, set art above love. Yet H.D. summarized Pound's mistaken idea that "'Love doesn't make good art,'" to which her autobiographic alter, Hermione, deftly rejoins that "love is art."[43] Frances probably feared her mother's control, and their poverty placed an artist's life outside her reach. Between Pound and Julia, the corpse of her love affair with H.D. awaited cremation. Frances chose returning to America with her mother. In October 1911, Pound and H.D. saw them off at Liverpool Station. After more than three months of excitement and bickering, disappointment assailed both sides. H.D. began regular studies at the British Museum in November.

* * *

Back in America in 1912, after hearing the lecturer John Cowper Powys, in Philadelphia, speak on distasteful conventions restricting sexual expression, Frances approached this unusual being, handing him her poem "Perché." Powys liked it and subsequently visited the Greggs' downtrodden flat on Derby Road. She found in him a secret-sharer, Heathcliff to her Cathy, in correspondence lasting two and a half decades. Yet he was the culprit that introduced Frances to Louis Wilkinson, a lecturer and writer, sent down from Oxford for membership in the Blue Tulip Club, known for staging parodies of Christian rites. A proponent of free love, Wilkinson wrote a supportive letter for the incarcerated Oscar Wilde.

In exchange for giving Frances children, Wilkinson bargained for complete sexual freedom. Agreeing to the pact, they married at St. Stephen's Church in Philadelphia on April 8, 1912, with Frances planning a reunion with H.D. Once in London, she invited H.D. on the continental "honeymoon," with Wilkinson lecturing against sexual taboos. Tempted to abandon her tenuous London roots, the day the newlyweds scheduled to leave for Brussels by way of Victoria Station, H.D. readied to depart with them. Her heart still throbbed for Frances. Shoving her into a cab, Pound banged his cane all the way from Oxford Circus to Victoria, browbeating her for ruining Frances' chance at happiness. In their youth, he had given her Balzac's novella *Seraphita*, with its "he-her." H.D. was perplexed by Pound's efforts to shut down unconventional sexuality. Yet she changed her plans when she spied Frances' "long tulle travelling veil."[44] Pound waited with H.D., watching the train depart, en route, it turned out, to Hades. *Paint It* admitted "[t]hey loved," that "theirs was a remote and impossible sisterhood."[45] H.D. later explained to her friend Viola Jordon about her "great shock" of loss, describing her crossing "in 1911 with a very dear friend, my most intimate with the one exception of Bryher."[46]

* * *

Pound's ambition was as fierce as the flammable kisses he gave muses, his singular aim to write "the greatest poems ever written."[47] Craving celebrity, his creative process was bound up with women as ideals or drudges, not agents or actors. Slashing at English Victorians and American philistines, denounced as sentimentality, he told his father that "the man's further and subtler development of mind puts a barrier between him & a woman to whom he has become incomprehensible."[48] Ultimately, modernist sexuality and art failed Frances Gregg. Characterizing herself "as real as a carrot" in contrast to the artistic set, she tracked Pound's decline as he "clung to his beret and velvet jacket and the flowing tie even when a round paunch and a ruddy countenance made them pathetic."[49]

Part of Pound's problem lay in his conception of the creative process as equivalent to ejaculation. He brashly asserted "the power" of "the phallus or spermatozoid charging, head-on, the female chaos; integration of the male in the male organ. Even oneself has felt it, driving any new idea into the great passive vulva of London, a sensation analogous to the male feeling in copulation."[50] This was perturbing masturbation to H.D.'s ears. Indeed, Moody surmises "that [Pound's] genius is to be the idealization of beauty, not the actual presence of a woman."[51] Altogether dismissive of "charging head-on," H.D. asked: couldn't muse and poet overlap like heavenly bodies, the inspiring and inspired, in a process of dynamic, re-creative metamorphosis?

* * *

Before H.D. voyaged to Europe, Bryher turned fifteen in 1909, and everything changed. In preparation for the birth of his son, John Jr., Ellerman purchased a mansion in Mayfair, 1 South Audley Street, close to Hyde Park and adjacent to the Dorchester Hotel. Bryher discovered her parents were unmarried. They slipped off to obtain a "Scotch marriage" to ensure the legitimacy of Bryher's expected sibling, covertly spending a compulsory twenty-one days in Edinburgh, from September 22 to October 14, with witnesses to corroborate their residency.[52] Scotland retained medieval canon law, conferring the privileges of marriage retroactively. In this way, they made the new baby a rightful heir. Without the "Scotch marriage," English law, which did not penalize cohabitation between adults, was merciless in its treatment of offspring and mothers. Elizabeth Gaskell's novel *Ruth* exposes the effect of the New Poor Law of 1834, requiring nothing from putative fathers.[53] Hannah was mute about the romance that led to Bryher's birth, but unlike Gaskell's Ruth, her suitor did not discard her. Legally, Ellerman might have easily denied mother and child any claim to his estate.

Bryher's childhood utopia, basking in her parents' love if not their understanding, abruptly ended with her brother's birth on December 21, 1909. Her parents focused on the baby boy, cooing over its future possibilities. Postpartum, Bryher's mother fell ill to unnamed ailments, unable to travel.[54] This shift threw the teenage Bryher into paroxysms, not only of anger and jealousy but, worse, despair, over her illegitimacy. Silvia Dobson, H.D.'s later London friend, imagined the wounding: "Bryher envied first boys, then men. She and Vita Sackville West had cause to do so. Had they been males they both would have inherited fortunes, great houses, ships, prestige."[55]

Reaching adolescence, Bryher described her sense of self as "[t]wo personalities uneasy by their juxtaposition. As happy together as if a sharp sword were thrust into a golf bag for a sheath."[56] She could not morph into her mother's ideal. A larger horror loomed—she believed she was the punchline of a terrible joke. Wishing to turn boy failed, the prospect of becoming a woman, unbearable. Seeking solace in her father's library, Bryher found a leather-bound William Hazlitt's *Dramatic Literature of the Reign of Queen Elizabeth*. There she met Bellario, whose identity, neither male nor female, was a unity. Bellario saved her mind.[57] Uneasy with the "signs," Lady Ellerman must have felt inadequate—Bryher knew she "presented a problem," wanting lessons in Arabic and drawing instead of clothes. Tending to stare through others, she "had only to enter a room to upset visitors."[58]

After several such upsets, her parents enrolled Bryher in Queenswood, originally a French finishing school for English girls, close to their Eastbourne home, twenty miles from London. Bryher was a day student. She prayed to die before the first day of school. Her closest allies had abandoned her. Miss Lillie J. Chudleigh ran the school with the help of her "partner," Miss Edith Johns, M.A., a classics scholar. The school was, however, "a terrific shock"; she "did not understand the school," and "the school did not understand [her]."[59]

The chasm between her childhood travels and this "violation" led her to dramatize her captivity in 1910 as being "sacrificed to the prevalent spirit of the age."[60] Yet the

Figure 4.3 Bryher on a ship, with notebook, 1912. Unsourced family photograph, Bryher Papers.
Courtesy of Beinecke Rare Book and Manuscript Library, Yale University.

school confirmed her rebellious spirit and autodidact self. On a brighter note, she met Doris Banfield. They began summer sojourns in Cornwall, sailing in the Scillies. During her mother's lying-in, she had discovered the blank space where her father's name should be on her birth certificate. Inspired by a trip with Doris, "Dolly" ritually took the name of an uninhabited island, expunging Annie Winnifred.

It is both odd and fitting that the school's history was written by a classmate, Dorothea Petrie Carew, *Many Years Many Girls: The History of a School, 1862–1942* (1967), dedicated to Bryher, "one Old Girl who wishes to remain anonymous but who generously defrayed all expenses for the considerable research required."[61] Carew decided the school performed the "slightly dangerous feat of actually educating girls on much the same lines as their brothers."[62] Yet when Bryher wanted to study archaeology at the University of London, her parents forbade it. Stuck at Audley supervising her brother, Bryher puzzled how to materialize an identity. A family shot shows the eighteen-year-old with her mother, clutching a sketchbook, wearing a resistant look (Figure 4.3).

5
Love & Art
Being Phantoms Together

Remaining in London, H.D. tried forgetting Frances Gregg. Pound introduced her to Brigit Patmore (1882–1965), an effervescent socialite with golden-red hair and pale gray eyes, who catalyzed sexual liaisons in several modernist circles. Her father abused her mother, whose "love of sorrow" haunted Brigit. Witnessing domestic violence as a child justified marriage on pragmatic grounds. Seeking entrance to literary circles, she wed John Deighton Patmore, a materialistic insurance salesman and philanderer. His grandfather, the Victorian giant Coventry Patmore (1823–1896), wrote the best-selling poem "The Angel in the House" (1854), teaching every good wife to cater to her husband.

After inviting her to the Piccadilly Club, Patmore called H.D. "the tall girl," "too fragile for her height and build," detecting "extreme vulnerability," with a "wild and wincing look in her deep-set eyes" and "a magnificent line of jaw and chin."[1] Brigit also introduced H.D. to Violet Hunt (1862–1942), who held salons where younger writers mixed with venerable ones, such as May Sinclair and Yeats, who admitted, "I was in all things Pre-Raphaelite.... We were all Pre-Raphaelites then."[2] H.D. met Richard Aldington through Brigit at Sinclair's home near the end of 1911. Born in Hampshire on July 8, 1892, Aldington grew up in Dover. Financially strapped, he attended only a year at University College, teaching himself French, Italian, Latin, and Greek. By early 1912, H.D., Aldington, and Pound were a gang of three, and Sinclair, taken with them, bequeathed 50 pounds to each.[3] Sinclair argued Christianity failed for "not being spiritual enough," recommending mystic detachment, a theory H.D. understood.[4]

Adrift and grieving after Gregg left, H.D. was an eager partner for Aldington's Poet's Translation Series. Together they studied Greek through "one of Imagism's sacred texts," *Select Epigrams from the Greek Anthology* (1890; second edition 1911), edited by J. W. Mackail (1859–1945).[5] H.D. left for Paris in May 1912; Aldington followed. That spring they became lovers and co-creators. From Brigit's line of sight, "[t]heir obsession with expression was almost like a drug."[6] They wrote in the Luxembourg Gardens, sketched at museums. H.D. imagined that "the thing between them, that they conjured up together," made them artists.[7]

After returning to London on September 26, 1912, Pound, at the British Museum tearoom, abbreviated Hilda's name to H.D. She recounted his response to her work: "'But Dryad' ... 'this is poetry.' He slashed with a pencil. 'Cut this out, shorten this line.' ... And he scrawled 'H.D. Imagiste' at the bottom of the page" of "Hermes of the Ways."[8] Notably, "Hermes" translated Anyte, "called by Antipater 'the woman-Homer,'" with its original in *Poems of Meleager*.[9] H.D. embraced the initials as a way to both hide and express; her small poem, however, grandly summoned the "thrice-greatest Hermes," a divine teacher of alchemy, invoking Pythagoras, persecuted for heretical wisdom and his hermetic texts.

In thrashing the nineteenth century's tendency to amplify, Pound found his ex-fiancée's lyrics ingeniously trim. His former muse now a poet, Pound wanted credit for making her one, forwarding her poems to *Poetry*'s editor, Harriett Monroe. The March 1913 issue showed Aldington and H.D. making Pound's theories praxis, capturing an "intellectual and emotional complex in an instant of time."[10] Imagism may have allowed H.D. canonical entry, but for her, the movement was exhausted, simultaneously with her becoming its *blueprint*.

* * *

In October 1912, H.D. rendezvoused with her parents and childhood friend Margaret Snively in Genoa. From there, they set off for Florence, Pisa, and Rome, enjoying the Vatican in December. Her father took Italian lessons; her mother shopped and sewed. On assignment for A. R. Orange's *New Age*, writing travel articles, Aldington joined the Doolittles in Rome. There, H.D. and Aldington studied Sophocles, Theocritus, and *The Greek Anthology*. He thought her a new Theocritus, a pastoral poet with small poems of contentment—not borne out in her poems' embodied awareness of a world about to crack open.

H.D.'s mother grew fond of Aldington, recounting his attentiveness; he escorted them to a Bach festival, scouted cafés, and guided them to Italian sites he was paid to review. "In Pompeii the bees hummed softly over the dwarf wild flowers among the ruins," Aldington relished, "while we rested and looked drowsily at the white smoke ebbing from Vesuvius. At Sorrento there were the freesias under the orange trees." The pair translated, swam, and made love, Aldington enjoying H.D.'s contagious, giddy responsiveness to art so that she "understands so perfectly, re-lives the artist's mood so intensely, that the work of art seems transformed. You too respond, understand, and relive it in a degree which would be impossible without her inspiration."[11] Already a medium, she transcended the roles of poet and muse.

In June, H.D.'s parents shepherded her from Capri to Austria. At Innsbruck, struck with a wordless imperative, H.D. backtracked to Paris to tell her parents she would remain in Europe. Arriving on July 8, Aldington's birthday, they decided to marry—or else face the world's scorn, or worse, H.D. would be pressed to leave London, her geographic-literary heartthrob. In August the couple headed there, occupying discrete units on Church Walk, H.D. at #6, Aldington at #8, with Pound at #10, and John Cournos, a Russian American journalist, at #14.

In September, the month before their marriage, the *New Freewoman* joined them under the banner "The Newer School." Aldington's "To Atthis," his Sappho adaptation, headed H.D.'s "Sitalkas," with "phonetically difficult" and "rare" references to Delphic Apollo, "protector of corn" and "northwest wind, the 'brightening' or 'whitening' wind of autumn."¹² After their "unofficial honeymoon in Italy," and before Pound's *Des Imagistes* appeared, the couple married at a registry office in London on October 18, 1913, her parents and Pound as witnesses.¹³ The couple moved to 5 Holland Place, while Gregg and husband settled into #6, the very flat H.D. and Aldington had vacated. With H.D. still etched on her heart, Gregg had married, and committed "to do it all, with [herself] as specimen in my soul's laboratory." Without H.D., she "was a woman dead."¹⁴ Enjoying Aldington's affinity, H.D. still remained emotionally bound to Gregg, now a phantom neighbor. In metamorphosis, H.D. was drawn to hurling seaweed, rock, sand crabs, flotsam, other animal life upon the shore.

* * *

H.D. and R.A., as H.D. called him, were excited by newly recovered Sappho fragments, "salvaged from among masses of illegible papyrus scraps coming to Berlin from Egypt in 1896." Successive excavations of an ancient tangible world startled modernists—Troy *had* existed. This was the same year that a German Egyptologist "bought in Cairo a manuscript" containing "the Gospel of Mary (Magdalene)," along with the *Secret Book of John*.¹⁵ Such findings raised hope that a sacred past could be reconstructed. One could follow the footprints of Jane Harrison (1850–1928), pioneering classicist, linguist, feminist, and the first woman appointed to any full-time academic post, at the progressive Newnham College, Cambridge. Her *Prolegomena to the Study of Greek Religion* (1903) traced Greek ritual and the placating of ghosts. Beginning with primitive sacrifices, the governing supernatural powers progressed from inchoate forces, such as sprites and demons, to gods; finally, ritual evolved into the "Mysteries," guiding humans toward the divine.

In 1913, *Poetry* printed three of H.D.'s poems, "Hermes of the Ways," "Priapus," and "Epigram." The last acted elegy for Gregg, with its phrase "Gone the dear chatterer." Pound placed Aldington's "To Atthis" in *Poetry*. In lines such as "I yearn to behold thy delicate soul / To satiate my desire," he condensed modernity's "sustained lament for an absence," Sappho "remembered across the sundering sea."¹⁶ R.A. ventriloquized Sappho and claimed all his girlfriends experienced cunnilingus with another woman.¹⁷ "To Atthis" entered Sappho's gymnasium, tantamount to a fashionable young girl's school, with a focal teacher in the arts, sparking others. In this way, H.D. and R.A. embraced Walter Pater's notion that "artists and philosophers" are not isolated "but breathe a common air and catch light and heat from each other's thoughts."¹⁸ By January 1914, H.D. and R.A. had plotted escape from Pound, with Aldington as co-editor to Harriet Weaver Shaw for the *New Freewoman*'s successor, *The Egoist*.

* * *

Receiving *Des Imagistes* in February 1914, Bryher, cocooned in Mayfair, read it eagerly, regretting her *Region of Lutany* appeared almost simultaneously, with one poem asking, "How shall I tune my lute to sing thy praise / Mysterious Sea?" Without an addressee in 1914, she recollected being "nineteen but incapable of action, split into three persons, an outer one trying to say yes and not at the right moment, a second self full of phobias as the direct result of such conformity and a third occasional layer of insight where I worked."[19] Among her phobias, she felt "queer numb apathy" and "terror of going even through strange doors."[20]

On July 17, 1914, Lowell organized a dinner party at London's Berkeley Hotel. Her plan to publish Imagist anthologies frenzied Pound. D. H. Lawrence attended, compensating for Pound's departure. The "group" now consisted of Lowell, Frost, Fletcher, Lawrence, Flint, H.D. and R.A., who noted they were "fed up with Ezra."[21] Threatening legal action, Pound demanded the Bostonian strike Imagism from her vocabulary. "It was a time of isms. And the ballet," H.D. reflected.[22] Playing diplomat, H.D. tried easing Lowell out of "Imagists" in her title: "Things gets worser and worser! Our great and good friend is taking up 'Imagism' again—don't you think *we'd* better drop it? R. wants to—H.D. wants to—Flint wants to—E.P. is making it ridiculous.... Poor Ezra—what blunderingly stupid things he has done!" Inspired by the six members of the Pre-Raphaelite Brotherhood, H.D. offered the title "THE SIX": "We would all be individual without being an ism and we would, in addition, be a group! ... *Our dropping the title gives him the satisfaction of feeling that he has secured—victory and gives us the exquisite relief of being free of him.*" Besides being attached to numbers, H.D. prized being an "individual" in need of creative collaboration as love.[23] After all, the Latin *collaborare* signifies "the work of a couple." Changing all of poetry, all of life, during Lowell's visit, on August 4, 1914, H.D. discovered her pregnancy the day Britain declared war on Germany after its attack on Belgium. The war, Kenner observes, "snuffed out the age of unrivaled prosperity and unlimited promise."[24]

* * *

The loss at Ypres on October 19 brought a flood of Belgian refugees to London. By December, Aldington, not yet mobilized, felt "war is killing us all" and "making us prematurely aged." In 1915, the couple moved to a larger flat at 7 Christchurch Place in Hampstead, further from Pound. Lowell published *Some Imagist Poets I* the same year, showcasing H.D.'s poems, among them "Sea Rose," "stunted" with "meagre" petal, withstanding flux, implying reader and poet could survive destructive forces. Good tidings also came from H.D.'s winning the Guarantor's Prize from *Poetry* for "Wind Sleepers," "Storm," "Pool," "Garden," and "Moonrise."[25] Depicting the limbo of war during her pregnancy, H.D.'s "Mid-Day," with "its hot shriveled seeds," appeared in the *Egoist* above Richard's "In the Tube."

H.D. internalized external events. Thus she believed Aldington screaming over the sinking of the *Lusitania* by a German U-boat on May 7, 1915, precipitated her stillbirth two weeks later. Ironically, the *Lusitania*'s cargo—1,248 boxes of empty shells,

50 tons of steel—came from Bethlehem Steel in her hometown. The ship's military freight was among the justifications for the submarine attack. Spared the sight of their dead infant, a distressed Aldington, after the fact, wrote Lowell newborn "was very sturdy but wouldn't breathe."[26] Lawrence, Sinclair, and Patmore visited at Prince's Gate Nursing Home, where the doctor warned H.D. against carrying another child.

The Germans' second Zeppelin raid, on September 8, 1915, caused more damage than all the year's air attacks combined. It "drifted" like a "Leviathan, a whale swam in city dusk, above suburban forests," H.D. narrated for Lowell, "the exciting night" with "the Huns."[27] Wounding her leg "terribly" but "refusing all aid or even sympathy," she rushed outside to catch a better glimpse at "the tip-tilted object in a dim near sky that even then was sliding sideways and even then was about to drop." Her wound was "annihilation itself" that "gaped at her."[28]

On November 1, 1915, "Choruses from Iphigeneia in Aulis," H.D.'s first translation of Euripides, emerged in the *Egoist*, its distinctive chorus heralding Iphigenia as agent: "Your name will never be forgotten." By scholastic standards, her command of classical languages was not profound—nor was that of R.A.—yet Eliot praised H.D. as the "exception" in Aldington's *The Poet's Translation Series I–VI*, singling out her "fresh contact," a poet needing "perpetually to draw sustenance from the dead."[29] In 1919, he would write his manifesto, "Tradition and the Individual Talent," which has drawn criticism from midcentury confessional poets; he actually supported H.D.'s own practiced method, developing "a concentration which does not happen consciously or of deliberation," yet saw no need for "new emotions"—they were simply scaffolding.[30] Yet H.D. did seek, if not novel feelings, then words for unnamed experienes.

Inspired, H.D. worked intensively on *Sea Garden* through 1915 for its American publication, and into 1916 for the British edition. She possessed a perfectionist's curse:

> The artist who is forever seeking the right colour or the right word or the right line or the right combination of angles and squares that may lead to a new optical instrument or to a new slant or level of an air-ship, is eternally tortured, till the thorns on his brow blossom into roses.[31]

Though written in 1943, this portrait spoke of lifelong pains to be both accurate and inventive; art required an engineer's precision and *vision*. During the Great War, H.D saw her quest: to express her thrill in natural processes and energies, foregrounding the unknowable, imperishable in them. She asked the orchard god, "Spare us from loveliness."[32] Ravaged flowers with spilt dye irradiate the volume. With surety, she *knew* Hermes as "more than the many-foamed ways / of the sea." The Egyptian god of writing, Thoth, doubles for the Greek Hermes, responsible for sacred writing and guide for those leaving for an afterlife. Impelled by Sapphic dactyls, H.D.'s "desperate sun" pierced "sea-mist" for "late ripened" apples.[33]

In January 1916, Houghton Mifflin brought out H.D.'s debut, *Sea Garden*, where "wave-lengths cut" through windy sea expanses as well as "leaf-mould and earth," part of a mosaic of elemental fragments,[34] "pebble and wet shells and seaweed,"[35] embracing both "waves" and "particles." Almost simultaneously, the *Egoist* printed "The Cliff Temple" for the New Year's edition, driving mortals toward the divine so that "[t]he world heaved—/ We are next to the sky," with "breath caught," being "lurched forward," at a cliff.[36] Repetition stalls the poem's pace, calling on a "daemon" to survive the natural devastation caused by man-made warring. She finally told Lowell they were "hard up," wanting a "little fund 'for desperate artists.' "[37] Lowell complied. By the end of February, the couple had relocated to 44 Mecklenburgh Square. The landlady, a prewar suffragette, wore George Sands trousers and jacket.

Before mandatory conscription, Aldington recoiled at the idea of someone "weaker" than himself at the front. In May 1916, he enlisted as a private in the 11th Reserve Battalion, Devonshire Regiment. The *Egoist* notified readers in June that "Mr. Aldington will shortly be called up for military service," giving "the assistant-editorship" to "Mrs. Aldington," steadily writing poems in 1916. With the backdrop of war, *Sea Garden* exposed an untamed world, its flowers "streaked" "marred" "flecked," and followed broken petals, troubled ecosystems. In March, "The Helmsman" recalled "we" who "forgot" that "we loved all this"—"enchanted with the fields," with a haunted sense of knowing an unnamed "*you* wanted us."[38]

Escaping London, the couple rented a cottage in Devon, soaking up the "wild and pagan" daffodils, violets, and snowdrops. H.D. readied *Sea Garden* for Constable, delayed by wartime paper scarcity. She found it "horribly uneven" due to its prewar and wartime genesis, this very hybridity satisfying.[39] By May, Lowell had published *Some Imagist Poets, 1916*, prominently featuring H.D. and R.A. H.D.'s poems made words elemental. "Sea God" conjured a "broken hulk of a ship," facing "sand—drift—rocks—rubble of the sea," where "[they] are cut, torn, mangled, / torn by the stress and heat."[40] H.D. took to the battlefield. The army promoted Aldington to lance corporal in August 1916, the same month H.D. admired Marianne Moore's poetic strategy "that holds, fascinates and half-paralyzes us, as light, flashed from a very fine steel blade."[41]

Receiving a "double check" from Lowell, H.D. was "very glad for [her] share of the swag."[42] In August, Aldington recruited the Clerk's Press in Cleveland to publish forty handmade booklets of H.D.'s *Iphigenia*, with a ship's insignia at the end, the pages even serrated, cut like choppy waves. Throughout 1916, Aldington felt doomed. H.D. edited and submitted his work so that he "feels he is not being forgotten."[43] In September 1916, R.A. joined H.D. at 44 Mecklenburgh. In October, H.D.'s "The Tribute," appeared in the *Egoist*, with the desolation of a city, a "heap of refuse / and the broken shards," while the boys leave for war.[44] She moved between numbness and dread. During Aldington's leaves, only a ghostly emanation survived their once finely tuned bond. From Waterloo Station on December 11, she saw Richard off and asked Lowell to assure her parents she was well.[45] (H.D. liked to communicate by proxy, otherwise finding it potentially overwhelming.) Aldington shipped out with the 6th Leicesters, a Pioneer Battalion, spending New Year's two miles from Calais, billeted near Loos.

* * *

Bryher worked on her autobiographical *Development,* rewriting it at least four times during World War I. After an air raid, she and Doris saw their "first bombed house," inspecting "the heap of glass swept into the gutter, tinsel, debris of a fête that even the wind had no use for." It was "unreal," "pre-historic." Smoke encircled men "dusting splinters out of ledges."[46] When Bryher "gripped the bannisters," "even the wood did not convince [her] of reality or that [she] was actually [herself]."[47]

While the world destroyed itself, Bryher was maroooned. Her father's vast fortune, estimated in 1916 at a staggering £55 million, dwarfed that of all other British subjects. His family consequently were targets of paparazzi as well as class antipathy, anti-Semitism, and German xenophobia. Of German extraction, Sir John fit the commonly held sterotype of the Jewish capitalist.[48] Anticipating public resentment, he bought up media shares, gaining the *Sphere* and *Tatler,* the *Illustrated London News,* the *Daily Mail,* the *Times of London, Sketch* and *Eve,* "an impressive slice of Fleet Street."[49] By the end of 1916 he had refurbished a hospital, paid for its equipment, defraying its operating costs for its first year. Opening on January 27, 1917, it admitted ex-army and -navy officers permanently disabled or paralyzed in combat. The press rarely mentioned Sir John. One paper he owned no interest in, the *Daily Chronicle,* decried his substantial wealth as a threat to national security because of his German and suspected Jewish ancestry.[50]

* * *

On the French battlefields, engaged in "grief duty," Aldington erected crosses and reconstructed demolished trenches, living "among smashed bodies and human remains in an infernal cemetery."[51] Lucky to get cold beef, he endured lice, unsanitary latrines, and mustard gas, learning the best defense was a piece of cloth soaked in urine pressed to his face. H.D. tried trusting there would be a "new-time" for "formative deep-sown earth-grains."[52]

Samuel Hynes describes World War I as "the first English war to be reported and photographed in daily newspapers, and the first to be filmed and shown to the public in cinemas," enlisting "those from the middle-class and upper-class volunteers, men who could read and write."[53] Asking H.D. to send *The Golden Bough,* Aldington watched his ideals crumble, blaming his parents' generation for their patriotic pandering to an imperialist culture. Bread rationing began in February 1917. Already excessively thin, H.D. had "flayed nerves," facing "the constant brutality of the present," "walking on a very, very thin wire,"[54] what Virginia Woolf later described as "the narrow plank of the present."[55]

The 1914 Defense of the Realm Act classified Lawrence's wife, Frieda, a Prussian, as an enemy noncombatant. In his rough boots and corduroys, Lawrence, with "his narrow chest, his too-flaming beard," stood just a tad shorter than H.D. From Cornwall, he urged her to "run her pencil down a page, or rather let it run for her." His initial enthusiasm led to "Eurydice" and "Pygmalion," published February 1, 1917. The latter inserted inspiration into artifact: "Which am I, / the stone or the power /

that lifts the rock from the earth?" "Eurydice" showed Orpheus compelled to turn back, only to lose her. The poem crackles, darkness providing definition: "What was it you saw in my face— / the light of your own face, / the fire of your own presence?"[56] Orpheus, representative male poet, achieved poetic fame by pressing his bride back into the underworld. H.D.'s Eurydice celebrated darkness, casting away Lawrence's sex theories that decreed "man-is-man, woman-is-woman."[57]

This helped H.D. differentiate from Aldington, telling Lowell her signature was "for poetic purposes," asking "to keep HD clear from RA, R has his career + it is best for him not to have me as an appendage."[58] One now asks, who was the appendage? In May 1917, Eliot, newly appointed editor of the *Egoist*, wrote his mother of his two female "colleagues": Mrs. Weaver, a "spinster," and "Mrs. Aldington, better known as 'H.D.', a poetess." He even sought out the courtyard at 44 Mecklenburgh, locus of domestic upheaval, "beautifully delapidated."[59]

In July 1917, Aldington attended the officers' training school in Litchfield, Staffordshire. In August, John Cournos asked H.D. if his love interest, Dorothy Yorke (1891–1971), an American fashion plate, could occupy H.D.'s room at 44 Mecklenburgh. With her jet-dark hair and eyes, the group's nickname for her, "Arabella" approximated her carnal appeal. Now an oversexed man showing off his uniform, Aldington returned to 44 to begin a full-blown affair with Arabella. H.D. could only repeat that Pound "just does not matter."[60] Later she pasted in a scrapbook several incarnations of Aldington, one in uniform, with a profile of Lawrence, looking askance (Figure 5.1).

* * *

While R.A. alienated H.D., Bryher embarked on a literary adventure, studying Elizabethan cross-dressing, and, convinced America was a poetry mecca, the culture-hungry Bryher introduced herself by letter in September 1917 to Lowell, who smoked cigars and lived openly with the actress Ada Russell. *Men, Women and Ghosts* (1916), she assured, accompanied "[Bryher] in all sorts of places, on boats, in a donkey cart, on the sands, recognizing it as one of "the great studies of loneliness." Bryher craved "a dreamed association with some mind, whose speech" corresponded "to every thought of the listener."[61] Praising Lowell's "In a Garden," innovative in its expression of female homoeroticism, "Bombardment" created the sense that "one was actually hearing the guns and the whir of the aeroplanes."[62]

Bryher bragged dodging institutions of learning, depending on her father's library. With no real friends but Doris, war kept her "from exploring new poetry." Fascinated by H.D.'s initials in "'A Sea Garden' [she] hope[d] to get next." Now twenty-three, Bryher sent Lowell *Development*, preemptively belittling it: "There is always the waste paper basket." Her brother, age eight, she wrote, loved being read "Roxbury Garden." Aside from tutoring John Jr., Bryher, tamped down, inhabited a household where "enthusiasm was a crime."[63] In the family shot in Figure 5.2, we see her with her brother. Wearing pearls, holding a book of poetry, she stuns, looking beyond the camera. Her

Figure 5.1 Scrapbook with clippings of D. H. Lawrence and Richard Aldington. H.D. Papers.
Courtesy of Beinecke Rare Book and Manuscript Library, Yale University.

brocaded empress-style gown was cross-dressing, from her point of view. Looking at her face, we spot imperious eyes, distress, a slight smirk, and a gloved hand over one with bare, possibly dirty fingernails. She sits, her young belted brother clasping her, already more inches than her head to torso.

Through corresponding with Lowell, Bryher began a lifelong passion: writing letters to distant friends. Reading *Tendencies in Modern American Poets* as "a series of love affairs with the great masters," and "especially" drawn to "the essay on H.D," Bryher trod carefully, with her essential desire not to hurt, calling H.D.'s writing "cold and hard" and "very beautiful and most interesting from a technical point of view." She seized on two sentences from *Tendencies*: "Her extreme sensitiveness turns appreciation to exquisite suffering. Yet, again and again, she flings herself upon the spears of her own reactions." Lowell depicted H.D. as willful masochist, not far from her perfectionist credo.[64] Bryher memorized *Sea Garden*, disagreeing on the "absolute disuse of inversion," admiring H.D.'s restitching of lines, making the end the beginning, reversing time.[65]

Lowell counseled Bryher to accept the fact of her family's wealth—"my father's in cotton, yours in ships"—also giving her the good news that Monroe accepted Bryher's poems "Wakefulness," "Rejection," and "Waste" without revision.[66] "Tease[d]

Figure 5.2 Bryher and John Jr., undated. Unsourced photograph, provided courtesy of the Schaffner family archives.

unmercifully over the failure of [her] attempt to be someone else," at her father's urging, she apologized for using an assumed name.[67] Not explicit about *missing* a male body, Bryher shared her anomaly of seeing consonants as colors, where "B" "represents a deep crimson, C is white, D black, F a rich brown, almost a red, sometimes, etc."[68] For her, poems, like illuminated manuscripts, glowed "in innumerable colors."[69] It took ten gratifying weeks for Bryher to write A *Critical Appreciation of Lowell* (1918), thanking her friend for giving her "a whole new world."[70] Lowell complained that her acolyte overlooked some of her best poems. Clement Shorter, a friend of Sir John's, editor of the *Sphere*, and author of the 1896 *Charlotte Bronte and Her Circle*, printed two hundred copies: sixty went to newspaper editors, the others sold.

* * *

The year 1917 tortured H.D. Evicted from Cornwall mid-October, the Lawrences decamped at 44, suitcases jammed against shelves, complete contingency. They displaced Arabella, who then shared the sitting room with H.D., who slept on a camp bed behind a partition, which the rival invaded to fetch the teakettle. Suddenly this new chaos in a tight dress demanded H.D. make way. H.D. hid her "Eurydice."

In late November, Aldington received a commission as second lieutenant; granted a year-end leave, he returned to 44. Musical rooms ensued. Lawrence scribbled, supped tea. Frieda knitted and smoked her pipe nonstop, toying with pursuing their friend, the half-Scot young composer Cecil Gray, who suffered a heart murmur, which kept him from soldiering. H.D. started seeing people as colors. Aldington compared H.D.'s poems, their "austere" and "profound passions," with "that beauty which only Platonists know."[71] But Plato's lofty forms crumbled as Aldington's mortality stimulated his longing for sex.

Shortly after his return, Aldington slept with Arabella on the top floor, leaving H.D. below in depression, devastated by his assertion "I love you & I desire—l'autre."[72] At her lowest ebb, she destroyed a ten-thousand-word poem. Then Cecil Gray arrived. Over his slightly flabby cheeks, his wispy hair stood on end; bookended with large ears, a beaked nose punctuated his face. Much too twee, he admitted being "bouleversé," stricken after hearing explosions. Walking together among soldiers, H.D. foresaw thousands of dead, unconvincing wartime songs reason enough to title her novel in process *Madrigal*, prose ode, the tentative title, a word perhaps raised by the musical Gray, signifying several voices counterpointed in Renaissance song. Gray invited H.D. to Cornwall early in 1918. In the New Year, Aldington returned to France as an officer in the 9th Royal Sussex Regiment. He saw his commanding officer killed and survived a gas attack in March. On a furlough, he raved in his sleep.[73] Fed up with Aldington, H.D., like a sleepwalker, arrived at Bosigran Castle in March 1918. Unmarried, in separate rooms in a square house, Gray lay pale after picking blackberries. Without real passion for him, she translated the chorus in *The Bacchae*.

Aware of her escape, Aldington asked after Gray's health.[74] While surrounded by "too many dead men," an "unending misery of all these thousands,"[75] he taunted her over "the beauty of those Cornish hills & the tranquility & comfort of a pleasant house," with "clean wind & flowers, and inside books & white linen and more flowers." H.D. likely said Gray provided some stability, for Aldington replied, "[I]f Gray can give you sanity from that marmoreal calm of his, then indeed he is not one that gives nothing."[76] By July 1918 Gray had left for London to escape conscription—and H.D.'s intensity.

Wandering alone, H.D. collected cyclamen and violets, climbed rocks, watched gulls, and took the road to St. Ives, with its anemones, gorse, and chamomile, sensing the "sacramental power" of Druid priests who fashioned circular stones like those at Stonehenge. Her stride convinced her she was breaking from a sex-obsessed crowd toward "a cold healing breath" that "enclosed" her "in crystal." But this wasn't just marriage woes. She cultivated her animist gifts while walking, tied to her "every breath," "charged with meaning," the falling mist "almost in separate particles." Shifting from logic, she gave way to heightened awareness, "filled literally now with the divine Spirit." As a "see-er at home in the land of subtle psychic reverberations," she considered "a pattern on a leaf ... holds the soul of the forest, as one salt drop, the ocean's." Being in Cornwall also redelivered her dear grandfather, herself acting botanist, in "heather country," where "tight bunches of heath were rock-plants from another continent," yet part of "remembered flora." Bosigran "loomed" "suddenly like a grey ship." She "rejoic[ed] in herself, butterfly in cocoon."[77] A sexual dalliance turned into spiritual reconsolidation.

"I love you too—too much," Aldington wrote, recalling his *Reverie: A Little Book of Poems for H.D.*, published by Clerk's Press in 1917. One poem cast the couple as "[we] two together in a land of quiet / Inviolable behind the walls of death." He had "hallucinations," one of which was "battling along," and seeing "Joan of Arc on her white horse in the barrage-smoke." He diagrammed their ordeal: "How does it seem from your angle of the triangle—or perhaps one should say acute-angled rectangle?"[78] While H.D.'s letters to Aldington at the front are missing, he recognized their "similarly framed & equipped" minds that made them poets rather than philosophers, moved by "the glory of the perishable—beauty, love, intoxicatingly, flowers, moods, the sea, all things that are transient and lovely."[79] Yet H.D. intuited an eternal dimension mirrored the ever-changing one.

* * *

Learning from Lowell that H.D. lived in England, Bryher "began to meditate an attack on her." In fact, H.D. was staying near Doris, in the very next village, "chosen instead of Scilly," off-limits in wartime; Bryher asked if she could visit.[80] On July 17, 1918, Bryher headed out as a storm brewed. With the door opening, Lawrence's "woman-as-woman and man-as-man theory" fell to pieces, H.D. instantly intrigued by this strangely familiar creature.

H.D. was drawn to Bryher's "enormous eyes" with a "commanding look," noting her head dragged down by "hair twisted in two enormous coils."[81] The look was commanding and prophetic and enabling for H.D., delighting in such idiosyncrasies. Bryher was "an extremely pretty creature, with eyes too intense for this generation, with bare feet too perfect, with slight arms too delicate, for all their wiry play of little nervous tendons."[82] They studied each other's faces and bodies like maps.

The week after this meeting, Aldington snarled at H.D. from "a hole 30 feet underground with a pint of water per diem," with "biscuit for food,"[83] wanting to know "more about this new admirer of H.D," adding, "She must be very wise since she can love your poems so much. Has she a name or is she just some anonyme?"[84] By now H.D. had guessed she was pregnant with Gray's child. An uncharacteristic two months passed before star-struck Bryher wrote Lowell about visiting H.D., casting herself as "a whirlwind disturbing a calm Sicilian day. We were both, I think, afraid of the other—till we got to the South and Greek." She would have gone to Cornwall "as usual" with Doris, sleeping "on a flat roof," her "very first experience of sleeping out in the open." She "was in pieces," not upset by Lowell's many criticisms volleyed at *Development*, just overcome by H.D., who promised Greek lessons. The Bostonian picked up the code.[85]

Thanks to Lowell's tutelage, the 1918 *North American Review* took two of Bryher's poems, having another "moment of pride"—"The Girl-Page in Elizabethan Literature," "immediately accepted" by the "Fortnightly Review," proving her desire to be a boy was not an isolated condition, with "no less than 30 examples" from "well known Elizabethan plays and it persisted in one form or another throughout literature."[86] Bryher's "passionate desire to make [her] dreaming real" spurred the essay, believing she spoke "Elizabethan" as a child, projected "as the little boy with puffed sleeves and a ruff that I had once seen sketched by a schoolboy on the pages of a Latin grammar."[87]

The autobiographical essay favored Middleton and Dekker's *The Roaring Girl*, based on the historical Mary Firth, a daring roustabout who broke the law, performing in men's clothing. During the Elizabethan Age, it was "impossible for any unprotected woman to travel alone, "save as a man," leaving "dramatists to fit their heroines with doublet and hose." "These girls," Bryher asserted, submitted to dangers when "food was not always easy to obtain," "where maps were scarce, and discovery was punishable as a crime." These girl-pages were Bryher's rescuers. She knew, of course, boys dressed as girls to play girls dressed up as boys, but this gender reversal satisfied. With Mary Firth, she found "the realist description of what a girl had to suffer directly she put on doublet and hose."[88] Meeting H.D. incited its swift publication, trying to substantiate a nonbiological gender.

* * *

After H.D. met Bryher, Aldington, likely from a trench, obsessed over the complications of H.D.'s pregnancy. Among his litany of instructions to her, he assured her not to worry, that he would "accept the child," yet insisted a biological father doubled as "spiritual mate." H.D. begged to differ. Then, withdrawing his offer to legitimate, he warned that no court would grant a divorce because of his adultery. Ultimately, he could not accept Gray's child, with the memory of their "sweet dead baby."[89] Freeing her "to have lovers & girl lovers," they could no longer be "imperishable sweet comrades."[90] But as self-judged gynecological expert, he advised H.D. to masturbate and to have "a sort of orgy straight off," to bring on what he hoped in August was delayed menses, though warning her to "only do it once or twice a week."[91] H.D.'s pregnancy exposed man-made customs as untenable. He was adamantly against abortion. "Look at Brigit," he wrote, "she is not the gay sweet creature she used to be."[92] By September he was offering his name again. H.D. evidently told him "to grow a shell," as he quoted her back.[93]

* * *

Early days, H.D. asked Bryher to assist Aldington through the critic Shorter, whom Bryher invited to a birthday party arranged for H.D. Aldington advised Bryher that Lowell "lacks something," juxtaposed to H.D.'s "restraint & dignity." Aware of Bryher's spectral relationship to H.D., he described the latter's "sharp edges and austere style," "near perfection," and moreover, was a "Theocritus only keyed up a note higher."[94] The same day, Aldington wrote excitedly to H.D., "Bryher realized what 'Captive' means." Her own *Development* had a chapter, "A Captive Year," describing her boarding school, "Downwood," as "a dust-heap of dead individualities. The girls filed out, face after listless face."[95] He told Bryher, well-read in Thucydides' *History of the Peloponnesian War* and the 413 BCE destruction of the Athenian fleet, she was *the first person* to understand his poem "Syracuse," meaning "the whole expedition, the fight in the harbor, the quarries."[96]

Aware of a "belle anonyme" in the fold, Aldington assured H.D. she was free "to make any kind of 'liaison,'" so long as "some sort of elementary social camouflage is used." Making space for Bryher, he nearly conferred his blessing, having "never worried about G," as in Gray, not Gregg.[97] Two months after meeting Bryher, the same age H.D. was when setting forth to Europe, she wrote Lowell:

> I met that Bryher girl in Cornwall. She is about 24. I think, too, shows great promise.... She comes from wealthy people. Do not tell her I told you as she is very queer about it. But her wealth could make no difference to you, nor to any real friend. She imagines any kindness & interest comes *only* because her father is reported "the richest man in England." Of course, one can understand, but if she is any good at all, her fathers [sic] position won't hurt her. (Her name is not Bryher.) Of course, I did not know this when I met her, and my interest was genuine.

Surmising Bryher as a "German jew (as you suggest) extract," H.D. glossed over her visitor's evident eager love of all the poet stood for: secret names, ancient cultures, psychic phenomena, the thorn of perfectionism. With her talent for crystalizing visions, she stared at candles, wearing a plain linen tunic, to improve focus. In October, H.D. began framing a future for Bryher, who, much like herself, had "a romantic idea that she wanted to be on her own."[98]

Armistice was declared on November 11, 1918, followed by jubilant chorusing and flag-waving. For Bryher, destruction left a greater impression. The London gas lamps, cleaned and relit, did not stop her imagining England might have lost the war; it and pregnancy and a possible new relationship battered H.D., who felt like "the froth or the nothingness of the crest of the black wave." In *Paint It Today*, H.D. crafted a Hellenic London, reenvisioned through love of a creature, "one with the small people with hummingbird claws"; Bryher was cast as Althea, "explain[ing] them to me."[99] Bryher's early attempts to explore matched H.D.'s. The war's "restraining fetters" only increased desperation. Wanting her hair very short and to wear boy's clothing, Bryher overflowed with attraction, erotic and intellectual, for H.D. and suspected Lowell thought her mad.

Slowly entangled, Bryher anchored one vertex of a triangle when H.D. learned on November 4, 1918, that her brother, Gilbert, had been gunned down in France in the battle of St. Mihiel on September 25, 1918. H.D. revealed her pregnancy to Bryher in December. This fueled a desire to help Aldington, who pressured Bryher *through* H.D., ordering, "Get Miss Ellerman down, tell her I have got this plan out, with work for her to do; & together sit on Shorter's neck."[100] A buffer from these fits of regret and rage, Bryher engineered a dinner for Aldington with her father. Impressed, Sir John wrote Bruce Richmond, editor of the *Times Literary Supplement*, recommending Aldington.[101] Thanks to Bryher, Aldington sold six articles on his wartime experiences, yet this cost her. The recently widowed man of letters was "queer in the head" from grief, and Bryher complained, "He almost spies on my every movement,"[102] probably encouraged by her mother, who "persecuted [her] to marry him" and now "hates the sight of [her]."[103] Shorter eventually married her friend Doris in 1920.

Writing H.D. steadily in 1918, Aldington understood shared mortality as a pathway to creativity. Knowing she functioned independently of her initials, Aldington proposed to Dooley, "Why not assassinate H.D."[104] Pound, he pitched, was uninterested in "humanity," arguing that "[o]ne acts & yet at the same time one reflects on action," a poet as much as a nonpoet, "simply because one is convinced that what happens to humanity happens to oneself."[105] Aldington dismissed "the dead-egotism of Pound," who cut himself off from "common humanity—which is fundamentally the same with who Christ walked with and Plato talked with & Villon played the scoundrel with." Ordinary lives belonged to "the true romance, that treats living truth which makes vital our love of beauty, our knowledge of dead worlds—here, I mean, on this earth." Bryher resonated with this "true romance." In December, H.D. wrote Bryher about a fantasized trip to Delphi, thinking she'd need "two years preparation," though, as if realizing she had met the person with whom she would spend most of her adult life, she modified, "we have many, many years ahead" of "expressing & scratching & writing."[106]

6
Romance of Rescue & "the Jellyfish Experience"

Early in 1919, Bryher was not the picture of stability. Frustrated at her daughter's rejection of women's clothes and finding a husband and her new fascination with a poetess who went by initials, her mother worried she was abnormal. Bryher ruminated about suicide and kept a bottle of rat poison, just in case. She feared her parents would block her fresh relationship. *Two Selves*, inspired by H.D., depicted veiled threats of a Harley Street doctor. Other respectable families used the hysteria card to manage wayward daughters, such as "[t]he girl round the corner" who sought escape: "They had shut her up. With two nurses." "If you spoke straight out your thought they called you queer," she telegraphed, "at all cost they would fight to break this."[1] H.D. was "the first real artist" Bryher knew, and H.D. quickly grasped Bryher's ensnarement.[2] After all, by Bryher's age, twenty-five, H.D. had roomed in New York and London, traveled, had a lesbian affair, married, lost an infant, and had an affair, resulting in pregnancy.

Demobbed in February, Aldington still considered himself H.D.'s primary reader, faulting poor spelling and excessive "inversions,"[3] warning "[D]on't submit your ms. *ever*" until he caught "little careless errors in spelling & syntax." He reminded, chillingly, "H.D. cannot afford to be anything less than perfection."[4] Bryher soon challenged him in an "erotic rivalry encrypted in ancient texts."[5] Before H.D. knew what to do next, she stayed with her girlhood friend, Margaret, then living at Speen. Dissociated, preparing to give birth, she dragged herself across Richmond Park, spotting "blue soldiers" wrapped in hospital gowns and sitting on benches. Writing on Valentine's Day to "Dear Girl," H.D. thanked Bryher for a bed coat, enclosing part of a new poem, "Thetis," the goddess-mother of Achilles. Calling *Development* "an inspiration," H.D. appreciated its "strength and real intensity & beauty," urging Bryher to send it to Havelock Ellis, and to Patmore, "so intensely interested in women who are more than women." Though still ailing, "inclined to crouch a bit over the fire," H.D. had "new plans," and they would "be a real incentive & stimulus to one another." This crouching was also emotional, invoking the snake, ambulant on earth, linked to the original mother. After rereading *Development*, finding "bits of prose, like poems," H.D. sent drafts of "Hymen," the title poem of a new volume she dedicated to Bryher and Perdita in 1921. Gratified Bryher understood "*Hymen* as a form," she had "already planned four or five others," wanting to know "[W]ould you call them masques?" She already trusted Bryher as androgyne authority, aware of subtle historical or poetic questions.

If H.D.'s "Eros" captured a lesson—"yet to sing love, / love must first shatter us"[6]—"Hymen" upended the marriage ceremony: the bride enters; no groom actualizes. Love momentarily arrives, departing with "a crash of cymbals." A band of boyish girls celebrate Artemis, with her "steel arrows." H.D. sent it to both Aldington and Bryher. He circled the word "'maidenhead,'" alerting it did "*not* signify virginity," while "'maidenhood'" meant "'sex of a maiden' in Elizabethan English." "Is that precisely what you wanted to say at that point?" he quibbled.[7] Learning this, Bryher pleaded that "[g]rammar never was poetry or prose, either," ordered her not to "alter a word to please him," for "maidenhead" with "maidenhood" revealed a happy off-rhyme, conflating "head" with "hood," male with female, present with past.[8] "For no reality whatever will [she] surrender,"[9] H.D. echoed back, securing "[t]hat all the wood in blossoming, / May calm her heart and cool her blood / For losing of her maidenhood."[10] Witnessing her husband's sex-crazed side, she craved tranquility. H.D. also sent her admirer "two songs," "Simaetha," her Sicilian "piece—rocks, smoldering fires, anemones, twisted olives—very wild and savage," and "Leda," the mother of Helen who hanged herself, "quieter in tone—birds, flowering grass & hyacinths."[11] Simaetha chanted "burn burn away / thought, memory and hurt!"[12] For *Hymen*, H.D. also penned "Evadne," one-time lover of Apollo, which expands its interpretation when we consider that Artemis and Apollo are twins, both queerly oriented on numerous occasions, and that H.D. saw Bryher as Artemis, goddess of both the hunt and midwifery; H.D. evasively superimposed these figures, likely addressing Bryher when she wrote, "I, Evadne," feminizing Apollo, with "crisp hair," "flower of the crocus," sinking into a "great arm-full of golden flowers." Bryher represented protection from males, who masqueraded as all-important sun-gods.

After reading *Development*, Aldington liked H.D.'s "little friend's book," "immature, but in some ways startlingly like you."[13] She possessed a "superb gift of realization of beauty & a clear imagist method of writing." "A prose H.D.," she had "pages of quite magnificent stuff."[14] H.D. read it, "an inspiration," at least six times.[15] The new pair began creating their own universe. Sending Bryher encouraging notes as she approached delivery, H.D. had to stem some of Bryher's "enthusiasm." This attention thrilled Bryher, whose "Adventure," in the *Bostonian* in February 1919, gasped, "Do not pass me like the wind."

By March 1919, Bryher was steeped in H.D.'s creative workshop. "Loss" led Bryher to "read dates and periods" as if "they are like an old vase or a piece of some statue to me." Bryher attributed H.D.'s "dangerous affect," upon her, surfacing in a dream.

> I watched the fall of Troy.—I was not in the city nor as far as I could make out either a Greek or a Trojan. I think I was standing near a work vat looking onto one of the highways in the city. In the distance I could see Troy burning and the Greeks plundering. Then a band of fugitive horsemen rode past.... It was *most vivid*. I looked on and thought both parties were fools to cause this waste etc. Hope I am not going quite mad.[16]

Greeks warring Trojans over a beloved ghost doubled with World War I, with the wreckage in King Arthur's countryside. H.D. stayed temporarily at a pension in Ealing. Early in March, she summoned Bryher, who took a long bus ride on an icy day, bearing scarlet anemones, only to find her first real *friend* in a small, freezing room. Congestion clouded one lung. Delirious, H.D. imagined walking the road to Delphi with Bryher when she recovered. As Bryher left for her return bus, the landlady inquired who will pay funeral expenses? Bryher caught her return bus. "Ashamed all [her] life," she attributed her abrupt departure to a nagging germ phobia, begotten by spotless Audley and aggravated by the 1918 flu pandemic.[17] The worldwide flu peaked in March, another wave spiking the following March, with 228,000 deaths in Great Britain alone.[18] People were literally dying in the streets. The dead and the living were never in air-tight chambers for her.

As in the years to come, Bryher quickly grasped historic reality: H.D. might be a casualty of the deadly virus spreading at rates that would exceed the death tolls of World War 1. Bryher convinced her father to help provide for the poet, and gave Patmore the funds to purchase necessaries, including a layette.[19] First, though, she arranged for H.D. to stay at St. Faith's Nursing Home, where trained medical staff attended to her. H.D. had a serious case of double pneumonia. Recovering, she attributed her resurrection to Byrher, whose "fruit and flowers ... persuaded [her] to pull through."[20] The rest of March, Bryher came "constantly with wonderful bunches of anemones," bearing an even thicker bed jacket to ward off freezing cold.

Although much less likely to die in childbirth than her mother had been, the thirty-three-year-old H.D. was not out of woods, especially with inflamed lungs. Before antibiotics, pregnancies posed serious dangers, and birth during this pandemic led H.D. to feel the violent conjunction of near-death and impending life, a paradox somatically recalled most every March. But Bryher beckoned, as H.D. portrayed it, "dragging her ashore ... blue eyes were working their horrible first aid," Bryher "call[ing] her back to war, to fight, to resist, to appeal. 'What do you think of Middleton?' "[21] This was one of the intellectual jolts Bryher offered to stimulate recovery. Though exhilarated to have found such a friend, Bryher still felt her condition was impossible, even more so now, and referred to drowning herself. H.D. preferred "sudden violent shattering rather than the suffocation of sheer drowning,"[22] cultivating morbid fantasies in third person: "If she woke up dead, after the baby, after the chloroform (is that the reason she wanted the baby? Legitimate suicide, she understood why the girl [Bryher] wanted to die, but with chloroform) if she woke up there would be no peace."[23] Not for a same-sex couple and baby.

At St. Faith's, H.D. had two "visions." Though he denied paying her a visit, the doctor transformed into a river-god, with chevrons on his khaki uniform. Chloroform lingering in her system, she believed her father visited her bedside. Unbeknownst to her, he died in the United States on March 2, 1919, during the pandemic. Bryher accepted H.D.'s visions as imagination's truth.

* * *

Having "never, never met so tragic a personality," H.D. sent Bryher to Dr. Ellis.[24] On March 20, 1919, Bryher met the gray-bearded Ellis in his frayed velvet smoking jacket at his Kensington home. Sitting beneath a portrait of Walt Whitman, he offered Bryher tea and lemon with a side of salted peanuts. Speaking of her "unfailing refuge," the Scillies, and desire to be a boy to travel with H.D., he laughed. Bereft by the recent death of his first wife, Edith, a lesbian, Ellis confided she too "was just like a boy."[25] Departing from Richard von Krafft-Ebing's *Psychopathis Sexualis* (1886), which pathologized aberrations, Ellis championed inverts as simply variants of the norm; their "congenital" "abnormalities," stemmed from "profoundly rooted organic impulses."[26]

Ellis met Arthur Symons at the Paris Exhibition in 1889 and read the famous critic's study of French poets, *The Symbolist Movement in Literature* (1898), influencing Yeats and Eliot. It doubled as a repository for unexamined visceral responses and an expanded sensorium, a spur for Ellis's encyclopedist seven-volume sexology studies, braiding science, literature, and multiple variations in identity, desire, comportment. Symons also prepared Ellis for H.D. and Bryher, leading him to develop the concept of "sexo-asethetic inversion,"[27] which dynamized the pair to go beyond Gregg's dismissal of aestheticism for failing to address common lives. For Ellis, sexuality itself was an inventive art. Bryher especially eschewed "Dolly's" clothes, intuiting a way to contour male identifications, H.D. referring to Bryher as "him" whenever possible.

Ellis clarified that cross-dressing did not always stem from fetishism but expressed "outward symbols of the inner state."[28] Such assertions tantalized our war-weary pair. When Bryher visited him, he provided a game-changing recognition:

> We agreed it was most unfair for it to happen but apparently I am quite justified in pleading I ought to be a boy—I am just a girl by accident. Then we got on to the "studies" and I said I thought everybody ought to read them. He smiled and told me about their being prosecuted. I wanted to know why the universe was narrow-minded.... I protested I had sat in a library so long I was afraid to get up and he asked me where my sense of adventure was. So I was silent.

The interview opened floodgates. That Ellis faced "prosecution," adjunct with H.D.'s fears, induced in Bryher the scary chance of being *seen*. Ellis recommended "a flat of her own." He thought America "sheer madness." Bryher assured him H.D. had taken "temporary charge of [her] education."[29]

The sex doctor nonetheless recommended Bryher read his *Studies in the Psychology of Sex*, volume 2. Psychoanalysis, he thought, removed "the upper layer of the psychic palimpsest," revealing a hidden layer. He anatomized various ways women could be together, naming "[h]omosexual passion in women" as kissing and "lying spoons" and "tribadism" as well as cunnilingus. The loaned volume supplied a multitude of women disguised as men, who lived with or even married other women, affirming Bryher's "Girl-Page," written the year before. Finally, he considered inversion as "not a localized sexual condition" but a "diffused one," though "firmly imprinted on the whole psychic state."[30] Bryher was living evidence. Her reading letters as colors, Ellis, through Symons, linked to "inverts," noting they were often "color hearers."[31] By August, Ellis was calling Bryher "Dear Boy."

* * *

Claiming to be H.D.'s "closet male relative," with his black velour hat and ebony cane, Pound hurtled into St. Faith's the day before H.D. gave birth. He mocked her dark laced cap, his "only real criticism" "that this [was] not [his] child."[32] Aldington brought daffodils. Although H.D.'s lungs stabilized before she gave birth, the doctor thought mother and child might die. As phantom father, Bryher agonized as H.D. delivered her baby on March 31, calling her "fire girl," after her sun sign, Aries (Figure 6.1).

Naming her baby Perdita Frances, H.D. deferred to Shakespeare to capture the poignant experience of near-death. Like H.D.'s daughter, the Perdita of *The Winter's Tale* "arrived on the last day of March with the 'daffodils, / That come before the swallow dares.'" H.D.'s autobiographic *Asphodel* gave herself the name of Hermione, also from *Winter's Tale*. In Shakespeare, the jealous husband-king falsely accuses Hermione of adultery, persecutes her despite oracles declaring her innocence, and banishes Perdita, a legal death. After a humiliating trial, Shakespeare's Hermione reportedly dies. Sixteen years later, almost as long as H.D. fretted over Perdita's paternity, Hermione returns to flesh.

For H.D., legal jeopardy and survival were both metaphorical and real. If barred from taking Aldington's name, Perdita would suffer erasure. H.D. worked to depetrify Richard's "bombastic Victorianism," only for him to act out again. He responded to her "Cookoo [sic] Song": "'Can't you understand that I tear it to pieces because I care for it.'—He said the same of your novel," his "method," "brutal—almost pathological."[33] During April, Bryher saw Doris in Cornwall, writing daily to check on mother and child. Most days H.D. went to Norland Nursery to breastfeed. Perdita thrived. H.D. agreed to travel with Bryher once her vital energy returned. Protective of H.D.'s creativity, Bryher dared speak of *their* future, jesting she would "even fight Perdita about it," promising "when she is older," they would "teach her to adventure."[34]

With his port and expensive cigars, Sir John welcomed H.D. to Audley during her recovery in 1919, and she never forgot this kindness, though Hannah thought the poet a bad influence on Bryher. By the end of April, Aldington was addressing letters to H.D. "c/o Miss Ellerman" at Audley. Before they rented a flat, they needed a plan, mock-configured in *Asphodel*; H.D.'s Hermione gazes into her lover's "wide eyes, bluer than blue, bluer than gentian, than convolvulus, than forget-me-not, than the blue of blue pansies," pleading with her not to threaten suicide and to promise to look after the newborn.[35] Bryher needed to grow up, and H.D. was herself child-like and believed Perdita could camouflage *and* suture their bond. Bryher found adventurous purpose in this custody arrangement.

Neither woman, postwar, knew what to expect. They fondly nicknamed Perdita "Pup," Bryher taking the name "Fido," urging Sir John to finance the towering, intense

Figure 6.1 H. D. and Perdita, c. 1919. Unsourced family photo, H.D. Papers.
Courtesy Beinecke Rare Book and Manuscript Library, Yale University.

H.D. with her sweet newborn, without revealing them as her new family. When she reached twenty-five in 1919, Bryher's income would amount to "about four hundred a year," approximately $1,450, a substantial sum. This helped materialize the alternative life H.D. promised, lending Bryher a masculine power. H.D. let Bryher arrange her healthcare, the baby's delivery, and separation from Aldington, shielding their new trio from the outer world.

While the Allies balkanized the earth during 1919, our couple consumed much of Ellis' work, mapping polysexuality. Both liked triangles; both became jealous. H.D. half-jokingly claimed, "The good doctor and father-confessor has forgotten me," asking Bryher to abscond on her next visit with "the most apropos [volume] at this moment," "his beloved VI," titled *Sex in Relation to Society*, one chapter addressing rest from lactation, another on the need for nakedness.[36] H.D. urged Bryher not to "go to pieces," freedom was "very near," devising a triangle with Dr. Ellis and herself, "planning to the very last sordid, practical detail." Bryher had to "keep strong" so *she* could go "on living."[37] H.D. buoyed Bryher with a planned adventure to the Scillies to quench Bryher's longing. Distressed that *Development* was not fully developed, Bryher felt she was "a book [herself]," provoking H.D. to say, " 'Little frozen being.' "[38] Thawing and unfolding passion, they crafted how to outsmart social conventions.

* * *

Unhappy in Soho's shabby Hotel du Littoral, Aldington, his body inflamed with boils, had intense headaches and insomnia. The lights from storefronts cast shadows of figures fighting on his wall. He threatened to consult a lawyer about his nonpaternity, but H.D. must have detected some opening for compromise because she left her bed, still unwell, to meet him. With Arabella present, he lost himself, vowing that if H.D. claimed the child as his, he would file a criminal complaint.[39] He tried shoving a stock-still H.D. and had to telephone Bryher, commanding, "Hilda must get out of here at once."[40] Bryher directed H.D. to call Richard's bluff. On May 6, 1919, in Middlesex, H.D. registered Perdita as Aldington's.

The inflammatory confrontation between shell-shocked veteran and new mother led H.D. to call Aldington "certifiable" to the Quaker illustrator George Plank, an early friend from New York.[41] To relieve some of H.D.'s ire, Bryher dubbed Aldington "Cuthbert," a word for an inglorious coward.[42] He insisted H.D. gain child support from the careless Gray. Goaded by Patmore, Bryher hunted "the Hare," as they called Gray, hiding behind his mother's skirts at Queen's Terrace; H.D. would have died except for Bryher, she told him, who "went green," claiming his people were penniless.[43] Patmore fantasized fathers becoming obsolete, where "women will soon propagate entirely without their aid & the poor men things will sink into a happy antediluvian [nullity?]!"[44]

Sending love to "Dear Girl," H.D. considered Bryher's handling the gossipy Patmore, petulant Shorter, and restive Aldington part of her education. Already committed to travel when she recovered, H.D. knew both were at the "breaking point." In May, Lowell, hurt that Bryher had not revealed Aldington and H.D.'s "personal affairs," complained that Lawrence had to tell her of H.D.'s childbirth. Flagging her penpal's immaturity, she heard from Shorter "it is to be called Perdita, so I now feel that I know something about the affairs of the family."[45] H.D. subdued Bryher's urgency to leave London immediately, reminding her they still had "Greek books & planning." Also Bryher had to ensure Hampstead Nurseries would care for Perdita while they traveled. H.D. discovered Bryher's passion to serve her in myriad ways.

Yet H.D. struggled with her new friend's distress over the necessity of "social camouflage." This no doubt increased Bryher's anger and sadness she was not born in the requisite body. "I Said," written in 1919, not printed until twenty years after her death, reflects a range of emotions, from anger to passion, frustration to encouragement.

Primarily, it coached Bryher to recognize "souls such as yours" at Marathon, a running event ignited when a messenger sprinted to Athens, alerting citizens of the Persian invasion. Despite its title, "I Said" became "we said," with the interlocutor's "I will not live, / I will not compromise." Welcoming Bryher as co-initiate in a secret world, the poem warned against indiscriminate coming-out, H.D. instructing Bryher as pupil; this shifted back and forth as time went on. But H.D. *knew* "open joy" was forbidden.[46] They could end up dead. H.D.'s warnings were similar to Lowell's earlier in the year, who wrote that Bryher would "stand a better chance walking through the streets of London in men's clothes than in one of our small Western towns. The speed with which you would find yourself in the lock-up would really astonish you."[47] Incarceration was still a possibility in 1919.

* * *

They embarked in late June to celebrate their first anniversary, July 17, 1919, in Mullion Cove, Cornwall. While they summered, Patmore visited Perdita daily. The couple consummated their love during this sojourn. The coast's wildness inspired H.D. to educate her "dear girl" in sensuousness. Perched on rocks, H.D. bathed, swam, and photographed Bryher, naked, more than meaningful to the sheltered heiress. From Mullion Cove, they traveled to St. Mary's, only eleven miles in diameter, the archipelago's largest island. They stayed at Tregarthen's Hotel, built by a sea captain who ran the mail packet; Tennyson wrote *Enoch Arden* there. H.D. sent a broken missive to Lowell on hotel stationary, dated July 19, 1919, musing on Aldington, Lawrence, and Pound, their "modern cult of brutality," covering over how matters stood with Bryher.

> Last winter seems all a blur—a dream of some sort. I was three months (an incredible time) in bed. But I believe, on the whole, the rest care was good for me and my little girl...—who not only survived but turned out an extraordinarily sturdy little creature—strong & over average in length & weight. It seems very queer to have her—a quaint surprise & treasure altogether—though I feel as if she were a little sister rather than my own infant.

Pause. Resuming, the "small" Bryher was "with her in Cornwall." H.D. found Bryher indispensable in creating a family based on "chosen kin."[48] More than female or male, Bryher acted out Gregg's and Aldington's better selves.

In this lush archipelago, after the Roman sun god Sulis, drawing most of England's sun, they basked in the warmth, donned pants, spent secluded hours roaming vibrant vegetation. The fecund landscape intertwined their imaginations. The islands came into H.D.'s "Thetis," where "you may dive down / to the uttermost sea depth" and sight "anemones and flower / of the wild sea-thyme" that "cover the silent walls / of an old sea-city at rest."[49] They thrilled at "open sea-flowers"—as if *Sea Garden* had found its stage, refreshing the enervated pair. Even the hotel's wallpaper mirrored ecological wonders, with "palm-trees, coral-plants, mesambeanthum," as if animated, "opened like water-lilies the length of the grey walls; the sort of fibrous under-water leaf and these open sea-flowers gave one the impression of being submerged."[50] Bryher drafted some of *Arrow Music* (1922), also guiding H.D. away from the wallpaper to favorite caves, lighthouses, the sites of shipwrecks, white sand beaches, starfish, abundant seals, dolphins, black-backed seagulls, puffins (which Bryher favored), rare corals, ferns, fields of narcissi.

Bryher's homoerotic "To Eros" asks the unnamed supplicant her desire, but "[w]ords died. All her body spoke its longing / but her lips could not utter her request." "Eos" then awakened physical contact:

Your eyes break Sleep!
I touch the pansy set below your heart;
Each kiss a star
that fades upon your body,
which is dawn.

"In Syria," the speaker "kissed her navel," so that "[a] queen was glad." The queen was H.D., tattooed with kisses, and in "Blue Sleep," Bryher praised "Aphrodite" for "at last [her] body is at peace." "The closed bud of dawn opens on your face," "Amazon" condenses. A short stanza recollects their imperiled spring: "I remember / Wind, April, the black rain." Bryher tenderly questioned, "Are my limbs but a sheath for your intensity, my love."[51] On this honeymoon, their writing assured of "diffuse" eroticism.[52] Bryher learned not to interrupt H.D., who tore pages to bits when her concentration broke.

During the stay, the pair had a peculiar experience, what "*Bryher called* the 'jellyfish' experience of a double ego," where "transparent glass spread over [H.D.'s] head like a diving-bell and another manifested from [H.D.'s] feet," which "insulated from the war disaster." H.D. mistakenly predated this event to their 1918 meeting, nine months before Perdita's birth, enabling the fantasy that she and Bryher had enacted parthenogenesis. H.D. even might "have dismissed it at once" had she been on her own, admitting again, "*It was being with Bryher that projected the fantasy*" (italics mine). Bryher coached, "No, no, it is the most wonderful thing I ever heard of. Let it come." H.D. relived childbirth, and "'let go' into a sort of balloon." Enclosed, she felt "safe but seeing things as through water." Writing *Notes on Thought and Vision*, dated July 1919, H.D. described a vibrantly sensate poetics, tentacles reaching everywhere.[53]

Switching to a more heightened state, H.D. underwent "grinding agony," a standard signal for shared "visions," and described "long feelers reach[ing] down and through the body" which "stood in the same relation to the nervous system as the over-mind to the brain or intellect," akin to "the long, floating tentacles of the jelly-fish." This jellyfish consciousness was "centered in the love-region of the body or placed like a foetus in the body." "[T]wo kinds" of vision existed: one "womb vision," "both centres... equally important." This embodied perspective has ecological reach,[54] though *Notes* essentially acted love manifesto for the new duo. When the "minds of the two lovers merge, interact in sympathy of thought," "[t]he love-region is excited by the appearance or beauty of the loved one," explained H.D.[55] Breastfeeding Perdita had stimulated oxytocin, a peptide hormone that fosters bonding, likely contributing to the pair's intimacy.

H.D. further dissected "the over-mind" experience with Bryher; it was "a cap, like water, transparent, fluid yet with definite body, contained in a definite space," or "like a closed sea-plant, jelly-fish or anemone," where "thoughts pass and are visible like fish swimming under clear water."[56] H.D.'s grandfather had, after all, taught that even a drop of water had "living and eternal life," was "complete," and "that where there is nothing, there is something."[57] In colorful coastal waters, the two saw themselves as a new species.[58]

H.D. called these "psychic experiences," later asking, "Are we psychic coral-polyps? Do we build one upon another? Did I (sub-aqueous) in the Scilly Isles, put out a feeler?" Turning, as she often did, from the purely human, she identified with coral with her keen awareness of herself as linked, as if by coordinates in a star map, to distant ecology. Besides, she knew from Papalie that coral reefs were made up of polyps, with translucent soft sac-like bodies, their mouths tentacles; through limestone skeletons, they connect to other such skeletons, becoming a single organism that grows, forming layers similar to tree rings, marking their thousand- to million-year presence. The "myriad-minded," already naturalist poet, identified with sea flowers, but here joined with Bryher as another polyp. Imagining themselves as inhuman natural phenomena was preferable to being "deviants"; they readily abandoned the "ego" for the "eco," with "super feelers," "elongated in fine threads."[59] H.D. downplayed *Notes* as "an interesting bit of psychological data." Yet she conceived it as a breakthrough, handing it on to Ellis, who, without explanation, dismissed this now classic in feminist poetics. Did he feel left out of this gymnasium? They were both hatching out, confirming each other's need for a quest, for life figured as a soul's journey enmeshed in living history. H.D. and Bryher faced each other as near mirrors, as an early photo of them facing each other in a later composed scrapbook, but in the moment, they turned shyly away from the camera, H.D., hiding under a signature sun hat, and Bryher with clenched fists (Figure 6.2).

Returning from the islands, H.D. imagined herself without Bryher, stumbling in London with "a baby" in her arms, dislocated, "sitting on the top of a bus," where "it might be anywhere with light snow drifting and little pink almonds all along the front of brick houses and behind rusty laurel hedges putting out pink fingers.... Eos the dawn. Eros. Someone, somewhere makes me think of Eros."[60] This "someone" was Bryher. While at St. Mary's, Bryher also wrote "Eos," the goddess with "pink fingers." *Notes* bears many traces of Bryher: "[t]he Galilean fell in love with things as well as people," a "young Jude with his intense eyes," who rested "along the shores." Likewise, H.D. now turned Bryher's raves, Boccaccio, Rabelais, Montaigne, Sterne, Middleton, de Gourmont, and de Regnier, listed in *Development*, into requirements: "If you cannot be entertained and instructed by [them] there is something wrong with you physically." H.D. essentially called for Bryher to enjoy her body, preparing for a

Figure 6.2 Scrapbook images of Bryher and H.D. posed, turning away, 1919–1920? H.D. Papers.
Courtesy of Beinecke Rare Book and Manuscript Library, Yale University.

second staging of Eleusinian mysteries, to "look into things with your intellect, with your sheer brain."[61] Both were in dire need of contact with the natural world.

Reminding that the Delphic charioteer had "an almost hypnotic effect on [her]," H.D.'s *Notes* relayed ecstasy between the lovers and confirmed the poet's aesthetic direction. Discovered at Apollo's sanctuary in 1896, the horse-driver, an ancient life-size bronze statue, with intact eyes, excepting silver eyelashes. H.D. saw herself as the tall charioteer, considering there "was enough beauty in the world of art, enough in the fragments ... to remake the world"; "two or three people," with "the right sort of receiving brains, could turn the whole tide of human thought, could direct lightning flashes of electric power, to slash across and destroy the world of dead, murky thought." *Reception* was key to H.D., invoking Marconi, decoding "the secret of dots and dashes," knowing by 1919 that "two individuals" acted as "receiving stations, capable of storing up energy." Her point that "[w]e *want* receiving centres for dots and dashes" boldly revised the creative process: art preexists or continues to exist, but we must use our over-mind, "like a lens," to truly re-envision art as message, to decode and reconnect the dots and dashes. For instance, her charioteer was "conjured" with "hard brain work."[62]

During this trip, H.D. also began her meditative essay "The Wise Sappho," enacting "one of the oldest purposes of poetry: commemoration."[63] Sappho's "sinister" face, its "living destructive irony," her "unhuman element," her "twisted" eyes and "bitter jeer," were qualities essential to H.D.'s own debunking male heroics and educating her girls. H.D. observed, "[T]his girl who bewitches you, my friend, does not even know how to draw her skirts about her feet," as if broadcasting Bryher's social awkwardness. Navigating their sailboat between islands, they taught each other, catching Sappho's poems as "magnetic, vibrant" remnants, geologic as layers, "broken sentences and unfinished rhythms as rocks." Sappho's fragments were "essence[s]," each a "scintillating star turned warm suddenly in our hand like a jewel, sent by the beloved."[64] Icy, and clasped.

From Mullion Cove, Bryher resumed correspondence with Lowell, after a hiatus of two months, making no mention of quince kisses or jellyfish, only brusquely remarking, "I hate infants but I make an exception in favor of Perdita," "so intelligent already, very like Mrs. Aldington with very beautiful eyes and a lot of soft hair." From Holgate's Hotel, Bryher described "sailing and fishing most days," everything "very wild." "I" shifted to "we" as they "land[ed] on uninhabited islands right among gulls, near pinks and puffins," assuring that "Mrs. Aldington" was not as impressed with puffins as she but was even "doing some work."[65]

Lowell begged Bryher to hire a full-time nurse, offering to defray the cost, warning against the London winter and the ongoing pandemic. Instead, Bryher became H.D.'s head nurse, agent, and lover. Once in London, she recruited a family doctor. H.D. was still quite weak, yet she assured Lowell she planned "to take [H.D.] South with [her] for the winter."[66] "Mrs. Aldington has all she needs" signified volumes. Envying Bryher's "all-day sails," Lowell again criticized *Development* as immature. "Do not let yourself be swayed all the time," she dug in, praising and disdaining Bryher's ability "to absorb atmospheres, places, etc. as you do. One cannot live transparently like the chameleon, a mere outline for other people's emotions."[67] Bryher was chameleon-like, but Constable wanted to publish *Development*, without knowing she was an Ellerman. But Shorter, behind her back, told the publisher she considered other presses. Though furious, Bryher finally claimed her *own* victory when Lowell reported Shorter praised her "genius." "I think I ought to explain," Bryher retorted, "he is romantically inclined towards me."[68] Lowell likely chuckled over Shorter's foolishness, and Bryher's.

* * *

The archipelago's jagged shores and "resonance of wind" helped the pair establish their "receiving station," amounting to an interlayering of texts in dialogue. One might say, with Jane Bennett, that the islands had a "geoaffect" through an "interstitial field of … human forces, flows, tendencies, and trajectories," the creaturely and the unhuman flux calling our pair.[69] Their texts and minds knitted together. "She Rebukes Hippolyta" addressed boy-like Bryher, dedicated "forever to you, Artemis, dedicate … / from out my reins, / those small, cold hands."[70] H.D. caught Bryher's "curious slouch forward that was her not wholly gracious movement, her hands, tiny, improbably fine, delicate as some delicate awkward flower-bud."[71]

Refashioning the bildungsroman that for women generally ended in marriage, H.D. envisioned *Paint It*, a "love poem" in prose, inspired by Bryher. H.D. was Midget, and Bryher, Althea, both among "the living spirits of the untouched, sacred virgins of Artemis," naked, wet bodies vowing mutual enchantment. H.D. set their scene after a swim: "they had spread their garments to dry in the other room"; naked, they discourse on mutability. "You and I change," Midget addressed Althea, "the creative mind does not alter." Through her character, H.D. imagined they will "grow old but never see [themselves] unsightly." She summoned "the visible world" that "exists as poignantly, as ethereally as the invisible," but with Bryher, she discovered "a combining of two worlds," visible and invisible, that made "another world." They discussed geographical differences after swimming, imagining some liberated future.

H.D. attacked Victorian schooling in *Development*'s vein—"Oh stop, stop, stop, parents, schoolteachers, professors, horde of the unredeemed." Or H.D. sought Bryher's essence, "her valiant outline blurred in the process of civilizing, of schooling, of devitalizing." H.D. loved outlines, footprints, words as "portholes." Bryher's incipient identity—the "child itself," doubled as "a nameless foundling sister of Princess Minnehaha, a bird or intermediate of a lost reptile race."[72] They stayed in the Scillies through July, gulping in fresh air, swimming, loving. Two photographs, one of lanky H.D. against a rock, the other showing a naked Bryher, expressing relief (Figures 6.3 and 6.4).

* * *

In late August, H.D. and Bryher took a flat in Bullingham Mansions, Kensington. Compelled to check in at Audley, Bryher spoke of her flat to Lowell, while H.D. referred to it as hers. H.D. wrote Cournos during their autumnal attempt to set up a household. Agitated, most likely by Bryher's shuttling between Kensington and Mayfair, H.D.'s frantic typewriting contained more than the usual number of crossouts. "I have again and again told [Bryher] that I cannot stand the strain of living with her and yet I *can not leave her*" (italics mine). Ironically, she was unsure *she was* ready to be "a philanthropist," referring to Bryher's so-called insanity, in equal parts projection of imbalance, internalized homophobia, and attraction to psychological terminology; recall H.D.'s dubbing Richard "certifiable," or herself "in bits." Seeking approval for choosing Bryher and their scandalous love affair, H.D. asked Cournos to

Figure 6.3 H.D. seated on a rock at Mullion, Cornwall, England, c. 1919. Unsourced photo, H.D. Papers.
Courtesy of Beinecke Rare Book and Manuscript Library, Yale University.

"*like Bryher*."[73] H.D. *chose Bryher*. She recorded the unusual state of affairs: "Richard comes to lunch at Bullingham Mansions and Ezra drops in. I finally, exclude both from the flat. Br. is back and forth from Audley Street, strange and uneven, but always staunch and loyal." Dependable Bryher met Pound when he visited their flat in 1920; with H.D. not present, he "put his arms round [her] shoulders." If she had been Elizabethan, she "would have screamed or snatched up a dagger." The "Leopard," her name for Pound, dismissed Bryher as "impossible."[74]

With their flat conveniently near Ellis, both turned to him as a confidante, and to theatricalize their "aberrations." He sternly counseled Bryher to let H.D. manage Aldington, somewhat galling in the face of how much she helped him. When Bryher

Figure 6.4 Bryher seated on rocks, c. 1919. Unsourced photo, H.D. Papers. Courtesy of Beinecke Rare Book and Manuscript Library, Yale University.

confronted her father about her illegitimacy, it only increased tension. Ellis thought it was good that Sir John knew *she knew*, yet advised her not to "drag the subject forward" too much,[75] also tutoring Bryher to mute her zealous love (i.e., her "insanity") because "Mrs. A. has an extremely sensitive & nervous temperament, a beautiful nature & much more experience than you." As if H.D. were a feral pet, he advised Bryher urge physical occupations for "her restless brain" that "works too much & exhausts her."[76] When H.D. visited *him*, he didn't overexcite her "by talking philosophy too much, & it seems to suit her."[77]

Yet Ellis did more than let H.D. rest, coaxing her into a psychological release, satisfying his "slight case" of urolagia—a desire to watch very particular tall women urinate, standing in a masculine pose. Crossing therapeutic boundaries, H.D. relieved herself, playing boy or charioteer, almost modeling gender elasticity for Ellis—what he described as a "rainbow stream" in "A Revelation" (1921), to him his best "sexo-aesthetic" writing. In fact, the "shower" evoked an aura for him—partly because it affronted Victorian morality; H.D. also enjoyed it, if we believe his recollection of her "drift[ing] into [his] room, like a large white bird hovering tremulously over the edge of a cliff, a shy and sinuous figure, so slender and so tall that she seemed frail," as well as "of firm and solid texture," while he witnessed "the glistering liquid arch, endlessly."

H.D. indulged her sense of statues having imminent life and queer expression: as Hyacinthus, male lover of Apollo, accidentally killed by him, but she asked Ellis not to publish "A Revelation," for the very reason she left *Paint It Today* unfinished and unpublished. H.D. thought certain moments best hidden from prying eyes. To the couple, Ellis was "Chiron," after the wounded healer, letting H.D. identify "with the hero," while "extricating herself from the paralyzing silence of becoming yet another male writer's muse."[78]

Bryher wrote Lowell on December 28 about escaping "the treacherous English Spring," recounting her pride in being "one of the very few favored ones that were invited to Perdita's first Christmas tree." Invited? Santa Claus Bryher bragged that Perdita "lay on the sofa and watched us and the tree with tremendously alert eyes," too "big for her age with a mass of dark gold curly hair."[79] Bringing H.D. a Greek testament, Ellis arrived to celebrate, along with Cournos. H.D. and Bryher modeled a clay bird and elephant for under the tree. This cozy scene sealed a modicum of stability. Yet the pair already plotted escape to Greece.

H.D. primed herself through "Islands," conceived in the Scillies, placed with the *North American Review* by Lowell in August 1919. With seven sections, it reiterated self-interrogatories: "What are islands to me, / What is Greece." The last section protested privately to Bryher—reversing "Eurydice," for here "without your gaze," their daring would be lost:

> What are the islands to me
> if you are lost,
> [...]
> if you take fright of beauty,
> terrible, torturous, isolated,
> a barren rock?
> [...]
> What are the islands to me
> if you hesitate,
> what is Greece if you draw back
> from the terror
> and cold splendour of song
> and its bleak sacrifice?[80]

LINE 2

BORODINO 1920–1928

7
Parting of the Veil

Greece, 1920 ...

Once home, an exhausted H.D. blamed the weather for her "going quite insane," with "sudden fits of depression." Her Puritan ancestors would have condemned her for having a child from an adulterous relation and for loving an ambiguously gendered woman, but she urged Bryher to "bully" her: "I am strong this evening & singing & shouting with joy. And now I feel we must go away next winter. Don't let me slide back, into our old despair. We *can* do what we want. We can do it, once we have a clear & final sense, of direction."

Fearing "*our* old despair," H.D. assured "dear, dear boy" that they "must escape" to Greece. She dreamed of "the sand & sleep[ing] under stars" and sharing "a great house—and the sun, the sun!—Flowers, and sudden realization that we are at one with the poems about us."[1] They invited Dr. Ellis as camouflage. At this point in their relationship, their decisions blurred. Bryher arranged for Perdita's board, obtaining the money they needed from her father. In October, the sixty-one-year-old Ellis signed on. Bryher kitted herself and H.D. with sleeping bags and bug repellent powder they never used. Passports, initiated in 1915, were difficult to obtain. In Bryher's long story "South," Dr. Harris, Ellis' avatar, concocted a study of Greek gynecology to get his visa.[2] Bryher metamorphosed her hair for a passport, eyes in their typical hypnotic stare (Figure 7.1).

Through winter, H.D. and Bryher read Fritz Baedeker's *Guide to Greece* (1909). It fused fact with mythology, plaguing moderns with a question: Where does myth end and reality begin? Baedeker wrote of the "history of Athens" with Theseus named its founder in 1259 BCE, forging other townships "into one common political society."[3] Reputed to have tracked and slain the Minotaur in his maze in Crete, Theseus violated Hippolyta, who birthed a son, Hippolytus, harkening back to an earlier Minoan culture. Battered by war, childbirth, and severe illness, H.D. thought Greece might offer "a final sense, of direction." Well before World War I, Hellenists journeyed to Greece and "staged encounters between ancient rituals and contemporary crises" as "a way of seeing ghosts."[4] Unable to trust postwar materiality, they found in the ancient world a sense of persistent incipience, glimpses into beckoning ruins. Studying Greece's map before leaving, H.D. saw it as a "rag of a country," "a hieroglyph." Foreclosing full comprehension of its magnetic topography, one must continually "begin all over, learning a cryptic language."

Figure 7.1 Passport photograph of Bryher, c. 1920. H.D. Papers.
Courtesy of Beinecke Rare Book and Manuscript Library, Yale University.

Packing Baedeker, they also consumed the underrated Pausanias (c. 110–180 CE), Greek geographer, author of *Description of Greece*, which pinned mythological stories and rituals to particular locales. During and after their trip, H.D. worked on "Pausanias," credited with the recovery of "the ghost of Greek beauty," learning from him that for "[g]hosts to speak, [one] must have sacrifice." Relics of the past "may not have perished but simply become invisible." Rapturing over Pausanias, uncovering miracles in the dust, H.D. saw a semblance in Bryher, like him, governed by "geographical emotions." He was "a little recording-machine" or "a sort of dried-up mummy of a traveler, seeing and recording, recording and seeing," taking in altars, marketplaces, "out-lying heaps of odd stones," "half-ruined temples and ... almost obliterated temples."[5] This helped H.D. cultivate, with Bryher, a poetics of transmission.

* * *

On February 7, 1920, Bryher, H.D., and Ellis, set sail on the *Borodino*. Built in 1911, the British commandeered it during the war as a mail ship and a kind of floating Harrod's—supplying the best available provisions to naval officers. To carry his daughter and companions safely over waters infested with "still floating mines," Sir John corraled the metal-lined vessel from ice-breaking duties in the Arctic. With its house flag JRE waving above the British one, Bryher took her first trip outside England without her parents. Although "very rough," the pair occupied "a small cabin but the best on the boat." A handful of other travelers sailed "as a special privilege."[6]

A few days out from London, while walking the deck, the threesome met Peter Rodeck, an archaeologist, fluent in ancient Greek, whose research into excavations, especially in Crete, fascinated them. Bryher's thwarted ambition to study archaeology led H.D. to think him a double for Bryher, "frustrated by the war and unable to express herself, cut off from her original Arabic and Egyptian research."[7] When H.D. met him again, years later, he was a priest.

They sailed through choppy waters, and passing through the Pillars of Hercules of the narrow Strait of Gibraltar, "the boat slipped into enchantment"; it took H.D. beyond material boundaries into uncharted waters. The moment suddenly "had no existence in the world of ordinary events and laws and rules."[8] After the winds quieted, H.D. leaned against the rail in reverie, staring at sunset light upon water, thinking Bryher "must not miss this," the water breaking into "a thousand perfectly peaked wavelets like the waves in the background of a Botticelli." Turning toward their cabin, she glimpsed Rodeck, without his thick-rimmed glasses and *without the scar* noted when first meeting him. On the ship's seaward side, he pointed toward "a chain of hilly islands," unveiling Atlantis or the Hesperides, then turned his palm down, drawing a dolphin up. He stood precisely "to [her] right" "at the head of the ship stairs."[9] Noting the violet hour, Bryher sought H.D., who then dressed for dinner, without time to speak of her encounter with the man "who was and was not Peter Rodeck." That came later. At the captain's table, Bryher faced H.D., sitting to the right of Rodeck, beside him a deaf lady from Canada; raising her voice, H.D. announced spotting dolphins; the captain emphatically assured that the wireless operator, an expert, had detected none. Rodeck said nothing. The Canadian retired to her cabin for the voyage's duration, making way for H.D. to sit beside Rodeck. Bryher gave her willing belief, thinking the story "seemed feasible,"[10] yet H.D. herself suspected the "quiet sea" and no engine noise, deducing her vision occurred outside time; the Rodeck at dinner had the "startling heavy scar" she had noted on his passport.[11]

Bryher knew her mate was highly sensitive and easily swept up in her imagination. Drawing on sea lore, her childhood treasure chest, Bryher said seeing dolphins, who rescued those in need, was a positive omen. This was the best she could do. Still the rail-side "presence" haunted H.D., or rather *them*, for over fifteen years. Bryher's open acceptance enchanted H.D., for whom this uncertainty was creative incitement, especially as she felt, if ever briefly, a potential oneness, outside of time, an "I Am," or the AUM in Sanskrit. H.D. thought Rodeck could possibly be a Christ emanation, with "X-ray eyes."[12] Recall, she was born in Bethlehem and watched a gardener cut a lily for her, an event her mother disputed. The key point: H.D. *never* disavowed this event, or any other "visions" that she, together with Bryher, generally relished and participated in. Each conjured the ability to cross between visible and invisible worlds, for them, not a pathology.

"Projection is the master metaphor of H.D.'s technique," Adelaide Morris asserts, claiming "[i]ts operations connect the material, mental, and mystical realms and enact her belief that there is no physical reality that is not also psychic and spiritual."[13] *Sea Garden* already possessed hallucinatory specificity, focusing on details and fragments, expressing linguistic exhaustion and repair. H.D. planned novelizing Rodeck in *Niké*, finally abandoned. By 1932, she had written "Mouse Island," with new vocabulary from astronomer Camille Flammarion's 1921 *Death and Its Mystery*, corroborating that Rodeck could have detached from his material body as an "astral double" into a "projected effluvial phantom." Publishing just a year after this voyage, Flammarion argued that "human beings possess fluid phantasms which may, under certain conditions, become visible and tangible."[14]

Facing more tumultuous weather, the boat docked at Gibraltar. With Rodeck, they took a side trip to Algeciras, walking in a cork forest, the ground "starry with February narcissus," Bryher excited by "herds of gold-brown pigs" among the flowers. Writing Lowell, she did not mention Rodeck. After docking a few days in Malta, the ship, plagued by storms, Bryher, mortified, was seasick. Increasingly dissatisfied with his self-absorbed companions, Ellis paced the deck, sighting falling stars.[15] He suspected Rodeck as a shipboard romance. In fact, Rodeck eased H.D. into "a marriage by proxy," the latter realizing he "got what Br. felt."[16] No matter how much they advocated modern sex, or adventure, this half-phantom made it aphrodisiacal for H.D. to enjoy Bryher all the more; by superimposing him, she assuaged the guilt of one bound, with another woman, to an ancient civilization.

* * *

When they docked in Athens on February 27, 1920, the clouds poured freezing rain. Bryher jumped through puddles at every corner. They checked into Hotel de la Grande Bretagne, centrally located in Syntagma Square, across from the Royal Palace and Gardens, redolent with oranges and oleander, with views of the Acropolis. Adjacent to the Rue du Stade, full of café life, one could purchase French and German newspapers, drink Turkish coffee, sip special "aerated" lemonade, and drop into the confectioner's for honeycomb from Mount Hymettos, crowded with bees and flowers. Ellis stayed at a pension on the city's outskirts.

A chill permeated their classy hotel. "How cold it was—wind from Siberia—there was a stove in the corner of our elegant drawing room, everything was ormolu and gilded mirror frames—no sticks, no coal," H.D. recollected.[17] No one knew how to drive; broken-down cars littered roads. American tourists were omnipresent. Faced with sky-high prices, Bryher complained that "everything is five times the post-war English prices. One literally pays to breathe." Only "the treasure of Marco Polo" would allow anyone "to live in Athens."[18] Their trip's duration depended upon how long Bryher's funds held out.

On their first day, they took a bracing jaunt to the high, rocky Acropolis, with crystalline limestone reaching 510 feet above sea level, reconstructed after many wars, believed home to Athenian kings, now shelter for ancient sanctuaries and ruins. Outside, they spotted the bespectacled Rodeck, who left them to venture alone. They prowled a steep staircase, decorated with fragments, dating back to the first century. Ascending toward Niké, Aphrodite's doves adorned railings, walls hinting where altars had once been. After their first visit, H.D. drafted "Hippolytus Temporizes," tracing the outline of "a beach / covers but keeps the print / of the crescent shapes beneath."[19] They returned several times for extended visits.

Highly attuned to Euripides, H.D. visited the "Tomb of Erechtheus," pivotal in her later translation of *Ion*. Steps led to a cavern believed to be the grotto where Kroeusa, the daughter of Erechtheus, surprised by Apollo, became "the mother of Ion."[20] Apollo's sister was Artemis, one of H.D.'s nicknames for Bryher, who became the goddess not only of the hunt but also of midwifery, which fit H.D.'s means of allowing Bryher to act father. Among their most notable sightings was the Temple of Athena Niké, looking through to the Aegean, the island of Salamis, as well as Piraeus harbor. Here H.D. envisioned Niké, adjusting her sandal. Keep this image of an-about-to-move goddess in mind; it recurred.

Early in the nineteenth century, the governing Ottoman sultan allowed Lord Elgin to take "incidentals," namely seventeen statues, 247 feet of the Parthenon Frieze, and four panels from the Temple of Athena, to the British Museum. Among the most notable absences was Phidias' statue of Athena Promachos (c. 456 BCE); this wingless defender of Athens, in full armor, reached thirty-seven feet, a landmark for mariners; destroyed by the Persians, now invisible. This absent statue prompted H.D. and Bryher to absorb the "not there," an invisible wonder, making it "the victory of the mind," inspiring H.D. to "keep [this Athena] on her firm rock." Studying absence compelled presence.

On March 1, they traversed the public garden to the River Ilissos, which has since sunk underground, the setting for one of Plato's dialogues, *Phaedrus*, that touched on man-boy love, madness, and rhetoric; speakers, reclining on the soft bank, listened to cicadas, arguing whether the gift of writing relived memory or was *only reminding*. Like lost statues, words were gates, lenses, "portholes," looking "out from our ship, our world, our restricted lives, on to a sea that moves and changes and bears us up." She saw "*through* the words."[21]

The lovers walked under the large plane trees, known for their medicinal bark, toward the stadium, returning by the river path to Rue de Byron. On its southern slope lay the Theatre of Dionysus, built to honor the wine god, patron of drama. Until 1863, the site was literally concealed by rubbish. They saw the stage, its extended wings; Bryher recited her "Hellenics" in draft, published in *Poetry* in December 1920: "O wild rose, bend above my face! / There is no world," "[w]hite moss," softer than her lover's feet, she yet invoked, "O peach-red lily of my love!"[22] H.D. busily scribbled her notes on "Euripides," keeping these from Ellis. Against the prevailing modernist preference for Sophocles, H.D. wagered one-fifth of Euripides' plays had been lost that were based on his "ultra-modern spirit." The playwright had "lived through almost a modern great-war period" with an intense desire for beauty. Her basic argument: Euripides, like Sappho, had a psycho-emotional intensity, subject to "censure," which she sensed, "precluded so many of [Sappho's] most exquisite stanzas." Fear of censure partly drove H.D.'s and Bryher's self-concealment. "Then," when Sappho, harvested into the margins, was "now."

H.D. insisted Euripides' works "were stained" with "erotic-emotional innovation," owing to Ionian island culture, which gained visceral reality when she and Bryher walked around the very amphitheater that showed his plays. Euripides vibrated with the books of Matthew and John, speaking the "I am of eternal beauty, of eternal striving toward intellectual and aesthetic achievement." Yet Christian monks had "burnt the odes of Sappho." H.D. radically asserted in her otherwise private "Notes" that "the words of Euripides and the writings of the disciples of Christ are in the same tongue," alongside Sappho and the Greek Testament, each spreading the idea "that the kingdom of beauty is within you." Her new formula asserted that "[h]appiness simply means sanity and spiritual attainment" and the love of "beauty and mysterious things."[23] This search for such "sanity" was rebellion against the commonplace notion of the acceptable. Figure 7.2 shows H.D. stepping out of Aldington's shadow, finding solace, self-fashioning with beads and amulet.

With wonder, they enjoyed a panoramic view from the broad hill of Lykabettos; its steep ascent took roughly an hour, accomplished by funicular. A favored spot of Ellis, he read among the plentiful anemones of early March.[24] But, unhappy with the couple's absorption in each other, he cut his stay short. H.D. and Bryher then ventured to Kolonos, the home of Sophocles. They took in the marble Tower of Winds and embarked on a long railway trip to Eleusis, to the Temple of the Mysteries, dedicated to Demeter. Eleusis called to them. During their stay, H.D. jotted lines for "Helios and Athene," laying out "[t]he Eleusinian candidate," who "at one stage of initiation, walked through a black cave, the retreat of snakes."[25] This was Eurydice too, but a renewed initiate.

Athens was crowded with refugees from Constantinople, postwar people "moving back and forwards and continually from Trieste and like places." One in every port, a friend of Sir John's, Mr. Crowe, advised them to venture to the Gulf of Corinth. With an epiphany that "aspects of antiquity seem more real than any modern happening," Bryher orchestrated more trips to the countryside, blooming with the "anemones of all colors and wonderful scarlet poppies."[26]

H.D. had longed to walk the sacred way with Bryher, who had done so with her parents, to the shrine of "Helios (Hellas, Helen)," where the oracle spoke through a medium, Pythia, a common woman, perched on a tripod over a chamber in the earth. The great mother goddess resided at the omphalos of Delphi, until Apollo decamped there. But when their boat stopped at Itea, they discovered "two ladies alone, at that time" were not permitted "to make the then dangerous trip on the winding road to

Figure 7.2 H.D., 1920(?). Unsourced photo, H.D. Papers.
Courtesy of Beinecke Rare Book and Manuscript Library, Yale University.

Delphi."[27] They gazed up from Corinth toward Mount Parnassus. One wonders if this forbidden journey helped provoke the pair's subsequent visions.

At the end of March, they set off from Piraeus for Corfu on a small Greek boat that belonged, Bryher told Lowell, "to some people [with] whom my father has business." On this journey, the two had a cabin to themselves, sharing the deck with a crowd of "pigs, hens, and all other varieties of animals." "The wilder things got, the more excited H.D. became," Bryher enthused over H.D.'s capacity to "thrive on adventure.[28] After leaving the Gulf of Patros, they spent the night in Santameri. No one spoke English.

On March 27, they checked into Corfu's Hotel Angleterre et Belle Venise, which Baedeker considered "a lofty and picturesque site," with a view of the Ionian Sea. Bryher herself had cultivated fantasies about this island in her own father-financed book of poems, *Region of Lutany,* with its 1913 "Corfu," its "red-sailed ships in the silver light"; it cast "a spell" from its "cypress-breast" and poppies.[29] Corfu captivated with its intense sunlight, its "small villages along the irregular coast where the water lay, for the most part, like a semi-transparent floor of aquamarine." An overcast sky and soft light made "the star-like clusters of the orange-blossoms outside the window" appear "dim and distant," with mist from the sea and "floating down the island-hills."[30] The hotel offered reduced rates for longer stays, justifying they remain five weeks.

The day after arrival, they walked to an ancient harbor, offering a view of Pontikonisi, dubbed "mouse-island" after its compact, rounded shape.[31] "Odysseus swept past," now "lit round the sides with white electricity."[32] In "Odyssey" (1920), envisioning Princess Nausica, kept in exile by Poseidon, on the island Scheria, H.D. envisions a capacious Athena, "her feet / clasped bright sandals ... / which lift her above sea, across the land stretch, / wind-like, / like the wind breath."[33] Through a concentrated trance method, repetition secured stepping stones to navigate unexpected visions.

Blessed with a bustling port, narrow streets, stone houses, Corfu was verdant in April through May, abundant with roses, oranges, and fig trees, fragrant with mingled oil, lemon, and eucalyptus. They had long evening drives in carriages on good roads and lost themselves in the small village of Pelleka, high above the Ionian sea, dense with olive groves and darker cypresses. On Perdita's birthday, they drove three hours to Paleokastritsa, a convent on a stone-studded precipice overlooking the sea. The sunlit waves below felt unreal.

During this retreat, Bryher told Lowell she was drafting *Two Selves*.[34] Set in London, it showed a search to be "[a] boy, a brain, that planned adventures and sought wisdom." Akin to H.D.'s visceral sense of herself as interned nun, Bryher discovered with H.D. her own defense to keep hidden. Bryher's plan to have a cottage in Cornwall, and other pleas for liberty, were quickly shut down by her parents' standard reprimand that they had sacrificed their lives for her. "Something had hit her very hard," leaving "numbness" and the sense that "the active section of her mind had been smashed by a heavy fist." What hit her was "like an axe" led her "to keep hidden in herself." H.D. lifted Bryher out of hiding as initiate in this love affair with Hellenism and geographic emotions, the latter calling Greece "the lover, the spirit, latest known of all lands, beautiful as a many coloured flower, a shell, the sea, the heart of a white gull."[35] Ecstatic with precision, H.D. observed "the olive groves and patch-work of tiny gardens, blue thyme, small dart iris under the cork-oaks, quince hedges with wide blossom." The world sang once more. H.D. "read" nature so that "a cluster of maple-blossoms in my outstretched flat palm, almost spelt words," and "almost spelt out an open-sesame to a strange continent" with "wild deer," "the god Bacchus."[36]

In late April, at the Belle Venise, in Bryher's east-facing bedroom, with tasseled maroon-velvet curtains, a "series of shadow—or of light pictures" on the wall greeted H.D., who carefully described the figures as "not shadow on light." She confirmed her images could not be shadows due to Greece's relationship to the equator, making for bright late afternoons. It was not too surprising that a "stencil or stamp of a soldier or airman," "*somebody*" (her brother, Gilbert, or Aldington?) "with visored cap," "square-shouldered," with his "cap pulled down over his forehead," arrived "as if he had stepped out of the cloud of sea-mist about us." Compelled, H.D. read the images; Bryher took dictation. Second, H.D. caught the "outline of a goblet or cup," a "mystic chalice," filling the "same amount of space" as the soldier's head. The third image consisted of a "circle or two circles, the base the larger of the two," "joined by three lines, not flat," and "in perspective." She considered it "a pun" on "the tripod of classic Delphi," "the venerated object of the cult of the sun god, symbol of poetry and prophecy" that matched their "old-fashioned wash-stand," "something friendly and ordinary."[37] Psychically, they transported Delphi to Corfu, later described by H.D. as a singular experience ("never before or since"), but "there were wings."

During the trance, H.D. paused, released from "clock-time," and knew this was a gift, her head "already warning [her] that this is an unusual dimension," anxious her "mind may not be equal to the occasion." After the first three images, she turned to Bryher, not "break[ing] the sustained crystal-gazing stare at the wall before [her]." Asking if she should "stop," "Bryher says without hesitation, 'Go on.'" But H.D. took an intermission, seeing "a sort of pictorial buzzing," akin to swarming midges. Suddenly New England pragmatist, she noted "it would be a calamity if one of them got struck in one's eye." The vision was *that real*. This "writing on the wall," she emphasized, "could not be shared with *anyone except the girl* who stood so bravely there beside me.... *It was she really who had the detachment and integrity of the Pythoness of Delphi*" (italics mine).[38] Detached from H.D.'s former crowd, Bryher strained her vision that "can last as long as the mind and eyes can endure rigid concentration."[39]

After the break, H.D. saw two distant dots that "faded in intensity as two lines emerged, slowly moving toward one another." Taxed, H.D. imagined herself as Perseus with "winged sandals and the cloak of invisibility." A number of rungs, a "series of foreshortened lines," like that of "a ladder." At this point, she "must not lose grip" or "so miss the meaning of the whole, so far painfully perceived." Each step on this ladder challenged. Bryher's assuring presence allowed another figure to came "quickly," who she called her "Niké, Victory," depicted as moving "from the last rung of the ladder and she moves or floats swiftly enough," through a "series of broken curves," forming a series of "half-S" marks. These marks doubled as pythons. Envisioning Niké's back facing her, H.D. climbed the ladder toward "a series of tent-like triangles." Through a porthole, H.D. saw Athena "on the rock of the Acropolis, to your right as you turn off from the Propylaea."[40]

After H.D.'s Niké traversed tents, vision "cut out," and another "explosion took place." Now H.D., head in hands, "relaxed, let go"; this time "[Bryher] saw what [H.D] did not see," "a circle like the sun-disc and figure within the disc; a man, she thought, was reaching out to draw the image of a woman (my Niké?) into the sun beside him." The image inscribed a classic union, with Bryher as "a man, she thought." Both passive witness and active in completing H.D.'s writing on the wall, Bryher sought "adventures and wisdom" and unexpectedly found them. "*Seeing it together*," how H.D. put it, "for without [Bryher], I could not have gone on." "[G]ranted the inner vision" herself, she modified to "'seeing' it together."[41] In their indoor cinema, Bryher acted Pythia, the so-called average woman, who received and interpreted "prophecies."[42] This smoothed jealousy over Rodeck, but also reinforced H.D.'s sense they could translate the "dots and dashes," almost down to the atomic particles, to conjure a "buried" life, whether the Delphic Charioteer or Athena, through intense focus, Bryher holding the reins.

Acquainted with Sir Arthur Evans' 1903 excavation of the Minoan snake-goddess at Knossos, both were also aware of the myth of Apollo seizing Gaia's temple when he killed the Python, or snake-goddess, central to matriarchal culture. Lewis Richard Farnell establishes that "the Delphian snake is feminine, as we should expect the incarnation of the earth-goddess to be."[43] Small wonder they wanted to peer into distant Delphi. They thought what had happened to Minoan matriarchies might happen to them. They found a past, needing an update. Bryher now had a lover who asked similar questions, such as "Had not the islands been the home of the sailors? Had not the Cretan ships linked Mycenae and further Greece with Egypt, with the East?" With H.D.'s aid, Bryher applied "early knowledge of the Nile, of Phoenician history," to "spell from painted vase and moulded weapon the tale of the rise of Knossos, the sack of the palace, conquest, the end of the island dominion."[44] This arrived as felt hallucination for Bryher. Believing in Bryher's psychic powers, independent of her own, H.D. let the Corfu experience stay "oracle," provocative mystery.

Neither wanted a quest with a single answer, a firm bond between them. In a trance, H.D. asked, "Was I singing or laughing, Gareth?," to which Gareth responded, "'You were doing both together.' So I had not dreamed it." Bryher participated in H.D.'s embodied visions, incarnating an ambisexual hieroglyph. In 1920, they cherished being caught "in the subtle joy of creation," their "Greek phantasies" part of "another world," distinct from poetry reviews and publicity.[45] The couple kept these fantasies as honeymoon secrets in order to protect them from those who they knew would judge them imbalanced. Still, Eliot encouraged the idea that true poetry was a "disciplined kind of dreaming," a voluntary cultivation of visions which, after Dante, "we have forgotten."[46] In Corfu, the pair experienced heightened "disciplined dreaming." As if facing the Gorgon's head, H.D. was stiff, so as *not to turn away*, deducing she was both Perseus and the Gorgon. *Sea Garden* possessed "god-stuff," where "each intense natural fact is the trace of a spiritual force; each charged landscape enshrines a deity."[47] Yet something changed after the war. H.D. needed Bryher as co-medium "to go on." Creating obsessive linkages across time and within herself, she might be accused of "apophenia," coined in 1958 by Klaus Conrad to designate "feelings of abnormal meaningfulness."[48] H.D. was trained to find patterns, global and cosmic asterisms through her astronomer father, and imbibed mythology, poetry, and spirituality—complemented by her mother's elaborate stitch work; Bryher was trained by history, mythology, shipping logs, and boy adventures. H.D. fashioned her new love with Bryher through *Notes,* born from their first escape together alone, proposing a receiving station (with two receivers) that could decipher telegraphic messages. Design and pattern, key to H.D., governed by a Neoplatonic sentiment to decrypt materiality as emanation of a preexistent ideal; her twist was: this ideal existed side by side with the fleshly, ultra-alive.

Passing the baton to Bryher, who "seems to appear, as she did in actual life, to take the place of Frances," H.D. relied upon Bryher's steadying presence, *completing* a vision. In the end, their outsider status probably enhanced intense susceptibility to altered states. H.D. found happiness in Corfu, inhaling orange trees and cypresses, with Bryher's "care of [her], [their] walks and drives," having "adjusted her to normal conditions of life," H.D.'s phrase, which Freud later corrected to "[n]ot normal, so much as ideal."[49] Secreted in a hotel room, unmoored, the co-created wall set the tone for the pair's future psychic and literary romance: the two were "we two" as never before. But the adventure was not over.

* * *

During their last nights in Corfu, H.D. acted out dance pantomimes. In a world that restricted the pair, she performed different genders and bodies: a Spanish woman, a South Sea Islander, a Japanese woman, a priest from Tibet, and Minnehaha; she enacted a pan-cultural tour de force. Intermittently, Bryher, as Gareth, stared into the room's mirror. This catalyzed H.D. into "acting." "My throat was like the frame of a harp, the strings had left it trembling," "personalities" arriving from elsewhere. While Bryher acted audience, H.D. intermittently queried her to gain assurance, for instance: "I said, 'It was a boy this time. He was talking, did you hear him talking?' Gareth said, 'Yes.'" She used the carpet as stimulus, counting and recounting its rose baskets, common strategies for entering trances, and here, caught the transcendent aspect of Bryher: "My audience looked at me, its eyes contained the universe of 'still waters' and great spaces between day-light planets. The eyes did not change, they were not flooded out with black pupil but remained fixed, like blue-glass eyes in the face of a statue." "'Go on,' Gareth said again." Bryher's austere "head was held high and she sat taut and eager on the edge of the bed."[50] H.D. admitted to feeling "a form of possession."[51]

In the "*tableaux-vivants*" that we re-called or re-invoked together," H.D. saw past lives as threaded together, and always present. H.D. heard as well "the laughter of trees," as if in eighteenth-century Bethlehem. Bryher acted receptive slate, an auxiliary catch, their union imprinted on the hotel wall. Yet the chasm between their wartime lives and their new freedom, tinged with residual guilt for taking this queer trip, with a year-and-one-month-old in London, led to a paradoxical purpose that included H.D.'s need to "dig down into the rubbish and the ruins of past centuries" in order to make "spiritual space around the jar or amphora."[52] Before they boarded the "psychoanalysis line," they conjectured that while they existed in an impermanent dimension, an eternal one also existed. Scared and thrilled over H.D.'s capacity to envision what was *not there*, Bryher was both worried and enchanted, though each took pride in surrendering to hallucination. With the fire just low enough not to burn, they frequently scared each other.

On May 1, the limp travelers, enervated by visionary theatrics, took the train back to London by way of Rome. Ellis filtered it: "Hilda went 'right out of her mind,' at

Corfu and Bryher had to bring her back overland."⁵³ H.D. thought Corfu her high point, as letters throughout the decades confirm. He thought H.D. (why not Bryher?) had lost her mind. The train was safer, traveling from Corfu through Italy, Sir John's recommendation. Of Italy, Bryher reported "innumerable adventures," safekeeping the "writing on the wall," dwelling on other matters important to her, such as Italy, "in an appalling state, no food, strikes, and complete unrest."⁵⁴ During their journey, Bryher received Macmillan's notification of *Development*'s acceptance. Taking her father's name to signal triumph, Bryher commanded in a cablegram to Lowell, May 15, 1920: "DEVELOPMENT WAITING PUBLICATION. CAN YOU SEND INTRODUCTION IMMEDIATELY. ELLERMAN."

* * *

After typing up their notes and poems, the pair returned to Mullion Cove to celebrate their second anniversary. Forwarded by one of Sir John's colleagues on Rodeck's behalf, a box containing a crystal ball arrived from Alexandria: "It was a *State Express* cigarette box. The ball was wrapped in silver paper and then in several layers of tobacco-smelling blue paper." Supplementing its uncanniness, the package, decorated by a crown and a sun aura, bore the cryptic 555 and the words *semper fidelis*.⁵⁵ The Latin phrase intimated that Rodeck doubled in a shadow marriage with Bryher, whom H.D. had named the "Fido," the faithful. H.D. smoked State Express cigarettes henceforth. The crystal ball manifested H.D.'s "vision or state of transcendental imagination." Emboldened, H.D. threw Imagism well overboard.

8
Questing America & Marianne Moore

After Greece, Bryher reported semi-regularly to Audley. The couple had a furnished flat at Buckingham Mansions in Kensington on 16 Church Street, as if H.D. had never left Bethlehem. H.D. struggled to match Corfu time to the quotidian, envying her intimate's ability to jump from "one world to another." After sighting "the wild rose of the sky," Bryher no longer felt like "eating one's own mind in a narrow room." H.D. translated Euripides, a satisfying challenge, while Bryher read her beloved's work almost as an illuminated manuscript, discovered most translated lines, not H.D.'s, were padded, perhaps "eleven words shoved in," with no sense of "the weight and smell of a word."[1] Bryher cut her hair like a boy's, a declaration of independence,[2] and subscribed to the *International Psychoanalytical Journal*, much later telling Susan Stanford Friedman, "[Y]ou don't read psychoanalysis, you experience it."[3] At this point, the unsettling, engaging experiences of Corfu led Bryher to investigate *their* "condition."

Sir John thought America uncivilized. Bryher fantasized it "as a place without a past, woods filled with flowers," assuring that "[e]verywhere is a bit queer now." H.D. wanted to see her mother, now a widow, and introduce Perdita and Bryher.[4] Still suffering aftereffects from the flu of less than two years earlier, H.D. contacted Marianne Moore, a classmate at Bryn Mawr, to tell her prospective plans: "shouting Poetry" might be unwise while her lungs were "busy digesting fog," though she committed "to survive somehow."[5] Moore remembered watching H.D. rapidly walking toward the science building at Bryn Mawr as an "athlete," "seeming to lean forward as if resisting a high wind."[6] H.D. toyed with repatriating, settling her small family, if Bryher was amenable, in California.

H.D. instructed Bryher to read all of Moore's poems she could find. "The Fish," published in the *Egoist* in 1918, gave a "sense of coral and sea horses" on first reading,[7] Bryher struck by "wade // through black jade / of the crow-blue mussel shells," which made her "prisoner for life."[8] Submarine explosions disturb the ecosystem of the poem's "defiant edifice." At last, H.D. alerted Moore and her mother, Mary Warner Moore, she would sail in the new year with "W. Bryher" and Perdita Frances.

Moore's mother, like Gregg's, had entered into an ill-suited match with a mentally unwell husband. She wove an imaginary cocoon around her children, Marianne and John Warner, ascribing magical *nonhuman* qualities to each: Marianne, "Rat"; John Warner, "Badger"; and Mary, "Mole," all taken from *Wind in the Willows*. Mole ailed when her children displayed independence. College provided semi-independence, though Moore confessed wanting "mothering by everyone."[9] Girl-on-girl crushes were the rage; Moore fell for Peggy James, William James' daughter. Sensitive to H.D.'s difficulties at college, Moore explained to Bryher that it was "peculiarly adapted to [her] special requirements," such as forging a self apart from her mother.[10] Mary Warner's breakup with a longtime lesbian lover, Mary Norcross, made her cling to her children. When John Warner married Constance Eustis, Mary Warner regarded it as betrayal; Marianne herself was angry Badger deserted Mary, who now maintained a "lover's" intimacy with her daughter. For more than thirty years, Marianne shared a bed with her mother.[11]

Sparked by Moore's ingenious poems, H.D. offered to try to publish a volume in London. Pound too goaded Moore to publish, inquiring whence she had "appeared." She quipped back, "I do not appear."[12] Shortly afterward, Moore published in the *Dial*, also placing several of H.D.'s poems, "Helios and Athene," "Phaedra Remembers Crete," and "Phaedra Rebukes Hippolyta," in the November issue. The first poem, inspired by co-visions, loosely linked prose assertions. "The statue of Helios on the Olympic frieze," not static, with its serpent "hatched from an egg like a swan," hinting at Helen's birth. She created a bisexual ideal, "merg[ing] in the softness and tenderness of the mother and the creative power and passion of the male."[13] Pound judged her new poems weak, telling Scofield Thayer, the *Dial*'s editor, that they were "part conceit—part nervous breakdown," judging "the quantum is exactly what it was in 1912—nothing added—nothing learned—no development possible."[14] Evolving with Bryher, these poems figuratively formed a coral reef of psychic maturation; if her "imagism" caught the ephemeral, after Rodeck and Corfu, H.D. had glimpsed a Hesperides-like eternity.

* * *

One and a half years old, Frances Perdita took her first voyage, on the SS *Adriatic*, arriving in New York on H.D.'s birthday, September 10, 1920, during an intense heat wave.[15] Perdita vaguely recalled being tipped to the side of the rail as Bryher was seasick. The small Bryher overheard travelers: one said Americans knocked down old houses every year for new ones; another praised the country's numerous bathrooms. This gave Bryher "shivers." So much for an untamed world. Among the travelers, a Polish Jew voiced Bryher's fears of war: "Yes, they will start again."[16]

Entering the "gates," New York beckoned as a "new lover."[17] Traveling from Boston, Lowell greeted her pen pal, with H.D. and child, at the dock. H.D. urged the small family on to the Belmont Hotel at 120 Park Avenue. Staying for only "a hectic five days," H.D. begged off the cab tour of New York with Lowell to stay with Perdita.[18] A pattern emerged: H.D. slimmed away from unnecessary socializing and "being seen."

Bryher started drafting her creative nonfiction, tentatively titled *Adventure* (published as *West* in 1925), almost as soon as they came into harbor. It snipped an image from H.D.'s own memory bank where "[t]he wind moved, the leaves, and the Indian bird-limbs of children, tall and graceful," where Hilda "had climbed the pear trees in childhood." Bryher saw her lover "flashed on the horizon, spear-length of gold," with a panorama of "moods to learn, changes of expression, sky-mood, city-mood, to caress and note." "Only an American had bade her live," Bryher credited H.D. with *her* resurrection.[19]

Bryher no longer elevated Lowell, portraying "Miss Lyall" prudishly knocking Greenwich Village. Lowell thought herself disappointed, not "the creature of [her] poems, young and in shot silk waiting for the sun to rise." New York was so modern she called it Egyptian. Riding as mummies, the fare still ticked up, the taxi maneuvering beneath overshadowing skyscrapers, Bryher mesmerized by the harbor's sheets of silver water. Once they crossed the Brooklyn Bridge, she felt caught in "a chain of continuous movement" in New York's "[w]heels. Whir. Whir. Wheels. Interlocked. Interchanging. Terrifying." She compared the experience to "a nightmare," as if seeing "refugees fleeing from a threat more ominous than a Zeppelin." Both H.D. and Bryher had lived through the First World War.

Two days after they docked, H.D. organized a meeting with Moore and her mother at the Belmont, with its quaint Palm Garden tearoom. The crystal chandeliers offset Moore's "austere boyish head, her flushed face above the prim white collar."[20] Bryher was immediately enthused by the poet, while both Moores were receptive to the queer couple. The foursome spoke of England—Mary nostalgic about a recent trip with her daughter. H.D. and Mary conversed, while Moore and Bryher, recessed in their chairs, recognized each other from a gender-defying species. A casualty of Moore's unusual charms, Bryher saw herself in this "prehistoric creature, half bird and half dinosaur, with her stiff head and penetrating eyes."[21]

Five-foot four, Moore stood several inches above her new friend, enjoying Bryher's cropped hair. Bryher masqueraded in dresses in New York, yet her likeness taken in Cornwall in 1921 captured a boyish defiance and pixie sturdiness (Figure 8.1). During the 1920s, Moore wore "a mannish suit that hung loosely on her shoulders and revealed nothing of her shape."[22] By the time of their Belmont visit, she was "the man" in her family. Both evident gender outsiders, Moore and Bryher, requested their intimates refer to them as "he" and "him." Moore later sent Bryher a shot of herself, looking particularly furtive and masculine (Figure 8.2).

During tea, Moore advised, "There is one cypress you must notice," as if sketching a treasure map, "ten miles to the south side of Monterey. You will know it by the twisted bough; it is on the right side of the path." Summoning Moore the next day, H.D. again offered to forward her poems to Weaver's Egoist Press.[23] If this plot collapsed, they would marshal other connections. The couple wanted to bring the thirty-three-year-old poet out of her mother's shadow. But Moore wasn't even sure *if* she wrote poems, thinking of them as forming an index. Yet she entrusted a sheaf of indices to Bryher.

The twenty-six-year-old Bryher thought Moore, only a year younger than H.D., a case of "arrested development." Far more virginal than the sexually experienced H.D.—or Mary Warner—Bryher and Moore both suffered "some strange repression"[24] and quickly began an intellectual courtship. Bryher spotted Moore as a girl-page in another key. Both adored boys' books, agreeing dolls were "the dreariest, tawdriest things in the world."[25]

Figure 8.1 Bryher in Cornwall, c. 1921. Bryher Papers.
Courtesy of Beinecke Rare Book and Manuscript Library, Yale University.

After the initial two meetings with Moore, the pair convened with Robert McAlmon and Williams, who knew H.D. Despite his literary swagger, McAlmon was "Piggy" to the Moores. With his penitentiary expression and single sapphire-blue earring matching his eyes, he looked lost. Bent on escaping his family, he had fled Clifton, Kansas. His father was a poor Presbyterian minister, the most redeeming fact about him for Mary Warner. In 1918, at twenty-two, McAlmon wandered to San Diego, enlisted in the Air Force for a year, only to enroll at the University of Southern California, then a single wooden building, studying with Carlyle MacIntyre, who wrote a book on Symbolist poetry. Dropping out less than a year later, he headed for New York, forging friendships with Williams and Moore. With Williams, he edited a low-budget journal, *Contact*, just begun in 1920, also working as an art model at Cooper's Union.

Figure 8.2 Marianne Moore, 1932? Unsourced photo, Bryher Papers.
Courtesy Beinecke Rare Book and Manuscript Library, Yale University.

He admired "the nice lines" of his own belly and thought art required one "to dig into the possibilities of oneself, and today without a past or future."[26] He raved to Williams about Bryher, "a small, dark English girl with piercing, intense eyes."[27]

* * *

In late October, the "family"—H.D., Bryher, with H.D.'s mother, "Beaver," and Perdita—departed for California. Bryher quickly bonded with Beaver, who nicknamed her "Bay," alternate to "Boy." The itinerary called for cross-country travel to Los Angeles, stopping at Santa Barbara, then to the Carmel Highlands, a rustic hotel "hidden in the pines."[28] In Santa Barbara, Beaver likely snapped the loving shot of two mothers, Bryher in semi-doublet and hose, holding the baby, with H.D. leaning in, under an oak (Figure 8.3).

During the trip, Bryher wrote both Moore and McAlmon, excerpting material from this correspondence for her "travel-novel." In *West*, Bryher cast herself as the adventurer Nancy, H.D. as Helga, and Moore, Anne Trollope, with McAlmon as the inflated pioneer Magnus West. Moore promised to approach "publishers in their reptile houses" with it.[29] Moore and Bryher flirted, while McAlmon courted Bryher, both interlocutors identifying with her. H.D. was relieved Bryher had two new friends.[30]

Moore recommended McAlmon read *Development*, the American edition appearing in December 1920. Having already observed its "intenseness" of language with "the force of poetry,"[31] it dramatized an impossible wish, that "if she hoped enough she would turn into a boy."[32] Moore praised it for "exposition of the baffled sense one has of being outside what it is one's birthright to enjoy,"[33] considering " 'the imagination of a child joined to the freedom of a boy' sums the thing up very well."[34] Moore wanted and feared that freedom too.

While the foursome traveled, McAlmon read *Development*. He, too, "hated [school] with an intense, brooding, vitriolic, contemptuous hate," portraying himself as possessing "the energy of a yearling stallion." He wanted someone as companion, for Williams was "so so so much married, married, married." Regarding Bryher's book, he sighed, "What is there to say? You record yourself. That is all anyone can do.... But you don't want to be a boy." He scrawled in the margin that *Development* "got him," ranking Bryher with T. S. Eliot, Wallace Stevens, and Moore.[35] Between them, hyperbole ran high. His quickly drafted letters lacked dates. From New York

Figure 8.3 Photograph of Bryher, H.D., and Perdita Aldington, 1920. H.D. Papers. Unsourced family photo.
Courtesy of Beinecke Rare Book and Manuscript Library, Yale University.

he scrawled a "we," ready for "volcanic eruption," and promoted *Contact* because we can *say* what we want there—and it needs to be said—."By now, he likely knew Bryher had the financial wherewithal to make the platform superb. While in California, H.D. enjoyed Bryher's interest in Moore and agreed that Bryher could marry McAlmon, establish a press together in Paris, and thereby throw her parents off *their* track. Both knew McAlmon was, at the least, bisexual. They rebelled through perverse conformity. Their plot sounds naïve and deceptive, yet it stemmed from real pressure from Bryher's parents that she marry or remain caretaker of her mother and, for the forseeable future, her brother.

* * *

Moore enjoyed *West*'s depiction of her as "boy scribe" and "pterodactyl," though thought the portrait of H.D. stilted.[36] Affection for Moore bubbled into *Arrow Music*, published in 1922.[37] Searching for more psychic compatibility, Bryher hypothesized herself in "Carthage watching elephants" and "fear[ed]" Moore would "prefer the thin lines of a herd of gazelles that merge in with desert and are swift and quiet."[38] In turn, Moore pictured Bryher horseback, unable to "imagine anything more delightful than riding through the woods by the sea, in California," adding, "[T]here is nothing I love more, than the concrete and there is an especial romance I think, about elephants."[39] In Santa Barbara, Bryher wearied of conspicuous consumption, everyone having "one, two or three motorcars, and there is no sign of wildness or freedom." It ranked a notch below London, since girls there could at least wear riding breeches in the country. Of Moore's poems, "all interested [Bryher] very much," singling out "Dock Rats," which asserted, "[S]hipping is the / most congenial thing in the world."[40]

Switching gears, Bryher scolded Moore that it was difficult for readers to find her poetry. While writing from Santa Barbara, she spotted "a few rocks, one or two shells thinking about the fish to be born perhaps in a million years; all sharp lines." "*I hope soon the poems will be collected into a volume*," she pressed, anatomizing Moore's aesthetics as based on "a world before the fish age where shells cling to a rock and whether the shell was just a shell knowing its own rock perfectly—the boundary of its own ledges—or whether the shell was the entire world."[41] Did she not know her limits, or know them too well? Moore crisply replied that she held intense "curiosity about the world before the fish age," "pleased to have reminded" Bryher of it.[42]

* * *

Once in Carmel, with no elephants in sight, three film crews invaded; the travelers felt "billeted." The production companies, setting scenes, fired guns and explosives. Bryher watched a journalist snapping photos of a filmed ocean rescue, overhearing a fan admire the star, Mary Pickford, for not removing her wedding ring.[43] Pickford had pledged in March never to wed again after a divorce six months earlier, though subsequently married Douglas Fairbanks the same month. Bryher speedily penned

"With Mary Pickford in California" in December.[44] Aware of her own parents' belated marriage, Bryher despised matrimonial illusions, and designing to marry "Piggy" pivoted on a desperate desire for freedom, yes, but it also covertly punished her parents for their after-the-fact-of-*her* marriage.

While H.D. and Bryher left Perdita with Mrs. Doolittle at the Carmel Highlands Inn, they cavorted in secret coves, photographing each other naked, as sculptures come to life—photos which Moore's mother enjoyed.[45] One shot, used later in a scrapbook, shows H.D. walking naked in the woods (Figure 8.4). Bryher gave Moore a Kodak before returning to London. With Carmel in mind, H.D. cast Bryher as one in "a group of girl priests" who "stood wild, half-savage beneath great trees" that "filled the woods with intense, powerful, intoxicating fragrance. They cried or

Figure 8.4 H.D. on wooded path, 1920. Unsourced photo, Bryher Papers.
Courtesy of Beinecke Rare Book and Manuscript Library, Yale University.

chanted frenzied paean to the goddess of ecstasy, Artemis."⁴⁶ H.D. situated Moore as "one of the tribe to which these two girls, Josepha [based on Gregg] & Midge [based on herself] belong." Further, she intended to "attach Dactyl & Bryher" in her *Paint It*, showing openness to their possible romance.⁴⁷

Returning to Los Angeles, they stayed at the Hotel Alexandria. The little family made a Thanksgiving pilgrimage to Monrovia, California, and Mr. and Mrs. Howard, H.D.'s distant cousins. Bryher wired home about Sir John's uncle, who had married an American, possibly Mr. Howard's cousin; she hunted to no avail. From New York, Moore praised Bryher's "Girl-Page," copying two paragraphs from it, while thanking her new friend for looking for places to publish her own essays.⁴⁸ Each conceived the other as possible conduits to publication.

Early in December, Moore was even open to being nicknamed by Bryher, a bold gesture outside her family, offering "a weasel, a coach-dog, a water-rat, a basilisk and an alligator and could be an armadillo, a bull-frog or anything that seems suitable to you."⁴⁹ Bryher called her Pterodactyl, *West* engraving it: "Anne leaned back, her hands folded on her lap, like some heraldic version of a pterodactyl stiffly watching from its Jurassic rock, sea anemones open and close to the rhythm of the tides." "Pool" of *Arrow Music* likely addressed Moore, as Bryher gazed into the "tides," beckoning her from her rock.

> Has no wing touched your cheek?
> Is there no bird
> to weave a nest between your sullen limbs
> and hatch a songster,
> (amber with lizard eyes)
> to chirp above your phrases: "Love, love, love…"

Like herself and H.D., Moore was either not yet legible or extinct, "prehistoric," "amber with lizard eyes." Bryher celebrated Moore's "submarine poems and her rock scratchings," and H.D.'s poetry evoked "[f]lower leaf and salt water and a mind like a bird, diving everywhere." Nonetheless, Moore dominated *West*, otherwise surveying American Prohibition, superficial friendliness, and "suburbia gone reckless." From Monrovia to the Mexican border, they came upon orange groves, billboards extolling Sunkist, inflated real estate, and boosters' slogans of "Come to California and Forget You're Forty" and "Plenty of Water. Plenty of Sun. Forget your Neurasthenia." Bryher poked fun at herself through H.D. as Helga mocking, "America is the future and … the only hope of the human race lies in the West. What has happened?"⁵⁰

The foursome returned to New York in December. Leaving the land of dreams and ripe fruit, they sped by Arizona on the Santa Fe Railroad, with its heat, red canyons, bleached cattle bones, and sage. They raced fields and a blizzard in Chicago. Upon return, Bryher met Moore for lunch in Greenwich Village. "The Dactyl waited. A hasty message had summoned it. It was disguised in an Alpine hat, a frog-green coat and skirt" was how Bryher described their rendezvous. "He" was transfixed by "his" (Moore's) "unmistakable Jurassic eyes," the way *it* "hunched forward" with decisive steps, fearful yet assured. Moore's body possessed "the *austere outline of a young scribe's form*," yet the elder poet turned the tables on Bryher's efforts: "Dactyls don't have to be rescued. They rescue themselves when the time comes." Bryher saw in Moore a "shrinking from life" as "a masculine rather than a feminine gesture," diagnosing Dactyl as stymied by "the *boy's denial of himself* for some misunderstood ideal" (italics mine).[51] This was both projection and reflection. Moore living with her mother as an anchorite was the very disaster Bryher tried avoiding, though even with the couple's flat, she was expected to show up for her own mother very regularly. Never far from her mother, Moore had a part-time position at the Hudson Park Library, exactly forty-two steps from her residence at 14 St. Luke's Place.[52]

Wooing Dactyl, Bryher offered a travel fellowship so she might record what remained of beauty in the wider world, and envisioned her falling from her rock to "enjoy swimming among the anemones."[53] Patricia Willis conjectures, "Bryher feared Moore was suffering the fate she tried to avoid while Moore felt alarm at Bryher's adventures to which she might have succumbed had her circumstances been different."[54] H.D. eagerly watched the two dance, much like Bryher watched H.D. in her Corfu embodiments. Bryher fantasized cutting Moore's luxuriant hair, H.D. wishing Bryher "could try the experiment."[55] Moore replied that "the pterodactyl" was tempted "to shortening its hair." She also lamented her lost opportunity at fencing,[56] feeling as "much excited to hear of [Sir John's] prowess, not to speak of [Bryher's]."[57] Moore sparred with the sprightly Bryher. Just as H.D. spoke of her poems as particles, so too Moore thought she had "some things to say about acacias and sea-weeds and serpents in plane-trees that will have to appear in fragments."[58] Moore both trusted and resisted Bryher, signing, "*Love to H.D. Your trusting but disobedient, pterodactyl.*"

With some glee, Moore told her brother that Bryher couldn't understand her "being cooped up and kept to work when she might be writing, or riding an elephant," noting also the extent of Bryher's devotion to her. H.D. let on to Moore that Bryher's father often sent her money for forwarding her "ideas and ideals." Finally, Moore revealed that turning down Bryher's offers for a Syrian expedition *was not entirely her own desire*, "work[ing] and liv[ing] here as much by choice as necessity."[59] Wanting to be a "good pterodactyl that will come out of its rock," Moore begged Bryher to be patient. But in the end, if "Mole's being more worried than benefited by [her] going," travel adventures were impossible.[60]

In February, Moore wrote Warner about "Piggy's" "bad crush on [Bryher]" and gossiped over Winifred's tempting words—"Dactyl if you don't take it [funds for a traveling fellowship] delicately with *a swish of your tail* it will be very awkward." In this way, Moore warned Warner she had a nonfamilial friend. She delighted in Bryher's story of verbal swordsmanship with Pound when she sat "motionless smiling brightly but saying nothing." The male bard offered to teach Bryher how to fence, then backed out because she was trained at a young age, with Bryher explaining that "fencing was too intimate, too revealing a thing to be done with any stranger." During this month, Piggy boosted Bryher, who courted Dactyl. H.D. observed Bryher's awkward, hasty efforts to socialize. At this point, on February 13, 1921, Moore had no idea Bryher planned to wear "a cute black silk dress with short sleeves tomorrow with a figured pattern of little flowers" with "a high, low neck cut square" for more than one occasion. Bryher's father had threatened to haul her home himself.[61] Hoping the Moores would comprehend this necessary "convenience," Bryher impulsively, with H.D.'s assent, married McAlmon on February 14.

Moore hosted a tea party that very Valentine's Day, gathering H.D. and Bryher, Scofield Thayer, Dr. James Sibley Watson, co-owner of the *Dial*, a pioneer in radiology, and his wife, Hildegarde, MacAlmon in absentia. H.D. beside her, Bryher in her gorgeous empress dress, announced she had wed McAlmon earlier at City Hall. She likely thought this experimental gesture might make necessary ripples; in effect, she cross-dressed to marry, showing the whole heterosexual imperative a joke. In shock, the group carried on with "conversation in a most strained and cold soup fashion." Bryher rammed the *Dial* as not modern enough, favoring the upstart *Contact*; McAlmon was as talented as Yeats or Joyce.[62] Thayer took both this revelation of marriage and her taste as personal affronts. Shaken, Moore called the nuptials an "earthquake."[63] Moore considered H.D., with her cool presence, the most "remarkable guest" and "the most dignified," foil to Bryher's raw declarations. This marriage both short-circuited her budding romance with Bryher and brought it to the surface. For herself, Mary Warner judged Piggy had stolen "*the choicest possession of Mayfair.*"[64]

Moore judged her friend's marriage a misstep, but for H.D. and Bryher, it represented potential creative cooperation—and Bryher spied a reflection of sorts in renegade McAlmon. To give him a chance to develop as a writer and to create a press, funded by Ellerman money and partly directed by H.D. and herself, she considered it fair that McAlmon act beard in exchange. They envisioned autonomy from the Ellermans, with Bryher and McAlmon eager to seek out avant-garde writers in Paris. Bryher's experiment with McAlmon was meant to guard her and H.D.'s freedom. While Bryher brought the Moores into the couple's "chosen family," she fostered a scandal, not the true scandal: her love of two women! Horrified by the press, Moore collected notices, "nauseous and not even racy," one even providing a photo of a fake younger couple as stand-ins for Bryher and McAlmon.[65]

Probably surprised that her wealth and nonconformity made her perfect tabloid fare, Bryher wanted her divergent desires and identity hid, and to have them too. On Saturday, March 12, nearly a month later, the *Times* reported, "Heiress Writer Weds Village Poet," the subtitle, "Bride Exploited as Daughter of Sir John Ellerman, to Who Burke's Peerage Credits Only a Son," sensationalizing Bryher's illegitimacy. Another article referred to "Winifred" as "adopted," alluding to queerness, having "their companion with them—Miss Helen Doolittle ... whom the Village remembers as having been Miss Ellerman's chum when she came here last winter."[66] "Miss Ellerman" had *not* come to New York "last winter." *Life* mocked McAlmon as "the first poet to earn ten million dollars a line for his verse."[67] Announcement of the nuptials spread to Indiana where one paper spoke of the heiress and mocked McAlmon finding "vers libre" "diverting but not fattening."[68] The press saw and didn't see the bride was queer, traveling with an intimate, Mrs. Aldington, and her illegitimate child.

H.D. and Bryher's whirlwind trip ended with a newly constituted family. Sir John arranged a bridal suite on the White Star liner the SS *Celtic*. Lady Ellerman eagerly awaited the newlyweds, relieved to greet a son-in-law. Her parents overlooked Bryher's most prized relationship: with H.D. After hearing that Bryher's parents were happy with McAlmon, Moore wrote H.D. that she could "only smile very ironically at Robert's harmonizing so nicely with the family, in his adaptability to Perdita." H.D. probably shared an ironic smile. Moore added that she was "suspended a moment" in thinking to accept Bryher's invitation to travel for a year, sharing a side joke that "[t]he dactyl is not an oracle—merely Bryher's problem." By late March, Moore was struggling to make the best of the inconvenient marriage, channeling her residual attraction to Bryher through their shared love of men's haberdashery, ties, suits, and riding breeches. She gushed over the husband's clothing, then lamented separately to H.D. that with such a "finely adjusted ... mechanism as Bryher, one's spiritual motive power is sure to receive a backseat."[69] It did, and didn't.

In May 1921, Moore wanted the revised *West* and asserted Bryher had "no means off [our Jurassic] rock; nor shall a husband share it with us."[70] The next invitation for an adventure led, unexpectedly, to the Dactyl's razor-sharp reply that she couldn't "leave the library unless it were to save a life." She would accept only if it "were so unbearable that by staying *there wouldn't be anything of me left to go when I did want to go*."[71] Keeping the door open, she sent Bryher a lock of her hair.[72]

Back in London, with input from H.D., Bryher funded and curated the debut publication of Moore's poems with Egoist Press for July, five months after McAlmon and Bryher wed. Moore's reactions to *Poems* replicated her response to their nuptials. While "feeling flattered and encouraged," she repudiated the publication, clarifying her original "no" did not mean "yes."[73] To McAlmon, she plainly stated she was more distressed than she had "ever been in [her] life."[74] H.D. from Lake Geneva in 1921, wrote Moore, discussing her work in progress, *Paint It*, wondering what Moore thought of her "distinguished little volume," *Poems*, meant to be "a sort of twins" with *Hymen*, part of their Artemesian world.[75] Moore accepted *Hymen* for possible review, then shifted to *Poems*. Mole slurred it as "Cretan twilight baby," *foreign, deformed, veiled*, and as if it was deformed, "offered it two fingers." She was grateful for H.D. and Bryher's intention[76] but admitted to Eliot that "it was no literary advantage to publish this work but Miss Bryher had been so optimistic as to disagree."[77] Frank with McAlmon and Eliot, a bit catty to H.D., she did not spare Bryher, a sign of her attachment.

Writing Bryher on July 7, 1921, she criticized *West* as too "hurried," and Macmillan's editor turned it down, repeating his words that Bryher would "regret having published it." Depicting herself as "*a pterodactyl with no rock in which to hide*," "a Darwinian gosling," "a variety of pigeon that is born naked without any down whatever," Moore asserted she "wouldn't have the poems appear now if [she] could help it." Moved "by the beauty of all the printing details," she felt deprived of affirming its readiness. Shifting to Frank Parson's *The Psychology of Dress*, she underscored her nakedness, referring to "[t]he cocoon style with small waist and two or three yards of ruffled train. (I explain this, my dear baby dactyl as you would not remember.)" The letter, a shadowy lover's quarrel with herself as "gosling," demoted Bryher to "baby dactyl," making Moore "mother dactyl" upbraiding a willful infant.

She had spotted at the Bronx Zoo, a favorite site of Bryher and Moore, a naked gosling, unready for flight, as well as "a white snake with pink eyes." "[I]t eats mice without any fur," she wrote, signing off, "Your now naked, Dactyl." She was being eaten. With ten copies sent her, her postscript betrayed desperation: "I don't know what to do with these and don't know what to do next." But Bryher literally understood from being with H.D. how lovely nakedness was after all the corseting clothes they had known, and stubbornly believed Moore needed this metaphoric jolt, comparable to much more injurious hurts H.D. gathered from flawed "heroes," spurring H.D. to dynamic expression. Moore still visited publishers with her friend's manuscript, recouping its memorial to their meeting, and forgave Bryher, sympathizing with H.D. for navigating around her overeager chum, whose efforts to please often obscured her own needs as well as the needs of those she loved.

Bryher offered another "writing fellowship" in 1921. Moore put Bryher's check into a bank account bearing her friend's name, arranging a passbook for her. The money represented a "large consolation," for "*without its actuality, I could not have known so well as I do, the strength of your friendship, its solidity and dependability*" (italics mine).[78] In March, Bryher sent Moore one of her signature wardrobe items, "collars." Wearing one, the recipient noted Bryher's "indomitable" manner of "vicarious collecting of choice possessions. Mother says *I bury every bone beyond recovery*; these I shall keep above ground," so great was her "pleasure in wearing the collar."[79] Bryher's frantic gift-giving shored up reminders of herself in others as a means of forging bonds.

Finally, Moore agreed with Bryher that Freud may have a point, that "our capacity for transferring energy from one field to another is almost infinite and the adjustments of one need to another," cryptically amending, "[A] thousand derangements are the result of our misunderstanding of the physical."[80] She told the truth, slant: the libido must out, whether through sublimation or actual contact. Letting her friend off the hook, Moore thought it "an outrage for anyone to marry Winifred Bryher in such a style so unromantic."[81] Yet the compulsory convenience of marriage had betrayed bachelorhood itself.

9
Inconvenient Marriages & Wanderlust

> How wonderful it would be if there were no family life.
> —Bryher, *Two Selves* (1923)

The next six years spelled restless travel—packing, unpacking, repacking. Bryher and McAlmon, their marriage a mirage, crusaded for freedom. As early as 1921, militant "blackshirts" blocked streets from Florence to Capri, yet modern fugitives, usually white and privileged, created a diaspora of their own pleasure. A decade later, refugees fled for their lives.

H.D. and Bryher believed their "deviant ménage" needed camouflage. Initially, Bryher stage-managed the newly orchestrated "family" at 1 South Audley for at least a month. With two "households," the marrieds allegedly in a service flat and H.D. nearby at 131 Prior's House, St James Court. Their situation was as *Paint It* puts it, a quest with a purpose *"they could not have put into words."* The couple's "joy" H.D. compared "to the heart when certainty is upon us, after hours of tension and enervating unsatisfied expectancy."[1] She had committed to Bryher.

During her marriage to McAlmon, Bryher came and went from the mansion to H.D.'s residence. Both preferred Riant Chateau in Territet, Switzerland, a hideaway, where Bryher established a pièd-a-terre at number 25 on the fifth floor to host H.D.'s mother, Perdita, Helen, and Aunt Laura, together dubbed "the Beavers." They were good for Perdita; in one shot, H.D.'s widowed mother at seventy-six bears a resemblance to the child (Figure 9.1). Bryher luxuriated in this circle, especially after visits to McAlmon in Paris.

H.D. sanctioned and encouraged her co-visionary to explore the Paris crowd. America, at first, dazzled Bryher from afar. Now Paris entranced, but Bryher did have a "back-set," as Moore predicted, but also a new stimulus. Bryher, like H.D., suffered periods of severe mental distress, though the former underplayed these, projecting a multicapable persona. In her autobiographical notes, H.D. recalled shared work from this period, when "[*we*] wrote at St. James Court, the unpublished novel *Paint It Today*. At Riant Chateau, *we* wrote two or three story sequences as for the war-experience in London and Cornwall; these, we later, destroyed" (italics mine).[2] The "we" of H.D. and Bryher permeated this novella, kept unfinished, unpublished until after their deaths. At Hyde Park, the pair had dialogues about differences between England and America. Instead of overfamiliar New York, London let one be "alone

Figure 9.1 Helen Wolle and Perdita, 1921 or 1922. Unsourced photo, H.D. Papers. Courtesy of Beinecke Rare Book and Manuscript Library, Yale University.

or with an escort," "equally shielded and apart." This early, H.D. identified with Delia, or the maid of Delos, anticipating her "trance" name assumed during World War II, when she wrote several novels with the name Delia Alton. Delos, another name for Artemis, at this stage implied fusion with Bryher, leading to the perplexing question "Do you think the goddess might be the mother of you and my lover and of me?" Mothers and lovers, they meshed.[3] With overlapping minds, the two both soothed and alarmed each other.

Dislocation defined their lives. Bryher may have attempted suicide with drugs procured in Paris or Berlin. At least, H.D. recalled Bryher "moaning" on a bed in *1921*, twenty-five years later, when explaining her own breakdown as partly a reaction to Bryher's instability. H.D. could get her dates wrong, yet it is quite possible, with H.D.'s note of destruction of joined writing, that Bryher was still depressed by her literal and internal split existence.[4] Gregg too had tried drowning herself. Bryher frequently talked suicide, nicknaming Dorothy Richardson, whose mother killed herself, after her code word for it, "Rat," incidentally Moore's nickname in her family. The couple did visit Sir John's favorite climb in Zermatt in 1922. Realizing the sad folly in marrying McAlmon, Byrher reverted to depressive states and suicidal ideation. McAlmon did not make Bryher's visits easy; he was in denial about his uncertain sexuality, while H.D. craved quiet, avoiding the spectacle of McAlmon's drinking and drug taking, with Bryher playing schoolmarm. To be fair, Bryher wanted McAlmon's press to publish H.D.'s work, her own, and that of whoever impressed while she styled herself to gallivant. Like the interlacing of life and death, the published, the privately published, and the unpublished were not strictly separate to this pair. Lives, and writings, were in painful process.

McAlmon found Sir John "surprisingly non-interfering," though recognized his repressive power over his daughter, who grew up without "proper pets or friendships." He was "appalled" at Bryher's twelve-year-old brother being forbidden to "walk across Hyde Park other than with a bowler hat." The chauffeur escorted John Jr. in a Rolls-Royce, if he went anywhere. His parents made him "helpless, as they had her, a girl," and thus "ruined her capacity for full self-expression and enjoyment of life." But McAlmon liked Bryher's mother, deducing that "the vigilance of Sir John and her deafness had made a closed-in person" out of a "spontaneous" and "affectionate" woman.[5] He aroused her "game streaks" and unexpectedly offered Bryher a grain of wisdom: Hannah's "early experiences got her frightened and cut her off," which now made her "turn upon what she thinks near her. You."[6] This marriage did not silence her mother's complaints about her daughter's lack of lady-like behavior or her neglect.

Painfully, McAlmon's dedication to fleeting pleasures ignited Bryher's "monomaniacal capacity to be rebuffed, screamed at, wept at, but to persist, long after one had forgotten the idea upon which she was insisting." Scolded for even reading in her mother's presence, Bryher's frustration was understandable. Wanting to rid the house of psychology books, Lady Ellerman relaxed with McAlmon. On drives to their home in Eastbourne, he rode with her and John Jr. in the Lancaster, while Bryher and Sir John took the Rolls-Royce. Roving between Paris, Munich, and Berlin from 1921 through 1924, the nomadic McAlmon chafed at the Ellermans' expectation of cables every few days. Bryher struggled to break her mother's "clutch," to break "the 'Dolly' complex."[7] "We buy freedom at the expense of feeling fugitive," he complained. Living apart, they "coincide[d] with [their] tales" to placate her mother, who loved hearing from "Bobbie."[8]

Bryher had at least three time-clocks to punch: in Paris with McAlmon, for her parents; and for H.D., Perdita, and the "Beavers." Initially giddy at being at large, Bryher expanded the entourage's circle, equipped to mobilize because of her father's gift, as if to make up for her tying the knot to please him and her mother, a gift of 2,500,000 dollars in London property. Without McAlmon, the little family spent Perdita's fourth Christmas in Florence in 1922 with Norman Douglas, whom H.D. had not yet met. Born in Austria in 1868, the queer polymath wrote *South Wind* (1917), a best-seller that brought many queers to Capri, loosely disguised as Nepenthe, for cruising and sensory indulgence. From Florence, Douglas wrote Bryher, observing her handwriting looked immature and that he wouldn't let an enemy's cat die in Territet.[9]

Over sixty, Douglas wrote separately to H.D. as "Unicorn."[10] Bryher sent him "exquisite shirts," handkerchiefs, and funds.[11] He advised H.D., "delicate *in the chest*," to avoid Sicily, where winds gusted fiercely.[12] As a "queer" who survived without labels, he cheered on their partnership. "What have you done with the unicorn? Are you together? Let us hope so, for it would never do for you to drift on alone. So very unhygienic, for one thing," he wrote, while mocking "R[obert] and his silly café haunting habits."[13] Perdita liked the "charming author," nicknamed "Oncle," recalling how she "romped and paddled and scrambled, rode on donkeys."[14] Leaving the couple to explore, Perdita stayed with Douglas, who read *Alice in Wonderland* aloud: "P often goes off by herself & reads & is very contented. The days slip by."[15]

With H.D. mostly residing in quiet Territet, Bryher sent gifts as simulacrums of herself. In forming a "chosen family," Bryher relished Helen's calm solidity, especially for Perdita's sake. Helen appreciated Bryher's "great kindness," gushing over gifts. For instance, writing "Bay dear" that "no words can flow from my pen to half express my love & appreciation & as I opened my eyes this morning my first thought was of you & then the gown & the first thing I did was to open the closet door to see if it was really there"; it was "*too too* beautiful for old Henrietta." This kind of response helped Bryher feel "real," her gift standing in for herself so as not to be forgotten. Asking for smelling salts for "Horse," H.D.'s nickname after the horse driver, Hippolytus, Helen did not "feel equal to doing it—as you do." "Doing" what? Purportedly, taming the wildness; H.D. had always been high-strung. As a famous trainer puts it, in another context, "Picture the most sensitive person you've ever known; a horse is ten times more sensitive. A horse is a naked nervous system, particularly a thoroughbred."[16] H.D. acted "thoroughbred," performing "escapades" in California for Aunt Laura.[17] "Horse" wrote Bryher twice a day, but Beaver observed her daughter "looks lonesome—no one to take your place—well, you are coming back to us—no 'ifs' this time."[18] H.D. often became sickly after Bryher left, and letters about McAlmon's antics didn't help. "Dear Baby Horse," one letter began, "Bobbie is so exhausted with a ten day bust," and "looks as if he had been trapped in a submarine."[19] Trying out freedom, Bryher now understood its grazing limits.

H.D. told Moore that Bryher, "intense & radiant," talked about "doing things with 'Dactyl.'" "A 'baby Macenas' I call her,"[20] she alluded to the patron of new poets under the first emperor of Rome, Maecenas (68–8 BCE), a "cultural minister." This was how H.D. framed Bryher's Paris search for new poets. Beaver appointed Bryher "leader" of their "little family,"[21] while McAlmon scoffed at Bryher's tutoring the not yet five Perdita, who readily named "all the continents, and main cities of the world."[22] Bryher tried getting her husband to see a psychoanalyst, Barbara Low, a translator of Freud's 1920 "Psychogenesis of a Case of Homosexuality in a Woman." He refused, and after meeting Ellis, dismissed analysis altogether.

London depressed McAlmon, though he was hardly ever there. Fully funded, his burden was his own. Paris intoxicated. A high point, he introduced Bryher to Sylvia

Beach's iconic Shakespeare & Co., the English-language bookstore, nexus for expat artists in Paris. Beach memorialized meeting Bryher, "a shy young English girl in a tailor-made suit and a hat with a couple odd streamers" like "a sailor's," with magnetic eyes, bluer than "even the Blue Grotto in Capri," who during their first meeting was "practically soundless." Beach took Bryher to meet her lover Adrienne Monnier, proprietor of the bookshop La Maison des Amis des Livres, just across the road. Meeting this couple somewhat redeemed Bryher's marital "inconvenience." "[S]tanding like a passenger from the Mayflower with the wind still blowing through her hair and a thorough command of French slang," Beach was Bryher's "guide."[23]

Beach bankrolled Joyce's *Ulysses*, battling prudish publishers in America and England who wanted it banned; Joyce ultimately diverted Beach's rights from the pioneering 1922 edition, selling them to Random House in 1934. Bryher inadvertently funded *Ulysses* by replenishing sums Beach doled out to Joyce. In late 1921, McAlmon pledged a "reform streak," even offering to send prewritten letters from "Dolly" to her mother from Munich.[24] Convinced his writing improved after leaving New York, he drank absinthe, white and red wine, chased with whiskey, taking Joyce to the finest bistros, tipping grandly, yet he missed his idol's publication celebration of February 2, 1922.

In 1922, Berlin attracted with its favorable exchange rates. Unable to tell the sexes apart "along Unter den Linden," McAlmon lived near Magnus Hirschfeld's Institute for Sexual Science, observing it on Bryher's behalf. He was hard-boiled toward "postwar privation," callously remarking, "People will starve to death; people will die; or kill themselves, or drink themselves to death." With this morbid viewpoint, McAlmon purchased a "massive bracelet that looks like a medieval anklet," inspired by a new pal, Djuna Barnes, who went in for jewelry, "a nice whim to make life appear more interesting than it probably is."[25] He remarked that Berenice Abbot, poet Mina Loy, and "even old Baroness Else Von Freytag," surrealist provocateur and lover of Barnes, each "stage moments of being."[26] Bryher couldn't, he implied.

Through 1922, McAlmon signed off confusingly from Pound's at 70 bis Rue Notre Dame des Champs, Montparnasse, in care of American Express, Charlottenstrasse, Berlin, Deutschland. He was itinerant. Finally, Beach set up Bryher's "post-office" service, "a fine, large sort of case, with pigeonholes marked with the letters of the alphabet," a "receiving station," keeping stories of togetherness intact. Beach apprized the newlyweds when Lady Ellerman asked their location, substantiating the couple's togetherness, when in actuality they barely spoke. Attached to "Bobbie," Lady Ellerman visited Paris in 1922, afterward sending from Brighton a bust of Shakespeare to Beach, a "most valued ornament."[27]

Bryher appreciated Hemingway, who, unlike McAlmon, boxed with her, though he often burst into tears; "sitting gloomily at a table near [her] and saying he would never find a publisher," he worked on *A Farewell to Arms*.[28] Of Stein, she observed, "Look, she seemed to say, this is a word but it has no simple meaning. It varies every time that it is used." The *Paris Tribune* raved that "the pulse of the Inner Circle of Montparnasse is beating much faster" after the arrival of the *other* shipping heiress, Nancy Cunard, apparently the only heterosexual in town.[29] Imbibing Bryher's encounters, H.D. aspired to "emotional wisdom," while Eliot told McAlmon to take Paris "as a place and a tradition, rather than as a congeries of people, who are mostly futile and time-wasting,"[30] Shy of Eliot but influenced by him, H.D. too *required* solitude and exquisite intimate connection, rejecting the weak bravado of self-destruction.

* * *

During August 1922, McAlmon attended all-night "owl" parties with Cunard in Hungerford, twenty-seven miles from Oxford, to escape H.D. and Bryher. By September, he had returned to Berlin, dipping further into its subculture. Occupying a large room at In Den Zelten 18, an adjacent flat to Barnes and her lover, the sculptor Thelma Wood, he "partied" with Isadora Duncan. In his whirl, he tantalized Bryher with "at least 100 cafés where ladies and gentlemen 'that way' congregate," describing "two cute girls of the type," "beautifully built, slender boyish things, one with a leonine head—magnificent as a noble man's head is. Quiet, calm, a lovely thing." He added a dig: "one must circulate to have circulation." Exploring cabarets and dance clubs, he often purchased cocaine, "[a] deck of 'snow,' " costing a mere "ten cents." Glib, he witnessed "a number of souls unsure of their sexes or of their inhibitions," while "several Germans declared themselves hermaphrodites." He warned Bryher not to force travel upon H.D., who struck him as "such a mixture of butterfly, hummingbird, giraffe and workhorse"; he admired H.D., who "seems surer of something worthwhile than anybody."[31] He meant it, but he also wanted to annoy Bryher.

In late 1922, McAlmon gave Sir John his stories, *A Hasty Bunch*, bluntly asking, " 'Gimme' cause I want to start a publish house [*sic*]."[32] Bryher softened his approach, though McAlmon sent Sir John "Abrupt Decision," a story featuring "a woman [who left no note] driven to suicide by the realization of what a hog of a man she's been married to and had children by, for nineteen years." Whether or not he read the story, Sir John invested the hefty equivalent of $50,000 for the couple's press, with *Hasty Bunch* its first publication. McAlmon published luminary experimental writers— Hemingway's *Three Stories and Ten Poems*, Mina Loy's *Lunar Baedeker*, Emanuel Carnevali's *Hurried Man*, Williams' *Spring & All*—in 1923, and Mary Butts' *Ashe of Rings* in 1924. Most accounts of Contact Press mistakenly champion McAlmon as sole engine.

Now a welcome visitor to Stein's salons, thanks to Beach, Bryher introduced H.D. to Stein when she came to Paris in 1923 to sit for Man Ray. His photo captured an arm defensively swerving upward, her face wincing, turning the other direction, while his photo of Bryher showed her elfish side, fists clenched and far-sighted gaze. Detecting a "glowing quality of life" in Alice B. Toklas, beneath her "apparent repose," Bryher aspired with H.D. to be like the two lifelong mates, maintaining "intact" personas.[33] Stein gave Bryher the opus *Making of Americans*, a successful "failure," striving to get to the "bottom natures" of everyone ever living. Accepting it for *Contact*, McAlmon threatened to destroy all unsold copies (it was, after all, almost a thousand pages), considering her work a jumble of "Hebraic, Sumerian, and primitive cultures, in the realm of incantations."[34] Secretly jealous of Stein, he joked that she could *not* do a cartwheel, but he could. He preferred Loy's *Lunar Baedeker*, with its delicious opener, "A silver Lucifer / serves / cocaine in cornucopia."

* * *

While "the marrieds" cavorted, Moore crystalized her hurt at Bryher's nuptials in her collagist poem "Marriage" (1923). She mused, "I wonder what Adam and Eve / think of it by this time, / this fire-gilt steel." Any harmony with McAlmon was null by 1922, though Moore's "Marriage" flirted with Bryher.

> Eve: Beautiful woman—
> I have seen her
> when she was so handsome
> she gave me a start
> able to write simultaneously
> in three languages—
> English, German and French
> and talk in the meantime.

Moore identified Eve with Bryher, often taken for a freakish genius, knowing English, German, and French, with McAlmon playing Adam.[35] The poem acknowledges "experience attests / that men have power / and sometimes one is made to feel it," and snipped from the eighteenth-century freethinker William Godwin, who wed his lover, Mary Wollstonecraft, that "marriage is a law and the worst of all laws." She was guilty, the contract "requiring all one's criminal ingenuity / to avoid!" For Moore and those outside compulsory heterosexuality, marriage "can never be more / than an interesting impossibility." Bryher was criminal in kind.

Keeping it from Thayer's *Dial*, "Marriage" came out in *Manikin*, edited by the homosexual couple Glenway Wescott and Monroe Wheeler. A friend of Moore's, Wheeler, open about his homosexuality, thought marriage inappropriate for those who needed to "avoid / it." Moore called Wheeler and Wescott's union "domestic," "able to maintain a relationship true to the spirit of marriage without the benefit of the social contract."[36] However, unbeknownst to Moore, Bryher financed its printing, this time in sworn silence, satisfied to sponsor a wounded and wounding poem about marriage.

Moore's exclamation "Unhelpful Hymen!" worked in cross-current with H.D.'s 1921 anti-epithalamium, *Hymen*, where H.D.'s prologue sighed over the dominant culture's loss.

> Ah, could they know
> how violets throw strange fire,
> red and purple and gold,
> how they glow

*gold and purple and red
where her feet tread.*[37]

H.D. claimed "ours is the wind breath" and "the bee's soft belly / and the blush of the rose-petal, / lifted, of the flower,"[38] rejecting "old desire—old passion" in "Fragment 113."[39]

* * *

In 1923, Helen, on behalf of Bryher, proposed a trek to Egypt, leaving McAlmon to gadfly. H.D. signed on, agreeing Egypt was next on their spiritual pilgrimage, providing "psycho-emotional" nourishment."[40] Helen promised Bryher she would carry smelling salts for H.D., if she should need the Victorian remedy. Merely glancing through Cook's brochures, Bryher smelled Egypt's palms and camels. Recently, in November 1922, after over a decade of digging in the Valley of the Kings, the Egyptologist Howard Carter had excavated Tutankhamun's tomb. Anticipating a swell of tourism, H.D., her mother, and Bryher resolved to visit Egypt in advance. Prior to embarking, H.D. and Bryher reviewed Sir E. A. Budge's translation of *The Egyptian Book of the Dead*, an anonymous text attributed to Thoth, the god of scribes, who measured each corpse's heart; if not light as a feather, the soul could not reincarnate. Depicted with reed and palate and his ape-headed dog, Thoth often accompanied Isis and her sister. Poor Budge, H.D. sighed sympathetically at his celebrated transmission: copyists replicated it with precision over a sustained period from 900 BCE to 1600 CE; in light of Tutankhamun excavations, the book needed revision. Without authorship, it echoed the duo's sense of being invisible scribes, advancing into the unknown.

Budge wrote of transformative incantations chanted to "ensure the well-being of the dead," hymns using "words of power by the deceased in the underworld." H.D. studied Isis, reassembling the jigsaw of Osiris' body through "means of magical words." Most hymns revealed every soul possessed a "ka," or double. After sighting "the man who was not there" on the *Borodino*, the "ka" deeply appealed to H.D., a shadow self that might escape its body to wander, or even "dwell in a statue."[41] "I was not dead in my sleep," says her speaker in "Fragment Forty-One" of *Heliodora* (1924).[42] Like Eliot, H.D. was influenced by the anonymous *Upanishads*, where an eternal "thumb-sized" "Self" or "Atman" (not to be confused with the "ego") witnesses the impermanence, and even in sleep carries on a unifying function.[43]

The trio arrived on January 25, 1923 in Cairo, checking into Shephard's Hotel, a famous nineteenth-century watering hole, its terrace's wicker chairs providing views of rare botanicals and the central boulevard. Heading for the Pyramids and the Sphinx in Giza the day after arrival, Bryher, jotting times and places in a journal, kept them on a hectic schedule. They took in the zoo, toured mosques, shopped bazaars. In stopping at all the same hotels and sites, they retraced the footsteps of Amelia B. Edwards and her compassionate friend, a woman physician, set forth in their two-volume *A Thousand Miles Up the Nile* (1878). H.D. cribbed phrases from it.

On February 1, they ventured up the Nile to Luxor and noticed ultra-subtle variations in light. Decades earlier, Edwards had observed, "The glow was in the stone."[44] Slicing light and shade, wheeling birds, crocodiles, hawks, and lizards reinforced H.D.'s own sense that "[e]verything in nature was inhabited by a spirit."[45] Edwards observed the Nile "greying, by some curious effect of reflected splendor," turning into "the most luminous of River of Revelations gold. The Nile flowed now straight into [my] imagination."[46] H.D. recast Edwards, calling "across that broad river of light, across that River of the Book of Revelations light."[47] Shadowing two women traveling without chaperone in the previous century reassured H.D. and Bryher, though they had Beaver.

Crossing the Nile from Hotel Luxor, they hitched a sand-cart across the Valley of the Kings to Tutankhamun's tomb. Edwards knew the avenue of sphinxes once lay from Luxor to Karnak, recording "colossal" sphinxes at ten feet, many "headless, some split asunder, some overturned, others so mutilated that they looked like torrent-worn boulders." Such enormity, though cut into, overwhelmed Edwards: it "strikes you into silence; that empties you, as it were, not only of words but of ideas." This sentiment set the stage for H.D. and company.[48]

Our couple thrilled blind fingers by touching raised word-pictures. They found the "crochet-like wave lines, with giant chick and bee," etched in tombs. They returned by way of Karnak, otherworldly yet homey, the sphinxes "cut out of butter, soft, lovable, mounded by this moon-light into soft pollen semblance of life." Releasing herself from strict Hellenism, H.D. uncovered an additive to her psychic cocktail. "Egypt offered anodyne, while she flamed up in Greece," the former softening pain, its heat like "soft snow melting in her brain." Not, thankfully, the snow McAlmon snorted. Greece made "you want to measure up to the ideal, to reach beyond yourself."[49] Egypt, Edwards had agreed, "made you silent, overwhelmed and drugged by realizing one's smallness within a monumental landscape," pushing the spectator into "the cool shade of unknowing,"[50] what H.D. desired, in her large sun hat.

Cruising down the Nile on the SS *Rosetta*, the trio took a side trip, first on a trolley, then in a rowboat, to an underwater island, Philae, recently submerged. They berthed at Aswan, staying at the Cataract Hotel, where they sighted gazelles. Bryher bought a scarab, and H.D. purchased a cat amulet to keep Perdita near, visually expressing their bond. Knowing Perdita often missed her, she explained that her writing had to be sustained, much like her "sampler." "So many stitches and just so many rows, day after day. If I miss even one day," she dramatized, "I drop a stitch and lose the pattern," difficult "to find again."[51]

Returning to Shepard's Hotel in Cairo, H.D. rose before her mother and Bryher, reading her Greek Testament. One morning, H.D. spied from a courtyard window where doves cooed, and saw her mother approach, bringing a book of poems and a bouquet of roses.[52] She deemed it a visitation when her mother did not materialize. While in Egypt, H.D. drafted "Secret Name: Excavator's Egypt (circa A.D. 1925)," the last panel begun first for her triptych novel, *Palimpsest*. With the presence of Helen, the title's "secret name" evoked faint memories of Mamalie's dossier, her father as well traced into "Secret Name," where Egypt is "simply another planet," "near, much nearer to the sun and stars."[53]

* * *

Bryher's *Two Selves*, finished after Egypt, emerged out of the same "we" of H.D.'s bildungsroman *Paint It*. Revising her manuscript, Bryher placed meeting H.D. last, rediscovering her "Egyptian" childhood while traveling with her poet-lover; it was "as if her whole being were concentrated into an eye" and "seeing straight through people and actions and conditions." With H.D., Bryher was "learning Greek" and, as if wearing her beloved's goggles, summoned "familiar if un-memorized phrases that had all the grit of sand in their sound, the silent padding of camels and the flash of hoopoe wings," glimpsing "the gold caravans of far off days that met and parted at Kom Ombo," with the Pyramids "less strange than the omnibus that jolted down the street, and olive and orange-flower more familiar than the buttercups." Sounding like H.D., Bryher saw her camera-mind as "a row of cells—a hive, open in the middle and dark. A line of a poem, an adventure, a new thought, opens one cell, many cells, and frees the pictures they contain."[54] After Egypt, Bryher reinstalled her "family" at Riant Chateau. May Sinclair visited, telling ghost stories to Perdita and Helen. Brigit Patmore also arrived; Beaver deemed her "too fast." "[One] evening P[erdita] 'knots' or 'weaves' velvet ribbons of a frock" out of material Bryher brought from Paris.[55]

Bryher engaged Maurice Darantiére of Dijon to print for Contact Press. After *Hasty Bunch*, *Two Selves* emerged in 1923, and McAlmon's *Village* in 1924. When visiting Paris, Bryher cultivated friendships with Beach and Monnier, Stein and Toklas, distancing herself from "Bob-Cat's" crowd. "Dear Baby Horse," Bryher wrote, reporting Mary Butts "got so drunk it's been too much even for Bobbie!!!," ticking off that "Djuna and Thelma are happy together. Williams returns here the middle of May. Oncle [Norman Douglas] is in an awful mess." Bryher dined with Mrs. Joyce and McAlmon at Boeuf sur les Toits, where she "saw the most alluring attractive puma, whom Robert had taken [her] there to meet." In this swirl of "smoke, jazz, scent, drunk Americans, scores of beautiful pumas all dancing together," she missed H.D., meeting many Bryher thought she should know, such as Jean Cocteau. She had "dinner with Man Ray and Kikki [*sic*].... Oh Horse... what's the use of seeing funny things if you're not there to be visibly shocked!" This Parisian adventure culminated with Stein, who called Bryher "the pure type of ethical Jewess." They "talked till eleven." She tried a cocktail, "no nourishment and pure fire."[56] McAlmon now scorned H.D. and Bryher as part of a "tri-feminat" with Moore. Stein was "too far removed from real experience."[57] As for Mole, she simply pitched *Hasty Bunch* in the "FIRE." He did mention that Cunard "got" *Two Selves*.

After hearing from Bryher that Mary Butts, who consumed "a whole jugful of drugs," made an advance,[58] H.D. proposed coming to Paris in "green corsets" to "lie on the bed done up in magenta scarves," having her "hair carrot-ed as a nice little surprise." Regarding it as a "gallant duty," she would "knock down" Mary if necessary. Offering to take an early train and "clutch [Bryher] in public" and sending "a thousand kisses and all my love."[59] "In public" underscored "clutching" took place in private. "If you just can't stand it, it would be wiser just to come back," H.D. advised, reminiscing on "loveliest associations" near Audley, their earlier years "an enthralling & enchanting story"; at Territet, she wanted to "know when [she] can see Fido."[60]

H.D. came on her longest visit to Paris at the end of September 1924, supporting Bryher's male identification after taking her everywhere, remarking, "I can never thank him enough just for being HE."[61] Williams and his wife, however, were dull. McAlmon imagined H.D. and Bryher were spying on him. Peeved by their coupledom, he quarreled with Williams, mortified his "marriage" was exposed as a sham by the couple's presence. He blamed Bryher for his closet and accused H.D. of duplicity, though the latter kept in touch with "Bobbie."

H.D. and Bryher returned to Riant Chateau with an invitation to tea with Dorothy Richardson in October. "Dorothy's great novel [*Pilgrimage*] was one of almost complete suppression of female independence," a fact Bryher "suffered herself."[62] Of Bryher's initial fan letter, Dorothy said it "read like a first chapter in a novel."[63] She hoped Dorothy might interest McAlmon in London, to quiet the caws of her mother for the couple's proximity. McAlmon preferred Cunard's parties.

* * *

Paris drained H.D.—yet it shaped her poetics, through Bryher, Beach, Stein, and others Bryher introduced her to.[64] H.D. published *Heliodora* in 1924, with poems interlayering Greece and Egypt. Inscribing a first edition "To W.B" "from H.D.," the poet quoted from its "Hyacinth" ("snow crater, filled / with first wild-flowerlets"). H.D. donned the role of love poet, missing her "inveterate / prodigal spender," admitting "all you have, / all, all I gladly give," for "the reach and distant ledge," longing for "the sun-smitten, / wind-indented snow," for their love nest at Riant Chateau.[65] Thawing, Bryher had "flowerlets," hopes for them and their art.

Heliodora's "We Two" configures a mutual "miracle" of H.D. and Bryher, in a world that saw them as a "blank wall," mistaking it for "a final resting place." Phantoms near tombstones, in other words. Recognizing that most *did not see* their relationship, "the two met within / this maze of daedal paths," with Ariadne's cord tautly between them. H.D. called up erased ancient female poets: among them, the epigramists Nossis and Telesilia, restaging Sappho's gymnasium. Heliodora, a poet, was Meleager's muse, and with H.D., recognized "fire or sunlight, not heat in the ordinary sense, diffused, and comforting," "another element containing all these, magnetic and vibrant." This was what it was like for H.D. to love, where the most commonplace event or object or person, "unhuman" herself, could live under a halo. Both icy and full of heat, Sappho gripped H.D,[66] hovering over *Heliodora*, a garland of her own.

In the first century BCE, Meleager thrived in Alexandria, which Eileen Gregory calls the epicenter for Hellenistic studies, possessing "sensual and yet intellectual charm." With the world's largest library, assimilative Alexandria was for H.D. a state of mind more than a place, "a city of heterogeneous texts and artifacts, of scholars and poets gathered in library and museum."[67] Being located on the Mediterranean brought the city robust trade with a mix of Greeks, Jews, and Egyptians. Meleager had "a Jew father, a Greek mother," echoing Bryher's suspected Hebraic ties. By displacing herself and Bryher upon Heliodora and Meleager, H.D. created a necessarily dynamic process, where "Love" is "mateless," "the rite, / the whole measure of being." Channeling Heliodora, H.D. asserts, "So I saw the fire in his eyes, / it was almost my fire," advising the poet to "surprise the muses," for "those ladies sleep." The poem proved a method, refined with Bryher where *intimate thoughts are kind / reach out to share / the treasure of my mind, / intimate hands* leading to "*sheer rapture.*" Demonstrating "in some subtle way" women as "co-workers with men," Meleager, H.D. believed, understood "the spirit of the 'courts of Love' and the chivalry of the Arthurian cycle," her reiterated through-lines—with King Arthur supplied in honor of Bryher.[68]

Sappho fragments, "re-worked freely," punctuate *Heliodora* as voice-over of H.D.'s drama with Bryher: "Fragment Thirty-Six" with "I know not what to do: / my mind is divided."; "Fragment Forty-One" with "thou flittest to Andormeda"; and "Fragment Sixty-Eight" with "even in the house of Hades." The poet of Lesbos was vibrantly modern, much like the girls H.D. now noticed with Joan of Arc haircuts more confident on London streets, and sang through Sappho's "simple" "I sing"— not to please any authority but "to sing beautifully like this, in order to please my friends—my girl-friends." Meleager mourned the lost work of Sappho: they are "little," but "all roses." For H.D., even if "[Sappho's] last line was lost," she was Plato's "Morning Star," another echo of her grandmother's memory of Native and Moravian peacemaking.[69] *Heliodora* held "Helen," bridging Greece and Egypt, its three short stanzas repudiating male mythic history as destructive desire. Warriors loved "only if [Helen] were laid, / white ash amid funeral cypresses."[70] For H.D., Artemesian love was impersonal, not scorching; the most anonymous, like Bryher, acted prosthesis for manifesting *inner* ideals; the pole star also played teacher, reminding H.D. that Helen was not in Greece or Troy but on the lam in Egypt, which Herodotus confirmed.[71] Eve wasn't even where she was supposed to be, as H.D. and Moore (in "Marriage") intuited. Indeed, new evidence shows humans descended from a "mitochondrial Eve" with "southern African origins," locating DNA inherited only through the maternal line.[72]

With *Heliodora* in press, H.D. returned to *Palimpsest*, shaped by cinema. In Montreux, the pair saw G. W. Pabst's *Joyless Street* in 1924, both star-struck with the film and Greta Garbo. Dating their cinema mania to this screening, H.D.'s "first real revelation of the real art of the cinema," while Bryher turned "late to the cinema," "because of *Joyless Street*."[73] Its Expressionist cobbled streets and alleyways tendered bleak survival, Garbo as Helen, an eternal figure of loss and repair.

By October 1924, McAlmon had booked tours in Egypt, Constantinople, and Athens; he was drying out, perhaps seeking rest in a sarcophagus, admitting "he was quite unprepared to grapple with what Egypt might mean to him had he read more"; he enjoyed "the smooth surge of the boat through Nile water," while the warmth "massaged his will and senses into passivity."[74]

* * *

Palimpsest began with a poem dedicated to Bryher, notably de-idealizing her. Like H.D.'s "[n]either honey nor the bee," she now boasted "stars" and "ships," calling up their fathers, negation creating an opening: Bryher, "not so rare as Hesperus," "not gracious as the Pleiades are, / nor as Orion's sapphires, luminous," yet the last stanza confirmed:

when all the others, blighted, reel and fall,
your star, steel-set, keeps lone and frigid tryst
to freighted ships baffled in wind and blast.

H.D. and Bryher each had "frigid" streaks. Through *Palimpsest,* H.D. was "baffled," freighted with Aldington—and Patmore, his new paramour. This autobiographical novel gave each of its main characters a "grinding labor," the phrase H.D. used to signal altered states. The first section, "Hipparchia: War Rome (circa 75 B.C.)," set after the conquest of Greece, gave the perspective of the "daughter" of the Greek female philosopher Hipparchia, who, exiled from conquered Corinth, witnesses a Greek theater built for Cicero, "watching like one risen from the dead, to attend the installing of some new religion." Like herself, H.D.'s character struggles with "some odd untranslatable fragment that after ceaseless modeling, remodeling" kept resisting her, for "Sappho in Latin" was "absolute desecration." Affirming "Sappho's singing" was *not* "sheer pain," H.D. connected her to Isis, "a blue cloud, exquisite that waited," a state of detached wisdom. Aiming to avenge "the whole lost and superseded civilization of the islands," Hipparchia unexpectedly meets Julia, not a poet but a historian of Alexandria, who knew her poems "all by heart," inviting her to travel lost history. Further winking at Bryher, Julia's father has "outposts in the islands."[75] The other two parts of *Palimpsest* focused on present anxieties.

As late as 1925, H.D. feared Aldington might claim custody of Perdita. Patmore had challenged Bryher three years earlier to dress as a man and meet Gray or to send McAlmon.[76] Finding it intolerable that having "a little freedom" meant "HE can come down on me. Perhaps just a PHOBIA,"[77] H.D. met Patmore several times for tea in London during 1925. "Mimosa" was the one who reiterated Aldington's impulse to divorce. Discovering Patmore's own passion for Aldington inspired *Palimpsest*'s second section, "Who Fished the Murex Up? (circa A.D. 1916–1926)." Patmore is likened to a "murex," a predatory sea snail that spilled purple ink, while the main character, Ray Bart (H.D.), fragmented together a modern poem.

After Greece, and now Egypt, H.D. identified as "a Graeco-Egyptian," "wandering across New Jersey marshes" until she discovered "[t]he laughter love in Isis and the laughter of wild Aphrodite" that emerged "from some exhaustless spring of which her shoulder blades, her shoulders and the bird-like smaller collar and throat bones seemed the rocks, the pebbles, the white and polished stones."[78] Mamalie thought laughter religious, and back in London she was on H.D.'s mind; Helen and Laura were with her in a temporary, small furnished flat at 37 Park Mansions, Knightsbridge for two months of summer. After her mother and aunt left in 1925, H.D. with Bryher rented a flat at 169 Sloane Street. H.D. recalled saying goodbye "in a suffocating white fog," regretful she and Bryher had not taken the train to Liverpool to see them off, forgetting to pack Bryher's gift to Helen of a fur coat.[79]

* * *

Early days, Bryher thought McAlmon might adopt Perdita, but he was not dependable. Besides, he asked to divorce in 1925. Still fearing Aldington could destroy her, H.D.'s new rune called for "strength of arm and throat," a more expansive love.[80] Close on the heels of McAlmon's decision to divorce, Pound wrote Bryher about his "secretismo," a mistress with child, asking her to assume "parental functions and look about for some suitable lying-in hospital or maternity home or whatever, in French Switzerland."[81] Dorothy wrote simultaneously about *West*, out in 1925, saying the book "decided in the negative—for myself—as to the USA but it was certainly right that you should try it."[82] Bryher was delighted *not* to answer such letters. H.D.'s *Collected Poetry* (published by Boni and Liveright in New York) was now out. The critic H. P. Collins, devoting pages to H.D. in his 1925 *Modern Poetry*, observed that as "a new classicist," her writing "depends upon a degree of self-revelation and self-abandonment."[83]

The same year in May, Frances Gregg's marriage to Louis Wilkinson collapsed. Gregg settled her family in a basement flat in a rundown London mansion, subdivided among several tenants, with the Macpherson family in the upper story: "Pop," or John Macpherson; Mrs. Macpherson; their eldest child, Kenneth; and daughter, Eileen. Frances fell for Macpherson, descended from a long line of naturalist painters. She thought this sensitive, handsome twenty-one-year-old might illustrate her writing. Her pen-pal, Powys, was pleased she found "someone's love to turn to." Macpherson was "something too light and sweet and caressing" that could remove "all the hurt out of all the past." Powys responded, "Love your boy. He will not fail you."[84] We already know the story's punch line. By return missive, Frances had relocated her family to a single room, informing her secret-sharer that she was once more let down.

After the "failure," Frances perversely sent Macpherson to H.D. to show off his talents. H.D. and Bryher were both drawn to his easy charm, detecting a new threesome. H.D. felt a spark in his indeterminate eroticism; her mate recognized in him a masculine role model. After blundering into the first marriage, Bryher now calculated what this one could achieve. Bryher hid queerness in plain sight so her parents *would not be hurt*. Her *primary sense of self* amounted only to a set of unmentionable facts.

At the end of the year, Macpherson took proofs of *Palimpsest* in Paris rain to McAlmon. H.D.'s poetic novel compared Joyce as self-consciously grafting the modern and the mythical, compared with her more capacious temporality, not just a double-decker affair. Instead, H.D. turned to modern science, that "[t]he past (she knew) was the future," and "[t]he present and the actual past and the future were (Einstein was right) one."[85] Space contracted, but expanded for our duo. Macpherson, like an emanation of Helios, convinced them that "they" could marry him, and then legally adopt Perdita. His warmth compelled H.D., depressed by her aunt and mother's departure; the "flowerlets" needed extra light. Elated by friendship with the ever-adventurous Bryher, Macpherson bubbled over with ideas about filmmaking, coinciding with our pair's newfound love of cinema. Bryher spotted Macpherson kindling H.D.'s creative energies; if he energized H.D., all would benefit. Besides, Bryher saw through to his queerness. The triangle, with McAlmon leaving it, shifted to H.D., Bryher, Macpherson—and the newly adopted Perdita.

After establishing Macpherson at Riant Chateau in 1926, Bryher started Pool Publications, a venue for film criticism and experimental work, its first book, eighteen-year-old John Jr.'s, *Why Do They Like It?*, attacking his schooling at Malverns. In March 1927, he accompanied his sister to Paris for her divorce. Beach sympathized with Bryher over the miserable breakup with McAlmon, who, after the date was set, at the last minute wired that "he want[ed] to drop the proceedings in Paris altogether." Unwilling to occupy a witness box in England, Bryher surmised an annulment could be forged "on the grounds of technical virginity," but preferred not "to bring up a lot of medical details." If divorce had been easy, H.D. would have long since disposed of her marriage to Aldington. "I wirelessed him to wireless me when he expects to land," Bryher wailed, extending her Paris stay another ten days.[86] McAlmon finally arrived.

Unlikely in all matters, Bryher made legal decisions based on an imperative to satisfy H.D., who waited anxiously for news. With Macpherson's almost imagined arrival, both women risked the experiment. H.D. wrote Bryher that she and Kenneth "had a lovely relationship on the strength of the talk about [her]," and Kenneth "wanted her 'to be HAPPY.'"[87] A repeat Rodeck, he grasped what H.D. and Bryher desired and mirrored in each other. In Paris on June 15, 1927, McAlmon divorced Bryher "on grounds of her indifference and abandonment," headlines reading, "Robert McAlmon Gets Paris Decree from English Shipping Magnate's Daughter." Fearing objections, she did not warn her parents. Hundreds gathered outside the French courts where three American couples also got divorce decrees. H.D. still worried over Aldington's reappearance. She began *Pilate's Wife* in 1924, featuring a woman trying to stop her husband from crucifying Christ.

The year 1926 marked the "illegitimacy act." Sir John offered to make Bryher retrospectively legitimate. Bryher determined "[w]e were all exiles." Richardson shared with her Miriam admirer that writing for her was "meeting a stranger in the form of a contemplated reality who has for the first time its own say."[88] H.D. and Bryher had met the stranger in Karnak, and in themselves. After Greece and Egypt, they beheld "two regions, two shining and slippery worlds, to be balanced carefully."[89]

10
Cinematics

We Three

> We're not three separate people. We're one.
> —H.D., "Narthex" (1928)

In 1927, H.D.'s mother died on the spring equinox, ten days shy of Perdita's tenth birthday. "Stricken," H.D. went "on as usual."[1] Three months later, in June, Bryher finalized her divorce, and bought a professional film camera. Over the grumblings of her parents, in September, the day before her birthday, the thirty-three-year-old Bryher married Kenneth Macpherson, eleven years younger, at a registry office in Chelsea. Bryher's mother asked, "[H]ow can you, a woman of your age, marry the poor young man?" To H.D., *said wife* blessed their life as "gilt openwork and one feels to complete it we should have Watteau panels."[2]

Seeing the peculiar new family off, the Ellermans, themselves married in secret, tucked Macpherson into a separate carriage. As H.D. put it, "K," "unraveled, critical," was with us, "'incog,' on a train at Victoria."[3] H.D. and Bryher enjoyed a separate compartment on the *Orient Express*, while Kenneth shared the stateroom with Perdita, who immediately liked the "tall and attractive" Macpherson, knowing Bryher's parents "disapproved of him." She missed Kenneth terribly when she was at Audley, knowing "he couldn't call." Understanding that H.D. and Bryher "probably saw him outside," Perdita increasingly felt excluded, this "the worst of being a child"— "[p]eople one cares for, just appear and disappear," with "nothing one can do about it." The triad neglected to see how Perdita, benefiting from the marriage, suffered their absence.[4]

The triad did not follow the heterosexual paradigm. Eve Kosofsky Sedgwick has famously teased out the dynamic of two men communicating their desire for each other through a woman. Here Macpherson was the object of two women, or three, if we count Gregg, who propelled H.D. toward him. Drawn to Macpherson, H.D. also desired Bryher, as "something more than woman." "Big dog" to "small dog," Macpherson reciprocated Bryher's boy-like crush, finding her "adorable," playing out his budding homosexual desires. In one shot, Kenneth poses with Bryher, their easy affection obvious as "Fido" leans into him (Figure 10.1).

Figure 10.1 Kenneth Macpherson and Bryher, 1927. Unsourced photograph, Bryher Papers.
Courtesy of Beinecke Rare Book and Manuscript Library, Yale University.

Each complementing the other, the trio innovated a creative process. The financial burden of maintaining what we might today call a polyamorous non-monogamous ménage fell upon Bryher, whose new grand schemes, hatched with Macpherson, was to release avant-garde films, crossing barriers between individuals and countries. This comported with the trio's vision. Macpherson's family also joined their lives: his mother, "Madame Macpherson"; his father, "Pop"; and his adrift sister, Eileen, nicknamed "Egon." Bryher pivoted from her mother's demands, who claimed she only *used* "Haudley," Kenneth's new coinage, as gateway to H.D., at Sloane. H.D. split her time between writing in London and living at Territet for film shoots and romance.

In multiple letters, H.D. addressed both Bryher and Macpherson as "dawgand-dawg." This nicknaming helped them undermine cultural hierarchies enforced by powerful white heterosexual men, who saw themselves as apart from feminized or "dark" natural forces. The "boys" barked for H.D., nicknamed (in this period) "Lynnix," "Kat," or "Mog," to return from her Sloane "basket"; every few weeks H.D. reported delays, while encouraging them "to keep their tails entwined." The proximity of "tails" probably involved physical solace. When at Audley or Sloane, Macpherson, having "queer hollowness," penned slobbering letters to "him" as "small Dawg." Bryher still exalted the now grieving H.D. and sent her a bottle of 4711, the perfume Beaver gave her, with "heaps of love." H.D. visited Lady Ellerman in London and thought, alone, she was "quite sweet," noting Bryher might, if she let herself, have a "heavenly time" at Audley.[5] H.D. played "Dolly" now.

Unable to regard their own families as "normal," Bryher and Macpherson became fascinated with other mammals. Bryher, not allowed animals as a child, saw her own body as idiosyncratic, found familitude and aggravation when by 1928, they had adopted eight monkeys, among them two gibbons and two dracouli, small "luminous creatures with owl eyes," Perdita dubbing them "Iddes" and "Eggles," after the Id and Ego; she was indeed Bryher's daughter.[6] Her favorite of the monkeys was "Sister." Both Bryher and Macpherson sought to reparent themselves through rambunctious pets. Reality punctured fantasy. The primates expanded domestic responsibilities, not the least of which: cleaning their cages. For Perdita, there "was a continual business of mopping and rushing frantically for bits of newspapers." Furniture was "covered with ominous stains," yet Perdita purloined Sister who slept between her feet, giving "an affectionate wriggle of furriness."[7]

In the so-called human world, H.D. turned to George Plank, the acclaimed Quaker illustrator, his Art Deco designs prominent in *Vogue*, as a father-confessor from the 1920s through World War II. She explained Bryher's sometimes intimidating manner, which stemmed from a "deep, almost suicidal reserve," having "walled (or had walled) herself so completely," she sometimes lets it "dominate HER," adding, that much like herself, Bryher was really a "funny shy elf sort of indefinite being, all hid away there." Macpherson was "like April sun-light."[8] Seeking to bridge the visible and invisible, she wanted a "hidden" and expansive light.

Together, the trio founded the Pool Group, their production and publishing company. They released "cinematographic" novels: Bryher's *Civilians* and Macpherson's *Gaunt Island*, portraying Gregg as "a dead satyr." Bryher's book poked at London's persecution of Germans living there during World War I; one of her cast, a German, works in the censorship office. From 1927 to 1930, the threesome made at least four films, the first, *Wing Beat*, mostly lost. They produced the first film journal in English, *Close Up* (1927–1933). Bryher assumed the bulk of the duties; Macpherson ran the editorial column. It published first translations of Sergei Eisenstein, experimental pieces by Stein, Moore, Oswell Blakeston, Robert Herring, Barbara Low, Hanns Sachs, Dorothy Richardson, H.D., Macpherson, and Bryher. Virginia Woolf turned down their solicitation; they rejected Pound, H.D. asking Fido to let him down easily, while she forcefully rejected Williams; Macpherson invited Langston Hughes, who didn't think he had anything suitable. *CU* remains a rich repository of still shots from now lost films. Anne Friedberg describes its enjambment, "situated symmetrically on the brink of two decades; at the threshold, as well as between silent cinema and sound film."[9] Both H.D. and Bryher were mad for cinema's "visionary" capacity to revive absence. With its ghosts, film could potentially heal war-tortured psyches through the frame's protective "holding." During its six-year run, H.D. wrote primarily for the journal's first three years, tying cinema to ancient writing; Bryher contributed twenty-two articles, on war films, censorship, distribution, and the availability of inexpensive projectors.

*   *   *

As a wedding gift, Lady Ellerman engaged the royal suite for Bryher and Kenneth for October, with a huge fire in the sitting room, when they first traveled to Berlin to scout out venues and contributors in October.[10] By then, they could carry their first issue of *CU*, July 1927, with H.D.'s "The Cinema and the Classics: Beauty," the film theater "a sort of temple": "Before our eyes, the city was unfolded, like some blighted flower, like some modernized epic of Troy town is down.... The true note was struck, the first post-war touch of authentic pathos, not-over-done, not over-exaggerated.... War and war and war." *Joyless Street* embodied Garbo as war survivor, "getting something to eat" "among execrating warriors, the plague, distress, and famine," with her "child's icy, mermaid-like integrity."[11] They also brought to Berlin their first film, the seventeen-minute *Wing Beat*, shot in early 1927, framing their aesthetic as both the "beat" and winging away, seeking to showcase Macpherson's animated drawing talents. Featuring stills of both Macpherson and H.D. in the July 1927 *CU*, the caption read, "A film of telepathy. The feeling of 'something about to happen' pervades the whole." They wanted to make the first free-verse film, with "actions of thoughts etched" on actors. Shutter action uncovered tensions between characters—conveying unspoken dread, connected somehow to "young men, caught... in the very tail of the blazing red war-comet," finding cinematic expression. She rejected "bird-stuffers," art straining for verisimilitude.[12]

This debut film scintillated with invisible communication. *Wing Beat* brought Robert Herring, a reviewer for the *London Mercury*, into their circle. The surprising intuitive rhythm reminded him of Jean Toomer's *Cane*. After *Wing Beat*, Herring became a regular contributor to *CU*, fell for Macpherson briefly, while acting confidante for H.D. and Bryher, almost a younger brother to both.

When they visited Berlin, Bryher and Macpherson sat for all-day immersions. Staying at the Hotel Adlon, Bryher, collecting mail in the lobby, looked up from H.D.'s letter to see her double, "a fat, middle-aged, but unmistakable manic-depressive Fido, looking worried and saying, 'Wo ist Herr Macpherson?' So I fell on him and said, 'Herr Pabst' and we fell almost into each other's paws." Having read H.D.'s analysis of *Joyless Street*, Pabst heralded the journal as "[t]he thing we all desire, the paper that expresses our inmost psychological thoughts [and] an Englishman has done it.... Ha ... ha ... ha. And tell me who is H.D.? Ah. How she understood *Joyless Street*. And poor little Greta Garbo.... And exactly who is H.D.?"[13] Chuckling at Pabst's praising "the English man," along with H.D.'s own routine question about "who she *was*" exactly, Bryher raved over the "honeycombed" palatial Berlin theaters, one "about the size of Regent's Park," decorated with "red plush, walls and red carpets. And miles and miles of entrances and exits." "Dawganddawg'" proclaimed they were "in love with Pabst."[14] Macpherson sent photos to H.D., "one of Pabst himself, young, very very very very Lesbian," or "[j]ust our Fido gone fat, rubicon and gayer, and a sweeping Germanic hospitality and generosity and cordiality that you just sink on to like a warm feather bed."[15] Urging H.D. to avoid the Greggs, he ordered, "DO see [Herring], he's a cute sort of ass."[16] Proud of *CU* and *Wing Beat*, H.D. flattered Fido, "a good little Herrnhuter," harking back to the Moravian family; she felt "little dog bristles really felt in the work."[17]

Pabst motored Bryher and Macpherson to Neubablesberg Studio, introducing them to lighting and set designers, taking them to lunch in Potsdam. Bryher learned *Joyless Street* took thirty-four days to film, Pabst's team behind the camera, working thirty-six hours straight. Macpherson and Bryher saw films of Eisenstein and Pudovkin before they were censored. In Berlin, Bryher noted they "were walking across a thin slab of ice. Fritz Lang and the perfect lunar landscape."[18] Pabst had also introduced them to the filmmakers F. W. Murnau and Lang. Bryher shared Pabst's horror at the sight of students taking up military traditions, while he believed in "pacifism, and psycho-analysis." Bryher especially appreciated finding "Turtle," her nickname for Hanns Sachs, one of the original seven psychoanalysts in Freud's inner circle. Pabst introduced them at a party on October 30, 1927, one of their last days this visit. Sensing Bryher's shyness, Sachs took her aside to discuss psychoanalysis, censorship, and education. Looking at shots of H.D. in *Wing Beat*, Pabst started "throwing stills at [them]," and screamed, "H.D. has understood, she has understood." Pabst's "great friend," Sachs, was soon to be Bryher's analyst.

H.D.'s second article, "Cinema and the Classics," subtitled "Restraint," clarified that partial images evoke emotion, that it was "not necessary to build up paste board palaces, the whole of Troy, the entire over-whelming of a battle fleet." Addressing an "everywoman," she encouraged, "[Y]ou and you and you can cause Odysseus with one broken oar to depict his woefulness." H.D. rearticulated her poetic mode suitable for cinematic clutter: "Someone should slash and cut."[19] Yet "cinema has become to us what the church was to our ancestors"; H.D. sought in the theater the "womb-mind," or at least a natal "sub-stratum of warmth."[20]

Sachs conceived of theaters as "nurseries" where spectators vicariously overcame inner obstacles. Bryher knew "films and psychoanalysis, in those experimental days were twins," directors "mak[ing] thoughts visible."[21] Believing film could "deepen consciousness," by "a process of concentration," akin to trance work in Corfu,[22] Bryher watched King Vidor's *The Big Parade* seven times, its rhythm exposing "the complete wastage and stupidity of war."[23] "The camera introduces us to unconscious optics," Walter Benjamin famously described, "as does psychoanalysis to unconscious impulses."[24] Before reading or meeting him, Bryher already understood Benjamin's "technique of the sudden shock," sprung from "the 'optical unconscious.'"[25]

While Bryher worked on *CU* at Territet, Lady Ellerman asked to meet her new son-in-law's London friends. H.D. introduced Herring, who heaped praise on Bryher's "uncanny and clever" discovery of film. After tea with Lady E. and Herring, H.D. reevaluated "mama" as "[a] sort of sweet old steam roller without the steam on. One rather liked her," noting Hannah's heart flutters after meeting cordial Herring. In March, H.D. urged Bryher back to London.[26]

After entrancing Bryher's mother, Herring sent H.D. a book on butterflies, proving antennae ubiquitous in relationships, revealing telepathy was rooted in natural science. He told her about driving down a country lane, looking in the rearview mirror while conversing with a companion, as a "crystal experience" of the present, past, and future, holding the three as one. Herring fit the Pool Group's dedication to crystalline, interactive, and queer forms.

* * *

Upon the advice of the London analyst Mary Chadwick, the trio sent Perdita to boarding school on a raw January 3, 1928, just after Lady Ellerman's birthday. Pup hated it, despising school as much as Bryher had Queenswood, or John Jr., Malverns. But Bryher still had close friends from her school, including Doris Banfield and Petrie Townsend, and probably convinced herself Perdita would benefit from escape from their monkey house. Hiding her tears when her two mothers left her at the station, she later generously excused them, for "time in Riant Chateau these days, was apt to be given over to intellectual problems and sheer hard work; Kenneth's films, H.D.'s intense bouts of writing, Bryher's morning-till-night sessions at her desk, typing, filing, trying to keep the editorial side of *Close Up* afloat."[27] H.D.'s perfectionist credo reveled in "chiseling and cutting, shaping and revising," leading to Macpherson's dismay when he drowned in celluloid strips.[28]

While her beloveds explored Berlin, H.D. used the trio's dynamic to translate Euripides. Mourning provided unexpected energy; she wrote in a cultivated trance. She adapted *Hippolytus Temporizes*. The hero's father, Theseus, founder of Athens, abducts and rapes Hippolyta, Queen of the Amazon, a mythological lesbian matriarchy. Upon discovery of his father's brutality, Hippolytus vows chastity, forsakes his paternal inheritance, seeking his dead mother through his patron goddess, Artemis. Enraged by his rejection of his Athenian birthright, Aphrodite plans revenge through the tragic, human Phaedra, Theseus' wife, making her fall in love with her stepson. To do this, Aphrodite casts Phaedra as an illusion of Artemis; in this guise, Phaedra seduces Hippolytus, who, after learning this trick, crashes his chariot into the rocks. His horror derives from sleeping with his stepmother, not from his desire for his mother *through* Artemis. In H.D.'s retelling, she chose a primordial drive: a search for a missing mother. Bryher could "play" Artemis, Hippolyta, even Hippolytus, while Kenneth played Hippolytus, "the boy," and H.D.'s roles were Hippolyta and the "stricken" Phaedra. She diagrammed a fluid playbill for three adults who questioned their own reality.

H.D. & Kenneth [Phaedra & Hippolytus]
  Kenneth & Bryher [Hippolytus & Artemis]
Bryher & H.D. [Artemis & Hippolyta]

Macpherson, one of H.D.'s "male virgins," like Hippolytus, doubling for Bryher, played both the violated mother and elusive Artemis. Each duet eroticized the absent one. H.D's adaptation left gaps in the play's narrative, as if rotating a camera, lending her words a whirring effect, "realizing a self" that "was an octave above [her] ordinary self." It "crystallized" the trio's free-floating eroticism in affectionate or embrace of unclaimed erotic desires.

Though coded, Macpherson wrote both women in spring 1928, wanting them "in his own big basket with all the butter for his tail, and the pussy willow prickles that the pussy puts beneath his tail." Whether fantasy or not, he needed the pair to stimulate his "tail," one with butter, the other with a pussy willow, one of the first woods humans used to make brooms, bats, wicker baskets, and dildoes. One way or another, "Kat" and "Fido" aroused "his tail."[29]

After finishing *Wing Beat* and *Hippolytus*, the trio traveled in May to Venice for their "honeymoon," which for H.D. relived a "pre-natal" memory of her parents' honeymoon there. Bryher was grouchy, wanting return to their mindset in Corfu. H.D. wrote "Narthex," almost on the spot, akin to Bryher's quick *West*, to celebrate Bryher and Macpherson. "Narthex" signifies a plant stalk used as a wand in a circle of initiates; she had them, with St. Mark's Cathedral its backdrop, siphoning off Gregg's intensity, lurking behind Macpherson's rejection of her and the one who made the triangle possible. The story shows Gregg "prematurely blighted," a "spiritual gynecologist," compared to Bryher, as Gareth, "singularly all along ... a spiritual successor." Gareth had "a needle to her intellectual compass, the thing that Garry was pointed true.... Follow your own achievement." Representing Bryher as well as either a snail that won't use its antennae or, more flattering, as a "child Buddha seated on a leaf regarding a spread lotus," with small hands tackling a teacake, putting "too much dynamic energy into everything," H.D. reckoned "years of intimate concord, conflict or communion (it didn't matter)" creating a loyal duet with "she and Gareth" as "a sort of composite person." Telepathic communication was "heaven," and she believed both Bryher and Macpherson got "(thoughts, sensation) across in some subtle way," making "this hieroglyph and language" between the trio.[30] Through Gregg's story "The Apartment," published in the 1928 *Second American Caravan*, Frances bid farewell to Macpherson, herself cast as "phantom."[31] H.D. had, in fact, never entirely shed her attachment to Gregg, empathizing with her financial distress, her divorce, especially after learning of Alistair Crowley's outrageous attempt to commit her.

On May 11, 1928, Bryher and Macpherson's adoption of Perdita was finalized. H.D. told Perdita her name was now Perdita Frances Macpherson, acknowledging her middle name derived from "a great friend," the name of her heartthrob as well as her favorite grandfather's. But for everyday purposes, she remained Perdita Aldington. To add to this hall of mirrors, H.D. heard from Nancy Cunard that "Arabella" introduced herself as "Mrs. Aldington," to which Cunard responded, "I know Mrs. Aldington, and she's not you."[32]

* * *

Letters between "Big Dog" and "Little Doglet" confirmed that Bryher, as boy, allowed Macpherson to fantasize a full-on homosexual relationship. "He misses him, he misses, he misses him ... empty and full of wanting his dog," he scrawled, while Bryher braved London. His moans paralleled his truncated love affair with H.D., surfacing as his ideal version of it in their next film, *Foothills,* shot in spring 1928, the plot bare-bones: a farmer (Macpherson) and visiting young city woman (H.D.) carry on a doomed romance. After shooting this lost film, Macpherson was desperate, uncertain whether he could finish it, admitting, "I am spoiling it." H.D. wrote Bryher, now in London, of Macpherson's editing anxiety; he feared distant shots were not sharp enough, and Fido might discover his "technical blunder."[33]

Originally full-length, only nine minutes remain at the Museum of Modern Art. Soft-focus meditative shots convey the city girl's resistance to village life. H.D. wrote Plank that it featured "a sort of idealistic encounter with the young intelligent lout who is K. in Vaudois farm clothes."[34] It led her to reexperience a "series of horrible phobias," with a sensation she was sliding into a "mild" nervous breakdown.[35] Thinking the "three" were one, her brief turn to Macpherson for sexual gratification, most likely begun with *Foothills,* derailed her.

Back in London, addressing both Bryher and Kenneth, H.D. diverted her libidinal attraction to Macpherson, to a camera, projector, and screen. Boasting she had "two hours of solid camera-vision," H.D. "worked [her] little lantern" with its "very nice lens." She bought it cheaply; it produced "loveliness" and could "project a clear round square of bright light" on a screen "bigger than ours at Territet." At Sloane, inspired by Eros, H.D. projected images on the wall from "10,000 tiny stamp-sized scraps," from which she chose "the best ones of these and the bigger clips to show when people come." Studying still shots, their "lovely quality of vision and a very king-projection of light," showed "for the first time" her path with Bryher, anchored in "the full reality of Greece," seeming to "sweep and swoop over me and down me."[36] This film apparatus reassured H.D. that seeing things that were "not there" in Corfu actually anticipated this new joyous medium. Her poem in *CU,* "Projector," let ghosts walk freely, objects freed from worldly use. "Don't come back. Not for a long, long time," H.D. signed off, erotically entangled with her "camera-vision," possible only through loving them both: "Darlings, I love you so, so much." Impersonal love interceded for art. Lady

Ellerman sent carnations, and H.D. got her phone to work—only there was a constant "Buzz."

Back in London in August, H.D., fortifying herself with champagne and a Bryher-supplied sedative, dined with the Ellermans. Grown up, nineteen-year-old John Jr. looked like a young guardsman. When H.D. told Sir John of Bryher's fluency in German, he replied, "'Dolly is a wonderful linguist. Dolly always was a wonderful linguist.'" Addressing her two beloveds as "Beauandbeau," H.D. now intensified her bond with Fido, "'vibrating away' in Berlin"; she was "living for [her]." "You are always my dear little Polestar."[37] Such singular expressions signified Macpherson could not substitute for Bryher.

That same August, Bryher discovered Eisenstein's *Potemkin*, "first shown in Germany in a censored version." Soldiers literally stopped it from screening; the "mutilated version was sent to America." At Territet, Bryher watched Eisenstein's *Ten Days* over and over, wanting to "run it through [the projector] a score of times," while finishing her *Film Problems of Soviet Russia*. As if echoing H.D., Bryher pointed to "the power of the single empty chair, which throws back at the receptive spectator whole cycles of history."[38]

In October 1928, Macpherson and Bryher again traveled to Berlin. After Pabst screened *Foothills* on Unter den Linden, Bryher relayed to H.D. that she had struck Pabst, who murmured, "Ach, Madame H.D, she is starkkkkkikkk." He praised Helga Doorn, H.D.'s stage name, saying she "showed up the utter futility of the Hollywood tradition." Macpherson nearly died with joy when Pabst arranged tea with Louise Brooks, the femme fatale who starred in Pabst's next film of 1929, *Pandora's Box*.

By late October, H.D. knew she was pregnant again. In cases endangering the mother's health, Germany had legalized abortion two years earlier. Forty-two, H.D.'s history of illness with pregnancy would convince most doctors she could not survive another birth. Yet losing her mother and, now, another possible life, were bitter blows. Tender but nervously cavalier about the conception, Macpherson wrote, "Now it's a Baby Kitten, please PLEASE not to worry. Dog is a sad, sorry & disillusioned Dog, but *we* have rung up Sachs," who would give "the latest 'dirt' on where to go." He underscored that "It [i.e., Kitten] is NOT NOT NOT UNDER ANY CIRCUMSTANCES to have the pup," that "Dog or Dogs" would "hound on & make arrangements." While urging her to remove "that star or starfish or star maiden or whatever it is," he relied on H.D.'s sympathy, for "Fido is most sniffy."[39] Bryher withheld her hurt, but H.D. knew it would take patience, otherwise it would be "prod[ding] a winkle from its shell."[40]

Never fond of Berlin, H.D. decided to face the abortion alone, venturing in December, entranced by snow and candles everywhere. "[E]verything is in order to go and all I do is to clearly come any time after 6 or 7," she wrote Bryher, remarking she lived in the blue fur coat just given her—plus enjoying the Duratz Lozenges and the Cibalgina, a mild sedative Bryher stocked her with. "I am tired and a little phobed," H.D. lightheadedly admitted, having just "talked to some German ex-war soldier." This was her third pregnancy, with two unliving, somewhat accounting for her distant mothering. Stricken by a trellis with a frost-edged rose in bloom, she asked Fido to thank Kenneth and Sir John for her flat's makeover.[41]

This same month Bryher began analysis with Sachs. Reaping creative benefits from the threesome did not protect her from injury. Bryher sent Macpherson to Sachs and stayed with H.D. during her recovery, then rescued Pup from Audley for a jaunt to Brighton. Perdita loved the slot machines and being with Bryher, yet was uncertain how long she could cope with Brickwell boarding school. Blocking out Perdita's, and Bryher's, sorrow, H.D. doubled "losing" Macpherson as losing Gregg again.

* * *

At the end of 1928, H.D. and Bryher followed the incendiary obscenity trial over Radclyffe Hall's *Well of Loneliness*. Ellis had written an introduction. Bryher informed H.D. that the magistrates wanted all copies burned. In a lecture prepared before the trial, Hall made very clear what Bryher herself believed: "Congenital inversion is caused by an actual deviation from the usual in the glandular secretions of the invert's body."[42] The distress was biological, not a sociological reaction. Every last invert could be killed; more would follow. H.D. and Bryher, along with many, among them Woolf and Vita Sackville-West, understood why this trial mattered, but it didn't make H.D. feel her prose any more acceptable. She recorded deviance, though not in Hall's plain style nor in the high incandescent style of Woolf.

Finished in 1928, not published until after H.D.'s death, *HER* addressed Gregg's reentrance into her life through Macpherson. Its ambiguous dedication, "to F ...... For Sept. 2," allowed that "F" could stand for "Fido" or Frances, both having the same birthdate. It likely stung Bryher that the former Pythian, that ghost, had not vanished. The autobiographical *HER* made Bryher Gregg's successor by answering a call that was "a bee shut up inside the telephone receiver, there was murmur of the sea, far places, ships shut up in the telephone receiver." "Her" knew "then" *now*, holding "to a tiny spar that sank with her yet held her safe. She was connected with ships, with people sitting around a table."[43] *HER* re-exorcised Gregg, forgave Bryn Mawr, which imposed "fresh barriers, fresh chains, a mesh here," and mourned her mother. This poetic prose resuscitated Helen as part of "the Mysteries"; where "Eugenia was not Hellenistic, she was Eleusinian. Eugenia is Eleusinian. My father is Athenian." During a storm, mother and daughter resemble "shipwrecked mariners" thrown into "profound intimacy," her mother's words superior to "textbooks," soothing with her "hypnotic movement of hands."[44]

In middle age, H.D. saw her mistake in letting Pound call her a Dryad, some "wood maniac," when she was "a TREE," or as one reaching with "octopus arm up into illimitable distance." Boldly, she set forth her youthful ontological crisis as one of tangible absence, "not of the world," "not in the world, unhappily she was not out of the world." Resurrecting her mathematically gifted half-brother, Eric, dead in 1920 from tuberculosis, she here raised his compass magnet that pulled together iron filings, a force comparable to the "cerebral-erotic affinities" between H.D. and Bryher.

H.D. now recognized that the "birdfoot violets" she loved "had far Alpine kinsfolk" through Eric's "theorem of general mathematical biological affinity." Nagged by a sense that "being" could not be located in one place, "affinities" was an answer. *HER* spelled rebirth—"God is in a word. God is in HER. I am the word AUM," Sanskrit for the primal sound of the world's creation, a "frightening" identification.[45] With Hall in mind, H.D. thought readers even more unready for her cymbal-crashing sense of interwovenness.

By the end of 1929, Perdita had returned to Audley with a "filthy trunk." Bryher prepared H.D., who awaited Pup at Territet. "Her trunk was in an indescribable condition," she began. "I am sending rescued manuscripts to you." Said trunk had H.D.'s letters "rolled up in boots or nearly." Vexed, Bryher railed, "Her manuscripts and lesson books and stamps are in a state of complete chaos scattered around trunk. Everything is in a state of filth, games, stockings thick with mud, porridge smears on clothes."[46] "For my sake," a request rarely made, Bryher channeled her wound from the affair into a litany on filth. H.D.'s response is a classic: "I regret the trunk."[47]

Another incident finally released Pup from school through what she called a "dreadful crime." Wryly commenting on her own ménage, Perdita described a family of mice nesting near the school's stable where "free love was encouraged," "producing countless offspring, minute pink objects, squealing vociferously on beds of cotton wool and straw." Demoted by her classmate "Daphne" to Musterseed, with only five words, in the school's *Midsummer Night's Dream* production, she took vengeance on her peer's mouse, Minnie, "expecting a large family." On "a pouring, wet, cold night," she "crept into the mouse shed," removing "Minnie from her box, and then flung her, full force, into an icy puddle. The next morning, Minnie suffered a miscarriage and "developed pneumonia and died a few hours later." By now, she knew H.D. and she herself could have died in 1919. At this point, "rodenticide" was a matricide-infanticide, venting anger over captivity and isolation; it also showed she had absorbed to some degree her origins in "free love."

Bryher sent Perdita to Chadwick, the very analyst who, in a kind of spectacle, daily fed fresh mice and rats to her new python, kept in her purse, leading H.D. and Bryher to nickname her "Python." Perdita received "three of [Chadwick's] prize litter in a biscuit tin; unknown to Lady Ellerman, they had spent the night under a washstand at South Audley Street."[48] Too distracted, neither H.D. nor Bryher saw Perdita's "crime" as a sign of her feeling cut off, literally staining her mother's letters, as if trash, sounding out an S.O.S.—*rescue me*.

A year after H.D.'s abortion, Bryher steered both Macpherson and H.D. to Chadwick for psychoanalysis. Striving to keep the trio intact, Macpherson pledged "infinite faith in the goodness and the goodness and the simple beauty of our lives together."[49] With this sanguine view, Macpherson advised H.D. to use her "silver curtain. Leave it down. Let it be a porticullis to your vulnerability." H.D. already knew that "Bryher has set up her own fortress. We all have to." Kenneth emphasized she needed to "be armed ... rely on your armies.... But you'll love Bryher nonetheless."

Figure 10.2 Scrapbook photomontage of H.D. and Bryher, undated. H.D. Papers.
Courtesy of Beinecke Rare Book and Manuscript Library, Yale University.

Figure 10.3 Photomontage of Bryher with Athena haircut, undated. H.D. Papers.
Courtesy of Beinecke Rare Book and Manuscript Library, Yale University.

Macpherson blamed not his own carelessness but "[Bryher's] genius father and crazy mother," a chemical potion of residual huffiness.

When at Territet, the experimental communal scrapbook held paste images of a ruined pair of Greek pillars over photos from the 1920 trip to Carmel of H.D. in ritual pose, balancing on a sea-splashed rock, and another of Bryher climbing down, spying a reflection in the water (Figure 10.2). The collages allowed them to see their lives as palimpsestic, breaking a false concept of linear development. Instead, by placing Greek pillars as ligature with the nude couple, the broken columns appear almost vulnerable, flesh-like, not impermeable art. Rather than extolling high culture through statuary, this collage links embodied awareness to "scrap." Bryher has several dramatic pieces in the scrapbook, one capturing Bryher with Athena haircut adjacent "two selves" of a more energized Parisian self (Figure 10.3). Macpherson also collaged multiple selves, one dressed in drag, another in lady slippers, poolside in Capri, and the made-up artiste. Yet another collage held H.D.'s fragmented Delphic Charioteer, embodying flight toward vision. The collages readied them for more cinematic splices—with an assault on "normative" film.

LINE 3
PSYCHOANALYSIS 1929–1939

11
Film Morphing into *Borderline*

H.D.'s film reviews called for restraint, yet the threesome worked on erratic emotions, projecting them onto celluloid. In 1929, Kenneth directed a whimsical short film, *Monkey's Moon*. Beginning with the release of the nocturnal monkeys, the dracouli frolic and dart beneath the moon; clouds pass; they meet for a flickering kiss, Bryher scrambling after them. The animals outwit the "humans." "The garden looks like a set for Verdun," an enervated Macpherson complained, and if the film "don't get done [*sic*], at least I have not been idle."[1]

Macpherson's and H.D.'s sexual relations ended with the abortion. Now Bryher covered her wound with a growing crush on the film star Elisabeth Bergner, enjoying an incomplete romance, much like H.D.'s with Gregg or Rodeck—or even herself. Bergner in *Fraulein Else* (1929) was "so cute in her boy's ski-ing things," so "coy in a ruffled dress," she wanted to "smack the Bergner," "pinch her behind for it." Fanning Bryher's crush, H.D. played self-combusting phantom, wearing "a lovely Bergner-length red, red dare-red, Jackmenot-red rose—red red dress. The color enflames me and heals me at the same instant."[2] They encouraged each other's phantom loves, Bryher even sending H.D. flowers, as if from Rodeck.

Bryher entered full-time analysis with Sachs in late 1929, a healthy risk for one who kept her feelings under tight wraps. Oversensitive and snappish after initial sessions, she uncovered her boy identity at age three. H.D. avoided the painful social obligation of "the Macphersons," staying with the Ellermans for New Year's and Lady Ellerman's birthday. Meanwhile, H.D. acted "nativity Madonna" for the monkeys at Riant Chateau.[3]

Using the first syllable of their first names, Kenneth and Winifred, Bryher envisioned "Kenwin," a Bauhuas overlooking Lake Geneva, as an open collaborative shelter, begun in 1929, completed in 1931; the September issue of *CU* provided a photo. Zurich's Building Commission required every modern structure to conform with an old roof. Over the next two years, Bryher worked with the architect Herman Henselmann. Calling it a "sadistic" time, she knew Sir John gave the astonishing sum of 4 million pounds to John Jr.[4]

Encouraged, Herring put together an issue of *CU* devoted to Black cinema, arguing for a "pure" Afro-American cinema, "[n]ot black films passing for white, and not, please, white passing for black."[5] He admired Paul Robeson in Oscar Micheaux's 1924 *Body and Soul*, with its all-Black cast, addressing the very duality the Pool Group struggled with. Learning that Paul and Eslanda Robeson had averted divorce, Bryher invited them to star in the trio's first and only surviving full-length feature, *Borderline*.

When the Robesons visited Territet during summer 1929 to consider an undeveloped scenario, they faced trouble renting a flat. Bryher immediately confronted the pension's manager as racist for overcharging them. From adjacent quarters, she saw Mrs. Goode, Eslanda's mother, watching over Paul Jr., who played on the roof, isolated and forlorn. Although they lived in an era when lynching and racial segregation were quite alive, Bryher, thoroughly disgusted, felt they had "out grown just here."[6] Their visitors gave Bryher new lenses for Territet. Through their eyes, Bryher spotted a racist community in their own backyard; the scenario quickly became a vehicle for exposing prejudice, using the locals as belligerent extras; they didn't even have *to act* to show they took offense at Black masculinity. Essie's diaries suggest they enjoyed sightseeing and dancing on their first visit and laughed over Macpherson and H.D.'s "naïve ideas of Negroes."[7] After they left, Macpherson meticulously plotted each scene, shot, and camera angle. Then, for respite, Macpherson pulled Herring and Bryher along to Norway in October 1929 (Figure 11.1). Bryher questioned, "WHY?" The answer was male bonding. Norway's awe-inspiring ice and rocks cracked, Bryher finding the colors of floes inexpressible.[8] H.D. ran to the phone whenever it rang.

Macpherson filmed *Borderline* during the last ten days of March 1930. Blending with its subversive racial politics, the storyline was pure melodrama: adultery, jealousy, and forbidden interracial love, culminating in a knife fight between husband Thorne (Gavin Arthur) and wife Astrid, played by H.D., or Helga Doorn, her stage

Figure 11.1 Bryher, Kenneth MacPherson, and Robert Herring in an alpine or glacial field at Advent Bay, Spitsbergen, Norway, 1929. Unsourced photograph, Bryher Papers. Courtesy of Beinecke Rare Book and Manuscript Library, Yale University.

name. Early on, Thorne readies to leave her, a hysterical racist, fearing her husband's abandonment for his mistress, the biracial Adah (Eslanda). Astrid collapses to the floor, playing dead. When Thorne checks her pulse, her eyes pop open. From cobra posture, she rises, seizing a dagger-like letter opener. The camera cuts to an old woman, played by their friend Blanche Lewin, sometime companion to Perdita, wagging her finger up at Astrid's window, with one of the film's few intertitles—"If I had my way not one Negro would be in the community"—meant to shock.

Back in the flat, Astrid cavorts around Thorne, nicking his face, binding this knife sequence with shots of Pete in front of a waterfall using "[t]he same sort of jagged lightening effect."[9] This instigated a desire to cut against the usual cultural exclusionary grains. The barmaid, with a knife between her lips, puts a rose behind Pete's ear, the montage quickly shifting to Thorne, who, after stabbing Astrid, cleans his blade in a bowl, then successfully pleads "self-defense" at the stamp-size police station, blaming the Black outsiders, played by the Robesons. After Astrid's death, the white café-goers insult Adah; Pete defiantly knocks down one, who looks conspiratorially to his mates, lifting fists in jeering coalition, forecasting Nazi brutality.

Borderline ends as Bryher, the café's butch cigar-smoking manageress, reads the mayor's order for Pete to leave (Figure 11.2). An intertitle voices helpless complicity: "What makes it worse is that they think they are doing the right thing. We're like that." Pete gets the parting shot, sardonically looking at her, then the camera, and

Figure 11.2 *Borderline* still of Bryher, 1930.
Courtesy of Beinecke Rare Book and Manuscript Library, Yale University.

us, saying, "Yes. We're like that." Herring, as piano player, tucks Pete's photo in his jacket's inner pocket. The last shot shows Pete at the train station, vulnerable, alone. Unprecedented during its time, the film crossed several borders: color lines, forbidden love, and gender lines.

"Antiblackness," the scholar Zakiyyah Iman Jackson writes, founds itself on a systematic "biocentric" racism that defines the human as distinct from animality, collapsed through "the onto-teleological terms of natural science and philosophy," rigidifying a distorting hierarchy.[10] This group, all queers, was aware of the discriminating cultural devaluation of bodies. White women fared better inevitably in this scheme than their Black counterparts. Gender rebels such as H.D. and Bryher, though socioeconomically buttressed, knew their relationship and identities were belittled in the cultural imagination and, if revealed, was proximate to abject Blackness. In 1930, anti-Semitism was fueled by and through anti-Blackness.

Jackson turns to Sylvia Wynter's notion of "sociogeny" to define "each culture's criterion of being/nonbeing," where Western socialization can "*artificially* activate the neurochemistry of the reward and punishment pathway *as if it was instinctual.*" This applies not only to the nervous system but to aesthetics, so that "the 'auto' of poesis" is rewritten "by the embodied self as a kind of openwork produced by a lattice of agencies rather than a primarily self-authored closed system." The Pool Group felt "lattices" of freedom and restriction, dramatizing identification and disidentification; the "sensitive" neurotic whites cause the racial trouble in *Borderline* in a self-conscious effort to rescript unheroic abjection onto white male bodies, such as the betraying husband, who has or "takes" an affair with Adah, and who, in one shot, slumps half-conscious on the floor while liquor spills over his face.

H.D. used her mediumship to perform the excessively unlikable Astrid. This proved cathartic. Her shawl, as prop, conveyed shifting moods. A jealous rage leads to her fatal fight with Thorne, which coded H.D.'s guilt over her affair, and ensuing disappointment in Macpherson, but it also exposed anti-Blackness in action, with the whites sticking together at the expense of those racially marked. Being knifed gave H.D.'s conscience a temporary rest.

Simultaneously, Macpherson was attracted to Robeson, discovering his exclusive desire for men and attraction to Blackness. Macpherson's camera caressed Robeson, amplifying his head against lofty clouds and mountains. The loving shot lingered on his hands. This worship showed the Pool Group's difficulty in disentangling their fetishizing inclusivity from their own desire to foreground a fragmented postwar body, making a film that was both honest and provocative, though hampered by its makers' own sense of existing as "an open-ended, looping indeterminacy, one whose terminus must necessarily be unknown." "The body is diffuse im/materiality, a bursting star; each particle interacts with external actants and forces," Jackson writes.[11] Both H.D. and Bryher willfully identified with the so-called abject—fragments, scraps, stones, roots, partial forms. They celebrated abjection, and non-linear development.

The trio were indeed naïve about race, but they poked at and tried undermining repressive practices. Remember H.D. grew up knowing that Native Americans had been

Figure 11.3 *Borderline* still of Paul Robeson, 1930.
Courtesy of Beinecke Rare Book and Manuscript Library, Yale University.

accepted by her Moravian grandparents, and on a short trip to the small nineteenth-century Bethlehem cemetery, Nisky Hill, the child saw burial stones inscribed with Native names and the graves of four Black Union soldiers buried beside whites.

For her part, Eslanda, as wronged woman, worried about her performance, though Bryher assured her she "stole the show" with her understated acting.[12] She exemplified walking the razor's edge of a racial borderline. The camerawork expressed the group's crush on Robeson, while H.D.'s "Red Roses to Bronze" sensualized the actor, sensing "underneath the garment seam / ripple and flash and gleam / of indrawn muscle," while wanting to be "something to challenge."[13] In one still, Robeson projects a mixture of sadness, pain, anger, hope; in another, Eslanda presents dignified composure in contrast to H.D., challenged, her character's frizzed hair and eyes bugging out. The brochure advertising *Borderline* showed the communal effort: Robeson, already internationally famous, predominated, with Garbo's head tucked under as well as a teeny Thorne, the offensive racist, perched on the idol's large head, fashioned to look like a mask; the design let whiteness recede through palimpsestic collage (Figures 11.3–11.6).

Unique for its time, this film affords a Black man complex subjectivity—more so perhaps than Robeson had in *Body and Soul*, in which he played the extremes of "bad" and "good," the film reinforcing tragic polarity. Here Pete expresses hurt at his wife's dalliance, tenderness, grief, and anger at the town's small-mindedness. He hits

Figure 11.4 *Borderline* still of Paul and Eslanda Robeson, 1930. Courtesy of Beinecke Rare Book and Manuscript Library, Yale University.

a white man, and shakes hands with another. Truly experimental, Macpherson, H.D., and Bryher wanted to free cinematic grammar from censorship, keeping white from Black, woman from woman, man from man.

After his obsessive directorial work on *Borderline*, Macpherson suffered a severe throat ailment, leaving H.D. and Bryher to edit the film; H.D.'s pamphlet still gave him primary credit. Painstakingly, the two women created electric, speedy clips, resulting in cascading images, which distinguished their work from the "mechanical superimposition of short shots." Their "clatter montage," quite masochistic, required "meticulous cutting of three and four and five-inch lengths of film and pasting these tiny strips together."[14] For Bryher, cutting was "far more important than the story." A pro with complex needlework, H.D. stitched in another medium. Their montage interrupted any "facile movement," deploying "a meticulous jig-saw puzzle technique in the best of the advanced German and Russian montage."[15]

H.D. promoted the film through her "Borderline Pamphlet," questioning borders: "When is an African not an African? When obviously he is an earth-god. When is a woman not a woman? When obviously she is sleet and hail and a stuffed seagull."[16] Astrid had a seagull affixed in her chamber, her shawl tassels echoing feathers. Taxidermy offset binary categories: this was an animal alive in death—a ligature to the white woman as "stuffed," trying to hold on to her wrecked white man.

Figure 11.5 *Borderline* still of H.D., 1930.
Courtesy of Beinecke Rare Book and Manuscript Library, Yale University.

Figure 11.6 *Borderline* still of Eslanda Robeson, 1930.
Courtesy of Beinecke Rare Book and Manuscript Library, Yale University.

Further at odds with popular films, sound technology was available in 1930, yet Bryher agreed with her friend and admired novelist, Dorothy Richardson's sense of silent film, "as a medium of communication" expressing itself like "innermost thought," while "voice" interfered with a free interplay of thought.[17] In the elections of September 1930, the Nazis received 18 percent of the vote, making them the second largest party in the Reichstag. The authoritarian screws tightened with strict, spat tones; no coincidence that Nazis learned much about raising terror after witnessing American anti-Black tactics.

To provoke the viewer from any inertia, Bryher encouraged conflict between shots, resulting in shocks, what Eisenstein thought induced somatic dissociative states through "[p]rojection of the conflict onto the whole expressive bodily system."[18] Eisenstein's techniques exaggerated cutting, perhaps why Pabst called *Borderline* "the only real avant-garde film."[19] Yet H.D. exalted Macpherson, with their Debrie camera, "all sinew and steel," making the "cinema-camera" a "renaissance miracle," "the delicate crystal lense [sic]." Comparing him to Leonardo, H.D. referred to Macpherson's "1,000" pen sketches, while he "sculpts literally with light." His father, John, worked "a spot-light as his son directed." Macpherson "sustained direction" primarily "THROUGH THE LENS." Without mentioning the duo's editing, H.D. configured Macpherson as Perseus, thieving their shared "eye," "a hard-boiled mechanic, as if he himself were all camera, bone and sinew and steel-glint of rapacious grey eyes."[20] Aware that their three-in-one was shifting orbit, she spotted a callous aspect of Macpherson's charm. Understandably, most of the actors suffered posttraumatic filmmaking disorder. Herring confessed to "a dreadful state of nerves," with "almost no identity at all." Finding it difficult to play a piano "no one could play," he suffered hero worship, for "one believes in Kenneth so absolutely, it kind of dopes one." He recognized H.D.'s "great strain," her "particular vibrancy," abandoning herself "in another dimension for [Macpherson's] work."[21] Finding this "frightening and responsible," Herring recovered from an infatuation with Macpherson, who was exhausted by his own shaky perfectionism.

* * *

Blocked by the American censor for its foregrounding miscegenation, *Borderline* first screened at the Academy Cinema in London in October 1930. Reviews were poor. British audiences were put off by its "unexplainedness—like something seen through a window or key-hole."[22] Adopting Bryher's new psychoanalytic vocabulary, Macpherson explained that "the film strip" was not static, that "[i]ts essential character is transferential, and it is this transferential character which alone has informed the structure."[23] H.D. and Bryher's cutting guided these "transferences," melding images that crossed psyches. While other critics complained Robeson did not appear more in the film, the *Chronicle* attacked its "misguided judgment," calling it a "cerebral bomb." H.D. suspected Gregg was responsible for this "brimstone and purge."[24]

The group—H.D., Herring, and Macpherson, without Bryher—went to Monte Carlo to recover. H.D. longed for Bryher to join them in the "blazing sun," more lovely "if only you were here." H.D., amused by Herring, told Bryher, "he WILL go shopping all the time," bringing his "TRUNK" for only two weeks. Monte was restorative, thinking it "open and public," and at once both "snob and democratic."[25] Macpherson reported Herring fit perfectly and "sprang into fancy dress" at "his zenith with a jade green sleeveless pull-on and cre de chine trousers."[26] Bryher resisted, remaining at Territet.

Returning to London, H.D. hosted Gregg at Sloane. The phantom complained about debts and bragged her son, Oliver, had "wonderful ideas of making queer poems with films," such as showing "the brain of a person in symbols," that only H.D. could understand. Gregg had spotted Macpherson in London, "looking puffed out and prosperous," "so gross and heavy," a real "Chesterton." Likely more unnerved by this visit than she stated, H.D. pictured Bryher "cleaning cages and cleaning cages and CLEANING CAGES" and, more surreal, "rows of Fidos and rows of red paws and rows of carrots."[27] Bryher responded with a "newsreel" titled "Light on the horizon"—but as the lunga bit the gibbon, she hired help; while "the menagerie increases, the goldfish swims happily." She craved H.D.'s return to Territet.[28]

Gregg meanwhile sent another letter H.D. planned to burn—but grew curious and read it. Her "ex" called her curtains ugly, praising her beauty, criticizing her feet. Bryher and Macpherson were gleeful H.D. "made [Gregg] cry" for she "asks for it." They suggested H.D. take "the Gregg to casino at Monte," where she'd "probably lose the last remnants of her rabbit-stew at Cannes, unless rescued."[29] They made a brutal team when it came to Gregg.

Emptying himself into *Borderline*, Macpherson suffered neurasthenia, the very postwar condition *Borderline* tried depicting. Still in Monte Carlo, he sank into a "state," occupying a flat supplied by Sir John. Showing her hurt had mostly healed, Bryher encouraged H.D. to revisit Macpherson. When H.D. arrived in December 1930, he didn't even come to the station; Miss Medford, their landlord, came. Macpherson was romancing Toni Slocum, a Black jazz musician, staying at the flat, whom he depicted as at the other end of the couch, book and cigarette in hand. H.D. thought, "K is almost unrecognizable."[30] Macpherson sunbathed and swam in Monte—indulging sensual pleasures. Staying in London through January, Bryher was compelled to attend her mother's birthday alone, while H.D. soaked in the orange blossoms. The smell conjured "always, always Corfu," prism for their devotions, and added tenderly, "O my little love, all that and the long days we have had."[31]

Herring, meanwhile, believed "in greeting the dawns with wide-open arms and clenched fists," advising that "danger" was "a sort of Frankenstein you invent and then can't control."[32] Once Bryher met Slocum, he predicted, all would be well. H.D. and Bryher concurred that "K." must find his own way. In 1931, Herring admired H.D.'s "rocklike compression of electric psychic magnificence" and asserted that others, like themselves, were equipped with "psychic invisible antennae, reaching into you from someone & showing you this light is really your own." H.D. struggled to stop feeling hurt by Macpherson. Herring's words, "one must as a kind of job, work not to be wounded," helped her heal. Both H.D. and Bryher found it hard to "be let down by anyone."[33]

Near the anniversary of Beaver's death, Macpherson divulged that Slocum had syphilis. This shocked the couple—yet the threesome remained friends. When H.D. accepted Toni, Macpherson appreciated "that nothing could be much wrong with life, or our lives and the elements surrounding it."[34] The following year, he brought the tubercular Black musician Jimmie Daniels to Kenwin, and H.D. paid for a year's treatment in a sanitarium. Bryher's worry over Macpherson was earnest: she wanted him to pursue his art, which he no longer believed in.

During March 1931, Bryher spent hours and days comforting H.D. Sachs thought their emotional complexities "enough for a dozen strong personalities or a hundred modern problem plays."[35] Early in April, H.D. started analysis with Mary Chadwick in London. Bryher comforted "Darling Kat"—she would "feel so different" after her first hour, underscoring, "I will always be there on hand if wanted; the situation with K. is quite other. *Whatever happens with him I will always want to see that the Kat has its proper basket with cream plate*" (italics mine).[36] H.D. and Bryher closed ranks, about to launch an analytic-visionary voyage.

After her first session with Chadwick, on April 9, H.D. admitted, "I am a wreck." Convinced she was fit only for secretarial work at the *CU* office on Maiden Lane, Macpherson, now living nearby at 6 Gerrard Mansions, did not help. Chadwick, herself a former patient of Sachs, judged H.D. was "too intellectual," advising her to "let go and drift."[37] H.D., she believed, needed to "wear out the top layer," to tap undercurrents. With Macpherson and his sister, Eileen, also seeing Chadwick, at Bryher's expense, H.D. gained another convert with her friend Cole Henderson, who arrived at Sloane in raptures of release. The circle was "a strange and touching little family," but H.D. found it jarring that the analyst went to "K[enneth] parties, to Wunderbar," distressed at mixing "ps-a," their shorthand for psychoanalysis, with palling around. That summer, H.D. saw Macpherson's mother lying drunk in her garden. Still, she felt her sessions "progressed like greased lightning."[38]

With Chadwick, H.D. first tackled her "inhibited" memory of acting Florence Nightingale to her father after his concussion, which explained why she had "clutched" Macpherson so tightly in Monte. The memory of subdural blood prompted the earlier memory of her father's accident. *Borderline* meddled with her unconscious, for if she looked traumatized in the film, it wasn't only acting; she was "torn and wrecked," triggered in the film by the man playing her husband washing blood from his hands. In essence, her sensibility was cranial and vulvic, as Bryher knew from the "jellyfish experience." Chadwick recognized the link between the film's basin and her father's bloodied head. Macpherson left for Monte Carlo again, but this time H.D. was fortified, knowing Fido had forgiven her, and traveled to Berlin for analysis. Sachs thought that her problems "centre[d] in aggressiveness," Bryher joking that "it came down to the fact that [she] should have been a contented professional boxer!!"[39] Sachs helped her remember that "almost as far back as memory" she felt "male," analysis focusing upon her brave "choice" to enact her masculinity.[40]

* * *

Following Germaine Dulac's dream-inspired *Seashell and the Clergyman* (1928), *Borderline* screened in Berlin in April 1931 at the Rote Muhle at midnight, creating mixed reactions of pleasure and anger. Some objected to its "deliberate slow tempo." Bryher brought her new friends, Lotte Reiniger (1899–1981)—innovator of silhouette films, among them the fantastical, *Adventures of Prince Achmed* (1926), considered the first full-length animation film—and her husband, Carl Koch, a documentary filmmaker who also wrote children's books. They "fell for Border," and Henselmann told Bryher that H.D.'s shawl work haunted him. Lotte made her films in a studio "the size of their Riant Chateau dining room, with a piece of glass, a Debrie, and electric apparatus." Bryher indulged in a family romance with the left-wing couple figuring as permissive parents. Lotte, Fido, and Pup cut out animal silhouettes. Reminding H.D. they never saw Berlin together, Bryher worried it would soon be too late.

Following the Austrian Bergner, "the Colette of the screen," Bryher kept clippings. Suffering sexual dysphoria and stage fright, the star submitted to two appointments with Sachs. Bryher recognized her own infatuation in *Maedchen in Uniform*, the 1931 film by Leontine Sagan, featuring Manuela's girl-crush on the teacher conveniently named Bergner. Other girls metaphorically tattooed their hearts with "Die B," the same nickname Bryher gave Bergner and the name of the film's lesbian soft-hearted teacher in a military-driven boarding school for proto-iron girls trained to produce iron soldiers. Reviewing *Maedchen* for *CU*, Moore mimicked the film's detractors: "No, we do not like loving [sic] pictures. We like any kind but love."[41]

In summer 1931, H.D. returned to London, while Bryher, in Berlin, grew in despair and anger. "The new N. uniforms appeared yesterday, rows upon rows of marching brown young males and woe betide you, if you happen to look dark," adding her desire to stand up to them, though they fiendishly "never go around in bunches of less than six."[42] Simultaneously, H.D. had a "stand-up fight with K," accusing him of violating the "loyalty to our situation as THREE people."[43] Confronting Macpherson with his early family dynamics, she "WANTED TO UNDERSTAND" but also knew "[t]hings would never be the same," for "vital things, are bound, by their own laws of vitality, to change."[44]

On July 9, H.D. ended analysis with Chadwick and had overcome her "fixation on HIM [Macpherson]," helped by knowing that finally Kenwin "satisfied something deep."[45] "The whole thing is so occult," she wrote, and "the whole house a dream."[46] Chadwick and her nephew, Dan Burt, visited Riant Chateau. Burt was H.D.'s "substitutional" fling. Distorted by memories of Macpherson overlaid with Bryher, their lovemaking was incomplete. "Dan and I are flung together," she recorded, as if the "fling" were foisted on her.[47] Inspired by the thwarted threesome, a truncated tryst with Burt, she started writing *Nights*, leaving for London in September, when Bergner and her "companion" qua secretary, Mrs. Williams, arrived at Kenwin [Figure 11.7].

Traveling from Switzerland to England, H.D. practiced occupying two places psychically. In late September, she stopped on the steps at the British Museum to read a note from Bryher. Having just reread Gilbert Murray on Greek religion, she found it "terribly Egyptian" that Bryher spoke of seeing a swallow. H.D. took Violet Hunt to meet Chadwick, and herself counseled Hunt to title her biography of Elizabeth Siddal *The Wife of Rossetti*. Though less disturbed by Macpherson, H.D. still felt unfit to care for Pup, just sprung from school; Perdita stayed at Audley.

By winter, H.D. was headed back to Kenwin, preparing for hours with Sachs during November and December. She traveled through Berlin, stopping in Prague to "prowl

Figure 11.7 Program for *Borderline, a Pool film with Paul Robeson*, 1930.
Courtesy of Beinecke Rare Book and Manuscript Library, Yale University.

into little coffee joints," then saw Sachs in Vienna. He pointed to her shock over her father's death and the fact she hadn't cried.[48] Sachs was "clever and comforting," but H.D. felt "a bit kicked in the ribs" by his treatment, though this did "[n]ot detract from its glamour."[49] On Christmas, feeling conspicuous dining alone, she listened to a wireless broadcast of Mozart and Strauss. Taking her last hour with Sachs on December 26 in Vienna, H.D. grew nostalgic for the time just before sailing on the *Borodino*, for the Christmas tree shared with Perdita and Bryher.[50]

* * *

Bryher hired Alice Modern, a young student from Vienna, where she studied languages, as Perdita's new governess, traveling with her and H.D. on a Delphic cruise in April 1932. "Speechless with happiness," Alice acted older sister to Pup, who loved the Parthenon.[51] Alice's pipe-smoking mother, very progressive, knew the "arrangements" at Kenwin, essentially a house of queers, only objecting to the cook, Miss Neuhold, who had a skin disease. Bryher acquiesced, hiring Dorothy Hull, soon dubbed the "Quex," who almost immediately displayed symptoms of inhibited homosexuality, according to Sachs. She moved between great reserve and overfamiliarity. The Queen's sister, C. Hull, visited. To her surprise, H.D. found her "direct, Lesbian in the Cole manner," "very decent and kind," who had "nervy states as she herself seems to be walking on eggs."[52] H.D. shared sedatives with her.

Bryher meanwhile now used *Close Up* to resist Hitler's militarism and bigotry. Writing for and running this journal was not without danger, with Bryher warning of fascism.[53] In August 1932, Bryher joined Sachs for the International Psychoanalytic Congress in Wiesbaden, honoring Freud's seventy-fifth birthday, celebrating his 1931 "Femininity." During the talks, Bryher doodled, finding her gaze distinguishing Ernest Jones from the numerous Jewish women, each training to be analysts as the "new woman" who "was to-morrow in a hundred years, you could see from the short black hair and her neck that had always been sunburnt that her myths and his must be different in texture."[54]

By autumn 1932, Bryher had gauged the political waters, doubting experimental cinema could emerge from Berlin: the "atmosphere" compared only to "any large city in 1914–1918." The studios let everyone go, including Pabst, an Austrian; only 100-percent Germans could work in the film studios. With groups of Nazis on foot or on motorcycles patrolling the streets in full uniform, "is it to be wondered that for the first time in many visits, the cinema lists are left unopened."[55]

* * *

Earlier in the year, on May 13, 1932, the Ellermans had visited Kenwin for Sir John's seventieth birthday. H.D. loved "1 + 3 = 4, her formula for 'SUN, for K, Br, and HD.'"[56] However, instead of joining the family, H.D. invited Rodeck to Sloane. He came on a bicycle, expressing a bias against psychoanalysis. Concerned the visit was "wearing on [Bryher]," upsetting her physically, H.D. reassured that he "is much more like his old Borodino self." Rodeck was entering "some sort of 'brotherhood' in order to finish his 'studies,' so, so ... you need not worry." The "ghost," "comical in the old Rodeck-ian manner on the subject of boy scouts, etc.," revived Corfu.[57]

When H.D. visited Monte Carlo again in 1932, everyone played yo-yo. She joked that if one could manage the toy, one could regulate one's fate. A constant remained, July 17, that was still "impossible to grasp the fact that fourteen years ago, you dug me out at Bosigran."[58] She haunted cathedrals, "got in, very deep with Bible," and asked for "the Grail book."[59] H.D. told Bryher she "was thinking in colors."[60]

In November, Sachs, soon to leave to join Harvard's faculty, advised Bryher to write Freud directly to accept H.D. for analysis. Based on her loss of creative urgency, nerves, and reclusiveness, he thought H.D. was heading for a breakdown. H.D.'s temperament was so capacious, he thought, only Freud could do her justice. Bryher and Macpherson had met Freud briefly in 1927. Bryher now wrote, asking he treat her "cousin," sending *Palimpsest*. A little over a week later, Freud very particularly addressed Bryher as "Sir"—not a sign of forgetfulness but playful permission, remembering "quite clearly the meeting with you."[61] After being accepted as an analysand, H.D. dove into the psychoanalytic journals Bryher stocked at Kenwin.

Wintering with "Quex" while waiting to hear exact dates from Freud in the new year, H.D. felt porous, vowing "to adopt an iron-clad exterior, towards all strangers," mandatory if one possessed "any psychic gifts." Ps-a might enable her to protect herself, agreeing with Bryher that there was currently "a terrible back-wash, like the backwash of a tidal wave, in England, the War-wave either drowned or carried forward, or carried back." H.D.'s "back-wash" reckoned that her generation already suffered their major war, but like Bryher, she thought analysis historically urgent. Chadwick had not really suited, as she told Ellis, having "no sex experience at all," lacking that "fine abstract quality that you get in a few women, in Bryher, for example."[62] Even before Freud, H.D. thought she had potential as a "psycho-hysterical visionary," stitching the roles of poet, patient and analyst in a soul's development.[63]

In December 1932 at Kenwin, H.D. read to Pup from Tennyson, Sir James Frazer, and the Grail—Bryher favorites. She lit Moravian candles to Bryher in her absence. "Wien is more than a gift, it is a resurrection," she thanked, wanting to see Bryher before leaving for Vienna. On Christmas, she retreated into one of Fido's annual gifts, a "*bed-coat* (you know I would)," affirming, "[W]ith you all the unc ties are RIGHT."[64] "Unc" was the unconscious in their language: H.D. tangibly with Bryher held to unworded "ties."

CU could not stop Hitler. But it insisted upon film's ability to "interact" with viewers, dynamically creating new thoughts or feelings. Bryher had been overly idealistic that consciousness-altering cinema might ward off fascism. Macpherson could not "paste up *Close Up*" when one knew "that everything's tumbling to ruin."[65] Art films, he believed, would not stand a chance for at least ten years.

The Austrian corporal began his hateful campaign, fourteen years in the making, in September 1919, taking the full reins of power in March 1933. Adolf Hitler fabricated the National Socialist German Worker's Party, the Nazi Party, advocating extreme nationalism and racial purity. It denounced non-Aryans, Jews, Marxists, sexual deviants, the democratic Weimar Republic, and the Treaty of Versailles. After gaining the support of prominent German industrialists, the growing fascist party pressured President Paul von Hindenburg, a general in World War I, to appoint Hitler as chancellor. On January 30, 1933, the SA and SS led ghoulish torch-lit parades throughout Berlin after Hitler took office. Following the Reichstag fire on February 27, 1933, ignited by the Nazi Party itself, Hitler got Hindenburg to suspend civil liberties. The Enabling Act, passed on March 24, 1933, granted Hitler emergency powers. He immediately outlawed all other political parties. In London that May, Herring encountered a right-wing rally led by Sir Oswald Mosley, heading a small, offensive party, the British Union of Fascists, jeering at his friends, who "hustled them onto Eros." He fumed, "Fascism don't fit, one doesn't go on in that way, wearing black, brown, or red shirts, standing on pavements, *here*." But Bryher was not so sure.

Nancy Cunard gave a party the same month to raise funds for her cause, the defense of "the Scottsboro Boys," nine Black teenagers falsely accused of raping a white woman. As the Nazis took power, this case raged in the press, fueled by more than three hundred years of American racism. With insufficient evidence, all-white jurors rendered a guilty verdict, overturned only thirteen years later for all defendants by the U.S. Supreme Court.

By June 1933, three months after H.D. arrived in Vienna, Bryher had published "What Shall You Do in the War?" Berlin had become "a city where police cars and machine guns raced about the streets, where groups of brown uniforms waited at each corner." Dislocated refugees with suitcases and bundles of household articles crowded train stations. Bryher exposed attacks "freely employed, both mental and physical," on Jews, who were being rounded up with homosexuals, the disabled, and the mentally ill. "Hundreds have died or been killed, thousands in prison, and thousands more in exile," estimating "six hundred thousand" persecuted Jews, "among the finest citizens Germany had, peaceful and hard-working, are to be eliminated from the community," including Einstein. German concentration camps existed for those with eyes to see, challenging readers to activism: "It is for you and me to decide whether we will help to raise respect for intellectual liberty in the same way, or whether we all plunge, in every kind and color of uniform, towards a not to be imagined barbarism."[66] The year 1933: a scary turnstile. Sir John's blood boiled as colleagues across the globe gave him news of unthinkable crimes. Watching him grow weak, with fainting spells, Bryher helped her overweight father up and down the stately stairs. The doctor told Lady Ellerman that her husband might become paralyzed. He asked for a holiday in Dieppe to convalesce.

12
Enter Freud

Dreaming through the Houses

Becoming Freud's patient, H.D. spotted a last chance to fill "curious gaps" in her "psychic being."[1] Essentially, falling for Macpherson and loving Bryher bewildered her. Urgency also came with Bryher's prophecies of global disaster. Richardson, in her sixties, didn't think analysis could help what life had already inflicted, believing "no one on earth" could stop current "political and racial passions unchained."[2] This made H.D. eager for "the weed slime depth,"[3] jazzily denoting ps-a as "un-UNKing the UNK or de-bunking the junk."[4]

Late in February 1933, Jules, Kenwin's chauffeur, drove H.D. and Bryher to Zurich, where they shared a thermos of tea, brandy, sandwiches, fruit. On the Vienna train, H.D. fantasized herself as Marlene Dietrich, performing husky femme for the customs officer. Arriving, she saw Nazi sympathizers marching.

Before her first session with Freud, she scouted out Berggasse 19, timing her walking route. Mistaken for an art student, she thought the "vibe" very "Philadelphia-Bloomsbury." The night before analysis, she slept restlessly, feeling alone and "cut off." She took from her Bryher-procured trusty tin of Cibalgina, remedy for insomnia and nerves and to calm her stomach, a drug with barbiturate-like properties. Excitable, on a quest, she reread Bryher's copy of Weston's *From Ritual to Romance* and believed, with Weston, Christian mythologies derived from mystery religions of the ancient Near East. "The grail is with us," she signed off. Craving connection, H.D. asked for two letters daily from Bryher, and the pair wrote to each other almost every day, for after her morning coffee and cigarette, "its [sic] falling down a precipice."[5] Freud and H.D. agreed upon two terms of analysis, the first to end in June. Initially, H.D asked Bryher to "Come to Wien … in lilac time" as "the hero of the hour."[6] But, confronted with patrolling Nazis, H.D. needed to find the hero within.

Sachs recommended H.D. stay at the centrally located Hotel Regina. Her room faced a cathedral. The first appointment was scheduled for March 1 at 5:00 p.m., her favorite time. In the waiting room, she spied Sach's photograph, "a beau of the nineties, with high collar, no chins, terribly dandy-of-the-period."[7] Ushered into Freud's sanctum, she glimpsed survivors from Pompeii among a substantial collection of Greek, Roman, and Chinese artifacts. Freud presented his small Athena (4 and 1/8 inches), a Roman copy of a Greek sculpture, without her spear; H.D. mused the goddess was "perfect" without it in "The Master" (1934). Freud "was not a person but a voice," emanating from antiquity. Situating her beside him, he noted he stood "nearly as tall" as she. She pet his pregnant Chow, Yofi, who affectionately rubbed against her. "[F]reud is terrible, dope and dope and dope," H.D. exulted, transplanting Bryher to the scene as they spoke about politics and Jewishness, existing only "in fragments." They "clicked like mad."[8]

Bryher scolded H.D. for her resistance to the couch: "How dare you not obey?"[9] H.D. succumbed, knowing she would end up sobbing. During an early session, she broke down. Through lingering tears, she chanced upon an old-fashioned café that sold white wine and apples, with tables facing a snowy courtyard. Drinking "coffee with five inches of cream," she read the *Daily Mail* and the *Sunday Chronicle*. She consulted Freud six days a week. Told not to record what went on during sessions, she rebelled for Bryher's and "history's" sake, striving to "collect and note all Papa's remarks, which may be useful ammunition against the world, for all time."[10] Freud "struck psychic oil," while Bryher's letter telepathically announced the "Oil O-Matic" arrived to heat Kenwin, with a sketch in the margins of a *"raving, shrieking mad"* Quex. Reminded by H.D. of Freud's birth in the Moravian town of Freiberg, Bryher boomed, "The GHOST," as in "the holy ghost," making him "just plain family."[11]

H.D. reported that Freud seemed "very interested in the Fido and its fido-mind," having given him a "very clear idea of the jelly-fish saga," and he praised Bryher, who, "by a miracle of love and intuition, understood what Dr. Ellis could never have understood." "So, you see, papa thoroughly approves"; H.D. situated Bryher " 'in' the analysis all along, via the first Greek trip and your rescue of the war-time stray-cat with cat on." With "the H.D.-Bryher saga" "well established," H.D. wanted Bryher to "put in an appearance."[12]

Not forwarding all H.D.'s letters to Macpherson, Bryher protected them for the "historical record."[13] H.D. described cafés with "separate little alcoves" so "full of Lllllllllls [Lesbians]," academics with stacks of papers, and herself wearing "oldest clothes, sit[ting] in bistros with a note-book and relays of sharpened pencils."[14] Bryher delayed visiting, but eventually came to Vienna twice, first from March 28 to April 17, and then June 3 through 17.

During this time, H.D. had an enormous dream, starring a regal lady, either Indian or Egyptian, at the top of a staircase, descending in "slow rhythm" toward a river. With "no before or after," she became the lady, not knowing why she was beside "a shallow basket or ark or box or boat" with a baby in it. "The Princess must find the baby," she thought, sure "that the baby will be protected and sheltered by her and that is all that matters." This reiterated the parable of Bryher rescuing her and Perdita. But Freud directed her to question herself: "Do I wish myself, in the deepest unconscious or subconscious layers of my being, to be the founder of a new religion?"[15] He "insisted" she "wanted to be Moses," "to be a boy" and a "hero."[16] Along with Freud, Bryher identified with Hannibal, standing up for the Carthaginians against Rome. This Moses and Hannibal wanted to save poetry, and the world.[17]

While Fido "transferred soil," planting trees at Kenwin, H.D.'s transference to Freud was maternal. Another version of Bryher as male mother, he didn't "like it," feeling "so very, very very MASCULINE."[18] Yet H.D. called him "hibou sacré" after

Athena's wise owl, also traced back to her father's gift of a stuffed snowy owl, sacred to indigenous female healers, and now endangered. Freud's pregnant dog occupied the therapy sanctum through May, fanning H.D.'s obsession with Pup's birth. So uneasy, she considered taking a room next to Papa's office. After two weeks, H.D. contacted Alice Modern, then writing a thesis. At first, H.D. dismissed her as a "sulky" student.[19] Alice's sister, Klara, "very, very pretty with blue eyes and the most entirely boy-face I ever saw in my life," resembled "a very decent straight boy."[20] Bryher clarified that Alice's weight loss and fearfulness stemmed from political thuggery. At last, H.D. observed the sisters "were simply shaking all over all the time," with everyone, "Papa" included, "horribly shocked psychically by Germany," and Alice "gasping S.O.S for Bryher."[21]

Dread leached the air; troops decamped on the frontier. With German refugees flooding the Swiss border and streaming into Vienna, H.D. resisted suggestions she leave. Bryher considered rescuing rather than visiting Kat, urging her to register with the British Consulate. Early in analysis, H.D. pegged Bryher as "the younger BROTHER," "something plus mother-object, must be small boy."[22] For them, the cerebral was erotic; the cranial was vulvic. They played familial roles for each other. Deemed all boy by Freud, Bryher woke up to find "an opened penknife in bed," "sheer codpiece of course," and "most dangerous."[23]

With Bryher's increasingly bleak outlook, H.D. asked her not to come *yet*. Wishing now to face it alone, H.D. lived in her "Jaeger coat"—"sit in it, work in it, all but go to analysis in it." She dreamed of Fido with "white stiff flea-whiskers,"[24] while Bryher dreamed of "a small Griffon" that would "fetch newspapers and carry them," only to transform into a Pekingese.[25] But she piggy-backed on H.D.'s dream. Norman Douglas, leaving Fascist Italy, "refugee-ing" it at Kenwin, discoursed on "living dangerously," while Bryher mock-snarled, "[D]amn lot of good it does for me."[26] Seeking to boost Bryher's male identification, H.D. sent risqué postcards from a shop "with some slime ones" of "die Bergner"; claiming to the proprietor she bought them on a friend's behalf. H.D. and Bryher cultivated each other's fantasies, even their sexual embitterment and redress. In turn, both cultivated incomplete romances.

Late in June, Bergner taunted Bryher, "Dearest, I am longing to see you."[27] Bergner called herself Mrs. Paul Czinner to mask her bisexuality. Poking at her through Macpherson, Bergner in trousers said she would come to Kenwin to see Pup and H.D. in summer, *if* Bryher did not push analysis. Husband and wife were both scared, Bryher was sure, reiterating that Pabst would be shot if he crossed the German frontier. "Terribly war-path," she wanted "to start an all exiles paper or something." H.D. loved Bryher's energy, but feared it too.

With Freud, H.D. quickly dropped into "earliest layers, with mother-transference," the pregnant Chow couch-side.[28] Hypnotized by her own queer potboiler, she conjured up "the moment in Corfu, in BED, and papa is licking his whiskers off for details."[29] Highlighting "BED," she entertained Freud, repeating in child-like tones that he had "never, no never, he went so far as to tell me, had such a subtle, strange, hair-raising combination of excitements." She set the 1920 stage: "Br and H.D. in Corfu with Chiron on the journey home and Rodeck in the oriental distance of the east," deferring to "we" when describing hallucinations. Freud called the scenario "more or less half-normal," sensing it "a poem sequence that was not written."[30]

Freud suspended disbelief in the Corfu adventure partly as his thinking in "Dreams and Occultism" (1933) reconciled telepathy and thought transference, acknowledging that "mental processes in one person" could be "transferred to another person through empty space without employing the familiar methods of communication." Transference might even be founded on an "original, archaic method of communication."[31] This encapsulated H.D. and Bryher's binding love story of communicating beneath the surface. In his youth, Freud could not have comprehended this pair, realizing only now that psychoanalysis had "[n]ot sufficiently understood that the girl did not invariably transfer her emotions [from her mother] to her father."[32] This was huge.

In London in 1932, H.D. had taken Perdita to see the prima ballerina of the Vienna State Opera, in *The Du Barry*. Stunned, H.D. now read in the café "picture-paper" that "[p]oor lovely Anny Ahlers" took large quantities of pills and sleep-walked out of her second-story apartment. Much like Ahlers, H.D. had worked hard, fearing the same fate. Bryher meanwhile backchanneled fifty pounds to Freud for a student in Berlin, Sachs a hundred for a "reserve fund," with twenty for Alice Modern. H.D. appreciated Bryher as "the means of so much good being done," especially her providing "this marvelous old Greek oracle." The seventy-eight hours with Freud were the same number of cards in a Tarot deck, H.D. tabulated.[33]

* * *

Nazi demonstrations blocked Vienna's streets during H.D.'s fourth week. Bryher reminded her how grim things were, receiving a "[f]rantic note in from [Ernö] Metzner to say he and Grace [his wife] escaped to Budapest at last moment."[34] Pabst had introduced Bryher and Macpherson to Metzner, a set-designer. Names of refugees kept increasing in letters. H.D. believed, as many did, things "could not be worse than in '14." She would stay put unless Bryher went "mad with terror, but it is good and deep and calm," only to add, "They did have the whole army out with machine guns."[35] H.D. and Bryher knew how to calm and to alarm each other. But all was not good, deep, and calm. Dreaming she had returned to Sloane, H.D. entered the downstairs hall, with men threatening her, until she screamed, "'Mother,' I am out on the pavement now. I look up at the window.... A figure is standing there, holding a lighted candle. It is my mother."[36] This dream revealed maternal transference with Freud comforted her.

Surveying Freud's book collection, H.D. told Bryher he did not have Sir Arthur Evans' pamphlet, published in 1931, after his excavation of Crete, providing evidence of the Minoan mother goddess, with its snake goddess surrounded by butterflies. Evans pointed toward a migration of Near Eastern religious imagery, from the Egyptian, Phoenician, Minoan into the Greek and Christian religions. H.D. wanted

Bryher to find "one of the little Crete snake goddesses" for Freud, though Bryher knew such a goddess would likely involve bribery.[37]

As if this absent goddess shifted something, Freud discovered in H.D. "a special kind of 'fixation,'" through earlier incarnations of the Minoan snake mother—prior to Artemis, prior to Aphrodite, prior to or contiguous with Rhea or Isis. Freud diagnosed she was "stuck at the earliest pre-OED stage," which elated her. "'[B]ack to the womb' seems to be my only solution. Hence islands, sea, Greek primitives and so on." Her erotic trajectory was a search for the mother. Missing the meaning initially, she "HAD the 'illumination,'" which was "you and me in Corfu (island=mother), with Rodeck always as a phallic-mother."[38] H.D.'s "FIRST layer" exposed Western culture's basic burial of the mother, though Helen returned with light in H.D.'s psychic window. Freud believed she wanted *to perform*, which explained why writing "made [her] feel like hell," "her dance and song turn" in Corfu," and her identification with Ahlers, who "did actually walk out of a window."[39] Preparing for Bryher's first visit, H.D. requested "ps-a dirt, nights," asking to be "re-analyzed by [Bryher]."[40] She planned meeting Bryher at the station with her "mother-fix." In spite of what she intermittently claimed, H.D. was not the only one who played mother.

* * *

Bryher arrived in late March, securing one whole hour with Freud and Yofi the day before the Chow traveled to the country to have her pups, three days before Perdita's birthday. In their meeting, Bryher asked Freud if she was suited to train as a lay analyst. Noting this "Hannibal" "was all fists," he provided Bryher a "shattering, true, and needful" corrective for her hyperenthusiasm, questioning whether she could "sit still six hours a day." Further, Bryher had "no trace" of Jewishness. Unlike her early consultation with Ellis, she talked back: "So I said rubbish I wanted to be a Jew because David was tiny but slew Goliath," her savior complex writ large.[41] Yet Bryher's rough-and-tumble kindness charmed Freud, and child analyst, his daughter, Anna, who recommended she train with Marie Bonaparte in Paris; that would not require the intensive residency among the "insane," the requirement that discouraged Bryher from training in Zurich. A social whirlwind from March 28 through April 17, Bryher attended Friends' meetings, charging her up. "I drop with dirt. And plan fifty volumes," the dirt being the rumors learned near the ground. Dining with the Moderns, Bryher also attended the cinema, loving Sachs' cozy family, asking Olga Barsis, one of his sisters, if she would take the soon-to-visit Mrs. Lewin, who acted the elderly racist in *Borderline*, to a music rehearsal. Olga consented, "unless there were a pogrom first."[42] Bryher made her mark—fun in her fury.

With Lewin, Perdita arrived for her birthday, fresh from Constantinople, eager to sit in cafés with cream. Contrary to H.D.'s belief her daughter was heavy, the ship doctor advised she gain weight. While suffering abdominal cramping as Yofi neared birth, H.D. told Macpherson, "Fido has made a great hit with F."[43] "Papa," however, appeared unaware of the connection between Yofi and H.D.'s "Pup" trauma, coinciding with the pregnant dog, tangibly in the analysis room. H.D. made Bryher's presence tangible as well.

On April 10, the whole gang—Lewin, Perdita, H.D., Freud, Anna, and Bryher—took "a fleet of taxis to call on Io-fi and the pups."[44] H.D. persistently inverted the Chow's name as Io-fi, sounding out "I owe fee," signaling her eruptions of guilt at Bryher's generosity. Bryher and Perdita played with the "two chow pups," "exactly like baby hippos, round and brown with short brown fur," until Yofi intervened. This blissful primal scene led Freud to offer Perdita her choice of the litter, causing turmoil for our pair, who knew they could not manage another pet.

The couple played analyst for one another, strictly not in Freud's rule-book. After her departure, H.D. thanked Bryher for "the treatment last night," making her auxiliary analyst. "It did me a lot of good," she confided, "maybe broke the actual P.R. (Rodeck) weight of connection."[45] Rodeck was the ideal "father" for Perdita in 1920; Bryher as father was even more ideal, crossing incrusted taboos.

In Fido's footsteps, H.D. visited an original Philadelphia branch of the Society of Friends (Quakers) on 16 Singerstrasse. Queasy, H.D. took brandy and bicarbonate of soda and read Dame Ethyl Smyth's outrageous sexual adventures in *Impressions That Remained* (1919). Still fathoming Bryher, H.D. found Smyth "a sort of ancient Bryher cum Mrs. Chiron, plus something else her own."[46] Uplifted by Bryher's visit, "such a good Corfiote time," she seized upon the cause of her stomach trouble. "The worst has happened," she began, "I feel like the Virgin Mary at the entrance of the dove." Deep into the "first layer," she shifted paternity to Bryher: "O, O, O, O Fido, why have you gone and got me in this awful mess??????" Writing both Macpherson and Bryher, she begged Bryher *not* to accept the "male twin." Feeling "about-to-deliver," she explained, "[T]he little dog represents a child, though he did most carefully present it to Perdita, I took it to be 'ours,' yours and mine."[47] Bryher reassured that planting over one hundred trees at Kenwin was her own Yofi.[48] In early May, H.D. wrote Bryher, "[Y]ou and I are literally feeding the light," excavating the unconscious stream beneath all life, striving to protect it.[49]

* * *

With Freud's upcoming seventy-seventh birthday, H.D. had distressing dreams she avoided discussing. She knew "the puppy equates death, impregnating and so on."[50] Two dreams followed, so vivid Freud called them "historical." Her success depended on her ability to stitch Freud's thinking to her own mythmaking. The doctor and most of the world, alongside her astronomer father, dismissed astrology, which H.D. yoked to both the mystical and the scientific. Interpreting her epic dream, she led Freud through astrological "houses," confronting her "fear and dread of the Scorpio, [her] father, a cold, distant, upright, devoted father," who gave her "a blind fear of space and the distances of the planets and the fixed stars."[51]

H.D. transcribed the initial dream for Bryher, dating it April 24 or 25. The numerous details of the whole are well worth studying.[52] Her so-called prologue situated her at a piano on a tilting boat, plunging toward a storm. Another boat, carrying a "number of women," capsized. Freud said it expressed "you and P., and a pity for the other women," endangered by "labor." The dream unrolled as she visited an exiled prince, whose unfurnished room had an "iron-railed balcony," similar to one she had at Kenwin. A fashionable woman wore "a green gown," a hat, and "pearl earrings of an enormous size," changing to "moon-stones," admitting it was "Bryher, all in all, but with the attributes of other women, as I love style, clothes and jewelry on OTHERS," so the "woman is Bryher plus certain frivolous attributes that I miss in her." The river started to "loom up like waves in the darkness," and "emerging from the water, numerous small white steers, bulls or oxen," echoing Freud's sun sign, Taurus the bull, with his birthday approaching. Together, Freud and H.D. bound the "sacrificial white bulls" to "the new life, the prophet, Joseph(a) in Egypt, the prince too in disguise," linked with "green" Bryher.[53]

The dream shifted back to the prince's castle (Kenwin?), H.D. calling it "The House of Marriage." Freud agreed she "wished to be a virgin, as [her] own 'house' is September Virgo." A church sale fit the "house of business" (Tenth House), with "two Siamese cats at large," and H.D. identified as the Chows in the "House of Twins." "You are the MOON and S.F. was the prince," H.D. told Bryher, making them "mother-bull and the father-cow." She decided, "The trio is you, Freud, me (and a child)."[54] Still unfolding her dream, H.D. created an altar on her hotel shelf with "narcissus in two jars, Fido on one side, papa the other, and J.C. from a catacomb drawing, in the middle."[55] H.D. was hell-bent on forming new triads to re-form the typical Victorian family.

In a follow-up fragmentary dream, she and Bryher gathered roses from an ancient garden, "the 'House of Pleasure.'" Several "gents" dissuaded them from picking roses. An "enchanted garden," equated with the mother. H.D. kept Freud purring, entertaining Bryher, who duly responded to "The Dream" as "an epic performance." Stunned, she "never saw such a thing, in no journal, in no volume and no text book!" H.D. now asked Bryher to allow *her* to "gracefully" dodge Freud's pup, while she "[was] on" the "operating table."

Freud suspected the couple had "evidently ... done some fish-tail stirring." Yet with her dream of "the father cow" and "mother bull" refiguring her father's "milky way," H.D. subverted the masculine and feminine principles as binary, making a queer family with Freud and Bryher as her parents. Freud's takeaway from the dreams was that penis envy assailed all women. Yet Freud had argued as early as 1905 that having "perversions of every kind is a general and fundamental human characteristic," and the infant's polymorphous perversity only *gave way* to species preservation.[56] Now, a quarter of a century later, he recognized a girl might remain fixated upon the mother or love another who was both male-like and mother-like.

* * *

May Day was often volatile, usually consisting of a parade of workers; this year the Fascists "stage[d] a patriotic celebration."⁵⁷ Freud was stunned when H.D. arrived on time for her appointment. Sent back to the hotel, she acted documentarian, with "the whole town one mass of barbed wire entanglements, and stacked rifles, really most, most effective." She boarded a tram, headed toward the opera house, detouring for miles, most streets cordoned off, while police patrolled with guns. Intending to cross "inside the barrier," approaching "a special lineup of soldiers" blocking the opera steps, the curtain had just gone up, so she slipped off for a beer and sandwich. "I must say it was marvelous, the way they were ready to shoot. The pavements were full of the usual confetti-signs and papers.... You would have loved it. Imagine the opera steps with soldiers and yet opera going on."⁵⁸

Bryher instructed her not to repeat this to Freud, while H.D. considered it "the most wonderful thing [she] ever did."⁵⁹ In artistic protest, she was a female bull gravitating to music. Bryher sent *J'Accuse!*, a pamphlet compiled by S. M. Salomon, published by the World Alliance for Combating Anti-Semitism, fifty-four pages of testimonials and photographs gathered from reputable news agencies and eyewitnesses, exposing torture, beatings, interrogation of Jews, normalized through hate articles and armed militias.⁶⁰ H.D. brought copies for "the she-Sachses" and Freud, overcome that the English produced it.⁶¹

After her May adventure, H.D. ventured for analysis to the Freud family's summer house, Hohe Warte, four minutes by car. She compared it to "a slice of Kew," with "long uncut grass in the English manner set with pansy beds and little squares of sheltered gardens," there crossing paths with Dr. J. J. van der Leeuw, a "tall young man" who "pretended not to see [her]."⁶² His analytic hour was before hers, so they often brushed elbows. In honor of his birthday on May 6, Freud's study was fit out "like a prima donna's first night," with "every sort of orchid and lily." H.D. thought him "a thin silver edge of flame, and so tired."⁶³

Bryher meanwhile watched her father ailing on his birthday, May 15, at Kenwin. She instructed H.D. to head for Zurich if the worst happened, semi-callously insisting she take care of herself first, then "take any of the Freuds with you if they don't delay you." H.D. was to contact Klara Modern every morning and to change money, keeping Swiss currency.⁶⁴ But H.D. felt invincible, having crossed barbed wire. She compared both Taureans, Freud and Ellerman, working like oxen, fearful to stop lest they perish, her own ethic mirrored back. Bryher bought a fifteenth-anniversary gift two months in advance, another fur coat. Drafting her will, Bryher provided H.D. a yearly income sufficient to ensure she and Pup were independent of Kenneth.⁶⁵

H.D.'s next pivotal dream in May took her "back to the womb" depths: one of three women, driving in the country, she spotted a gigantic moon, "rainbow colored and like a pool of rainbow in the sky," and "a dim figure of a woman in the moon," draped in rainbows. Envisioning herself as "Greek" and Artemis, she was stunningly "VIRGIN but pregnant." In fact, there are two figures in antiquity named Artemis: the most familiar, sister to Apollo, a virgin huntress; the other, the Artemis of Ephesus, whose temple, stupendous in size, is situated on a marshland. The latter, a great fertility goddess, wears upon her breast a zodiac necklace from fourth-century Babylonia, her torso draped with mounds, often interpreted as testicles. This stitched back to her bull dream. She shouted at the moon, then "a bird crossed the surface, a dark pigeon, a dove." "The moon, of course, equated mother," and the three women "a sort of band of sisters, the Graces or Fates." This dream took her "a step forward into the pure homo layer," its aftereffects restorative; she "slept for two hours like dead," evaluating her "high water mark was Corfu," where she performed both genders.[66]

In this psychoanalytic quest, while her "star-stuff" met with Freud's snorts and the Chow's snores, she clarified that she was not "a sloppy theosophist or horoscope-ist, for astrology was a whole other-science." Freud had "to stick to his scientific guns," while she to hers. Led to oceanic mother-love, she realized "we can't, no matter how we idealize the mother-idea, get rid of the father," her interruptive clause separating "we can't" from "get rid of the father," mother safe between commas, for now.[67] The dove, after all, called up Mary's immaculate conception, linked to "fantasies of female parthenogenesis and/or lesbian procreation."[68]

* * *

In late May, Bryher sampled Bergner's cat-and-mouse game for H.D.'s amusement. Staying near Audley in Mayfair, she commanded, "[R]ing me up at ONCE." When Bergner answered, she stole the conversation with details of her busy schedule. As if entertaining *her* mother, Bryher repeated Bergner's antics for H.D., then dreamed she "poured boiling tea in a fencing glove." "Very text book," she acknowledged.[69] Still, she gave Die B. a wooly little blanket, at Macpherson's suggestion, as affectionate transitional object.

Lady Ellerman and Bryher had Bergner to tea that May. Gushing over Bryher's parents, the star chuckled mercilessly over the portrait of a young "Dolly." Bryher shared her collection of 118 Elizabethan cross-dresser plays for her "Girl Page in Elizabethan Literature."[70] While with Herring and Bergner, Bryher received a letter from Heinrich Mann addressed to "Herr Bryher." Herring and Bergner laughed, imagining Bryher as "a fat old gentleman with a beard." His communication was sobering—his books burned by the Nazis. Bergner planned Kenwin for June; Bryher warned H.D. not to mock the star for her smallness.[71] As expected, Bergner failed Bryher. An unbreakable contract led to her canceling Switzerland.[72] Forbidden in Germany in 1934, making the film *The Rise of Catherine the Great* terrorized Bergner, yet Bryher could not lure her into analysis. The star wrote on June 23, admitting, "I need you too." Alice Modern arrived to supervise Pup, while Bryher returned in June to Vienna. Sachs asked Bryher to help the son of Karl Abraham, Freud's first pupil, work at Bergner's studio, Elstree, as an extra.

Finding both Freud and H.D. ailing, the latter with an eye infection, Bryher, at this point, supported "six adopted refugees" and might "flatten like a pancake."[73] She woke every morning in horror. During this second visit, the Austrian Nazis concocted a week of terror she did not dare communicate to Bergner, who complained Bryher sent no real news of her birthplace. On June 13, armed officers stopped the couple's tram, searching for a bomb. Before H.D. and Bryher headed back to Kenwin, Freud explained to Bryher that ps-a was a "philosophical system that could influence the great wave of life," yet was not an absolute antidote. Sachs recommended to Freud that Bryher train in Austria, "to bind you closer to our cause," again thinking "the most liberal" and appropriate training group in Zurich.[74] Bryher, in the end, was too late, swept up in her "mad dog" state, living in proximity to the Germans. H.D. thought she would reenlist Freud later in the year. Sachs came to Kenwin in July, and H.D. booked sessions to consolidate her new findings.

* * *

In July 1933, Bryher's mother took the ailing Sir John to rest at the Hotel Royale in Dieppe, a holiday spot, familiar from his youth, but his health deteriorated. The Kenwin group scrambled for timetables. A train departed in ten minutes. Instead, Bryher chartered a two-seater airplane. Perdita thought it "microscopic," watching as "[s]omebody strapped Bryher into a leather coat and goggles"; Bryher looked "at once very capable, and very tense and pathetic."[75] Her flying "off in a gypsy-moth" during a storm wrecked H.D., who waited up, "not knowing if she had crashed," until hearing from Bryher, who arrived too late.[76] H.D. wrote McAlmon to comfort Lady Ellerman. Sir John succumbed to a second stroke at age seventy-one, on July 16, 1933, a day before H.D. and Bryher's fifteenth anniversary.

On the heels of his death came an explosion of publicity. The *Daily Mail*'s headline read, "Britain's Wealthiest Man Dead."[77] One obituary stated that he "desired no publicity" as "magnate," which he was.[78] A media circus greeted Lady Ellerman upon reaching England with her husband's body. During the funeral, a heat wave hit London. Black dye bled from Bryher's clothing; Perdita wore stockings for the first time; and H.D. was absent.[79] Six captains of his shipping companies acted pallbearers. Dozens and dozens of colleagues and well-wishers came. Perdita described South Audley Street as "full of weeping friends and relations, and solemn business men from the city, all dressed in black, all talking in whispers."[80]

Dowager Ellerman, however, wrote the *Times*, protesting, "At the cemetery men with cameras ran beside us, leaping over graves and vying with one another to be first on the scene. As the coffin lowered, the silence was broken by the clicking of cameras."[81] Making her private loss public, the press tried ferreting out Sir John's secrets. For a woman with shadowy beginnings, her letter boldly rebuked journalistic crassness.

Macpherson, impressed by Bryher's "loveliness and loyal, gallant courage," told H.D. that the funeral was "gorgeous but simple."[82] Honored to serve in the city memorial for Sir John, he helped Bryher through her delayed reaction, letting her cry in his arms in the evening. H.D. now urged Ellis to contact Bryher.[83] Nearly a member of the family, Herring was thankful Bryher did not, as expected, "sort of slid[e] into herself, withdrawing from contact." He hailed Bryher as having a knack for "being bigger than the moment, of suddenly becoming huge."[84] He admired Sir John's "humor, the gnome-quality, the abstraction," observing in Lady Ellerman "a touch of Bryher's greatness." Her father's death left a vacuum. Unable to face the funeral, when they spoke by phone, H.D. noted Bryher's "strange exultant mood."[85]

The press continued to plague the widow. If newspapers recognized Bryher's existence, they referred to her as "adopted." Journalists discovered Sir John's will, a public record, spanning more than eighteen thousand words, requiring an index.[86] Papers around the world valued his estate between £17 and 40 million. Recent surveys of the Inland Revenue estimates it at £37 million—by far the largest in British history.[87] His will reveals a meticulous mind, calling for strict adherence to his promises. Sir John valued capital as a force with intangible powers. He gave his employees of more than fourteen years, whether afloat or ashore, a month's wages, and granted outright bequests of £15,000 to needy former employees, their widows, or dependents; £10,000 to every London hospital; and sizable gifts to household servants. He allocated £50,000 each to McAlmon, and Macpherson, who privately raged to H.D., insisting he deserved better.[88]

Along with a tax-free lifetime annuity of £30,000 per annum, Lady Ellerman received £150,000. Granting Bryher £500,000 in London real estate as a New Year's gift in 1930,[89] the will gave her £600,000 outright and £600,000 in trust; it left John Jr. £600,000 in cash, with £2 million in trust along with the estate's residue, approximately £20 million, placing John Jr. at the helm of Sir John's empire.[90] Sir John's bequests followed expected patriarchal expectations. Shortly after the funeral, John Jr., now twenty-one, announced he would marry Esther de Sola, from a well-off Canadian Jewish family. Bryher thundered at his desertion of their grieving mother and his nonchalance toward their father's business interests. Instead of stepping in as protector of their mother, near deaf and increasingly needy, he wanted to leave the continent; Bryher essentially saw herself in Moore's position when her own brother married. As early as 1925, the *Sunday Referee* sub-headlined "Secret of the Millions His Son Does Not Want."[91] Preferring amateur theatricals with Esther and friends, John Jr., rebelling against being a Junior, once aspired to be a ticket agent rather than direct a vast shipping enterprise. He watched Bryher's manic loyalty, wanting greater independence. Yet her insistence, which could be difficult to withstand, that he postpone his marriage and grieve with their mother led him to hurl a chair at her. They never spoke again. Keeping a low profile, he penned tomes on rodents.[92]

Sachs arrived, judging John Jr.'s announcement unbecoming, spoiling the solemnity. Macpherson confirmed, "John alone is contemptible."[93] Two weeks after the funeral, Bergner dealt Bryher another blow, rejecting her outright. Claiming intimacy with only one person, her husband, except for a week she would never repeat, her single emotion reduced to "jealousy."[94] Pound wrote H.D., not to offer condolences but to pressure Bryher for money.[95] H.D. stormed over his "mad, wild, frustrated letter."[96] Pound, she knew, lacked something "fundamental," was blind to "the creative drive that touches one as birth and death do."[97]

Still blocked in her writing, H.D.'s "Woman in the Moon" dream liberated a series of poems under the title *A Dead Priestess Speaks*. This priestess, a witch-doctor, writing a prize-winning epitaph "to a dead soldier," finds "winter-green / and ripe oak-leaf" to "stay" suffering from plague, but kept "circumspect," having "wings they saw not," and "never shone / with glory." Ultimately, this "Delia … / run wild" was H.D., who

> far, far, far
> in the wild-wood,
> they would have found [her] other
> had they found
> [her], whom no man yet found.[98]

H.D.'s "ka" pushed her inward.

In September, Bryher gave notice to housekeeper Quex, whom Sachs insisted was dangerously repressed. She reacted badly, but the rupture did not end in a triple murder. Elsie Volkart replaced her. Consistent with the couple's boundary-crossing in analytic situations, she became a friend, nicknamed "the Vee." H.D. summered at Kenwin, "tidying" her manuscripts, returning to Sloane for September. She heard from Conrad Aiken, who needed analysis badly. Anna Freud wrote Bryher her father had had a heart attack but was now out of danger, also conveying that the Chows were meant to be a "pleasure," not an "obligation."[99] Freud hammered in what felt like false reciprocity to H.D., "I could not take Aiken and I am sorry you could not take the 'twins,'" which he had to separate.[100] Thanking the heiress for sponsoring the Sachs Foundation for training analysts, Freud warned Bryher with gruff warmth that "an inoculation against guilt complexes ought to be officially forbidden."[101] Bryher had to face her guilt over her inheritance, harnessing it for a more peaceful future.

* * *

Grief-laden, Bryher attended Bergner's opening night of *Escape Me Never* in Manchester that November. Bergner asked for moral support. Bryher already en route, Bergner telegraphed Audley: "REHEARSING ALL SUNDAY AND ALL WEEK WITH NEW THIRD ACT PLEASE DONT COME LOVE = ELISABETH." Sachs had warned Bryher, who rushed toward disappointment, seeking anonymity among the audience. Once in Manchester, Bryher put on her best analyst glasses and saw Bergner "shook herself into such hurricanes that even her rescuers lost themselves." Intransigently, Bryher identified as a rescuer. After the performance, she attempted to join the entourage, but Mrs. Williams, the assistant, blocked her. All repressed lesbians H.D. and Bryher coded as "Mrs. Williams," but then *what* did that make Bergner?

Quickly transmuting her experience into art, a repository for hurt feelings, Bryher started a longish story, *Manchester*. Her main character, Ernest, a travel agent, did precisely as Bryher did; pulling out his portable typewriter, he exposed gritty details of jobless working-class women in Manchester. Having come to launch a futurist "commercial" airline, open to travelers unable to summon a Moth, he planned "a penny-a-mile airline," a cheap flight for weekend sunbathing in Portugal. Knowing Bergner's crippling anxieties, Ernest, Bryher's male prosthesis, portrays the nerve-wracked Cordelia, doubling for H.D., "the second half of himself."[102] Essentially, Bergner represented an emotional self, lacking H.D.'s psychic, intellectual dimensions.

Bergner scolded Bryher from the Midland Hotel Manchester for not easing her stage fright. Then she telegrammed Audley two days before Christmas: "WILL DO MY BEST TO ESCAPE AND SEE YOU ALL MY DARLINGS MONDAY AFTERNOON AT SIX." In all fairness, Bergner played sold-out shows in London and acted mentor for Perdita, who visited her backstage. As Freud recognized, writing was performance for H.D., who saw with Ahlers and Bergner a connection to herself—she had "dressed up," using the stage props "left to [her] mother by a retired prima donna who had taught singing at the old school."[103] She too identified with Bryher wanting Bergner, even once dreaming she herself "violently kissed E.B."[104] But H.D. knew Bryher's unerring fidelity and Bergner's "impossibility."

In December 1933, someone broke into H.D.'s flat and stole a suitcase, underpants, and the shawl she wore in *Borderline* as well as a gift from Freud, which he dubbed the "Rodeck wallet," representing the very security H.D. found in Bryher. Sergeant Detective Fish blamed the burglary on "the stiletto thief" and explained that "he-she always takes a suitcase."[105] *Fish!* H.D and Bryher's very code word for psychic matters. The unexplained sawdust in the kitchen made it even creepier. The "he-she" burglar led H.D. to imagine a former, less secure self, until, as she put it to McAlmon, Freud gave her "a sort of radium-burning to the back of [her] brain."[106]

13
Death Drive & "the Perfect-Bi"

In the new year, H.D. rode "the actual woof and heave and surge and wave and flow and flood and ebb and tide of the UNK."[1] This coincided with overcoming her writing block and meeting Silvia Dobson, a twenty-six-year-old aspiring writer, living with two friends, an opera singer and Una Cheverton, a violinist and poet, at 29 Edith Grove. Cheverton introduced Dobson to H.D.'s poems. They struck her as "tender fiery miraculous," and she sent an exuberant letter to "Atlantis." H.D. invited her to "[c]ome and see [her] but telephone first." She gave her address, "above Jaegers shop 26 Sloane Street," lowering her fan's expectations: "Use the side door beside a window bulging with bras, panties, stockings, suspender belts. I like the Atlantis touch, but this is a prosaic world." This prose world included climbing to "a scruffy landing," turning right, with the bell "out of order."[2]

Teaching grammar school on Chester Square, Dobson could visit only after 4:00 p.m., and H.D. offered tea. Bryher was at Kenwin. On February 15, Dobson knocked, the door opening to "reveal H.D.'s long slender hand," the arm next, and then the memorable "whole." Dobson was immediately overpowered by "those magnetic sea-green eyes under wide level brows, the high-domed forehead, planes and power of jaw and throat."[3] A spark ignited.

Welcoming Dobson into her exotically decorated flat, with its gold Buddha, Persian rug, and "sweeping damask curtains," H.D. served Earl Grey tea, dubbing Dobson "Dragon," after the motif on the bone china cups they drank from. The host wound and unwound a string of amber beads until it broke, both on their knees, picking up the glittering pieces. Dobson recognized in the fragments "someone's astrology chart," music to H.D.'s heart.[4] Curious about sexual "deviance," she confessed to H.D. that she was named Silvia Herbert Dobson, giving her leeway, she thought, to choose between being boy or girl.[5]

Dobson constructed birth maps for H.D., a compatibility chart with Bryher, and eventually a chart for H.D.'s circle, concentric ones, with Rodeck at the center as the eldest, and Peridta at the perimiter, Dobson the second furthest ring. It seemed to explain why Dobson and Herring never got along, thought H.D.: he was sturdy Taurus; she a sensitive Cancer. H.D. poked fun at Bryher's mother, born under the sign of the Goat, a Capricorn, gossiping that Lady Ellerman saw a viper in the fields at Cornwall, noting "how the UNK will allure the most drastic symbols of its own affinities." Besides, this viper sighting allowed Doris and Bryher to walk the fields, escape "the goat-storms." Asking for a birth chart exclusively for Rodeck, H.D. thought it would be "neat and Virgo-like to label [Rodeck], after 14 years," having "never found out whether it was a sort of 'astral' double actually of the man, or another person."[6] Dobson even accompanied her to Rodeck's miracle play at St. Clement Dane City Church in early March.

H.D. and Dobson began a lifelong correspondence. Addressing Dobson as "Cher X," H.D. confided her lost passion with Gregg, superimposing Dobson upon her.[7] Recall H.D. superimposed Gregg upon Bryher as well, and that imprint held. Here she matched Bryher's unrealized erotic desire for Bergner with this new friend. Less than a month later, H.D. invited Dobson to travel to Venice for her Easter break. Busy with refugee work, Bryher booked her rival "a sleeper on the Orient Express," and "in [her] cantilevered womb-tomb," Dobson caught "glimpses of La Belle France." H.D. supplied a gondola for the journey down the Grand Canal to their pension. Dobson's room was on the fourth floor, H.D.'s on the third. Every morning they met at 11:00 for coffee at Florian's, and later for sunset teas at Quadri's. Calling themselves "inveterate candle-lighters," H.D. guided Dobson to "the fabulous Ca D'Ora, all the Tintoretto's, all those churches," through cul-de-sacs, over bridges, to the Plaza di San Marco. They climbed 325 Campanile stairs at St. Mark's Square, H.D. instructing that from there, one could spot Venice's labyrinth "from a series of rising altitudes and angles," "the perfect circle, a fish biting its own tail." Life "advanced in a spiral," H.D. repeated. Mesmerized by Venetian glass, Dobson nursed a short-lived fantasy they could be a couple. They never spent a whole night together, though Dobson intimated sexual pleasure took place, feeling "changed, changed, becalmed, invigorated, blessed, sanctioned, recreated." Santa Maria dei Miraculi "did do a miacle for [her]."[8] The trip ending, H.D. taunted that Bryher had memorized *all* of her poems.[9]

Dobson sent H.D. her short story about a woman failing in an attempted suicide, provoked by a crisis in sexual identity. H.D. told her she needed to let the writing carry her wherever it would.[10] Declining the role of writing mentor, H.D. readied for Kenwin; she didn't "write letters as a rule" (not true), but responded incisively to her friend's notion that sexuality could be pinned down: "It is hardly a question of you being, as you say A2 or B3 Lesbian. It is doubtful what you are at all.... [I]t's a matter of something infinitely bigger than Lesbian A2.... The Lesbian or the homo-sexual content is only a symbol-note." In warding off labels, H.D. imparted a classic. "*How* you love is more important than W H O you love. And how that love helps or hinders you," she advised, convincing Dobson that instead of either an erotic affair or a writing apprenticeship, she needed psychoanalysis, which would help "catalogue [her] various selves a little. Yes—catalogue them. Shiver if you will. It is an enthralling task."[11] Bryher had met the Austrian psychoanalyst Dr. Walter Schmideberg, a "former captain of the hussars."[12] H.D. recommended him as perfection itself. Dobson resisted, but decided analysis, even if supplied by Bryher, kept her in H.D.'s world.

Educated at a Jesuit school in Carlsberg, Schmideberg studied psychology, fought in World War I in the Austro-Hungarian army, and was interned as a prisoner-of-war. After the war, he supplied food when Freud's family suffered malnutrition. Fourteen years Melitta Klein's senior, Schmideberg married her in 1924; Melitta, a training analyst herself, escaped her influential mother, Melanie Klein.[13] H.D. and Bryher nicknamed Walter "the Bear," and Melitta, "the Bearess."

In June, Bryher took H.D. to preview her new residence-to-be, sequela of the prior year's break-in, and Bryher's inheritance, 49 Lowndes Square, part of "four modern six-story blocks," not ready until the end of 1934. Meeting Dobson, Bryher too thought she should consult Schmideberg. Dobson cast Bryher's persona as dual, "a larger-than-life Napoleon" and "timid cabin-boy." Resentful Bryher *had* H.D., as early as 1934 she wrote, "Bryher was spending her fortune rescuing Jews from Hitler's brown-shirted thugs"; she was "a life-preserver, a 20th Century Scarlet Pimpernel." Bryher helped Jewish psychoanalysts emigrate to England, which made finding them patients a logical consequence. Dobson was an "early victim." Offering to finance a degree in Boston, with Sachs as analyst, Bryher tried, without success, removing her from H.D.'s path.[14]

H.D. and Bryher worried Macpherson drifted and wanted him too in analysis. Refusing to "genuflect" to ps-a, Bryher's "religion," he scrawled from Monte Carlo, "Vienna highly dangerous and the last spot I'd want to find myself if the old war bomb explodes again."[15] If he wanted to abandon their joined lives, Bryher required "a separation"; if not, a divorce; she had responsibilities, among them answering "begging letters."[16] Economics plus fondness led Macpherson to balk at divorce and continue analysis, though it was boring as "an advanced course in algebra."[17] For himself, Herring thought "Freud & writing must be just the two things worth having."[18]

Macpherson designed a protocol of three months on with Schmideberg, three months off in Monte, three months on again, and the next trio of months in New York. Two years later he thanked Bryher, who "bludgeoned [him] toward a means to such consciousness" of what he called "Home Blight."[19] Bryher suspected Macpherson gave his parents money as "a sort of polite blackmail," to buy his freedom so he could gallivant in New York and Monte.[20]

At Kenwin through September with H.D., Bryher persuaded her to publish recent writing with a Dijon press in fifty to a hundred limited editions, knowing they were not dead-ends and would be republished when the time beckoned. Beginning with *Kora and Ka* (1930), H.D. wrote two other "Ka" books, *The Usual Star* and *Mire Mare*. Macpherson enthused over the latter, set in Monte Carlo, as "a Garbo in prose," catching "the best qualities of the coast."[21] "*K and K*" shed light on psychic intertwining—as "Kora is everything. Without Kora, Ka would have got me." Kora was Bryher. Working on *Nights*, her fourth "Ka" book, gave H.D. "a sort of convalescence,"[22] though it also expressed something of what she recovered from.[23]

Tempted to show *Nights* to Dobson, H.D. retracted it as "pretty emotional stuff."[24] Its second part, written *first, before* seeing Freud again, was divided into twelve sections, like astrological houses, organizing her psychic self. Skating on the melting Lake Leman, her protagonist, Natalie, a lyric poet, strives to make two lines meet in infinity, leaving "a dark gash on the luminous ice-surface." A shadow suicide, Natalie placed her watch on her sweater on the lake's bank, as if to leave clock-time behind.[25]

At Kenwin, the tumult across the frontier frightened H.D. and Bryher. From June 30 to July 2, 1934, the German SS and Gestapo carried out a series of extrajudicial political assassinations to consolidate Hitler's power, the intrigue, known as the Night of the Long Knives or the Ernst Röhm Putsch, after the purge's best-known victim, a reputed homosexual seeking "a second revolution" for workers. With chaos restricting travel, Dobson pined to visit Kenwin, while H.D. still labored on *Nights*.

H.D.'s narrative of myriad sex scenes, all unfulfilled, has Natalie masturbating; "after [David as Dan Burt] left, [she] excited [herself] more," with premature ejaculation cherished as "almost sexless ... White and lavender. It was radium." Natalie glimpsed her "hand out of ashes, Pompeii," "terrific electricity," where the "crystal" broke. *Nights* showed love and death working in tandem so that "the bed clothes were banked like the dim lining of a tomb. Was bed, tomb; womb?"[26] Rejecting the genres of potboilers or popular arch novels, Natalie—and H.D.—broke taboos that stifled creativity, and though she loved Kenwin, it sometimes felt too vacuum-cleaned, too bare in its pristine isolation.

Just before the anniversary of Sir John's death, Dobson planned a July hiking trek through the Black Forest with her friend Sheila Barnard, stopping at Kenwin. Bryher instructed them to leave Germany as fast as possible for Bern. Signaling a depressive state, H.D. asked Dobson to forecast "the time and manner of her death" and invited them to come "for a bath and rest," that they "would need NO other clothes, we live like pigs, and eat berries and roots."[27] Jules drove Dobson and Barnard from Bern in August, motoring around hairpin turns. Welcoming them, Bryher showed off her rock garden, rare plants, and lake views. Built above a stone quarry, Kenwin, with its "huge lofty main living area" looked "across garden green and dazzling blue lake water to snowcapped peaks in France, often reflected in double image on Lake Leman." A powerful thunderstorm rocked the canton. Sighting the visitors after a walk, jealousy seized H.D., seeing Barnard's dazzling red hair and youthful glow; she bid her "play with [her] rocking horse" and reproached Dobson for flaunting "a young lover."[28] Bryher booked a pension down the hill for the visitors.

Repairing disharmony, Bryher funded Dobson for travel to Schaffhausen Falls and Konstanz. A geopolitical error. The assassination of Austrian chancellor Engelbert Dollfuss the previous month emboldened the Nazis, who were congregating along every border. Venturing into southern Germany to see Lake Constance, a steamer took the travelers to the fairy-tale town of Lindau, then hosting a Nazi Youth festival. Barnard, Jewish, was terrified. When they crossed the border to the closest Austrian town, Bregenz, officials questioned them. Dobson made up fictitious hosts, Hanns and Greta, who lived in a pink house with a "swastika flag."[29] From Austria, they took the long way home to London. H.D. apologized to Dobson two months later for being "so ill" and "trying to pretend [she] wasn't and that is worse than the real collapse."[30]

* * *

Between August 22 and 31, 1934, Bryher attended the very vexed and vexing 13th Annual International Psychoanalytic Congress in Lucerne, addressing the very "death drive" H.D. explored in *Nights*. Bryher reunited with Sachs, missing him after his emigration to Boston. The Congress elected her to the Executive Committee of Verlag Press. Among those Bryher admired, Ludwig Jekels was a "'double' for papa," with real "liberty of thought."[31] *Everyone* was either "terribly aggressive, or mournful."[32] "Germany was boycotted," she told Herring.[33] Before the Nazi takeover, the Berlin Psycho-Analytic Society had blossomed. Leaving Freud's circle for the Berlin Institute, Wilhelm Reich, Otto Rank, and Sándor Ferenczi created a "the third hub" of psychoanalysis. The Berlin Institute trained the Freud translators James and Alix Strachey, along with other theoretical innovators, including Klein, Karen Horney, and Erich Fromm, who sought to explain the fear of freedom.[34] In 1933, the Nazis forced Jewish psychoanalysts to resign, including Schmideberg's mentor, the Russian-born Max Eitingon, who also attended this conference, campaigning the IPA to actively resist Fascism. It didn't. Bryher's romance with the IPA wilted.

At Lucerne, contention arose over the "death instinct" and Freud's landmark 1920 *Beyond the Pleasure Principle*. Rebelling against Freud's fundamentals, Reich favored "social repression" or "orgasm anxiety," contending "fear of punishment" disturbed metabolism, causing neurosis. To the contrary, Freud maintained that the ego, "the mental apparatus," "precariously caught on the borderline between outside and inside," necessarily turns "towards the external world."[35] The ego must contend with the social world, filtering both "anxieties from within" and from "without," on a narrow footpath. As if describing H.D., Freud dramatized the ego as "a little fragment of living substance" that was "suspended in the middle of an external world charged with the most powerful energies," incapable of survival, "if it were not provided with a protective shield against stimuli."[36] Indeed, in the summer of 1934, H.D. felt besieged, writing dammed. No wonder Perdita wrote that Kenwin was "fraught with personality clashes," making it an "echo chamber for arguments."[37]

H.D. and Bryher, indeed, were mending from Macpherson, and H.D. truly mythologized Bryher, who deviated from all ordinary measurement and with whom her cerebral-erotic relationship was a fixed star; yet they argued. Insecure about her writing at this insecure historical moment, H.D. fielded McAlmon's anger at Bryher for getting "all the raps … as one who married for money," while Macpherson did not. Bryher and H.D. were aware of the false economy of a gift as a burden that had to be repaid.[38] H.D. occasionally identified with McAlmon and Macpherson, shadows of the original "husband-wife." *Nights* was unsparing, sharp, crystalline, and not written *to repay* Bryher.

Freud thought "artistic play carried out by adults" does "not spare the spectators (for instance, in tragedy) the most painful experiences," who also find them "highly enjoyable." Without catharsis, the desire to reclaim "the original state of things" motivates compulsive repetition of a trauma, giving the impression "of being pursued by a malignant fate or possessed by some 'daemonic' power."[39] *Nights* had that "backwash" feel. D.W. Winnicott later called this phenomenon the "fear of breakdown" and ensuing unplaced anxiety over a trauma that has already occurred but is "*not yet experienced*."[40] H.D. feared dissociating from her demons; Freud was her chance to face them.

At the IPA, Bryher observed Marie Bonaparte acting like "Mae West," delivering "Essential Female Masochism," arguing it governed all female sexuality. Bryher impishly sketched the faces of Anna Freud and Sachs, giving her "sadism" a healthy outlet. She already knew British psychoanalysts Barbara Low, whose "Nirvana Principle" designated emotional homeostasis, and Edward Glover, to whom Bryher sent patients and funds. They joined Anna's contingent against Melanie Klein's. Observing "the Jones-Klein group," angry that her money supported the "Anna-Sachs training fund," Bryher pleasured in Ernest Jones fulminating. Masochistically satisfied, Bryher wrote, "[I]f looks could kill I'd be in morsels."[41] She "licked lips and giggled."[42] Anna Freud, with the British group, wanted "dollars" to resist Melanie Klein's emphasis on the child's "sadistic desire," originating before the Oedipus conflict set upon robbing "the mother's body of its contents, namely, the father's penis, faeces, children, and to destroy the mother herself."[43] Bryher sighed, psychically robbed by both her parents!

Sitting next to a man with an indiscriminate cough, arousing her germ phobia, Bryher mocked herself to Herring, "leap[ing] to hind legs," making a "long speech on the subject of advertising and publicity," based on "long experience of journalism." Bryher chuckled with Herring about Dorian Feigenbaum's "Morbid Shame," a case study of a woman's humiliation in owning only one pair of pants. On the last day, Bryher praised the American contingent, which swept the field, struck particularly by Karl A. Menninger of Kansas, who spoke on "attenuated suicide" and "accidents as suicide prevention."[44]

* * *

By September 1934, H.D.'s "slight breakdown," indeed her fear of one, had lifted. "Deep in old Mss as usual," she asked after Dobson's progress with Schmideberg, reminding that ps-a did not end after a session; material from the "sea-bottom" had to reconstellate.[45] A month later, H.D. was pleased that Macpherson had "started with [Dobson's] man [Schmideberg]."[46] However, H.D. plummeted after Freud notified her in mid-September that J. J. van der Leeuw, a Dutch theosophist, flying his own plane from a conference in Johannesburg, had "crashed in Tanganyika."[47] Previously, Freud linked the two patients in 1933, and even sent H.D. a note in June with a card from "v.d. Leeuw," hoping he would "safely arrive at the Cape."[48] Having learned of Rodeck's ordination as a "priest," this pilot fit in the same "vibration." She knew he had "a strange experience in India," as she and Bryher had in Corfu.[49] She tabulated "two summer shocks" between the Freud sessions: in 1933 the death of Sir John; in 1934 the death of van der Leeuw,[50] triggering return to Freud. Between these deaths, H.D. was taut, the mysterious fallen pilot giving her a new Rodeck to stitch herself to.

Born in 1893, the year before Bryher, Johannes Jacobus van der Leeuw joined the Theosophical Society in 1914, was ordained as a priest in its liberal Catholic Church in

1921, and published *The Fire of Creation*, a classic, in 1925. Ensuring his "excommunication," his 1930 lecture, "The Conflict in Theosophy," revealed the movement's militarism, its hierarchical "Masters." Groomed by theosophist thinkers, Krishnamurti, born in British India in 1895, also rejected theosophy's lack of free thought. Hearing him lecture in India, van der Leeuw wrote *Conquest of Illusion* (1928), holding that "reality" was constructed through "concepts," artificially divorcing the individual from a preexistent oneness. By the time H.D. passed van der Leeuw on Freud's stairs, he sought to bridge Eastern and Western thought, pivoting on Einstein's theories of relativity. His efforts resembled H.D.'s own: he flew too high; she dove too deep. With Dobson, H.D. created initials for another self, "A. von. R," for "a sea change."[51] Now she thought it "better be R.I.P."[52] Freud blamed himself for missing the possibility of "reckless flying," in light of van der Leeuw's "intimate phantasies"; he urged H.D. "to take his place," a terrific honor.[53] *Nights* almost predicted her doppelganger's crash with a poet's suicidal accident while striving to make parallel lines meet.

* * *

H.D. posted to Chiron "two little prose volumes" (*The Usual Star* and *Kora and Ka*) that "Br had set up for [her] as a birthday present."[54] "I have gone on propheting," she punned, recalling Ellis misunderstood "Fish Notes" (*Notes*). She feared disappointing her friends Silvia, Cole, Viola, and evidently Gregg, who got copies. While she hid it well, H.D. engaged in intermittent epistolary and in-person contact with Gregg during the 1930s, letters handed off to Dobson to protect them from Bryher's eyes. In fact, injury in 1934 from Frances, addressing "sweet Hilda," "delighted that [H.D. was] using prose as a medium." She liked the stories, and then came a dig—urging her "to write for a larger public."[55] Plank, however, convinced H.D. that it was "entirely worthwhile to go on and go on spinning." It was her "necessity."[56] Bryher slipped Plank H.D.'s children's book, *The Hedgehog*, to illustrate; written between 1926 and 1927, its story a timely antiwar message. "How T E R R I B L E of you," H.D. mock-scolded Bryher, who in fact shored up H.D.'s ego with such publications.[57]

En route to Vienna on October 28, 1934, H.D., burst out, "O—Fiend": "I have had my first *real* fan letter from a woman—Marianne, of *all* people!" Assuming she would be offended at *Night*'s overt sexual language, H.D. quoted for Bryher Moore's words, which she wanted emblazoned in "gold": " 'never doubt from such worms as myself the admiration which the shining face of your courage evokes!' " H .D. credited Bryher for this exchange, having "Y O U to thank for all this, Fido!"[58] Moore understood *Nights* as "torture" conveyed with razor "accuracy."[59]

Bryher left for "golden hours" with Sachs in Boston almost immediately, sending H.D. a watch, as if replacing Natalie's timepiece to indicate a "new time." H.D. and Bryher created code words to indicate safety or lack thereof while apart: Bryher chose "Jane" to signal trouble, H.D.'s "magnificent roses" denoted "things are VERY good." This horticultural signage coincided with Bryher's purchase of a bulb farm, Trenoweth, in Cornwall, operated by her friend Doris, remarried to the agriculturalist

John Long. The "FARM" delighted H.D., Bryher "flooding" Plank with iris roots and bulbs.[60] Cornwall, associated with Corfu and Demeter's bounty, revitalized H.D.

* * *

When H.D. again arrived in Vienna, pro-Austrian nationalists guarded the frontier.[61] She consequently resisted probing "the father-brother war-accident layer, not pleasant."[62] Freud was "drilling away like mad ... worse than Haudley or Kenwin put together."[63] With Trenoweth in mind, H.D. agreed with Bryher that "roots" spoke to psychological and geographical mindsets, with Macpherson all water, and Bryher, earth, a rock. In October, Freud told H.D. that he suspected the charming Schmideberg was a homosexual. "Don't worry about Kex," H.D. in turn reported to Bryher. "He is having the time of his life. And Sch is too, I shouldn't wonder."[64] Bryher's intuition that "Schmide" made an ideal "father" substitute for Macpherson proved correct. When Macpherson lived in New York, Herring "filled in" as analysand. Dobson too was analyzed, resenting the language barrier, with "Mr. S." flipping through dictionaries, failing "to notice [her] psychic slips."[65] Her fantasies of what she could buy with what he charged counterpointed with H.D.'s frantic fear of "get[ting] stuck in a back-water," signaling creative stagnation if "Papa" couldn't set her on track.[66] She *had* her war. The world threatened to get "stuck" in Nazi barbarity, the death drive incarnate.

In 1934, H.D. received potent letters from Gregg; she passed their "electric current" to Dobson for safekeeping, classing them as "very mad, and sort of cruel," trying "to analyse [her] backwards."[67] Dobson, H.D. told her, might find "a clue" to H.D.[68] Learning "that the roc egg had hatched at last," Gregg alluded to Bryher's inheritance. "These stories are very good," Gregg offered. "GET these things decently and honestly published." She implied Bryher's binding her beloved's work as somehow indecent, massaging H.D.'s insecurity that she wrote for "her keep," though she had untouched American funds.

This ghost lover, Gregg, gave a barker's call, while she ate a sausage, and her son, "the god," slept:

WALK UP. WALK UP LADIES AND GENTS TO SEE THE ONLY DOUBLE
SOULED WOMAN. THE ONLY WOMAN IN THE WORLD WHO HAS TWO
PERFECTLY DEVELOPED SOULS   WALK UP   WALK UP[69]

This letter in capitals actually anticipated a dream H.D. narrated to Bryher on November 11, headed "Shades of Armistice." "I am riding a black horse ('dark horse')," she began, and then it "suddenly turns into two horses or a two-headed horse, pulling both (opposite) ways.... I then drive the animal to a station near Bethlehem, Pa."[70] With Freud, she discussed Plato's *Phaedrus*, Socrates' allegory of the charioteer steering two horses. Without mentioning Gregg, H.D. missed Bryher, signing off "ever and ever and ever."[71]

In another letter, Gregg thought her son Oliver suited Perdita; if they met, they would "spit and shoot electric sparks at sight," a vision repellent to H.D., who had alluded to her summer depression, for care bled into the next hysterical response: "WHO nursed you? Where were you? Are you all right now? ... How did you ever bring it about that we are as separate as all this?" She evidently forgot she had deserted H.D. after their trip abroad. "I am really all the mother you have now."[72] Gregg struck H.D.'s heart, and as if to erase her old flame's identification of herself as mother, she dreamed Bryher was "Beaver" or "Mrs. Doolittle." H.D. wanted to flee the couch, but Bryher insisted this was a "false economy," especially since Freud had now located the father-terror complex. With Freud listening "to wave-lengths," H.D. could "find no words" for "the happiness of the quest," certain there existed "a formula for Time that has not yet been computed."[73]

* * *

Determined this trip to Freud would uncover what kept her searching, she swore off alcohol and drank so much coffee she was "turning into a coffee bean." Lightness aside, H.D. had a breakthrough dream placing R.A. (Aldington) and Bryher in bed together, "evidently married and ... R.A. shoots you. Then shoots himself." " 'Bryher is killed,' " she apologized with her quirky humor, adding she "had to get some one with a gun." Substituting Bryher for herself, "the father or husband, R.A., 'kills' the mother by shooting her in the head in bed."[74] As a military man, R.A. represented a "killer" of the maternal. Aldington still held the legal weapon of charging H.D. with perjury, a fact that truly terrified her. For H.D.'s socially trained mind, she suffered guilt over being able *to have and to be* both genders. She escaped to Europe to liberate herself from the "terrible" father, while her grandfather stood for the maternal church. Rodeck, the "astral father," was a smokescreen for Bryher, freeing the couple to nurture a sun-baby, or the mystic androgyne that Bryher projected on the Corfu wall.

With this dream, H.D. reached her real "bed-rock" ties to Bryher, representing to her "food, help, support, mother, though of course, it mixes into father too. It is really reversible." The social norms of her day had disengaged her from her dual identity, "really," quite simply, "reversible." Given the clarity of her dream, she still wondered "W H O I am in this puzzle"; Bryher was both father and "in the REAL scene, you are the 'hurt' or martyred mother," admitting Bryher "did all the work" with Perdita.[75] H.D. openly called her daughter a projected self, often asking Bryher communicate to Perdita on her behalf, now wanting her to "[t]ell old Pups how important to my unc she is, and has been—rather as MYSELF," not a solacing confession.[76] Yet her "primal scene" dream led to life-changing assertions: "He says, 'you had two things to hide, one that you were a girl, the other that you were a boy.' It appears I am that all-but extinct phenomena [*sic*], the prefect-bi."[77] This thrilled her to no end.

Uncertain of her next move, H.D. obsessed over Kenwin as a "half-way house" during the last month of analysis, signing off to Bryher with "much much love."[78] From 49 Lowndes, not yet ready, Macpherson dangled tidbits of work in progress, such as "a divine kitchen, just one mass of built-in cupboards enameled in primrose, and tiles with a yellowish tinge," with the "divans chez Sloane" reupholstered.[79]

Nearly "extinct," in Freud's view, H.D. now recognized that Gregg raised a pathogenic belief she was a horse "in a stable," in this sense confusing Bryher with "the [paying] father." Agonizing over Bryher's generosity to Freud, and influenced by Gregg, H.D. committed herself to being more independent. "PLEASE, Fido, if you love, and love my work," she began, "leave that to work its own will in its own way." If she could "go on her own two rails, it will be all right," otherwise her creative drive might die. Conveying a dramatic, satisfying realization, she wrote, "I am not, except in certain hours of writing and in certain hours of FORGETTING writing, ever free. Let me write, then let me FORGET my writing." What H.D. didn't say was her fusion with Bryher, who she configured as alter ego, who urged her to publish.

H.D. planned working "on a sort of ps-a re-hash of the Greek scene," which she would "publish when ready." Not only two-souled, H.D., with two rails, was a psychic hermaphrodite; female rail plus a male one equated with her "grail." Being "the perfect-bi" had hindered her on certain occasions, finding it "so hard to be at Audley for more than a few hours." Acting the part of a lady for several hours led to "terror of claustrophobia" and an urgent need "to get to an intellectual retreat, book or pages—to prove I am man. Then I prove back again." She required "the cloak of invisibility," and Bryher to hold her identity puzzle together.[80]

Twenty years earlier Freud might not have recognized H.D.'s perfection. His research *had* concluded the child usually "decides in favor against one or other parent, or identifies himself with one." Addressing her "Fiend," "it was simply the loss of *both* parents, and a sort of perfect bi-sexual attitude arises, loss and independence." "I have tried to be man, or woman but I have to be both," she declared. After this realization, H.D. assumed a "male" persona, writing Bryher and Macpherson together about her flat, arranging a room for each occupant—Pup, Kenneth, and Bryher, the latter assigned the large room to entertain. Before leaving Vienna, H.D. was jubilant about Bryher's investment in Lowndes and the Trenoweth Farm as well as the Hanns Sachs Training Fund as a "symbol to old Papa, the Gold, Frankincense and Myrrh touch."[81]

While H.D. labeled her psychic compartments, Dobson visited Perdita and Lady Ellerman at Audley, and H.D. wrote her friend that "mama" was "indeed one of the sole survivors, and one must hand it to her—she has kept the 'modern' at bay. But it makes one understand Br—how did S H E happen???????"[82] Not only an endangered species, Bryher existed as improbable accident. Enjoying the precision of herself as "a sort of split-infinitive, or split dual personality," H.D. aimed "to get the two together." The female rail versus the male one corresponded to the "ideal, and the real," "on quite separate rails, all the time." Celebrating female generativity, there was "Rummel-Rodeck" as " 'ideal,' plus F.G. and you [Bryher]"; the male rail, "Ezra, R.A., Cissie [Gray]," the father of Perdita, "sadistic," constructed to favor men, each getting away with it. She decided her "problem is to get the two rails going together," her sacred, mechanical-sounding task. Pronounced "finished," she exclaimed, "O, Fido, I do feel we are ALL going to be so much happier in 1935."[83] At Kenwin, she worked her male rail as John Helforth, her "author" prologue framing the death-driven *Nights*.

14
"Group Consciousness" & *Ion*

In the new year, Doris at Trenoweth Valley Farm, located in St. Keverne, Cornwall, a small village ten miles from Mullion Cove, assured Bryher that their "Hyacinths are all out in the ground. The Mother bulbs have been planted in prepared beds with a good base of sand and peat."[1] With its thatched roof and swamp, Trenoweth was a rustic refuge. Bryher and Doris cultivated roots and bulbs, preserved fruit, and raised turkeys, preparing for the worst.

After wintering at Kenwin, letting her "perfection" settle, H.D. moved into 49 Lowndes. To the north of her flat, two roads invited entry to Knightsbridge: Albert Gate led to Hyde Park; from the south, a road extended to Belgravia and Kenneth's flat. The fourth-floor dining-room window overlooked flower-bordered paths, lush "plane and pine trees, blossoming May, Lilac, Cherry, Laburnum, syringa, rising from dense laurel, privet, hydrangea bushes." From her bedroom and kitchen, H.D. peered over Victorian mansions. Crediting the "furnishings arranged by Bryher & Kenneth for Christmas 1934," it was no doubt a fine basket.[2] Mrs. Louisa Ash agreed to "do" for them.

With Gregg's "surcharged" letters, Dobson felt entitled to criticize H.D. for not providing Perdita with more mother love. Such jabs enraged her. Couldn't Dobson understand her annual crisis of 1918, when war turned rebirth? "Pup was just about beginning, it all works out to the mystic snake-biting-tail."[3] Two days later, to Bryher, she celebrated their "consummation 15 years ago"; she was "drunk with the ether—intoxication of that faint, lovely scent—smelling of water and rain and shelves of moss."[4] Writing Dobson she was not mother to the entire group (Kenneth, Bryher, her, etc.), her nineteen question marks underlined 1919, then shifted perspective; the lines, indenting like a stanza, reversed position:

You see???????????????????
    Well, perhaps I   A M[5]

H.D. believed Perdita had plenty of mothering from Bryher, "mama," and herself.

As a lay analyst in spirit, she opened her door to Dobson and to her neighbor, Cole Henderson, twice a week at Lowndes, which she called "a regular sort of high diplomatic intrigue green-room."[6] She sifted what had emerged with Schmideberg. Recognizing the difficulty in "being [Silvia's] analyst and friend," H.D. practiced with Cole, "now nicely on the couch," frustrated in her creativity, just needing someone "to finish her off."[7] Once, sauntering into Lowndes, Cole imitated Schmideberg in a

Garbo voice.[8] Schmideberg detected Cole's "negative transference" with H.D., who attained both art *and* motherhood.

At times, excessive appreciation of Bryher made H.D. resist. Cole "howled" that Bryher "had saved her life." H.D. protested that Bryher would still be stuck at Audley if not for her.[9] When Macpherson padded off for the boat-train with Bryher and Perdita, he spoke of "Schmide" as a "she," proof enough analysis took.[10] From within his own closet, Schmideberg treated queers like Macpherson and Herring. Meanwhile, H.D. asked Bryher for some jewelry (sounding out her "female rail") as well as all "ps-a vols" to be sent: "our ps-a centre, after all, is HERE."[11]

Ignoring Freud's advice not to consult about "cases," H.D. asked Ellis for guidance in being "semi-professional."[12] She relayed the curious case of M.C. (Murray Constantine, aka Katharine Burdekin, 1896–1963), who published *The End of This Day's Business* (1935), a science fiction novel set in a matriarchal culture, looking upon Fascism from a long distance. Although M.C. lived with a "sort of Bryher," a "masculine woman," when psychoanalysis came up, she screamed. M.C. "works like a steam-engine," a process resembling H.D.'s own so much it "annoyed," and H.D. diagnosed M.C.'s trouble as mediumistic "depersonalization," herself feeling "*almost* out of herself, or in the hands of a 'control,' " while writing.[13]

In 1935, H.D. posted *Pilate's Wife* to Ferris Greenslet at Houghton Mifflin. If he liked it, her "male rail" would oblige him to publish Bryher's *Manchester*, a work she "approved of thoroughly." "I loved the end of *Manchester*, if it is the end. It is terrific in its concentration," H.D. reiterated.[14] Sachs read *Manchester* as evidence of "dangerous repression," advising Bryher rewrite it. Perdita remained the story's greatest fan.[15] Bryher told H.D., "Richardson is re-writing Manchester!"[16] Soon both were rejected.

On her front, Bryher received a "mile long telegram" from her Queenswood chum, Theo, Petrie Townshend's nickname from Queenswood, asking if she wanted to buy *Life and Letters To-Day* for £1,500.[17] H.D. approved, and Bryher purchased the monthly, insisting their names not appear on its masthead, making Theo business manager, and Herring literary editor. H.D. left for Kenwin in April, aware that Vaud, Kenwin's canton, was isolated, forcing her to "weave a sort of garment for the naked spirit, the Ka, if it is to survive at all," compared to Bryher's "rare and dangerous gift of bringing the soul to life." At this junction of their relationship, *without* Macpherson, H.D. reemphasized their astrological likeness: "[Y]ou and I have Sun and Mercury (writing) in Virgo," and "[you with] the dear virgin-dog have your virgin-marriage also in Virgo."[18] Again, she firmed up Bryher as Artemis, the huntress-midwife.

Bryher warned the British Government of ongoing German atrocities. She badgered consulates, yet officials said her photos were "doctored," or "those exiles" deserved it. Acting in concert with the Friends organization whenever possible, Sachs first helped with lists of analytic students in need. In multiple reconnaissance visits to the States, Bryher arranged affidavits to aid refugees needing work. Venturing to Vienna and Prague to interview the displaced, she brought necessary papers obtained from embassies through vigorous persuasion and cash, so they could apply for visas.

Evading close scrutiny of such documents, she folded them into the *London Times*, allegedly pro-Fascist.

Late in 1935, Bryher, Theo, and Herring gave a *Life and Letters*' launch party at a large drawing-room near St. George's Hospital in Knightsbridge, marking its first sold-out issue. Garnering new and established writers, the journal published Gide and Kafka and emergent writers like Muriel Rukeyser, May Sarton, and Moore's young prodigy Elizabeth Bishop. Bishop's "Man-Moth" appeared in 1936, describing a creature who rides the New York subways "always facing the wrong way," aware of "a disease / he has inherited the susceptibility to." Authored by a closeted lesbian and alcoholic, it expressed frustration at her "disease," which Bryher understood, only a tad more comfortable in her body than the "man-moth." Bishop's poem followed Bryher's story of her frustrated affair in *Manchester* in *Life and Letters*.

* * *

Planning to visit Macpherson in New York, and then to Boston to consult Sachs, Bryher was indecisive, hoping to avoid Bergner's Broadway debut in *Escape Me Never*—but Perdita persuaded her to attend. The fifteen-year-old had first seen Bergner at the Apollo in London the year before, sitting with Lady Ellerman, H.D., and Macpherson in "a peculiarly uncomfortable box," while Bryher "perched in the back of the dress circle." Perdita saw the play four more times, wore her hair like Bergner's, and adopted a "slightly husky, Viennese manner of speech." Macpherson arranged for Bergner to meet Paul Robeson, making with Perdita a foursome. Acting out Bryher's own longing, Perdita escorted Bergner to the Apollo; in full view of an adoring public, the actress kissed Perdita goodbye.[19]

Bryher's travel mania became a sore point between her and H.D. as well as fodder for jokes. Bryher wished H.D. "didn't hate the States so much" but expected she would "never leave Le-owndes." In January 1935, Bryher and Perdita sailed from Southampton on the SS *Olympic*. Bergner and her cast were aboard. Watching Bergner as Gemma, mother of an illegitimate child, in *Escape Me Never* one too many times, Bryher joked to H.D. that on deck she performed "a cross-dressed Gemma in old age in my best Cornish clothing."[20] Bergner rarely stirred from her cabin. Perdita caught her in "a peculiar red velvet suite known as The Adam Rooms," playing solitaire.[21]

Nostalgic over H.D. in New York circa 1911, George Plank, then in the city, greeted Bryher and Perdita at the pier. Fifth Avenue enthralled Perdita. Bryher told H.D. that Pup "just fits in here as you do in London," and "atavistic memories come over her."[22] H.D. urged Perdita, "[H]ave a good time and lick off the cream—but come back to Britannia Rules the Waves." H.D. visited Lady Ellerman, "in terrific form."[23]

In Boston, Bryher and Pup stayed at The Vendome, a hotel overrun by "old dames," as Bryher affectionately called them. Perdita complained that everyone "wore little lace capes," the bedrooms all had rocking chairs and Bibles, and "the sitting room radio was tuned to one religious service after another." Bryher's design for living— "mornings ps-a, afternoons typing letters, and lights out at nine"—cramped her style.²⁴ However, Bryher had an epiphany through Sachs. As an infant, he proposed, she apparently "passed into the Greek state" identified "as 'ecstasy,' and wished to remain unaltered." This was distinct, "completely other than the usual disassociation." Discovering in analysis an inner wholeness, an UNUM, Sachs picking out her early "undifferentiated" "attitude" that merged her parents, preemptively losing them, *seeking* independence, beset by guilt for running away so often. Feeling "finished," Bryher cut her hours with Sachs, returning to Manhattan for a week's stay.

Moore was unchanged, "except that she has become purely a giraffe," her hair "as gold as ever."²⁵ Perdita sent postcards from the Empire State Building, bought a new handbag at Saks, and squeezed in a Ginger Rogers film. On January 21, 1935, Perdita and Bryher attended the opening night of *Escape*. Their box had a pillar blocking the stage. Bergner performed Gemma, pregnant with one man's baby, sought out by his richer brother, portrayed as a "delicate swan" and "poor little waif," without coincidence that H.D. assigned the illegitimate Ion this endearment in her now incubating translation of the play.²⁶

They returned to Boston during its worst blizzard since 1890. Marooned, Bryher and Perdita had electric shocks from "magnetic disturbance, due to snow."²⁷ Reversing course again, Bryher rushed back to New York so Macpherson could show his "daughter" the town, spending an extra week at the fashionable St. Moritz, where Bergner conveniently stayed.²⁸ Their room offered a full view of Central Park. With Macpherson, they saw Bea Lillie in the Rainbow Room, danced at Harlem's Savoy Ballroom and the Coq Rouge. Scouring Liberty Music shop, they swooned over Cole Porter's "You're the Top" and "I Get a Kick out of You" which they played on Perdita's portable gramophone, handily collapsing to the size of a Kodak. Bryher and Macpherson went wild at *Anything Goes*, which portrayed antics on an ocean liner cruising from London to Manhattan. They heard Ethel Merman sing, bought a Duke Ellington record, and went to Marie Harriman's gallery, exhibiting Isamu Noguchi's photography. Mrs. Goode, Eslanda Robeson's mother, visited Bryher in hysterics—bullies had prevented Paul Jr. from skating, and she wanted to take him to Russia for his education. Bryher warned of food shortages.

Insisting on meeting the trio after a performance, Bergner cabled. With customary bad timing, she narrowly missed Bryher, Perdita, and Macpherson, just leaving for the play *The Old Maid*, its subject "the awful sin of having little ones unless married." Bryher thought Judith Anderson's acting was wonderful but the play itself horrible. After her father's death and her brother's substantially greater inheritance, Bryher knew what her own illegitimacy signified, while witnessing H.D.'s struggle, fearing for Perdita, due to outmoded social customs. Meanwhile, in London, H.D. invited Rodeck to tea; he accepted, but never arrived.²⁹

After seeing *Old Maid*, the trio scouted the stage door to the Shubert. The play still in progress, the dresser motioned with his finger—and to Bryher's distress, they were practically on stage, stranded in what Bergner called "the station waiting room," with a light in wire cages, "like lamps in barns." Bryher noted a chintz-covered couch, and the rug she had given, paraphrasing the actor's mood for H.D.'s benefit: instead of autumn, she had to say fall, the theater was too large, taxis banged her head, and her stockings had static. Perdita, visiting Bergner's dressing room, wanted to be an actress or a "female Noel Coward," asserting H.D.'s own duality.[30]

On March 1, Macpherson saw Bryher and Perdita off; back in London, they went to Trenoweth to survey the farm's modern milk-sterilizing equipment. H.D. sent "kindest thoughts to Doris, your co-partner in this miracle of Cornish moss and rain and wind and I can ever hear the gulls—O Fido." She linked Cornwall to Corfu, "mixed up" with "taking flowers to Nisky Hill,"[31] while Bryher fretted over her commitments—to *Life and Letters*, impossible without Herring, and "couldn't do it, run the family, St. Keverne," along with Kenwin, while her responsibility to refugees escalated.[32]

Missing Bryher terribly when at Kenwin, Perdita stood in for her at Audley, seeing H.D. by appointment, not enough for the adolescent's liking. H.D. described one session with Perdita, "I had a good time but she tore my insides. I felt terrible, she has evidently fallen in love with me, in good Maedchen in Uniform manner," when she brought, "as from you, a heap of panties, stockings, shoes, bathing dresses. I hate to think of it. I got her some late lunch and she went off to Audley with her bags."[33] Addressing Bryher as "most adorable flea," Perdita herself chronicled seeing H.D. for their "permanent psychologist's conference date every Friday afternoon" before her tap-dancing class. Boosting Pup, "Mama Haudley" was "definitely cheerful," "trot[ting] around quite gaily," excited she would accompany Perdita to see "STOP PRESS tonight," with Maurice Chevalier, at the Adelphi.[34]

Perdita reconciled herself to stay part of the summer at Cornwall, "if [she] live[d] till then.... Trenoweth is the best place for me." Besides, she wanted "to meet the cow and fish for sharks with Doris and Doreen!"[35] As it transpired, she enjoyed sailing, fishing, eating bowls of fresh cream, and practicing Juliet and Miranda monologues.[36] Yet bounced between households, Perdita felt the time keenly. Finally, hope came in the form of Bryher's friend Lotte, the animator, who knew a London producer, Tyrone Guthrie, with a drama school, The London Theatre Studio. Practicing for her audition on ducks in Hyde Park, Perdita recited mother-longing:

I do not know
One of my sex: no women's face remember,
Save, from my glass, mine own.

Mama E., wearing all black, laid out special strawberries for her breakfast. Perdita circled the theater, swilled coffee, smoked, girding for audition. She started lessons on May 30 at the Old Vic, hired out for the summer course. Perdita's teacher, Michel St. Denis, based all acting on identification with inanimate objects, sounding like H.D. herself, where "one must be able to do things with things which weren't there."[37] Perdita acted out being a tree—so the audience believed it.

Before starting *Ion*, H.D. relived "new terror" with Macpherson gadding in New York. By 1935, H.D.'s personal three-in-one had broken down, regarding Macpherson "as a sort of younger lover-son," now diagnosing that "both those children [Kenneth and Eileen] were blighted" by their parents. She shifted responsibility to Bryher for opening their circle to them, telling Plank, "Br doesn't pick up just crooked sticks, she has a magic sort of power, she should have been a surgeon or biologist—she GETS such people, wants to help them—they break."[38] H.D. might have recalled he hailed from Frances, and that she herself tried fixing people, such as the "frustrated" Cole. Bryher's farm, *Life and Letters*, and her Anglo-American transits, all hot spots, gave "community" a wider resonance, especially in the context of the U.S. willfully ignoring Hitler in Nazi Germany and signing neutrality acts.

* * *

Gertrude Stein and Thornton Wilder motored to Kenwin in late July to visit H.D. "I like them both so much. [Wilder] wants me to finish up a Greek play for him to take back to America," she wrote Bryher, though doubted she "will be able to do it!" Stimulated by her visitors, H.D. surprised herself with "beating out Greek Prologue to more or less chant rhythm, a new method." "*The syllables of these first lines*" were "*to be stressed like a gong*," joking it was "a wonderful idea, I just thought of it, as Stein would say."[39]

In translating *Ion*, a project begun when she met Bryher, H.D. veered from exactitude through embodied reception, using introductory notes like these before the play's dialogue:

> Parse the sun in heaven, distinguish between the taste of mountain air on different levels, feel with your bare foot a rock covered with sea-weed, one covered with sand, one washed and marbled by the tide. You can not learn Greek, only, with a dictionary. You can learn it with your hands and your feet and especially with your lungs.... Realize with some sixth sense, the sea; know that it is there, by the special quality of the shimmering of bay-leaf or some hinted reflex from the sky-dome.[40]

This elemental "sixth sense," serving as medium "for the gods," linked her back to Cornwall 1918–1919, and she was "glad the Stein and T.W. poked [her] in the psychic tummy."[41] She channeled backward to imbibe fragrance, soils, plants, statues, stones.

Avoiding "long dialogues" for "which no translation can do justice," she captured essence over substance, rhythm over plot, her choral translations "the spiritual element" set beneath notes. Her childhood choirs turned her to the community of choruses. Amplifying the estrangement felt by the play's characters, H.D. relied on Leconte de Lisle's three-volume translation of *Ion*. By way of French, she arrived at her own transfusion. *Ion* was a "good old classic melodrama" where "his mother shall know him," "the god's act hid," and "the child shall be happy." "Now risen," the illegitimate Ion became the founder of Ionian island culture, a "matrix," liberating a more gender-fluid civilization.

The drama began with a flicker, a coupling in Athens: "there, Phoibos loved Kreousa." In her girlhood fancy, Kreousa expects marriage, though Phoibus (Latin for Helios, cognate with Apollo, all used by H.D., and brother to Roman Diana, Greek Artemis) conceals the pregnancy from her father, Erechtheus, the archaic Athenian king; she is freed from "the stones, midwifed by Athene," the "motherless" "virgin." Fearing her mother's judgment, Kreousa left her baby "on those briderocks," "exposed to death" in a "deep basket," with "the serpent-necklace: / gift to each true-born Athenian infant."[42] Without Kreousa's knowledge, Phoibus saves Ion, with Athene, delivering the babe to Delphi; the Pythoness rears Ion. Claiming spiritual lineage as more significant than biological "lines," H.D. associated the Pythoness in the innermost temple with Bryher, watching over Perdita. Bryher was also Artemis who kept her brother in check; Helios, we recall, was one of Macpherson's early aliases, and surely their aborted baby belonged to H.D.'s complex response to Ion, this abandoned child she identified with, beset by mother longing and guilt.

Convinced *Ion* would break "the backbone of her H.D. repression," the sense that she was delimited as "imagist," it was, as Eileen Gregory remarks, a "writing cure."[43] She ambitiously undermined the cultural forces forbidding lives of nonheterosexual eroticism. *Ion* mirrored her own grievances, not just with Macpherson but with legal loopholes that let Cecil Gray, like Helios, simply flee. H.D. set the play in nineteen sections, mirroring the birth year of Perdita; 1919 had two "19s," equating 1 + 0, the rails of male and female, real and ideal, writing and forgetting. *Ion* represented "our Greek-Corfu thing, and the pre-Pups, and is most important to the unk, that it was 'wanted.'"[44]

The couple, Kreousa of Athens and her husband, Xouthos, a non-Athenian who won her "as a prize of combat," arrive at the Delphic temple to ask the oracle if they will remain childless. Kreousa, now middle-aged, longs for her son, realizing she has "hidden too long this truth."[45] Acting as steward, Ion sweeps the shrine with a laurel broom, maintains friezes, and fends off birds, whose songs he loves. He is stranded in a "psychic hinterland of loss, doubt, loss of personal identity, terrible groping depersonalization."[46] Kreousa does not recognize him, while he almost does, as "something akin to himself," *but "with a start,"* notes "her eyes are fast shut."[47] The oracle tells Xouthos that he fathered Ion after a drunken night with a Maenad.[48]

Enraged at her husband's cavalier adoption of this discarded son, Kreousa turns to one of Athene's gifts of a vial of deathly dragon blood to avenge herself upon Helios and the temple's keeper, not yet known as her son. When Ion is about to drink from the goblet, a priest calls for fresh wine, dashing the liquid to the ground. A dove sipping the spilled drink immediately dies. Kreousa takes refuge in the temple. Emerging out of "the inviolable altar of justice-beyond-justice," the crone-like Pythia appears: "It was against the veils of her early novitiate that his small hands had clung. The frozen body of the deserted waif was warmed before the brazier. . . . His feet and hands were laid with holy water. And by whom? By the Pythoness of Delphi."[49] The Pythoness, addressed as "mother of my spirit," negotiates between mother and son; invoking the infant's basket as evidence, Kreousa names its objects, among them an "embroidery" not yet finished and an olive branch. Ion softens to his "mother, / most dear," admitting he had been "alive / and dead," a condition H.D. knew well.

"Group Consciousness" & *Ion*   191

For dialogue, H.D. forged a unique vers libre, resembling *Borderline*'s "clatter montage" as "broken, exclamatory or evocative," showing slippages in recognition. By translating "two-line dialogue, throughout the play," H.D. created "sustained narrative." By "concentrating and translating sometimes, ten words, with two," she strove not to "depart from the meaning," but to catalyze it. "[S]on and mother" tell their "same story in suave metres," as "skilled weavers throwing and returning the shuttle of contrasting threads."[50] H.D. orchestrated their dialogue, losses synchronizing, as in this early segment:

KREOUSA: —but your mother?
ION: I am maybe—
KREOUSA: —no; what fine stuff—
ION: —robe of a priest—
KREOUSA: —but your parents?
ION: I have no clue—
KREOUSA: —ah, the same hurt—
ION: —what hurt—tell—
KREOUSA: —I have come here—
ION: —you have come here?
KREOUSA: —for a friend's sake—[51]

The Pythoness tells Ion, "I have loved you / as much as any mother, / yet / you must find her."[52] Mother and child needed catharsis.

Translating *Ion*, H.D. understood why she obsessed over it so long, recalling a teacher named Helen reading "from a myth book [Hawthorne's *Tanglewoood Tales*], with pictures—one of a boy, I thought was a girl"; this struck her as "the last period of 'phallic' hope." That the boy was really a girl was a shock, yet re-created hope for misapprehension. *Ion* was "a sort of fancy-dress edition" of this fantasy.[53] This bi-gendered vision gave Kreousa a special independence, self-sighting a woman "about to step out of stone, in the manner of the later Rodin."[54]

H.D. found a kindred spirit in Gilbert Murray, whose *Euripides and His Age* argues that "the poet or philosopher or martyr who lives, half-articulate, inside most human beings is apt to be smothered or starved to death in the course of middle life."[55] Murray pointed out the "repressions" that plagued his Victorians. Likewise, H.D. believed Euripides liberated her to "speak through his boy-priest, Ion, with his own vibrant superabundance of ecstasy before a miracle; the sun rises."[56] This illegitimate child chimed with Bryher's discovered *ecstasy*, a "UNUM"—Latin for Ion, a oneness.

Through an ancient past, H.D. predicted "a new culture, of an aesthetic drive and concentrated spiritual force," a time when the incipient post- or pre-Oedipal woman broke from marble. H.D slipped into *Ion* a fragment of her dreams from analysis, "you saw three sisters dance; / grass swayed," disabling the idea of a purely masculine godhead. Ecstatic with her draft, she claimed achievement: "I went through such an inferno that I seem to have come out the other end and to say to myself I am, I am,

I AM a P O E T and you know I never said that before." H.D. thanked Bryher "for having held me together all these years."[57] Now fifty, she understood many sides of mother love and hurt. She dedicated *Ion* to B.M. and P.M.—for Bryher in 1920, and for Perdita in 1932, for their travel to Delphi. Playfully grumpy about Bryher to Plank, H.D. knew Fido was almost too idealistic and imagined a "little temple" for her as "an under-sized Pallas Athené. She wears her helmet & nothing can break it—or her."[58] In fact, when Athene "steps forth," imposingly real, with "intellect, mind, silver but shining with so luminous a splendor," Ion momentarily confuses her for Helios—H.D. again underlining the nonbinary.

Bryher urged H.D. to stay at Kenwin if trouble should erupt, but H.D. remained because she "felt FISH had [her] by the tail or [she] had fish by the tail." While translating, she broke her day into sections, divided by swims, taking Elsie Volkart ("Vee") with her at night, "a sort of sudden maenad mania," assuring "perfect control and decorum among the maenads."[59] To Dobson, she noted that "things outside" contributed to analysis "in a most uncanny way."[60] While writing of the poisoned dove, she discovered a very tiny bird in "the triangle pink-bed" in the garden, still alive. Volkart nested the bird in a small cage. H.D. nursed the bird, settling it near her desk in straw, and while typing, her "tummy went through all pre-Pup emotions." She wrapped one of Perdita's green garments around the cage to calm it. Vee "turned into an Eluesinian priestess and began talking to the brute in a pure-fish bird-tongue—all terribly odd." H.D.'s mother reappeared in a dream; "the sea was near," thinking that with *Ion* she "was probably re-creating 'mysteries,' all very odd and birds in my bed and bed-room."[61] Bryher and Perdita meanwhile saw swallows in Cornwall, venturing to haunted Bosigran.

Satisfied with *Ion*, H.D. replied to Bryher's questions about plans for "hiding" in case of an invasion, with a "defense" of her work, striking up an odd poetic manifesto: "1. My work is creative and reconstructive, war or no war, if I can get across the Greek spirit at its highest, I am helping the world, and the future. It is the highest spiritual neutrality." H.D.'s second practical point was that her "fans" wished a return to Greek themes, and her "actual inner urge" coincided. Her third point was that this work might provide "the sort of America I did not have in my youth." Point 4 claimed *Ion* as "a sort of counter to P.R. [Rodeck] and his church—this is my church." Point 5 reiterated the basis for *Ion*, worked at "after the first confinement and during pregnancy with old Pups," which "linked up with [her] physical creative force." Yet while "the Greek" held "[her] to [her] centre," she "could N O T face the loneliness if there were trouble."[62] H.D. could be very independent, if in a creative whirlwind.

On her crossing with Perdita to America on the *Normandie* with Charles Henri Ford on deck in November 1936, Bryher realized, "[T]his year everyone is writing poetic plays, and reading Yeats. For heaven's sake, get right on to Chatto about *ION*—if you miss this moment, it will be awful next year, because then plays as you know, wont [sic] be done. Everything this year is poetic drama, please, please, please, Kat, write Chatto about it."[63] Insistent, Bryher struck a premonitory note; in 1937 the British edition of H.D.'s *Ion* emerged in the lovely wrapping of Chatto and Windus. She sent it to Freud, who was "moved by the play" and by the notes, "especially" their extolling "the victory of reason over passions."[64] He read her backwards. The "victory" was the survival of emotion and rationality together. If he had read *Ion*, with its mother needs, not *Oedipus Rex*, as model for human sexuality, would his theories have played out differently?

* * *

During this fragile time, H.D. worried over Bryher's money spent on analysts for their circle and for herself, while Moore and her mother suffered extreme financial hardship. Bryher came to their aid, which Moore called "supernatural," Bryher an "agent of solicitude and unselfishness."[65] As Pythoness, Bryher cloaked her gift of an annuity as something she herself required. Moore belonged to a group "under a covenant," so accordingly "[t]his is a business rather than a personal matter." Invoking laws that helped relatives living elsewhere, she could avoid high taxation, and if Moore checked it, the covenant was "duly reposing in Coutts Bank." Moore belonged to the couple's chosen family.[66]

In the depths of the Depression, Moore, describing herself as "a frenzied miser" who "could not have been more desperate," experienced "the sense of support," the greater part of the gift.[67] Bryher learned to circulate money as a kind of liberating energy; H.D.'s childhood community taught giving was receiving; asking, praying. Bryher also convinced Moore to publish a "posy" of poems in a limited edition through a sideline press, Brendin Publishing Company. Gorgeously illustrated by Plank, *Pangolin and Other Poems* was published in February 1936.[68] Bryher showed it at the 1936 Exhibition of Books in Paris, with Monnier and Beach.[69] Her investments—the farm, the journal, people, "Pups"—all were sound.

Anna Freud resisted Bryher's generosity almost as much as Moore. True, she accepted funds earmarked for others. But in 1937 she accepted a personal cash gift from Bryher, using it for manure, echoing her father's analogy of feces to lucre and the notion of its being the child's first "gift." She joked that "20 cartloads of old and well-rotted cow manure [was] the only sensible thing to spend money on." Anna claimed Bryher was "the only person in the world" she had ever "accepted a money-present from," as her "first impulse always was to give it away again."[70] One of Anna Freud's case histories (1937) referred to a patient whose generosity (giving sweets and other items) was a means by which she "made over to other people the right to have her wishes fulfilled without hindrance."[71] The patient, in being "lavish" with others, identified herself with the gift's recipient, "betrayed by a sudden warm sense of a bond between them." Caught in perpetual gift-giving, Bryher also sent palliatives. Moore replied, "I felt immediate improvement from the calf-foot jelly; and the Port although we administer it almost with a dropper," feeling "reassurance that we have it."[72]

* * *

Writing from Kenwin, Bryher accepted her "fraternal duties" and would not go to the States, unless her super-ego forced her. In other words, her guilt would not let her miss a stitch in rescue work, now her primary focus. As if performing in *Ion*, Bryher knew Perdita needed her birth mother, that Pup longed for "the healing touch, the magic moan, ah, that, that, only her dear mama can give." The separation was "killing her." Finally, Bryher advised H.D. send an S.O.S. to Schmideberg that "whirl wind may descend" because "a good twelve stone of vigorous Pup is about to be launched on you, whether here or there." H.D., so thin, agonized over Perdita's weight, not really a problem. Proving Euripides very modern, Bryher dug in: Kat could not escape for "she means to track you down, and it might upset her unk not to." Bryher penciled a postscript that she had "just been kissed on both ears," and part-ironic, articulated she could "not understood" the young adult's desire for "a mother's heart."[73]

Bryher's frustration with her own mother's standoffishness at her boyish persona led to sealed-up longings, hoping to quench them first with H.D., then Bergner; now it was unexpectedly Lady E. herself who, through her love of Perdita, showed Bryher that it was, sometimes, a "mother's heart" Bryher missed. Lady E. "wants to discuss Pup," H.D. wrote, dating her letter four days after Bryher's request that H.D. show Perdita more affection. At the same time, H.D. tugged at "mama" to let Perdita celebrate her sixteenth birthday at Lowndes, but then relented. Claiming her own sense of *real* independence, H.D. "love[d] Pup in large surroundings, Kenwin etc.," discovering her "UNK, as I write, is in love with the Pup, or with its UNK." Exaggerating, she admitted "guilt, lest I make love to her or she to me." This was "the mother situation."[74] With her pages flying, H.D. explained, she lacked energy for Pup. *Ion* convinced her that mother longing had an erotic element, sensitizing H.D. to a mother and child's dual needs for security and independence, confessing to a bisexual fantasy of her aunt, very kind to her when her mother focused on her younger brother, Harold, explaining her own "mother fix." Perdita was in a similar "fix."

By late March, Bryher had "destroy[ed] everything that might compromise [her] in an invasion!"[75] She redrafted her will and sent H.D. an anniversary gift of "fur coat by Kuhl," in case of capture. So worried, she moved Vee from Kenwin, freezing all winter, buying her a tiny flat where she would live with two apes. "Much cheaper" and "far less lonely," she decided.[76] Bryher's silhouette filmmaker friend, Lotte Reiniger, recommended a comic antidote, *Modern Times*, which both saw eight times for its elaborate seamless rhythm.[77]

* * *

Dobson moved from Edith Grove to 30 Tite Street in Chelsea, letting Perdita room with her and her sister, Mollie. It was rumored that Cecil Gray and even Louis Wilkinson had lived there once. The "ghost" inhabitants did not deter Dobson—or Bryher from finding a solution amenable to the seventeen-year-old and H.D. Giving Perdita her bedroom, Dobson slept in the living room, a "Grand Central Station," the flat's occupants crossing to get to the front door. Installed, Perdita lined up photos: Katharine

Hepburn, Ginger Rogers, Bergner, and the Marx Brothers eating pancakes. Bryher sent pineapple juice and daffodils from Cornwall. Every morning, Perdita went to Maiden Lane, to be taken under the wing of Miss Voules, the advertisement manager of *Life and Letters*. Perdita rang strangers with the line "The London Mercury cost two shillings, Life and Letters only one."[78] Working with Herring gave her structure; reading hundreds of submissions, she also worked on an autobiography. When the Spanish Civil War broke out, Bryher numbered the atrocities for Perdita, dedicating a whole *Life and Letters* to expose Franco's Fascism, and sent introductions to Beach and Monnier for the young activist Muriel Rukeyser, in Paris on her way to document atrocities of the war.[79] H.D. asked Dobson, awed by the documentarian's "fiery" experiences, to entertain Rukeyser on her way through London.[80]

Dobson also taught Perdita to drive. Herring accompanied Perdita to the showroom, where, with Bryher's checkbook, she settled on a blue Flying Standard Twelve. Mollie Dobson and Perdita sped off to Cornwall for a test run.

15
Abdication, Aggression, Anschluss

Much of London suffered paralytic denial of Hitler's early atrocities. Public attention fell elsewhere. King Edward VIII, taking the throne on January 26, 1936, announced his desire to marry the American divorcee Wallis Simpson. As Perdita put it, "Wally burst over every headline."[1] By the end of the year, he was the first English king to abdicate because of opposition to his marital choice. With Bryher and Pup heading to New York, H.D. and Lady Ellerman were at Audley, glued to his speech. Her Ladyship blamed the abdication on "that woman, Lady Cunard," "a symbol of vicarious sacrifice," holding "all resentments or unloved romances."[2] "It rained yesterday for the reign," H.D. remarked, feeling "like a battery that lost the other wire."[3] Later it was learned that the husband and wife were Nazi sympathizers. On May 12, 1937, Edward's brother, George VI, was crowned, ruling until his death in 1952.[4]

After Sir John died in 1933, Bryher threw herself into rescue efforts. H.D. both feared and adored Bryher's zealotry, though H.D. forwent ventures to the States. This stalemate kept them together, in the end. H.D.'s *Ion* was a timely portrait of dislocation from one's origins; Bryher knit herself into the visceral abyss faced by those forced from their birthplace; and H.D. didn't want to run "home." Naïve when they met, political barbarism now led them to resist, to love, to rage—even to go mad.

Monnier sent Bryher Walter Benjamin's landmark "Work of Art in the Age of Mechanical Reproduction" in February.[5] In May, the polylingual Bryher met him at one of Monnier's book parties and dined with him, along with the filmmaker Jean Renoir and André Gide. In June, Bryher sought an English translator for "L'Oeuvre d'art," grateful her *Paris 1900* was translated by Monnier into French.[6] "Life is getting quite desperate," Bryher admitted. The French the year before had rather unscrupulously "invited all refugees in, without papers at the beginning, and as soon as they spent their money, deported them."[7] Volkart put down the aged monkeys, who threatened her in nightmares.[8] In these tough days before Paris fell, Bryher understood Benjamin's dire predicament, sending him increments of 500 francs, in every note urging he plan an exodus.[9]

* * *

While the horrifying political backdrop was never far from her mind, the manic Bryher took a small respite to raise the morale of her *Life and Letters* staff by staging a wedding for her Queenswood chum, Theo (Petrie Townshend), marrying Major Robert John Henry Carew on July 25, 1936. The wedding pleased "mama," while

Bryher secretly rebelled by inviting all her queer friends. Asked about gifts, the bride sent a hefty registry. The jumble so amused Bryher she shared it with H.D.: large cocktail shaker, toilet case, handbags, garden furniture, all house linen, opera glasses, tortoiseshell lorgnettes, a fur coat, a folding canvas boat—the list spiraled endlessly. The illegitimate Bryher decided "on either a refrigerator or a wardrobe trunk," and hosted three hundred guests—Church of England services with a reception afterward in the "Haudley back drawing room and ALL the ps-a set."[10] Macpherson designed H.D.'s gown, Herring acted usher, and the queers wallowed. Among the attendees were Melitta and Walter Schmideberg, who planned a trip in August with Bryher to attend the Psychoanalytic Congress in Marienbad.

After the nuptials, Bryher pressed H.D. to join her caravan to Marienbad with Alice Modern and the "Bears," inviting Herring and Dobson. As for holidays, Bryher thought Lapland, or they might venture to Sweden. Sensing Bryher's panicky travel bug, H.D. decided on an "inner vacation" instead of "'flight from reality' to Stockholm." Staying at Kenwin with Perdita through early September, she shifted from "tidying papers" to a "restoration mania," compiling works in progress.[11]

Preparing for the 1936 Psychoanalytic Congress in Marienbad, Bryher impishly proposed a paper on "the polar bear controversy," jesting that "the future of the psycho-analytical movement is dependent entirely upon the[ir] case histories," shocked too "to learn from Miss Freud, that she feels a successful analysis could not be undertaken in a Zoo." Earnest Anna provoked Bryher's irreverence. Look out, Marienbad! From the Hotel Carlton, Bryher scrawled that they "met the Princess [Marie Bonaparte] and gave her a lift in car!" En route, they picked up Lotte, who guaranteed "a constant rushing and hiding," while Schmideberg "promised an escort of Viennese men-at-arms." Bryher outlined "the sad story of the bear that dies under the attack of Wien. As puppets perhaps, silhouettes on a film."[12] Passing through Vienna, Bryher found the Freuds in bed with grippe. Marienbad was "the sweetest mixture of Boston and the Riviera."[13]

Bryher no longer idealized ps-a *as it stood*, but attended Jacque Lacan's groundbreaking debut paper on the mirror stage at the conference. There, Sachs shared the first issue of his new journal, *American Imago*, with Freud's article in German, posing the question "was Moses an Egyptian?" H.D.'s Moses dream, Bryher thought, contributed to Freud's query. Finally forgoing an analyst's "collar," Bryher defined herself as "a sort of superior guinea-pig, able to sympathize with analyst and guinea pig alike," akin to H.D.'s "semi-professional" capacity.[14]

After Marienbad, Bryher received Benjamin's signed essay "Eduard Fuchs, Collector and Historian," describing the "toil of the anonymous." "Great geniuses," he observed, depended on invisible toilers, while "no document of culture" exists without being also "a document of barbarism."[15] This formulated H.D. and Bryher's own sense of history. The latter readied for the U.S. without H.D., who tried quelling anticipatory worry by accepting, "[I]f the war comes, it comes, and I will run to another cushion if I have time. But trust God, please do, and keep your powder dry, ye good old 1776-ers." Her rooms at 48 Lowndes Square became a group fort.

H.D. reinforced Bryher's "duty to live for the state, the one and indivisible UNITED STATES of the WORLD. We will all stick together, little band of the faithful, e pluribus UNUM, ever and ever, darling Fido," adding she was "nicely fur-licked in the UNK," claiming her new-old trinity: "You and Pup and self . . . indisolvable."[16]

In October 1936, H.D., slightly jealous of Bryher's bond with Schmideberg, to whom she could tell "the worst," called him "a good community fur-conductor between our unks, so all is well." With him, H.D. tapped into a "pre-conscious," distinct from the unconscious, "almost like having a house with one floor hermetically sealed tight." Having heard Lacan's argument, proposing a bodily ego, whole only in fantasy, Schmideberg considered H.D.'s "externalization of the 'hidden phallus'" through art.[17] Unable to completely accept her mate's sometime-claim "I am your husband," because it dragged up Aldington, H.D. advised Bryher see "himself" as Pup's progenitor, offering proof of fertility—"take one long look at the PUP in PERSON."[18] For H.D., the biological widened to spiritual affinity.

Expecting Bryher to be rattled after hectic New York, H.D. boasted "ear-flaps and a diving helmet," wanting to be "a sort of punching-ball" to "stabilize [Bryher's] UNK." Their practiced, complementary polarity was now exaggerated by global challenges. While bragging of "eight generations of New England back, or other seven and one mid-west false move[s], our covered wagon generation and seven N.Y. upstate and New England States," H.D. defensively invited Bryher to "charge at the whole solar system," only wanting her "small secure footing" at Lowndes. She would wander "the States as a Prague fortune teller" if more pressure was applied for her to repatriate.[19]

Early in November 1936, Perdita, Macpherson, and Bryher sailed to New York on the SS *Normandie*. Before the crossing, Bryher had repeating nightmares, losing her visa and passport in the first, then one with a shipwreck, followed by confinement in a cargo cage full of dogs. In all, she was a "prisoner."[20] H.D. eased Bryher's chains by helping with "dear mama," easier to get along with alone, creating an entirely "different space and vibration."[21]

During the voyage, Bryher was seasick, "huddling uncomfortable into a crumpled rug" like "an unacclimated marmoset."[22] Yet she managed to reread H.D.'s *Hedgehog*, published in 1936, written for Perdita, complete with her own avatar, "Madge" (a name linking Perdita to Midge [H.D.] in *Paint It Today*), who called her "magical" mother Bett (Bryher), with short hair, also recognizing in her "a maddening mother, overly concerned about dark woods, deep currents, snakes, and boots." Beyond biology, Bryher was "really Madge's mother."[23] The children's book also called for cosmopolitan equality between "French children and German children and Serbian children and Turkish children," "all a sort of odd little brothers and sisters." *Unum.* H.D. led Perdita to "the fortunate half-children of Olympus," Madge accepting "only a Father-which-art-in-Heaven for a father."[24]

New York wore neon petals of WRIGLEYS and COCA-COLA. Bryher and Perdita settled Kenneth into his 64th Street flat. He took them to parties in Harlem and to hear Jimmie Daniels play piano; they talked Jerome Kern and driving. Perdita climbed the Empire State Building and wept when she heard Franco had toppled Madrid. Bryher wrote Schmideberg, "American papers do not spare us, in Britain's ostrich manner."²⁵ On this trip, Bryher and Perdita took a psychic-geopolitical tour of H.D.'s early landmarks. Bryher received letters she could not read while rushing through Penn Station. In a taxi, they passed Friends Central School, Bryher naïvely scribbling, "Is here where you went?" Bryher visited the Quakers, headquartered in Philadelphia, who supplied the most efficient aid to refugees. After exploring the city's museum, with its "miles" of exhibitions, they met Mary Herr, H.D.'s chum from Bryn Mawr, at the Bellevue Stratford, who "whisked" them off to Rittenhouse Square, then gave them a tour of Bryn Mawr. Bound to her eighty-eight-year-old father, Herr could spare only two hours a day. Bryher gleaned that she was both terribly fond of and a bit scared of H.D. Bryher and Perdita went on to Lancaster, seventy miles outside of Philadelphia, with its "brown grasses, woods, a lovely sunset, tiny Swiss looking towns." Bryher exclaimed, "Give me Pennsylvania, if I have to be out of New York." They drove to the oldest Moravian church in the United States, "exactly like a little Czech town church, with the round bell effect on roof," which "felt distinctly home."²⁶

Back in New York before their departure in December, they attended a cocktail party where Bryher met Nella Larsen. Teasing H.D. that the writer "fell into her arms, and she into mine," she added, "[S]he is so quiet, and so interesting. But do not worry, she is elderly, with two grown up, over twenty, sons." Larsen was a "color hearer" like herself and interested, like Bryher, in "the Scandinavian influences on Beowulf." At that night's party, she again met "Miss Nelly," and Bryher chatted up her companion, Eleanor "(whom [Bryher] should not at all mind as a girl friend)."²⁷ The Swiss were digging fortifications when she arrived back home.

* * *

In the New Year of 1937, Aldington asked for a divorce while aboard the MS *Lafayette*, headed to England, warning "Dooley," his erstwhile nickname for her, he was "madly in love." Having romanced Brigit Patmore after breaking with Arabella in 1928, he was now in "true love" with Brigit's daughter-in-law, Netta, one of "our lot." He hated hurting either Brigit or H.D., pleading, "Lovers are selfish. They have to be. The world is against them. Don't be against us. Let us have our life together."²⁸ H.D. even wrote Gregg that Aldington "dropped a bomb from mid-ocean," that the bride-to-be was young enough to be his daughter, "but it would be like that." She decided "a real bonefide wife for R" would stabilize her, after years of nagging fear of his return.²⁹

H.D. dreaded the Temple Courts and made "tracks for the trenches in Kenwin," "homesick" for it, "with or without bombs," to prepare first notes for the court.³⁰ "Arabella was Mrs. A, of course. Everybody is Mrs. A. It is a sort of Greek chorus," she bitterly laughed, presuming herself "the leader of the chorus," wanting to step aside before "the final curtain." After her first draft, H.D.'s "head [was] like ice, [her] chest ... like [a] black crater."³¹ By February, Bryher had coaxed H.D. into a less melodramatic narrative. Perdita would remain "Baby X." H.D. described an "oversexed" Aldington, his demobbing from the army, wanting "intercourse more often (even during the day) than [she] could manage as [her] health had never really recovered from the effects of [her] confinement in the spring of 1915." Aldington refused to give up his affair, and Cecil Gray invited her to Cornwall "for about six months during which time misconduct took place between [them] on several occasions."[32] Her lawyer thought it a good case if she didn't "collapse in the witness box." Bryher coached H.D., who recounted "every little detail," making herself "far guiltier than the guiltiest criminal alive."[33] Born in the 1880s, H.D. suffered a divorce phobia reinforced by social norms and ancestral inheritances.

The case's formal notice, entitled "Yourself and Aldington," Bryher thought would be "a marvelous title for a book." Aldington's editor at Heinemann, and her own, H.D. saw him off with his bride to Florence, exclaiming, "[S]uch cards, so happy, O, such joy, such happiness, a changed being. The miracle of lo-oo-ve!" H.D. could laugh that R.A. was on his "4th honey-moon in the heel and toe of Italy and environs."[34] Bryher directed interested parties to Somerset House, where Perdita's adoption documents resided.

H.D. recovered at Kenwin from "the last land-slide of the Inner Temple" and underlined to Dobson, "*Br remains the benefactor, spiritual and temporal to all of us Bears and Pups and Dragons and Virgo-s. It is good we have her like a pin in the centre of the whirl.*"[35] Yet the "centre" kept coming and going. Bryher got a boxer, Claudi, as well as a new Airedale puppy, Taro, who tugged her over hill and dale. With her divorce finalized, H.D. was inspired, even "rush[ing] to [her] machine [typewriter] as to a morphia cupboard," relieved with R.A. at Capri—no "sour grapes."[36]

At the end of May, Sylvia Beach visited Kenwin for the first time, a perfect guest who "disappears in traditional manner all day on long walks." Before Beach left on June 5, Taro barked loudly, and Bryher saw an apparition, whose "date was uncertain—no clue, might have been eighteenth, nineteenth or this century," looking as though he had eaten "a good dinner and feeling cheerful."[37] Bryher even asked Beach to gaze at the suspect room. Someone dropped out of time, H.D. diagnosed, but the vision probably emerged from exhaustion, from stressful efforts at the Zurich Consulate, noted repeatedly in her diaries. Bryher was "annihilated" more than once, one woman raving, for instance, over Mussolini as "a great man who has 'cleaned things up.'"[38]

At last, after Marienbad, Bryher formalized ps-a's present limitations. Freud addressed an almost extinct concept, that of "the Victorian idea of the family." Psychoanalysis, to survive, needed to discard the image of the Victorian family. She preferred Dr. Ludwig Jekels' idea of a band (like H.D.'s chorus), alternative to hierarchical families. A main quarrel stemmed from a personal one: p.s-a was blind "with regard to the girl who is really a boy," though it "profoundly influences daily life," anticipating twenty-first-century nonbinary gender and transgenderism. Bryher also disliked that analysis catered to those with money, jettisoning it "from the life, the living part"; the only hope lay in affordable brief analysis of two to three months for workers, or "badly paid intellectuals."[39] Finally, she protested requiring analysts to be doctors. A growing trend relied on tests, photographs, specimens, while psychoanalysis functioned best as "vers libre."

That September, Bryher's mother confused her own birthday with Bryher's, and in cutting the cake, wounded her own hand, reflexive of Mama's uneasy symbiosis with "Dolly." Bryher called herself "a middle-age Oedipus," her father having entrusted "mama" to her care.[40] She dodged a reception and meeting Elizabeth Bishop at Beach's bookstore. Sounding like H.D., Bryher, "unable to cope" with an "electric atmosphere," wanted "anti-guilt pills."[41] Schmideberg diagnosed that Bryher "feared everything dear to [her] would be taken from [her]," leading her to lose preemptively, which "only increases the feeling of having lost so much, and the fear of having to lose more still."[42] These words rang true, but they didn't stanch Bryher's painful need to be invisible *and* be seen as masculine.

* * *

On November 16, 1937, H.D. joined Bryher on the SS *Normandie*, crossing to America to celebrate Christmas with Macpherson in New York. The precocious Perdita sailed on her own, met upon arrival. She turned to dry martinis instead of tomato juice, listening to Richard Rodgers and Lorenz Hart's "Where or When," tracing a deja-vu of a love story, on Kenneth's gramophone over and over. With *Ion* published, the couple met Norman Holmes Pearson, a Yale graduate student eager to interview H.D. In 1937, he was twenty-eight, coediting *The Oxford Anthology of American Literature* with William Rose Benét. Bryher planned to suggest a new edition of H.D.'s poems.

Born in 1909, the same year as John Jr., Pearson, suffered tuberculosis as a child, resulting in a sore on his hip that impeded walking. He attended college in a wheelchair. He went first to Yale, then Oxford, then studied German history at Kaiser Friedrich Wilhelm University. In 1933, he had a short-lived "fit," believing the Nazi Party might relieve Berlin's poverty. By this point, he was eagerly disseminating works by American poets with what Annette Debo calls, "his gift for cultivating writers."[43] Gathering American expatriates into his anthology, it turned out, made him perfect for intelligence work.

Pearson wanted to understand the creative process in H.D.'s delicious early poems. Besides calling them "finished fragments," she refused all questions in "A Note on Poetry." "Poetry? you ask. I am to say, why I wrote, when I wrote and how I wrote these fragments"; she almost admitted mediumship, saying "I am afraid I can not."[44] Still, Pearson's *Anthology* held "Garden," "Orchard," "Sea Gods," "Oread," "The Pool," "Leda," "The Islands," "Fragment 36," "Fragment 113," "Song," "Lethe," "Lais, "Helen," and "Hippolytus Temporizes." H.D. bonded with Pearson through their New England ancestry and his obsession with early American history, later signing a letter, "very (your) Cotton Mather."[45] Bryher, for her part, believed it her mission to "provide information about German refugees or French literature of an experimental type to anyone who wants it," finding in Pearson someone willing to talk politics and who might advance H.D. Bryher asked Herring to send the latest *Life and Letters* to Pearson.[46]

With Mary Herr, H.D. guided Bryher through Bethlehem on December 9, including showing her Nisky Cemetery. Back in New York, Bryher shut her windows and, without thinking, turned on the gas in her room. "Evidently my unk was in two minds," she told Schmideberg, "because I suddenly started sniffing and wondering what in the world was happening." Her unconscious was "a hedgehog," abusing her "worse than usual."[47] Bryher's spines turned in just now, unable to avert atrocities. Likely overwhelmed by Bryher's frantic affidavit work and her "accidental" gas attempt, H.D. sailed with Perdita on February 5 on the SS *Île de France*, built after the first World War, decorated in Art Deco. Meeting Pearson for dinner at the Four D, Bryher recommended Stein and Moore as two others for his *Anthology*.

Bryher prized Benjamin's letter of December 19, 1937, thanking her for *Paris 1900*, which reverberated with his own *Berlin Childhood around 1900*. Comparing *Paris 1900* to *Alice in Wonderland*, with its disjunctive scale, he called it a "rein-gestimmler Text," a perfectly tuned text; he understood her terror when a "painted clown" stepped out of a side path and spoke to her, noting a "danger of being beyond the imagination." He identified with the precocious child, armed with "silent, martial determination." His compliment went deep.[48]

Before leaving New York, Bryher wrote Benjamin she researched the French Revolution in Switzerland. "Unfortunately I'm never away from history," she remarked, hoping he was now naturalized in France, sending him another 500 francs.[49] Bryher also saw Moore at their favorite spot, the zoo, telling Schmideberg she was "one of the best writers of her generation" but "so mama-dominated." The Moores served peppermint tea and vitamin biscuits. With "a lecture on deep breathing," they prayed aloud.[50] That same day, accompanied by Virgil Thompson, she attended a boxing match, and later wrote H.D. of Moore, who looked "like an old, old lady, with a lovely face but quite withered."[51] While in New York, she wrote Pearson of "a boy—introduced to her by Beach, Jacques Mercanton, from a rather famous Vaudois family, now teaching at the University of Lausanne," "desperately anxious" to work in England or America. People in Lausanne refused to speak to him because he was not a Fascist.[52] And so on. Bryher provided her most "usual safest address" as *Life and Letters*, 26 Maiden Lane. A week later, she learned Pearson did "something" for the Mercanton boy. The reciprocal good they did each other persisted.

Already back in London, Perdita scouted with Silvia Dobson a country house and found Woodhall, a round two-story oast, designed for kilning hops. It had a "large raftered ceiling," "sloping brick floor, an Aga stove, a huge copper for boiling clothes." The small blue room was Perdita's. Twenty-nine miles from London, Woodhall had fruit orchards and a large garden where Dobson planned cultivating vegetables. H.D. came several times before war began, taking a bay leaf from the gate as she left. Dobson put up Bryher's exile Ernst Modern, brother to the Modern sisters, who worked as a laborer in this bucolic corner until his visa arrived.[53]

* * *

Once more, on February 11, 1938, Bryher sailed for London, this time on the *Queen Mary*, a Cunard White Star vessel, missing her "dear Normandie," unhappy to break a vow to her father to forgo the Cunard line. Isolated in her Cassandra role, she returned to Kenwin and became "desperately busy," having elderly Austrian friends "who clung to their environment."[54] Bryher's geographic temperament both helped her cope with dislocation and drove it home.

Few shared Bryher's dark vision; H.D. did, and did not, unable to grasp humanity had not graduated from world war. After aiding refugees from Berlin and Prague, Bryher felt "like one of those bits of petrified rock that are cold even in full desert." Past lives seemed more palatable, Bryher supposing she "once had too good a time in Carthage."[55] Moore's "Pangolin," with its Plank illustrations sponsored by Bryher, gave words needed about humor: it "saves a few steps, it saves years."[56] Wintering at the bulb farm, the very moment Bryher heard "Anschluss," Austria's annexation on March 13, 1938, her adrenaline sky-rocketed. With Nazi flags hurled up, Bryher lamented the loss of "her Berlin period," 1927 to 1931, meeting Sachs, Pabst, Lotte, among many, picking up Berlin slang.[57] Her requiem. Bryher insisted readers of *Life & Letters* know their dire condition: "you will just go and water the lupins, you are making it a little more certain that you will lose eventually, your garden, your home, and your life."[58]

Perdita encapsulated the group's sense of disjunction: "Crocuses popped out all over the park, and Hitler walked into Austria."[59] Bryher's mother was "astoundingly interested and sympathetic" but definitive that she would "not outlive another war," so best not even to talk about it.[60] Perdita moved to her own flat at Portsea Hall, and H.D. came to Kenwin for Perdita's birthday there, encouraging her idea of going to "April in Paris," to follow the song, with chestnuts in blossom, and courageous citizens facing "the political situation."[61]

Bryher reached out to the Austrian Schmideberg and called to see if the Freuds needed help.[62] Feeling Kenwin imperiled, she worried about Alice Modern, who received a postcard stamped with a giant swastika.[63] She asked Schmideberg to send Alice's sister, Klara, now in London, to "one of the strictly-Freudian refugee analysts." Drowning in obligations, she advised him to rush his naturalization papers. What she communicated to her interlocutors was that they did not have to be cheerful "or pretend things are calmer than they are." With H.D. she muted her agonizing fears. Scavenging more French gas masks, better than English ones, she assessed at this low ebb they'd be confiscated from her.[64]

After reading French headlines in March announcing Freud's arrest, Bryher learned Jones and the Princess Bonaparte were with him. Martin Freud (1889–1967), Freud's eldest, ignored Bryher's urgent advice, several weeks prior, to transfer Verlag funds, her refugee money, to Coutts Bank in London.[65] He put it in an Austrian bank. She vented, "I must try and discover something in the garden to smash."[66] Bryher reminded Anna Freud she could use the income from capital from the fund for Sachs in Boston for railway tickets.[67] The "underground" "transport" was now more urgent than analysis. She next cabled Sachs about Maidi Fournier, analyzed by Otto Fenichel; Maidi believed it was her duty to stay through the bombing of Prague. By May 18, Bryher had arranged analysis for the analyst in London.

Sachs' sister, Olga, and his nephew, Max, anticipated leaving Vienna soon, but his other sister, too sick to travel, stayed on with her brother-in-law. Sachs asked Bryher to "take care of them as soon as they have passed the frontier," warning that "they may be penniless."[68] He told Bryher of "a young doctor /: female:/ who left at the last possibility," boarding with him, who just learned of her father's sudden death in Vienna"—you know what that means."[69] Peril kept Bryher zigzagging from one embassy to the next. Months, years earlier, she had warned Austrian friends they should apply for U.S. visas, boasting that "Alice has all her papers bar one for entry to the states." Trains arrived late, and everyone with money was hauled on to the frontier. The leavetakings were breathtaking. Bryher's cables rattled off: Brecht was leaving Denmark, with another friend who *must* move from Paris to the States, likely Benjamin.[70]

In May, Benjamin sent Bryher his *Berlin Childhood around 1900*, in response to her *Paris 1900*, written to "make [him] immune against homesickness to the city" as "Impfung" (vaccination) against loss.[71] He described himself as "a mollusk in its shell," with his "abode in the nineteenth century, which now lies hollow before me like an empty shell." The moon wears a "widow's veil which the day had torn off."[72] Bryher praised Benjamin's prose as "so quiet, so clear," noting he "adjust[ed] every little thing together, mat[ted] them, as a picture of many colors, where none are more important than the other," thinking "such writing is not easy."[73] She could live only moment to moment.

Perdita drove to Cornwall on her own, staking out coves and rocks, visiting Kenwin for Easter, happy for Alice Modern, now married to Franz Alt. Bryher tied up loose ends in their paperwork, the couple emigrating before summer.[74] They were readied weeks in advance of the Anschluss, and thus were at the top of the consulate's lists. The Modern sisters were part of H.D. and Bryher's "chosen family." Alice and Franz reached New York in May 1938, losing no time in finding acquaintances who might supply affidavits for those in exile. Unable to find employment in his field, Franz studied insurance mathematics and served in the U.S. Army from 1943 to 1945. "I am glad Alice Modern-Alt's husband was allowed to leave Vienna," Moore commiserated, "uprooting is very sad, and persecution, worse than death." America's gain was "already perceptible—by the courage and magnificent minds of those driven here."[75]

* * *

H.D. faced her official divorce on May 13, 1938. So much depended upon, as Bryher told her by telephone, the court's humor that day. H.D. fretted all night about incriminating letters. Herring accompanied her, laughing that the judges filled their ink jars with whiskey. They broke for lunch, and she had a "white lady" with Herring at Romano's bar. When two cases dropped from the docket, they rushed back, and it was all over very quickly. The courtroom was "charming," "a lovely old room, like a school-room with a huge clock."[76] Stunned at the mess he made of other people's lives, Aldington asked to see H.D. after the trial; she consented, with Dobson present.

Shocked at the appearance of the writer of *Death of a Hero*, Dobson described him as "a plump, middle-aged business-type cynic," who sat at Lowndes for over two hours, drinking endless tea, chain-smoking, his new wedding ring tight on his plump finger. Agonized over Netta's extremely small pelvis, possibly necessitating a cesarean, he begged for the divorce decree to be legal in May instead of June, possible only if H.D. helped with costs, who, freed from the haunting of this marriage, felt "a halo pinned to [her] hat."[77]

H.D. saw *Dark Victory* twice: it features Bette Davis going blind while planting bulbs, the terror of losing one's bearings fitting the world's mood.[78] Perdita recalled going to a comedy she watched without smiling, the fade-out treating her to the stark warning "Citizens of Westminster were to get their gas-masks, last fitting on October 1st, after which No Fitting, No Gasmask."[79] H.D. renewed her passport, and Bryher gave Schmideberg over $4,000 so Melitta could study juvenile delinquency in New York. Everything was urgent: "Only lose no time. It may be impossible to rescue anybody."[80] Her mantra became *Quickly, quickly*.

Bryher informed Pearson of H.D.'s official divorce, confiding her own trauma, with no time even to touch a book, summing up that she "had to move four friends to the states entirely [herself], to help three others, to get two more to England." She obtained in New York an affidavit for them, "strictly illegal, because an English citizen can't give an affidavit for the States." Bryher enjoyed outsmarting officials but was increasingly overwhelmed with people "dropped on [her] literally from the skies," necessitating "wild dashes and phone calls and booking tickets." Closer to her heart, Bergner was rumoured to be in a sanitarium in Prague, she told Schmideberg.[81] Even after many rescues, her heart sank to hear of a surgeon working as a street cleaner in Vienna. Late in May, while Bryher tinkered with Kenneth's projector at Kenwin, a young man, Sergei Feilberg, surprised her. She thought he was a Nazi, but Anna Freud had sent him.[82] Like a twin, he was small like her, gazing despairingly. Sergei described three migrations, form Riga to Berlin to Vienna, "re-touched," as if "by an electric wire," by Hitler.[83]

Freud and his immediate family reached London by May 1938. Marie Bonaparte shipped his antiques to Hampstead, where Martin Freud resided. In June, H.D. visited Freud, finding him much the same. During the 1938 International Psychoanalytical Association congress in Paris, Bryher visited Heinrich Mann in exile in Nice, and Sylvia and Adrienne, and Natalie Barney. Beach took Bryher to Gisele Freund's photography studio; Freund, a German-born French woman, had taken a likeness of Benjamin, and Woolf's; she now captured Bryher, hair slicked back, hands clutching each other, leaning in, eager to fight inhumanity (Figure 15.1).

Bryher traveled to Prague in August to help refugees, writing Benjamin that the city was "so full of hope and faith," thanking him for a Brecht manuscript.[84] After his dismissal for being a half-Jew, the poet and historian Johannes Urzidil, friends with Kafka and Franz Werfel, left for London with Bryher's help. During this hectic time, Bryher kept vigil for arriving refugees, among them "Edith Taglicht, a second of three Prague friends," who made it to Paris, sailing for the States on October 1.[85] Bryher

Figure 15.1 Photograph of Bryher by Gisele Freund, 1938.
Courtesy of Beinecke Rare Book and Manuscript Library, Yale University.

approximated aiding about 105 refugees, but there were likely more, her funds often traveling in place of her.

In September at Kenwin, H.D. revised her story of World War I. In Munich on September 28 and 29, the leaders of Britain, France, Germany, and Italy decided the fate of Czechoslovakia. After commencing border incursions, Hitler issued an ultimatum, that unless the Sudetenland was ceded, the neighboring Czech territory would face full-scale invasion. The French and English forced Czechoslovakia to capitulate. Chamberlain hailed the agreement as "peace for our time," but Bryher termed it a "betrayal, though foreseen," "still shocking."[86]

Pearson apologized for not writing either H.D. or Bryher sooner. He occupied a bed in the hospital at the University of Chicago. On a trip to Colorado, he "went lame." His Chicago doctors made a bone graft that was disintegrating, so a new one to keep his hip mobile was needed.[87] Like a mummy wrapped in plaster from the top of his left toe to his torso, he was unable to meet this year in New York.[88]

In Paris on November 7, Herschel Grynszpan, the seventeen-year-old son of one of the families of Polish Jews expelled from Germany, assassinated a German diplomat, leading to a day and night of barbaric violence, Kristallnacht, or the Night of Broken Glass, across Nazi Germany. On November 10, thugs set synagogues on fire, destroyed Jewish shops and stores; stormtroopers raged through the streets, smashing windows, beating up Jews, and subsequently arresting about thirty thousand, among them teachers, doctors, bankers, lawyers, and shopkeepers, sending them to concentration camps.[89] This tragic night motivated British Jewish and Quaker citizens to appeal to Chamberlain to admit unaccompanied Jewish children to England. By December 2, the British Parliament had let in ten thousand German, Polish, Czech, and Austrian minors.

Bryher arrived again in New York two days before Kristallnacht. Mourning with Sachs and Macpherson, she met with "a group" working on "the refugee problem privately," guiding others in rescue work. Only briefly there, Bryher visited the Alts and Jekels, met Alfred Stieglitz, and had her photo taken by Carl Van Vechten on December 22. He caught her sober gloom, while Freund caught her fermenting energy. During Bryher's absence, a "blue Standard" nearly ran Schmideberg over, spotting Perdita and H.D. speeding toward Hampstead to visit Freud.[90]

* * *

By May 1939, Bryher's year-long boarder, Sergei, was living on pills; he had "an assortment of every known pill," Bryher determined to "wear one of each round [her] neck," a macabre necklace for emergencies.[91] In summer that year, Bryher traveled to Lapland with Sergei, dubbed "Marmot," and Herring, wearing matching berets, identifying with the Resistance. A baret was now Bryher's signatory accessory. Perdita encouraged them to "track down the midnight sun."[92] They were detained in Sweden by the police, but not for Bryher's refugee work: Sergei's cargo of a kitten in a basket was strictly forbidden.[93] Briefly locked up, the travelers reveled in amber sands "that smelt of pine and salt." Bryher wrote Benjamin of Sweden as a possible refuge.[94]

"I was and always was, absolutely consciously, scared to death of my mama," Bryher wrote at the Baltic Hotel, knowing that "to want something" was to have it "taken away" or "forbidden." Her mother was upset she spent time with Sergei and Herring in Lapland. From Helsinki, Bryher complained her trip would end at Audley, where she would not be able to read, write, or telephone, only "sit and talk," most subjects taboo.[95] She had always wished her family *understood* her; their love couldn't satisfy. In July, back at Kenwin, H.D. lit her candles, "celebrating" their "twenty one year" anniversary.[96] Perdita, inspired by Bryher, took off to the fjords in Norway, hopping steamers, traveling on "quite a miniature Normandie, with carpets and futurist mermaids."[97] Bryher worried to Pearson about Perdita's future, hoping her multilingualism could serve to stop war, while noting Stein's sense of a blackout of everything we believe in.[98] H.D. and Bryher would live their war together—marking an unprecedented period for their wisdom search, H.D.'s writing, seared and searing, and for Bryher, recalibrating as a writer.

LINE 4

BLITZ 1939–1945

16
Twilight Zone & "the Combined UNK"

After the Land of the Midnight Sun, Bryher returned to H.D. at Kenwin. Perdita arrived in London from her Nordic adventure at the end of August. King's Cross was "shrouded in screens and blue light," and she saw "frantic and busy people who didn't seem to be of this world at all, at least not of the world" she knew. The ghoulish streets, devoid of taxis, presented air raid shelters, stacked sandbags, and vehicles emblazoned with "Stretcher Party." Chandeliers at Portsea Hall, "fitted with blue bulbs," lost their sparkle.[1] After the summer of 1939, suspense stopped the breath. Bryher understood Benjamin's inertia, but, odd for her, she didn't predict war *this year*,[2] sending francs; if war was not declared, she promised more when he was settled.[3]

H.D., Bryher, and the Schmidebergs were at Kenwin on September 1, 1939, when Hitler invaded Poland. Two days later, Britain, France, Australia, and New Zealand declared war. The rupture that brought them together recurred. Bryher reenvisioned 1919, "as if the intervening years had been wiped out with some dark sponge."[4] H.D. felt "the last 20 [years had] simply dropped out, simply gone."[5] Lady Ellerman, fitted for a gas mask the year before, excessively weak, cabled Bryher from Trenoweth, hoping fresh air might help. She rallied upon Perdita's arrival. "How drastically difficult everything is," she wrote on Bryher's birthday.[6] When the seventy-one-year-old Lady Ellerman worsened, Doris took her to Truro Hospital, where she died peacefully on September 17.

For forty-five years, Bryher had been psychically tethered to her mother. While out walking, a last letter, delayed in transit, arrived from Lady Ellerman, whom H.D. regarded as "a land-mark gone," regretting they had "so much on [their] minds—and one did little and felt so much—too much." Bryher's eyes "got too big sometimes," she told Plank.[7] Unable to face her mother's death or funeral, Bryher dove into more refugee work, aware "we were so few."[8] Urging Benjamin to write his American friends for affidavits,[9] she assured, "[N]'ayez pas peur que je vous oublie."[10] Her grief over her mother's passing blurred with her despair over those exiled.

H.D. knew that "bottling up" leads to "bottling back," but Herring considered Bryher's choice not to attend the funeral wise, so as not to rattle the "unk in its associations before unk has had time to come to surface."[11] Perdita spoke for Bryher at the funeral, and though "unmolested by the Press," John Jr. was very "nervey and elusive," ignoring her.[12] Freud too died during the pair's birthday month in 1939. H.D. admitted that "the shock of Lady E., and now Professor Freud has been a good deal for the combined UNK."[13] Bryher merged her mother's death with Freud's; hearing a wireless report, she condoled Anna a second time, "because my mother died exactly one week before your father."[14] Sachs, with H.D. and Bryher, could not imagine a world without Freud.[15]

The Schmidebergs took the stunned griever on long walks, yet Bryher arranged their French visas, booking a car. H.D. stayed on, thinking she would accompany Bryher to London to attend to her mother's effects. The "combined Unk" threw itself into more turmoil than necessary. H.D. could have repatriated to the U.S. with Perdita: she had relatives, including Harold, her brother accountant, who supervised her dollars; Bryher too might have joined Macpherson in New York. Herring wistfully assumed Bryher would leave for the States—though knew she was never long in any one place.

Just two days after her mother's death, the British consul general in Zurich sent brusque condolences, assuring that she "must go to England," adding, "[W]hilst this war lasts and probably for some time afterwards there should be work for you here," though not "on a strictly official basis," promising that after the war she could facilitate "the interchange of prisoners and the gravely wounded."[16] For Bryher, dread crystalized. By now, modernism's giddy claims for freedom in the 1920s grimaced back at those about to endure another war.

Stamped "October 20," a postcard from Sylvia Beach told of Benjamin, now an enemy alien quartered temporarily at Nevers (Camp des Travilleurs Volantairs), accepting what Bryher sent: chocolate, tobacco, and sweaters.[17] Eager to join Londoners, having soothed as much as possible, H.D. finally left on the *Orient Express* for London, November 8.[18] Herring prepared for the returnees gas masks, gloves, and small bags with first-aid medicines. Chalked sidewalk edges lessened stumbling during a raid. Air wardens commandeered the streets during this "War in the Dark."[19]

Perdita missed Bryher, wanting a world "populated by Bryhers, and more Bryhers, and nothing but Bryhers," adding, "Just one Bryher sitting alone in Kenwin is far, far too little."[20] Yet Bryher lingered, helping, among others, the Austrian physician and psychoanalyst Annie Reich to leave for New York. Her mother's death, she told Reich, was "mercifully swift," but "the whole of Europe is collapsing," and looking toward France, she could see only "a sudden darkness."[21] Bryher had "a pound of documents in weight to carry everywhere."[22]

In London, Herring, unfit for fighting, volunteered at All Souls Emergency Hospital with Edward Glover, a member of the British Psychology Society in 1921, who added a Psychological Aid Centre for patients "suffering war neurosis." Herring advertised the clinic in *Life and Letters*. Thirty-six, he knew it was harder for Perdita's crowd, "first war-ites," with "between lives," the era's gestalt.[23] He promised loyalty to *Life and Letters*, a "sort of energy using up aggression" until "the last moment," regarding the journal "of national importance."[24] Grateful for his interwar analysis, he admitted to Bryher, "I cry over Finland—but also, we did go there. We *know* what we're crying for."[25] Meanwhile, practicing escape, Bryher took four flying lessons, each flight "really like making a poem," until the Lausanne aerodrome barred civilian pilots.[26]

Back at 48 Lowndes, H.D. spoke of streets "full of attractive girls in long blue trousers," others with "short skirts and short hair," "the ambulance drivers" in "their blue pants, like yours and Pups," "very familiar and sea-shorish." Euphoric, she had "many chats with people in shops and everywhere. We in the city are very much at one."[27] "[E]xpecting Br., end Nov or early Dec.," H.D. told Dobson she was "hale and hearty, moving about like a fire-fly," perversely feeling "the black-out very beautiful and exciting."[28] Perdita herself couldn't stop swearing and observed that H.D. had "one of those poetic, detached natures which see the best in all," so that "the emergency lamps are like fairy candles," air wardens in "tin helmets like at a fancy dress party."[29] She tried luring Bryher back with "Mexican dishes from tins" and her "lowest surrealist jazz."[30] H.D. fretted about how Bryher, "a little Atlas," would fare.[31] By December 1939, Bryher had obtained a visa to travel through Paris to London on December 4. She spent the night at Monnier's flat. For the last time, she saw Benjamin, who walked her to the train station.

At Lowndes, Perdita and H.D. comforted her. Herring, asking for Christmas gifts for hospital patients—"Scarves, Razor Blades, Darts, Pencils. Nothing is Too Small"—threw a "Lights Out London" party with "snow artificially guaranteed" and "special barrage balloons." After a bomb hit near his Chelsea flat, Bryher bought Herring a cottage in Eastbourne whose "bulge" ensured its safety, inspected by H.D. Seeing it through her eyes, he thought she suited its spacious lightness. "I want to study the stove, and sink," he reveled, decorating one room as a covered wagon to induce in Bryher a "feeling of en voyage."[32]

After storing her mother's belongings, cringing at Audley's closure and her brother's inheritance and though Perdita and H.D. asked her to stay, Bryher returned to Kenwin on January 29, 1940. Herring wired that the journey "must have been perilous."[33] Soundlessly grieving, Bryher's activism flirted with danger. In February, Kenwin had no heating, and while walking Claudi, Bryher blacked out. In March, reading Benjamin on Baudelaire the flâneur, she admired his "concept of history," recommending he reach out to his former supporter Theodor Adorno, who had made it to New York.[34]

H.D. and Bryher experienced different initiations into war life. They still worked in tandem, but Bryher focused on last-minute refugees, mostly strangers, while H.D. sought new ways of "feeding the light," creating a special fund for those in extremis, and meeting Perdita for regular lunches at The Warming Pan, the central locale in Bryher's Blitz chronicle, *Beowulf*. Seeing herself as "analyst poet," H.D. especially wanted to help those like her, enduring a *second* world war. Every day in February and March 1940, H.D. wrote Bryher as war demoralization set in. She also met a new friend, Elizabeth Bowen, a mere forty to H.D.'s fifty-three.[35] Knowing it would tantalize Bryher to learn Bowen volunteered as an air raid warden, H.D. marked six dates with Bowen for tea in February and March, with seven visits already scheduled through May.

On March 6, Bryher obtained a Swiss reentry visa, put in for a French one, planning to leave on Good Friday by the *Orient Express*. Then, paralyzed, she couldn't leave. Her words were not cohering: "My prize sentence of yesterday was: May, she ate five eclairs before the tea commenced." "In case of trouble they say all English will be dumped in France," she grimly put it, and she needed "to provide straw if evacuees come." Aware that British mail was stalled by the censor, she observed, "Cherry trees in flower. Deep green lake with flakes of foam."[36]

While H.D. supped tea with Bowen, Bryher dined with the Swiss poet Charles Ferdinand Ramuz, totally marooned.[37] For Perdita's birthday, Bryher sent twenty-one roses, a fur coat, a telegram, and a letter. Perdita congratulated herself and Bryher on nearly simultaneous trips to Norway and Finland,[38] while Herring was frantic.[39] "OH! Bergen gone! Norway. Thank god Norway declared war. O Bergen, Oslo taken, the rest," he etched a geographic memorial, "Bryher, just somehow that lobster-claw—that overhanging bit which said 'Norway' and meant US, that loveliness and sparkle ... gone."[40] Friends with Perdita, he was pleased *he* had *at least* ten non-Nazi years at her age.[41] Near Lowndes, target practice started in an empty lot, and H.D. dreamed "the songs of the birds drowned out the guns," hoping it "prophetic."[42] Days lost continuity; H.D. begged Bryher to return.

Churchill became prime minister on May 7, 1940. Fight, and fight on they must; he convinced the public to face disaster head-on. H.D. regularly listened to the BBC, finding sustenance in the minister's firm gruffness.[43] After Norway's capitulation, on May 10, 1940, the Nazis invaded Holland and Belgium. British and French troops crumbled under the Luftwaffe, which moved into the low countries; enemy forces corralled the majority of Allied troops at Dunkirk. Bryher missed part of what Churchill called "the Battle of Britain." Air Marshall Hugh Dowding commanded the RAF, birthed in World War I. Headquartered in Bentley Priory, "the Dowding System" used radar, relaying information about incoming German planes by radio to airborne British fighters, anti-aircraft guns, and searchlights. England's smallish three thousand Allied crew fought off the relentless Luftwaffe. Churchill acknowledged the debt "owed by so many to so few." Behind the "few," thousands of volunteers manned observation posts and drove barge balloons. By mid-1940, the Home Guard, running with the likes of Plank and Bowen, kept total chaos at bay.

During the critical days from May 26 to June 4, 1940, Churchill commanded all private and commercial boats of any demonstrable size in the evacuation of Allied forces at Dunkirk. The thunderous response heartened H.D., binding herself to Churchill and the air marshall, leading his "boys" into action. This rescue was religious spectacle, "something out of all time, wonderful.... Tugs were all taken off the Thames, all fire-boats, trawlers, fishing smacks, lifeboats and so on, took that terrible trip over and over."[44] Fewer than an eighth deployed for Dunkirk perished; these "boys" haunted H.D.

H.D. held Lowndes "for [Fido], first and foremost, a little fortress." This was her "chief raison-d'etre. Then Pup."[45] H.D. had forgotten Bryher's code for suicide was "rat" when Schmideberg's patients begged for it.[46] Imagining invasion with "crab-tanks that may crawl along the channel sea-floor," H.D. envisioned "steel claws up the white cliffs of Dover," while Perdita, whose death-fear expressed itself in her wearing Lady Ellerman's fox furs, drafted her will. After exuberance over Dunkirk faded, H.D. grew impatient: "You said early June, then mid-June, then just June!"[47] Bryher watched the frontier, her last note to Benjamin in June, sending him 1,000 francs,[48] gaining "posthumous fame," as Hannah Arendt called it, after "the darkest moment of the war," the fall of France, when Hitler and Stalin set up "two of the most powerful secret police forces in Europe."[49]

On June 9, Sylvia Beach offered Bryher Adrienne's cellar. The German tanks moved toward the French capital. On June 14, while gunned down and bombed, civilians fled Paris en masse. By mid-June, Bryher joked of her hysteria, "I gallop from here to Geneva and back and have collected visas from nearly all the unknown countries in Europe!"[50] On June 22, 1940, France signed an armistice with Germany, leaving a small unoccupied zone. That month, stock markets crashed. H.D. framed the war as "truly for all, a spiritual rebirth. If ones bodies [sic] stand it."[51] British propriety collapsed; people wandered about with coats over pajamas; women stopped wearing stockings. Spotting women in short skirts, H.D. cut Bryher's dresses in half, though it felt like "castrating" Bryher![52]

From the country, Edith Sitwell considered, "[T]he last fortnight has been on such a gigantic scale, that everything in history since the Crucifixion seems dwarfed—only Shakespeare could do justice to it."[53] The "scale" pushed H.D. toward shorter stories. "Before the Battle" (1940) reframed the coral polyps of 1919, standing "shoulder to shoulder, living bodies, *like* the bodies that make up coral-islands." Through a "rhythm of terror" and "birth-pangs," she saw the collective "begetting this new age." Prayer, she decided, was "asking," and "act[ing] like a charm sometimes, it dispels fear and opens doors." Opening doors, we may recall, was an early Bryher phobia, one diminished by H.D.'s aesthetics of invocation. She braided Nisky Hill with England's dead, thinking she and her dead mother might "belong in dream, out of time ... to some religious order," as she almost did with Bryher.[54]

* * *

When André Gide recruited Bryher to prepare an intelligence report on the French Resistance, "some hush-hush work (unpaid)," H.D. was unsure if Bryher would "jump at it or not."[55] Jump she did not, entirely. Bryher drafted an unofficial report, "My Communications with Non-Occupied France, June–September 1940," supplying anecdotal evidence of "a general feeling of intense depression." One testimonial came from Norman Douglas, now seventy-three, informing that Fascists looted villas near the Italian frontier. There were "extraordinary rumors, such as Italy was in a state of revolution, England and Italy had concluded a separate peace, London had been utterly destroyed." Bryher knew Beach's "business was ruined." Her next eyewitness, "a refugee, a scholar, Jewish, by birth German," "a resident in France," waiting for an American visa, granted at last, yet without other necessary permits. "I have not heard whether he got out or not. I fear not." Referring to Benjamin, she later scrawled in pencil, "(He was killed at frontier)."[56] This tortured her.

That July, Bryher gave 50,000 francs to His Majesty's vice-consul at Montreux "for assistance to distressed British subjects"; she even received a thank you from

Lord Halifax. Ever-expanding her cache of comrades, glad Alice had arrived safe in New York, Bryher bonded with Klara Modern in London, who evacuated young children, and, unlike Alice, her brother-in-law, and her "sweet mother," would willingly sacrifice herself for "mother England." Klara thought Perdita was "getting larger and larger," unlike her mother's gazelle figure, and imagined Bryher "completely stranded in this little island, called Switzerland."[57] Klara sounded H.D.-like: "if one has taken joy and comfort from a country, one does not want to leave it when there is trouble about."[58] She made a distinction between "us ordinary people" and the fleeing of "some of the intellectuals and rich people."[59] The Royals at Buckingham Palace solidified H.D.'s and Klara's steadfastness. "The King and Queen are just here, as if nothing has happened and they go around and visit the bad districts," Klara wrote Alice. A family planted a Union Jack on their ruins, and women "with garden shears capture Nazi pilots": "one was captured by a dustman, which after all is the proper procedure for them."[60] The radio linked H.D. and Klara and myriad others across England. Willing to be interred in a camp if it would help defeat "the Nazi beasts," Klara preferred working with traumatized children. Perdita drove a canteen, providing tea to some stuck among rubble.

With the fall of France, mail between H.D. and Bryher arrived late or not at all. From New York, Moore sent H.D. Bryher's June letter, arriving July 2, about Claudi's she-puppies, animals she adored. H.D. communicated through Moore to Bryher that they were all "living in this burning light of LIFE," so that "every day one is grateful for the wall about one, the roof, the unbroken windows." Accustomed to epistolary contact when unable to telephone, H.D. made sure "the wire is open or the ground or the sky or whatever it is."[61]

Expecting the British to capitulate, Hitler paused, giving Churchill a small window to bolster Dowding's resources. Then, on July 10, 1940, the dictator ordered raid after raid. The Blitz, with its grand-scale night attacks, started on September 7 and continued until May 11, 1941. Depending on high-quality wax earplugs from Lausanne, H.D. considered herself a "private air-warden."

On June 4, Herring's mother died, and he asked Bryher not to be "sorry" for him. His mother's cancer began with a blow she had received in an air raid during the previous war, and now there was an air raid, unbearably loud, the night before the funeral. He wanted no flowers, directing any donations to war charities.[62] H.D. gave money to the Red Cross on behalf of her and Bryher. Most Londoners by now had got into the fighting spirit. With Dover "a mass of ruins," Herring fitted out his basement with jigsaw puzzles, tin hats, barley sugar, books, cards, candles, chairs. H.D. and Perdita joined him for sherry underground.[63]

"Numb with anesthetic with only half of one unconscious and the other rawly aware of what's being gouged out," Macpherson wrote on the couple's anniversary, July 17. Distressed that Bryher was still at Kenwin, he observed, "Wave upon wave of refugees are here because of her and she—typically somehow—is the one to be stranded." Bryher sent Macpherson "heartrending envelopes full of fragments," with "lilies and her arms filled with puppies." He safeguarded "these treasures" "to hold scripts for a future: a sort of early stirring of a life to be reconstructed."[64] Schmideberg acted Bryher's current receptacle for grimmest truths: "Never say consulate to me again, I have LIVED in them."[65]

By early September, heavy air raids hit Croydon and Wimbledon. Bombers struck central London as the couple's birthday week commenced. Shopping between sirens, H.D. recognized the "big gun, our special Big Ben and feel very comforted when it booms off."[66] After "three weeks of constant hammering," she acclimated to a "nine o'clock symphony." "Every morning," she wrote Moore, "is a sort of special gift; a new day to be cherished and loved, a DAY that seems to love back in return."[67] Fealty to England gave her a fervor that "gives new life to the very bones."[68] Proximity to death expanded H.D.'s capacity to love—and to resist.

* * *

Bryher sleepwalked through visa motions. In late July, Swiss radio warned of possible immediate invasion, instructing citizens "to turn hoses of boiling water on the enemy." Embassy officials advised she make haste. But she could not leave. The sun shone, the lake gleamed, swans glided. Rumors swirled that foreigners would be interned. Her ability to help would be severely limited, and if tortured, she feared endangering others.[69] Volkart offered Bryher her identity card and basement. But Bryher scrupulously avoided creating complications for others.

No stranger to the consulate, officials offered her a plane to Belgrade. Limited to a single suitcase and £100, she had to turn this down because it would not accommodate her latest refugee. What had Bryher possessed? Particular green and white colors, clouds, grapevines, summer's healing light. She bought passports on the black market without a sliver of guilt. Aid finally came unexpectedly—a Swiss travel agent, a Mousieur Kocher, who received through Bryher's help a textbook from Monnier's bookshop that his son desperately needed. In August, Kocher obtained Spanish, Portuguese, and French visas for her, booking two seats on a coach for businessmen so she could also evacuate Grace Irwin, twenty-two, a Jewish student in Lausanne.[70] Her mother was Lady Ellerman's "best friend." Bryher packed one book, Tyall's *Twenty-Five Languages*.[71]

Bryher and Grace assembled at 6:00 a.m. at the end of August with a group of forty-four passengers, carrying one suitcase and a rucksack of food. The first leg in "unoccupied France" consisted of miles through Provence. Bryher focused on the lavender fields, recalling easy drives enjoyed when visiting Gertrude Stein and Alice Toklas in Bilingin. Now Nazis whizzed by on motorcycles. After long cramped hours, the coach left Port Bou on the Spanish side. The passengers boarded trucks that rattled along to the next frontier, using the very route those fleeing Franco took in their last days. Stalled in Barcelona, her own remark in 1936 that the Spanish Civil War was "simply a dress rehearsal for their own destruction" made her inwardly wince.[72] In Lisbon, everyone was a double agent. Cabling Macpherson for dollars, and Moore to reassure H.D. she was safe, Bryher saw men shrivel with hunger, and two Nazis break a man's hands with rifle butts.

While Bryher trekked to London, the most devastating air attacks occurred. The Germans struck over seventy-one cities in England, leaving gigantic piles of rubble. On September 7, German planes swarmed over Kent, heading toward Southampton, the first of many near misses of Dobson's farm. By dusk, the East End was in flames, bricks falling into smashed glass, thick ashen air. Chelsea and Victoria were heavily bombed. In the third major raid, September 9, the Woolfs' house and Hogarth Press were utterly destroyed. Bombs rained day and night on H.D.'s birthday. Two days before Bryher's return, H.D. claimed she now knew how to shop, cook, and do housework.[73]

Landing during an air raid at Poole in a German plane with an Italian pilot, in "the middle of the Blitz," was ludicrous. Rail damage stopped Bryher's train to London several times. On September 28, Bryher sat on the stairway at Lowndes. At forty-six, with no illusion the war would end by Christmas, she felt "forced back into the cage and misery of the first war."[74] H.D. had ducked out for lunch at the Warming Pan.

Coming upon Bryher, H.D. extended her hand, guiding her toward the sand piles that put out incendiaries. Like one sleepwalker to another, H.D. initiated Bryher into war-ways. Perdita was staying in Bryher's room. Sirens started up; they climbed down to the lower floor. H.D. told Bryher she had once left Lowndes only in pajamas for a shelter; finding no one there, she returned to hear Schmideberg ringing her that he had been on a lovely walk. The next day Bryher confronted the "war made new." "So you made it," Herring commented it was "a fabulous time at which to drop in. Congratulations."[75]

Stunned, Bryher could not believe "what the people are enduring—most of them sleeping on the ground in excessively damp shelters or sitting up on chairs under the staircase or parked in the tubes."[76] Moore knew her friend felt out of commission and reminded that she was not alone in being frustrated. Pearson thought he could hustle up a possible post in Washington, D.C., but Bryher was unable—because of H.D. and Pup—expressing to Pearson her willingness to die for the island but her distaste for living on it.

Nearer Bryher's age, Bowen, "more often exhilarated than afraid," wore her air warden's hat, whistle, and respirator.[77] She reported that Oxford Street "glitters with smashed glass," and "bodies shed blood, buildings shed mousey dust," only "paper rooms."[78] But Londoners now unbuttoned their mouths. On a foray to obtain the necessary identity card and ration book, Bryher was stopped by the porter, once an acrobat in Switzerland, who said he knew Lake Leman "upside-down."[79] She talked "incorrigibly to people in the street," "acquiring a mass of miscellaneous knowledge," conveying to Annie Reich, "[O]ne friend of mine is over sixty and suddenly decided that she had to make munitions."[80]

The H.D. whom Bryher rejoined had endured weeks and weeks of the Blitz; the Bryher who rejoined H.D. had her eyes forced open in brutal ways. Here in London, unpredictable noise patterns coiled around them. Bryher convinced H.D. to spend an October weekend in Cambridge; it soothed, gliding down the river. "A very good change," she admitted to Dobson, tasking her to cancel a regular veg and flower delivery.[81] In Cambridge, they visited the damaged Inner Temple, where Shakespeare had presented a play to Queen Elizabeth. Whether or not H.D. spotted Shakespeare's "fair youth," wearing "firm sort of boots," almost a "young pilot," in Cambridge, is uncertain, though she put it in a diary.[82] Bryher feared "Shakespeare would go silently out of mind and Chaucer would be violently destroyed."[83]

On November 9, Neville Chamberlain, the infamous appeaser, died of colon cancer. Mourners gathered in an Anglican church in Westminster.[84] The day of his funeral, November 14, was marked on the 1940 calendar with an empty circle, signifying a full fiery Hunter's Moon, renamed "Bomber's Moon." Coventry, not central London, got the worst. Relying on pathfinder planes to drop flares, timed by radio waves, German fighter pilots were guided to targets. The attack began on munitions factories, then, devastatingly, Coventry Cathedral was bombed. By 8:00 p.m., the enflamed city could be seen from Warwick, seven miles distant. Fresh bombers appeared at midnight, interrupting surgeries, knocking out windows.

Compared to London, the bombing of Cambridge had been slight. "Death becomes the one important idea," H.D. admitted, happy with fog "on us," making "the city foolproof," for fog, she knew, congealed to ice "above and the Nazi wings can't take it."[85] War or no war, Bryher sent Moore Woolf's biography of Robert Fry.[86] The bombing persisted through December. Many called these intense raids "the Second Great Fire of London," resonant for H.D., whose ancestor preached through the first one.

In October, a time bomb hit the *Life and Letters* office. There were no casualties, but "ceilings fell on desks."[87] Maiden Lane was gone, but "not a proof was lost," even rescuing "not only file contents & subscriber's lists, etc but typewriters, duplicators," and Bryher's hoarded paper.[88] Learning of three nearby unexploded bombs, Herring abandoned his adored Eastbourne flat. Osbert Sitwell knew Bryher and took in Herring, with all his recovered equipment, until *Life and Letters* could be reestablished elsewhere. Herring stayed a month; awed by the Sitwells, he had jitters.

* * *

Set in a park of yew trees, Renishaw estate resided in North East Derbyshire. One wing of the house had eleven bedrooms, and under its cracked ceilings it was decorated with tapestries, portraits, and furniture from all periods. Guests were given kerosene lamps. Upon Herring's arrival, Osbert looked pale, and his lover, David Horner, who joined the RAF in August 1940, greeted him, leading him to Edith, "charming & friendly," who "look[ed] like an Elizabethan ghost in folds of the period's primrose brocade."[89]

Osbert invited Bryher to Renishaw for the second week of October, Herring urging her to come to this "certain loveliness" and provide a "background" that might make sense of his being there at all.[90] Bryher's friendship with Edith grew. She revealed to Bryher that her mother had displayed "rages so violent that they would lead to a sort of cataleptic state," culminating in "an immobility which was terrifying." Any affection her mother possessed was given to the elder Osbert. Knowing well the differing treatment of siblings, Bryher tried to "mother" Edith, who responded to lace Bryher gave her as "so lovely that [she] look[s] at it at least twice a day."[91] H.D. sought new language for higher love, while Edith thought a "completely new vocabulary" was required "to express one's grief, and our rage."[92] Bryher gave her new friend a first edition of *Windsor Forest* and *The Rape of the Lock*, regarded as "living creatures." "Poetry, sometimes,—or the writing of poetry, is very like rough-riding, don't you think?" she asked Bryher, who sent *Development*. Edith empathized with Bryher's thwarted aims, speculating they led to "lightning insight into other people," due to her proximity to deep inner hurt.[93]

Bryher gave Osbert, Edith, and David Horner each £500, and knowing Edith was dependent on Osbert, Bryher bought her a house in early 1942, one formerly owned by Dr. Johnson, in Bath, on 8 Gay Street, a piece of England fast disappearing; the "very idea of it" lifted Edith up. Requisitioned during the war, she never spent a night there, but it increased in value. Victoria Glendinning, Edith's biographer, judges "Bryher's saintliness was that of St. Teresa of Avila."[94] Osbert enthused over Bryher's "kindliness," "a thing that one could not have believed *could exist*."[95] Bryher's generosity assured kinship with distant friends.

In November, Herring, with Bryher's aid, bought a house in Eckington, the "best house" on the "second best street," No. 18 Station Road, near Renishaw. Three minutes led to open country on the left, while two minutes to the right led to Sheffield's bus station. Built of local stone, with a green slate roof, it had five bedrooms, the surrounding landscape draped in holly, with streams "simply hurtling along and everywhere masses of little waterfalls." Herring discovered a nearby Druid's hill and sensed presence in the stones among a "blasted heath" of pines, scarred by lightning. The soil was ancient, "more like lava dust."[96]

Eight miles away, Sheffield, blasted on December 12, 1940, endured more high explosives the next week. Kindling toward war poems, Edith felt "every second or so would be our last."[97] Bryher accompanied Herring into town to survey the damage; icicles froze ash, giant holes pocked the town, and very few stores were open. The pair wore funny caps and used poles Herring procured, reviving their Nordic adventure.

* * *

Wearing her signature beret and leather coat, Bryher wrote from a window ledge at Lowndes, creating her satiric novel, *Beowulf*, conceived as *Comrade Bulldog*. It featured Selina and Angelina, based on Miss Venables and Miss Docker, who ran the tearoom H.D. cherished. They used only farm eggs, not powdered egg rations, struggling to keep their food high quality and simple. After patrolling ruins, Bryher's Angelina places a plaster bulldog in the shop's hearth, which ironically survives the tearoom's demise. The joke on the foundational warrior Beowulf reminded that there were no supermen or superwomen, only humanity, which fared no better, or worse, than plaster when bombs fell.

Writing Dobson on New Year's Eve 1940 from the Bull Hotel in Cambridge, H.D. wished "a happier 1941." They were "heart-broken over 8 wren Churches reported gone!" Christopher Wren (1632–1723), an astronomer and mathematician, rebuilt fifty-two churches after the Great Fire in 1666, among them his masterpiece, St. Paul's on Ludgate Hill.

In January 1941, Bryher expressed her dissonance, never "sure if one goes out ... the house will still be standing" when one returns.[98] Herring asked for paintings, fenders, fire screens. Bryher sent seeds to Herring to grow parsnips, mint, and peas, as well as garlic bulbs. Osbert gave Herring two washstands with Morris tiles. Drawn to the cragged mountains in Eckington, Bryher pleaded with H.D. to join in a visit, while Herring tried attracting her with State Express cigarettes. With H.D. still at Lowndes, Bryher walked from Herring's to the Sitwells', tramping through snow for more than five miles. Osbert, she reported to H.D., "look[ed] magnificent in corduroys," Edith "superb in a black quilted gown," and David "in civilian top and flying fleece-lined boots to his knees."[99]

After she left, Herring assured Bryher that "[i]f [she] found it gay, that was largely due to [herself]," making the worst part of setting up house into "a kind of Finnish holiday."[100] Station Road had a "caravanserai feeling" of communal refuge.[101] But H.D. could not imagine herself in Eckington. Her story "Blue Lights" explained, "It unnerves me to make another move," tied to "the only real thing now," the "enemy wings above," which at least while she heard them, lessened her worry over who "is getting it now."[102] The multilingual Perdita visited before starting a job, recommended by Pearson, "unscrambling codes for British Intelligence," not a small responsibility.[103] Perdita enjoyed Herring's collage of items from Cheyne Row, Audley, Eastbourne, the office, and the warehouse where Lady Ellerman's belongings were stored. Herring kept Station Road "spick and span" for H.D.[104]

March saw the worst bombing in London. On March 28, 1941, Woolf took her life, walking into the River Ouse in Sussex, her body not found for three days. Woolf's aura made "[e]verything seemed worthwhile, important and beautiful," Edith recalled.[105] In May, H.D. was still struggling with Woolf's suicide, conveying to May Sarton her complex reaction: "stricken to think she got away like that, just when really everything is very exciting and one longs to be able to live to see all the things that will be bound to happen later."[106] H.D. envied her escape, but this act of self-annihilation frightened her.

At last H.D. spent the end of May until June 12 at Station Road. She was not sure she would last. After two days, she needed to feel she could "just pop back to London" and not be accused "of NOT being 'fluid.'" She equated any distance between herself and Lowndes as letting her guard down. She assumed Herring wanted the radio off; he told Bryher he missed it. H.D.'s fragility visible, her toughness was harder to see. She wrote that "either Bud [Herring] does Harlequin acts or goes into complete suicidal depression."[107] Talk of raids at Renishaw, she thought, disturbed Herring, while he cringed for her sake when Osbert's boyfriend mentioned undetonated bombs. The phone was out of order, the pink cherry in bloom, and Herring weeded his bean rows.

H.D. read Donne, a "cozy" choice to him, "knocked sideways with [the poet's] sonorous strangeness," but in the spirit of Bowen's *Heat of the Day*, he evaluated his generation as one "made to feel it had muffed the catch."[108]

Bryher lunched with Bowen, while H.D. dared Eckington, and was "anxious to learn about Bow-en. I visualize a very stutter-y scene and then you rushing her to the Bear[Schmideberg]!"[109] Herring presided over tea with H.D. and Edith, who was quick to advise about remedies for ash-induced eye infections. Herring raved that Edith was "very masculine, in the best feminine way; the way that only very few men can be."[110] Osbert hosted H.D. at Renishaw, a palace barely hiding its profound flimsiness; he pointed out the garden's unwrapped statues, in sacks of dead leaves. Statues always excited H.D., prone to animate them. Inside, a painting drew her to it, as if by jellyfish tentacles, her favorite, "the pink youth" to which Osbert happily responded, "[T]hat is the ghost."[111] They discussed Crete, invaded on May 20, 1941. Herring found the Sitwells therapeutic; H.D. agreed.

Like her other 1941 stories, snapshots lifted from a sizzling scroll, "The Ghost" peered into a two-paneled eighteenth-century Venetian mirror with its "silver-grey" frame, "grey-green" surface—one of Osbert's "treasures." Bryher even wrote Pearson about it.[112] The flawed mirror was a " 'booby trap,' " a phrasing Horner injected, and if H.D., identifying with Woolf's course, did *not see herself* in the mirror, she expected "a flash, a white-hot searing iron," then "no more, not ever any more, pain." She "earned" it, for she "had not died once in London, but fifty times at least." "Her death was a sign of failure, or not?" she asked of Woolf. "Had she done her work?" Herself guilty even for this short jaunt, she challenged an unseen populace, "How many blitz-nights, did you spend in London?," echoing Bryher's "What Will You Do in the War?" There was "no note-book, no text-book, no religious manual, no prayer-book"—all items dear to H.D—to direct the body, for "[t]he whole skeleton had come alive, a skeleton in the cupboard; everyone in London had it."[113] H.D. sought guidance from the skeletal.

H.D. enjoyed the English countryside as much as "almost anywhere—it combines USA and Suisse and even Greek walks," she admitted to Bryher, asking her to greet Mrs. Ash, their dependable and now-well-named housekeeper, whose intense industry contributed to the pair's survival.[114] Osbert, Edith, Herring, and H.D. took a road trip to Sherwood Forest to see "Major Oak," green erupting from its monumental frame. In the giant hollow tree, H.D. picked up an aura of aged furniture from a much earlier century. Herring chirped, "H.D. responded."[115] Troops encamped nearby; mythical Robin Hood (Robert Herring liked the initials) exerted an androgynous force-field. Already packed, H.D. slept through a raid her last night. The day after she left, Edith wrote Bryher about lunching with H.D. "look[ing] really better": "[H]er eyes have lost that look of needing to *bleed*. Poor thing, how she looked when she arrived first."[116] H.D.'s eyes almost saw themselves in a poem by Donne's contemporary, Richard Crashaw, "A Hymn to the Name and Honour of the Admirable Saint Teresa": "Why to show love, she should shed blood."

17
Walls Falling & the Drive Inward

H.D. was anxious at Renishaw, slightly competitive with Edith, until she experienced the fragile grace of the Sitwell siblings, which fostered her self-perception as a war poet, exploring what might buttress her adoptive country against obliteration. When in London, Edith would drop in for coffee and chats with H.D., urging her back to Renishaw. T. S. Eliot's editorial, sounding Churchillian, in the February 1940 edition of the *New English Review* issued a call "to keep alive aspirations which can remain valid through the longest and darkest period of universal calamity and degradation." A month later, on March 21, 1940, Eliot published "East Coker," sounding out a "via negativa" inspired by Underhill's *Mysticism*: "I said to my soul, be still, and let the dark come upon you / Which shall be the darkness of God."[1] Eliot prepared readers for long suffering and false starts. "East Coker" was reprinted, selling "nearly 12,000 copies."[2] He held up the luminous paradox of St. John of the Cross: "In order to possess what you do not possess / You must go by the way of dispossession. / In order to arrive at what you are not / You must go through the way in which you are not."[3] A formula for knowing oneself by fearlessly releasing spurious foundations. Eliot's "Dark Night" reverberated with H.D.'s eclectic and syncretic dark nights, tinged as much by Saint Teresa as by the heretical *Gospels,* among them "*Acts of John,*" which instructed, "Learn how to suffer and you shall be able not to suffer."[4]

In following Eliot's lead, H.D. vigorously modeled an interactive experience with the fertile "void." She even, prematurely, announced the coming of "[t]he Aquarian age," "a woman's age and we must stick together."[5] This was her premise, albeit blurry, for survival; she hesitated mentioning to her friend Viola Jordan her search for a divine female power that might supplant war. To her mind, Christ was androgynous or "nonbinary," if you will, in line with Euripides and Sappho as spiritual emanations. Watching the "rain of incendiaries," H.D. also absorbed the fourteenth-century anonymous *Cloud of Unknowing*, increasingly aware that "interior work proceeds through lack of knowing, patience, and love."[6] Feeling her age, unable to volunteer as a fire warden like Eliot or Bowen, through prayer and enforced fasting, interchanges with Bryher, Lowndes Square became a "core of burning cerebration."[7] Readying their "receiving station" after checking her "spiritual bank-account," she wanted to transmit gnosis, hidden experience, and joined vulnerability. Led to re-incant "ancient rubrics," H.D. turned communal suffering into art, facing the outside from the inside to uncover those fleeting, experiences of being "the music/ While the music lasts,"[8] between bomb scares, Bryher lunged into the community, alleviating suffering, acting witness and recorder.

In July 1941, Mary Herr solicited H.D.'s "Letter from England" for the *Bryn Mawr Alumnae Magazine*, criticizing her country's neutrality. "No one I believe has hated war more than myself," yet "morality" should spark Americans to join forces with England.[9] Her "Letter" addressed Aldington too, now in New York, who wrote her of his 1941 edited collection, *The Viking Book of Poetry of the English-Speaking World*, containing five of her poems.[10] Macpherson told Herring he envied their struggles, to which Herring snarled.[11] H.D. described Bryher's "prophetic way" as "very wise and comforting," assuring Plank that "Br. thinks USA will, this year, just have caught up to our blitz-period without the stimulation and excitement of the real blitz to carry them through."[12] H.D. clutched her Dunkirk jubilance.

Both mothers celebrated their daughter's war effort. Set between Oxford and Cambridge, Bletchley Park was a drab town, the building "one of the most hideous baronial halls in England," Perdita herself "at the bottom of the slave ladder, copying stuff, decoding, translating unrelated bits and pieces. Boxes within boxes."[13] Barbed wire encircling the Victorian Tudor-Gothic mansion, the spyworks hid in plain sight.[14] After a month, she felt as if "forty years" of "normal life" was over, telling Bryher, "[T]he house where we work is a desperate secret." Billeted four miles away, her cycling skills were "on the Marx Bros. Level." The chief drove her in.[15]

H.D.'s "war" resulted in *Trilogy*. "East Coker" and Sitwell's "Still Falls the Rain" readied her first sequence, *The Walls Do Not Fall*, its title more affirmative, perversely contradicting the "reality" of falling bricks. Oxford University Press released it with two additional sequences in successive years, 1944, 1945, 1946, when such publications were near zero. *Walls*, completed in 1942, was pivotal in H.D.'s career—and pilgrimage, "proud and chary // of companionship with you others," establishing spiritual agendas, rejecting blind patriotism as "crumpled rags, no good for banner-stuff."[16] Before finishing *Walls*, H.D. had at least one visitation, marking "you others" as both those enduring war with her, like those she greeted every day, and those ghosts—no longer living.

* * *

H.D. did not travel to Trenoweth Farm in Cornwall directly after Eckington with Bryher in July, avoiding triggering memories from the "old war." Despite this, she worked "on some of the Scilly notes," transported to "back in July 1919, where we were there—about now—together. Those two Julys were so important to my body and spirit." H.D. braced for their twenty-third anniversary, "the great 17," the guarding 1 and the mystic 7.[17] Bryher called London to Cornwall, "a refugee train,"[18] inserting Schmideberg's remark that "if Hilda gets into her basket, she is very difficult to dislodge."[19] Bryher rode in a packed compartment, the corridors jammed as well. H.D. should bring her identity card for venturing on cliffs. With the Schmidebergs and Doris, Bryher walked to Pup's favorite spot, where the "hedges are simply one mass of flowers."[20] Doris lodged thirty Home Guard and boarded evacuees, requiring victuals. H.D. was to visit Melitta at Gloucester Place, obtain a parcel, and give it to

Perdita, who "MUST bring it down with her."[21] Bryher and company stayed at the nearby hamlet of Tregonning—"an old farm house, the site dates back to 1201 … a farm attached to a monastery, we look out of the windows on to apples now gradually changing color and to a little stream."[22] Bryher thought that if "sacred ground" failed to attract H.D., a catalogue of heather, roses, delphiniums, sweet williams, mimulus, owls, deep purple heather, white bell heather, and "general loveliness everywhere" might work; she repeated a rumor to avoid London in September, then comforted, "[D]on't—don't—worry." As July ended, Bryher warned H.D. if she didn't leave London soon, she'd "be snowed under with jobs."[23] Perdita came on her own, with bacon and tea, carrying extra cigarettes for H.D., whose faith without faith, however, was challenged when Silvia Dobson's sister, Ethne Dobson, was shot down in a naval plane over northern England. The crash dismembered the bodies. They were given a military funeral, eleven coffins lowered into the ground while the "Last Post" played.

This tragedy led H.D. to visit Trenoweth. Daily news of death rubbed up against Cornwall's splendor, sparking her survivor's guilt, "ashamed of ones [sic] life of ease— or comparative ease and safety," reveling in "the luxury" of "melons and ripe corn and grapes and lovely apples from Bryher's orchard."[24] H.D. even stayed until after the September birthdays.

One of H.D.'s rare "narrative" poems, "R.A.F," in twelve parts, dated "17 September, 1941," emerged from the return train journey, re-creating her encounter with an airman. "He said, I'm just out of hospital, / but I'm still flying," it begins. Existing in two dimensions, the convalescent is still in "action." Reliving their proximity after reinstalling at Lowndes, she had read his gaze, at first as a pick-up look, not "knowing / what fire lay behind his wide stare." The pilot stammered, and "his speech failed / altogether." The brittle poet detected the force in his eyes as "congealed radium, planets // like snow-flakes." Having witnessed worlds destroyed in seconds, the RAF pilot was otherworldly. The poem shuttles between the pilot visiting H.D.'s desk (II–V) and the train (VI–XII). In casual tones, the poet knew "he would come again," not knowing "he would come so soon." Another Rodeck, an astral self "stood by [her] desk," not in uniform: no wings, no flying helmet. Difficult dialogue ensued: "he had said, / I did nothing, // it was the others." "Persistent," herself stammering she "was there the whole time / in the Battle / of Britain," and now committed to remember him as his comrades flew overhead. A second visitation led H.D. back to the train, looking from the window to "this field, that meadow" altered by this encounter, the English countryside, "branded" by a "new cross." This pilot put himself in harm's way, and many like him, she knew, spent sleepless nights, so more would not die.

At her desk, the pilot manifested, and "again" "he did not speak." While she kept one foot in Lowndes, the other in the moving train, he sat "huddled / in the opposite corner, // bare-headed, curiously slumped forward." When the train stopped, "[their] knees brushed," igniting contact; "we were very near; // we could not have been nearer, / and my mind winged away." Her mind became "*our minds*" (italics mine) that "are winged." The wounded pilot ushered in a vision "of sea-blue, emerald, violet, // the stone-walls, prehistoric circles," all "that [she] had just left / in Cornwall,"

Trenoweth with its "camellia-bush, / the stone-basin with the tiny lilies // and the pink snails," which ushered back "other islands, / the isles of Greece," with even more ancient "sun-circles," where "the invisible web, / bound us."[25]

In England, the war's onset fed the Spiritual Movement. One of its main proponents was the RAF commander himself, Hugh Dowding, papers hailing him as the savior of "civilization." H.D.'s own "R.A.F." imagined herself and pilot as having "crossed over," "already dead," *and* living with heightened perception: "we had already crashed, / we were already dead." She even credited herself with "some inch of ribbon." By this point, H.D. had redefined herself as "recording instrument," summoning "wave-lengths of sound, vibrations of light," exploring "that medium for which we have few descriptive phrases." After this RAF encounter, she cultivated more absent presences.[26]

Radio was central to wartime life, with such programs as Stephen Spender discussing Whitman, alongside Churchill's steady riling tone. Voices came and went, invisibly. Eventually, H.D. believed Dowding was working on a secret "psychic radio."[27] On December 8, 1941, the day after Japanese planes bombed Pearl Harbor, Roosevelt declared war on Japan and Germany. H.D. invoked the "pearl of great price" throughout *Trilogy*.

* * *

While H.D. etched *Walls*, Bryher set off to visit the writer Compton Mackenzie and his wife, Faith, living on the remote "wee" island of Barra, only eight by five miles of dry land, in the Outer Hebrides off Scotland. Admired by Henry James and F. Scott Fitzgerald, Mackenzie's *Sinister Street* (1914) met success, with his current *Red Tapeworm* satirizing wartime economics, aptly descriptive for Bryher of how minds hooked up, while waiting in queues, often to obtain some document that required other documents or sold-out food items. Bryher kitted up, obtaining field boots in Knightsbridge. At Cook's they warned this adventure might prove strenuous, but "IF" she returned, to "give them details." Bryher phoned "La Bowen," who "said at once 'And Hil . . lll . . . lll . . . da is she well.'"[28] H.D. resisted Barra, worrying its "enchantment" would "un-floor" her, then refrained that we all "carry our own light within ourselves."[29]

Lacking central heating, the Mackenzies' modern house made sleep difficult, so they paced, bundled. The tension between the couple was palpable. Faith confided their imminent breakup due to discovering Compton was queer. Faith had Poe-like visions that reminded Bryher of their visions, "not mercifully as you had them," she wrote H.D., suggesting that their balancing of real and unreal in Corfu was a more unflooring ordeal than they had let on to Freud. Bryher saw what H.D.'s agonies of concentration cost her. Simultaneously, however, H.D. entered another such agony through "R.A.F." Grateful for two letters from H.D. at Barra, Bryher kept dreaming she tried returning to Lowndes; frontier after frontier kept her back.[30]

Once back at Lowndes, Bryher was unaware the second Corfu chapter had already begun. After hosting the RAF pilot in her flat, H.D. started to envision and hear *Walls*.

On November 10, before honing a vatic *and* public style, she ventured on her own to the International Institute for Psychic Research (IIPR), whose members had included Lewis Carrol and Henri Bergson, and now included Air Marshall Dowding. Bryher rated it as more intellectual than other psychical societies, calling it "eminently respectable."[31] The IIPR did not advance a specific spiritualist belief but promoted the scientific investigation of psychic events.

Dowding's *Many Mansions,* published in 1943, after H.D. joined the IIPR, claimed he was "an ordinary man speaking to ordinary men." Listing Moses, Buddha, and St. John "as powerful mediums," he admitted "discarnate spirits, and their power of manifesting themselves" through "human beings by means of apparitions, physical phenomen[a] or intelligible communications."[32] H.D. sought confirmation for her recent "mystical" encounters. She learned that some members feared the "Old Witchcraft Act," still law,[33] though she signed up to meet a seer, Arthur Bhaduri, a frail fire warden whose father was a Brahmin in India. Shortly before Christmas, Bhaduri gave H.D. a private session, during which he *saw* her mother. Surprisingly, he advised her to throw all the work she had done on the *Borodino* "over the deck-rail," helping *Walls* materialize; she could reenter Egypt, the open-roofed shrine.[34] Not alluding to Bhaduri, H.D. wrote Pearson that Perdita was "using her languages in war work" and, as though all was as usual, praised Bryher as "very good and adaptable," creating "fun days" for shopping and housework.[35]

* * *

The couple had not lived together during such a sustained, stressful time before. They were claustrophobic on occasion, though H.D. thought Bryher "exciting." To Jordan, she claimed they got on like "Spratt and Mrs. J.S." from a 1638 nursery rhyme: "Jack will eat not fat, and Jill doth love no leane. / Yet betwixt them both they lick the dishes cleane." Continuous war was enervating. Bryher survived by doing "local" good whenever possible. Still feeling a "paralyzing terror" from her trip back to London, bombs did not frighten her. She admitted her "morale was low" and "fed [herself] the nicest morsels [she] could find, for who would collect the rations if [she] cracked?"[36] Bryher played parent, with none more precious to her than H.D.

Eighty-year-old Violet Hunt died of pneumonia in her cottage in an enclave of Chelsea in January. In April, Cole's husband, Gerald Henderson, named Hunt's executor, accompanied Bryher to the estate auction. Matted papers stuck to outdoor cat pens. Bryher bid for Hunt's tripod table crafted by William Morris. Ever a lover of his poems and belief in handmade goods, quality furniture, stained glass, alongside his desire for an economic utopia like the one Bethlehem fostered for a short while, H.D. revered Morris, who combined utility and beauty, using machines as "helping"; he emphasized work as play or vocation, imagining a communal life *without* the words "rich" or "poor." His "two islands," England and a utopia, found a groove in H.D.'s mind. Later, H.D. recalled Cole and Bryher delivering what to the poet represented a "spirit" itself, emanating from the very hands of Morris, to Lowndes, Cole warning, "Don't let it keep you awake nights."[37]

As did their practice, which did not fully develop until the following year, 1942 moved slowly. While Bryher and Perdita trekked Cornwall, H.D. visited Woodhall for a several-day reprieve in September. Another of Silvia Dobson's sisters, Nanny, her London room bombed out, stayed. H.D. overflowed with spiritualist talk, confiding in Dobson about Bhaduri. Nanny wanted to get in touch with Hildyard, their elder brother. "Mis-trusting psychic side-stepping," Dobson rejected H.D.'s invitation to their forming a "home circle," later regretting the decision.[38]

H.D. poked around Kent, musing about another abode; the countryside entered her writing. She considered making up "bouquests" as "war-work," garlanding London. In spite of these inspirations, she suffered "general exhaustion."[39] At Dobson's, H.D. missed Bryher at Trenoweth. She felt "starved at times," complaining of "NO snacks."[40] Feeling "such a pig to sneak off and make myself chock," she deemed herself a criminal, squirreling away sweets.[41] H.D.'s staples—chocolate, coffee, biscuits, and cigarettes—were primarily supplied from Bryher's foraging and from Jordan's parcels from the U.S. Woodhall was too proper: none of the girls, Nanny, Silvia, Molly, smoked; she reminisced about having sherry at the monastery with the Bears. H.D. "picked apples to the sound of channel-bombings," while watching Silvia's beekeeper ply his trade.[42]

A raid near Trenoweth rattled Bryher, provoking her to reconsider how best to protect H.D., advising her that England's guns would be noisier now and reminding her not to confuse them with the enemy's.[43] Recover for as long as possible, was Bryher's refrain, sending supplies through Mrs. Ash, who instructed the former to shed all clothes with war debris sticking after helping clean out disasters. Once home, H.D. and Bryher eagerly resumed work with Bhaduri. "Br seems happy here," H.D. wrote Plank, "after the monkey house chatter down at Woodhall, it is bliss to be on ones [sic] own again and to have Bryher's steadfast help."[44]

* * *

During 1942, H.D. wrote *Walls Do Not Fall*, not intending a tryptich. *Walls*, mostly in couplets, excepting the initial poem in tercets, had forty-three parts. A stunning opening situates the reader in at least four places and times, Bethlehem, Pompeii, Egypt, the present: "the shrine lies open to the sky, / the rain falls, here, there / sand drifts; eternity endures," even with "ruin everywhere."[45] Adelaide Morris observes that *Trilogy* "instructs us in values crucial to individual and social survival, provides models of conduct by which we can regulate our lives."[46] H.D. converted "dark nights" into dialogues with the invisible, "surrounded by companions / in this mystery."

Dedicating this sequence to Bryher "*for Karnak* 1923" and "*from London* 1942," a pivotal arc in her "search" recalled enclosure "in a small space" during 1923: "in a short time, the sky, that February night in the Temple, seemed to shower down its stars upon us," and "twenty years later, the Cloud of Witnesses" showed that a child "could understand the message." She ecstatically explained to Pearson that *Walls* was "'[p]rotection for the scribe,'" clarifying her "assurance back of it of the presence of the God of the Scribe,—Thoth, Hermes, Ancient Wisdom, AMEN," with her "'job' as 'householder.'" "[We] do not know if we live to tell the tale,'" she understood, but insisted "we still cling to our standards—to this, I mean, our P R O F E S S I O N." The poet was medium, both "householder" and "the original rune-maker."[47] "Protection" was not so much *for* herself as for cadenced language, its apostrophes, chants, the embedding of words in other words, such as her Osiris-Sirius-Isis anagrammatic circuit, or finding in "Sirius" the "Dog Star," derived in Greek from words for "glowing" *or* "scorching." One glows with love, or burns alive. H.D. set forth potential force-fields for safeguarding cultural and spiritual traditions, working alongside "carriers, the spinners // of the rare intangible thread" that connected humanity to "ancient wisdom." "Not old enough to be dead," H.D. self-consciously addressed those who considered poets "useless," with the exception of trying times, when as "bearers" of "living remnant," they existed in silent witness with other citizens. H.D. was giddy for the "true-rune, the right-spell," where "amulets, // charms" existed in "the dream parallel"; as was customary, the poet saw double.[48]

The war community suddenly felt like a "queer" community, "initiates" signaling each other, prodding each other to "re-dedicate" themselves "to spiritual realism," "enchantment" rather than "sentiment," whether to "scrape a palette, / point pen or brush, // prepare papyrus or parchment," or simply "offer incense." She substituted "resurrection myth" with "resurrection reality." *Walls* enacted a chorus on an intrepid ship, finding vibrational effects in treaties, maps, ship logs, or "folio, manuscript, old parchment." Setting forth her linguistic serpent biting its tail, "there was One // in the beginning, Creator, / Fosterer, Begetter, the Same-forever // in the papyrus-swamp / in the Judean meadow."[49] H.D. bound readers to syncretic oneness, a million deaths paralleling a million resurrections or reincarnations. Even as "we were powerless" against the "*zrr-hiss*," H.D. sensed "a wing" covering them, "though there was whir and roar in the high air, / there was a Voice louder," its speech "lower / than a whisper." This was sublanguage, god-stuff, "indelibly stamped / on the universe somewhere, // forever." Words as energy could pry open, recrystallize "underground" wisdom of "the original great-mother."[50]

A key section of *Walls* enacted a "worm-cycle," appearing in *Life and Letters* in 1942: poem 6 shows *persistent* natural cycles and powers. Bhaduri, H.D., and Bryher spoke of the lowly and lordly worm, and of past lives. War chastened, trimmed lives. H.D. addressed her sharers: "you have a long way to go, / walk carefully, speak politely // to those who have done their worm-cycle." The implication was that H.D. began her "worm-cycle" by writing the poem. A carefully segmented piece, H.D., as "industrious" worm, "spin[s] [her] own shroud," holding to regeneration. In this definitive section, "I" flags itself, couplet after couplet, of two- or three-stress lines, the worm warding off elemental danger, "I escaped, I explored," actively turning at the semicolons that cut and connect, even obtaining ecstasy, with pragmatic cunning: "I profit

/ by every calamity; // I eat my way out of it."[51] H.D. might have thought of her Woodhall "snacks."

Sly humor too—her meager diet may have inadvertently opened doors otherwise shut. Casting some light on H.D.'s condition, Eliot noted Pascal's idea that "debility, ill health and anaemia may produce an efflux of poetry," viewing them as favorable for religious illuminations.[52] Eliot believed that poetic composition could not be consciously controlled, a point H.D. herself made, writing *Walls* almost effortlessly after preparatory vigils.[53]

No one during the war knew if they would survive—and no one knew if the barbaric air raids of 1940–1941 would return. H.D. resisted with grim humor and manageable emblems: the common "worm," having "gorged on vine-leaf and mulberry," was yet eternal. *Walls* ranged from below ground to vast seas to distant galaxies, with a paean to lesser known stars that "blaze through the clear air." Possessing a hermaphroditic life cycle, a single worm can birth more worms in burrowing tunnels, rejuvenating the soil. Her tunnel imagery was stark and accurate for shelters where "*dust and powder fill our lungs*": humans, metaphorically the legless, eyeless, unhearing, without lungs, dexterously searched for food and shelter. Moreover, earth worms distinguish light from dark by detecting vibrations of nearby creatures; it is believed that dung beetles are guided by the Milky Way, so her binding stars to the activities of the tiniest creatures was intuitive. From her father, she could name "Sirius, Vega, Arcturus" (the latter the fourth star from the sun, its name meaning in Greek "Protector of the Bear," [24]), (she punned on H.D. and Bryher's nickname for Schmideberg), and then in [50] the "the higher air / of Algorab, Regulus or Deneb," their very names vibrations one might sense.[54]

In a related poem to her worm paean, H.D. offered another emblem of resistance from her trove of sea imagery; here a "craftsman" creates unsealed walls. In twenty-three interlocking stanzas, poem 4 enacted defense: "There is a spell, for instance, / in every sea-shell" protecting it from "sea thrust," "powerless against coral, // bone, stone, marble / hewn from within by that craftsman." With refined sensing equipment, mollusks create shells patterned on Fibonacci sequences of proportional increase, spiraling outward, then back inward. Needing to remain in its own orbit, her mollusk, "prompted by hunger," gains sustenance by opening "its portals / at stated intervals." It—and by extension H.D.—rejected "infinity" as too dangerous. The shell and its occupant were guided by stars. "I sense my own limit, / my shell-jaws snap shut," if overwhelmed by "ocean-weight." Obsessed with the "Parable of the Pearl" (Mathew 13:45–46), H.D. saw hard-won interiority as "living within / you beget, self-out-of-self, // selfless, / that pearl-of-great price."[55]

Dobson sent cowslip bath essence to H.D., along with her Christmas packet of fruit and flowers; learning horticulture's "enduring cycles of natural growth and decay," she observed "thousands of other country dwellers" had "picked rose hips from the hedges so that every child in England under five could have rose syrup for vitamins."[56] Their cauliflowers and cabbages may not have been well-formed, but the Dobson farm produced strawberries, honey, celery, mushrooms, lettuces, and large brown eggs. H.D. asked for a copy of an astrology chart Dobson had made in 1934, casting the gestalt of H.D.'s circle. Dobson noted that Rodeck was out of orbit, and Macpherson, now in Peggy Guggenheim's New York apartment, "broken from all of them."[57] Staunch Bryher wished those in the armed services found sustenance in the pages of *Life and Letters*. At last, Pearson arrived in 1943, looking like an Oxford or Cambridge don, to help poetry persist.

18
Séance Nights

H.D. finished her autobiographic novel *The Gift* in late 1943. First, our pair lived it in the new year. When bombs fell, they often lay with their heads covered by rugs to block out the thunder of the bombing.[1] H.D.'s ancestral past leaped into this present crisis. "It was sinking and I was sinking with it.... [T]his was January 17, 1943.... The papers would be burnt, that is what Mamalie had said," she wrote. This terrible and terrifying raid seeded a "final draft" that year of *The Gift*, which contained her grandmother's secret "plan for peace" between white "colonizers" and indigenous peoples. This writing held such value for H.D. she wanted it out of London, fearing its incineration, sending an "untidy copy" to Houghton Mifflin in the spring, "glad to hand it over to" Pearson for "[his] collection," telling him it was "a thing [she had] worked at, off and on, for 20 years—but it only finally snapped into shape after I had scrapped all early efforts, during the bad raids."[2] Twenty years with Bryher.

During this January raid, Bryher shut doors to bedrooms and kitchen that H.D. counted and recounted, a form of self-hypnosis. They sat in their chairs with guns going off, until Bryher said, "[I]t's nothing," trying to calm H.D.'s terror, "it's just practice." H.D. "heard her words though the noise of little bricks," followed by "a terrible quiet that was worse than the roar of the guns." She "knew it was not practice." *The Gift*, besides much else, caught the couple's joint terror and endurance, Bryher striving to keep "her face quiet," hearing "walls" crumbling. H.D. compared the journey into the bedroom to retrieve a handkerchief to *Borodino*-like difficulties, "like going below, from an upper deck in a sudden storm."[3] Shattered glass and debris covered the street outside their windows.

H.D. called "1943–1945" her "vintage year" for good reason, not only for its numeric 4 + 3, her mystic 7, and 43 the number of pieces in each volume of *Trilogy*, writing as well *The Gift*, *Majic Ring* (addressing the pair's séance work), and *Tribute to Freud*, serialized in two issues of *Life and Letters* in 1945. *The Gift*, dedicated to her mother, memorialized "Bethlehem, Pennsylvania 1741 / for Chelsea, London 1941 *L'amité passe meme le tombeau*." True friendship extended beyond the tomb. Nearby, bombing in Chelsea anchored a cord to 1941, stretching back to the Moravian founding of Bethlehem in 1741. She called it "a story of *death and its mystery*," based on the astronomer Camille Flammarion's title, *Death and Its Mystery*, probing bilocation and the porous boundary between the living and the dead. Admitting "[*The Gift*] is autobiographical, 'almost,'" she gave psychic credit to Bryher, having "worked the story of myself and [Bryher] into my own family and made my grandmother reconstruct a strange psychic experience." With Bryher steadying her, H.D. now dropped down "through the grandmother's submerged consciousness" to talk with Mamalie about "torture and death by burning."[4] Her grandmother feared being called a witch for mixing female divinity and indigenous spirituality.

With Bryher's help, H.D. called upon "curious chemical constituents of biological or psychic thought-processes" to "develop long strips of continuous photographs, stored in the dark-room of memory," to watch people coming and going from rooms and, moreover, "to watch the child watching them." H.D. reverted to child-witness, admitting *not knowing* "how it works, when it will work or how long it will continue to work." After a first wave of bombers, she watched their first Christmas tree at Lowndes reverberate with its glass ornaments, and she clutched an intact tinsel star as a second wave brought "giant-propellers over our heads." Bryher sat "with her head slightly too heavy," and "whatever she said would be prophetic though she would say it to me slowly ... so *that I would not know that she knew I was afraid.*" With Bryher "accepting the fury, we could accept the thing together." The pair tiptoed around each other's automatic defenses. In the aftermath, H.D. "remembered [her] grandmother's words exactly," admitting they "could not achieve the super-human task of bringing back what had been lost."[5]

H.D. acutely imagined the "very worst terrors," seeing herself "pinned down under a great beam," aware of fearful children in underground shelters, zooming in upon a cat caught in "bricks and mortar." Like Bryher's *Beowulf*, starring a plaster bulldog in a hearth surviving the destruction of the Warming Pan, H.D. equated herself with the cat, thrilled she could "rise again." On this occasion, during a ferocious "third wave," Bryher had to convince H.D. the terrible sounds were "outside" her mind. Bryher then telephoned Cole and Gerald Henderson. H.D. suffered "a new sort of pain," seeing a "half-frozen person drawn inwards near a fire."[6]

With this new year, and H.D.'s crystalizing *The Gift*, the couple started keeping "Séance Notes," opaque and associative, one reason scholars have largely shunned them.[7] Both women preserved the messages received. Hunt's William Morris tripod table was thought to have been for "his paint-pots and brushes." Their group séances kept the creative drive alive and functioned "as a sort of safety valve."[8] Table-tapping went on during raids, the "rocking houses and furrowed pavements," an "overfamiliar wail" of sirens, bells, engines, explosions, and even more disturbing, "absolute, uncanny quiet."[9] H.D. trusted the table because it was a Morris, a hero of adolescence. H.D. and Bryher, with their 1920 "writing on the wall," now decoded messages, possibly from the beyond. During wartime London, it was not "considered insane or socially stigmatizing to consult mediums," yet neither woman publicly alluded to their séances.[10] Arthur Bhaduri and his mother, May, made a foursome for their séance nights. Both trusted and liked the seer, his first name not lost on them in their quest motif.

Beginning with some invocation or prayer or an image, they held hands in the dark and waited for taps. One tap meant "yes," two "no." H.D. was aware certain muscular twitches or reactions might create taps, yet the séances sustained the couple. Bhaduri sometimes had spontaneous visions, formed by questions asked at the table, answered by his "control" or spirit guide. After some painstaking practice, H.D. counted the taps to form letters, a strenuous, meticulous study, as grueling as stitching *Borderline* together. She took rapid notes in the dark, using a "rough pencil," sometimes writing over other writing on the same page.[11] The messages were "either commonplace and pedestrian or else over-stimulating." As a novice, H.D. felt "pulled sideways," as though on an ocean liner; May found it "routine work," while "[Bryher] surprised [H.D.] by her own understanding," though she sensed they were "in water-tight compartments." Bryher initially received most of the messages and "seemed to give and get"; she was "physically as well as psychically so much stronger," while H.D was "more sensitive." Bhaduri, they were sure, "was seeing through and into things."[12]

H.D. took the name "Delia Alton" to emphasize mediumship. After writing *Majic Ring* (1943–1944), for the first time she signed off, "H.D. (Writing as Delia Alton)." While their flat heaved with almost a continuous year of bombings, Bryher received two reassuring messages on "January 7 1943": "Delete all hurry. Leave all in hands of God." As the séances progressed, Bhaduri relied upon two guides, one, Kapama of "ancient Vedic India," who "possessed" an "intellectual cerebral intensity," echoing our couple's.[13] Like fragmentary poems or partial visions, the séance messages obeyed their own logic. Kept up into 1944, the home circle occupied them, as did their so-called Lowndes Group, Dobson, Plank, the Hendersons, Herring, with Pearson. Only the foursome participated in the séances, though Pearson was a Sunday guest for "dinners."

Bryher's green curtains over the black made the séance evenings entrancing. Setting candles in sconces, their light glinting off crystals and a propped mirror, Bryher was addressed twice in January and every week in February, March, and April. On February 12, Bhaduri tendered his "spirit guide's" introduction: "I am just agent for God." On February 19, the foursome tapped out "Elizabethan stage urgent. Travel Soon." Another message to Bryher instructed, "Uphold tests. You were very well. Play you rose. Elizabethan go on tune open very much. Read Persian too." Already studying Persian from a ninety-year-old woman, Bryher passed "tests" of love and scoured the London Library for Renaissance texts.

On April 2, Sir John swooped in: "Egypt blesses you. John here, Pater. Good girl. Each together Egypt. All is well, be happy, rely on us." The message spoke "To all present." More distinctive assurance came for Bryher in April: "Seal of Cornwall good. Keep land. Trade good. Land ten times more valuable." May 4 brought Schmideberg, the refugee Austrian analyst, to the horizon: "Pray for him. He will recover on his own." That he was dangerously addicted to alcohol H.D. and Bryher did not yet know.

* * *

H.D. was ill in fits and starts during 1943 and 1944. Herring reminded that even soldiers needed leave from the trenches. Bryher "pumped" herself "full of inoculations" and "managed to keep on her feet," H.D. told Dobson, and while she herself was "much better," the couple felt "the dark and mist."[14] Through February, Perdita, ailing with the flu, went to Cornwall, where Doris fed the "miserable specimen" tomato juice, and daffodils came up fast. On Valentine's Day, a bomber hovered over the farm; the broccoli crop came up.[15]

At the April 2 séance, a message tapped that "Sitwell will play big part in future." As it happened, Osbert organized a poets' reading, but might not Bryher have learned already he sequestered the elegant Aeolian Hall on New Bond Street for April 14? He found a Victorian lectern at the Caledonian Market and enlisted H.D., Edith, Edmund Blunden, George Bottomley, Eliot, Walter de la Mare, John Masefield, and Vita Sackville-West, each to read something new. Dobson always regretted missing the event. As Her Majesty's literary adviser, Sir Osbert Sitwell, invited the Queen with the two princesses, Elizabeth and Margaret.

A fundraiser for the Free French, the reading was scheduled for 4:45. Bryher took H.D. in her newly fashioned black gown, tailored by one of Lady Ellerman's old friends, from material bought with eight coupons H.D. had set aside. She wore her "mother-*not-in-law*'s" fur cape and beret.[16] The Royals sat in the front row. Walter de la Mare was too short to reach the stand. Towering, H.D. read "Ancient Wisdom Speaks to the Mountain," carrying her listeners into an "outer space"[17] with conversational and oracular cadences:

she knew our fear,
and yet she did not falter
nor cast herself in anguish by the river:
[…]
winter and summer,
summer and winter
… again … again …

The blue-cloaked protector, Demeter-like, against self-drowning, welcomed "empty frames" that "praise [her] name."[18] Herring beside her, Bryher sat near an aisle, in readiness in case H.D. needed her. Eliot read "What the Thunder Said," newly appropriate, "London bridges falling down," earning giggles from the princesses. By reading this post World War I poem, he re-keyed himself for this *second* war. "What the Thunder Said" is the only section of *The Waste Land* that Pound did not edit; here Eliot turns to the *Upanishads,* and invokes his knowledge of Sanskrit, calling out for "Shantih shantih shantih." Words then were not only vibrational for H.D.; Eliot was a secret sharer.[19]

After the reading, lowering her head, Bryher readied to extract H.D., who greeted the princesses. Writing Moore, H.D. noted the "two little girls exceptionally well-shaved and charming."[20] Early in May, H.D. raved to Pearson, "[W]e forgot the war for a whole week" and "wanted to go on forgetting it—four years is too long!" Bryher was "a wonder with her good deeds and constant care." When H.D. accompanied her on prowls, it "is one triumphal procession. Someone's teeth here, someone's gout there, someone's baby there, someone's son in the near-east somewhere else."[21]

H.D. created techniques for listening *above* bombs, but these efforts, lasting daily for many months, made Bryher watchful.

Definitely energized, H.D. finished *Tribute to the Angels* between May 17 and 31, methodically writing two to three installments a day, séances on temporary hold. "Since moons exist only on reflected light, you and Bryher must be my suns," H.D. wrote Pearson when Bryher and H.D. made lists of unassembled writings to his request for "tiny things, out-of-the-way things."[22] With letterhead "in c/o the American Embassy," he hoped H.D. didn't mind "this pawing over [her] literary body."[23] She sent Pearson her Doolittle history, linking her by "one remove" from Paul Revere, even suggesting "a contest reading Paul R," as she noted Bryher at "a distance and the clock in the steeple is about to strike."[24]

By June 1943, Bryher was following promptings from their séances, letting Gerald Henderson, the librarian at St. Paul's, provide a historical tour. She saw a "wilderness of flowers," over fifty varieties, growing where streets and houses had been and where fire burned the ropes holding the Bells of Agincourt. Her soles possibly mixing with the dust of smashed bells, Bryher walked to the London Library. Almost led to it, she came upon T. W. Baldwin's *The Organization and Personnel of the Shakespearean Company*, and "as if the thunderbolt of Zeus had struck," the book mentioned a one-part actor, James Sands, who played her favorite, original girl-page, Bellario. While Bryher underplayed her psychic capacities, this experience resembled earlier "flashes" of intuition.[25]

Bryher now germinated a novel, written in the next decade, nursed through the war, with James Sands starring as *Player's Boy*. On May 28, she had another message from the table: "Great personalities under influence of present cycle. You are Elizabethan England to be used for an end." Prompted by these telegraphic phrases, Bryher searched Silver Street for Shakespeare's house in Aldermanbury, walking on fire-black stones to St. Mary's Church, burned in the Great Fire in 1666, rebuilt by Wren, and bombed by the Luftwaffe on December 29, 1940.[26] Bryher envisioned an Elizabethan congregation and admired the duo John Hemmings and Henry Cordell, actors and officers at St. Mary's who collected the first folio of Shakespeare's plays. A Home Guard officer knew the destroyed home of "the Folio chaps," directing Bryher to its foundations. Benches surrounded Shakespeare's bust, set there in 1896; it was plaster, and "for that reason it was one of us, it did not have to be stored in the country or muffled up with sacks."[27] Like her plaster bulldog in *Beowulf*, it abided. She contributed "A Note on Beaumont and Fletcher" to *Life and Letters*, explaining that they "wrote in the middle period between the Spanish defeat and the Civil War." Bryher saw her girl pages reincarnating, for "not one Bellario but hundreds, drove ambulances or sat at telephone switchboards quite unmoved by any falling bombs." Reflecting upon thought transferences with H.D., she asked of Beaumont (one séance told Bryher to read all of his work), "[S]urely the style of the one influenced the thought of the other?"[28]

* * *

Perdita's OSS boss, James J. Angleton, who loved Eliot, was erratic and fussy, his adrenalin pushing the office from "crisis to crisis"; she had long hours, checking footnotes, carbons, and insertions for his reports. When their office was hit, busting a window, leaving "glass in every cranny" of her typewriter, he was nonplussed. In this chaos, she also discovered a side of beef in their filing cabinet, which he offered as unexpected prize.[29]

After settling Perdita with two other Foreign Office girls into 29 Ovington Street in July, Bryher returned to Cornwall. Transferring at Plymouth, two soldiers leaned from a window to haul her small body into their packed car; standing for hours, she was stuck among three civilians, four soldiers, and a child needing the lavatory. Bryher read her pocket *Tamburlaine*, grateful she had Ernest Freud's sleeping tablets, dreading the ride back. These details amused H.D.—small wonder she resisted taking a packed train for approximately 262 miles.

When first in the Scillies, Bryher felt "an instantaneous falling in love," superannuated by meeting H.D. at Bosigran.[30] Now wire blocked the sand beaches, though the overgrown Cornwall "lanes were open." The landscape planted seeds for *The Fourteenth of October*, her historic novel that took time-traveler Bryher to the turnstile of 1066. Bryher conceived her Saxon boy, Wulf, as having "the sight," foreseeing the Norman Invasion five years before the Battle of Hastings. The possibility of current defeat preyed on her mind, though Cornwall embodied the continuity of cottage life, fishermen, and "sight," necessitated by dangerous rocks and shoals. With a "blue leather coat" nearly torn "to pieces with old age," Bryher asked H.D. to forward "a perfectly new one in cupboard."[31] Mist softened most evenings.

At Lowndes, H.D. conceptualized the war as the need "to shed a skin or husk, once so often—a biological process—in fact, the whole race has got to slough-off, out of it—the past." She regarded herself as a "new creation" with others, "glued to their rocks,'" laying out the couple's efforts: "If two such transitional beings meet and can not clutch at each other across the abyss, then life ends, all life!" They clutched. The war was "a trial of endurance—such as is put on dedicated novices in any vocation," which led Bryher, another "novice," to "going on too."[32]

* * *

Séance life was more intense later that year. *Majic Ring* kept up with the Morris table as another modern machine, where "the telegraph or the messages conveyed by the tapping of one of the tripod-feet upon the carpet of my flat in Lowndes Square in London, was sustained, logical. It could be renewed at any moment, given time and opportunity."[33] Writing *Majic* in 1943 and 1944, relying on séance notes, diary entries, and letters she sent the retired hero Lord Dowding, dated November 5 through December 12, 1943, followed up with journal entries dated December 17, 1943, through January 26, 1944, reestablishing Corfu in 1920 as "initiation."[34] *Majic* cast the pair's psychic credentials anew in 1943. Dowding impelled this composition, H.D. pitting herself against another male authority.

On September 3, the anniversary of war declaration, and a day after her birthday, Bryher received news of Sir John through Bhaduri: "Father with Buddhist monks in yellow robes," "grateful" for his "chance to repose," to contemplate "esoteric doctrine." Bryher's mother sent "practical help," advising, "Sign nothing with Cornwall." Bryher typed and kept these pages. September 9 messaged "H": "Great peace. Angel with laurel crown and white cross. Rhythmic breathing. Scientist helping. (A shaggy old worker.) Edith (a sister)." These messages drew upon H.D.'s keen awareness of Einstein, the "shaggy old worker." Breathing instruction sounded solid advice for coping, and Edith was, in fact, a "poetic" sister.

September 17 issued "H" a more substantial message, addressing "John Wesley preaching under a tree." This "John," not Sir John, was a Methodist theologian whose life spanned the eighteenth century (1703–1791). At Oxford, he launched the "Holy Club" for seeking grace within. Founding the Methodist Church, he left for the colonies, soon returning to join a society of Moravian Christians during a dramatic shift in thinking, requiring the so-called irrational to hide underground, among the Moravians. On September 24, news came to H.D.: "Peace be in your heart. We are very near. Get busy," "November will be time of real result. (Writing)." Then the message shifted: "Tribes gather together. Okita-hama-tele-na. Great Spirit blesses you." The table tapped advice on October 15: "Scatter not energy.... Be of merry heart for this is the gateway to illumination. Very good future for you all." Each "had a part" in a "plan," helpful to H.D., who wondered why she was saved and another, like Goldie, an ambulance driver, commemorated in her "May, 1943" poem, died at her ambulance wheel.[35] Survivor's guilt fueled the couple as amanuenses for the dead.

The séance nights swerved after Bhaduri gave H.D. and Bryher his tickets to hear Dowding speak at Wigmore Hall on October 20, 1943. The place was packed. Like most of England, H.D. idealized Dowding, awarded the Knight's Grand Cross of the Order of Bath, among England's highest military honors. His special relationship with his pilots, who called him "Stuffy," led to triumph. H.D. later wryly considered that "[he] said one outstanding thing": "At this time of conflict and confusion, Beings of a higher order could and would enter regions (which otherwise they avoided)," inspiring H.D. with *his* urgency that "[n]ow was the time, if ever, to strive to attain some sort of attitude that would make possible the work and effort of the higher spheres." H.D. took his remark "Strike and strike quickly"[36] to heart and contacted him almost immediately about her group's envisioning a Viking ship with Bhaduri *before* she attended this lecture, excitedly proposing that her small group join his circle.[37] "Mrs. Aldington" was brushed aside, with a crumb, that if he were tempted to "enlarge a 'circle,'" he would consider it, but foresaw "no immediate probability of this."[38] The powerful man's letters rejected H.D. from his circle's "special sort of work."[39] Such dismissals inspired her to protest that "the voices and the presences ('they spoke, they laughed, they crowded around the table')" were "more enduring than all the high explosives."[40]

Dowding's talk and H.D.'s response electrified the Morris table. A detailed message on November 4 began like a telephone call: "Halbard calling." Shipboard, Hal (Prince

Hal?) "sounds a note and there is chanting and singing," while "a gentleman," presumably Dowding, "is influenced and has been influenced by unseen forces he does not realise." H.D. thought the ship came for obvious reasons to Bryher, who was reading Norse sagas, then reconsidered it came "as well as for [herself]." With a "light-hearted vibration," Hal noted "a stone altar near a wall" with "a cross in a circle" and a "gold goblet," objects familiar from Mamalie's distant ramblings.[41]

When H.D. placed Dowding's first letter in Bhaduri's hands, "Oh there's music here," he broke out. He intuited Dowding as one whose "real self has not been expressed in this life"; he might have been an actor—instead, he was "an instrument," a "lone eagle," his conventionality causing an "inward ache." After two rejections, H.D. *again* wrote Dowding. She presented their basic practice: she wrote notes in the dark with difficulty, tossing aside pages as messages often speedily came. Transcribing the November 4 séance, she insisted it had relevance to the RAF.[42] On his Viking ship, Hal led the séance circle across "the North Sea," "right across to another century, 16th or 17th century." Bhaduri then saw a priest, a "Quaker type," who lived "among North American Indians," and sighted "women as well as men" in the vessel. The message wavered between question and confidence: "Extreme north, link with Norway lost to settlement. Harald?—All connect—long dark ship.... [T]his date roughly 50 B.C. to 50 A.D. Figure of the sun disc and wings from disc line hull of boat." These "wings" replaced the "flying shadow /of high wings" from *Walls*. The sun disc recalled Bryher's Corfu hieroglyph completing H.D.'s.[43]

The next day, November 5, Bhaduri channeled "Kapama": "Hilda, I greet you. All is good. On you is help being rendered. Indian contact powerful. They gather here. A-B-C-D. Three times. A-B-C. (long) Abode (quick). Get used to beat. (Alert and guns). God is near—no harm ever comes if Faith is true."[44] Such fragmented messages boosted H.D.'s confidence; *Majic* played corrective for 1920: "The 'veil' had parted for me on the *Borodino* and I had had a glimpse of perfection ... the 'absolute' of beauty—the lost Atlantis."[45] The palimpsest of eternity existed beside war wreckage. H.D. confirmed "[a] Dolphin led the way." *Majic* set the *Borodino* in its proper "key," doubling as a ship for "the priests who sailed from Crete to Delphi."[46] During winter 1943, séance work, as collaboration every other week, gave H.D. and Bryher renewed intimacy to start their "whole machine." But Bryher as Gareth in 1920 was not the post-Lisbon one facing H.D. now.

Bryher had insulated the live wire, while H.D. entered multiple embodiments, and now reevaluated her "possessions"—among them a medicine man, a "grass-clothed island-girl and the pretty china-doll of a Japanese with her mirrors and her scent bottles and her sashes and her one tall stem of jade, the iris-stalk in a crystal vase," H.D. catalogued. "All these are dead."[47] The sitters, she surmised, "travelled along a certain degree of longitude, a little below the 40th parallel" that led "to Japan and on again to northern India or Tibet." Though Japan was now an enemy, these women channeled, she was convinced, "other phases of [her] psychic past."[48]

Obsessed with the séances, H.D. in a letter drafted "Nov. 19" practically demanded Dowding recognize their "Viking Ship": its "sun-disk on the seal," with "the centre of the disk" as "two wings spread, not outside, but *in* the sun," resembled the RAF symbol of "a circle and crown with wings as a sort of sun-symbol."⁴⁹ Such attenuated subtleties put Dowding off; metonymic association was one of her poetic signatures. He had no light to shed on the ship or the notes, but thought H.D.'s group may have glimpsed "the veracity of past lives." H.D. captured the couple's banter about former lives in *Majic*: "She [Bryher/Gareth] said, 'I was a boy.' I said, 'You can't always be a boy. You say you were a boy in Elizabethan England,' with the response, 'I was a man in Egypt and probably a woman as well but I was a boy before that.'"⁵⁰ Dowding himself believed he was a "Mongol chief in a previous life."⁵¹

Two days later, H.D. wrote again, insisting they were not "fly by night"; she kept a strict record at "the little private wireless station," mentioning "a soldier out of a Detroit hospital" who flew in from the "psychic-air" to say "I am dead, I am helping."⁵² She pointed to Bryher again, whose "people actually had shipping interests and she herself travelled in Iceland," perhaps too fiercely insisting "the Ship was hers, *had come because of her research.*" "Viking" meant *to adventure*, and *research*, this couple's necessity. H.D. dug in: "[I]t is *N O T* delusion. It is *fact.*"⁵³ Dowding simply recoiled.

A séance on November 18 reclaimed the "Viking ship," ending with another message for "H" from an "old man like a monk," offering "fruit on a flat dish." Bhadhuri brought comfort: "Now B.'s father is here, I think he was very fond of you, H. He pats you on the shoulder." Like Doolittle and Dowding, Sir John "was a lone wolf." They asked the guide what to do. "Pray. He is worried about B," the reply was. Bryher, by this point, resisted H.D.'s obsession with Dowding. On November 19, a séance handily set H.D. on track to her "WRITING." "To H. I have this message for you. Prepare the way. Your writing must go on—keep it going—keep a record. Answer this person's notes. Answer and do notes. Formed by spirit." The table started sounding like Bryher.

By December 18, H.D. had reframed their purpose, not "fundamentally, to *help* anyone." They were "more like painters or poets, intent on the creation of something out of nothing; we actually, are held together, more like petals of a flower, that ne-nu-far that opens for nobody and for nothing except the workings of divine law." Mingling spirituality and science, her "pearl of great price" was "the product of an amorphous elemental creature ... far below that of the glistening, leaping sea-fish, in the scale of biological evolution."⁵⁴ On January 20, 1944, the words tapped out were "I am the Fish," warning her to withdraw from Dowding for "later full opening. Rest, relaxation—come back fresh. Lovely water." Bhaduri would not touch the hero's latest letter, dismissing him as otherwise absorbed.

A message came with "[t]wo gates opening out" beside one, a "Rose tree," but "the flower to be plucked is still in bud." The "rose-bud" opened to an underwater "early paradise-Aegean." The table tapped out H.D.'s desire "to go under that sea" and "walk on bottom of sea-old buildings—across (Crete to Yucatan?) Isthmus—up river-stone of sacrifice—not human sacrifice." The séance connected Crete to the Yucatan, "C" to "Y"—an imaginary city, resembling a diverse cosmopolitan Alexandria. Bhaduri's guide praised "H": "These Indians love you. You represent BELT cutting across Asia Minor"; coached "H": "You will live to achieve so much. It may seem crazy—all a big work—no delusion—mountains to scale." Then the table acknowledged "Beaver,"

H.D.'s mother: "knowledge through understanding—beaver—understanding through patience—patience through realization of what is to be." Bhaduri's guides—and his circle—were spiritual analysts, and quite talkative.

* * *

Pearson manifested in January 1944 at Lowndes with two bananas, two oranges, and a pineapple. They had not tasted fresh fruit for two years. H.D. believed it merited a party. "Be merry," the séance instructed. Bryher telephoned, sending notes to about twenty people, packing their living room, cutting the fruit "into tiny mouthfuls." She also finished *Beowulf*, formerly *Comrade Bulldog*, on January 18, read aloud during blackouts to H.D. and Perdita. Bryher knew the English would have none of it, with its criticism of unpreparedness and unnecessary food shortages, while H.D. told Pearson Oxford University Press wanted an American copy of "W A L L S."[55]

H.D. had two major dreams during Holy Week. A friendly voice on April 11 told her she was dead, lying in a coffin in the living room; Bryher told her such dreams signaled "awakening." Presences surrounded. "I had been welcomed out of my body, by friends," particularly "[t]he personality of [Bryher]," as "absolute," " 'all there,' materialized and familiar. She and I were together in this new life, though she herself was not aware of this transition."[56] H.D., fused with Bryher, interpreted her dream as being reborn as a couple, their trials and endurance producing a metamorphosis. Perceiving in her dream only one section of a coffin, she presumed the other was for her alter ego. On Easter Sunday, H.D. had "another dream, very real." Bhaduri turned into "a patriarch type," an Osiris, wearing a pharaoh's cap, intuited as nonbinary: "This person is Love itself, he is mother, he is father." Then she "melted into" this entity as "a small drift of snow" that "melted back into the original snow-cloud."[57]

These dreams added to H.D.'s sense of being a revenant. Pearson observed that Bryher wrote inward from actual experience, while H.D. did the opposite, herself framing this dialectic as complementary. Yet a dogged fixation on Dowding drove a gap between them. Rebuffed in efforts to shepherd H.D. from London, Bryher tried not complaining about "Food Control." Being "exo" equated to waiting in queues, wandering in rubble, picking up the less ideal side of human nature. Lately, Bryher noted, not everyone behaved in lines.

* * *

Tribute to the Angels, written between May 7 and 31, 1944, featured angels and ladies, drawing upon the so-called Secret Book of John, denounced as heresy by second-century Christians.[58] In 1896, a German Egyptologist discovered several copies of John's book as well as the Gospel of Mary, both texts repressed by the Catholic Church and both understood by H.D. to be part of the "wisdom tradition," a Gnostic, an Alexandrian "attitude"—her "The Poet" summed it up well in the image of a skull-shaped snail singing, and wailing, whose "nerves are almost gone," "its small Coptic temple" with a candle and altar nearby. As medium, she needed protection.[59]

During this world war, H.D. confronted the persecution of Moravians in *The Gift*, but in *Trilogy* she identified with wisdom seekers, such as John, and Magdalene in the next sequence. Poem 3 of *Angels* enacted bold ventriloquism: "*I John saw. I testify*," he "of the seven stars."[60] According to Elaine Pagels, the "Secret Book" opens with Christ's offering "to reveal" to this apostle "the mysteries" and "things hidden in silence."[61] Dedicating the poem to the "hidden," H.D. made a modernist joke on modernism. "*I make all things new*," no longer modernism's "making it new," the spirit was alive, just unseen.

H.D. told Pearson that a "voice to quell the re-gathering / thundering storm," a phrase from Poem 40 of *Angels*, came to her on a bus, when she "really DID feel that a new heaven and a new earth were about to materialize."[62] She created multiple versions of a "Lady," a goddess-Mary-cum-Saint-Guinevere, to engender "the blank pages / of the unwritten volume of the new."[63] Bryher initially objected to the "Lady" as too archaic, and Dobson saw this sensualized memory as inspired by their Venice romance, visiting St. Mark's Coptic Basilicus:

and I remembered the bell-notes,
Azrael, Gabriel, Raphael,

as when in Venice, one of the campanili
speaks and another answers

until it seems the whole city (Venice-Venus)
will be covered with gold pollen shaken

from the bell-towered, lilies plundered
with the weight of massive bees . . . [64]

H.D. had heard beneath all the bell notes "an un-named, resurging bell, // answered, sounding through them all."[65] "A N N A E L," an angel to give an "old Testament" quality, she explained to Pearson, while the word secondarily signaled the alchemical subjection of heat to glass, cooling slowly to avoid brittleness, to toughen a surface. It reverberated with "Anna, Hannah or Grace," recalling some "Hannah" riding to Putney.[66] *Angels* praised, "never, never / was a season more beautiful, // richer in leaf and color."[67] Weaving in English paganism, H.D. replaced the apple tree with the May tree, depicting resurrection as living possibility.

Halfway into *Angels*, "the Lady knocked."[68] Claiming a choral vision, H.D. toured "cathedral, museum, cloister":

we have seen her head bowed down
with the weight of a domed crown,

or we have seen her a wisp of a girl
trapped in a golden halo.[69]

This female emissary cropped up everywhere. One only had to look, was H.D.'s bid, making fresh hybrids: "we see her hand unknot a Syrian veil / or lay down a Venetian shawl."[70] The sequence created a composite of stills, each addition bearing slight modifications—"the Child was not with her" in 32, while in 35 "she looked so kindly at us // under her drift of veils"; this "new Eve" "brings the Book of Life, obviously."[71]

Of her next installment, already dedicated to Pearson, H.D. wrote, "I haven't the foggiest of what the 3rd is to be about and am rather harassed and wrote the 2nd under compulsion—I don't know where I am. Do you have any inspirational ideas?????" Disorientation was the very condition afflicting "initiates." *Walls,* the first sequence, arrived in published wrappers from Oxford, its "green-green glass on the brown-green and Nile green texture of the same said figs" reverberated with Herring's gift of a calendar, correlating Pagan and Christian festival days. The birthday "octave" corresponded with "Sept. 2–10 to Ceres and the Greater Eleusinian Mysteries—and the 10th itself to Arthur, King of Britain and the Round Table as Last Supper symbol and zodiac." H.D.'s synthetic imagination embedded circle in circle, like Major Oak's deep time.

After a Sunday dinner, H.D. thanked Pearson for cooking "the corn for us—real Eleusinian. I hope Br did not raise your hair too much with her horrors—she is wonderful, I am half the time shivering with goose-flesh, a wonderful ghost-story feeling she gives me, she is usually right but her [doses?] are very strong!"[72] Both of their doses *were* strong, supplemented now with Dobson's observation of "heavy vehicles, gun-carriages, tanks, huge transport lorries" moving into their district, "stashed in woods under camouflage nets."[73]

England's bombers "pounded Dunkirk and Calais, hoping to fool the German generals into thinking the invasion would be staged there." Early in June, H.D. and Bryher saw *Winter's Tale* in Regent's Park, glowing with chestnut blossoms. They learned that Sylvia Beach had been taken into custody August 1942, sent to an internment camp at Vittel, at a hotel, "a shabby, dirty old building, with bad plumbing and dirty water."[74] Some interned women lost their minds. Monnier visited on the one day permitted each month, bringing under her cape a can of condensed milk.

H.D., Bryher, and Herring huddled, hearing that 160,000 Allied troops landed in Normandy on June 6, the largest amphibious operation in history. Over the next months, the Allies pushed into Paris. Herring was excited, as "one always purrs at Navy," diagramming the couple's sense of history, calling this akin to "the Battle of Hastings in reverse."[75] The Normandy victory, however, was followed a week later by gruesome new weaponry. V-1 bombs, called "doodle-bugs," subjected victims to piercing sounds. Bryher called them "Christmas Tree Raids," distinguished by their colored flares, millions of strips of tinsel-like aluminum tape disrupting radar. Consequently, anti-aircraft gun crews fought blindly. Osbert cautioned Bryher, "Your duty now is to get Hilda away. The Germans have got a new missile and you are right in the center, near the park. Take her to the country at once."[76] Pearson was in London throughout the V-bomb attacks: 6,080 Londoners died, and 40,000 were injured.

H.D. spent the first terrible night alone, while Bryher started for Cornwall but immediately returned to endure the doodles with H.D., who persisted in "taking it," with many close calls in their neighborhood. On July 5, they "heard a 'doodlebug'" aimed at Lowndes. Both lay on the floor. Silence "followed by a terrific explosion" led Bryher to worry about the Hendersons. Telephoning, she discovered their flat had been split in two. Cole was in the hospital with jaundice. Bryher rushed immediately to the "final clean-out," for "unless possessions were rescued quickly, the acids in the dust destroyed them." She even absconded with a saucepan and a dress. A bloody handprint covered the staircase wall as Gerald fled, and "Cole's sofa, where she usually sat, had vanished," leaving "not even a fragment of wood." Gerald lost an eye.[77]

Even more now, H.D. needed her routine, as séances instructed, but after this horrible loss of a friend's eye, she was ready for Cornwall. Gerald had been writing a history of London streets, now impossible. Pearson assured Bryher that "the crack within Germany may have begun," sending a carton of cigarettes to keep her "in puffs during [her] holiday," saying he'd "prefer to see Germany just split apart, so that we can walk in without bothering to pick up the pieces." On July 20, the pair finally retreated to Cornwall. Sculpting intentionally caricatured gender roles and pragmatic selves, Bryher reported, "Our Hilda seems happy and trots around patting bushes and doing her embroidery. I stalk in a boiler suit and a mackintosh with a hoe." Still, H.D. indicted herself for leaving "bomb-alley."[78] "Puritan," Pearson's code name, referred to "spirits like ours." Intercepting his letter to Bryher, H.D. told him she "very naughtily has hidden [Bryher's cigarettes] from [her]" until she finished her stash; in a trio, he told Bryher "[t]hat definitely is not as it should be. Smoke twice as fast, and two at once, one from each corner of the mouth."[79] On August 5, H.D. "bathed and lay out on the rocks." A week later, she still fretted over London, Bryher soothing her "as much as possible at this minute."[80]

June 6, D-Day, put Bryher and H.D. back in contact with Monnier and Beach in Paris. H.D. sent Monnier "a greeting across the abyss"[81]; Bryher finally could send Beach a care package, "a gift that redeemed the bitterness of the closing season."[82]

Weakened German air power allowed the Allied forces to break through German garrisons on August 19, and on August 25, the Resistance, with General George S. Patton's forces, cornered the German military and liberated Paris. Crowds flocked to the cinema to watch the Liberation. The next day, H.D. told Dobson about her two marvelous months in Cornwall. Bryher planned a trip to Eckington, while H.D. decided to visit Dobson at Woodhall, making embarrassment into a joke: "This is terrible—I blush—

BUT
    if you have a spare
        POT

I would be most grateful."[83]

At Woodhall, H.D. enjoyed saplings with wide trunks, spied a fox at dusk, and in the relative silence heard the cuckoo, nightingales, and doves cooing in the brush. During her visit, a Nazi pilot dropped from a plane. He was stuck, Dobson reported, "up a *very* tall tree all night." All too Mrs. Miniver, they gave him tea, and the military took him away.[84] Herring missed H.D., "the way [she] gallops up to one like a deer in a wood once she makes a clearing."[85] To Pearson's wife, Susan, H.D. confessed, "There comes a moment when one cannot absorb any more intensity or drama, and yet I would not have missed this time for anything."[86]

19
The Writing on the Wall

After her birthday in 1944, H.D. wrote *Tribute to Freud*. Dobson suggested she "slam it out," and she did. She began psychoanalysis "in order to fortify and equip [herself] to face war," and if it came, "to help in some subsidiary way" those "war-shocked and war-shattered people." Herself war-shattered in 1933 and 1934, she could not really address her "1914–1919" trauma, when she feared for Freud's fragility. Then her "own personal little Dragon of war-terror" had no chance but had "growled and bit on his chains and was only loosed finally, when the full apocryphal terror of fire and brimstone, of whirlwind and flood and tempest, of the Biblical Day of Judgement and the Last Trump, became no longer abstract terrors." Horrors happened almost continuously "to [herself] and [her] friends, and all the wonderful and all the drab and ordinary London people."[1]

H.D. and Bryher had caused Freud to modify his theories of sexuality; now H.D. prepared to adjust his stance on mortality. Knitting, with firmness, Freud into the chosen family, she wrote, "Count Z was an Austrian, we were called Moravians, Professor Freud was an Austrian, born as it happened in Moravia," thus a direct "descendent of the Brotherhood."[2] Psychoanalysis was her search for inward illumination, but, she explained, "there was an argument implicit in our very bones." During analysis, she wished to split her remaining years with the elder Freud. Now she *believed* Freud *had* continued on, though he had "really no idea that he would 'wake up' when he shed the frail locust-husk of his years, and find himself alive," similar to H.D.'s sense that she and Bryher would "go on." She knew this was audacious. This was section 30 of *Tribute to Freud*, of this forty-four-day project started on September 19, 1944, finished after the Day of the Dead, November 2. A last group séance with Bhaduri on October 19, 1944, made Freud focal. Transcription took on the "master's" voice: "My best work was trodden in dust crucifiction (*sic*). Eyes know everything—marriage fulfillment." This shifted attention to the imminent wedding of Bhaduri, whose other guide, "Zakenuto," tapped out, "Respect for you—attached—mind keen at end—you are placing yourself at disposal of a greater mind—you are the instrument—you will prove the work of this Master did not represent a finality but a THRESHOLD. Not science, only lever that opens door—way cleared, then work begins." This was part of the couple's new "work." In a trance state, H.D. ventriloquized Freud letting go, "as Spirit will hold on. I am breaking door—I enjoy it—necessity—everything breaking—doesn't matter. A design—necessity—everything breaking." Another chilling "telegraph" arrived with "[c]rucible—things burnt—as instrument being used." This astral Freud knew a "dose given too quickly will make sick—compromising—convention."

Their "wireless" communicated he enjoyed "pleasant occupation—fruit." Pleated into eighty-four small pieces, *Tribute* unraveled Freud's belief that immortality was only "conventionally mosaic."[3] Its "Writing on the Wall" H.D. published in *Life and Letters* in May 1945, laying out the Corfu visions. Anyone who knew H.D. knew Bryher, she wrote, assuring collaboration, supplying their prognostication credentials in this wartime memoir.

After the First World War ended, H.D. had thought, "rung by rung or year by year," she would "be free," set "in another, a winged dimension." The tent shapes that flashed on their Corfu wall, originally interpreted as "past battle-fields," were now "shelters to be set up in another future contest." In 1944, "semi-permanent" residents lived in tube stations. With World War II *not yet over* but France regained, H.D. suspected the Corfu visions had predicted this war. Even H.D. took her visions as akin to "madness." Imagining Freud's early training with Charcot at the Salpétrière, she discovered a "border-line" with "hysterics and neurotics on this side and the actual insane on the other," with "a wide gap for all that, an unexplored waste-land, a no-man's land between them." This comforted H.D. Freud observed the "apparently unrelated actions" of some patients, enacting "a sort of order," was "like the broken sequence of events in a half-remembered dream."[4] H.D. advocated a broader "border-line" to accommodate "seers" like Freud, herself, and Bryher. She even imagined the wife of a patient with a Caesar mania, wondering what *the wife* suffered. In what follows, all of H.D's words and punctuation are lineated in her "rhythmic prose," laying out Freud's identification—like her "I, John" of *Trilogy*:

> There is Caesar behind bars—
> Here is Hannibal, here am I, Sigmund Freud
> [...]
> I, Hannibal—not Caesar.
> I, the despised Carthiginian, I,
> the enemy of Rome.
> I, Hannibal.
> So you see, I, Sigmund Freud,
> myself standing here,
> a favourite and gifted,
> admit it, student of Dr. Charcot,
> in no way to all appearances deranged
> or essentially peculiar, true to my own orbit—
> *true to my own orbit?*
> True to my own orbit,
> my childhood fantasies of Hannibal,
> my identification with Hannibal,
> the Carthginian (Jew, not Roman)—
> I, Sigmund Freud, understand this Caesar.
> I, Hannibal![5]

During analysis, H.D. discovered "Mignon," her child-self that Freud "raised," along with other "dead hearts and stricken minds and maladjusted bodies." Like Bryher, Mignon "did not fit its body." The sister lost a brother in the First World War. Now she reflected on "the great many" that "have fallen since," all the "[n]umberless, poised, disciplined and valiant young winged Mercuries [who] have fallen from the air, to join the great host of the dead." Love, she held, always overcame death.[6] After analysis in 1934, H.D. composed "The Dancer," vibrating with this challenge:

Dare further,
stare with me
into the face of Death,
and say
Love is stronger.[7]

* * *

Osbert reviewed *Walls*, with words like "trap-doors" and a coolness that came "with an immense relief."[8] Now H.D. asked what she had left unloved. Having to "carry on from the black tunnel of darkness or 'initiation,' at least toward the tunnel entrance," she appraised that heaven appeared on earth, "lasted as you know, for a few weeks— then D-Day!" After revisiting Freud, she began *The Flowering of the Rod*, calling upon more angels, as Wim Wenders imagined them consoling postwar Berliners in *Wings of Desire* (1987). The opening piece spoke of "the anger, frustration / bitter fire of destruction," though "higher beings" had "done all [they] could," compelling one to "mount higher / to love—resurrection."[9]

One of the gnostic texts discovered in Cairo in the late nineteenth century, the Gospel of Mary, "interprets the resurrection appearances as visions received in dreams or in ecstatic trance," while the Gospel of Philip contends not only that individuals must "receive the resurrection while they live" but also that "the companion of the [Savior is] Mary Magdalene [whom Christ loved] ... more than [all] the disciples, and used to kiss her [often]."[10] With Magdalene in mind, H.D., as mystic poet, sensualized this "rain of beauty" returning to "the cloud." She sang, "I go where I love and where I am loved, / into the snow: // I go to the things I love," trusting she went "where I belong, inexorably."[11] As "migratory flocks," "we must be drawn or we must fly, / like the snow-geese of the Arctic circle, // to the Carolinas or to Florida," to rediscover "what we once knew."[12] The geese possess "the will to enjoy, the will to live," remembering Hesperides; they don't "swerve," "for there is the hunger / for Paradise."[13] H.D. herself was quasi-scientist, deciding her own flight was "[n]o poetic fantasy / but a biological reality," herself "an entity / like bird, insect, plant // or sea-plant cell; I live; I am alive." This warned readers to "shun" her, for "this reality / is infectious-ecstasy."[14]

Flowering recasts the myth of Magdalene's "loose" life challenging male Church authorities as "a female counterpoint to the male deity."[15] If Magdalene greeted Christ after the crucifixion, such reality bore "infectious-ecstasy," knowing love won over death. H.D. set forth *we two* as "a frozen Priestess, a lonely Pythoness // who chants, who sings / in broken hexameters."[16] Dowding resembled disdaining Kasper, who "whispered the secret of the sacred processes of distillation," because "they knew— / no secret was safe with a woman";[17] looking toward "the half-open door; // she understood; this was his second rebuff."[18] Bryher assured H.D., as had Bhaduri, that Dowding's hurtful rejection was war strain. But to escape hurt, H.D. practiced dangerous dissociation from her body, having "to detach herself," so as Mary M., "when stones were hurled, / she simply wasn't there."[19] In H.D.'s gnostic vein, Christ had already returned a second time, speaking to Magdalene first. Crucified, Christ showed that even in the material world one could enjoy the "kingdom within" on earth. Kaspar disdained "the feasting, the laughter." The laughter of H.D.'s ancestors' Moravian feasts echoed therein. *Flowering* reached through Magdalene to "Ge-meter, De-meter, earth-mother // or Venus / in a star."[20] *Trilogy* emerged after three roughly three-week intervals of illumination.

* * *

A quiet uneasiness growled after Paris was liberated. No one knew when exactly peace would be declared; others feared more raids.[21] H.D. watched Bryher enter "a state of permanent rush, hysteria," playing everyone's Santa. Dobson joined the United Relief & Rehabilitation Administration, helping displaced persons in Egypt. H.D. reiterated her choice to stay in England. With "no word from K," she accused Macpherson of "hiding his head in the New York desert-sand." Grateful for the purring central heating, she admitted they were "in a frightful toil and moil or grumble, G R U M B L E I think we are all just TIRED!"[22] Satisfied that Dobson enjoyed her "Freud Notes," H.D. herself called them "a great triumph." But H.D. and Bryher both dreamed of escape. H.D. felt Tibet-minded, though knew it was fantasy.[23]

Dowding visited H.D. and Bryher in February 1945. H.D. insisted on Bryher's presence with the lord and tea. The hero dropped his overcoat, immediately tackling reincarnation. Bryher said nothing, staring through him as she had Pound. She even tried to get away. H.D. confessed, "I shoved my chair over so she couldn't get out."[24] Bryher smoked, bored with the mighty, and referred to Perdita traveling to "Western Europe," "resplendent in American uniform."[25] After Dowding left, H.D. was disappointed, Bryher scoffing. In March, Perdita rode her bicycle along the Seine, enjoying her "new GI Angle." With her map clutched in one hand, she drove excitedly with her parcels of sweets, cigarettes, and Spam to Rue de L'Odeon, greeting Sylvia and Adrienne.[26]

With Roosevelt's death on April 13, H.D. conveyed to Susan Pearson the immense gratitude everyone felt for him.[27] Perdita thrilled at "HITLER DEAD," as a *Stars and Stripes* headline announced. Assuring her two mothers that blackouts were over, "the first Peace Scare passed [her] over."[28] Waiting for "official" peace, Herring, Bryher, and H.D., as a trio, enjoyed a weekend at the end of April in Stratford for Shakespeare's birthday and St. George's Day, walking slowly in a procession, Bryher finding it "a religious experience." While at Avon, they saw John Webster's *The Duchess of Malfi*. Establishing some psychic "landmarks," H.D. began her "Shakespeare" poems, first grouped as "Good Frend," published in *Life and Letters* in 1946. H.D. returned to Stratford alone later in the summer.

At least twice Bryher left large sums of money for H.D. at Lowndes: the first for £30,000, then £20,000, meant for H.D.'s dream cottage, should she find it, setting off guilt tremors. Bryher felt guilt too, but hers was because she found London unbearable. Bryher thought H.D. might resume her Lowndes-Kenwin bilocation, though Bryher predicted postwar London would be intolerable.

Herring, H.D., and Bryher together heard the news of unconditional surrender on May 8. Three days earlier, Bryher had complained the bread had gone stale waiting to celebrate. H.D. covered her windows with a huge U.S. flag, while Bryher procured a "Welsh Dragon and a Union Jack." Bakers stayed open for an extra hour on May 8; Bryher rushed out for another loaf after sending H.D. ahead to Chelsea with Osbert for Churchill's broadcast at 3:00 p.m. Taking a jammed bus to St. Paul's, Bryher walked to Shakespeare's bust, tracing the footprint left by Roman London, and then headed to Herring's flat, where he had draped every possible Allied flag; for days, stores had been sold out, but he cleverly bought flags whenever a major disaster transpired. Bryher hopped on a bus, delighted by Wrens with cockades in their hats. Children covered the paws of the Landseer lions at Trafalgar Square.

When Bryher arrived at Herring's flat, H.D. was already there, savoring a tempered ebullience. Back at Lowndes, ripping down the curtains, turning on lights, the first time in almost six years, they shared with Pearson the last of their "hoarded fruit juice." The next day Herring heard Churchill conduct popular songs at Whitehall, and even danced with a policeman. V-E Day, with Japan still hostile, "was a dreadful anti-climax." Bryher stumbled over a corpse at the entrance to Lowndes.[29] On June 8, Clement Atlee declared the Labor Party triumphant *before* the election. H.D. hoped "the poor dear old fellow gets in again."[30]

After seeing *As You Like It* in Regent's Park, Bryher imagined being among "an original audience of apple sellers and citizens," slipping back to the age of exploration and high anxiety and, in an instant, "understood the words instinctively, through the heart, not the mind." Still "two selves." Bryher kept her "psychic powers" under wraps, yet she slipped in and out of time during these suspended days. Early in June, she was wandering among stones and wildflowers when an "empty building" manifested. "It was just a mid-Victorian house leaning drunkenly towards a by-now nonexistent neighbor," she wrote, becoming "aware of a room cluttered with dark, massive furniture and two elderly ladies sitting beside a fireplace," the atmosphere holding "deep apprehension in the room." Bryher dismissed this vision as war strain; diagnosing it beget "hallucinations," driving "us back to the blank spaces of our beginnings."[31] Imagined as stuck in a backwash, the two women in Bryher's vision manifested her anxiety.

Beset by weakness and headaches, H.D. saw Dr. Ernest F. Blumberg, who diagnosed low blood pressure and anemia, treating her with vitamin injections. As a holiday, she planned Stratford to consult a new doctor friend who loved astrology, Elizabeth Ashby, living in Gloucestershire, part of the Cotswolds, home to an eleventh-century cathedral. In June, H.D. set off on her own, while Bryher described her day: London Library, loads of laundry, "galloping around like a squirrel."[32] H.D. stayed at the "Swan's NEST," thinking of Helen's conception.[33] Bryher, happy that H.D. was "in the Elizabethan vibration,"[34] reread Morris, screened visitors, avoided the phone, and monitored the shell-shocked Cole, suffering from shingles.[35] H.D. returned to Lowndes on June 15, Bryher still installed, an unusual reversal, though she would visit Cornwall for the election drive.

Bhaduri visited Bryher in Cornwall on June 28 for the actual election. For H.D.'s sake, Bryher tried to forestall his marriage to a girl his mother thought "wrong," and besides, he wouldn't have time for séances.[36] In one of their last summer meetings, he "saw" a boat, with two women aboard; one sent "signals," the other landed on a cliff looking back. H.D. and Bryher thought it was them. Finally, they let the seer find his way.

Before writing *The Fourteenth of October*, a preparatory vision inspired Bryher, as the "Norman Conquest" almost "repeated itself in 1940." History taught that Normans brought "high culture," though they actually "were the Nazis of their time." While she wandered Cornwall, invasion "*unrolled itself*, with the regular movement of the waves across the sand, exactly as if it were happening in front of me." Bryher *saw* armored invaders, ships, warfare, occupation, much like her dream of the Trojan War after she first met H.D.[37]

At the end of June, then, H.D. found herself alone at Lowndes, tempted by the Morris table, surprised that it awoke under her solitary presence. H.D. asked the table, "Is there anything I can do?" It answered affirmatively.[38] Leaving for errands, she then hurried home to the table, stopped answering calls, telling friends and even Bryher she was working on notes.

In July, H.D. returned to the Swan's Nest, but, as Bryher reminded, the local regulations permitting war-weary tourists only a maximum of four nights, so sent telegrams, cobbling together several stays. Donning a Sir John persona, Bryher started "corresponding like mad" with her lawyer's "man combing the district," arranging for H.D.'s stay at a Mrs. Denny's rooming house—she could even rent it for six months if desired. By this point, Bryher, eager to see and talk to H.D., suggested mid-August as "indicated" for an Avon meeting.[39] H.D. roomed at Cygnet's Repose for their anniversary. The couple exchanged letters. The day before, Bryher sent "[a]ll my love for the 17th," regretful they could not "be together that day," but shared her "gratitude for all the years especially the blitz years, London would have been quite unendurable without the Kat and I doubt if I would ever have found my way to our work sans Kat."[40] Trance work was "our work."

H.D. discovered, while away, G. Wilson Knight's *The Olive and the Sword* (1944), arguing that Shakespeare shored up the "golden age," and after Hitler, "Europe will be saved by an English 'messiah' Shakespeare."[41] She agreed that *The Tempest* was "the most perfect work of mystic vision in English literature."[42] Further excited, she told

Bryher that Shakespeare made "*war* a background for even the light comedies—& comedy-tragedy!" She felt at home with theater people. With Bryher in Cornwall, H.D. diagnosed to Dobson, then in sweltering Rome, that "separation is good, in fact, a necessity," a remedy for claustrophobia, though they would both be back "before their Virgo birthdays."[43]

H.D. invited Bryher for a weekend. "Our thoughts must have crossed," responded Bryher, who remained in Cornwall, writing it was a "[q]uestion entirely of rune."[44] H.D. was with Shakespeare, Bryher relived Norse legends, Perdita was in Paris, and Pearson returned to New Haven. The same month H.D. was at Stratford reading Pearson's glowing review of *Angels* in *Life and Letters*, calling them "victory or peace" poems, comparing the two sequences to Eliot's poetry, sharing "the same single affirmation of the strength and endurance of the civilian in war, who through Apocalyptic fire gains integrity, and through integrity rebirth."[45] Receiving proofs from Herring, she wrote from the Noel Arms, calling the review a "treasure." H.D. basked in Avon territory, visiting Ashby, who took her on a trip to Stow-on-the-Wold, a small market town, where many roads converged, once dominion of the Normans for plunder and trade. Susan Pearson sent H.D. lovely chocolates "wrapped in their stork paper," which she devoured between plays. Vibrating in Stratford, with strangers asking her for directions to Shakespeare's house, she strolled by the river, steadying "reality."[46]

On this journey, H.D. resumed "Good Frend" poems, sparked when she laid roses for Shakespeare with Herring and Bryher. These poems rescued Claribel, not in the *Dramatis Personae*, encrypted in *The Tempest*: "Read for yourself," she told readers, "[s]he is not there at all, but Claribel, / Claribel, the birds shrill, Claribel, / Claribel echoes from this rainbow-shell."[47] Shakespeare's Alonso, King of Naples, marries his daughter, Claribel, to the King of Tunis, launching a ship to carry the bride to her groom. Robbed of his throne and exiled by his brother, Alonso, Prospero conjures a shipwreck. Key for H.D., Alonso finally regrets marrying off his daughter. The King's brother, Sebastian, taunts, "You were kneeled to and importuned otherwise / By all of us; and the fair soul herself / Weighted, between loathness and obedience." Claribel married against her will, the last trace of her before H.D.'s resuscitation. With this in mind, Bryher explained H.D.'s identification with this figure, having been "born in Pennsylvania, married to an Englishman in 1913 but treated throughout the First War almost as if she were an alien, and now in the second one 'come home'" to offer tribute to Shakespeare.[48]

H.D.'s *Good Frend* became a fifteen-plus-eight-stanza poem, amounting to twenty-three, marking the bard's birthday, the first part "*The Tempest*," the second, "Rosemary," the memory-botanical. H.D. absorbed Bryher's talk of famed explorers Raleigh and Drake, who enacted a "politics of empire."[49] She paused over colonial exploits that *The Tempest* itself addressed: "They'll come to no good, / (No one ever did) in that colony, / What d'you call it? Virginia?" All rivers, Avon included, were "Indigenous" ones, conquered.[50]

H.D.'s Claribel never marries the King; she weds her soul, akin to Eurydice's inner garlanding. "I plotted to efface myself / To steel in un-noticed to the rail," H.D. spoke through Claribel, sensing "the music in the stone," able to "touch the letters and the words, / reading the whole as the blind read." H.D. relied on the stubborn optimism of her ancestor, who knew flowers and herbs healed; she upheld midwives, "witch women," witches, and deliberately speaks for her, uncertain why the bard chose "[t]he invisible, voiceless Claribel."

> I only threw a shadow
> On his page,
> Yet I was his,
> He spoke my name;
>
> He hesitated,
> Raised his quill
> Which paused,
> Waited a moment,
>
> And then fell
> Upon the unbolted line;
> I was born,
> Claribel.[51]

Without a foothold, Claribel drifts among lilies, attends a funeral. H.D. was simultaneously aware of Bryher's experience of "unrolling" images from the distant past, "[d]im shapes or shapes seen and sensed clearly / ... / Unrolled mysteriously / Into the future." H.D.'s Claribel "wandered near" and "wandered far": "The others thought that I had lived, / The others thought I had died."[52] Readying to join H.D. for a weekend play, Bryher found herself, strangely, immobilized in Cornwall.

* * *

Although the Allies hammered away with all-out aerial firebombing of Japan, the emperor remained belligerent. Einstein, a pacifist, had warned Roosevelt in 1939 about the possibility of Germany engineering such a weapon. Roosevelt ordered a top-secret project to build one in the remote New Mexican desert, the Los Alamos Laboratory, run by Dr. J. Robert Oppenheimer, who conducted the first atomic test on July 16, 1945. When "Trinity," a plutonium bomb, detonated, a hundred-foot steel tower evaporated. Such absolute obliteration put H.D.'s beloved invisibles at hazard.

President Harry Truman presented an ultimatum to Japan on July 26, 1945, after the Potsdam Conference: surrender or face a "Rain of Ruin." Calling it "the greatest achievement of organized science in history," Truman ushered in the "age of atomic energy."[53] Destruction *was* confirmed, although terrible aftereffects were not. The first strike, a uranium bomb, hit Hiroshima, a well-placed port with large military and industrial installations on its periphery. The *Erie (Pennsylvania) Daily Times* headlined, "HIROSHIMA IS WIPED OUT." Only three days later, with no sign of a Japanese surrender, Nagasaki was bombed, this time with a plutonium implosion bomb. Truman's ultimatum gave little time for the Japanese to assess the destruction; plunged into an "[i]mpenetrable cloud of dust and smoke," no one could see, at first, much less measure, the damage.[54] Documentary footage later showed victims scorched by radiation burns, unspeakable mutilations, radiation sickness and cancer, as well as despoiled lands. The longed-for peace gripped world consciousness, leaving many disassociating from its horrific price, a blinding luminescence, not resurrection, not a poetics of *Trilogy* or *Four Quartets*.

Particulars of the devastation slowly leaked out, yet H.D.'s unconscious, like that of many people, absorbed it, already primed by a sympathetic chord with the East, believing herself to have "incarnated" selves from Tibet, Japan, and India. Bryher could not shield H.D. from this huge world-changing catastrophe. Revealing how slow, unwilling, and shocked Bryher was to comprehend the attacks, there was no "daily" letter on August 7, but she wrote every day following, encouraging H.D., "[Y]ou would be wise to go on staying there," safe with Shakespeare, and finally, reducing the incomprehensible to an admission, "Was astounded to get your postcard of the burst waterspout! I can't help feeling that with all this new atom bursting we shall shatter the weather! I think the possibilities are very terrifying though I am told it is also for good."[55] A bit like telling H.D. *Those guns were our guns*.

The same day, the day before Nagasaki, a weary Herring hoped this "atom business won't upset H.D." too much. Bryher recalled Doris coming in with a newspaper, announcing that "thousands were dead, the war in the East was virtually over," though she couldn't respond.[56] No one could. Declarations of peace passed over H.D., unable *not to* incorporate the suffering of "enemy" civilians, and "watched in [her] imagination, migrations of hordes of starving people, driven like cattle in search of pasture. It was only food that mattered."[57] V-J Day was declared on August 14, 1946, not the Helios H.D. imagined.

After six years, Herring felt "the election and the atom bomb had drained" joy. Over a hundred thousand died instantly, as if swallowed by the sun. H.D. wormholed her way into incandescent bodies. Soon the phrase Bryher heard on the street resounded: "They should never have let it happen." Herring incanted "tomorrow never comes" with acute understanding. The war consolidated his friendship with Bryher; he was grateful for her keeping their troupe together, for her "inexhaustibly unrationed sympathy, good humour & sense."[58] Such war bonds were bittersweet.

Writing Pearson, H.D. felt trapped: "I wonder if we ever W I L L get away?"[59] All doors closed. On August 14, still in Trenoweth, Bryher was bleak, but shot out a tentacle to H.D. at Lowndes, with all "so desperately uncertain" over when "the Victory holiday begins." The official unconditional surrender of Japan was announced on Bryher's birthday, September 2. Edith planned "a monster birthday" for them on the 17th; they went, everyone feeling half-dead.

Dowding visited H.D. on the anniversary of the war's beginning, September 3. During tea, she described one of "their" airmen, Ralph, whose first words were

"*Advallon*," and "love all." But Dowding blanched, caught off guard by H.D.'s intensity. Letting down her defenses, she told him his boys wanted to communicate with him, encouraging Dowding to "set up a sort of inter-communicating radio."[60] After all, the hero had set up "Chain Home," a series of transmitter-receiver stations to detect high-flying aircraft, and himself believed he had contact with astral beings. Dowding, though, recoiled, even positing that her messages came from "a lower order of beings."

At the end of September, Bryher went to Eckington for relief from the strain of peace and H.D.'s accelerating obsession with Dowding. Herring's garden flourished with "last roses and great big scarlet dahlias," and his pig "look[ed] very fat and scrubbed." But the real kicker was Bryher momentarily dropping epistolary guard, relaying she had "an interesting talk with Z. last night. It is uncertain, he feels, whether we will stay in England or not. He does not feel we can decide for a year or two." This recounted contact suggests she either had a solitary encounter or wanted to comfort H.D., but it was likely both. This "Z" also thought Herring would "probably find a friend." Herring, she told H.D., was "even more pessimistic" than her about London, "so it may be Avon, Arizona, after all!"[61]

At this crucial moment, Bryher was blind to the extent of H.D.'s shattered psychological state. H.D.'s purpose in Stratford evaporated when faced with the great catastrophe. The details of the A-bomb were released by the time H.D. rejoined Lowndes; Bryher thought she should see Ernst Freud for calming tablets. They tried going duo on the Morris table, but it refused to respond; they spoke of the danger of going solo, but H.D. secretly trekked to the table—recalling coldness at earlier séances, finding her private ones induced "cold fever." Her "chest seemed stuck to [her] backbone," something she felt once when a V-2 dropped in Hyde Park. "Frozen," she was "like a tree that bends over in an ice-storm."[62]

In late September, Bryher left with Herring to "tear around the Cathedral" in York, gathering material for her Norman Conquest novel. York had gone downhill, "all cheap, trippery shops"; it took two visits before the verger opened the crypt. They unearthed a Mesopotamian horn from a festival of Mithra, an Indo-Iranian "god of light," linked to friendship, oaths, and bonds. With Bryher away, H.D. sat back, pulled the Morris table to her. She received messages from those self-identified pilots who died under Dowding's command. They craved contact. Perhaps this gave H.D. control over chaos, yet she sat with a searching, overcaring mind. The table became analyst, tapping into fears of nuclear annihilation. She summoned pilots, and H.D *through* Delia began narrating *Sword*: "It was as if they had been waiting for a new telephone-girl to learn the technique of the switchboard, before they manifested." The pilot Ralph, her dearest, confided, "Lost we are found." Strong stuff, with Lad, Larry, and John, their "burning intensity" matching her own.[63] She recorded "numbers and letters" with her right hand, while her left "held on to the table or to *them*." Without Bryher, she "felt like a battery, negative or positive … that had to be completed by another."[64] She had nearly wept blood for over five years; now Dowding dismissed the airmen who contacted her with messages that she thought might deter a Third World War.

Behind the scenes in summer 1945, Pearson contacted Bryn Mawr's English Department, encouraging a sponsored lectureship for H.D., with her "five war-shattering years," "anxious to visit her own country and relatives again." She scrawled teaching notes between her private table sittings. In November, she received an official invitation for spring, surveying modern poetic tendencies, and immediately put out feelers to friends to select a dozen poems they liked best for her to muse over as models. "You must not let me down about this," she challenged Pearson. "Think it out; it takes some thinking or feeling rather. What would you take across Lethe if you were RATIONED as to memory, about 12 short poems." Anxious, she told Pearson she couldn't "L I V E with people, if possible; want to be private," to gain "her bearings."[65] Mentioning Lethe, she packed for a sarcophagus, decorated with loved poems. She applied to several ministries for her visa, Bryher submitting them.

H.D. and Bryher joined the Dobsons on the eleventh day of Christmas, at H.D.'s notion, where they speculated on "the not known."[66] As if sensing something amiss, Herring wrote Bryher, "[Y]ou and Hilda—and I are 'real fighters' not because of our *guts*," but rather, "One fights to be soft and gentle, and you and Hilda tangibly do."[67] But H.D. was unable to fight for softness during this "peace" year. *Flowering* caught the group portrait: "we are voyagers, discoverers / of the not known."[68] H.D. read *Lost Horizon* with its "lovely shelter Shangri-La."[69] Sizing up the novel's paradise as corny, she was to find herself, as Bhaduri predicted, high in the mountains, as if declaiming: *I, Claribel*.

LINE 5

VIKING 1946–1961

20
Losing One's Mind to Find It

Bryher counted on accompanying H.D. to Bryn Mawr in February 1946. Pearson wrote he was traveling to the Yucatan to "see ruins made by something other than bombs, and a civilization which has simply disintegrated, not [been] blasted to hell."[1] Herring chorused, "The new age has gone wrong."[2] The grotesque dissonance between what H.D. imagined as postwar joy and the violent outcome led her to a breakdown. Addicted to counting, she "re-lived the first war, the second war and pre-visioned a third war."[3]

H.D.'s Claribel poems written in Stratford simmered as she entered a "death in life" condition. Bryher rescued a case of Veuve Clicquot Ponsardin 1926 from her mother's storage, but the bubbly did not drown H.D.'s anguish. That January, the U.S. indicted Pound for treason; pleading insanity, he was committed to St. Elizabeth's Hospital. Bryher was blunt, saying he was "lucky to be an American" because "the two British accused" of treason "were both hung." After witnessing Nazis murdering her friends, "one a Quaker lady and the other an elderly man," she could not forgive.[4]

The December before, "Ralph" among the several self-identified the airmen who visited her, prompted Bryher to type their séance notes to send with a letter from H.D. to Dowding, who predictably responded that *he* relied on "Z" in his home circle. On Valentine's Day, he returned the pair's notes, with no encouragement. H.D. sank into a depressive paranoia, induced partly by excessive weight loss, spiraling into agitated grief. She accused her nearest and dearest, Bryher and Perdita, of espionage, tapping the phone. Deluded that St. Paul's Cathedral was blown to smithereens by a small atom bomb, H.D. rushed to the roof, under which she had spent most of the past six years, and hurled a fur coat from Bryher to the pavement, poised to jump. H.D. finally raced back into her flat, shutting herself in her room.

Dr. Ernest F. Blumberg initially diagnosed H.D. with meningitis, an acute infection, often called "brain fever," the very malady that had afflicted Mamalie. H.D. rejected Bryher, associated with bombs and séances, sending her to "the martyrdom of the cave," their basement shelter.[5] Although Bryher kept H.D.'s condition under wraps, hoping for recovery, Dobson suspected something was awry. Late in February, Dobson delivered her "weekly flower arrangement" to Dr. Blumberg, and he explained meningitis drove H.D. to the roof, "meaning to throw herself down." He ordered absolute quiet for the patient. Dobson now reread H.D.'s Valentine greeting as a farewell, referring to "the past years" as "all so full of change and terror too, of those war years. *Just take this little note with love to all*" (italics mine).[6] Bryher finally told Dobson the humiliating truth, that a doctor and a nurse had taken her place by H.D.'s side.

In March, Bryher confided in Pearson, telling him H.D. kept repeating "[Y]ou see, I have a Puritan spirit," wanting to be present for V-E Day, which had already passed. Bluntly, she told him H.D. had had "a complete nervous break after all the years of the war."[7] Rooming in the basement, Bryher engaged Dr. Dennis Carroll and a team of nurses and sought Sachs' input. Nine days later Sachs reassured that "such delusional episodes often are apt to disappear as surprisingly as they come." He advised that Dr. Schmideberg step in "to help and heal in a difficult and responsible situation."[8] The latter proposed Kusnacht Nervenklinik, where Nijinksky and Joyce's daughter were treated.

After having "shared five years and a half of the Blitz and its hardships together," Bryher crept from Lowndes while H.D. slept, the nurse asking her not to wake patient.[9] The pair lost regular contact from April through August, their first major gap in communication. Early in April, Herring brought H.D. an amarylis; he was the only one she allowed in, which he chalked up to his being in the country during most of the war. The Hendersons called, and Herring asked if he should "shut them up." "I can't think how you went through the last month," Herring commiserated, assuring Bryher she "did everything right all along the line."[10]

Dr. Carroll tried extricating H.D. in March on a Red Cross plane Bryher arranged. She resisted moving from Lowndes. The doctor took the plane himself, exploring treatment at Kusnacht. On Herring's next visit, H.D. invited him into her room, pottered about, tidied books, and offered tea, though she waited until he drank his before touching her cup. Unaware of the full Dowding saga, Herring thought H.D. needed "to persuade herself that the war really *is* over." Osbert and Edith remained "naive" and "passionately sorry for her," but had no inkling of what H.D. "might be feeling," while he considered her "a prophet" who "feels 'in touch,'" only in a nightmare "about a tenth of the time." After all, Herring published "Writing on the Wall," which gave him insight into the deliberate quality of her visions, readying herself to "serve as instrument of warning as to what is ahead." His more down-to-earth calculation was that the "strain of war plus the atom has sort of short-circuited something." Only Perdita, Herring, Schmideberg, and Pearson knew the scale of H.D.'s breakdown. Herring, Bryher wrote Pearson, was "kind beyond words, slept at the flat when the night nurse failed [to appear] once, did our shopping."[11]

Back in London, Dr. Carroll sent a more clinical report to "Mrs. Macpherson" about "Mrs. Aldington," both husbands in absentia.[12] "[H.D.] continued to be deluded & hallucinated in much the same way as before," though "the delusions have been less frightening & have not involved anything at all likely to produce violence—either defensive or offensive." H.D. was plagued by sudden urgencies "to look for something, to tidy something frantically," engaging in the very obsessional rituals she attributed to those in *Tribute*. The difficulty lay in the sedation initially induced "to lessen the danger to life when continuous war crisis began."[13] Dr. Caroll persuaded H.D. against moving heavy furniture. Tenants in the building had already complained of "noisiness." He warned he might be forced to institutionalize her.

Dr. Carroll ordered glucose in orangeade with sodium amytal, a powerful barbiturate, synthesized by the Germans in 1923, not to be given indefinitely. Insulin-shock treatment to reduce motor activity was used in the prior decade to treat some schizophrenia. In fact, it produced half-dead coma-like states, followed by confusion, but the thinking was that with increased injections, equilibrium could return. In April, H.D. told Dr. Carroll, as if she staged the event, that if she slept she would leave her body for two years. Deciding against "over-prolonged sedation to avoid certification," the doctor saw two clinical avenues: either find a "home" in England, or "she go to Switzerland so the stigma of certification would not follow her," where "[the certification] would be temporary only & terminate on arrival." Dr. Carroll knew Bryher wanted H.D. safe—and uncertified. Patient from March onward, he finally maneuvered H.D. mid-May into a biplane headed to Zurich.

* * *

Shortages in fuel precluded anyone living full time at Kenwin. Bryher and Schmideberg moved in with Elsie Volkart in her small cottage in Pully, near Lausanne. Schmideberg greeted H.D. when she arrived in Zurich, while Herring visited Bryher, still grazed by rejection; they sought comfort hiking at Zermatt, Sir John's favorite spot.

From Kusnacht, Dr. Theodore Brunner withheld all communication from Bryher, and she was not to visit. Inevitably, H.D. asked who paid for all the loveliness, the excellent food and coffee. He asked Bryher, "Was sol ich ihr antworten wenn sie wieder fragen nollte?" (What shall I answer when she asks again?)[14] The doctor repeated Bryher's fairy tale that the "British Bureau" covered it.[15] Extremely gracious, H.D. told Dr. Brunner that something "outside" influenced her, in a good sense; she denied hearing voices. At the end of May, Perdita arrived and had a more or less successful, if truncated, visit.[16] By June, H.D. had improved, even napping after lunch an hour or two. Only occasionally a "black feeling" returned, like the one suffered in London. Dr. Carroll had always brought two cigarettes, a custom Brunner resumed. She asked for an inexpensive watch. Enclosing a bill for 69 francs, he asked Bryher how many "side expenditures" the patient could make.[17]

By mid-June, Dr. Brunner considered Dr. Carroll's diagnosis of "paranoid schizophrenia" overreaching, though H.D. continued to fuss over various pieces of jewelry, clothing, toothpaste, powder—but providing objects a metaphoric valence was her usual poetic practice, now magnified. At the end of June, Dr. Brunner assigned H.D. an apartment at Seehof, a more private ward that had one room for herself, another for a caretaker. However, H.D. remained convinced the war had ended only three months earlier. She penciled a note to Dobson that she had "walks about the garden," remarking on each rose variety, sure "*we* will all be much happier and able to continue writing in *real* content and security."[18] H.D. could not pin down *why* she was at Kusnacht, or *why* Bryher had vanished.

Recovering was almost worse than the illness. As H.D. gained clarity, she suffered a loss of "family," Bryher, almost a "second mother."[19] On July 18, the day after their hitherto sacred day, H.D. heard voices warning that her caretaker was a bad person. She requested to see Schmideberg, who visited and managed to alleviate some of her delusions.[20] Later that month, though she walked to the village on her own, she frantically knocked on the doors of other patients.[21]

Dr. Brunner allowed H.D.'s letter of August 9 to get to Bryher. The patient had been unaware letters were held back. The doctor's censorship widened the gulf between her and Bryher, who now trod carefully: "delighted to get your letter and to know that you are enjoying being among the mountains," "feeling better and enjoying the good air."[22] H.D.'s *Flowering*, just out from Oxford University Press, enjoyed a fine success.[23] A week and a half later, not sleeping or eating, H.D. had a relapse. The maid locked her in, trying to persuade her that her life was not in danger, as she believed. Dr. Brunner thought H.D. needed a private nursing home, unless she quieted.[24]

As if from behind a screen, Bryher cared for H.D.'s affairs, her flat, her possessions, her writing. Faulting Bryher, readers seize on H.D.'s "a sort of shock treatment" and her initial fury at "captivity."[25] The insulin treatment was terrible to endure, yet, again, it was as if she and Bryher, together, had been peculiarly saved from London's postwar scarcities, and likely from electroshock treatment, available in Great Britain by 1939.

After initial contact, our couple tread carefully. H.D. wrote, "Today is your birthday," after their twenty-sixth "birthday octave," the first without fanfare. "Perdita wrote me, saying she hoped we would soon be together again," one parent's plea to another. "You are catching up, though my brand new 6 0 still makes me the grandmother," H.D. rebooted.[26] For H.D.'s birthday, Perdita sent flowers, bonbons, and pralines. Watching "sudden Byronic thunderstorms" from "the shelter of [her] old-fashioned, wooden shuttered, oak-framed window," she sealed her letter to Bryher "with so much love." H.D.'s mental health improved after communicating with Bryher and Perdita, yet she still refused food. Bryher visited on September 19, bringing fresh clothes; H.D. complained that the visit was too short, yet she dated her recovery to this anchoring reunion.

Dr. Brunner read his patient's letters before sending them, discovering H.D. sent out a feeler to Dr. Carroll in London: "This dreadful time we have all had—but I am sure, the beautiful things suffered only a temporary eclipse, and since the war ended, three months ago, they have returned."[27] The same day, she wrote "Dearest Bryher." Then, through September, H.D. plotted escape. Though rapprochement was slow, H.D. recognized Bryher's love, sending "just the right things," among them her "Norway shawl & your beautiful faun, embroidered house-jacket," connecting her to "memories of travel and happiness." She savored her "sleeveless blue-checked hemwork" that magically "merged into the landscape," a brightness "after the dark & drab of London." Grateful for her comfortable "over-whelming duck-bed," she noted a "washstand, with soap dish, à la corfu," insisting she missed Bryher, keeping cigarettes for her in a box beneath her bed.

Eager to rejoin Bryher, H.D. asserted she was cured, craving contact, now willing to move anywhere, wherever Bryher decided, even the U.S.A.[28] During the second half of September, in her more private room, she regained strength, gratified she now could contact Bryher and Perdita, wanting "just to keep in touch & let you know how grateful I am for everything that you did for me—both of you, all the time." "How they feed one here. And the coffee is so good," she assured, walking among apple trees, nearly stuffing some "fragrant cammomile" in her envelope, then "thought better of it." Sealing it, she was "surprised to find [her] fingers reminded [her] of the Acropolis."[29] Dr. Brunner may have flagged this communication as hallucinatory, but in fact it reassured her family that H.D.'s usual method of hitching herself to landmarks of Corfu and Cornwall was intact.

Bryher strategically directed H.D. back to her creativity, to her "Good Frend," inspired by their trip to Stratford; it worked. After Bryher's initial visit, H.D. reread her Claribel poems. They provided realignment, but as expected, the more she recovered, the more she probed what "had happened." Bryher slowly divulged details. H.D. didn't understand why Schmideberg had to "clear" her for release. This led the relentless Kat to dig. Ultimately, digging led to greater empathy for Bryher, who repeated that after these years, H.D. had "to gain some weight and strength before London is possible again." Slowly emerging from hell, like her stealthy worm in *Walls*, she "ate" her way out. Normalizing her situation, Bryher observed that "thousands of English have come out here to have a good meal," with hotels across Switzerland booked.[30]

Eager for communication, "Kat" wrote "Darling Fido," giving the number to Seehof, planning to wait downstairs near the office after breakfast at 10:00 a.m. and 5:30 p.m. after tea. H.D. was "heart-broken," unaware why they "made this fearful effort to pull away from England." Simultaneously, she assigned her "frenzy" to their separation. This initial contact released in H.D. a range of contradictory emotions: frustration, anger, and gratitude. She missed "those evenings, when you polished & I stitched & Pup was in & out." Apologizing for acting "an all-around pest," H.D. wanted "the old 'family romance' on its feet again." The same day, at 6:30 p.m., she shifted course. Agonized by the memory of sending Bryher to the "CAVE" and "God—if only I had known," she admitted she went "too far with the table & all that," and it was "clear fixation—dissolved now completely."[31] She remembered rushing down one night to burn the séance notes, thinking they drove a wedge between them, then faintly recollected "the wars super-imposing & Pup going away—& then, both of us so very very sick.... *Why* did it ever happen?" H.D. "nearly died of heart-failure & love when [she] heard" Bryher's voice, and promised "to go on writing. Don't be afraid at all."[32]

But Kat was impatient, threatening escape by train and the return of all Fido's gifts, if not rescued soon. As usual, Bryher bundled her in "a rug that [she] live[d] in." With residual anger at the "shock treatment," she decided it jolted her into wanting "no more injections," so the "shock" was "good too." Glimpsing a return to things as they were, and might be again, H.D. penned five notes to Bryher on September 21, eager to "keep the connection, now that it is made again." After a "huge breakfast," she posted herself in the office in case Bryher called.

H.D.'s second note was sent at 9:30 a.m. Getting better, she imagined herself in a *Magic Mountain* setting, where patients convalesced from tuberculosis. Knowing Bryher's germ phobia, she taunted, "Why me, darling Fido?" Bryher's reluctance to visit resulted from hurt and the very phobia that precluded she train as analyst, fear of insanity! In her third note, at 11:00 a.m., she thought phone wires were cut, preventing Bryher's calls. Kusnacht was lovely "but without contact, perilous," a place with no familiar inhabitants. With Bryher a "good object" again, Kusnacht turned "trap." By her fourth note, at 1:30 p.m. that afternoon, she was on a "rampage," concocting a plan for Bryher and Schmideberg to kidnap her. "*I will not stay,*" she insisted. A sense of menace shaded into a noir script. By 5:15 p.m., unaware this was the doctor's method of severing H.D. from war associations, *thirty* letters from Bryher had never been given to her.

If things were not so terrible, H.D. would have realized, as she later did, her kidnap plot was hilarious: "Come right up to my room. The Bear knows the way. Park the car where you can keep an eye on it." She identified with the persecuted, having all the dramatic cues in motion. More fantastically, she suggested Schmideberg "bring his gun and some extra gun-men—if necessary." They would lunch in her room, then, while Brunner was distracted, Bryher could provide her British passport; she had "signed no papers" and "asked no questions."[33]

In fact, H.D. recollected flying "10 hours over the weirdest country I have ever seen." Dr. Carroll apparently helped her "visualize a gentle cross-channel flight." But for all she knew, they headed to Tibet. Her arrival at Kusnacht was "'better' than the most lurid film," locked in a room with barred windows, with "three hefty men and a nurse," who she thought "were trying to kill [her]." The treatment reinforced her paranoia, especially when "[a]n enormous prize-fighter, weighing a ton, ordered [her] to lie down." Another man, who she called "the waiter" for his lighter build, apologized after "shocking her."

Airing such details of her experience bridged H.D. toward stability. Complaining about "slippery note paper & no ink," using a pencil, "like ploughing through rock," she explained her refusal of food was due to her pathogenic belief that Bryher and Perdita had "written [her] off." Now she knew "we will laugh soon & I feel dear Fido, I can now discuss with you, intelligently the *Tibetan Book of the Dead.*" H.D. grasped she left her body between April and August, approximating a "bardo" state, marked by the *Book of the Dead* as the first forty days after death. "What dreams, but once out, how we will laugh," she rounded out.[34]

The next day, H.D. dedicated each volume in *Trilogy* to Fido, and insisted of *Beowulf*, "*The book must come out*, even if I publish it myself.... *I don't like this obscurity* of lovely scenes & images & historical imagination like yours!"[35] No longer focusing on grievances, H.D. now walked by the lake, watching boats dock, flattered the landscape, feeling "wonderfully restored." Finally, she asked, "Could you put me up, somewhere else, if you are too crowded there?"[36]

In late September, H.D. still had paranoid thoughts. In one instance, she believed Bryher fought her case on the outside, so wrote, "Fido *you must not come here*. They may trap us both & then I would never be free. Trust *no one . . .* nor *anyone*," deciding it was best Bryher remain "free & outside—looking after Perdita," repeating, "*Please do not come.*"[37] Common enough during "regular" communication, *Come right away* usually changed to *Don't come yet* to *Come now*. But these shifts were now heightened.

H.D. returned to a kidnap plot. Schmideberg knew "the little lane that turns into the Seehof gate." She asked they bring dark glasses. Bryher and Schmideberg visited on September 26, though H.D. was disappointed they did not kidnap her, writing Pearson nearly nine months after her mania began, "[W]e were both a little crazy but I dont [sic] yet fully know why I was brought to this place."[38] Her mood shifted back to grievance. She scolded not having time even to give three apples she saved for Bryher, who "hurried so." H.D. now claimed she "spent 30 years" attempting "to give [Bryher] freedom." Nearing sanity, she struck out, "*I am not free*. Could you send me a pencil sharpener."[39] While "seeing" Bryher had "changed everything," in a three-page letter H.D. was still unsure how she arrived at Kusnacht or why she received no visitors or calls at Lowndes. Who gave Dr. Carroll "authority" to "charter a biplane?" She was sure the plane landed in "two countries," and questioned, "Are they enemy territory?" Although the sanatorium was scenic, the staff and doctors spoke German. Dr. Brunner's son crassly asked her where she had been "confined for insanity in England," which dialed H.D. back to her appearance at the Temple Bar, so she knew she could testify "here or in England." With habits returning, she catalogued the causes of her breakdown, making "anxiety as to [Bryher's] welfare" initial, followed by "famine neurosis," based on real deficits. H.D.'s angst now was that she had to be "cleared" of insanity. In a more quotidian fashion, she noted everyone had "bad colds." The same day a coloring kit arrived.[40] Dr. Ashby also helped by reassuring H.D. that "much of [her] apprehension" stemmed from "language trouble." H.D. also learned of other patients coming "for shelter, after 'our' atrocities on Dresden."[41]

In late September, Bryher gently restated the "reality" of their situation: "You have to eat a lot, gain weight, sleep well, and listen to no voices other than those of Dr. Brunner and his staff, then very soon they will send for me and we can have the happiest of times together again. *I am waiting for that*" (italics mine). Painfully sensitive to H.D.'s sense of disunity, Bryher added, "Do eat, my love, and sleep and very soon we can be together again." H.D.'s letter, bombarding her with questions, crossed with this one, forcing Bryher to clarify matters over and over until frustration broke out: "[Y]ou want to know what has happened and why you are at Kusnacht. Last February you were taken very ill and for a time I think you did not know any of us." Dr. Carroll, Bryher explained, was unable to obtain a plane for just herself, thus H.D. shared it with a woman and her children. They flew to Paris, landed to refuel, and that was it. Bryher underscored there were no enemy countries now. H.D.'s papers were safe, Perdita expected "full recovery," and it was "not a question of sanity or otherwise, it is just that you, like hundreds of other English people, have suffered a terrible strain through the war."[42] There was no case, no trial, no defense, not even a diagnosis; she was simply one of many in Switzerland there to eat and to recover—these repeated words were balm.

H.D. replied to "Darling Fido" that she loved her new pencil sharpener, turning to her *Book of Verse*, ready "to forget all this misery." She reassured she did "nothing but remember, scenes, pictures, from the first hour I met you at Bosigran, to the last, when I met you & Bear here." Withdrawing from heavy sedatives, she regained her sea legs, inspired by "the thought of seeing [Bryher] again," "able, at last, to turn round & explore this lovely neighborhood." Vowing not to grumble, she walked halfway to Zurich, regaining confidence in her physical ability. After being "in Purdah," she asked if Bryher could send a "house-coat" as transitional object.[43]

In October, Bryher wrote daily on half-sheets of Kenwin letterhead to ensure she *could* write every day, without seeming parsimonious. Mrs. Ash, Bryher reiterated, had packed up her clothes, protecting them from moths. Happy to have mad-money again, H.D. found a lovely tea shop and would eat, she reassured. Bryher left for London at the end of October, telling H.D. that Mrs. Irwin, who stayed at Lowndes, only had "one egg in five weeks." Once Dr. Brunner gave the green light, Bryher promised to "gallop to fetch [her]."[44] H.D. walked to the train station every day. She cherished a new bag, "soft faun suede linings with the little Fido-band (signifying their enduring bond) tucked inside," handmade by a "little man in Vevey," fondling it while reading *Merchant of Venice*.[45] She packed and repacked her "Rosalind Robin Hood bag," "eternally grateful" that Fido "*took all this trouble, to get me in touch with the only possible means of saving my life.*"[46]

Bryher advised H.D. return to Claribel poems, mostly drafted before Kusnacht. To her own surprise, H.D. launched a second half, a lyric essay meditating on Elizabethan poets, to companion the poems, together titled *By Avon River*. Pumped up with reunion, she drafted this essay during her "protected" time between Bryher's visits to Seehof, bearable with their "line" repaired. With two manuscript copies of "Good Frend" in *Life and Letters*, she rededicated it, "Remember, the whole is for you."[47]

"[R]econvening *Claribel* all morning," she reassured Bryher, adding, "Do not worry about *Voices*, Fido dear. That is all over now. But there is still the common-or-garden voice of inspiration & of love—may I keep that?" Admitting she had gone "too far," she observed her ego rising from ashes, and imagination, defined as "inspiration & of love," arrived. She asked about friends, especially Bhaduri, who came to Switzerland before returning to London with new fleece slippers by way of Lugano.[48] What about "his voices," H.D. wanted to know? Bryher couldn't answer. Natural for H.D. and trying for Bryher, the former was overeager to "pick up the old thread & to keep in touch with everybody, for Perdita's sake & yours." H.D. knew now that tranquilizers prescribed in London, according to Ashby, were a "two-edged weapon," like most things in H.D.'s life—they can trigger "dream states, & imaginative terrors were apt to follow the treatment."[49]

H.D. found Kenwin too isolating and would likely, Bryher knew, prefer living partly alone and sometimes together, their "normal" style. H.D. was jubilant that she would be "installed in Lausanne," where they could have long teas and talks. She thought

Schmideberg might help her "work out why [she] was so ill."[50] The irony of this will emerge later. A link to Freud, he visited again, putting to rest H.D.'s "phobia" about Bryher's next London trip, explaining he also needed to see two patients; he brought an "exquisite flowering cyclamen" from Bryher. H.D. listed her needs: "1 Umbrella 2 raincoat 3 bed jacket 4 Stockings 5 Scarves 6 Clothes brush." At last, Bryher's letters "meant everything" to her, explaining her "melancholy" arose "because [she] felt so cut off";[51] now she was freed to get "busy with Elizabethan 'Notes.'"[52] Reentering the visible world, H.D. wanted all news, even about politics. Bryher was excited "that you really are so much better."[53] In mid-October, Bryher rejoiced to Pearson that "with a bang dear Hilda came to herself." At last, H.D. "remembered [her]," though "dreadfully sad" because "she implores me to take her 'out' and of course that I cannot do."[54] *Not yet*, at least. H.D. wrote Dobson she felt "a little snappy and cross," "forgotten by the great world," and missed "gossip of fruit trees."[55] Justifying not writing earlier, she believed censorship was in force. From London, Bryher gave H.D. gossip of Trenoweth's quince crops and cheered her with Herring's compliments about her Stratford poems.

At the end of October, Bryher cleaned shelves in Kenwin, making a library nook for H.D.'s books.[56] H.D. again insisted that "something really *must* be done about [Bryher's] own MSS."[57] Something was being done, Bryher announced: "My Beowulf is coming out in France," after Sylvia and Adrienne now found a translator.[58] During their bitter separation, H.D. learned, Bryher fine-tuned the manuscript. Venturing to London in November for two weeks, she explained there was greater difficulty getting there these days "than to travel around the world," reiterating she had been in constant contact with Dr. Brunner, listing Dobson, Doris, Cole, May, and Bhaduri, each wanting to see her in London, "but we had to send them away," now all were pleased "that at last you are better again."[59]

In retrospect, Bryher's visit on September 19, initially unsatisfying, H.D. dated as "resurrection." H.D. "gained a ton to Brunner's delight," writing "The Body's Guest," a "general resume of 100 Elizabethan poets," to form *Avon*. She now believed that "the whole (almost) of poetry following Herrick is a reflex or reflection or simply the crest of the wave, broken, spreading & loosing its intensity." "I hope I am not trespassing on your 'period,'" H.D. credited Bryher's writing as inspiration.[60] This was the H.D. that Bryher knew. Giving her 200 francs until her return, Bryher hailed H.D.'s title, "The Body's Guest," as psychically joining "Girl-Pages in Elizabethan Literature" from 1917.[61] A few days later, Perdita celebrated that H.D. would soon "be prowling at large" until "a nice Cat's Home can be found." Noting the sanatorium was "ideal," with its "change of air and mountains," Perdita knew her mother prized independence.[62]

H.D. asked Bryher, while in London, to locate her "huge brown" bag containing her tapestry work with "smaller pieces," some "big needles," and one of Perdita's tapestries.[63] The moment Bryher heard of a revived desire to weave, she sent "a heap of the most beautiful wool." H.D. used it to savor their past, "going over & over & over the separate strands & colors." Sated enough with Bryher booking rooms at Hotel Glockenhof in Zurich for November 20 and 21, she refined "Body's Guest."[64] They agreed Lausanne would calm Hilda's "unk." After surveying hotels, Bryher booked Hotel Alexandria, for at least a month, until they decided what was best; the residents of Pully "were just down the road, it will be as if we were together."[65] H.D. decided against an extra room added to Volkart's, for proximity's sake, especially after she saw the "tiny" rooms.

Anticipating Bryher and Schmideberg's arrival at Kusnacht on November 19, H.D. gaily wrote, "The Guest progresses. I want to dedicate it to Bryher. The dates framed September 19 1946–November 19 1946."[66] She conceived her essay as "going to a party" with these Elizabethans.[67] Defying chronology, she moved among fifty-six poets whose themes echoed the couple's own: creativity as counterforce to war, the exiling of those too inspired or those who loved unconventionally. The essay intimated what H.D. struggled with at Kusnacht:

> Remembering Shakespeare always but remembering him differently. Reach from your bed in dark night, half in dream or delirium. What do you seek. Your hand, touching the bed-table, remembers the telephone—but that was in your room in London. You are somewhere else; you want something? There are no friends near. You murmur a number, 1-5-6-4 and follow it with another, 1-6-1-6. But that is no telephone number.[68]

Birth and death dates entered as codes, combinations unlocking lives, set her free to communicate again. From this opening, she shifted to the plague's height in 1600, with Sir Philip Sidney "(b. 1-5-5-4)" fighting in one of the period's "small wars," killed in battle September 1586. From a distance of three or four hundred years, H.D. found kinship with wartime poets. With Bryher, she turned to Sir Walter Raleigh, who supplied the essay's title. While in the Tower, he wrote, "Go, Soul, the Body's guest." With the status of a Dowding, Raleigh put down the Spanish Armada.

Bryher reported long queues in London; Lowndes was "desolate" and "odd" without "Kat," she unguardedly wrote. The Irwins, mother Norah, an old friend of Bryher's mother, and her daughter Grace (who trekked back to London with Bryher in 1940), sent love, and Cole confirmed London was "very shoddy & sad & drab."[69] That winter of 1946 everyone in London had the flu. Bryher was "ravenously hungry all the time and there is literally NOTHING to eat."[70] H.D. felt guilty not to share the "distress in London" and begged to read *Beowulf* in French, urging publication in English.[71] Bryher prepared H.D. that she planned divorcing Macpherson in New York in the New Year; she looked forward to seeing him, "that is all," "quite independent. I stay with Pup."[72]

H.D. had an "undulation Froide" (a permanent) and trusted Bryher would help her exist in her breakdown's aftermath.[73] She combed over notebooks for "early notes & the Viking sequence & our trip to Greece." Of course, "Dowding came in," now realizing his "work" was not, as he himself said, "the same sort of thing" as theirs. He sent her his latest book, *God's Magic*, which she dismissed as uninspired. Aware that obsession with Dowding had contributed to her breakdown, she told Bryher, "I was quite all right, the minute I saw you or the minute after, though I was ill and furious before that, to think of the waste of time & anxiety."[74] H.D. and Bryher had to work their reunion carefully, like tapestry; their history of intimate exchange held during this suspended animation, this tense intermission. Something had broken, but once more, they were spared.

21
Tidying Up Modernism

H.D. literally "wrote herself out" of the sanatorium, seeing herself in William Morris, his writing "nagging at him constantly like one of his compulsive physical activities, a mental equivalent of his netting or his weaving."[1] For such word-weaving, she required monk-like solitude and a "wire" attached to Bryher, who needed to come out as a writer, and to tend to others, helping Perdita settle in New York. H.D.'s stop after leaving Zurich was the Hotel Alexandria in Lausanne, ten minutes from the small house in Pully where Bryher and Schmideberg boarded.

Once established, H.D. described for Dobson "odd French parties, all rather hectic," comparing herself to the "sleep-walking English," who "stand agape before shop windows, trimmed with boughs & red, green & silver balls."[2] Our couple celebrated Christmas, Bryher bringing wooden "WISE MEN" as well as "two new, marvelous Zurich scarves" and a box of chocolates in a "pine nest."[3] Before venturing to New York, Bryher left behind several Hermann Hesse books to nurture the idea of H.D. nesting part time in magical Lugano, an Italian-speaking Swiss town, then known for its quaintness, warmth, and tropic plants. Hesse lived in the nearby mountains. Both H.D. and Bryher luxuriated in Lugano, a "postwar land of peace and color where without restrictions we could do what we wanted."[4]

After Kusnacht, H.D. temporarily shed her initials for "Delia Alton," signaling her writing as mediumship. Animating Claribel, she started hunting out "lost, hidden or invisible characters," observing her "little flaire [sic]" for it. Bryher inspired H.D. crossing "the Rubicon" through *Avon*. "It [Avon] belongs to you," she established Bryher as buoying her from sickness back to health.[5] H.D. had penned another "invisible's" story in *Pilate's Wife*, sent out in 1934 and rejected. Returning to *Pilate's*, she named the wife not Claudia Procula, her actual name, but Veronica, after the woman who apparently gave Christ, before his crucifixion, her handkerchief to wipe his face, which returned with the image of his face imprinted. This transfer enthused H.D., whose quest progressed through psychoanalysis and then, peculiarly, through the couple's war endurance and séance work. In *Pilate's Wife*, H.D. compared Christ, a Jew, to the Eleusinian, calling to "mind the grain, its sowing, its reaping, the manifold beauty of its various stages of growth ... its final medium-death, or new life, which completes re-birth on the earth-plane."[6] Now, in 1946 through 1948, she probed other invisibles and rebirths, notably Elizabeth Siddal, fashioned as a kind of Magdalene in Violet Hunt's *Wife of Rossetti*. H.D. plucked out the tragic love of Gabriel Dante Rossetti and Elizabeth Siddal for her next novel, *The White Rose and the Red*, knowing "poetic insight" itself could "reveal the true self, or soul, of the loved one," discovering Rossetti failed at this task.[7] Bryher saw the novel as gothic Victorian in the best sense.

More memories returned alongside Hunt's biography. When May Sinclair died on November 24, 1946, she left Pound, H.D., and Aldington select titles from her library. Bryher established a cabinet at Pully devoted to these books, teleporting the poet back to prewar times.[8] Pound's *Spirit of Romance* arrived, leading H.D. to reread Dante. In anticipation of Lugano and meeting Hesse, she spent early 1947 in Lausanne, delighting in Dante, which she read in German and Italian. The latter language her weakest, she practiced on Hesse's "Blauer Schmetterling" (Blue Butterfly), using her "little four-barrel dictionary, three by five inches."[9]

The new year sent Bryher to New York to see Perdita, Pearson, and Macpherson, planning hours with Sachs, only to learn he died from heart failure on January 10, 1947, just before she arrived; again "just too late."[10] Grieving her analyst's death, she divorced Macpherson, gave him a villa in Capri, and together they enjoyed *Annie Get Your Gun*.[11] The Moores "terrified" Bryher, who learned Marianne would not eat because her "Mother could not." As a result, Marianne suffered kidney trouble and rashes.[12] New Yorkers were "mildly surprised over our interest in food." Bryher assured H.D. that Perdita looked "wonderfully well."[13] This visit culminated with Bryher's deed poll application, the legal means to make a name change, legitimating her invisibility, H.D. congratulating, "Much much love to Deed Poll B R Y H E R."[14]

In Lugano by May, H.D. further touched up *Sword*. Hesse's poems inspired her to see fig tree leaves as butterflies "just out of the cocoon," and she heard herself "clatter[ing] across the rough stones of the market-square in Ticino sandals."[15] Plotting outings in Lugano, "about a hundred pilgrimages to be taken," making "a list of the hundred shrines and churches that [she] wanted to see,"[16] she drafted "Dante and His Circle," notes never published, and revealed Beatrice, as the male poet made her abstract screen, while as a bisexual writer, spiritual love required shared ecstasy and dual gender, at the "circle" all seekers occupy, partaking of "inspiration & the gifts of illumination." Here, she reaffirmed the "soul or mind as spirit or ... anima, & the *Sanctus Spiritus*, the church, is feminine."[17]

H.D. lived at Lugano's Minerva Hotel from May through September 1947, while Bryher entertained guests needing postwar relief in Lausanne. Mrs. Ash came to Lausanne, bringing H.D.'s case of "tapestry work, all wool." Bryher thrilled at witnessing her guest's enjoyment of "Switzerland with a passionate intensity,"[18] also hosting Doris, Herring, the Glovers, Miss Voules from *Life and Letters*, and the Irwins. But when Grace Irwin, who traveled with Bryher on her way back to London in 1940, and her mother arrived in Lausanne, "poor Grace" had "a sort of nervous collapse, a little like your illness," she told H.D., "she was almost unable to speak."[19] Grace's mother, a survivor of two world wars, also succumbed to mental collapse. This left Bryher to arrange their care. "You couldn't do better than the Brunners," H.D. chimed in, who were "a sort of miracle to [her]."[20]

Still basking in Lugano on her first solo trip, she had "four weeks of solid bliss," grateful for "an orgy of bells yesterday evening."[21] Perhaps a counterintuitive choice,

H.D. revised *Sword* to explore *what happened to Dowding*. He occupied a partly destroyed home "near the air-fields" and confessed during his Valentine visit in 1946 a lack of will to live. Did this despair stem from her "letters from the dead," saying they were *his* boys, who "wanted to live and had gone on living"? She had envisioned pilots "wandering about the air-field," chanting, "*No one wants us round, / Walking on the ground.*" The couple's séances were "wave work."[22] As a true obsessive, or traumatophile, H.D. returned to the very experiences that pushed her over the edge; she walked a razor-fine borderline.

With Dowding calling his spirit guide "Z," *Sword* distinguished the couple's "Z differently" as "Z was a graph on a map," "really a bee-letter or the bee-letter." "Words are not necessary," and "the airmen could have dictated a graph on a map," or "zzz-ed a detailed line-drawing." Echoing her grandmother's musical transposition, H.D. thought she could have "transcribed the rhythm, the up-and-down, the pause and beat of ruled music-paper." Differentiating Dowding's afterlife of "summer-land felicity" from her own, she was sure no music sounded "more compelling than the zzz-zzz of a great bumble-bee in the summer grass," indicating that "now" was confluent, adjacent to eternity, or the ample imagination of poets, lovers, and assorted Gnostics. For the quotidian, H.D. read the London *Times*, although usually a week old when it arrived. From London, Bryher confirmed the Morris table was "nicely polished and made secure," looking forward to "Summerdream," the second installment of *Sword*.[23] Although H.D. had burned notes in her frenzy, she cannily kept carbon copies.[24] In Lugano for their anniversary, Bryher loved the hotel's "gay rooms" and "unforgettable piazza," stoking H.D.'s regained well-being.[25]

* * *

Aldington reignited correspondence with H.D. in early 1947. She sent him the first part, *Wintersleep*, of *Synthesis of a Dream*, her initial title for *Sword*, later the subtitle. Treading carefully, he admitted that "the assumed name [Delia] is punk." She'd lose her "H.D. reputation in sales"; if she wanted "real secrecy," he instructed, this wouldn't do it.[26] Two months later, she asserted that "*the five year 'reality' of bombs, fly-bombs and V2 was by far the less stable or 'real' than the world of the imagination.*" "Delia" acted as "a sort of protection," explaining, "[I]t does not really matter WHO wrote DREAM! It stands or falls or fades on its own merit or its own 'message'": those in authority "could do something with the atom—better than smashing cherry orchards" (italics mine).[27] Her creativity depended upon being nourished by the unknown.

Aldington recognized H.D.'s allusion to Morris' poem "Golden Wings" in *Sword* and offered to send Mackail's Morris biography. Several days later, Bryher herself sent the biography, saying it provided dates "at any rate."[28] Almost as much as Bryher, Aldington raged that Pound might have left Italy after Pearl Harbor but instead chose to "go against America."[29] Yet Pound had introduced H.D. to Morris, whose utopian 1890 *News from Nowhere*, with its unkind look at the nineteenth century, imagined

1955, when ancient buildings were demolished.[30] Indeed, postwar Europe was recovering from war wreckage of "ancient" things well into the 1950s.

From Sinclair's stash, volumes of Henry James arrived. H.D. concluded he put "Victorian America right on the map," representing a London vanishing, coming into being, and now gone.[31] James further inspired H.D. to texture Morris into Siddal's story in her emerging *Rose*. She shared Aldington's "long breezy letter, re the private Morris" with Bryher. He pointed to "declining energy," though Morris walked every Sunday to breakfast with Edward Burne-Jones. Although a socialist, he "inherited shares in a copper mine" and "was preaching revolution while laboriously reprinting Chaucer at 40 guineas a copy."[32] Reminding Aldington that she "gave [Violet Hunt] the title [*Wife of Rossetti*]," his visceral facts electrified H.D.—"such magnificent material for a PLAY," drawing her back to this second-wave Pre-Raphaelite. This very name of the Pre-Raphaelite Brotherhood spelled time-travel, as if asserting "before Raphael, came I." Those in the movement conceived themselves as part of a Round Table, devoted to gallantry and love, a boys' club until Morris revived it. H.D. thought she could "toss off the biography" in spare moments.[33] "I can SEE these people, and hear them talking. All you have to do is a little home-work.... An idea?" She defined her sensory imagination as akin to "[w]atching a play, reading a book or hearing an old mystery-story is, living it, if one has the artist's passion." This was the quality in H.D. Aldington admired when they were lovers. She even envisioned this creative nonfiction as screenplay, with Garbo playing Siddal, and Laurence Olivier, Rossetti.[34]

During September, the couple began sorting their papers for what H.D., amazed, called Pearson's "redoutable redoutable H.D-Bryher shelf" at Yale (she wanted "table" to recall the Morris vehicle); the professor asked for *all* the "H.D./Bryher correspondence."[35] Salvage and reconnection occupied them. With only the short tram ride between them, they met regularly, taking stock and discussing their writing and traveling plans. Late in November, Bryher went to London, and then the West Indies with Herring and Perdita. Writing from "Ocean View Hotel, Barbadoes," Bryher enchanted Kat with "[g]reat sweeping seas all speckled with surf, green water, blue water, white sand, and patches of rocks and thyme and sapphire," along with "the dwarf yellow plant."[36] H.D. could vicariously reenact enchantment, seeing Bryher in "the summer-sea that you took me to in July, 1919."[37] Her echolalia of love notes anchored them in time.

* * *

On New Year's Day 1948, the Order of Merit, "the highest award if not the highest, ever given in England," was conferred upon T. S. Eliot.[38] Bryher supposed H.D. should congratulate him. Then H.D. read in the February 20, 1948, *Lausanne Gazette* that Pound, at St. Elizabeth's, won the first Bollingen Prize for *Pisan Cantos*. The *New York Times* headline read "Pound in Mental Clinic, Wins Prize for Poetry Penned in Treason Cell." Shivers, muted empathy, and fear comprised H.D.'s myriad responses to the devolution of her old beau's genius.

From London in February, Bryher assured H.D. that "Summerdream" (the second half of *Sword*) read like "a series of poems"; she wanted to discuss its gorgeousness when back from grisly London.[39] On Valentine's Day 1948, H.D. asked Bryher to greet the Morris table, its "circumference" that "turned from a nightmare to the Summerdream." Bryher gave the "inspiration and help that made [it] possible, the keeping faith."[40] H.D.'s dedication embedded Bryher's "secret name" and words:

FOR GARETH
This isn't lost, it will go on somewhere.

Bryher hoped notice of Pound's award would not derail H.D., whose closest contemporaries had achieved accolades she deserved, so Bryher thought, especially for her masterpieces, *Trilogy* and *The Gift*. H.D.'s willful imagination, changing to Delia as amanuensis, made her impervious to fame. If anything, these public awards redoubled H.D.'s fascination with "invisibles" like herself and Bryher, feeding H.D.'s revision of *Wife of Rosetti* as a modernist Victorian potboiler.

* * *

On April 18, 1948, Monnier's Mercure de France published a French translation of Bryher's *Beowulf*. When its translator, Helene Malvant, expressed uncertainty over the title, Beach said, "If the French have never heard of Beowulf they are going to do so now."[41] London publishers rejected its wry exposure of Blitz conditions. After a reception for "Beowulfians" on April 28, Sylvia heard "loud praise" from Madame Paul Valéry and others, "all thrilled and charmed by [Beowulf]."[42]

While H.D. enjoyed Lugano, Beach and Monnier boarded their first airplane in May 1948 to London, also visiting Oxford and Stratford. Bryher spared no expense, putting them up at Grosvener's Gardens, booking them seats at the Palladium; if that were not enough, she endowed an annual sponsorship for a French writer of Monnier's choice to travel in England, although she couldn't fathom why anyone would care to do so.[43] On this "historic trip," Rita Winsor, Bryher's trusty travel agent, handed them each £10 for pocket money at the station. Herring cooked dinner, and Beach thought he'd make a fine matrimonial catch.[44] They made a pilgrimage to Lowndes and to the site of the bombed-out *Beowulf* tea shop, and influenced the BBC to broadcast the novel.

While Bryher's novel traveled with Monnier and Beach, H.D. reread Violet Hunt's 1932 biography that started with her lineage with one of the Brotherhood, William Holman Hunt. Rosetti's story was known, Violet boasted, but not "the truth about the woman he married." After her additional research on Dante and nineteenth-century spiritualism, H.D., in May 1948, launched *Rose* in earnest, setting it during the Crimean War (1854–1856) and the American Civil War (1861–1865). In a shadowy "pre-incarnation," she wrote, "'I am Elizabeth Siddal,' she said to herself, and I can't remember the last war.'" Hunt strongly implied Siddal committed suicide due to

Rossetti's neglect; H.D. made war terror causative. Borrowing details from *Wife* about Siddal's poverty, dislocation, and invisibility, H.D. emphasized her penumbral engagement to Rossetti for nine years, granting her more mobility and intellectual freedom than being a wife. Hunt wrote, "Lizzy was probably the first woman to live by herself in a bachelor's flat."[45] At Chatham Place, before their marriage, the couple read Wilkie Collins' *The Woman in White*, its author a laudanum addict like Siddal. The Brotherhood's John Everett Millais nearly gave her pneumonia, staging her as Ophelia in a chill bath with soggy drapery.

Musing she herself might *have been* oversensitive Swinburne, H.D. paired the poet as likeable companion for Siddal. She configured Pound as once Rossetti, and Swinburne, once Shelley. Lives haunted, reblossoming into other lives. Not yet aware Gregg had died in a raid in Plymouth in 1941, she was the electric current engendering her version of Siddal or "Sid," misused by a cavalier lover. *Rose* enacted H.D.'s "realistic" turn, as she exposed industrialism's ill effects, rampant pollution, disease, and class disparities. During the Pre-Raphaelite Brotherhood's existence, cholera raged in England, coinciding with the attraction to the color red. Rossetti, as Hunt reminded, ignored dust and dirt, craving fresh paints and models, not a clean house.

Bryher, meanwhile, longed to meet Mr. Ruskin in H.D.'s novel; he rated Siddal's own drawings better than her husband's.[46] Siddal finished a tapestry with Morris in the "book-within-the-book" (the meeting between Morris and Siddal that did not happen), the element Pearson most admired. Morris, central to her sense of Siddal's merging art and love, left Oxford as a "budding parson" for "art, in place of—or because of God."[47]

Researching Rossetti, H.D. "found the clue, not only to Dante and his School of Love, but to the whole subject of psychic communication," discovering Siddal and Rossetti went to a famous medium on Sloane Street, where "Sid" was spotted alone as well. Séances like hers and Bryher's happened a hundred years prior. *Rose* crossed geographies, pivoting between London's "Academy" for Spiritualism and the U.S., where the persecuted psychic Fox sisters fled to a Connecticut farm and smuggled runaway slaves to freedom in Canada. Their grandmother, H.D. improvised, "was what in the old days they called a wise woman, what in older days, they burnt for witches."[48] H.D. attributed these discoveries to "dear old Beowulf," which "has brought back to [her]" fantasy and realism.[49] The pair stitched themselves back together through writing—and war writing.

At Lausanne's Hotel de Paix during winter 1948, H.D. was still "deep 'communicating' with the Pre-Raffs."[50] By June, she had uncovered spiritualists in the mid-nineteenth century through Jean Burton's *Hey Day of the Wizard*, Bryher's gift that H.D. credited for saving "[her] life and [her] Red Rose." Burton tracked the American medium Daniel Home, with his extraordinary telekinetic powers, "a Swedenborgian" who believed in "a future world where like found like, its inhabitants grouped by affinities."[51] Although her husband remained skeptical, Mrs. Browning was devoted to séances and Home himself. In Home's agonizing trances, furniture spontaneously moved, bells rang without his "doing anything." When he moved to London, friends set him up at the Spiritual Athenaeum at 22 Sloane, H.D's old street.[52]

H.D. now saw that nineteenth-century spiritualism *premeditated* modernism. Spiritualists in America and England, "overwhelmingly anti-slavery, felt that they played a very definite part in determining the outcome" of the American Civil War.[53] This gratified H.D., feeling similarly about Bryher and her own presence in World War II, "feeding the light." She told Bryher that Napoleon III "wallowed" in spiritualism, and Hawthorne, not a full believer, found the very atmosphere of Florence "induced transcendental speculation."[54]

In July 1948, H.D. reread most of Eliot, recalling Bryher spoke about "some sort of 'initiation,'" with *Four Quartets* sculpting "a new set of values." H.D. understood Eliot's rest cure in Lausanne in late 1921 while composing *The Waste Land*, with his double-sexed Tiresias. He might have "overdid it" too, "putting down dreams, messages, circle experience," having two years training in Sanskrit, as well as partaking of "the mazes of Patanjali's metaphysics" under James Wood.[55] Further regrouping, Bryher suggested H.D. grant Pearson power of attorney over her literary estate, with Harold, her brother, executor of American funds.[56] They spent their thirty-year anniversary at Hotel Minerva in Lugano, coinciding with a telegram on July 17 from Pearson that Macmillan had accepted *Avon*.

* * *

H.D. concluded she belonged "to the Henry James, Pound, Eliot vibration—in time, I mean."[57] Emphasis on "in time." Her *Rose* pitted itself against both Pound's and Rossetti's creative process. Not a huge leap, as Pound had early styled himself on Rossetti, with outlandish attire and addiction to Italian tapestries and illuminated manuscripts. "Gabriel was reputed to be the most selfish man in London.... But Gabriel Rosetti had his moments," sentences reflexive of H.D's sense of Pound.[58] The war drive shaped these artists, abusive to the women in their lives.

Through *Rose*, H.D. puzzled "what DID HAPPEN" to Pound through Rossetti. Finding Pound's early *Spirit* "unaffected," she assumed the "change" arose in London during World War I but not "IN it."[59] Sponsoring his son's travel to London, his father begged H.D. "not to drop" Ezra. The couple put Ezra "on the couch" in October, his birthday month. After having "re-read all Ezra's poems very solemnly," Bryher pinpointed "flashes of extreme beauty, an extreme coarseness, an obsession with 'fame,'" unable "to surrender anything to a living human being," concluding, "Eliot has pity, Ezra the lightning of genius and the desperation of narcissistic mania,"[60] "a strange dis-humanity."[61] Liking Bryher's diagnosis of Pound, H.D. asked to repeat it to Aldington. "By all means," Bryher replied, reformulating the treasonous poet's "equation" of "gold=fame" led to "disintegration,"[62] while her money shored up lives in danger of extinction, particularly her beloved's, whose *Sword* acted part-cure.

Herring believed in *Sword*, writing H.D., "You hold about fifty threads all at once, and you 'establish' each one so deftly and vividly." Writing next about *Rose*, he connected it with Bryher's *Wulf*, both turning to "the period of Hastings by going BACK to it, but by leading one FORWARD from the times before ... terrific living freshness ... All most moving."⁶³ H.D. met up with Bryher at Hastings in *Rose*. At the same time, Pearson continued to want "Elizabeth as the truly central focus."⁶⁴ Encouraging him to reread it, H.D. hollered, "William Morris was as bored and distressed by Crimea as you are by atom-bomb."⁶⁵ Pearson wanted her to modify her novel, though H.D. was now "in no hurry to get" either *Sword* or *Rose* published.⁶⁶

Engaged in "a real, grand tidy-up," wintering in Lausanne, H.D. readied herself for her sixty-third birthday, counting as her "NINTH" sabbatical, if divided by seven.⁶⁷ She "grieved" that McAlmon sold an "ordinary, friendly little note."⁶⁸ Bryher thought McAlmon burned all her letters,⁶⁹ explaining to Pearson that before 1924, she and H.D. telephoned or were together, while the latter reviewed "all the Bryher letters," sending everything except a train scrawl, with "only the Seehof gap," a lacuna explicable through a note indicating the doctor forbade letters.⁷⁰ Faced with loose ends, Pearson's loyalty cheered H.D. as "the only ONE person to mention in the same breath with W. Bryher." "No one else."⁷¹ He convinced them that "[t]he important thing is to keep the mass of material in one spot" for "critics" and "historians."⁷²

H.D. set her lands in order—"a great chore, a back-break, a head-ache at first," but having "the old MSS boiled-down, dated and re-typed," very satisfying.⁷³ Threatening a bonfire, in April 1949 she revived *Madrigal*, conceived after World War I, giving her "a new lease on life." Still guided by Victorian discretion, she assured Bryher, "[Y]ou and Perdita do not come in," not wanting either to feel exposed.⁷⁴ Writing "finis" to *Sword*, *Rose*, and *Majic*, among her personal favorites, they awaited readership.

* * *

During 1949, H.D. resided at Lugano's Hotel Croix Blanche from April through October. Every day she frequented Café Saipa for coffee at 10:00 a.m. and 3:00 p.m., penciling notes to Bryher. In July, H.D. met Hesse, who lived off the beaten track. Taking a bus to his village, Montagnola, she found "the last red house on earth." Rendering this in *Sword*, she "brushed through the tangle of spiraea," scrambling up slopes, breaking "a branch of wild oleander."⁷⁵ She almost turned away, but then she spotted a "large notice," reading " 'Bitte, keine Besude' (please no visits)."⁷⁶ Clutching her invitation, she walked behind the house, coming upon Frau Hesse, who was at least twenty years younger than her husband, with "Bowen's age, black hair, cut short," and "slightly aggressive." H.D. joked she expected "to be asked next for [her] passport." Then the tall Hesse in his summer suit and large straw hat appeared. Almost immediately, he rushed away to get a book, a Powys in German, excited that H.D. had met him once with Gregg. The Hesses led her through woods filled with lilies, oleanders, and cats, arriving at a stone bench, where the couple occupied their "rustic chairs or thrones" before a "perfectly wild" and "cared-for" tea house built by a friend as " 'gift for life.' "⁷⁷ While H.D. relished "a most remarkable apricote-cum-cream cake," Hesse located himself among "the first writers" to incorporate Freud's ideas in his work.⁷⁸

Fierce hot rains hit Lugano, while H.D. wished Bryher "happy *Avon*" from Saipa, where she read *Paradiso*. When Bryher telephoned, H.D. felt her presence "in the room."[79] Not up to meeting Pearson, Perdita, and Bryher in July in Venice as planned, nor ready to plan August in Florence, H.D. remained in Lugano.[80] All she could "cope with" was an hour and a half talking about manuscripts. Long discussions and walks were out for now. Sending regrets to Pearson, she encouraged Bryher to take him sailing and sunbathing and for Bryher to visit en route.

Pearson's research on Hawthorne sparked Bryher's interest; her mother had kept *The Marble Faun* by her bedside.[81] They arrived in Florence during a Liberation Day celebration and witnessed "lots of men turned out in white and scarlet" with "long leather boots and two in coats of mail." Pearson "went off his head"; we gather Bryher did too. It was "the first time in [Bryher's] life [she] had a suit of chain mail in [her] hands."[82] They saw Botticellis, newly cleaned, "hung on a plain ash-grey background," their colors screaming. At the Nationale, she was awed by a "wonderful ninth century Anglo Saxon ivory carving" that Pearson spotted, "very strange with horse headed figure—most exciting for me." Although museum treasures had been well-preserved, Bryher noted, "[T]he bridges have gone except for the Ponte Vecchio." While H.D. was reinforcing *Rose*, Bryher wrote her from Florence, "[T]he mood is Browning": people rose late, wandered in moonlight, drove to the Duomo. "[E]normous green melons" lined stalls, yet the "rubble—shells of houses" was omnipresent.[83]

On the same trip, Pearson, Perdita, and Bryher visited a villa Hawthorne had rented for two months, which "Norman photographed wildly." A lady told Bryher in English that the Allies had destroyed her family home of over four hundred years, then guided them to "Donatello's house in the Marble Faun." Pearson loaned Bryher Hawthorne's unpublished journals, and she discoverd "the Browning group did nothing but have séances and try to contact Dante." Now they "were off to fence and Montegufoni," "Corfu-like." On her desk, H.D. perched postcards from her "suns." The porter at Croce Bianca recognized "Mrs. Bryher's" voice when calling, which she did nearly daily. Pearson deemed *Avon* ideal for Christmas gifts. Bryher's *Wulf* was still unfinished.[84] Before arriving in Lugano, Bryher sent H.D. a new blue dress needing no alteration. H.D. celebrated their "years and years," feeling "younger and happier than 31 years ago, when you miraculously came in through the Bosigran front-door."[85] She enshrined Bosigran as her awakening.

In August, Melitta arrived in Lausanne to accompany Schmideberg to the Psychoanalytic Congress in Bellagio. That very day, he collapsed from "drinking hard." Sending them off to Bellagio, Bryher took Pearson to lunch at Hotel Paix, showing him the dining room where they celebrated Christmas dinner, as if laying the groundwork for H.D.-Bryher scholarship. Bolstering H.D., limpid from a sirocco and storms, Bryher reassured that Pearson deeply admired *Sword*.

In September, H.D. *invited Bryher* to meet Hesse, offering to wait in the pub near the bus stop while she interviewed him. The Hesses knew "a lot of refugees in the U.S.A., probably some of your bunch," H.D. referred broadly to Bryher's interim-war work.[86] Bryher, she advised, would have "to go so carefully, as he is well entrenched," "really a frail giant." Only Freud measured up to Hesse's "character, intellect, perception."[87] Eventually, he ran "down the path as if we [H.D. and Bryher] were doing him a favor by coming to see him."[88]

H.D. reread *Rose*, frustrated with Pearson's requests for lists of poems already written: "I do not see why N[orman] holds [the Rose] up."[89] Bryher too reread it and, in fact, believed it to have "best-seller" material, reading like an early Richardson; when she arrived for their birthdays in the next month, they would discuss it.[90] H.D. was, however, accurate that the year she finished this time-travel novel was an ideal time: 1948 marked the centenary of the "Pre. R. Brotherhood," coinciding with a Whitechapel Gallery exhibit of their work. H.D. sent both *Sword* and *Rose* to Macmillian in September; both were rejected. She judged *Rose* to be "purely romantic, with no personal catch, like *Sword*." Yet there was a catch: both books likely stalled because of H.D.'s insistence on "Delia Alton." Paradoxically, her confidence swelled: "[*Sword*] is really a tour-de-force & tells the history of the 'table.' ... [I]f ever a book was fool-proof (with *Avon*) it is *White Rose & the Red*."[91] H.D. finalized "Delia's" version by September 1949.[92]

Amid dirt and mess, Bryher altered the Pully residence's "scaffolding"; "the front is done," she felt, as if H.D. were in the room with her, "Yes, unk, probably wished you were here to see the new façade."[93] Bryher didn't want H.D., in her fragile state, to unwittingly run into "Melitta in a funiculaire" and would play Frau Hesse to "ring [Hilda] round with protective beacons so that the masses who appear to converge on Lugano are kept off."[94] Perdita visited H.D. in September; they were just talking about Bryher when she called. H.D. kept thanking Bryher, almost painfully, "from way back in the beginning-of-time," admiring her Saxon chapters for *Wulf*, loving especially the Morris-like little wooden houses.[95]

Back in Lausanne, Bryher dove into "trade," keeping her father alive. First, she converted H.D.'s annual allowance of £1,200 to Swiss francs "at the full rate," proudly announced the next day, when the pound dropped from 17.80 to 11.50.[96] The same day she alerted Kat about a transfer of 1,000 francs to her bank, insisting there was "no need for [H.D.] to economise in any way." By September 21, the Swiss were in a panic about the franc, so Bryher told H.D. to stuff a thousand francs in her trunk and not to say anything to the bank.[97]

Detached from money, H.D. fretted about the atom bomb.[98] Fearful herself, Bryher wrote, "[E]ven with a devalued pound you can still stop among the pomegranates."[99] A trade frenzy helped Bryher cope with the fact that "the Russians exploded an atom bomb near Persia on July 10th."[100] She aligned geopolitical events with economies, finding in the atomic testing "the reason for this unprecedented summer."[101] Kenwin's lawn was scorched brown. More sanguine than in coming years, desperate to soothe H.D.'s nerves, Bryher claimed to be "quite cheerful and as you know pre the war I was not."[102] These obsessional letters reached a manic crescendo when Bryher took "precautions last night," changing H.D.'s pounds to francs: the dollar skyrocketed, worth three francs ninety, and, caught up in her wizardry, Bryher enthused, "now four francs fifty!"[103]

In October, Bryher, off for London, invited H.D., who was not up to its "crowds and vibrations." Bryher visited Dr. Edward Glover "to carry with her to Switzerland 100 tablets [of Veronal] for use of Mr. Walter Schmideberg, a patient of mine," to treat his delirium states due to advancing alcoholism.[104] After Bryher returned to Pully, Schmideberg suffered a hernia, had to wear a harness, and stop smoking—and heavy drinking.[105]

In June, H.D. started a "Prague sequence," entering the eighteenth century for *The Mystery*, tracking Moravianism to its reincarnation from underground. Bryher sent a reference book, *Herrenhuters*, in 1949, fueling H.D.'s renewed interest.[106] "The document is fascinating beyond words, and one could write a volume on it," H.D. responded to the even more stunning gift of a letter from Count Zinzendorf.[107] Indeed, his letter spawned *Mystery*. Understanding H.D.'s appreciation of letters, alive with vibrations, Bryher also sent a valentine from the Count's son, Christian Renatus.[108] After H.D. finished *Mystery*, she reversed gears: "NO—I want my books to wait a bit, possibly the last one, later as for Moravia 1458 (I think)—some time off—as for 500 years—as N. suggested, that is 1958," all three in "the W. Morris tradition."[109] She packed for La Paix, stuffing her manuscripts into several largish bags, asking Bryher not to manifest until she readjusted from Lugano.[110]

As part of her tidying up, Bryher settled an annuity on Beach, as she did with the Moores, and later Aldington and his daughter, Catha. No one knew what the world was hurtling toward. Tottering under "vast benevolent works" and "Bryher-power," Beach often sent a "fierce bear hug."[111] Of her friends, Beach and Herring knew best the extremes Bryher went to make lives more livable. The former called her gift-giving a form of "clairvoyance," an intuitive ability to recognize need.[112] Bryher was a "fairy with a wand,"[113] a "guardian angel," a "Mr. Santa Claus."[114] Yet Beach was not enthusiastic about *Wulf*, now *Fourteenth of October*. With H.D., Bryher anticipated publishers rejecting its "preoccupation" with the less "visible world,"[115] though showing more confidence in distinguishing between the English who liked *Beowulf* from those preferring the not yet published *Fourteenth*.

H.D. and Bryher presided, sorting and handing on, Pearson officiating their pre-wake. Bryher had to disappoint him about her mother, who "burnt all her letters before she died."[116] By 1950, Bryher had entrusted her letters to Pearson, after removing "one or two things best destroyed," H.D.'s practice as well, perhaps hoping the lacunae in their lives would call out to readers. With their "Chevalier," they trusted the future to weave their lives together.[117]

22
Cold War Romances

I am sailing on with *Helen*.

—H.D. to Bryher, September 30, 1952

In September 1949, Bryher wrote H.D., "I am not at all worried or alarmed."[1] Yet Bryher's own persecution fear as an unrecognized transgender being persisted. Her mother's displeasure with her, her father's tremendous power and almost pathological need for privacy, cast long shadows. No matter how sorted the couple's papers became, Bryher rotated between manic anxiety and intense fear of atomic war—as if living out more of the panic that led H.D. to Kusnacht.

Pearson wrote that Yale was "dickering for [his] return," promising "the directorship of a new undergraduate department of American studies," "bait" for his Hawthorne passion, and patriotism, after his wartime role.[2] Pearson groomed Yale undergraduates for the CIA, formerly the OSS. Wearing broad suits too big for him, walking with a limp, he energized recruits.[3] Pearson's own terror that the Soviets aimed to control the world heightened Bryher's phobias.

H.D., meanwhile, settled into a large room in "the middle of the new wing-corridor" at La Paix for the same price, more "chez-moi here than anywhere since leaving Lowndes," with a sauna that helped her rheumatism.[4] Bryher and H.D. renewed their intimacy, meeting nearly every day in the first half of 1950 to "ad-lib" at Mutrux Café for tea, long lunches on Sundays, meetings "all the winter."[5] They looked forward to warmer days and nights under its "many bright umbrellas, fish in a pond and a lovely crazy-pavement garden."[6]

In New York, Perdita worked as a stenographer and fell in love with her boss, John Valentine Schaffner, thirty-six, a prominent literary agent who represented Alice B. Toklas and Sheila Graham, to name two.[7] Before establishing his own agency, Schaffner served in World War II and worked for *Collier's* and *Good Housekeeping* magazines. Our couple was especially pleased to discover that his father was a tree specialist, publishing an Imagist-like report on "the redheaded pine sawfly," a caterpillar whose infestations caused tree defoliation.[8] Perdita announced her engagement on her birthday, March 31, 1950, matching her age of thirty-one. Though "a little shattered at the thought of Maine," where the wedding would take place, H.D. relished the idea of "the forest-father," John's father who worked for the New Haven Forest Insect Laboratory. Both "mothers" remained in Switzerland, Schmideberg telling them they "were not being urged and were not invited to Maine."[9]

Before H.D. left the hotel to meet Bryher at Mutrux on June 24, 1950, Pearson's letter of "Midsummer Day Wedding Day" arrived, regaling Perdita's "soft blue dress," bouquet of "white flowers rimmed with yellow roses, and white lace."[10] He gave away the bride. H.D.'s minimalist message to Perdita—"What Can I say but I L O V E Y O U"—glowed.[11] H.D. felt the wedding freed them "from certain inevitable anxieties."[12] Overflowing on July 17, she wrote Bryher in her "bless-you-for-all-the-years letter. *I am seeing you in an hour so will try to say something, but it is never possible. Just that DAY changed the course of my life, of Perdita's, and I might almost say, of history—my feelings are so strong, so vivid about it all*" (italics mine).[13] "You have opened such doors to me," H.D. repeated.[14]

A month after the wedding, Perdita was pregnant. Bryher visited in July, supplying washing machine and crib for the household, plotting *next year's* trip to visit the grandchild, who would be named Valentine, after Shaffner's father's middle name, suiting either boy or girl. After meeting John, Bryher recognized some of Kenneth's affability, and also assured H.D. he was "very soft, and Germanic and yet knows what he wants." Moreover, "John would come if necessary to Europe to rescue us." They lived in a "most charming little house, very olde New Yorke, with trees behind."[15] She sensed "[e]verything has dropped away from Pup," "all of Europe, she might be a young Beaver." H.D. toasted Bryher with "ember-flowers," for "Valentine on the way, herself-himself owing you all!"[16]

Bryher was not alone in fearing Russians threatened Europe in the 1950s. After all, they had successfully repelled the Nazis. After the war, the Soviets gobbled up thirteen countries in Eastern Europe and infiltrated Africa, the Middle East, Latin America, and Cuba. The covers of *Life* and *Time* displayed bombs exploding, fallout shelters, and spreading menace. In late 1950, Bryher shared her terror with Pearson of "an era of appalling danger" from the Russians, who were "enlisting hundreds and even thousands of Chinese," successfully because of food scarcity. Europe had "little future," although it was "just possible that something of England will survive, because of its geographical position." Reliving "the early thirties" with "inevitable war creeping on us," Bryher wove this fatalism into *Fourteenth*.[17]

The next year, though H.D. feared flying, she hoped to get to Ireland, "then 'hop' (Bryher's word) to Canada, then down to N.Y." Explaining her new twin residences to Viola Jordan, H.D. paralleled her usual "50-50 between Suisse and London."[18] H.D. and Bryher went to Geneva to renew their visas, swearing "not nazi, communist or Falangist."[19] Her fingerprints, taken in 1946, were now "mislaid." She haunted herself in every metonym. Bryher ticked off documents for visiting their "children," taking H.D.'s "birth certificate," so in "utter emergency" U.S. citizenship could be restored and they could return "permanently." If matters worsened, "we'll have to await till the last moment and as the Russians approach take rat poison!"[20] Bryher relived, on a less visible scale, H.D.'s fear of extinction. Considering Switzerland unsafe, for "defenses here would be nil, as the fighting would be from the mountains," Bryher kept such dire details from H.D., who "simply can't stand the idea of another war."[21] As if rehearsing for a breakdown, she acted "slowly and cautiously to get [H.D.] across [to New York] without mental hurt." And now wherever she went with H.D., she also needed to rescue Schmideberg in an emergency, compelling explanation of what no one understood: her loyalty to the psychoanalyst, "born European, land locked." Though intensely "scared of Russians," Schmideberg couldn't face a fourth dislocation.[22]

Aware of H.D.'s intense birthing traumas, Perdita and Bryher tricked H.D., telling her the baby was due a month later than it was. The next year, the pair stayed at the Beekman Hotel from April 1 to 20 for the christening of Valentine, a boy born February 21, 1951. With Bryher, H.D. visited the Schaffners, saw Moore, went to Bethlehem with Mary Herr, and met new friends, Horace Gregory and the poet Marya Zaturenska, who introduced Pascal Covici, an editor, urging H.D. to do "straight biography," as she told Aldington.[23]

With Yale the inevitable haven for their papers, H.D. and Bryher had a positive sense of entwinement. Wryly, H.D. thought the early "indiscreet" Aldington correspondence "read more vividly than any of his novels."[24] H.D. increasingly suffered "tummy germs." Bryher, for her part, started "saving" money to move her whole entourage. Her paranoia mounted. The Swiss were "terrified" of "foreign agents," a fear massaged by Schmideberg himself.[25] And alongside communism's threat, Swiss banks shielded German investments.

Nonetheless, Bryher was pleased Lugano served H.D. as an ideal writing retreat; a new hotel, the Bristol, more comfortable than the Minerva, had spacious rooms with balconies facing the lake. H.D. bought "20 runs" for the nearby funicular, noting it close to Bryher's favorite dock, inviting her for extended visits.[26] Food was "more tomato and imagination," H.D. thinking of Bryher "at every corner and under every arch."[27] Forming summer plans slowly, she imagined Bryher "popping in and out of [her] own balcony."[28]

Convinced *Sword* was timely, H.D. sent it to Covici, summing up his reply for Bryher, that the novel was "a mass of delusions," and "(it and I) need discipline." Discipline was the least quality she needed. Laughing, she asked Bryher to preserve the letter: "I value it highly."[29] Learning of Covici's rejection, Herring fired off that *Sword* was "difficult," but "how ANYONE can say that 'the events you indulge in'—my dear Hilda, they were the *raids*; did you *indulge* in them very much, or did you face them and surmount them," thinking that "if the reader IS left, as he says, in a vacuum—mightn't that not be a bad thing?"[30] Herring saw *Beowulf* with *Sword* as a group portrait of war.

Bryher finally finished *Wulf*. Pearson recommended it to Kurt Wolff, an Austrian emigré, who with his wife, Helen, established the publishing house Pantheon in New York in 1942. Wolff accepted it as *Fourteenth of October* in 1951.[31] Imbued with H.D.'s poetic restraint, its stark language and ghost-like scenes marked her entry as historical novelist.

With Perdita a mother and Bryher publishing, H.D. thought her "SWORD and ROSE [were her] MAGISTER LUDI grand finale." She regarded these works as infants. Memories of Corfu and the Scillies she mapped on to Lugano. Even her room boasted a "little tin tripod" with "the famous recorded wash-stand" from "Writing on the Wall." They spoke on the phone before H.D. dreamed of geranium cuttings and pearls, all signatures of Lady Ellerman, who turned into Queen Mary and "she herself."[32] Spreading out a new scarf from Bryher, she re-created a scene of shells, fish, seaweed, their bedrock.

A born synthesizer, H.D. extravagantly linked Perdita's "V" (Valentine) to Beaver, Sir John, Lady E., now "grandparents" to Perdita, making Bryher genesis of "Valentine himself," "for without your wisdom and foresight, dear old Pup might have got entangled in the drab, sad English picture." Now she formed another holy triad with "the turn of the tide—Ludi (after Hesse's famous 1943 *The Glass Bead Game*, otherwise known as *Magister Ludi*) the Professor, the Bear, all of another world and inspiration."[33] Precisely, Bryher thought, watching that other world fast eroding.

Dr. Glover pegged Schmideberg as a pioneer, who may or may not have been a practicing homosexual; he was a male mother, suitably "Bear." He helped many troubled neurotics between the wars, yet H.D. caught him gazing at the "operatic moon" on his last trip and diagnosed him returning to "old Vienna in his fantasy" and "only completely himself at a café table. It could not go on."[34] Yet his lugubrious unfitness drew our pair's empathy. In *Fourteenth*, Bryher's Latif, an exile, soon to sail for Byzantium, "transformed into a conical tower." Schmideberg, like Latif, stood drinking and smoking for lengthy stretches on the piazza in Lugano. Like H.D.'s devotion to Freud, Bryher believed she was keeping faith with Sachs—and Freud. Among the first to befriend Bryher in Berlin, he was the prototypical displaced person, steadily unraveling.

Through *Fourteenth*, Bryher overcame her fear that writing something successful would spell ruin. Zooming in on a single day in the Battle at Hastings, Wulf's small party met defeat in a "landscape of death," facing an invader, a "dark substance," quickly forming masked and shielded fighters, a gilt-work steel "wall" of men, "riders, lances, all moved as one, and the great, multi-coloured banner fell into serpent folds." Her hero enacted her key defense mechanism; studying a "tuft of moss," he was beset by a sudden impulse to uproot it, burn it in the courtyard "before it was shattered by a flying stone." This free-fall riddled Bryher's psyche, expressed in her hero's cry "[H]ow can we help everybody?" "*They can't ask more of me.*"[35] Moore called it a "gallant book," one with "temperate objectivity," possessing the quality of "a Bayeux tapestry."[36] Bryher breathed life into this earlier England, showing *what might have happened had the Nazis proved victorious. Fourteenth* ended with profound suture: "[T]he five years, from landing to leaving, were as a single July rose."[37] Perhaps July 17.

* * *

Schmideberg increasingly hounded Bryher, who had no intention of remaining in one place long. He used his nightmares to manipulate his keeper. In one, he located her at a mountain resort, but by his arrival she had left "for another place called Aventurer."[38] Relieved that Melitta would spend four weeks from mid-July to mid-August with her husband at Kenwin, Bryher half-joked to Pearson that she was "retraining her escape routes" of 1940.[39] Bryher summered in the Scillies to recoup. Schmideberg blamed his ailments on Melitta, who spoke incessantly about the damage psychoanalysis did.[40] Promising to arrive sober in Lugano, he visited Bryher's room every morning.[41]

Observing the fireworks' "grand finale" in Lugano, H.D. worried over Bryher's plan to bring "Master Valentine." With a blistering heat wave in July, H.D. thought it too much for an infant. Looking for other "tots," she found "none quite so small as Master V." With violent hot thunder and screeching swallows, H.D. could not concentrate on Thomas Mann's *Faustus*.[42]

Bryher sent the Schaffners to Venice, while "Master V" stayed with Volkart at summer-warmed Kenwin. Invited to join Herring in Rome, H.D. desisted, especially when a gala birthday celebration widened to join Macpherson and his new lover, the photographer Islay Lyons.[43] H.D. decided she "must just SEE and BE this month," horrified at Kenneth's idea of her being "chaperoned by a German baroness or having a maid or anything." Pragmatically, she reminded of stress from overheat and mosquitoes and awaited John and Perdita in mid-August. John enjoyed his balcony at the Bristol, grateful Elsie stayed behind to care for Valentine.[44]

Meanwhile, Bryher convened with Pearson, Macpherson, and Islay in Rome, restating one of the couple's tenets, that "the present can sometimes be expressed only in the terms of the past."[45] Perhaps not in "search of her mother," as Freud conceptualized the 1919 trip to Greece, Bryher excavated broken stones and battered mosaics, research for her next novel, *Roman Wall*, a view of third-century invasions of Vaud. The publication of *Fourteenth* renewed Bryher's courage. Joining Pearson and Bryher vicariously, H.D., deciding against lavish parties, asked Bryher to visit for "their birthday octave." Turning sixty-five, she reserved September henceforth for replenishment and would greet Bryher at the station. They enjoyed a small private celebration before returning to Lausanne. H.D. unpacked at Hotel Paix, then ventured to Kenwin, before Bryher left again for Cornwall.

The "Schaffs" convened at Kenwin in early September, with John returning to New York on his own, giving H.D. an opportunity to stay with Perdita, Valentine, and Schmideberg, while Bryher looked after Doris, ailing at Trenoweth. At Kenwin from September 17 until after Bryher's return mid-October, H.D. cut roses and pottered, indulging her grandmother role with "V."[46] Perdita and baby left in early October, heading to Lowndes Square, met by a party of twelve, Bryher, Cole, and Herring among them, with H.D. at Kenwin, busily "re-assembling self and all impressions."[47] She looked longingly into Bryher's room.[48] Picking up Bryher's gusto for sending people on needed vacations, H.D. sent Volkart to New York—with Perdita.

* * *

Inevitably, the whole group had to become more independent. In fact, being in Lugano by herself helped H.D. rediscover the "old H.D." in *Helen in Egypt*. On New Year's Day 1952, H.D. and Melitta recommended Bryher send "Bear" to Dr. Brunner.[49] Bryher took Doris to New York in July, H.D. eager for reactions.

Keeping in touch with Dr. Brunner, Bryher learned of a shift toward parapsychology, the term, coined by biologist Berthold P. Wiesner, first applied by psychologist Robert Thouless in 1942.[50] The nineteenth-century parapsychology movement reckoned with apparitions, hallucinations, telepathy—all centerpieces in H.D.'s writing and the couple's relationship. Herring recommended Robert Ambelain's *Dans L'Ombre Des Cathedrales* early in 1952, which reached him from Monnier, and Bryher followed the same year with Ambelain's *Practical Kabbalah* (1951).

For most of the winter, Ambelain, a new companion, echoed H.D.'s own explorations. His principles play out in her poetics, insisting upon a generative Void, absorption in the "En-Soph," literally meaning "without end," "the ultimate center of reality and the intangible source of the tangible world." The En-Soph evades all images. In *Palimpsest,* Isis is "a blue cloud" "without attributes." Friedman explains, "Sometimes the seeker experiences the En-Soph as a blinding white flame, and sometimes as an endless dark night, black as ink."[51] Ambelain referred to kabbalah's creation myth as the Infinite striking the Void with the "sound of the Word," a point of light that set forth "ten emanations." These paired masculine and feminine principles, resolving in androgyny, in the One that was two. In *Trilogy*, H.D. wrestled with opposing forces of love and war, and already instructed an unconditioning practice, to produce more emotional and spiritual freedom: in *Tribute to the Angels,* she had wanted "to minimize thought, //concentrate on it / till I shrink, // dematerialize / and am drawn into it.[52] Not yet written, *Helen in Egypt* would dramatize H.D.'s dialectical lenses, transferring love through hate, distilled back through love, in alchemical refinement, where "nothing" *is* creative *concentration* or plentitude, not to be confused with intellectual achievement. In another way Ambelain called attention to what she had intuited all along: her belief in a *Soul,* "a Principle" that "through a mysterious magnetism, ... is attracted to a Higher Plane with which it joins."[53] Her notion of the soul's path had always meshed with a larger collective; what particularly appealed was his emphasis on scorned theurgy, on ceremonies, rituals, and invocations as means of expansion. These were H.D.'s very poetic forms.

* * *

The year 1952 began momentously, with two deaths: the first, Norman Douglas. Macpherson and Islay went to Capri to help him die in 1952; in constant pain at eighty-four, he took a bottle of pills. Wading through his myriad matted papers was a nightmare. His death on February 8 marked a generational shift, overshadowed by news flooding in of King George VI's death on February 6. Reluctant to take the throne, he had bravely conducted himself from the time of his brother's abdication in 1936 through World War II.

"Everyone here takes the King's death, personally," H.D. wrote Bryher the day of his death. She wrote several times that day, in "Letter II. Communication 6," thanking Bryher for "making possible that Reading and my contact, our contact, with the little Royals."[54] They remembered the small princess, now, the day after her father's death, coronated as Queen Elizabeth II. The Pathé newsreel showed bewildered mourners at Buckingham Palace, the newscaster announcing no loss of continuity. Volkart arranged her clothes so she might die in the night like the King.

With Bryher dashing to New York in February, H.D. "caught" her, teasing that she learned she was "going USA *sub Rosa,*" as if to a deceptive child, "who may do it yet."[55] On route, Bryher sorted Lowndes, with H.D. guiltily wanting to help. "The whole store is yours," she extravagantly marked their work as joint venture. While Bryher was away, H.D. had an array of excitements, but three stood out. C. J. Furness's biography of Robert Louis Stevenson, *Voyage to Windward,* she knew from Bryher's "boy-books," delighted to learn that "R.L.S. was soaked in Baudelaire," along with "the old story too, of laudanum and opium."[56]

Also in February, stamps celebrated "100 years of electricity" (Figure 22.1). H.D. purchased several sheets for each of them, illustrating their electric love, communicating across distances, distinguishing their love story. They "celebrate so much—so much 'communication' that we have had together," H.D. satisfied that "all worked out for [her]." She described a hotel guest, a French lady with eight furs, and a woman called "Spider," who knew Lady Ellerman and inquired about Bryher's brother, who could "save civilization." H.D. supplemented a dash of commiserating spite—"if the RAT would ever emerge." She drank in Bryher's "huge fan-mail" for *Fourteenth.*[57]

Brooding on her "hatched chicks" that "need nothing" (i.e., publication) during her now annual sojourn in Lugano, H.D., as usual, worried about visitors, concerned that Ashby might visit during Perdita's stay.[58] Perdita, pregnant again, was to come to Lugano after London in June. John worried about her return home, but H.D. had already enlisted Volkart again as "chaperone." This time, the matriarch thought Lugano's tropical climate for a pregnant woman was unsuitable, but Perdita visited anyway, in July, H.D. having trouble keeping up with her when they ventured to nearby Locarno, as she had with Bryher on their previous visit, partaking of Roman ruins, recently discovered. Her intestines knotting this trip, H.D. "screamed at the oleander TREES."[59] Trying "to hide it," later in Perdita's visit, her "tummy distended, as if [she] were having [a baby]."[60]

H.D. found pages and pages of "luminous, stained glass" from Fabula, Bryher's *Roman Wall* in 1954, evincing the "same quality as *Fourteenth,* "ivy and wild grasses." Sitting up in her nightgown, sweating and reading, she thought her own "War I and War II volumes" "cloudy beside this." Incubating her "War I" book, H.D. tried to "'fix' the impressions in Cornwall," to discover the "emanation" from 1918 to 1920, casting Bryher as cherished invisible, saturating her writing off-stage. Thankfully, H.D. repeated their legend, given its significance: "Perdita and Valentine both owe their lives to you. How glad I am that John really sees this."[61] What she meant was that John

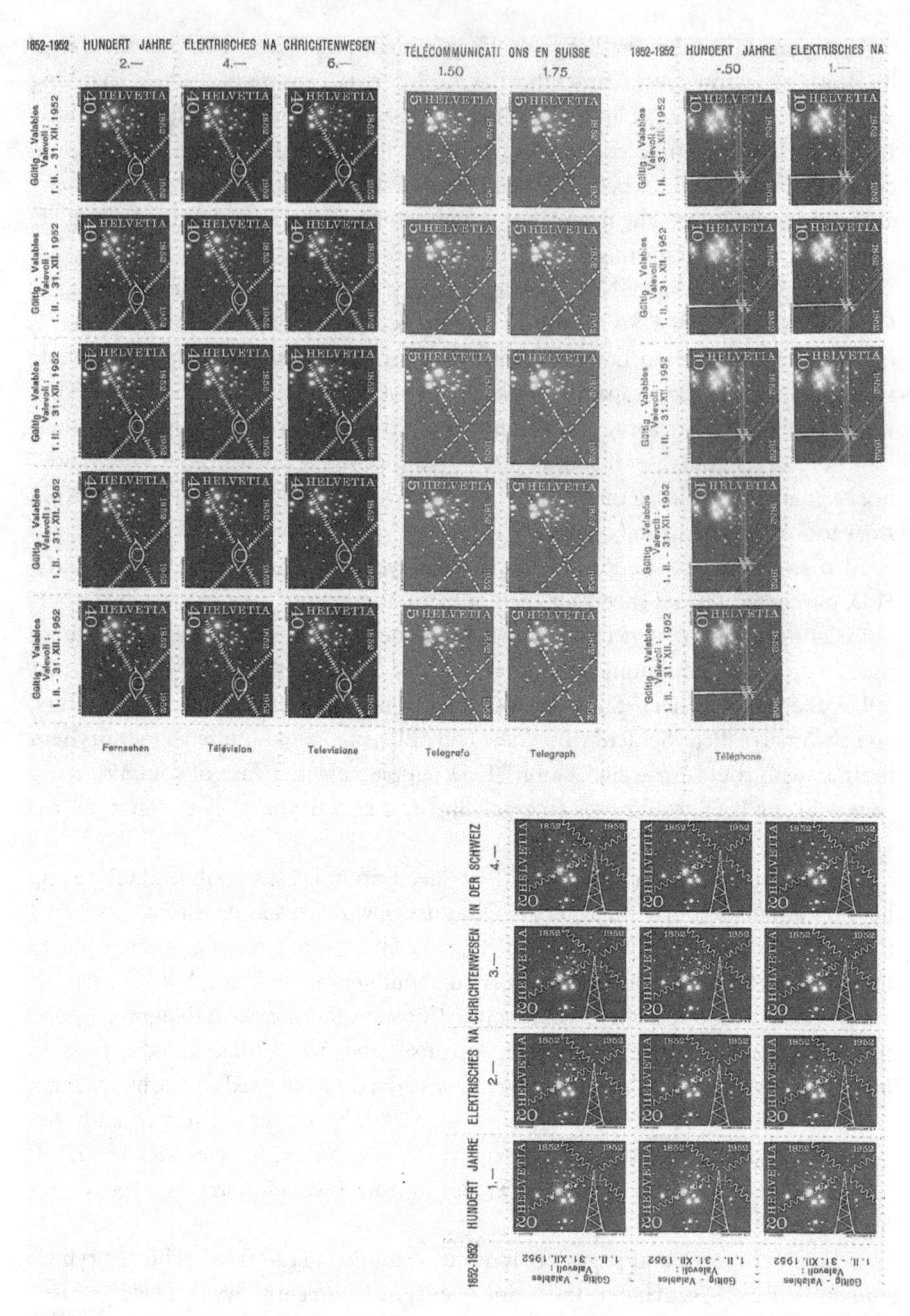

Figure 22.1 Swiss stamps celebrating one hundred years of electricity, 1951. Purchased by H.D. in Lausanne, Switzerland.

recognized Bryher as coparent, without any qualms. H.D.'s insistent expressions of gratitude stemmed largely from lacking an "officially" legible relationship.

In their "July month," Bryher sailed the Scillies with Doris, staying at Tregarthen, where she and H.D. had roomed in 1919. H.D. wrote Iris Origo, author of *Allegra: A Short Life of Byron's Daughter* (1935), intrigued by its look at Byron's illegitimate daughter, birthed by Claire Claimont, stepsister to Mary Shelley; abandoned, she died in a convent at five years old. H.D. worried over childbirth, thus her unnecessary anxiety for the robust Perdita, while her Morse memory stitched from St. Mary's island to Lugano, affirming "vistas of memories," urging Bryher to translate the islands into her novels. H.D.'s near-hallucinatory memory unfolded "palm trees, the coral flowers" growing "like water-lilies from the walls, the very fat, very, very white and huge gulls on the stone-roofs and ledges, your saying it was like Sweden in bits and my being sure it WAS the ISLES OF GREECE."[62]

Volkart accompanied Bryher and Perdita to New York. Alone, H.D. imagined that Bryher was *with her*, linking geographics of Lausanne, Greece, Cornwall, and New York. The "Vee" was enchanted by the city as much as by the Schaffners' modern kitchen in their Victorian wooden house. When Bryher phoned H.D. from the Schaffners on September 18, inspiration seized the poet, "so *beseigered* mit Troy." H.D. announced a breakthrough, "dreadfully happy, setting a *Helen*," also responding to Pearson's request for the "early H.D." Her "suns" provoked this sudden "embarcaton [sic] on the good-ship Helena for Egypt." Holding Bryher present in her absence allowed H.D.'s persistence, and likewise gave the zigzagging Bryher tangibility: "I am with you ... every time I go places, I am with you and re-living it all."[63] About to relive the Trojan War, H.D. peeled back her version of a "defenseless people," asking if Achilles "sacked Knossos."[64] The Trojan War, as it had for Sappho, "came to represent the war not to end, but to start all wars."[65]

The Sicilian poet Stesichorus (sixth century BCE) retracted Helen's presence in Troy during battle. H.D., following suit, configured Helen as "project[ing] herself out," sending a phantom, while living her corporeal life for ten years in Egypt. Stesichorus inspired—but both he and Euripides offered less extreme versions of Helen's purported stay in Egypt than did H.D., who did not depict her as waiting a husband's rescue.[66]

It was "good to meet Helen face to face, for men and poets have visualized her so crudely," H.D. wrote in 1920; now she dismantled these very crudities. Her Helen, "beautiful as a skull or as a bird's swift, destructive beak is beautiful."[67] Simultaneously, H.D. wrote excitedly to Bryher and Pearson. In three days, she set her "*Helen* sequence" in motion, with eight poems. She typed them herself, editing as she went along, not risking the spell by a delay in sending pages to the couple's typist, Miss Woolford.[68] Besides, she had "a sort of superstition" she must type it herself.[69] The couple talked of the "fourth dimension" and a possible "barrier"; this long poem, in process, dynamited the "fourth wall"— ultimately pleated into a montage of dramatic scenes, with prose "script" set above.

"Dazed" by her inspiration and "*out-of-time dimension*," H.D. relied on an old pad of paper Perdita had left to catch vivid outpourings. In her matrix, she fused with Bryher, and with Perdita, for creative inspiration. Though typing challenged her, this poetry necessitated tapping keys. She sifted memories from her and Bryher's "Greece and Egypt," the latter like Lugano, with "blazing sun and like a pool of miraculous warmth."[70] The next day, she typed her remaining draft, consulting Bryher and Pearson, unusual for her to send work "hot off the griddle," even to her "suns."

By telegram, responding to the first eight poems, Pearson wrote, "SUPERB!" and "A DEEP BOW WITH A SWEEP OF MY PLUMED HAT."[71] These initial pieces revealed a "synthesis of a new richness on the old," a highly developed "sensibility and understanding."[72] "New poems" appeared, "as though [he] read ectoplasmic waves from [her] vitality."[73] Disoriented by "[her] MUSE," who "comes along to Porch or inspires me in bed, the Helen, it could go on forever." H.D. cast her earlier poems as "just stepping-stones." Swinburne's unfinished novel *Lesbia Brandon* also fanned her flame. Bryher had sent Randolph Hughes' edition of it earlier in 1952, almost giving her an "electric coma."[74] Part and parcel with Cold War suspiciousness, the *Times Literary Supplement* called *Brandon* a fake. H.D. extended epistolary solidarity with Hughes.[75]

In late September, H.D. asked Bryher "to confirm or correct" certain facts, questioning if "the Samoan plain" as battlefield before Troy was the "correct expression."[76] Bryher sailed with her through the "*Helen II* sequence, 17 typed poem-pages, in all." H.D. remembered Freud and Sir John to Bryher, those magnanimous patriarchs—stand-ins for her dual "Amen (or Zeus)" of poem I of *Helen in Egypt*. "[S]ailing on with *Helen*," she counted on Bryher to "inform" her about the Schaffners or political danger, while she dove into the material, dominating her for several years.[77] Returning to an earlier self, she could write "anywhere," "like [Bryher's] sketch vibration," from under tables, her smallness a help, compared by H.D. to Brueghel, who obscured himself to absorb scenes.[78] Fearful to lose her new ghost, H.D. carried a rough copy of *Helen* in her purse wherever she went, penning "GOD BLESS FIDO."[79] Outfitting Perdita for her second "event," Bryher encouraged H.D. to delay returning to Paix.

On October 6, H.D. was thrilled, having completed the first part containing four "books" of eight poems each, beginning with "Palinode," in Greek, a defense, that became seven books; two other parts followed, "Leuké" of six books and "Eidolon" of seven, each a long section of "books," not "Cantos," as Pearson called them, when finished two years later.

H.D. sent Bryher the whole "30 typed pages" of Book I, asking her to read slowly. A window beckoned collaboration. Bryher was to "indicate in pencil at side, any mistakes in spelling etc. or general queries." Toning down a bit after Bryher recognized her "wings theme" from *Sword*, H.D. said, "[A]nyhow, it opens the door." Too busy to answer letters, Bryher "always the exception," she let "ghosts" actualize on stage.[80] Pearson's emphasis on the line made her "iambic conscious." And if thinking of Bryher's *Fourteenth*, she decided on a metric "jog-trot" in order "to get in battle movement," with " 'the roar of the chargers.' " She read *Fourteenth* for inspiration, noting their shared "strand"—"that is freedom," the need for liberty. "Is it your UNK or mine?" she reaffirmed joined imagination.[81]

The last poem in Book II, cataloguing Achilles' war deeds, presents "an enigma": "I ask not, nor care to know / what is or is not the answer," Helen insists. Achilles stole children "here and there, everywhere," "luring youth in to battle";[82] Helen wonders why, but "will refuse to consult the oracle but will find the 'answer' or 'answers' " in memories and stone pictures."[83] Bryher praised the last poem of Book II as "a concentration of the rest." After straining to retype *Helen,* H.D. sent the whole to her confirmed alter ego to retype, though typing "just this lot" led her "back to the old vibration."[84]

Often regarding her daughter as a sister, H.D. felt some rivalry at Perdita's announcement of a second birth. Bryher's retyping and publishing with Pantheon, Pearson asking for "H.D.," and new correspondence with Aldington, all took her back to poetry, now on course to have at least a book every nine months. With Perdita pregnant again, H.D.'s opuses sequenced with the births and Bryher's publications.

1951: Valentine born
    1952: *Fourteenth* published
        September–October 1952: *Helen in Egypt Book I*
1953: Nicholas born
    1953: *Player's Boy* published
        Summer 1953: *Helen in Egypt Book II*
    1954: *Roman Wall* published
        1954: *Helen in Egypt Book III*
1956: Elizabeth Bryher born

Childbirth and writing, an easy comparison—but our couple greeted a chorus of new babies and books. Between 1956 and 1960, H.D. recorded sections of *Helen*. Perdita's youngest, Timothy, was born on February 28, 1960. The new family members were emblematic survivors of the traumas H.D. and Bryher endured, which explained Perdita's shifting the month of births, easing transmittable "birth pangs." H.D. stitched herself in, feeling "so near to you and old-times," with "new-times with Helen."[85] She was "anxious to keep it by me or by you, until I get on with this second sequence," sensing a need to "rein in the inspiration."[86] At last, H.D. begged Bryher to cease typing; it aroused her too overwhelmingly.

In mid-October, H.D. readied to depart, but Bryher kept her there by responsive queries, resending Gilbert Murray on Euripides and *Iphigenia*. Touched by telepathic gifts, H.D. wasn't sure "HOW [Bryher] could have been so inspired."[87] Suggesting subtle changes in punctuation, Bryher questioned whether H.D. relied too heavily on repetition, while observing her canny use of internal rhyme.[88] This method created "more clarity," she explained of her tercets, that needed "to break a line or repeat a phrase, or run on a line, an uneven length." With it and repetition, she reestablished her poetic DNA; "life runs in a spiral," knowing she had to go back, through repetition, to move gears forward. This spiral form was "a sort of controlled free verse." Glad she remembered Nephtys, sister to Isis, H.D. wanted to compare them with siblings Helen and Clytemnestra.[89]

Finally, doped with Lugano sun, "its long corridors of lotus-bud," H.D. decided to leave for Lausanne by the end of October, trying "to keep away from *Helen*, but it simmers on the hob." Bryher retyped H.D.'s messy "script," the pair in tune, while H.D. cried, surrounded by packing cases, "Do, do go easy on script.... [W]ith packing and so on—you do too—greatly inspire me." These excitatory long-distance exchanges oddly juxtaposed with new hotel guests. H.D. was "frightfully upset" about "troublesome sex maniacs who have dinner in the room about nine and play games on till toward mid-night."[90] Three days later, she had the blueprint of "Palinode," deciding "to run it along, six sections, eight poems each," "enough of a 'contemplation' for now."[91] She posted sections five and six, not knowing how "this did happen."[92] An accidental birth fated into being.

* * *

Before she invented short prose descriptions to double the topography of the book's labyrinth, the poems spoke for themselves. Adrift near a temple, Helen surveyed the empty scene and her sudden solitude in "long corridors of lotus-bud": "I hear their voices, / There is no veil between us / Only space and leisure."

H.D.'s "Helena, Helen hated of all Greece" goes incognito, taken, with Zeus' help, to an unknown seascape to meet the soldier Achilles, sparse language distilling:

few were the words we said,
nor knew each other
nor asked, are you Spirit?

are you sister? Are you brother?
are you alive?
are you dead?

The harpers will sing forever
Of how Achilles met Helen,
Among the shades,

but we were not, we are not shadows.

Helen and Achilles are threshold figures, mortal and immortal, sharing suspended animation, H.D. balancing a timely and timeless perspective. She dwelled upon Achilles' "mortal" part, his "wounded heel," and the "sea enchantment in his eyes / of Thetis, his sea mother." Sensing his "stricken" foot as though she "had withdrawn /

from the bruised and swollen flesh / the arrow from its wound," Helen must "melt the icy fortress of the soul, / and free the man." She sighted "the dim outline," while "the new Mortal, / shedding his glory, / limped slowly across the sand."[93]

Drawn to maladapted figures, H.D. seized on Swinburne with his epilepsy, Pearson with his impediment, Bryher, too short, herself, too long and tall, her Helen attracted to a "limping" man who discovers Thetis "within." She endowed Achilles with tenderness. "When Achilles asks which was the dream, which the veil, it is my own effort to get the two together yet separate," she explained to Bryher, their relationship's dynamic as well.[94] They had to be "together yet separate."[95]

Using her syncretic spiritualism, a mythology to demythologize, the only response left, after two world wars, H.D.'s Achilles had to shed imperviousness. Put simply, H.D. brought the warrior face to face with the "real" Helen, not the phantom he fought to abduct again. In this "pause" in temporal flow, Helen believes herself among the shades, coming upon Achilles "drifting without chart / famished and tempest-driven." "Few were the words we said," Helen narrates, though their words "minted on gold." He assembles his "human" tangibles, "finding an old flint in his pouch," saying, " 'I thought I had lost that.' " *Helen* sang for Pearson because it "moved" back and forth and was "all very much of our time."[96]

The first sequence shows Helen drawing Achilles toward the temple to read the hieroglyph of Isis, the "life-symbol," praying to "*love him, as Thetis, his mother,*" a generous leap, considering a warrior-hero catapulted her exile. This maternal circuitry, "*the primal cause of all the madness,*" jump-cuts to Achilles hallucinating Helen as the "femme noire of antiquity," Hecate, yet another repository for disowned irrationality in H.D.'s palimpsestic overlaying. "*Can you throttle a phantom?*" asks the notes, charting Achilles' futile rage against difference.[97]

Thrilled with H.D.'s start in 1952, Pearson fanned *Helen*'s continuation: "I asked for poems, and I got a masterpiece." He recognized "the calmness and certitude of the eternal and love," depending upon "the narrow verse limits you have set yourself," heralding "a fresh H.D."[98] Already curating her for lasting, he guided, "We must work this out carefully, shape it like a vase," perhaps unaware of the absolute appropriateness of this aesthetic spur to otherworldly adventures. The vase opened like a chalice to the Void. Returning to the Greek scene, she saw "the old serpent of Gnosis, biting its tail."[99]

By the time H.D. returned to Lausanne to celebrate Christmas with the "family," Macpherson and Islay were staying a floor beneath her at Paix. H.D. crafted holiday games, like "split proverbs."[100] Book I of *Helen* near her, she suffered severe stomach cramping and underwent a medical emergency. Her innards torqued. Bryher admitted her to Hirslanden Clinique Cecil, where she underwent surgery on January 27, 1953. Bryher explained to Pearson that "[t]he trouble turned out to be that with great height and narrow hips," she did not have enough "room for all the organs and a bit of intestine suddenly turned itself into a knot for lack of space."[101] An X-ray showed a pebble in her bowels after the operation. Recuperating at Kusnacht, she described Dr. François Perret, wearing a "green semi-transparent X-ray coat and close-fitting rubber cap," a "Mephisto image."[102] He stretched his long arm to show the length of intestine removed, akin to Freud shooting out his arm at an epiphany. Under sedation, she overheard another doctor exclaim, "[A] brilliant surgical-opus—shall we say?" H.D.'s operation occurred the day before Perdita delivered her second child, Nicholas, on January 28.

Roads converged. *Madrigal*, sent to Aldington, shared the loss and anguish it described. He begged off reading the whole because of a high fever, but offered to scout for a publisher.[103] Even in a hospital bed, H.D. worried over this autobiographic war novel. Although she called her room a "heavenly place," she half-considered Aldington to blame for their lost baby: "they say I have been dragged down for years + years by some internal tangle, they have straightened now inside—an unexpected shock."[104] After recovering from his flu, Aldington contacted Bryher; after the long gap in their epistolary friendship, he addressed her formally as "Mrs. Macpherson," writing that he was "shocked and grieved" about H.D.'s health, that "her shaky handwriting" made him "guess she was bad."[105] He recommended *Madrigal*'s title be *Bid Me to Live*, "much better," in the *Avon* vibration, with Herrick's phrase more dramatic. Bryher thought H.D. should convalesce in Zurich; Aldington agreed, and further, it was excellent they had Mr. Pearson, waiting for *Bid*.[106] Bryher sent a scarf to Aldington's daughter, Catha, who "showed it off" at school.[107]

Until released to Bryher, H.D. convalesced on her back. Weak, she could write only with pencil. By April, H.D. and Bryher were headed to New York, staying at Beekman Hotel. Though she found it a trial to travel, H.D. wanted to greet the newborn she fantasized as Miranda. Back in Lausanne by May, she worked toward the second section of *Helen*, entitled "Leuké," importing the island in the Black Sea, "hence pomegranate seeds to strike a note."[108]

As it turned out, H.D. needed another operation at the Clinique, checking herself in on May 30, taking room 70, choosing it based on "Nurse D's" recommendation, avoiding the "frightful" noise of the "best rooms" facing the avenue. She alerted Bryher, then in New York, that her small room had a garden view, reminding her of Riant Chateau. Before the operation, she wrote, "[B]ut O, my heart is in every word, in every letter." She told Fido not to waste energy writing her while with the Schaffners. Dr. Perret judged her "bowels" might be "massaged in, a minor op. without cutting, on Tuesday at dawn, after fasting & praying." "Less of a shock," with the doctor "not doing the outside stitch-work till end of week."[109] Bryher sent roses, sweet peas, peonies, iris, carnations, and for the coronation of Elizabeth II, signed off "God save the Queen!"[110]

Recognizing Bryher's internal resources were stretched, H.D. released her from coming "at once" and avoided complicated explanations to Perdita or Bryher on the telephone. She even schemed *not* telling either of them, though the operation was not without risk at sixty-six. H.D. convalesced at Paix, feeling "frustrated." The operation had lasted one and a half hours; Aldington called it "prehistoric."[111] H.D. asked Bryher to communicate to Perdita that she was fine, "just bored with enforced convalescence." Elizabeth II was coronated on June 2, 1953, and Bryher treated Dobson and Perdita to see "the WHOLE PROCESSION," while she looked after H.D., immobile until late June.[112] Still shaky, H.D., with Bryher, thought Kusnacht might serve for further convalescence—and as writing retreat, with nurses on hand should further troubles occur with her abdomen and its scar. Situating her there in July, Bryher whooshed off to the Scillies, with H.D.'s blessings.

23
Recovery & Illuminations (1953–)

> The art of the poem, like the mechanism of the dream ... is a cathexis: to keep present and immediate a variety of times and places, persons and events. In the melody we make, the possibility of eternal life is hidden, and experience we thought lost returns to us.
> —Robert Duncan, *The H.D. Book* (2011)

Returning to Kusnacht in July 1953, after seven years, H.D. re-created it as monastery. Dr. Brunner was Father Brunner, the nurses, all Sisters. The bells chimed every half-hour. Taking stock of the private lane to Seehof and the "giant sail-cloth umbrellas" on the terrace, "perched like a ship's deck, just above water," H.D. sensed the air somehow "softer" in Zurich than in Lausanne.[1] Her large room at Am Stram faced the lake, "the 'Father Doctor's' private house." She voyaged with *Helen*, the "mechanism of dream" joining multiple places and times, allowing "breath-taking encounters / with those half-seen."[2] It verged on "heterotopia."[3]

On July 7, she met thirty-two-year-old Dr. Erich Heydt, a tall, gaunt man with domed forehead in a white coat, his first question, "You know Ezra Pound, don't you?"[4] When the dreamy-eyed doctor jabbed her with a hypodermic needle, she likened it to an arrow of Venus. His name harkened back to her half-brother Eric, who died in 1920, a link to her father's astronomy dome. This Erich inspired stark words: "I knew you / who would know you anywhere."[5] Dr. Heydt had interned at St. Elizabeth's but had not met Pound. In Zurich, he studied with Medard Boss, innovating existential psychotherapy, focused on "being" as a process, with patients helping other patients. This often required forgetting history—something H.D. and Bryher shunned. With his angular wolf-like look, Heydt played exquisite Mozart; Ivan Nagel, his lover, the Frankfurt music and theater critic, had hid during World War II and taken a Christian name.[6] Heydt cloaked his queerness. The closet was de rigueur, for homosexuality in the 1950s was suspect, even more so than in the 1920s.

H.D. read Jean Chaboseau's *Le Tarot* (1946), admitting she did "not delve very deeply but [she thought she] found the answer." Sensing herself a "Phoenix, rising from the discarded ashes of the burnt nest," she seized upon the word *dépouillé*.[7] Almost immediately, she took pencil to paper, scrawling notes to Bryher, charting the latter's zigzagging travel. Inevitably, she celebrated "the day" at St. Mary's, its "eternal" memory of "swathes of calla lilies!" H.D. "found Bryher for [Heydt]" on the Scillies postcard she sent.[8]

H.D. metamorphosed Heydt into Paris for the second book of *Helen*, "Leuké," tearing down opposing camps of Trojan and Greek, where Helen's "first lover / was created by [her] last."[9] Not only a "subtle genealogy," this was H.D.'s effort to bridge the vast rift between allies and enemies during the war. In Homer, after the prophecy at his birth that Paris would cause the Trojan War, the gods left him on Mount Ida; after being suckled by a she-bear, he returned to civilization. Dr. Ashby ferreted out Heydt's astrological aspects; he was born on December 7, 1920, in Stuttgart, and his sun sign, Sagittarius, the Archer, revealed what she already detected: secrecy, abruptness, emotionalism, all "complicated or intensified by the Uranian X-ray."[10] "Uranian," Karl Ulrich's 1860s designation for a "third sex," H.D applied to an unarticulated queerness.

H.D. and Bryher wondered how Heydt had survived the war. "'[Heydt] must have been a Nazi.' ... Did I say it or did Bryher."[11] But he was half-Jewish. *Helen* needed this postwar encounter between former "enemy" civilians. Paris "the slayer" transforms into "the son of the slain." Transference love approximated the creative process.

"Father Brunner" headed a long wooden lunch table, with Heydt in the middle, where "general harmony depended on the group."[12] In late 1953, H.D. and Bryher met Ivan, engaging in "long table" repartee. He tried translating H.D.'s "Mid-Day" into German, but admitted failing to achieve his ideal for it. His selection captured her vision of life as quest, where she might "perish on the path / among the crevices of rocks," striving toward the poplar that "spreads out, deep-rooted among trees."

In August, Bryher joined the table, confiding in Heydt about Schmideberg, her unofficial patient.[13] To Heydt, H.D. clarified this attachment to the Austrian exile, who checked on the couple after bad air raids, as one of their chosen family. Bryher jokingly called him "boyfriend," one of her group of gay men. Heydt praised Bryher's intelligence and goodness, insisting she "must have help."[14] As it was, Bryher lived like a gypsy, at Kenwin for only brief stints, otherwise roving between London, Cornwall, New York, Pully, and Zurich. H.D. needed several more weeks of bed rest, shunning Kenwin for its isolation, should her scar open. Dr. Brunner judged her well, if too thin.

Between Bryher's first visit and return in late September 1953, H.D. had an exhilarating experience. Six weeks into convalescence, while taking coffee on "the old oak table in the hall," she saw Heydt in an elegant red velvet smoking-jacket. Later, she asked about his colorful attire. He rushed her into his closets, disgorging drawers, holding up a brown coat, H.D. insisting August light could not have made his brown deep rose. Once more, "the invisible had been made visible."[15] While enumerating lovely dresses and underdresses, she praised Bryher, who "adorned" her "like a bride."[16] Intuitively, Bryher had sent a "double," a reversible coat that could be worn turned inside-out, with "that beautiful deep-rose complete with second set of buttons."[17] Heydt became her "Rosenkavalier," supplementing "Chevalier" (Pearson), Bryher, still "magnet, a lode-stone, a lode-star."[18]

Before Heydt left for vacation on September 14, he showed "scant sympathy" toward H.D.'s "story of the R.A.F." When she explained 1946 and her breakdown, Heydt "turned on her," telling her she couldn't possibly believe such fantasies. Hadn't he read her case file? She told him, "[T]he young pilots of the group I spoke of, were all dead by the end of October 1940. They had nothing to do with—with Dresden—or whatever came to your mind."[19] In his absence, the scholar E. M. Butler's *Faust* sent her flying with its depiction of Goethe's "Helen problem," his fear of destroying her. With his mesmerizing voice, Heydt became a perfect "model" for the abducting Paris.

H.D. continued "in [her] two compartments or capacities, the withdrawn, satisfied, creative artist," slowly persisting with *Helen* stanzas as "the still half-convalescent guest of Doctor Brunner." Dr. Heydt returned in full-transference mode, taking "these people into himself, like a mother, then, actually, they are born again."[20] By October, they were sharing regular 4:00 tea. Due to heavy snows, Bryher called that winter of 1953 "the great frost."[21] The insulation of snow led H.D. to project herself as "Helen," living with Paris on the island of Leuké, as "L'isle Blanche." The lake had "waves like ocean breakers."[22] H.D. tried helping Heydt reconcile himself with a paradox: "Yes, I am a German. Mozart was a German."[23] An inner voice asked her, "[D]o I love War?," deepening her awareness. "I crossed the frontier," H.D. now wrote.[24]

Spoiled by Bryher, she shared, if not a circle, a long table, with others, mostly from other countries, who had "struck out" in the "reality" game; she settled for "relative reality." Here, as in Lugano, she came "alive in the *Helen* sequence," her practice depending upon her "meditation-hour," a trade secret where she would "crawl back to bed" and "go round and round the clock-dial of the symbols and find a new reading and get caught into a semi-trance state. This state is life to me; at night too, before sleeping." The clock was imagined as a kind of tarot wheel. Such trances were what Yeats called "reveries" in his "Autobiographies."[25] Such states safeguarded her.

September brought H.D., lingering at Kusnacht with her "margin to heel, at last," "typing out the new Helen." Starting poems for "Leuké," the day after Bryher's birthday, she shared her plan "to meet and complete her life or after-life there with Achilles, but have her meet Paris instead."[26] With "the Trojan side of it," she gave "Paris and Helen, more 'reality.'"[27] "We both seem to take to early fighting," H.D. remarked to Bryher, the latter scripting H.D. as Fabula in *Roman Wall* who taught "immortality" as "a state of seeing."[28]

H.D. read American poems to Heydt, who confided difficulties with patients, putting H.D. "more or less in charge of Madame Herf's reading."[29] Assigned to ensuring H.D. ate enough, Herf was convinced she had caused the war. She had been comatose, and her American relatives had left her for dead; Heydt spoke German to her softly month after month for seven years until she awoke, contributing to H.D.'s conviction that Heydt wielded magical powers. What better co-patient for H.D.'s meditations on Helen—loved, blamed, exiled. Yet when asked to take Herf to "a film in Z," H.D. was relieved someone else volunteered.[30] Bryher visited for their birthdays, leaving H.D. "exalté, writing the new poems, seeing you," "tearing away" with *Helen*.[31]

Like Bryher, Heydt accepted H.D.'s visions as part of her creative process. Once he proposed they go to Egypt, or the "mountains of Arabia," or "as Bryher said, 'the sea-coast of Bohemia.'"[32] H.D. dodged other guests, believing Heydt and herself advanced on a path where she acted co-analyst.[33] As Helen, "tired of memory of battle," she escaped with Paris to a sturdy yet vulnerable self.[34]

I wanted to hear the wind, to feel
snow, to embrace an ancient
twisted pine, so I walked
a long way up a mountain.[35]

Helen clutched a veil to break her fall from stairs, "spiral, like a snail shell." Paris "lived / on my slice of Wall, / while the Towers fell."[36]

* * *

In December 1953, Bryher maneuvered Schmideberg to Kusnacht, wondering if she should check in as well. He was in a semi-coma with pneumonia, his heart and liver weak. After he dried out, his yowls and threats to report his kidnapping to the British Consulate began. At Christmas, Herring visited, charmed by Heydt, agreeing that he looked "like the early Conrad Veidt."[37] After four and a half weeks, Schmideberg's depression worsened, though H.D. visited him twice daily; he compared Heydt, whom H.D. called "clairvoyant," to Bhaduri.[38] An X-ray showed "a coin" stuck "in the deepest bronchus." Jeering he was a "money-pig," he wanted Bryher to have it, "[having] harbored it so long in my chest."[39]

With Bryher in London, H.D. encouraged Schmideberg to translate poems into German. Dr. Heydt recognized "the psychology of the addict" and found out the patient obtained extra drugs in Lausanne. Acting realist, H.D. said "no one could have checked-up on this," reiterating to Bryher, "[T]here is nothing you can do."[40] Finishing "Leuké" on January 15, 1954, she felt it had been delivered to her. Father Brunner told H.D. that Bryher could "stay here," "home away from home," but H.D. knew Bryher needed distances (they both did), so instructed, "Clear OUT and FORGET everything."[41] H.D. awaited the last section, "Eidelon."

By the end of January, Bryher had plotted "extreme adventure" with Macpherson and Islay in Pakistan,[42] after arranging with Beach a photography exhibit for Islay before she left, who sent the "ok" once she saw images of the Khyber Pass.[43] H.D. promised to "rattle the dear rose-wood beads, Bryher-rose beads," whenever she felt "the least bit cut-off."[44] Bryher left behind a prop, boots that were "huntsman's boots," which H.D. worked into "Leuké," turning from Paris to Theseus, speaking for Bryher, "absent on a mad adventure."[45]

While Bryher trekked in Pakistan, H.D. danced with Heydt in the snow, "amazed, with rheumatism in me feet," to have "scittered around like this."[46] Schmideberg came on several outings, one on a trail to a gorge. He waited behind as H.D. and Heydt climbed, but they spotted him, heading to a "hut" that served punch. He claimed he sought a match.[47] While writing assuring notes to Bryher, H.D. confided in Pearson being "battered at times, with the Bear," but glad to "act as a buffer-state" for Bryher. She could not "stand his blindness as to his own condition."[48] Shocked after the fact that he was the one who had to clear her to leave Kusnacht in 1946, H.D. glimpsed Bryher's hidden suffering.

* * *

All was not smooth sailing with Dr. Heydt. H.D. let Helen forgive Paris, an aspirational metaphor for the Allies and their enemies. Impersonal love, almost a metaphoric Marshall Plan, might, H.D. thought, transcend endless retribution. But Paris had to change, as had Achilles. The former shot his arrow at Achilles, so that Helen "lost the Lover, Paris / but to find the Son" in Achilles. "[B]righer than the sun at noon-day," yet "whiter than snow" or "dust of shells." Theseus, a more mature version of Heydt, offers "rest" and "safety," advising Helen return to her mother, finally letting "Thetis / the goddess hold" herself and Helen "in this her island, her egg-shell," her stability depending on being able "to crystalize" the poem into being. She started recognizing Heydt as a Macpherson update; H.D. turned her terrible fixation on the latter into "the memory of molten ember."[49]

Early in February, Schmideberg "was very expansive and affable at table," holding forth in German.[50] Except in arguments with Melitta, H.D. never heard him speak the language. Wearing dark glasses, H.D. played games with "Bear," calling Heydt "Spy 1" and Ivan "Spy II." Her Palm Sunday letter to Bryher mentioned Ivan three times, once that he was with Heydt, another that he spoke of Bryher and that he would still be there when she returned.

In March, Bryher, back from Pakistan, tried selling Kenwin, as if to auction off the rough times with Schmideberg—and the lost times with H.D. She asked Charlie Chaplin to buy it for its wonderful projection room; he declined. She then moved many of her own and H.D.'s books and papers, among them a tapestry box carefully packed by Mrs. Ash, into an attic at Kusnacht. With Kenwin coming to Kusnacht, H.D.'s diary notes let out, "Dear Lord of Hosts! Bryher packed eight cases and had them sent here. She is trying to sell the Villa and wants to make preliminary clearance."[51] This transfer of goods sparked abandonment fears: what would Bryher do next? Writing Aldington, anxious about Bryher "on the loose," with a new dislike of Switzerland, "I am upset for her," she expressed, feeling deprived of her "help and stabilizing now," the kind of help Bryher usually unsparingly supplied.[52]

By renaming the "dormer room" a "poet's corner" located "at top of the house, under a slope of roof,"[53] H.D. decided the extra space knit their stories together. Her patience was worn thin after sittings with Schmideberg, and she begged Bryher's return: "[T]here is quite a gap at table, but you must fill it in."[54] Staying in March in the small side room, Bryher planned for New York in late April to see the Schaffners, with H.D. unsure she could manage it.[55] She needed dental work, touched that the clinic prepared liquid drinks with eggs and fruit especially for her. She recalled splitting a tooth, forced to see Freud's specialist, Dr. Pichler, about a third her size, with "a light on his forehead so one gets a sort of Borderline sensation, and electric-ray treatment at the same time."[56] "Love is a martyrdom," *Pilate's Wife* articulated, the couple living it. Bryher visited again in April, firming up H.D.'s proximate ineffability.

With Heydt, H.D. discovered a layer of trauma *not* uncovered with Freud—the reason she resisted finishing her World War I novel, *Madrigal*; until she uncovered *what* was buried, she was unaware what blocked the book's birth. Heydt coaxed her to confront her miscarriage. A repressed memory surfaced of Aldington loudly screaming at her, "[D]on't you realize what this means. Don't you feel anything? *The Lusitania has gone down*." Slyly, H.D. set this confession into surety by parenthesis: "(But this never happened. Surely, this was fantasy.)"[57] This "earlier unremembered shock, when the first child perished under her heart," nestled deep, brought into light, enabled *Bid Me to Live*.[58]

* * *

Bryher's Sapphic apprenticeship with H.D. manifested in *Player's Boy* (1953), dedicated to H.D. Less stark than *Fourteenth*, with "its lovely reconstruction of Hastings,"[59] *Player's* rendered the theater as temple. The novel unfolds from May 1, 1605, as James Sands faces his master's death. Besides teaching him fencing, singing, and lute playing, at the final performance, "momentarily hushed citizens had become his phantoms," enabling Sands to see "not taffeta, but the cold glory of the stars."[60] The book touched Moore, especially moved by Raleigh's approach to the scaffold, discovering "an unforced eloquence that is poetry" "lovingly integrated, not imposed.'"[61]

In July 1954, Bryher brought *Majic Ring* to Kusnacht, memorializing their séances and Corfu experiences. When H.D. tried to pack it for Lugano, Bryher said it was "a winter book." Though Bryher had it typed, she worried it could trigger H.D., who now wrote only two hours a day, one in the morning, the other before dinner, resenting her "forced siesta." "Amazed," H.D. pursued *Helen*, enjoying reprieve form the "ps-a whirl at Z."[62] Sending "so much love, dear, dear Fido," H.D. exposed that distance never lasted; she arranged rooms for Doris and Bryher, who visited on August 10; H.D. "loved our à trois."[63]

That summer, with Dr. Heydt and H.D. away, Schmideberg went wild, wishing "to fetch" Bryher from airports, calling Kusnacht a "concentration camp."[64] In August, Heydt turned up with Ivan in Lugano. H.D. dubbed them the "boys" or "the Dioscuri"(Castor and Pollux, whose mother, like Helen's, was Leda). They swam at the Lido, went to Salvatore, and met H.D. for coffee at Saipa, all a "great surprise." Recognizing the Discouri were lovers, she preserved Heydt as a mythical one. Bryher returned to Lugano for the birthday octave, which H.D. called "the best visit of all the wonderful times—the *best*."[65]

Thriving on incompletion, H.D. turned down Heydt's invitation to Venice. On his return later in September through Lugano, he dined with the "family," H.D., Perdita, and Bryher, the latter craving a group bus trip to Rome. H.D. resisted "the big undertaking." Farewells growing harder, she asked Bryher not to see her off at the station in Lugano. She needed to be alone for "the last few days" with her "intense concentration" that "requires a sort of almost trance-like detachment," explaining her trick more carefully: "[T]his is all very clear and very simple. The last days, if I am alone, I am really GONE from the spot and so slide off with no ties whatever." Dissociation was a life's practice. H.D. now thought *Helen* "a sort of tapestry-piece" that, when complete, she "could do a sort of dissertation on it all."[66]

* * *

H.D. cabled Bryher in Pully the news that Schmideberg died on September 22, 1954. Grief and relief ensued. Hearing of his former psychoanalyst's demise, Herring tried honoring "the Bear that IS, and not the pale ghost he WAS after the war."[67]

H.D. and Bryher left for Rome in December, comforting each other for their mutual loss. Irritability cropped up. Bryher was sad that Heydt currently held the bulk of H.D.'s attention, while H.D. regretted how much energy Schmideberg had drained from Bryher—as did Herring. Heydt had his own manias, confiding to H.D. "extraordinary ideas" and little to no sleep. Bryher was surprised he "had not broken under the strain, months ago," for "training-analysis" in Zurich "often penetrates to a dangerous depth."[68] Walking from the train in the snow to Kusnacht, Bryher complained about slush and cold. That same December, Heydt left to see Ivan, "his Hungarian friend," during Christmas; they loved London, and *Trilogy,* wishing a translation for those bombed in Dresden.

Back at Kusnacht, H.D. took Bryher to the nearby Café Saluz, where Schmideberg once enjoyed treats. Mothering a bit, H.D. selected two chocolate eggs that he had savored. She feared Bryher might disappear again, and Heydt dissolve. In 1955, she dreamed of Dowding "clinging to a spar in the dark sea, slips off—is gone"; Bryher corrected that "he did not drown, he is buried." As for Helen, "[s]he is lost, to be found again."[69]

By now, Bryher seemed fated to send friends to Kusnacht. In April, Doris, Bryher's oldest friend, asked her to sort her sister, Ethel's, crisis. Ethel's daughter, Joan Leader Waluga, suffered a mental breakdown when her fiancé failed to show up for their Argentine wedding. Afterward, she couldn't speak or eat. Heydt assigned Joan to H.D., who knew her as a child in khaki shorts with hunting knife. This let Bryher travel with Macpherson and Islay to Capri in late April, posting descriptions of jasmine and orange scents.[70] Late in April 1955, Bryher drove Madame Herf, Joan, and H.D. to a flower show in Zurich, and in the front seat, wearing sunglasses, H.D. sensed "timeless-time," nearly blinded by "luminous flood-lit tree-fern and orchids":

> [T]here is a stranger wave of reality; all the dim, rain-washed world outside, the grey lake, dripping beeches, give me the impression that *that* outside exists in a

secondary dimension, but a fountain (we pass it) becomes a classic feature on stage, set for a just-laugh perception; *everything outside can be lighted, renewed by this within.*[71]

The "outside"—nature, artifacts—turned eternal when inner sight haloed it; H.D. continually adjusted transcendent and relative rails.

While Heydt vacationed during spring 1955, Joan's depression wore on H.D. The Discouri fiendishly sent a postcard from Capri, depicting Aphrodite "urging Helen to love Paris," anticipating *Helen*'s second section. Heydt then vacationed in Rome with Ivan, convening again with Bryher, Macpherson, and Islay, a virtual queer convention. H.D. sensed Heydt seemed "to 'know' Kenneth," especially after he read "Narthex," which led him to ask about Bryher sulking in a tin chair at St. Mark's Square: "Did [she] mind?" Surprised, H.D. replied that Bryher "made the story," successor to Gregg, and much more.[72]

* * *

In November 1954, Pearson arrived to produce sound recordings of *Helen* poems. In the studio with Pearson and Bryher, H.D. rediscovered her "alter-ego or [her] double—and that [her] mother's name was Helen," now herself "Helen out of the body, in another world." On the circular record, "there I, there Helen lives out her war—her wars." The other side of the disc memorialized Helen cavorting with Paris. She "warmed [her] hands and heart at the glow" of this creation, reinstating another triad: "it is you and Fido who gave me the courage to go on with it." *Helen* was "strictly I N N E R and esoteric and personal," with no need to blow "her tin horn," for "you [Pearson] and Fido chiefly did that for me."[73]

"Caught up at last," H.D. explained to Dobson her epistolary "absence," boasting "161 poems in sequence in 3 books, with notes in addition. Well over 200 pages in type-script. I have spent 3 years on it."[74] For five days in November, H.D. created prose captions, "mounted B E F O R E [each] poem," much as she had with *Ion*. She seized two rails. On February 2, 1955, Heydt drove H.D. to the Zurich studio to finish more recordings, providing "a self-assurance that [she] generally lack[ed]."[75] Heydt and her "suns" summoned the recordings.

In June, Beach confided to Bryher that Monnier had "la maladie Meniere," suffering spells of terrible vertigo, dizziness, vomiting, her life unlivable.[76] Finally, on June 19, 1955, Monnier took her life with pills. Bryher and Doris had long imagined a euthanasia club, then strictly outlawed. H.D. wrote Beach to "accept [her] heart's devotion—a double devotion."[77] With losses stacking up, she appreciated Bryher anew, who "not only brought her own little typewriter but in a sense has mended my own shattered mechanism." During July storms in 1955, H.D. woke up with her nightgown soaked in blood. Her abdominal sutures, not completely healed, had torn open. On September 17, she checked into Zurich's Luxor House, the echo not lost; the doctor "dug out another whole stitch."[78] She then joined other semipermanent convalescents living at Kusnacht's Villa Verena; Bryher, the ambulater, occupied an adjacent maid's room when there.

* * *

H.D and Bryher, taking Doris along, visited Perdita and her new baby, Elizabeth Bryher, born June 30, 1956. Although fretting about the journey months in advance, H.D. felt sustained by the two houses, Schaffner's and Pearson's. In New York, H.D. adored the infant, whose clothes combined genders, even countries, "like a Dresden doll" and "such funny, outgrown, tiny chiffon full-skirted, puffed sleeves," "with all the other-utility-yet very pretty rompers and ruffled over-pants." Staying again at the Beekman Tower Hotel, H.D. delighted in Pantheon's ad for *Tribute to Freud* and *Beowulf*. The caption for the half-page ad read "The meeting of two creative minds." She wrote Dobson, "We combined our books," and celebrated with Pearson.[79]

A photograph of H.D., Pearson, and Bryher sitting in front of Yale's Sterling Library in 1956 shows each one debilitated by war and, of course, time (Figure 23.1). It "was almost too much," attending the exhibition of her very old manuscripts and photographs on display at Yale for her birthday month. "Yes—we do belong there," she voiced. New York was "modern Alexandria" with "powerful attractions."[80] Bryher guided H.D. toward her citizenship, to ensure she always had an extended family near.

On November 6, back at Verena, H.D. pranced into Dr. Brunner's office and slipped on "the highly waxed" parquet floor, skidding on a small rug. Her leg fractured at the hip. She saw it as punishment for her pleasure in New York and New Haven. Alerted by Bryher, Aldington learned that H.D.'s efforts at "premature walking" complicated her fracture. He empathized, "[T]he thought of Hilda being lame is dreadful."[81] Pearson comforted, himself knowing "what it is to lie abed this way," comparing it to a spiritual retreat.[82]

After H.D. penned a fan letter to E. M. Butler the previous month, the Cambridge scholar dedicated *Byron and Goethe* to her because of the usual "dead silence" around her academic books.[83] She invited Butler to Kusnacht, but the scholar demurred. Still bedridden, H.D. saw her own drama playing out through Goethe, an "impassioned Hellenist," who faced an enormous "obstacle blocking the path to the completion of his masterpiece [*Faust*]." Driven to "introduce Faust to Helen," Goethe fearing distortion of her beauty had "turned [Helen] into a heart-hauntingly lovely ghost."[84] Music to H.D.'s ears. Studying Goethe prompted another poem.

From April 5 to May 13, 1957, H.D. wrote *Vale Ave*, confronting the final departure as arrival, a prelude to losing Heydt. Collapsing temporal and spatial realms as well as making palimpsestic typologies of those she knew with those long dead, she dedicated it to Bryher: "To: *Amico*. Kusnacht, Spring 1957." Introducing the poem in a sequence with Adam and his first wife, Lilith, she asked, "Is she the Serpent who tests the *androgynat primordial?*" This referred to the splitting of original psychic wholeness, materialized through her own and Bryher's split psyche and body. Setting forth a procession "through time—specifically, late Rome, dynastic Egypt, legendary

Figure 23.1 H.D., Norman H. Pearson, and Bryher in front of Sterling Library, Yale University, 1956. Unsourced photograph.
Courtesy of Beinecke Rare Book and Manuscript Library, Yale University.

Provence, early seventeenth-century England, and contemporary London," "herself and Aldington" joined pairs of doomed heterosexual couples. The seventeenth-century couple Raleigh and Elizabeth Dyer, niece of the court astrologer and poet Sir Edward Dyer, acted centerpiece.

Earlier, H.D. almost wrote a story of reincarnation: *I am Elizabeth Dyer, come back to tell you all*. Raleigh, like Bryher, was frequently at sea. But Raleigh "chose the way of love" and "found himself (and with her) in the Tower"; this compelled H.D. The delirious "Lizeth" thought an angel "paced" about her bed, but "Hugh" (as in Dowding) presumed it "was a devil," thus failing in love. The one "to free her," Bryher as "Amico," was present as H.D.'s doctor detailed, "some of my cases / have to wait a year; we can later fortify / the pin, the wedge with a cross-wedge."[85] Heydt sent H.D. gardenias when he left for America in August 1957. Still hobbling, H.D. began *Sagesse*, telling him her "room is fragrant with enchantment, with the flowers he left."[86] A taunting gesture. With other Kusnacht residents, she still feared his "escape" to America.[87] "Amico" complained that Heydt dominated H.D.'s world, yet Bryher also rewarded Heydt's efforts to help H.D., giving him $3,500 that December.[88]

* * *

H.D. told Horace Gregory that *Helen* functioned as "a wish to make real to myself what is most real," confirming an amorphous existence, necessary disorientation, at least for her art: "Where are we? / and what is the answer?"[89] Now Bryher, Heydt, and Pearson were H.D.'s main support system. Beach comforted Bryher, repeating Toklas' words that Stein "thought [her] a Napoleon," herself regarding her friend "as someone taking over Heaven, and running it efficiently after the lord's weak management of it all these centuries."[90]

Bryher let Aldington back into the fold. He was suffering a mild crack-up after his 1955 biography on Lawrence of Arabia. Shattering reviews killed his book that unmasked Lawrence's homosexuality. The ethos of the 1950s weirdly resembled the Victorian age; Cold War lenses often held spies and queerness as interchangeable.[91] H.D. liked his attempt to "debunk a legend," though faulted him for "basking on Sunset Boulevard" during the Battle of Britain. H.D. foresaw T. E. Lawrence at the glorifying film of himself, "crouched or craning forward in a crowded theatre, secretly watching himself in heroic splendor."[92] Bryher offered Aldington "assurance of aid" because of his boycotted books "following [his] exposure of the [Lawrence] legend."[93] Netta Patmore had abandoned Aldington and their child, Catherine (Catha), in 1950. The Patmores, he explained to H.D. in 1957, extorted divorce damages of £5,000, which "they knew he didn't have," in order to make "the decree absolute (so that C. would not have been illegitimate)."[94] Aldington now understood what "legitimacy" meant.

* * *

Saved from a trial for treason, Pound was found mentally unfit for his own defense in 1945, though a campaign to release him began well before his discharge on May 7, 1958, and after spending nearly thirteen years at St. Elizabeth's, he headed back to Italy. Upon debarking in Genoa, the remorseless Pound issued a Fascist salute to the press. In spring of 1958, Pearson, who supported Pound's release, urged H.D. to preserve their early bond for the future. With some reluctance, she acquiesced, starting *End to Torment*, dedicated to Pearson, comprising a daily record, a nonlinear meditation, from late spring 1958 to Pound's landing on July 9. It did not leave Pound unscathed, even on light points. She suffered "excruciatingly from his clumsy dancing," code for feeling trampled. She relived the time "almost fifty years ago," "when Erza left for Europe," asserting "he would have destroyed the center they call 'Air and Crystal' of her poetry."⁹⁵ Bryher was fearful Pound would show up at Kusnacht.

H.D. lived, she told Dobson, "[her] travels through [Bryher]."⁹⁶ Both Bryher and Pearson came for the birthday week, with final paperwork for regaining H.D.'s U.S. citizenship.⁹⁷ Divorced, and friendly with her ex-husband, H.D. fantasized a life in California, especially after the beat poet, Robert Duncan, wrote her. Bryher thought San Francisco an attractive city for them, as "[e]verybody" "among the refugees" told her it was "the one place they would like to live in."⁹⁸ But H.D. was increasingly frail.

Then Heydt visited on November 3, 1958, to announce his engagement to his analyst, Dori Gutscher. His pale face told all. H.D.'s congratulations were stilted. Bryher sadly complained to Pearson that she had spent almost half a century with H.D., who now fixated upon Heydt. Bryher urged H.D.'s memoir, *Thorn Thicket* ("Bryher tells me that it must be said"), akin to the purge of Pound in *End to Torment* or Dowding in *Sword*.⁹⁹ With wobbly legs, Bryher pulled the arrow from her own wounds, realizing H.D.'s turn to authority figures and to apparitional queers, like herself, Gregg, Macpherson, Heydt, and maybe even Rodeck, to confirm her gifts.

For the sake of her sanity, Bryher had to consider her gift-giving process profoundly akin to what Marcel Mauss uncovers in his famous 1925 sociological study of Maori culture, the discovery that "the spirit of things" existed in the "hau," "the god in the goods," "alive and active, a part of the donor that travels along with the thing given and eventually draws the gift ... towards its sources," and Morris further summarizes, "if the hau were simply a spirit that compels return, gift exchange would require just two stations," and the Maori have three, the gift increasing with its handoff to a third.¹⁰⁰ Both H.D. and Bryher believed in transformative alchemy, and they had expected an Aquarian Age. It had not come. Human dominance on earth seemed fated to extinction, through the wars and then the atom bomb.

Bryher invited Aldington, the not so spruced solider of yore, his chivalric patina cracked, to make an unannounced call on H.D. Viewing himself as "a neurotic" and "in a rather feeble state," he was at first "startled at [Bryher's] suggestion."¹⁰¹ True to her role as deus ex machina, Bryher orchestrated a reunion with a humbler Aldington to rally H.D.'s spirits. He brought Catha to meet H.D. and Bryher, staying from December 16 through 18, 1958. The timing was right. After seeing Aldington's physical troubles and meeting his motherless daughter, Bryher, hinting at an annuity, sent him the enormous amount of 200,000 francs.¹⁰²

The next day our couple made their congratulatory call on Heydt and Dori, although H.D. could hardly manage the stairs. Dori met them halfway up. Bryher eased H.D.'s disappointment that Heydt wasn't, like H.D., reversible. Bryher, with Aldington, helped her face daylight reality, to "remember" *Helen* on "a beach," searching for "a bead, a bowl / half-filled with sand / after a wreck."¹⁰³ Disturbed that Heydt had abandoned Ivan, H.D. repeated Bryher's knowing remark, "Make no mistake about it." Leaving Kusnacht in maudlin mode, Erich and Dori sailed to America for their nuptials in August 1959. Heydt sent gardenias again before departing. They "did not palliate ... the separation."[104] Eventually, H.D. learned sexual taboos necessitated Heydt's compromise. Apparently a distraught Heydt, wanting to settle there, visited Melitta (the Bearess) in New York in 1957, fearful his German roots and his attraction to men would count against him in America, a visit she imparted to H.D. to ameliorate unnecessary hurt. Henry Abelove describes the 1950s need to shield "difference" by escaping through travel, imposed exile;[105] no wonder Macpherson and Islay went with Bryher to Rome and Capri.

The tale of H.D.'s war-torn marriage, preserved in *Bid Me to Live*, was accepted for publication in 1959. With H.D. for the birthdays, Bryher informed Beach when they heard.[106] To H.D.'s dismay, Grove took the book as "H.D.'s"—when it followed "the *D.A.* series." She considered the Delia Alton novels the "'blood + tears' etc. to get the formula." Her ironic side described the novel as "*Marriage* 20 years later, with another war." *Bid* meanwhile raised her former self as H.D. with Aldington, though "compar[ed] to them [Erich and Dori], we are old people, compared to us, ... they are old people."[107] Repeatedly, H.D. and Bryher, in phantom marriage, witnessed the discounting of women and "deviants." Their loving faith in one another spanned their adult lives: their erotic early years, their intellectual duration, and their familial, even ancestral sense of relation.

In February 1960, H.D. won the American Academy of Arts and Letters Award, following W. H. Auden, Saint-John Perse, and Jorge Guillén. Bryher offered to join the ceremony on May 25 at Yale, but H.D. preferred facing it alone, though she took Brunner's granddaughter, Blanche, as bodyguard. Wanting specifically to center herself, she drew upon her own "quite considerable" American funds. Her brother Harold wrote Bryher, who repaid these sums, already allocated, as Bryher saw it, to Perdita. He was "still at sea," puzzled by *Bid*.[108]

H.D. and the twenty-one-year-old Blanche flew Swiss-Air from Zurich. Bryher set her clocks to New York time. Robert Duncan popped in to pay her tribute at the Stanhope Hotel. He praised her valedictory *Vale Ave*, sent to him by Pearson. The long poem, she explained to Duncan, was "the descent into matter or the final acceptance of the material aspects of life and the struggle to survive."[109] The survival of materiality had inversely led to transcendent poetry and prose. Her skeletal slightness, her angular body mediated her breathy poems. *Selected Poems* pulsed through Grove in 1957. "Bryher was my heritage," H.D. wrote in *The Gift*, and Duncan well recognized the unnamable union of two women, possibly enacting a new model for rethinking sexual and familial ties. Before meeting H.D., he surveyed literary history for queers—teachers still taught Whitman as straight. As early as 1944, he wrote "The Homosexual in Society and Politics," hailing resistance to dominant culture as obfuscating identity itself.[110] He looked to our contemporary opening up of gender identifications; meanwhile Heydt disappeared into queer anonymity.

Bryher cheered H.D. on from afar. At the ceremony, Pearson counted three thousand in the audience, noting that three hundred had "to be turned away."[111] Blanche detailed for Bryher H.D.'s performance as "perfect," "strong and intense," so that "everybody was deeply touched."[112] Upon H.D.'s return, Heydt supplied gardenias she did not want. He was in the wrong story. "The perfection of the fiery moment cannot be contained, or can it?" H.D. asked Dobson, who recognized both H.D.'s and, ultimately, Bryher's capacities for grand articulations and actions. As for aesthetics, Aldington celebrated the "beautifully formed thought and speech" of *Helen*. Pound and Eliot, he thought, "pushed her into the background, after stealing what they could of her discoveries and techniques."[113] By the end of *Thorn* (1960), H.D. had returned to the pole of Egypt, discovering that "Bryher and [her] mother were in a sense, myself, in the mysteries, Karnak, Ko Ombo and the rest, my alter-egos."[114]

Behind the scenes, Heydt worried that H.D. flirted with a breakdown similar to the one she suffered in 1946. Bryher stood vigil. Meanwhile, Beach planned an American Embassy exhibition, a retrospective of Americans in 1920s Paris, and wanted to include "H.D.'s Man Ray" and the "most beautiful photo of [Bryher] for [her] memoirs."[115] Dobson sent H.D. Lawrence Durrell's *Reflections on a Marine Venus* for her birthday, which Bryher warned her not to read without her.[116] Durrell put his finger on the couple's sensibility. Returning to Rhodes after World War II, he proposed a "disease as yet unclassified," denoted as "*Islomania*," for those who "find islands somehow irresistible," as if "direct descendants of the Atlantans."[117] He even spotted a dolphin near the Pillars of Hercules. Bryher arrived "for [H.D.'s] birthday," celebrating what they could hardly believe: *Bid Me to Live* out in 1960.[118]

H.D. stayed at Villa Verena until May 1961, when Brunner's son, Rudolph, decided to sell Kusnacht. A terrible shock for H.D., precipitously transplanted, along with other regular semi-incapacitated guests, who were notified of an August "eviction" that arrived in May. Bryher conveyed to Dobson the shock for Verena residents, one nearly driven to suicide by this removal. Until they could determine their best course, H.D. resided at Zurich's Sonnenberg Hotel, where Bryher attended her, attributing H.D.'s subsequent stroke and heart attack on June 6 to the abrupt dislocation.

Moved to the hospital, Roten Kreuz Spiral, H.D. suffered paralysis on the right side; she regained mobility in her legs and hands, though her speech was slurred.[119] She slowly began walking on crutches, but her throat muscles kept her from speaking, except sparingly. Her precarity was a kind of triumph. Her last posthumous poem, *Hermetic Definition*, captured the inevitability of blossoming, death, and rebirth: "the reddest rose unfolds; // (nobody can stop that …)."[120] Bryher imagined them moving to New Haven near the Pearsons, she told Dobson, warning that H.D. had "lost tremendous ground" due to gastric flu and not eating.[121] On the twenty-seventh day of her most productive month, September, in 1961, H.D. died in her sleep.[122]

* * *

Set in Cornwall, the site of their first meeting, *Ruan* (1960) was Bryher's pre-death adieu. In it, her cabin-boy-sage adventured in the Scillies. Mary Renault, already a celebrated historical novelist, found the book possessed "a magical quality of pause, of waiting for the kaleidoscope of history to shift to its next pattern." She applauded its ability "to communicate this blankness of expectation to the reader."[123] This "blankness" resonated with the "wall" in "We Two," H.D.'s early poem articulating obstacles to visibility. If ever in the same location, Renault hoped to meet Bryher, who sent *Helen* as a historical poem.

After H.D.'s death, Pearson, Bryher, and Perdita began contending with the critics, who sought to probe the "mystery" of H.D. Susan Stanford Friedman was among the first to develop a friendship with Perdita. Writing *Psyche Reborn*, Friedman corresponded with Dobson, Pearson, and Perdita. Bryher published three other acclaimed historical novels—*Coin of Carthage* (1963), *January Tale* (1966), and *Colors of Vaud* (1969), accompanying *Ruan, Gate to the Sea, Roman Wall, Player's Boy, Fourteenth*, each released before H.D.'s death. Her memoir, *Heart to Artemis*, a lesbian classic published in 1962, downplayed gender struggles.

Perdita cherished Bryher, hosting her visits to the Hamptons, fitting out a room like a ship's cabin.[124] Bryher had to contend with all and sundry asking her for money, including a letter from Hamilton College to fund a Pound lectureship; the associate professor wrote that it "was a custom," "this care of past men," salting her wound that H.D. had not the attention "great men" duly received.[125]

In the years leading up to her death in 1983, Bryher suffered grave memory loss, and Perdita's genius "other" mother was getting "vaguer and vaguer." In 1980, Perdita communicated that Bryher, the producer of thousands of letters and telegrams, could not even send a postcard; on a phone call with her, "she spoke of 'Perdita'—an alter ego extension right there at her side as well as the U S A," and though Perdita found it "traumatizing," it reiterated H.D. and Bryher's pattern, believing they communicated through wavelengths.[126] In 1982, "as her next of kin" and with power of attorney, Perdita took the terrible responsibility of declaring Bryher "mentally incompetent," enveloped by persecution fears, the product of war neurosis. Max Reugg, her latter-day accountant, reported that Bryher, the adventurer, had retreated to a single room in Kenwin.[127]

Thus, by the time her biographer Barbara Guest arrived, Bryher was losing her grip—even walking in the garden was too difficult. Though the interviewer wished she could have received more testimonials about H.D., Bryher had testified, for the better part of her life, with and apart from H.D.; she kept her "beat" safe, while H.D. celebrated Bryher's transgenderism. After Bryher's death on January 28, 1983, Perdita told Friedman that senility had spread "chaos," and it took two full days with her son Nicholas, born on the same day in 1958, to organize Bryher's papers and tidy Kenwin; it marked the "end of an epoch."[128] The *Gay Literary Supplement* hailed Bryher in February 1983 as "[p]assionately valued by a few, unknown by most. Bryher who died five weeks ago was one of the most remarkable lesbians of this century."[129] "Lesbian" was the only available word. On November 30 of the same year, Perdita's husband John died of cancer.

Perdita reviewed in 1987 Gillian Hanscombe and Virginia L. Smyers' *Writing for Their Lives*, showing H.D. and Bryher creating an edgy modernism, with large photos of each and the caption "They lived to write."[130] Bryher, her main invisible, makes them both visible. Both were larger than life. Without Bryher, H.D. might have lost her creative drive; without H.D., Bryher might have done herself in. One might say H.D. acted "closet," shielding the transgendered, hidden Bryher.

A trio met again at Shakespeare & Co. with the Man Ray photo of H.D. posted on the wall between the then still living Beach and Bryher, kindred ambassadors of modernist creative inspiration (Figure 23.2). The photo expresses the unfettered devotion of Beach and Bryher, mostly regarded as anonymous aids to Joyce and H.D., respectively.

H.D. and Bryher *consciously* defied the category "woman." It is not who you love, but how you love. Poetry was a transcript of the ephemeral doubling with "timeless-time," H.D.'s phrase throughout *Helen*. This pair's untold love story is necessarily incomplete—as was *Paint It*, key in H.D.'s early grappling with her polysexuality. The love story of modernism was one of destruction and incipience, wrestling with unknown modes of living, hatching out of invisibility, surviving two wars. Their shared lives and creative work, their resistance to labeling, their lifetimes expanding and reconfiguring modernism itself, but equally important, what it means to be human. This story will go on somewhere.

Figure 23.2 Sylvia Beach and Bryher with a photo of H.D., undated. Unsourced photograph.
Courtesy of Beinecke Rare Book and Manuscript Library, Yale University.

Notes

Chapter 1

1. William D. Rubenstein, *The Richest of the Rich* (Hampshire: Great Britain, 2007). He states, "Ellerman was easily the richest man in Britain by the 1920s" (125).
2. H.D. to Bryher, July 13, 1918, All letters to and from the couple used here are from the Beinecke archives unless otherwise stated. See abbreviations for location of archives.
3. H.D., "Sheltered Garden," *CP*, 51–55.
4. H.D., "Sea Rose," *CP*, 5.
5. H.D., *CP*, 7.
6. H.D., *Paint It*, 18.
7. Bryher, *Two*, 289.
8. Bryher, *Heart*, 23.
9. Susan Stanford Friedman, interview with Perdita, unpublished notes, 1978, in author's possession.
10. Bryher, *HA*, 17.
11. H.D., *Paint It*, 18.
12. H.D. to Bryher, July 17, 1951.
13. H.D., *Paint It*, 92 n. 9. Laity cites this translation from an anonymous Latin poem: "*Cras Amet qui numquam amavit, quique amavit cras amet!* (Let those love now …)."
14. David Paternotte, "Disentangling and Locating the Anti-Gender Campaigns in Europe," *Politics and Governance* 6, no. 3 (2018): 6–19.
15. Heather Love, "Modernism at Night," *PMLA* 124, no. 3 (May 2009): 744.
16. Bryher to H.D., November 16, 1934.
17. H.D.'s grandson, Nicholas Schaffner, authored *Beatles Forever* in 1977. Born January 28, 1953, Bryher died on January 28, thirty years later. Nicholas died of AIDS in 1991.
18. Bryher, "Clippings," box 127, folder 4433.
19. Daniel Bergner, "The Struggles of Rejecting the Gender Binary," *New York Times*, June 4, 2019, https://www.nytimes.com/2019/06/04/magazine/gender-nonbinary.html. Still, for clarity's sake, I often use the pronoun "she" for Bryher, though this in itself enacts her violated boyhood.
20. H.D., *Gift*, "H.D.'s Notes," 248.
21. Hilary Clinton's eulogy for Eve Windsor, lead plaintiff in the case decided by the U.S. Supreme Court, legalizing gay marriage and creating marriage equality. *Daily Beast*, September 15, 2017.
22. Susan Stanford Friedman to Norman Pearson, March 9, 1978, SSF.
23. H.D. to Bryher, September 21, 1947.
24. Pearson to Susan Stanford Friedman, May 9, 1978, SSF.
25. Tobias Chruton, *The Gnostics* (New York: Barnes & Nobel, 1987), 52–53.
26. Celina Kusch and Rebecca Walsh created the digital resource H.D. Biography Wiki.

27. New Directions has kept much of H.D.'s work in print (*HERmione, Helen of Egypt, Hippolytus Temporizes/Ion, Hermetic Definition, Tribute to Freud*, and *Collected Poems, 1912–1944*). Other publishers have contributed to H.D.'s twenty-first-century renaissance. The most notable is the University Press of Florida; its current catalogue includes *The Gift* (1998), *The Sword Went Out to Sea* (2007), *Majic Ring* (2009), *The Mystery* (2009), *White Rose and the Red* (2009), *Bid Me to Live* (2011), *By Avon River* (2014), *Within the Walls* and *What Do I Love?* (2014). Additionally, ELS Editions, produced by the University of Victoria, has focused on H.D.'s late prose, publishing a single edition of three collected texts, *Magic Mirror, Compassionate Friendship*, and *Thorn Thicket* (2012), and a scholarly edition of *Hirslanden Notebooks* (2015).

    Bryher's resurgence has paralleled H.D.'s. Schaffner Press is out with a fresh *Beowulf: A Novel of the London Blitz* (2020). University of Wisconsin collected *Development* and *Two Selves* in a single volume in 2000; Paris Press has published two of her novels (*Visa for Avalon: A Novel* [2004] and *The Player's Boy* [2006]) along with her influential memoir, *The Heart to Artemis: A Writer's Memoirs* (2006). All H.D. and Bryher scholars owe a debt to Susan Stanford Friedman's magisterial edition of the letters between Freud, H.D., Bryher, and their circle, *Analyzing Freud*, published by New Directions in 2002.
28. Barbara Guest, *Herself Defined: The Poet H.D. and Her World* (New York: Doubleday, 1984). Janice Robinson, *H.D.: The Life and Work of an American Poet* (New York: Houghton Mifflin, 1982) wrongly alleged D. H. Lawrence was Perdita's father.
29. Susan Stanford Friedman to Perdita Schaffner, February 22, 1983, unpublished letter, SSF.
30. Guest, *Herself Defined*, 115.
31. "H.D." predominantly refers to Hilda Doolittle. To show levels of intimacy, I use nicknames when a particular fondness needs marking. See "Dramatis Personae."
32. Viola Baxter Jordan, introduced by Pound in 1905, gave H.D. Evangeline Adams' *Astrology: Your Place in the Sun* (New York: Dodd, Mead, 1927). See Friedman, *PR*, 166–170.
33. H.D., *Paint It*, 86.
34. Rachel Plau Duplessis, "Romantic Thralldom in H.D.," *Contemporary Literature* 20, no. 2 (Spring 1979): 178–203.
35. H.D., *CP*, 55.
36. Michael Schmidt, *Lives of the Poets* (New York: Knopf, 1999), 620.
37. H.D. to Bryher, May 3, 1933. *AF*, 238. This phrase "feeding the light" comes up across H.D.'s letters to Bryher from this time forth.
38. Susan Stanford Friedman, "Interview with Robert Duncan about H.D.," December 28, 1979, unpublished notes, SSF.
39. Lawrence Rainey, *Institutions of Modernism: Literary Elites and the Public Sphere* (New Haven, CT: Yale University Press, 1999), 155; Rainey makes factual errors, calling Bryher an "only child"; she was illegitimate. He alleges that in 1933 Bryher helped Walter Benjamin escape from Berlin (167); Bryher and Benjamin did not meet until 1936.
40. Rainey, *Institutions*, 148.
41. Susan Stanford Friedman's notes from interviewing Pearson, July 1979, SSF.
42. H.D., *Hermetic Definition*, 116.
43. Hugh Kenner, *The Invisible Poet: T.S. Eliot* (New York: McDowell, Obolensky, 1959), xi.
44. H.D., *Helen*, 21.
45. Bryher, *Beowulf*, 53.

46. H.D., *Walls*, 24.
47. T. E. Hulme, "Romanticism and Classicism" (1911), in *Speculations*, edited by Herbert Read (New York: Harcourt, 1934), 116.
48. Perdita Schaffner to Susan Stanford Friedman, January 23, 1984, unpublished letter, SSF.
49. Perdita Schaffner, "Running," *Iowa Review* 16, no. 3 (1986): 7.
50. H.D. to Bryher, November 27, 1934.
51. H.D. to Bryher, August 30, 1936.
52. Marianne Moore to Bryher, August 9, 1935, *MMSL*, 351.
53. Marcel Mauss' famous sociological study *The Gift: The Form and Reason for Exchange in Archaic Societies* was published in French in 1925, translated into English in 1990.
54. Adelaide Morris, *How to Live/What to Do: H.D.'s Cultural Poetics* (Urbana: University of Illinois Press, 2003), 82.
55. H.D. to George Plank, September 25, 1939.
56. H.D., *Gift*, 50.
57. Dorothy Richardson, *Pointed Roofs* (New York: Knopf, 1967).
58. H.D., *Notes*, 22.
59. H.D., "Notes to *Gift*, 217.
60. H.D., "Euripides," box 43, folder 1103.
61. H.D., *Tribute*, 56.
62. H.D., "Euripides."
63. H.D., *Thorn*, 190.
64. H.D., *Majic*, 47.
65. Bryher, *HA*, 5.
66. Gayle Salamon, *Assuming a Body: Transgender and Rhetorics of Materiality* (New York: Columbia University Press, 2010), 55.
67. See Heather Love, *Feeling Backward: Loss and the Politics of Queer History* (Cambridge, MA: Harvard University Press, 2007).
68. H.D. to John Cournos, n.d. (1919?).
69. Bryher to H.D., March, 20 1919.
70. Walter Benjamin, "Some Motifs on Baudelaire," in *Illuminations*, edited by Hannah Arendt (New York: Schocken Press, 1968), 112.
71. H.D., *Tribute*, 77, italics mine.
72. H.D., *Pilate's*, 86.
73. H.D. to Bryher, November 27, 1934. Bryher Papers.
74. Robert Dreyfuss, *Devil's Game* (New York: Henry Holt, 2005), 31–32.
75. H.D., *Gift*, 113–114.
76. H.D., *Gift*, 50.
77. H.D., *Walls*, 47.
78. Leigh Wilson, *Modernism and Magic: Experiments with Spiritualism, Theosophy and the Occult* (Edinburgh: Edinburgh University Press, 2012), 5–7.
79. Joel Martin and William J. Birnes, "Who You Gonna Call? Edison's Science of Talking to Ghosts," *Salon*, October 8, 2017, https://www.salon.com/2017/10/08/who-you-gonna-call-edison-and-the-science-of-talking-to-ghosts, excerpted from Joel Martin and William J. Birnes, *Edison vs. Tesla: The Battle over Their Last Invention* (New York: Skyhorse, 2017), citing *Modern Mechanix Magazine*, October 1933.
80. H.D., *Gift*, 51.

81. T. S. Eliot, "*Ulysses*, Order, and Myth" (1923), in *Selected Prose of T. S. Eliot*, edited by Frank Kermode (New York: Harcourt Brace, 1975), 177.
82. H.D., *Majic*, 135.
83. H.D., *Majic*, 131.
84. Diary entry of Piotr Qwiazda in *James Merrill and W. H. Auden: Homosexuality and Poetic Influence* (New York: Macmillan, 2007), 61.
85. H.D., "Advent" (1933), in *Tribute*, 153.

Chapter 2

1. Francis Wolle, "A Moravian Heritage" (Boulder, CO: Empire Reproduction and Printing Co., 1972), 21. Francis was Hilda's cousin.
2. William J. Murtagh, *Moravian Architecture and Town Planning: Bethlehem, Pennsylvania, and Other Eighteenth-Century American Settlements*, (Philadelphia: University of Pennsylvania Press, 1998), 6, n. 21.
3. H.D., "Advent," 124.
4. H.D., *Tribute*, 32.
5. H.D., "Notes to *Gift*," 232.
6. Aaron Spencer Fogelman, *Jesus Is Female: Moravians and Radical Religion in Early America* (Philadelphia: University of Pennsylvania Press, 2007), 78, 85.
7. Murtagh, *Moravian Architecture*, 6.
8. H.D., "Excerpts from a record by Agnes Angelica Seidel Howard written for her son," in "Genealogical Notes," box 48, folder 1221. H.D. Papers.
9. H.D., *Gift*, 68.
10. H.D. to George Plank, February 5, 1944. H.D. Papers.
11. Joseph Mortimer Levering, *A History of Bethlehem, Pennsylvanian, 1741–1892* (1903), 7–8.
12. Elaine Pagels, *The Gnostic Gospels* (New York: Random House, 1979), xxi, xxiii.
13. H.D., "Notes to *Gift*," 247–248, 266, 265, 263.
14. Fogelman, *Jesus Is Female*, 73.
15. Pagels, *Gnostic Gospels*, 49, 66–69, passim.
16. Fogelman, *Jesus Is Female*, 77–78, 79–80, passim.
17. H.D., *Gift*, 164, 156; "Notes to *Gift*," 233, 270.
18. H.D., "Notes to *Gift*," 240–243, 262.
19. H.D., "Notes to *Gift*, "262, 271–272, 271; Levering, *A History of Bethlehem*, 193.
20. H.D., *Gift*, 154. She imagined herself "the last bee in the bee-hive."
21. Fogelman, *Jesus Is Female*, 80, 89.
22. H.D. to George Plank, February 5, 1944; Levering, *A History of Bethlehem*, 28, n.3.
23. H.D., *Gift*, 35–36; "Notes to *Gift*," 229.
24. H.D., Gift, 133, 152, 166–167; "Notes to *Gift*," 231.
25. H.D, *Gift*, n. 30; "Notes to *Gift*," 280.
26. H.D., "Notes to *Gift*," 231–232.
27. H.D., *Gift*, 41; "Notes to *Gift*," 228.
28. H.D., *Gift*, 179; " Notes to *Gift*," 229.
29. See Charlotte Mandel, "Magical Lenses: Poet's Vision beyond the Naked Eye" in *H.D.: Woman and Poet*, edited by M. King (Orono, ME: National Poetry Foundation, 1986), 301–317.

30. H.D., "Advent," 115; H.D., *Gift*, 95.
31. H.D., "Advent," 178.
32. H.D., "Notes to *Gift*," 251.
33. H.D., "Notes to *Gifts*," 252, 253.
34. H.D., "Advent," 178–179.
35. R. H. Tucker, "Charles Leander Doolittle," *Astronomical Society of the Pacific*, March 20, 1919, 103–104.
36. Charles L. Doolittle, "An Address Delivered for the Alumni Association," Lehigh University, June 17, 1885, 5, 30.
37. Tucker, R.H. "Charles Leander Doolittle," 104.
38. H.D., "Notes to *Gift*," 253.
39. H.D., Advent," 142.
40. Thomas Hardy, *Two on a Tower* (Oxford: Oxford University Press, 1993), 34–35.
41. H.D., *Gift*, 96.
42. H.D., *Paint It*, 5, 4, 6.
43. H.D., *Tribute*, 33.
44. Perdita Schaffner, "Running," *Iowa Review* 16, no. 3 (1986): 9.
45. H.D., *Gift*, 116.
46. H.D., *Gift*, 175; see John 20:15. The lily turns communion chalice.
47. H.D., "Advent," 121.
48. H.D., *Gift*, 151.
49. H.D., "Notes to *Gift*," 222.
50. H.D., *Gift*, 158–159.
51. H.D., *Gift*, 161.
52. H.D., *Gift*, 165.
53. H.D., *Gift*, 173.
54. H.D., *Trilogy*, 159.
55. H.D., "Notes to *Gift*," 259, 246, 265.
56. H.D., *Gift*, 166.
57. H.D., "Advent," 118. In 1932 H.D. visited Alchemist's Street in Prague.
58. H.D., *Tribute*, 106–107.
59. H.D, "Advent," 118.

Chapter 3

1. Bryher, *Two*, 211.
2. Bryher, "Family Papers," box 147, folder 5032.
3. Guest, *Herself Defined*, 110.
4. Bryher, "Family Papers," box 152, folder 5145.
5. John R. Ellerman in entry for Mary Butlin, 1871, "England and Wales Census, 1871," Family Search online database with images, accessed December 10, 2017.
6. John Ellerman in household of Ellen Ryland, Edgbaston (Warwick), Worcestershire, England, "England and Wales Census, 1881," Family Search, accessed December 12, 2017; "1881 England, Scotland and Wales Census," Find My Past online database and images, Piece/Folio 2956/18, 27; National Archives, Kew, Surrey; Family History Library microfilm 101, 774, 837.

7. Bryher, "Family Papers," box 151, folder 5111.
8. Bryher, "Family Papers," box 151, folder 5114.
9. Ian Collard, *Ellerman Lines: Remembering a Great Shipping Company* (Stroud: History Press, 2014), 17.
10. Bryher, *HA*, 20. Morgan apparently generally did not take cash.
11. Collard, *Ellerman Lines*, 17, 34.
12. *London Times*, July 18, 1933.
13. *Daily Mail*, July 18, 1933.
14. Ben Fenton, "Was This the Richest and Most Secretive Tycoon Ever?," *Daily Telegraph*, May 22, 2006.
15. The cemetery clerk had no record of interment for Hannah Glover Ellerman when I visited Putney Vale Administration during the Havelock Ellis Conference, July 2011.
16. Bryher, *Heart*, 4.
17. The *Times* obituary made it clear that Glover was Hannah's father's name: "In 1908 he married Hannah, the daughter of Mr. George Glover, and had one son, John Reeves, who was born in 1909, and who succeeds to the title as second baronet." July 18, 1933.
18. Based on census records of 1871 and 1881, economic historian and Ellerman biographer William D. Rubenstein communicated that his research assistant, Ann Haydon, found another Hannah Glover, born and baptized in February 1866 at Fillongley, Warwickshire. See "Astrology" folder in H.D. Papers, box 47, folder 1145. Hannah left sparing traces to her past.
19. George Glover, 1875, "England and Wales Death Registration Index 1837–2007," Family Search, accessed December 31, 2014; "England & Wales Deaths, 1837–2006," Find My Past accessed 2012; "Deaths," Birmingham, Warwickshire, England, General Register Office, Southport, England.
20. Bryher Papers, "Family Papers," box 151, folder 5105.
21. Bryher, *HA*, 19.
22. Ginger S. Frost, *Living in Sin* (Manchester: Manchester University Press, 2008), 1–2, 5.
23. Frost, *Living in Sin*, 4.
24. Bryher, *HA*, 17.
25. Bryher, *HA*, 15. I use "they" here to accentuate Bryher's nonbinary identification, as "she" rings incorrectly, reverting to "she" for clarity.
26. Bryher, *HA*, 19.
27. Bryher, *HA*, 17.
28. Bryher, *Heart*, 14.
29. Bryher published these memories in *Paris 1900* with Adrienne Monnier's La Maison Des Amis Des Livres in 1936, translated into French.
30. Bryher, *HA*, 25.
31. Bryher, *HA*, 40.
32. Bryher, *HA*, 41.
33. Bryher, "Composition Book," box 147, folder 5040.
34. Bryher, *HA*, 62. Bryher's daily diaries note the need for a "prick" from the doctor.
35. Gustave Flaubert, *Flaubert in Egypt: A Sensibility on Tour*, edited and translated by Francis Steegmuller (London: Penguin, 1979), 29.
36. Bryher, *HA*, 75.
37. Bryher, "Arabic Notebooks," box 147, folder 5018.

38. Bryher, *HA*, 65.
39. Bryher, "Arabic Notebooks," box 147, folder 5018.
40. Bryher, *HA*, 70–71, 72–73.
41. Bryher, *HA*, 98–99.
42. Bryher, *HA*, 101.
43. Bryher, *HA*, 29.
44. Bryher, *HA*, 110.
45. H.D., "Advent," 146.
46. Bryher, *HA*, 145.

Chapter 4

1. William Carlos Williams to Edgar Williams, *Selected Letters of William Carlos Williams*, 8–9.
2. William Carlos Williams, *The Autobiography of William Carlos Williams* (New York: New Directions, 1967), 51, 57.
3. James George Frazer, edited by Robert Fraser *The Golden Bough* (Oxford: Oxford University Press, 1994), 9.
4. Emily Wallace, "Athene's Owl," cited in Louis Silverstein, "H.D. Chronology, Part One (1605–1914)," accessed August 19, 2018, http://www.imagists.org/hd/hdchron1.html, 21.
5. Interview with Perdita Schaffner, 1978, SSF.
6. A phrase H.D. used to answer a Bryn Mawr questionnaire, nd. HDPBM.
7. Wolle, "A Moravian Heritage," 56.
8. Pound included "Psychology and Troubadours" (1916) in a revised edition of *The Spirit of Romance* (New York: New Directions, 1952), 92.
9. H.D., *Paint It*, 7.
10. Frances Gregg, *The Mystic Leeway*, edited by Oliver Marlow Wilkinson (Ottawa: Carleton University Press, 1995), 139. A Blitz attack destroyed Gregg's flat, killing her and her mother and daughter in 1941. She had the foresight to lock this memoir in an army-navy vault.
11. Gregg, *ML*, 55, 21.
12. Wolle, *A Moravian Heritage*, 56.
13. H.D., *Paint It*, 8.
14. H.D., *Paint It*, 9.
15. Wolle, *A Moravian Heritage*, 56.
16. H.D., *Paint It*, 10.
17. Gregg, *ML*, 65.
18. Christine Dell'Amore, "Dung Beetles Navigate via the Milky Way," January 24, 2013, blog.nationalgeographic.org.
19. Keats to John Taylor, February 27, 1818, in John Keats, *Selected Letters of John Keats*, edited by Grant F. Scott, rev. ed. (Cambridge, MA: Harvard University Press, 2002), 87.
20. H.D., *Paint It*, 10.
21. H.D., *End to Torment: A Memoir of Ezra Pound* (New York: New Directions, 1979), 36.
22. Gregg, *ML*, 69, 65.
23. Gregg, *ML*, 70, 115.
24. Gregg, *ML*, 69, 70.
25. Quoted in Moody, *Ezra Pound* 1:87.

26. Gregg, *ML*, 84.
27. Gregg, *ML*, 115, 130.
28. Gregg, *ML*, 156.
29. Gregg, *ML*, 130.
30. Helen Carr, *The Verse Revolutionaries: Ezra Pound, H.D. and the Imagists* (London: Jonathan Cape, 2009), 338.
31. H.D., *Asphodel*, edited by Robert Spoo (Durham, NC: Duke University Press, 1992), 9. The autobiographical novel covered this first European travel, revealing her split sexuality, her break from Aldington, and union with Bryher.
32. Gregg, *ML*, 15.
33. Gregg, *ML*, 109.
34. H.D., *Asphodel*, 19, 22.
35. Gregg, *ML*, 122. Gregg wrote, "[w]omen gestate in all that they are" (146).
36. H.D., *Asphodel*, 26.
37. Gregg, *ML*, 59.
38. Gregg, *ML*, 59.
39. H.D., *Asphodel*, 25, 28.
40. Gregg, *Ml*, 147.
41. Gregg, *ML*, 109.
42. Gregg, *ML*, 151–152.
43. H.D., *HERmione* (New York: New Directions, 1981), 149.
44. H.D., *End*, 11.
45. H.D., *Paint It*, 9.
46. H.D. to Viola Jordan, March 1932, Jordan Papers.
47. Moody, *Ezra Pound* 1:13.
48. Ezra to Homer Pound, September 1909, Pound Papers.
49. Gregg, *ML*, 17.
50. Pound's translation of Remy de Gourmont's *The Natural Philosophy of Love,* for which he devoted a special issue of *Little Review* in 1919. For de Gourmont, the brain functioned as a repository of seminal fluid that charged and recharged creativity.
51. Moody, *Ezra Pound* 1:8.
52. Bryher, "Family Papers," box 151, folder 5113, 1909.
53. Frost, *Living in Sin*, 9–11, 12.
54. Bryher, *HA*, 113.
55. Silvia Dobson, "Mirror for a Star," unpublished manuscript, box 6, Dobson Papers,. This box holds letters received from H.D. and Bryher and stashed letters from Frances Gregg in the 1930s, best hid from Bryher.
56. Bryher, *Two*, 114–115.
57. Bryher, *HA*, 117.
58. Bryher, *HA*, 114.
59. Bryher to Amy Lowell, September 14, 1917, Amy Lowell Papers.
60. Bryher, *HA*, 154.
61. Dorothea Petrie Carew to Bryher, July 22, 1957.
62. Carew, *Many Years*, 142.

Chapter 5

1. Brigit Patmore, *My Friends When Young: The Memoirs of Brigit Patmore* (London: Heinemann, 1968), 48, 5, 6.
2. W. B. Yeats, *The Collected Works of W.B. Yeats*, vol. 3, *Autobiographies*, edited by William H O'Donnell and Douglas N. Archibald (New York: Scribners, 1999), 114.
3. Richard Aldington, *Life for Life's Sake: A Book of Reminiscences* (New York: Viking, 1941), 7.
4. May Sinclair, *A Defence of Idealism: Some Questions and Conclusions*, (London: Macmillan, 1917). She paralleled the mystic and the hysteric, declaring, "[T]he one indispensable condition of mystical experience, is, primarily and essentially, a state of dissociation" (259).
5. Carr, *Verse Revolutionaries*, 796.
6. Patmore, *My Friends*, 66.
7. H.D., *Bid*, 10. She told Norman Pearson that she began *Bid* "in situ, Cornwall, 1918." September 14, 1959, *BHP* 244–245.
8. H.D., *End*, 18.
9. Collecott, *H.D. and Sapphic Modernism*, 214.
10. Ezra Pound, "A Retrospective" in *The Literary Essays of Ezra Pound* (New York: New Directions, 1954), 4, originally published as "A Few Don'ts," *Poetry* 1, no. 6 (1913).
11. Aldington, *Life for Life's Sake*, 116, 101.
12. Eileen Gregory, *H.D. and Hellenism* (Cambridge: Cambridge University Press, 1997), 138.
13. H.D., *End to Torment*, 5.
14. Gregg, *ML*, 117, 103.
15. Pagels, *Gnostic*, xxiv.
16. Hugh Kenner, *The Pound Era* (New York: New Directions, 1971), 59, 56.
17. Caroline Zilboorg, *Richard Aldington and H.D.: The Early Years in Letters* (Bloomington: Indiana University Press, 1992), 43.
18. Walter Pater, *The Renaissance: Studies in Art and Poetry*, edited by Donald L. Hill (Berkeley: University of California Press, 1980), xxiii–xxiv.
19. Bryher, "Elizabethan Notes," box 72, folders 2862–2863.
20. Bryher, *Two*, 189.
21. Aldington, *Life for Life's Sake*, 126.
22. H.D., *Bid*, 1.
23. H.D. to Lowell, December 17, 1914, Lowell Papers.
24. Kenner, *Pound Era*, 6.
25. Aldington to Lowell, December 1914, Lowell Papers.
26. Aldington to Lowell, May 21, 1915, Lowell Papers.
27. H.D. to Lowell, October 7, 1915, Lowell Papers.
28. H.D., *Bid*, 3, 4.
29. T. S. Eliot, "Classics in English," *Poetry* 9, no. 2 (November 1916), 101–104.
30. T. S. Eliot, "Tradition and the Individual Talent" (1919), in *Sacred Wood*, 33.
31. H.D., *Majic*, 102.
32. H.D., "Orchard," in *CP*, 28.
33. H.D., "Hermes of the Ways," in *CP*, 37–38.
34. H.D., "The Helmsman," in *CP*, 6.
35. H.D., "The Shrine," in *CP*, 7.
36. H.D., *CP*, 26.
37. H.D. to Lowell, January 20, 1916.

38. H.D., "The Helmsman," in *CP*, 5, 7.
39. H.D. to Marianne Moore, April 15, 1916.
40. H.D., "Sea Gods," in *CP*, 29, 30.
41. H.D., "Marianne Moore" (1916), in *The Gender of Modernism: A Critical Anthology*, edited by Bonnie Kime Scott (Bloomington: Indiana University Press, 1990), 126.
42. H.D. to Lowell, August 30, 1916, Lowell Papers.
43. H.D. to Lowell, October 13, 1916, Lowell Papers.
44. H.D., "The Tribute," in *CP*, 59, 60.
45. H.D. to Lowell, December 11, 1916, Lowell Papers.
46. Bryher, *Development*, 229.
47. Bryher, *HA*, 167.
48. See Philip Beresford and William Rubenstein, eds., *The Richest of the Rich: The Wealthiest 250 People in Britain Since 1066* (Petersfield: Harriman House, 2011).
49. Taylor, *Ellermans*, 79.
50. Aldington to H.D., April 30, 1917.
51. Aldington, *Death of a Hero*, 366.
52. Zilboorg, introduction to *Richard Aldington and H.D.*, 31, 24.
53. Samuel Hynes, introduction to Rebecca West, *Return of the Soldier* (London: Penguin, 1998), viii.
54. H.D., *Bid*, 22–23.
55. Virginia Woolf, *Orlando* 309.
56. H.D., "Eurydice," in *CP*, 48, 51.
57. H.D., *Bid*, 83.
58. H.D. to Lowell, March 5, 1917.
59. T. S. Eliot to his mother, in *The Letters of T. S. Eliot,* vol. 1: *1898–1922*, edited by Valerie Eliot and Hugh Haughton (New Haven, CT: Yale University Press, 2011), 200.
60. H.D. to Lowell, September 19, 1917. Lowell Papers.
61. Bryher, *Appreciation*, 19, 13.
62. Bryher to Lowell, November 14, 1918. Lowell Papers.
63. Bryher to Lowell, December 15, 1917. Lowell Papers.
64. Lowell, *Tendencies*, 257.
65. Bryher to Lowell, December 9, 1917. Lowell Papers.
66. Lowell to Bryher, November 28, 1918. Lowell Papers.
67. Bryher to Lowell, October 15, 1918. Lowell Papers.
68. Bryher to Lowell, December 15, 1917. Lowell Papers.
69. Bryher to Lowell, September 14, 1917. Lowell Papers.
70. Bryher to Lowell, May 26, 1918. Lowell Papers.
71. Aldington to Lowell, November 18, 1917. Lowell Papers.
72. Aldington to H.D., May 20 1918; Zilboorg, *RAHDEY*, 49.
73. Zilboorg, *RAHDEY*, 40.
74. Aldington to H.D., May 6, 1918.
75. Aldington to H.D., May 28, 1918.
76. Aldington to H.D., June 29, 1918.
77. H.D., *Bid*, 88, 89, 90, 91, 92.
78. Aldington to H.D., July 9, 1918.

79. Aldington to H.D., July 4, 1918.
80. Bryher to Lowell, August 12, 1918, Lowell Papers.
81. H.D., *Asphodel*, 168.
82. H.D., *Paint It*, 71.
83. Aldington to H.D., July 23, 1918.
84. Aldington to H.D., July 28, 1918.
85. Bryher to Lowell, November 14, 1918, Lowell Papers.
86. Bryher to Lowell, December 30, 1918, Lowell Papers.
87. Bryher, "Elizabethan Notes," box 72, folders 2862–2863.
88. Bryher, "The Girl-Page in Elizabethan Literature" (1920), box 89, folders 3295–3296.
89. Aldington to H.D., August 4, 1918.
90. Aldington to H.D., August 5, 1918.
91. Aldington to H.D., August 12, 1918.
92. Aldington to H.D., August 31, 1918.
93. Aldington to H.D., September 1, 1918.
94. Aldington to Bryher, September 22, 1918.
95. Bryher, Development, 114.
96. Aldington to Bryher, September 22, 1918.
97. Aldington to H.D., August 14, 1918.
98. H.D. to Amy Lowell, September 1918, Lowell Papers.
99. H.D., *Paint It*, 69, 89.
100. Aldington to H.D., December 13, 1918.
101. Bryher to Lowell, May 6, 1919, Lowell Papers.
102. Bryher to H.D., October 7, 1918.
103. Bryher to H.D., April 22, 1919.
104. Aldington to H.D., June 21, 1918.
105. Aldington to H.D., July 1, 1918.
106. H.D. to Bryher, December 23, 1918.

Chapter 6

1. Bryher, *Two*, 286, 288.
2. Bryher, *HA*, 186.
3. Aldington to H.D., January 6, 1919.
4. Aldington to H.D., January 3, 1919.
5. Diana Collecott, *H.D. and Sapphic Modernism* (Cambridge: Cambridge University Press, 1999), 203.
6. H.D., "Eros," in *CP* 175.
7. Aldington to H.D., January 3, 1919.
8. Bryher to H.D., April 22, 1919.
9. H.D. to Bryher, April 19, 1919.
10. H.D., "Hymen," in *CP*, 108.
11. H.D. to Bryher, February 14, 1919.
12. H.D., "Simaetha," in *CP*, 116.
13. Aldington to H.D., October 6, 1918.

14. Zilboorg, *RAHDEY*, 145 n.1.
15. H.D. to Bryher, February 1, 1919.
16. Bryher to H.D., March 1919? Excitement outstripped Bryher's usual precision with dates.
17. This is the exchange as Bryher remembered it in *HA* 186–187.
18. In gauging a complex vaccination season in 2021, Ed Yong reports that the 1918 pandemic killed about 100 million people worldwide. "Where Year Two of the Pandemic Will Take Us," *Atlantic,* December 29, 2020, https://www.theatlantic.com/health/archive/2020/12/pandemic-year-two/617528/.
19. Bryher to Brigit Patmore, March 25, 1919. Bryher Papers.
20. H.D. to Bryher, April 10, 1919.
21. H.D., *Asphodel*, 182.
22. H.D., *Hedylus* (Redding Ridge: Black Swan Books, 1980), 37.
23. H.D., *Asphodel*, 180.
24. H.D. to John Cournos, 1919?. H.D. Papers.
25. See Phyllis Grosskurth, *Havelock Ellis: A Biography* (New York: New York University, 1985).
26. Havelock Ellis, *Studies in the Psychology of Sex* (Philadelphia, PA: F. A. Davis, 1915), 2:328, 325.
27. Havelock Ellis, "Sexo-Aesthetic Inversion," *Alienist and Neurologist* 24 (1913): 156–167.
28. Ellis, *Eonism and Other Supplementary Studies*, 53.
29. Bryher to H.D., March 20, 1919.
30. Ellis, *Studies*, 2:305, 257–258, 327.
31. Ellis, *Studies*, 2:318.
32. H.D., *End to Torment*, 7, 8.
33. H.D. to Bryher, April 19, 1919.
34. Bryher to H.D., April 21, 1919.
35. H.D., *Asphodel*, 206.
36. H.D. to Bryher, April 10, 1919.
37. H.D. to Bryher, April 10, 1919.
38. Bryher, *HA*, 189.
39. H.D., *Asphodel*, 201.
40. Starting with this initial break, it seems unlikely Aldington and H.D. "were always to regret their parting." Zilboorg, *RAHDEL*, 205.
41. H.D. to George Plank, February 1929. H.D. Papers.
42. Guest, *Herself Defined*, 112.
43. Brigit Patmore to Bryher, February 2, 1922.
44. Patmore to Bryher, February 25, 1922.
45. Lowell to Bryher, May 28, 1919. Lowell Papers.
46. H.D., "I Said," in *CP*, 323, 322.
47. Lowell to Bryher, January 7, 1919. Lowell Papers.
48. Adalaide Morris, "A Relay of Power and Peace," in *Signets: Reading H.D.,* edited by Susan Friedman and Rachel Blau DuPlessis (Madison: University of Wisconsin Press, 1990), 56.
49. H.D., "Thetis," in *CP*, 117.
50. H.D., "Advent," 130.
51. Bryher's *Arrow Music* (London: J & E Bumpus, 1922) is available online through Emory University at http://womenwriters.digitalscholarship.emory.edu/toc.php?id=bryher_arrow.

52. Susan Stanford Friedman considers 1919 and 1924 their "most intimate" years. *Penelope's Web: Gender, Modernity, H.D.'s Fiction* (Cambridge: Cambridge University Press, 1991), 227.
53. H.D., "Advent," 116, 130.
54. F. D. Rudhyar writes that "in the total field of the Earth-organism a definite type of culture inherently corresponds. Each region is the 'womb' out of which a specific type of human mentality and culture can and sooner or later will emerge. All these cultures—past, present and future—and their complex interrelationships and interactions are the collective builders of the Mind of humanity." *Directives for New Life* (1971), quoted in Christopher Stone, *Do Trees Have Standing?* (Oxford: Oxford University Press, 2010), 30. *Notes* envisions an emerging womb-vision, interacting with the dynamic sea. She would agree with Stone that trees have standing—as do jellyfish.
55. H.D., *Notes*, 19, 20, 21, 22.
56. H.D., *Notes*, 18, 19.
57. H.D., *Gift*, 41.
58. Mandel, "Magical Lenses," 302.
59. H.D., "Advent," 133, 116.
60. H.D., *Asphodel*, 204–205.
61. H.D., *Notes*, 28, 31.
62. H.D., *Notes*, 27, 26.
63. Collecott, *H.D. and Sapphic Modernism*, 10.
64. H.D., *Sappho*, 59, 60, 57, 58.
65. Bryher to Lowell, July 16, 1919. Lowell Papers.
66. Bryher to Lowell, September 7, 1919. Lowell Papers.
67. Lowell to H.D., July 28, 1919. Lowell Papers.
68. Bryher to Lowell, September 15, 1919. Lowell Papers.
69. Jane Bennett, *Vibrant Matter: A Political Ecology of Things* (Durham, NC: Duke University Press, 2010), 61.
70. H.D., "She Rebukes Hippolyta," in *CP*, 138.
71. H.D., *Hedylus*, 37.
72. H.D., *Paint It*, 84, 85, 80, 5, 4.
73. H.D. to Cournos, 1919. H.D. wrote Pound in 1938, "Don't let Cournos come to see me," writing she "simply turn[s] [his letters] over to Bryher as to a lawyer." Pound Papers.
74. H.D., "AN," box 47, folders 1181–1182; Bryher, *HA*, 190–191.
75. Ellis to Bryher, September 7, 1919.
76. Ellis to Bryher, August 1919.
77. Ellis to Bryher, September 7, 1919.
78. Friedman, *AF*, 52.
79. Bryher to Lowell, December 28, 1919. Lowell Papers.
80. H.D., "The Islands," in *CP*, 127.

Chapter 7

1. H.D. to Bryher, dated Autumn 1920 by a library archivist, but likely written in Autumn 1919, before they traveled to Greece in February 1920.
2. Bryher, *South*, box 87, folders 3221–3233, 3.

3. Karl Baedeker, *Greece Handbook for Travelers* (Leipzig: Karl Baedeker, 1909), 17.
4. Vassiliki Kolocotroni, "Still Life: Modernism's Turn to Greee," *Journal of Modern Literature* 35, no. 2 (2012): 2.
5. H.D., "Pausanius," box 43, folder 1112.
6. H.D., "Advent," 155.
7. H.D., *Majic*, 107.
8. H.D., *Majic*, 161, 152.
9. H.D., "Advent," 160.
10. H.D., "Mouse Island," in *Narthex and Other Stories*, edited by Michael Boughn (Toronto: Book Thug, 2011), 38.
11. H.D., "Advent," 154.
12. H.D., *Majic*, 94.
13. Adelaide Morris, "The Concept of Projection: H.D.'s Visionary Powers," in *Signets: Reading H.D.*, edited by Susan Stanford Friedman and Rachel Blau DuPlessis (Madison: University of Wisconsin Press, 1990), 413.
14. Flammarion, *Death and Its Mystery*, 66, 39.
15. Grosskurth, *Havelock Ellis*, 297.
16. H.D. to George Plank, 1935.
17. H.D., "Advent," 168.
18. Bryher to Lowell, February 29, 1920. Lowell Papers.
19. H.D., *CP*, 121.
20. See Baedeker, *Greece*, 39–59 for some of this information.
21. H.D., "Euripides."
22. Bryher, "Wild Rose," in *Arrow*.
23. H.D., "Euripides."
24. Grosskurth, *Ellis*, 297.
25. H.D., *CP*, 326.
26. Bryher to Lowell, March 20, 1920. Lowell Papers.
27. H.D., *Tribute*, 49.
28. Bryher to Lowell, April 14, 1920. Lowell Papers.
29. Bryher. *The Region of Lutany* (London: Chapman & Hall, 1914).
30. H.D., *Majic*, 104–105.
31. Baedeker, *Greece*, 262.
32. H.D., "Mouse Island," 29.
33. H.D., *CP*, 98.
34. Bryher to Lowell, April 14, 1920. Lowell Papers.
35. Bryher, *Two*, 183, 267.
36. H.D., *Majic*, 105–106.
37. H.D., *Tribute*, 45, 46.
38. H.D., *Tribute*, 44, 48.
39. Bryher, *Two*, 175.
40. H.D., *Tribute*, 55, 54, 55, 56.
41. H.D., *Tribute*, 49.
42. Joseph Fontenrose, *Python: A Study of Delphic Myth and Its origins* (Berkeley: University of California Press, 1959). He attributes the Pythia's messages to gaseous fumes rising from a break in the tectonic plates beneath her tripod, her prophecies hysterical babble.

43. Lewis Richard Farnell, *The Cult of the Greek States* (Oxford: Oxford University Press, 1896–1909), 1:9–10.
44. Bryher, *Development*, 129.
45. H.D., *Majic*, 113, 73.
46. T. S. Eliot, *Selected Prose of T. S. Eliot*, edited by Frank Kermode (New York: Harcourt Brace, 1975), 209.
47. Morris, "The Concept of Projection," 415.
48. Sandra L. Hubscher, "Apophenia: Definition and Analysis," Digital Bits Skeptic, LLC, November 4, 2007, online.
49. H.D., "Advent," 168.
50. H.D., *Majic*, 111.
51. H.D., "Advent," 173.
52. H.D., *Majic*, 121.
53. Grosskurth, *Ellis*, 297.
54. Bryher to Lowell, May 16, 1920. Lowell Papers.
55. H.D., *Majic*, 82.

Chapter 8

1. Bryher, *Two*, 284.
2. Bryher, *HA*, 6.
3. Bryher to Friedman, October 1, 1971, unpublished letter.
4. Bryher, *West* (London: Jonathan Cape, 1925), 20.
5. H.D. to Moore, July 6, 1920, RML.
6. Moore to Bryher, July 7, 1921, *MMSL,* 164–165.
7. Bryher, *West*, 36.
8. Bryher, "My Introduction to America," *Life and Letters To-Day* 26 (September 1940): 237.
9. Donald Hall interview, in Hall, *Their Ancient Glittering Eyes: Remembering Poets and More Poets* (New York: Ticknor & Fields, 1992), 301.
10. Moore to Bryher, August 31, 1921, *MMSL,* 175.
11. Linda Leavell, *Holding On Upside Down: The Life and Work of Marianne Moore* (New York: Farrar, Straus & Giroux, 2013), 108.
12. Moore to Pound, January 9, 1919, *MMSL,* 124–125.
13. H.D., "Helios and Athene," in *CP*, 326–329.
14. Pound to Thayer, November 8, 1920. Pound Papers.
15. Schaffner, "UA."
16. Bryher, *West*, 10, 11.
17. Bryher, *West*, 21.
18. H.D. to Viola Jordan, January 16, 1921. Jordan Papers.
19. Bryher, *West*, 21, 20. She invoked Herrick's poem "To Anthea, who may Command him Anything," with its "Bid me to live, and I will live." More than twenty years later, Aldington suggested *Bid Me to Live* as the title for *Madrigal*, H.D.'s World War I novel.
20. Bryher, *West*, 26, 33, 27, 33, 35.
21. Leavell, *Holding On*, 40.
22. Leavell, *Holding On*, 165.
23. Leavell, *Holding On*, 39, 36, 180.

24. Bryher, *West*, 37.
25. Moore to Bryher, November 29, 1920, *MMSL*, 136.
26. Robert McAlmon, "Post-Adolesence," in *A Selection of Short Fiction*, edited by Edward N. S. Lorusso (Albuquerque: University of New Mexico, 1991), 5.
27. Williams, *Autobiography*, 176.
28. Bryher, *West*, 61. Now Carmel Highlands Inn is a corporate hotel, with time shares and none of the privacy H.D. and company enjoyed.
29. Moore to H.D., July 26, 1921, *MMSL*, 171–72.
30. Letters to McAlmon from this period have vanished.
31. Moore to Bryher, November 29, 1920, *MMSL*, 136.
32. Bryher, *Development*, 24.
33. Moore to Bryher, November 29, 1920, *MMSL*, 137.
34. Marianne Moore, *Dial*, May 1921, 70.
35. McAlmon to Bryher, c. 1921, Bryher Papers, box 35, folder 1259.
36. Bryher, *West*, 35.
37. These erotic poems, "Wild Rose," "Eros," "Blue Sleep," and "Hellenics," all published in *Poetry* 17 (December 1920).
38. Bryher to Moore, September 24, 1920, RML.
39. Bryher to Moore, October 15, 1920, *MMSL*, 133–134.
40. Marianne Moore, "Dock Rats," in *Becoming Marianne Moore: The Early Poems, 1907–1924*, edited by Robin Schulze (Berkeley: University of California Press, 2002), 247.
41. Bryher to Moore, September 24, 1920, RML.
42. Moore to Bryher, October 17, 1920, *MMSL*, 134.
43. Bryher, *West*, 88.
44. "Mary Pickford in California," Bryher Papers, box 91, folder 3358; the title bears the date of December 25, 1920.
45. Leavell writes that the photos "enhanced Mary's esteem" (*Holding On*, 185).
46. H.D., *Paint It*, 17.
47. H.D. to Moore, April 11, 1921, RML.
48. Moore to Bryher, November 29, 1920, *MMSL*, 136, 135.
49. Moore to Bryher, December 13, 1920, *MMSL*, 157–158.
50. Bryher, *West*, 39, 52, 123, 69, 48.
51. Bryher, *West*, 145, 159.
52. John Flood, "Marianne Moore and the Short Commute," April 1, 2009, Nypl.org.
53. Bryer, *West*, 148–149, 15.
54. Patricia Willis, "A Modernist Epithalamium: Marianne Moore's Formal and Cultural Critique," *Paideuma* 23 (2003): 276.
55. Bryher, *West*, 102.
56. Moore to Bryher, December 13, 1920, *MMSL*, 138.
57. Moore to Bryher, January 10, 1921, RML.
58. Moore to Bryher, December 13, 1920, *MMSL*, 138.
59. Moore to John Warner Moore, January 23, 1921, *MMSL*, 140–141.
60. Moore to Bryher, January 23, 1921, *MMSL*, 141.
61. Moore to John Warner Moore, February 13, 1921, *MMSL*, 143.
62. Moore to John Warner Moore, February 20, 1921, *MMSL*, 144.
63. Bryher, *Two*, 145, 205.

64. Moore to John Warner Moore, February 20, 1921.
65. Moore to Bryher April 18, 1921, *MMSL*, 153.
66. "Heiress Writer Weds Village Poet," *World* (New York), November 10, 1921.
67. *Life*, April 14, 1921.
68. Herald Democrat, Greencastle Indiana, April 15, 1921.
69. Moore to H.D., March 27, 1921, *MMSL*, 149–150.
70. Moore to Bryher, May 9, 1921, *MMSL*, 159.
71. Moore to John Warner Moore, May 3, 1921, *MMSL*, 157.
72. Leavell, *Holding On*, 188.
73. See Cyrena N. Pondrom, "Marianne Moore and H.D.: Female Community and Poetic Achievement" in *MM: Woman and Poet*, edited by Patricia Willis (Orono, ME: National Poetry Foundation, 1990), 384.
74. Moore to Bryher, July 8, 1921, *MMSL*, 167–168.
75. H.D. to Moore, May 1921.
76. Moore to Bryher, July 7, 1921, *MMSL*, 165–166.
77. Moore to T. S. Eliot, July 15, 1921, *MMSL*, 171.
78. Moore to Bryher, June 26, 1922, RLM.
79. Moore to Bryher, June 13, 1922.
80. Moore "Dactyl" to Bryher, April 18, 1921, *MMSL*, 153.
81. Moore to John Warner Moore, April 4, 1921, *MMSL*, 152.

Chapter 9

1. H.D., *Paint It*, 83.
2. H.D., "AN," H.D. Papers, box 47, f. 1181–1182. Switching from "we" to a more impersonal, passive voice: "Two-thirds of the MSS was destroyed, re-typed and now called MADRIGAL." H.D. also marked the manuscript *Asphodel* "Destroy."
3. H.D., *Paint It*, 79, 56, 79, 72.
4. H.D. to Pearson, September 26, 1946, *BHP*, 58.
5. McAlmon, *BGT*, 4–5, 2, 3, 58.
6. McAlmon to Bryher, March? 1924, Bryher Papers, box 35, folder 1261.
7. Smoller, *Adrift among Geniuses*, 2.
8. McAlmon to Bryher, 1921, box 35, folder 1258.
9. Douglas to Bryher, January 1921.
10. Douglas to Bryher, December 20, 1922.
11. Douglas to Bryher, May 2, 1922.
12. Douglas to Bryher, December 19, 1921.
13. Douglas to Bryher, May 2, 1922; June 9, 1922
14. Schaffner, "UA," 3.
15. Douglas to Bryher, March 24, 1925.
16. Steven Pressfield, *Turning Pro: Tap Your Inner Power and Create Your Life's Work* (New York: Black Irish Entertainment, 2012), 95.
17. Helen Doolittle to Bryher, August 8, 1922?
18. Helen Doolittle to Bryher, June 14, 1923.
19. Bryher to H.D., 1922?, box 13, folder 81.
20. H.D. to Moore, April 11, 1921.

21. Helen Doolittle to Bryher, July 15, 1924.
22. McAlmon, *BGT*, 53, 200, 2.
23. Sylvia Beach, *Shakespeare & Company* (New York: Harcourt, 1959), 25, 99.
24. McAlmon to Bryher, 1921, box 35, folder 1258.
25. McAlmon to Bryher, 1921?, box 35, folder 1258.
26. McAlmon, *BGT*, 14, 15.
27. Beach, *Shakespeare & Company*, 102.
28. Bryher to Lowell, October 7, 1921, Amy Lowell Papers.
29. Lois Gordon, *Nancy Cunard: Heiress, Muse, Political Idealist* (New York: Columbia University Press, 2007), 94.
30. Eliot to McAlmon, May 22, 1921, in T. S. Eliot, *The Letters of T.S. Eliot*, vol. 1: *1898-1922* (New Haven, CT: Yale University Press, 2009), 563.
31. McAlmon to Bryher, 1921?, box 35, folder 1258.
32. McAlmon to Bryher, 1922?, box 35, folder 1259.
33. Bryher, *HA*, 210-211.
34. McAlmon, *BGT*, 207.
35. Willis, "A Modernist Epithalamium," 203, 282.
36. Schulze, *Becoming Marianne Moore*, 464.
37. H.D., "Hymen," in *CP*, 109.
38. H.D., "White World," in *CP*, 131.
39. H.D., "Fragment 113," in *CP* 131.
40. H.D., *Palimpsest*, edited by Harry T. Moore (Carbondale: Southern Illinois University Press, 1968), 177.
41. E. A. Budge, *The Egyptian Book of the Dead* (1899; New York: Penguin, 2008), 4-5, liv, lix.
42. H.D., *CP*, 181.
43. Eknath Easwaran, trans., *The Upanishads*, Blue Mountain Meditation Center (Tomales, CA: Nilgiri Press 2007). "Of the unseen, eternal," which "is awake even in our sleep," from *The Katha Upanishad,* only one of many of H.D.'s echoes of this sacred text (87).
44. Amelia B. Edwards, *A Thousand Miles Up the Nile* (London: G. Routledge & Sons, 1877), 155.
45. Budge, *The Egyptian Book of the Dead*, 10.
46. Edwards, *A Thousand Miles*, 187.
47. H.D., *Palimpsest*, 202.
48. Edwards, *A Thousand Miles*, 199.
49. H.D., *Palimpsest*, 207, 202, 211.
50. Edwards, *A Thousand Miles*, 177.
51. Perdita Schaffner, "The Egyptian Cat," afterword to *Hedylus* 142, 145.
52. H.D., *Thorn Thicket*, 183.
53. H.D., *Palimpsest*, 226, 213, 229.
54. Bryher, *Two*, 191, 192, 173.
55. H.D, "AN."
56. Bryher to H.D., June 14, 1923.
57. McAlmon to Bryher, (1924), box 35, folder 1261.
58. Virginia Smyers interview, December 18, 1979, quoted in Virginia L. Smyers and Gilllian Hanscombe, *Writing for Their Lives: The Modernist Women 1910-40* (London: Women's Press, 1981), 10.

59. H.D. to Bryher, June 12, 1923.
60. H.D. to Bryher, August 24, 1923.
61. H.D. to Bryher, September 26, 1924.
62. Bryher, "Dorothy Richardson," box 169, folder 3595.
63. Gloria G. Fromm, *Dorothy Richardson: A Biography* (Urbana: University of Illinois Press, 1977), 164. Before even meeting Dorothy, Bryher gave her and her husband, Alan Odle, "10 days in glorious Paris!" Landing at the Dome on April 30, 1924, they stayed at Hotel de le Havre Loire on the Boulevard Raspail, enjoying breakfast in bed.
64. Shari Benstock, *Women of the Left Bank: Paris, 1900–1940* (Austin: University of Texas Press, 1986), 311.
65. H.D., *Heliodora & Other Poems* (London: Jonathan Cape, 1924); "Hyacinth," 116–120, in *CP* 165.
66. H.D., "The Wise Sappho," 57–58.
67. Eileen Gregory, *H.D. and Hellenism* (Cambridge: Cambridge University Press, 1997), 50–51, 33, 50.
68. H.D., "Notes on Ancient Lyric Poets."
69. H.D., "The Wise Sappho," 62, 68.
70. H.D., *CP*, 155.
71. Herodotus, *The Histories*, translated by Aubrey De Selincourt (London: Penguin, 1954), book II, 127.
72. E. K. F.Chan, A. Timmermann, B. F. Baldi, et al., "Human Origins in a Southern African Palaeo-Wetland and First Migrations," *Nature* 575 (2019): 185–189, https://doi.org/10.1038/s41586-019-1714-1.
73. James Donald, Anne Friedberg, and Laura Marcus, eds., *Close Up, 1927–1933: Cinema and Modernism* (Princeton, NJ: Princeton University Press), 106, 56. Unless noted, all references to *Close Up* are taken from this edition.
74. Smoller, *Adrift among Geniuses*, 143.
75. H.D., *Palimpsest*, 75, 72–73, 92.
76. Patmore to Bryher, February 25, 1922.
77. H.D. to Patmore, February 18, 1925.
78. H.D., *Palimpsest*, 220.
79. H.D., *Thorn*, 183.
80. H.D., "Fragment 113," in *CP*, 131.
81. Dorothy Pound to Bryher, February 26, 1925.
82. Pound to Bryher, February 28, 1925.
83. H. P. Collins, *Modern Poetry* (London: Jonathan Cape, 1925), 115, 144.
84. Jack Powys to Frances Gregg, February 6, 1925, and May 19, 1925, in Oliver Marlow Wilkinson, ed., *The Letters of John Cowper Powys to Frances Gregg* (London: Cecil Woolf, 1994), 1:.
85. H.D., *Palimpsest*, 165.
86. Bryher to Sylvia Beach, March 14, 1927.
87. H.D. to Bryher, March 4, 1927.
88. Bryher, *HA*, 203.
89. H.D., *Palimpsest*, 176.

Chapter 10

1. H.D., "AN," box 47, folders 1181–1182.
2. Bryher to H.D., July 1927.
3. H.D., "AN," box 47, folders 1181–1182.
4. Schaffner, "UA," 60.
5. H.D. to Bryher, October 28, 1927.
6. H.D. to George Plank, June 12, 1928.
7. Schaffner, "UA," 88
8. H.D. to Plank, August 31, 1927.
9. Donald, Friedberg, and Marcus, *Close Up*, 4.
10. Macpherson to H.D., October 21, 1927.
11. H.D., "The Cinema & the Classics I Beauty," in *Cinema and Modernism*, 109.
12. H.D., "Wing-Beat," typescript, box 43, folder 1111.
13. Bryher to H.D., October 28, 1927.
14. Bryher and Macpherson to H.D., October 27, 1927.
15. Macpherson to H.D., October 29, 1927.
16. Macpherson to H.D., October 25, 1927.
17. H.D. to Bryher, November 12, 1927. "Herrnhuter" was the guardian of the dogs in Moravian-speak.
18. Bryher, "Notes on Berlin," 1927, box 72, folder 2855.
19. H.D., "Cinema and the Classics II Restraint," in *Cinema and Modernism*, 111, 112.
20. H.D., "The Mask and the Movietone," in *Cinema and Modernism*, 116.
21. Bryher, "Notes on Berlin." Unpublished.
22. Bryher, "Westfront 1918," *Close Up* 7, no. 2 (August 1930): 105
23. Bryher, "The War from Three Angles," *Close Up* 1, no. 1 (July 1927):16, 48.
24. Walter Benjamin, "The Work of Art in the Age of Mechanical Reproduction," in *Selected Writings*, vol. 3: *1936–1938*, translated by Michael W. Jennings, edited by Howard Eiland (Cambridge, MA: Harvard University Press, 2002), 37.
25. Laura Marcus, *The Tenth Muse: Writing about Cinema in the Modernist Period* (Oxford: Oxford University Press, 2007), 332.
26. H.D. to Bryher, March 25, 1927.
27. Schaffner, "UA," 71.
28. Donald, Friedberg, and Marcus, *Close Up*, 111.
29. Macpherson to Bryher and H.D., 1928.
30. H.D., "Narthex," 44–45, 66, 67, 55, 82, 55.
31. Frances Gregg, "The Apartment," in Arthur Kreymborg's *Second American Caravan*, 1928, 286.
32. H.D. to Bryher, June 22, 1929.
33. H.D. to Bryher, March 28, 1928.
34. H.D. to Plank, June 12, 1928.
35. H.D. to Bryher, July 1928.
36. H.D. to Bryher, July 7, 1928.
37. H.D. to Bryher, August 1, 1928.
38. Bryher, *Film Problems of Soviet Russia* (Territet: Pool, 1929), 32, 37, 38, 39.

39. Kenneth suggested that a certain "V.S. is a dirty old blunder to suggest you should go through. But she's just a smelly old sadist.... Don't let any windy old gas-bag talk you down." No one, so far as I know, has tracked down "V.S." with certainty.
40. H.D., "Narthex," 77.
41. H.D. to Bryher, December 7, 1928.
42. Diana Souhami, *The Trials of Radclyffe Hall* (New York: Doubleday, 1999), 155, 122.
43. H.D., *Her*, 102, 103.
44. H.D., *Her*, 31, 88.
45. H.D., *Her*, 73, 71, 8, 19, 32.
46. Bryher to H.D., December 1929.
47. H.D. to Bryher, December 1929.
48. Schaffner, "UA," 127.
49. Macpherson to H.D., 1929.

Chapter 11

1. Macpherson to H.D., 1929.
2. H.D. to Bryher, October 8, 1929.
3. H.D. to Bryher, December 1929.
4. Bryher to H.D., May 1930.
5. Donald, Friedberg, and Marcus, *Close Up*, 34.
6. Bryher to H.D., October 28, 1929.
7. Martin Duberman, *Paul Robeson* (New York: Knopf, 1988), 131.
8. Bryher to H.D., October 12, 1929.
9. H.D., "*Borderline*: A Pool Film with Paul Robeson," in *Cinema and Modernism*, 230. The "pamphlet," as they called it, was published by the Mercury Press (with Herring's help as a former editor there) in London in 1930.
10. Zakiyyah Iman Jackson, *Becoming Human: Matter and Meaning in An Antiblack World* (New York: New York University Press, 2020), 159.
11. Jackson, *Becoming Human*, 169, 192.
12. Duberman, *Robeson*, 131.
13. H.D., *CP*, 212–213.
14. H.D., "Borderline," 227.
15. Bryher, *Film Problems*, 14.
16. H.D., "Borderline," 223.
17. Dorothy Richardson, "The Film Gone Male," *CU*, no. 9 (March 1932), 37.
18. Sergei Eisenstein, "Dialectical Approach," in *Film Form: Essays in Film Theory*, translated and edited by Jay Leyda (New York: Harcourt, Brace, 1949), 153.
19. Donald, Friedberg, and Marcus, *Close Up*, 389.
20. H.D. "Borderline," 226.
21. Herring to H.D., 1930.
22. Kenneth Macpherson, "As Is," *Close Up* 7, no. 5 (November 1930): 381.
23. Kenneth Macpherson,, "As Is," *Close Up* 7, no. 1 (July 1930): 296.
24. H.D. to Macpherson, October 1930.
25. H.D. to Bryher, August 1930.
26. Macpherson to H.D., August 1930.

27. H.D. to Bryher, November 1930.
28. Bryher to H.D., November 1930.
29. Macpherson to H.D., October 1930.
30. H.D., "AN."
31. H.D. to Bryher, January 10, 1931.
32. Herring to Bryher, January 13, 1931.
33. Herring to H.D., February 1931.
34. Macpherson to H.D., 1931.
35. Bryher, "AN."
36. Bryher to H.D., April 11, 1931.
37. H.D. to Bryher, May 17, 1931.
38. H.D. to Bryher, June 25, 1931.
39. Bryher to H.D., April 23, 1931.
40. Bryher to H.D., April 27, 1931.
41. Moore, *MMCP*, 303.
42. Bryher to H.D., June 31, 1931.
43. H.D. to Bryher, June 1, 1931.
44. H.D. to Bryher, June 2, 1931.
45. H.D. to Bryher, June 23, 1931.
46. H.D. to Bryher, June 25, 1931
47. H.D., "AN."
48. H.D. to Bryher, June 25, 1931.
49. H.D. to Bryher, December 1, 1931.
50. H.D. to Bryher, December 24, 1931.
51. Alice Modern to Bryher, April 8, 1932.
52. H.D. to Bryher, August, 1932.
53. Marcus, *Tenth Muse*, 325.
54. Bryher to H.D., (August) 1932.
55. Bryher, "Notes on Berlin," b. 72 f. 2855, Bryher Papers.
56. H.D. to Bryher, May 16, 1932.
57. H.D. to Bryher, May 23, 1932.
58. H.D. to Bryher, July 19, 1932.
59. H.D. to Bryher, September 2, 1932.
60. H.D. to Bryher, June 13, 1932.
61. Freud to Bryher, November 13, 1932; Friedman, *AF*, 7.
62. H.D. to Ellis, December 27, 1932.
63. H.D., *Palimpsest*, 203.
64. H.D. to Bryher, December 25, 1932.
65. Macpherson to Bryher, November [nd] 1932.
66. Bryher, "What Shall You Do in the War?" *Close Up* 10, no. 2 (June 1933): 188, 189, 190.

Chapter 12

1. H.D. to Ellis, January 17, 1933; Friedman, *AF*, 14.
2. Richardson to Bryher, October 1933.
3. H.D. to Bryher, March 11, 1933; Friedman, *AF*, 75.
4. H.D. to Bryher, May 2, 1936.

5. H.D. to Bryher, November 20, 1934; Friedman, *AF*, 489.
6. H.D. to Bryher, March 1, 1933; Friedman, *AF*, 35.
7. H.D. to Bryher and Macpherson, March 4, 1933; Friedman, *AF*, 45.
8. H.D. to Bryher and Macpherson, March 1, 1933; Friedman, *AF*, 34–35.
9. Bryher to H.D., March 9, 1933; Friedman, *AF*, 67.
10. H.D. to Bryher, March 10, 1933; Friedman, *AF*, 68.
11. Bryher to H.D., March 3, 1933; Friedman, *AF*, 41.
12. Bryher to H.D., March 5, 1933; Friedman, *AF*, 48.
13. Bryher to H.D., March 4, 1933; Friedman, *AF* 47–48.
14. H.D. to Bryher, March 5, 1933; Friedman, *AF*, 49–50.
15. H.D., *Tribute*, 37.
16. H.D., "Advent," 120.
17. Bryher's *Coin of Carthage* narrated, "To be free, to be able to walk at will to the river as alright, this was the only thing that mattered." Bryher, *Coin of Carthage* (New York: Harcourt Brace, 1963), 78.
18. H.D. to Bryher, March 10, 1933; Friedman, *AF*, 69.
19. H.D. to Macpherson, March 4, 1933; Friedman, *AF*, 46–47.
20. H.D. to Bryher and Macpherson, March 11, 1933.
21. H.D. to Bryher, March 17, 1933; Friedman, *AF*, 107.
22. H.D. to Bryher, March 14, 1933; Friedman, *AF*, 91.
23. Bryher to H.D., March 11, 1933.
24. H.D. to Bryher, March 5, 1933; Friedman, *AF*, 50.
25. Bryher to H.D., March 8, 1933; Friedman, *AF*, 64.
26. Bryher to H.D., March 14, 1933; Friedman, *AF*, 93.
27. Friedman, *AF*, n. 48, 117.
28. H.D. to Bryher, March 16, 1933; Friedman, *AF*, 104.
29. H.D. to Bryher, March 17, 1933, Friedman, *AF*, 108.
30. H.D. to Bryher, March 19, 1933; Friedman, *AF*, 115.
31. Freud, *Standard Edition*, 22:39, 55.
32. H.D., "Advent," 175.
33. H.D. to Bryher, March 19, 1933; Friedman, *AF*, 117.
34. Bryher to H.D., March 20, 1933; Friedman, *AF*, 126.
35. H.D. to Bryher and Macpherson, March 21, 1933; Friedman, *AF*, 127.
36. H.D., "Advent," 174, 175.
37. Bryher to H.D., March 23, 1933; Friedman, *AF*, 138.
38. H.D. to Bryher, March 23, 1933; Friedman, *AF*, 142.
39. H.D. to Bryher, March 25, 1933; Friedman, *AF*, 149.
40. H.D. to Bryher, March 26, 1933; Friedman, *AF*, 152.
41. Bryher to Macpherson, March, 31, 1933; Friedman, *AF*, 163–164.
42. Bryher to Macpherson, March 31, 1933; Friedman, *AF*, 163–164.
43. H.D. to Macpherson, April 6, 1933; Friedman, *AF*, 171.
44. Bryher to Macpherson, April 9, 1933; Friedman, *AF*, 173.
45. H.D. to Bryher, April 18, 1933; Friedman, *AF*, 181.
46. H.D. to Bryher, April 23, 1933; Friedman, *AF*, 188.
47. H.D. to Bryher and Kenneth Macpherson, April 26, 1933; Friedman, *AF*, 200–201.
48. Bryher to H.D., March 26, 1933; Friedman, *AF*, 153.
49. H.D. to Bryher, May 3, 1933; Friedman, *AF*, 238.

50. H.D. to Bryher, April 27, 1933; Friedman, *AF*, 203.
51. H.D. to Bryher, April 28, 1933; Friedman, *AF*, 212.
52. See Friedman, *AF*, 208–214.
53. H.D. to Bryher, April 28, 1933; Friedman, *AF*, 209, 210, 213.
54. H.D. to Bryher, April 28, 1933; Friedman, *AF*, 209, 210, 213.
55. H.D. to Bryher, April 28, 1933; Friedman, *AF* 214.
56. Freud, *Three Essays on Sexuality*, 1509.
57. Friedman, *AF*, 225.
58. H.D. to Bryher, May 2, 1933; Friedman, *AF*, 232–233.
59. H.D. to Bryher, May 6, 1933; Friedman, *AF*, 247.
60. World Alliance for Combating Anti-Semitism, *J'Accuse* (London: Salomon House, 1933).
61. H.D. to Bryher, May 16, 1933; Friedman, *AF*, 284.
62. H.D. to Bryher, May 6, 1933; Friedman, *AF*, 248.
63. H.D. to Bryher, May 7, 1933; Friedman, *AF*, 251.
64. Bryher to H.D., May 16, 1933; Friedman, *AF*, 282–283.
65. Bryher to H.D., May 23, 1933; Friedman, *AF*, 311–312.
66. H.D. to Bryher, May 28, 1933; Friedman, *AF*, 324–326.
67. H.D. to Bryher, May 28, 1933; Friedman, *AF*, 331.
68. Friedman, *AF*, n.3, 324.
69. Bryher to H.D., May 21, 1933; Friedman, *AF*, 304.
70. Bryher to H.D., May 27, 1933. Friedman, *AF*, 330–331.
71. Bryher to H.D., May 31, 1933; Friedman, *AF*, 336.
72. Bryher to Bergner, June 23, 1933.
73. Bryher to Bergner, June 9, 1933.
74. Sachs to Bryher, June 14, 1933.
75. Schaffner, "UA," 158.
76. H.D. to McAlmon, July 20, 1933; Friedman, *AF*, 363.
77. "Britain's Wealthiest Man Dead," *Daily Mail*, July 18, 1933.
78. *Daily Mirror,* July 18, 1933.
79. Perdita to Bryher, July 23, 1933.
80. Schaffner, "UA," 160.
81. Lady Ellerman, letter to the editor, *London Times*, July 19, 1933.
82. Macpehrson to H.D, July 1933.
83. H.D. to Ellis, July 13, 1933.
84. Herring to H.D., July 18, 1933.
85. H.D. to Bryher, July 13, 1933.
86. "The Remarkable Will of Sir J. Ellerman," *Straits Times* September 17, 1933.
87. Rubenstein, *Men of Property*, 43.
88. H.D to Ellis, August 30, 1933.
89. *Daily Telegraph*, July 18, 1933.
90. Tim Carroll, "The Lost Tycoon," *Sunday Times*, October 22, 2006.
91. *The Sunday Referee,* May 2, 1925;Box 152, f. 5147.
92. John Jr.'s works include *The Families and Genera of Living Rodents*, volumes 1 and 2 (London: Printed by order of the Trustees of the British Museum, 1940); *Checklist of Palaeartic and Indian Mammals 1758 to 1946; Supplement to Chasen (1940)*; and *A Handlist of Malaysian Mammals*.

93. Macpehrson to H.D, July 1933.
94. Bryher to H.D., July 25, 1933.
95. Bryher to H.D, August 26, 1933.
96. H.D. to Ellis, August 30, 1933.
97. H.D. to Viola Jordan, June 1, 1934.
98. H.D., *CP*, 369–377.
99. Anna Freud to Bryher, September 18, 1933.
100. Freud to H.D., October 27, 1933; Friedman, *AF,* 387.
101. Freud to Bryher, October 27, 1933; Friedman, *AF,* 388.
102. Bryher, "Manchester," *Life and Letters To-Day* 15 (Summer 1936): 81–82.
103. H.D., "Advent," 184.
104. H.D. to Bryher, November 14, (1934); Friedman, *AF,* 473.
105. H.D., "AN."
106. H.D. to McAlmon, August 6, 1933; Friedman, *AF*, 366.

Chapter 13

1. H.D. to Silvia Dobson, March 25, 1934.
2. H.D. to Dobson, February 28, 1934; Tinker, "Friendship."
3. Dobson, "Mirror," 3,4.
4. Dobson, "Mirror," 4–5.
5. Dobson, "Mirror," 9.
6. Dobson, "Mirror," 10–11.
7. H.D. to Dobson, February 28, 1934.
8. Dobson, "Mirror," 14.
9. Dobson, "Mirror," 14–15, 28.
10. Dobson, "Mirror," 30–31.
11. H.D. to Dobson, May 31, 1934; Tinker, "Friendship."
12. Bryher to H.D, August 29, 1934.
13. Phyllis Grosskurth, *Melanie Klein: Her World and Her Work* (New York: Knopf, 1986), 112.
14. Dobson, "Mirror," 30–31.
15. Macpherson to Bryher, August 1934; Friedman, *AF, 405*.
16. H.D. to Pound, August 19, 1933; Friedman, *AF,* 367. Without a secretary, Bryher herself "meticulously" answered endless letters for funds, aiding "scientists and students in Vienna."
17. Macpherson to Bryher, August 30, 1934; Friedman, *AF,* 416.
18. Herring to H.D., April 13, 1936.
19. Macpherson to H.D., April 25, 1936.
20. Bryher to H.D., November 12, 1934.
21. Macpherson to H.D., September 24, 1934.
22. H.D., *Kora*, 26.
23. H.D., *Nights* (New York: New Directions, 1986). Perdita Schaffner's introduction asked, "Who, to begin with, is this John Helforth ... author of *Nights?* He doesn't exist. He never did.... [H]e is H.D.'s alter-ego" (ix).
24. H.D. to Dobson, May 1934.
25. H.D., *Nights*, 5.

26. H.D., *Nights*, 63–64, 71.
27. H.D. to Dobson, July 18, 1934.
28. Dobson, "Mirror," 43.
29. Dobson, "Mirror," 43–44.
30. H.D. to Dobson, October 10, 1934.
31. Bryher to H.D., August 29, 1934.
32. Bryher to Herring, August 28, 1934.
33. Bryher to Herring, September 1, 1934; Friedman, *AF*, 419–420.
34. Veronika Fuechtner, *Berlin Psychoanalytic: Psychoanalysis and Culture in Weimar Republic Germany and Beyond* (Berkeley: University of California Press, 2011), 10.
35. Freud, *Standard Edition*, 19: 2728.
36. Freud, *Standard Edition*, 19: 3731.
37. Perdita Schaffner, in H.D., *Nights*, xiii.
38. McAlmon to H.D., October 3, 1933; Friedman, *AF*, 385.
39. Freud, *Standard Edition*, 19: 3732, 3753.
40. D. W. Winnicott, "Fear of Breadown" (1963?), in *Psycho-Analytic Explorations: Donald Winnicott*, ed. Clare Winnicott, Shepherd, and Davis (Cambridge, MA: Harvard University Press, 1989), 91.
41. Bryher to Herring, August 28, 1934.
42. Bryher to H.D., August 28, 1934.
43. Grosskurth, *Melanie Klein*, 203.
44. Bryher to H.D., August 28, 1934.
45. H.D. to Dobson, September 12, 1934.
46. H.D. to Dobson, October 10, 1934.
47. H.D., *Tribute*, 4.
48. Freud to H.D., June 1934; Friedman, *AF*, 403.
49. H.D. to Dobson, September 16, 1934.
50. H.D., "AN."
51. H.D. to Dobson, September 26, 1934.
52. H.D. to Dobson, October 10, 1934.
53. Freud to H.D., September 24, 1934; Friedman, *AF*, 422.
54. H.D. to Ellis, September 26, 1934.
55. These letters from Gregg are in Dobson Papers, box 6; without month or day noted, they appear written in autumn and winter 1934.
56. H.D. to Plank, October 16, 1934.
57. H.D. to Bryher, November 17, 1934; Friedman, AF, 482.
58. H.D. to Bryher, October 28, 1934; Friedman, *AF*, 427–428.
59. Moore to H.D., January 6, 1935; *MMSL*, 340.
60. H.D. to Plank, November 18, 1934.
61. H.D. to Bryher, October 31, 1934.
62. H.D. to Bryher, November 8, 1934; Friedman, *AF*, 452.
63. H.D. to Bryher, November 7, 1934; Friedman, *AF*, 452.
64. H.D. to Bryher, October 31, 1934; Friedman, *AF*, 439.
65. Dobson, "Mirror," 69.
66. H.D. to Dobson, November 10, 1934.
67. H.D. to Dobson, November 23, 1934.

68. H.D. to Dobson, December 17, 1934.
69. Gregg to H.D., November 8, 1934.
70. H.D. to Bryher, November 11, 1934; Friedman, *AF*, 460.
71. H.D. to Bryher, November 11, 1934; Friedman, *AF*, 460.
72. Gregg to H.D., November 1934.
73. H.D., "Advent," 145.
74. HD. to Bryher, November 19, 1934: Friedman, *AF*, 484–485, 33.
75. H.D. to Bryher, November 19, 1934; Friedman, *AF*, 486.
76. H.D. to Bryher, November 20, 1934; Friedman, *AF*, 489.
77. H.D. to Bryher, November 27, 1934; Friedman, *AF*, 503.
78. H.D. to Bryher, December 5, 1934; Friedman, *AF*, 518.
79. Macpherson to H.D., December 5, 1934.
80. H.D. to Bryher, November 24, 1934; Friedman, *AF*, 498. "Bisexual," once common to all, left "behind only a few traces of the sex that has become atrophied." Freud, *Three Essays* (1905), in *Standard Edition*, Vol. 7, 1405.
81. H.D. to Bryher, November 27, 1934; Friedman, *AF*, 503–504.
82. H.D. to Dobson, October 24, 1934; Tinker, "Friendship."
83. H.D. to Bryher, December 15, 1934; Friedman, *AF*, 520.

Chapter 14

1. Doris Banfield to Bryher, February 1935.
2. H.D., "AN."
3. H.D. to Bryher, March 21, 1935.
4. H.D to Bryher, March 23, 1935.
5. H.D. to Dobson, December 20, 1934.
6. H.D. to Bryher, December 5, 1934.
7. H.D. to Bryher, November 29, 1934.
8. H.D. to Bryher, February 1, 1935.
9. H.D. to Bryher, August 26, 1935.
10. H.D. to Bryher, January 30, 1935.
11. H.D. to Bryher, April 17, 1935.
12. H.D. to Ellis, November 25, 1934.
13. H.D. to Bryher, December 20, 1934.
14. H.D. to Bryher, January 16, 1935.
15. Bryher to H.D., January 31, 1935.
16. Bryher to H.D., February 6, 1935.
17. Bryher to H.D., April 13, 1935.
18. Bryher to H.D., May 27, 1935.
19. Schaffner, "UA," 196, 178.
20. Bryher to H.D., January 9, 1935.
21. Schaffner, "UA," 198.
22. Bryher to H.D., January 16, 1935.
23. H.D. to Bryher, January 28, 1935.
24. Perdita to H.D., February 1935.
25. Bryher to H.D, January 23, 1935.

26. Bryher to H.D., January 20, 1935.
27. Bryher to H.D., January 19, 1935.
28. Bryher to H.D., January 16, 1935.
29. H.D. to Bryher, February 1, 1935.
30. Bryher to H.D., February 15, 1935.
31. H.D. to Bryher, March 5, 1935.
32. Bryher to H.D., April 21, 1935.
33. H.D. to Bryher, June 8, 1935.
34. Perdita to Bryher, June 15, 1935.
35. Perdita to Bryher, July 3, 1935.
36. Schaffner, "UA," 212.
37. Schaffner, "UA," 230.
38. H.D. to Plank, May 2, 1935.
39. H.D. to Bryher, August 7, 1935; Friedman, *AF*, 527.
40. H.D., *Ion* (New York: New Directions, 2003), 158.
41. H.D. to Bryher, August 11, 1935.
42. H.D., *Ion*, 151, 152.
43. Gregory, *H.D. and Hellenism*, 205.
44. H.D. to Bryher, February 26, 1936.
45. H.D., *Ion*, 210.
46. H.D., *Ion*, 234.
47. H.D., *Ion*, 171.
48. H.D., *Ion*, 187.
49. H.D., *Ion*, 239.
50. H.D., *Ion*, 174.
51. H.D., *Ion*, 177.
52. H.D., *Ion*, 242.
53. H.D. to Bryher, August 7, 1935; Friedman, *AF*, 528.
54. H.D., *Ion*, 172.
55. Gilbert Murray, *Euripides and His Age* (New York: Henry Holt, 1913), 20.
56. H.D., *Ion*, 145, 156.
57. H.D. to Bryher, August 7, 1935.
58. H.D. to Plank, May 9, 1935.
59. H.D to Bryher, August 26, 1935.
60. H.D. to Dobson, August 31, 1935.
61. H.D. to Bryher, August 26, 1935; Friedman, *AF*, 531–532.
62. Bryher to H.D., August 25, 1935; Friedman, *AF*, 530.
63. Bryher to H.D., November 9, 1936.
64. Freud to H.D., February 26, 1937.
65. Moore to Bryher, January 18, 1936.
66. Bryher to Moore, June 9, 1936.
67. Moore to Bryher, January 18, 1935.
68. See Marianne Moore, *Adversity and Grace: Marianne Moore, 1936–1941*, edited by Heather Cass White (Victoria: ELS Editions, 2012).
69. Moore to Bryher, November 7, 1936; *MMSL*, 368.
70. Anna Freud to Bryher, December 30, 1937.

71. Anna Freud, *The Ego and the Mechanisms of Defense* (London: Routledge, 2018), 127.
72. Moore to Bryher, March 14, 1936; *MMSL*, 337.
73. Bryher to H.D., February 1936.
74. H.D. to Bryher, February 7, 1936.
75. Bryher to H.D., March 26, 1936.
76. Bryher to H.D., May 19, 1936.
77. Bryher to H.D., June 6, 1936.
78. Schaffner, "UA," 329, 261.
79. Bryher to Schmideberg, July 8, 1936.
80. Dobson, "Mirror," 196.

Chapter 15

1. Schaffner, "UA," 255.
2. H.D. to Bryher, December 17, 1936.
3. H.D. to Bryher, December 14, 1936.
4. Dobson, "Mirror," 198.
5. Bryher to Benjamin, February 11, 1936, published in Werke und Nachlaß. (Work and Estate) 16 (2012): 545–547. Bryher wrote three postcards and twenty-nine unpublished letters between 1936 and 1940, WBA folder 33.
6. Bryher to Benjamin, June 24, 1936, WBA 33.
7. Bryher to H.D., May 1, 1936.
8. Bryher to Schmideberg, October 26, 1936.
9. Bryher to Benjamin, August 5, 1937, WBA 33.
10. Bryher to H.D., May 30, 1936.
11. H.D. to Bryher, July 11, 1936.
12. Bryher to Schmideberg, March 14, 1936.
13. Bryher to H.D., August 10, 1936.
14. Bryher to Schmideberg, October 8, 1936.
15. Bryher to Benjamin, August 15, 1937, WBA 33. Walter Benjamin, "Eduard Fuchs, Collector and Historian," in Benjamin, *Selected Writings*, 3:267. Bryher later gave this article to Erich Heydt's boyfriend, Ivan Nagel, who had it with him when I interviewed him in Berlin in 2011.
16. H.D. to Bryher, August 30, 1936.
17. H.D. to Bryher, October 23, 1936.
18. H.D. to Bryher, November 3, 1936.
19. H.D. to Bryher, October 25, 1936.
20. Bryher to Schmideberg, October 28, 1936.
21. H.D. to Bryher, November 23, 1936.
22. Schaffner, "UA," 259.
23. Schaffner, Introduction to H.D., *Hedgehog*, xii.
24. H.D., *Hedgehog*, 27.
25. Bryher to Schmideberg, November 1936.
26. Bryher to H.D., December 7, 1936.
27. Bryher to H.D., December 18, 1936.
28. Aldington to H.D., January 15, 1937.

29. H.D. to Gregg, February 10, 1937.
30. H.D. to Bryher, January 31, 1937.
31. H.D., Draft for "Petitioner's Statement," box 48, folder 1201.
32. H.D., Draft for "Petitioner's Statement."
33. Bryher to Schmideberg, April 17, 1937.
34. H.D. to Bryher, February 6, 1937.
35. H.D. to Dobson, February 20, 1937.
36. H.D. to Dobson, March 2, 1937.
37. Bryher to H.D., June 1937.
38. Bryher to Schmideberg, May 2, 1938.
39. Bryher to Schmideberg, July 6, 1937.
40. Bryher to Schmideberg, September 9, 1937.
41. Bryher to Schmideberg, July 1, 1937.
42. Schmideberg to Bryher, October 30, 1937.
43. Annette Debo, "Norman Holmes Pearson, Canon-Maker," *Modernism/Modernity* 23, no. 2 (April 2016): 443.
44. H.D. to Pearson, December 12, 1937.
45. H.D. to Pearson, February 5, 1938.
46. Bryher to Pearson, December 21, 1937.
47. Bryher to Schmideberg, January 26, 1938.
48. Benjamin to Bryher, December 19, 1937.
49. Bryher to Benjamin, January 14, 1938, WBA 33.
50. Bryher to Schmideberg, January 17, 1938.
51. Bryher to H.D., January 17, 1938.
52. Bryher to Pearson, January 17, 1938.
53. Dobson, "Mirror," 222, 281.
54. Bryher to Pearson, February 18, 1938.
55. Bryher to Schmideberg, February 1, 1938.
56. Moore, *MMCP*, 119.
57. Bryher to Schmideberg, March 13, 1938.
58. Bryher, "The Crisis: September," *Life and Letters To-Day* 19, November 1938, 1.
59. Schaffner, "UA," 300.
60. Bryher to Schmideberg, March 19, 1938.
61. Schaffner, "UA," 306.
62. Bryher to Schmideberg, March 13, 1938.
63. Bryher to Schmideberg, March 17, 1938.
64. Bryher to Schmideberg, March 13, 1938.
65. Bryher to Schmideberg, April 30, 1938.
66. Bryher to Schmideberg, May 18, 1938.
67. Bryher to Anna Freud, May 31, 1938.
68. Sachs to Bryher, April 18, 1938.
69. Sachs to Bryher, May 12, 1938.
70. Bryher to Schmideberg, May 17, 1938.
71. Walter Benjamin to Bryher, December 19. 1937.
72. Walter Benjamin, *Berlin Childhood around 1900*, translated by Howard Eiland (Cambridge, MA: Harvard University Press, 2006), 114.

73. Bryher to Benjamin, May 16, 1938, in Werke und Nachlaß. (Work and Estate) 11, no. 2 (2019), 368–369.
74. Schaffner, "UA," 301.
75. Moore to Bryher, June 10, 1938; *MMSL*, 391–392.
76. H.D. to Plank, May 18, 1938.
77. H.D. to Plank, June 11, 1938.
78. H.D. to Bryher, May 1, 1939.
79. Schaffner, "UA," 305.
80. Bryher to Schmideberg, May 1938.
81. Bryher to Schmideberg, March 1938.
82. Bryher to Pearson, May 31, 1938.
83. Bryher to Schmideberg, May 31, 1938.
84. Bryher to Benjamin, August 28, 1938, WBA 33.
85. Bryher to Schmideberg, September 1938.
86. Bryher to Pearson, October 14, 1938.
87. Pearson to Bryher, October 30, 1938.
88. Pearson to H.D. and Bryher, October 30, 1938.
89. Martin Gilbert, *Churchill and the Jews: A Lifelong Friendship* (New York: Henry Holt, 2007), 147, 148.
90. Schmideberg to Bryher, December 2, 1938.
91. Bryher to Schmideberg, May 20, 1939.
92. Perdita to Bryher, June 6, 1939.
93. Bryher, *HA*, 283.
94. Bryher to Benjamin, May 19, 1939, WBA 33.
95. Bryher to Schmideberg, June 26, 1939.
96. H.D. to Bryher, July 17, 1939.
97. Perdita to Bryher, June 15, 1939.
98. Bryher to Pearson, December 17, 1939.

Chapter 16

1. Schaffner, "UA," 369.
2. Bryher to Benjamin, August 21, 1939. "Ich glaube nicht, personlich, das wir Krieg haben warden, dieser Jahr." My translation: "I do not think, personally, that we will have war this year."
3. Bryher to Benjamin, August 26, 1939.
4. Bryher, *HA*, 288.
5. H.D. to Plank, September 25, 1939.
6. Perdita to Bryher, September 2, 1939.
7. H.D. to Plank, September 25, 1939.
8. Bryher, *HA*, 278.
9. Bryher to Benjamin. September 25, 1939.
10. Bryher to Benjamin, October 13, 1939, postcard. "Do not fear I will forget you."
11. Herring to Bryher, October 6, 1939.
12. Herring to Bryher, September 21, 1939.
13. H.D. to Plank, September 25, 1939.

14. H.D. to Plank, October 7, 1939.
15. Sachs to Bryher, September 30, 1939.
16. British consul general to Bryher, September 19, 1939.
17. Beach to Bryher, October 20, 1939.
18. H.D. to Dobson, September 25, 1939.
19. Herring to Bryher, September 21, 1939.
20. Perdita to Bryher, October 26, 1939.
21. Bryher to Annie Reich, September 24, 1939.
22. Bryher to Pearson, November 13, 1939.
23. Herring to Bryher, October 14, 1939.
24. Herring to Bryher, October 6, 1939.
25. Herring to Bryher, October 20, 1939.
26. Bryher to Pearson, November 17, 1939.
27. H.D. to Bryher, November 11, 1939.
28. H.D. to Dobson, November 16, 1939.
29. Perdita to Bryher, November 14, 1939.
30. Perdita to H.D., November 14, 1939.
31. H.D. to Plank, November 14, 1939.
32. Herring to Bryher, December 20, 1939.
33. Herring to Bryher, February 2, 1940.
34. Bryher to Benjamin, March 2, 1940.
35. H.D. to Bryher, March 5, 1940.
36. Bryher, Diary 1940, box 148, folder 5059.
37. Bryher to H.D., March 1940.
38. Perdita to Bryher, April 1940.
39. H.D. to Bryher, April 6, 1940.
40. Herring to Bryher, April 9, 1940.
41. H.D. to Bryher, April 25, 1940.
42. H.D. to Bryher, April 26, 1940.
43. H.D. to Bryher, May 16, 1940.
44. H.D. to Bryher, June 5, 1940.
45. H.D. to Bryher, May 31, 1940.
46. H.D. to Bryher, May 22, 1940.
47. H.D. to Bryher, May 30, 1940.
48. Bryher to Benjamin, June 11, 1940.
49. Hannah Arendt, *Men in Dark Times* (New York: Harcourt, 1955), 153.
50. Bryher to H.D., June 18, 1940
51. H.D. to Bryher, June 7, 1940.
52. H.D. to Bryher, May 1, 1940.
53. Edith Sitwell to Pavel Tchelitchew, June 6, 1940, quoted in Richard Greene, *Edith Sitwell: Avant Garde Poet, English Genius* (New York: Virago Press, 2011), 284.
54. H.D., "Before the Battle," in *Within*, 145, 150–151. Debo's edited *Within the Walls* contains fourteen stories written between summer 1940 and spring 1941.
55. Hogue and Vandivere in H.D., *Sword*, xlix, n. 48.
56. Bryher, "My Communications with Non-Occupied France, June–September 1940," 2, 3, 5, box 72, folder 2877.

57. Klara Modern to Alice Modern, June 19, 1940, in *Dearest Family*, 84, 85.
58. Klara Modern to Alice Modern, June 19, 1940, in *Dearest Family*, 84, 85.
59. Klara Modern to Alice Modern, August 4, 1940, in *Dearest Family*, 91.
60. Klara Modern to Alice Modern, August 22, 1940, in *Dearest Family*, 94.
61. H.D. to Moore, June 1940.
62. Herring to Bryher, June 8, 1940.
63. Herring to Bryher, August 25, 1940.
64. Macpherson to H.D., July 17, 1940.
65. Bryher to Schmideberg, July 18, 1940.
66. H.D. to Bryher, September 2, 1940.
67. H.D. to Moore, September 24, 1940.
68. H.D. to Harold Doolittle, September 1940.
69. Bryher, *HA*, 293, 294–295.
70. Bryher, "Report: The Journey from Geneva to Lisbon," box 72, folder 2870. These experiences are retold in *HA*. I draw upon both sources.
71. Bryher, *HA*, 295.
72. Bryher, *HA*, 303.
73. H.D to Bryher, September 26, 1940.
74. Bryher, *HA*, 307.
75. Herring to Bryher, September 30, 1940.
76. Moore to Bryher, October 14, 1940, RML.
77. Lara Feigel, *The Love-Charm of Bombs: Restless Lives in the Second World War* (London: Bloomsbury Press, 2013), 21.
78. Elizabeth Bowen, "London, 1940," in *The Mulberry Tree: Writings of Elizabeth Bowen*, edited by Hermione Lee (New York: Harcourt Brace, 1986), 21, 23.
79. Bryher, *Days*, 8.
80. Bryher to Annie Reich, January 5, 1941.
81. H.D. to Dobson, October 30, 1940.
82. H.D., *Compassionate*, 120.
83. Bryher to Pearson, December 10, 1940.
84. William Manchester, *The Last Lion: Winston Spencer Churchill, Defender of the Realm, 1940–1965* (New York: Bantam, 2013), 212.
85. H.D. to Moore, November 1940.
86. Bryher to Moore, December 8, 1940, *MMSL*, 406–407.
87. Bryher to Pearson, December 5, 1940.
88. Herring to Bryher, December 1940.
89. Herring to Bryher, October 1940.
90. Herring to Bryher, October 7, 1940.
91. Edith Sitwell to Bryher, December 26, 1941.
92. Bryher to Edith Sitwell, April 20, 1941.
93. Edith Sitwell to Bryher, September 1, 1941.
94. Victoria Glendinning, *Edith Sitwell: A Unicorn among Lions* (New York: Knopf, 1981), 226.
95. Osbert Sitwell to Bryher, January 11, 1942.
96. Herring to Bryher, November 22, 1940.
97. Greene, *Edith Sitwell*, 1.
98. Bryher to Pearson, January 15, 1941.

99. Bryher to H.D, January 26, 1941.
100. Herring to Bryher, February 6, 1941.
101. Herring to Bryher, February 14, 1941.
102. H.D., "Blue Lights," in *Within*, 119.
103. Schaffner, "Running," 10.
104. Perdita to Bryher, March 23, 1941.
105. Greene, *Edith Sitwell*, 283.
106. H.D. to May Sarton, March 30, 1941.
107. H.D. to Bryher, May 27, 1941.
108. Elizabeth Bowen, *Heat of the Day* (New York: Knopf, 1948), 24.
109. H.D. to Bryher, May 28, 1941.
110. Herring to Bryher, June 12, 1941.
111. H.D., "The Ghost," in *Within*, 144.
112. Bryher to Pearson, January 1941.
113. H.D., "The Ghost," 144, 136–137, 140–141, 139.
114. H.D. to Bryher, May 1941.
115. Herring to Bryher, June 12, 1941.
116. Edith Sitwell to Bryher, June 13, 1941.

Chapter 17

1. T. S. Eliot, *Four Quartets*, (New York and London: Harcourt Brace Jovanovich, 1971), 27.
2. Lyndall Gordon, *T. S. Eliot: An Imperfect Life* (New York: Norton, 1998), 353.
3. Quoted in Gordon, *T. S. Eliot*; see his citation of the translation Eliot used to base his lines upon from *The Ascent of Mount Carmel I. xiii*, translated by E. Allison Peters (in Eliot's library), 350.
4. Pagels, *Gnostic Gospels*, 74, quoting from the Acts of John. Pagels refers to ancient codices discovered in Upper Egypt in 1945 in "a red earthenware jar, almost a meter high," containing multiple texts, including poems, and several "secret gospels," among them the Gospel to the Egyptians, the Gospel of Thomas, and the "Secret Book" of John. *Gnostic Gospels* notes the 1896 discovery of Mary Magdalene's book.
5. H.D. to Viola Jordan, July 2, (1941?), Jordan Papers.
6. Gordon, *T. S. Eliot*, citing Anon., *Cloud of Unknowing*, 352.
7. H.D., *The Walls Do Not Fall*, in *Trilogy* (New York: New Directions, 1973), 42.
8. T. S. Eliot, *Four Quartets*,44.
9. H.D. (Hilda Doolittle), "A Letter from England," *Bryn Mawr Alumnae Bulletin* 21, no. 7 (July 1941): 22.
10. Aldington to H.D., April 30, 1941.
11. Macpherson to Herring, September 1945.
12. H.D. to Plank, July 1941.
13. Elizabeth P. McIntosh, *Sisterhood of Spies: The Women of the OSS* (New York: Dell/Random House, 1998), 124.
14. Robin Winks, *Cloak and Gown: Scholars in the Secret War, 1939–61* (London: Harvill Press, 1987), 270.
15. Perdita to Bryher, May 1941.

16. H.D., *Walls*, 19.
17. H.D to Bryher, July 18, 1941.
18. Bryher to H.D., July 19, 1941.
19. Bryher to H.D., July 26, 1941.
20. Bryher to H.D., July 20, 1941.
21. Bryher to H.D., July 27, 1941.
22. Bryher to Pearson, July 31, 1941.
23. Bryher to H.D., July 31, 1941.
24. Dobson, "Mirror," 306–307; H.D. to Dobson, September 7, 1941.
25. H.D., "R.A.F.," in *What Do I Love?*, reprinted in *Within*, 165–172.
26. H.D., "The Ghost," in *Within*, 140.
27. H.D. *Sword*, 35.
28. Bryher to H.D., September 12, 1941.
29. H.D. to Plank, September 5, 1942.
30. Bryher to H.D., September 22, 1941.
31. H.D., *Sword*, 6.
32. Hugh Dowding, *Many Mansions*, (Guildford, UK: White Crow Press, 2013), 4.
33. H.D., *Sword*, 9.
34. H.D., *Majic*, 66, 67.
35. H.D to Pearson November 19, (1941), in *BHP*, 20.
36. Bryher, *Days*, 54.
37. Dobson, "Mirror," 314.
38. Dobson, "Mirror," 326
39. H.D. to Bryher, August 1, 1942.
40. H.D. to Bryher, August 3, 1942.
41. H.D. to Bryher, August 3, 1942.
42. H.D. to Bryher, August 13, 1942.
43. Bryher to H.D., August 19, 1942.
44. H.D. to George Plank, September 9, 1942.
45. H.D., *Walls*, 3.
46. Adelaide Morris, "Signaling: Feminism, Politics, and Mysticism in H.D.'s War *Trilogy*," *Sagetrieb*. 9, no. 3 (1990): 129.
47. H.D., "H.D.," 187; H.D. to Pearson, 1943, in *BHP*, 32, 31.
48. H.D., *Walls*, 24.
49. H.D., *Walls*, 48, 54.
50. H.D., *Walls*, 14, 58.
51. H.D., *Walls*, 11–12. It appeared in *Life and Letters* (Fall 1942).
52. T. S. Eliot, *The Use of Poetry and the Use of Criticism* (London: Faber and Faber, 1933), 144.
53. Peter Ackroyd, *T. S. Eliot* (New York: Simon & Schuster, 1984), 261.
54. H.D., *Walls*, 33, 50.
55. H.D., *Walls*, 8–9.
56. Dobson, "Mirror," 327.
57. Anton Gill, *Art Lover: A Biography of Peggy Guggenheim* (New York: Harper Collins, 2002), 325.

Chapter 18

1. Bryher, *Days*, 131.
2. H.D. to Pearson, August 9, 1943, in *BHP*, 26.
3. H.D., *Gift*, 209–210.
4. H.D., "H.D.," 212.
5. H.D., *Gift*, 49–50, 216, 214.
6. H.D., *Gift*, 215, 219, 221.
7. "Séance Notes" includes Bryher's, covering September 2, 1943, through January 20, 1944, with messages to the group, joining H.D.'s notes from January through April 1943, gathered in H.D. Papers, box 23, folder 682, discreetly labeled "Source Material" for *Majic*. Bryher typed these notes December 9, 1945. Demetres Tryphonopoulos provides H.D.'s "last note" in the séance sequence in *Majic*, n. 118, 222.
8. H.D. to Mary Herr, February 1944.
9. H.D., *Sword*, 12.
10. Hogue and Vandivere introduction to H.D., *Sword*, xxvi.
11. H.D., *Majic*, 176. H.D. revised her "Séance Notes" in 1954 to include describing her practice.
12. H.D., *Sword*, 10, 21.
13. Hogue and Vandivere introduction to H.D., *Sword*, xxv, 137.
14. H.D. to Dobson, February 1943.
15. Doris Long to Bryher, February 20, 1943.
16. Bryher to Moore, April 18, 1943, RML.
17. Bryher, *Days*, 82.
18. H.D., *CP*, 483.
19. T.S. Eliot, *The Waste Land*, *Complete Poems*, 50. In an early review of Hindu philosophy in 1918 in *Complete Prose* v.1, n.3, 705, clarifies his two year study of Sanskrit with eminent Charles Lanman, and under James Wood, he studied Indian grammarian Patanjali (150 BCE), unifying body, mind and spirit in *Yoga Sutras*.
20. H.D to Marianne Moore, April 18, 1943.
21. H.D to Pearson, May 2, 1943, in *BHP*, 22.
22. Pearson to H.D., August 25, 1943, in *BHP*, 27.
23. Pearson to H.D., May 14, 1943, in *BHP*, 24.
24. H.D. to Pearson, May 11, 1943.
25. Bryher, *Days*, 98, 100.
26. Bryher, *Days*, 103.
27. Bryher, *Days*, 106.
28. Bryher, "A Note on Beaumont and Fletcher," *Life and Letters* 36, no. 65 (January 1943): 5, 8–9.
29. Perdita Schaffner, "Glass in My Typewriter," *East Hampton Star*, May 15, 1975.
30. Bryher, *Days*, 110.
31. Bryher to H.D., August 6, 1943.
32. H.D to Pearson, August 26, 1943, in *BHP*, 28–29.
33. H.D., "H.D.," 199.
34. Demetres P. Tryphonopoulos, editor of *Majic*, xxix.
35. H.D., *What Do I Love?*, in *Within*, 155–164.
36. H.D., *Sword*, 13.

37. H.D. to Dowding, October 21, 1943; H.D., *Majic*, xxxi.
38. H.D. to Dowding, October 27, 1943; H.D. *Majic*, xxxi.
39. H.D., *Sword*, 14.
40. H.D., "H.D.," 198.
41. H.D., *Sword*, 11.
42. H.D., *Majic*, 174–175, n. 10. The note records H.D.'s lengthy description.
43. H.D., *Majic*, 11.
44. H.D., *Majic*, 176.
45. H.D., *Majic*, 116.
46. H.D., *Majic*, 132.
47. H.D., *Majic*, 128.
48. H.D., *Majic*, 129.
49. H.D., *Majic*, 15.
50. H.D., *Majic*, 10.
51. Leo McKinstry, "Revealed: the bizarre life of the RAF's Battle of Britain supremo,"*Daily Mail*, November 21, 2007.
52. H.D., *Majic*, 8. Not all séance messages were typed up, and some were integrated into *Sword*.
53. H.D., *Majic*, 9.
54. H.D., *Majic*, 64–65, 44–45.
55. Bryher, *Days*, 117, 118.
56. H.D., *Majic*, 164.
57. H.D., *Majic*, 165.
58. Pagels, *Gnostic Gospels*, xv, xxxii.
59. H.D., *CP*, 462, 464.
60. H.D., *Angels*, 65. The passage refereneces Revelations 1.20 to denote "the seven stars" as "the seven angels." n. 8, 185.
61. Pagels, *Gnostic Gospels*, xv.
62. H.D., *Angels*, 66.
63. H.D., *Angels*, 103.
64. H.D., *Angels*, 78.
65. H.D., *Angels*, 107.
66. H.D. to Pearson, December 5, 1944, in *BPH*, 45.
67. H.D., *Angels*, 80.
68. H.D., *Angels*, 89.
69. H.D., *Angels*, 93.
70. H.D., *Angels*, 95.
71. H.D., *Angels*, 97, 100, 101.
72. H.D. to Pearson, September 11, 1944, in *BHP*, 43.
73. Dobson, "Mirror," 363.
74. Sylvia Beach, "Inturned," *PMLA* 124, no. 3 (2009): 943.
75. Herring to Bryher, June 13, 1944.
76. Osbert Sitwell to Bryher, June 18, 1944.
77. Bryher, *Days*, 132–133, 139.
78. H.D to Pearson, July 31, 1944, in *BHP*, 43.
79. Pearson to Bryher, August 2, 1944.

80. Pearson to Bryher, August 16, 1944.
81. H.D. to Monnier, October 19, 1944.
82. Bryher, *Days*, 146.
83. H.D. to Dobson, August 26, 1944.
84. Dobson, "Mirror," 362.
85. Herring to Bryher, October 2, 1944.
86. H.D. to Susan Pearson, September 12, 1944.

Chapter 19

1. H.D., *Tribute*, 94.
2. H.D., "H.D," 190.
3. H.D., *Tribute*, 91.
4. H.D., *Tribute*, 77, 78, 118.
5. H.D., *Tribute*, 80.
6. H.D., *Tribute*, 157.
7. H.D., *CP*, 448.
8. Osbert Sitwell, review of *The Walls Do Not Fall*, by H.D., *Observer*, May 28, 1944.
9. H.D., *Flowering*, 114.
10. Pagels, *Gnostic Gospels*, 11–12, xv. These texts belong to the *Nag Hammadi Library*.
11. H.D., *Flowering*, 115.
12. H.D., *Flowering*, 116.
13. H.D., *Flowering*, 120.
14. H.D., *Flowering*, 125.
15. H.D., *Tribute*, 16.
16. H.D, *Flowering*, 126.
17. H.D., *Flowering*, 133.
18. H.D., *Flowering*, 134.
19. H.D., *Flowering*, 131.
20. H.D., *Flowering*, 145.
21. Bryher, *Days*, 147–148.
22. H.D. to Dobson, December 15, 1944.
23. Dobson, "Mirror," 429.
24. H.D., *Sword*, 18.
25. Perdita to Bryher, March 28, 1945.
26. Perdita to "Darlings," March 2, 1945.
27. H.D. to Susan Pearson, April 14, 1945.
28. Perdita to H.D. and Bryher, May 3, 1945.
29. Bryher to Pearson, June 12, 1945.
30. H.D. to Dobson, June 5, 1945.
31. Bryher, *Days*, 149.
32. Bryher to H.D., June 12, 1945.
33. H.D. to Dobson, June 5, 1945.
34. Bryher to H.D., June 6, 1945.
35. Bryher to H.D., June 10, 1945.
36. Bryher to H.D., July 6, July 7, July 11, 1945.

37. Bryher, *Days*, 166, 167.
38. H.D., *Sword*, 27.
39. Bryher to H.D., July 25, 1945.
40. Bryher to H.D., July 16, 1945.
41. Laura Vetter, *Curious Peril: H.D.'s Late Modernist Prose* (Gainesville: University Press of Florida, 2017), 108.
42. Collecott, *H.D. and Sapphic Modernism*, 231.
43. Dobson, "Mirror," 425; H.D. to Dobson, July 20, 1945.
44. Bryher to H.D., July 27, 1945.
45. Norman Pearson, "H.D.'s *Tribute to the Angels*," *Life and Letters*, 46, no. 95-96 (July-September 1945), 26-27.
46. H.D. to Pearson, July 29, 1945; Hollenberg, *BHP*, 46.
47. H.D., "Good Frend," in *Avon*, 6.
48. Bryher to Schmideberg, August 9, 1945.
49. Vetter, *Curious Peril*, 217, n.19.
50. H.D., "Good Frend," in *Avon*, 9.
51. H.D., "Good Frend," in *Avon*, 10, 15.
52. H.D., "Good Frend," in *Avon*, 17, 25.
53. "Rain of Ruin," *New York Times*, August 7, 1945.
54. Barton J. Bernstein, "The Atomic Bombings Reconsidered," *Foreign Affairs* 74, no. 1 (1995): 150.
55. Bryher to H.D, August 8, 1945.
56. Bryher, *Days*, 169.
57. H.D., *Sword*, 47.
58. Herring to Bryher, August 10, 1945.
59. H.D. to Pearson, September 1, 1945, in *BHP*, 47.
60. H.D., *Sword*, 32.
61. Bryher to H.D., September 26, 1945.
62. H.D., *Sword*, 34.
63. H.D., *Sword*, 29.
64. H.D., *Sword*, 31.
65. H.D. to Pearson, December 27, 1945, in *BHP*, 49.
66. Dobson, "Mirror," 442.
67. Herring to Bryher, December 29, 1945.
68. H.D., *Walls*, 59.
69. H.D. to Dobson, December 10, 1945.

Chapter 20

1. Pearson to H.D., January 23, 1946, in *BHP*, 51.
2. Herring to Bryher, August 8, 1945.
3. H.D., *Sword*, 67.
4. Bryher to Viola Jordan, January 12, 1946.
5. H.D. to Bryher, September 20, 1946.
6. H.D. to Dobson, February 14, 1946.
7. Bryher to Pearson, March 1, 1946.

8. Sachs to Bryher, March 9, 1946.
9. Bryher to Pearson, April 1946.
10. Bryher to Pearson, April 14, 1946.
11. Bryher to Pearson, April 18, 1946.
12. Dr. Carroll to Bryher, April 30, 1946.
13. Dr. Carroll to Bryher, April 20, 1946.
14. Dr. Theodore Brunner to Miss Macpherson, May 25, 1946. Brunner's letters reporting to Bryher are in her archive, untranslated; Marjorie Perloff kindly translated these letters for me.
15. Brunner to Bryher, May 17, 1946.
16. Brunner to Bryher, May 25, 1946.
17. Brunner to Bryher, June, 5 1946.
18. H.D. to Dobson, June 22, 1946.
19. Jane Augustine, introduction to H.D., *The Gift*, 24.
20. Brunner to Bryher July 18, 1946.
21. Brunner to Bryher, August 6, 1946.
22. Bryher to H.D., August 9, 1946.
23. Bryher to H.D., August 9, 1946.
24. Brunner to Bryher, August 20, 1946.
25. Nephi J. Christodoulides, citing Guest's biography, *Herself Defined*, writes, "[They] virtually kidnapped her and took her to the Nerven clinik." Nephi J. Christodoulides, "Reflections on H.D.'s *Majic Mirror*," *H.D.'s Web Supplemental Newsletter* 2, no. 1 (Summer 2008).
26. H.D. to Bryher, September 2, 1946.
27. H.D. to Carroll, September 16, 1946.
28. H.D. to Bryher, September 16, 1946.
29. H.D. to Bryher and Perdita, September 17, 1946.
30. Bryher to H.D., September 18, 1946.
31. H.D. to Bryher, September 20, 1946.
32. H.D. to Bryher, September 21, 1946.
33. H.D. to Bryher, September 21, 1946; notes at 11:00 a.m., 1:30 p.m., and 5:15 p.m.
34. H.D. to Bryher September 21, 1946.
35. H.D. to Bryher, September 22, 1946.
36. H.D. to Bryher, September 23, 1946.
37. H.D. to Bryher, September 24, 1946.
38. H.D. to Pearson September 26, 1946, in *BPH*, 58.
39. H.D. to Bryher, September 26, 1946.
40. H.D. to Bryher, September 20, 1946.
41. Ashby to H.D., October 6, 1946.
42. Bryher to H.D., September 28, 1946.
43. H.D. to Bryher, September 30, 1946.
44. Bryher to H.D., October 3, 1946.
45. H.D. to Bryher, October 6, 1946.
46. H.D. to Bryher, October 5, 1946.
47. H.D. to Bryher, October 13, 1946.
48. Bryher to H.D., October 16, 1946.
49. H.D. to Bryher, October 6, 1946.

50. H.D. to Bryher, October 10, 1946.
51. H.D. to Bryher, October 14, 1946.
52. H.D. to Bryher, October 12, 1946.
53. Bryher to H.D., October 14, 1946.
54. Bryher to Pearson, October 16, 1946.
55. H.D. to Dobson, October 15, 1946.
56. Bryher to H.D., October 22, 1946.
57. H.D. to Bryher, October 23, 1946.
58. Bryher to H.D., October 28, 1946.
59. Bryher to H.D., October 8, 1946.
60. H.D. to Bryher, October 16, 1946.
61. Bryher to H.D., October 18, 1946.
62. Perdita to H.D., October 22, 1946.
63. H.D. to Bryher, October 24, 1946.
64. H.D. to Bryher, October 24, 1946.
65. Bryher to H.D., October 21, 1946.
66. H.D. to Bryher, October 18, 1946.
67. H.D. to Bryher, October 28, 1946.
68. H.D., "The Guest," in *Avon*, 31.
69. Bryher to H.D., October 31, 1946.
70. Bryher to H.D., November 8, 1946.
71. H.D. to Bryher, October 29, 1946.
72. Bryher to H.D., November 7, 1946.
73. H.D. to Bryher, November 9, 1946.
74. H.D. to Bryher, November 2, 1946.

Chapter 21

1. Fiona MacCarthy, *William Morris: A Life of Our Time* (New York: Knopf, 1995), 75.
2. H.D. to Sylvia Beach, December 14, 1946.
3. H.D. to Bryher, December 26, 1946.
4. Bryher, "Writings," n.d., box 90, folder 3332.
5. H.D. to Bryher, June 6, 1947
6. H.D., *Pilate's*, 65.
7. G. Wilson Knight, *The Mutual Flame: On Shakespeare's Sonnets and "The Phoenix and the Turtle"* (London: Methuen, 1955), 40.
8. Bryher to H.D., April 25, 1947.
9. H.D. to Bryher, January 10, 1947.
10. Bryher to H.D., January 11, 1947.
11. Bryher to H.D., January 18, 1947.
12. Bryher to H.D., January 20, 1947.
13. Bryher to H.D., January 8, 1947.
14. H.D. to Bryher, May 21, 1947.
15. H.D., *Sword*, 147.
16. H.D., *Sword*, 140, 146.
17. H.D.'s "Dante and His Circle" was written in Lugano during 1947–1948.

18. Bryher to H.D., April 26, 1947.
19. Bryher to H.D., May 29, 1947.
20. H.D. to Bryher, May 31, 1947.
21. H.D. to Bryher, May 15, 1947.
22. H.D., *Sword*, 148, 153, 158.
23. Bryher to H.D., May 16, 1947.
24. Vandivere and Hogue, in H.D., *Sword*, xxi.
25. Bryher to H.D., July 20, 1947.
26. Aldington to H.D., April 6, 1947.
27. H.D. to Aldington, June 6, 1947, in *RAHDLY* 92.
28. H.D. to Bryher, August 16, 1947.
29. Aldington to H.D., August 7, 1947.
30. As a utopian socialist, Morris appealed to both H.D. and Bryher. His sense of the future as despoiling the past led to Bryher's novel *Visa for Avalon*, which pivots on the bulldozing of country cottages to make way for "linoleum" and the ultra-convenient.
31. H.D. to Bryher, May 21, 1947.
32. Aldington to H.D., August 7, 1947.
33. H.D. to Aldington, August 24, 1947, in *RAHDLY*, 103.
34. H.D., *Compassionate*, 127.
35. H.D. to Bryher, September 22, 1947. Herring sent a butterfly book the same day.
36. Bryher to H.D., December 6, 1947.
37. H.D. to Bryher, December 8, 1947.
38. Bryher to H.D., January 1, 1948.
39. Bryher to H.D, February 13, 1948.
40. H.D. to Bryher, February 14, 1948.
41. Sylvia Beach to Bryher, January 28, 1948.
42. Sylvia Beach to Bryher, May 3, 1948.
43. Sylvia Beach to Bryher, May 22, 1948.
44. Sylvia Beach to Bryher, May 29, 1948.
45. Violet Hunt, *The Wife of Rossetti* (New York: E. P. Dutton, 1932), 60.
46. Bryher to H.D., May 14, 1948.
47. H.D., *Rose*, 89.
48. H.D., *Rose*, 65, 78.
49. H.D. to Bryher, Novermber 29, 1948.
50. H.D. to Bryher, April 20 1948.
51. Jean Burton, *Hey-Dey of a Wizard*. New York: Knopf, 1944, 28.
52. Burton, *Hey-Dey*, 96.
53. Burton, *Hey-Dey*, 184.
54. H.D. to Bryher, April 21, 1948.
55. H.D. to Bryher, July 19, 1948.
56. H.D. to Pearson, August 14, 1948.
57. H.D. to Pearson, April 20, 1949.
58. H.D., *Rose*, 64.
59. H.D. to Bryher, October 12, 1948.
60. Bryher to H.D., October 12, 1948.
61. Bryher to H.D., October 14, 1949.

62. Bryher to H.D., October 17, 1948.
63. Herring to H.D., November 28, 1948.
64. Pearson to H.D, November 1948.
65. Pearson to H.D, September 22, 1949.
66. H.D. to Bryher, December 1948.
67. H.D. to Bryher, January 8, 1949.
68. H.D. to Bryher, December 3, 1948.
69. Bryher to Pearson, February 8, 1949.
70. H.D. to Bryher, July 5, 1949.
71. H.D. to Pearson, April 1, 1949.
72. Pearson to H.D., August 28, 1950.
73. H.D. to Bryher, March 11, 1949.
74. H.D. to Bryher, April 18, 1949.
75. H.D. to Bryher, July 14, 1949.
76. Bryher, "The Years of the Quest," box 77, folder 2993.
77. H.D. to Bryher, July 14, 1949.
78. H.D. to Bryher, July 15, 1949.
79. H.D. to Bryher, June 18, 1949.
80. H.D. to Bryher, July 23, 1949.
81. Bryher to Pearson, July 3, 1949.
82. H.D. to Bryher, August 9, 1949.
83. Bryher to H.D., August 7, 1949.
84. Bryher to Pearson, March 7, 1946.
85. Bryher to Pearson, August 29, 1949.
86. Bryher to H.D., August 13, 1949.
87. H.D. to Bryher, September 5, 1949
88. Bryher, "The Years of the Quest," Box 72, f.2881.
89. H.D. to Bryher, August 17, 1949.
90. Bryher to H.D., August 18, 1949.
91. H.D. to Bryher, August 18, 1949.
92. H.D. to Bryher, August 28, 1949.
93. Bryher to H.D., August 20, 1949.
94. Bryher to H.D., August 26, 1949.
95. Bryher to H.D., September 17, 1949.
96. Bryher to H.D, September 19, 1949.
97. Bryher to H.D., September 20, 1949.
98. H.D. to Bryher, September 29, 1949.
99. Bryher to H.D., September 30, 1949.
100. Bryher to H.D., Septmeber 24, 1949.
101. Bryher to H.D., September 25, 1949.
102. Bryher to H.D., September 26, 1949.
103. Bryher to H.D., Septmeber 27, 1949.
104. Glover to Bryher, October 16, 1949.
105. Schmideberg to Bryher, September 11, 1949.
106. Bryher to H.D., May 1, 1949.
107. Bryher to H.D., August 20, 1949.

108. H.D. to Pearson, December 18, 1948.
109. H.D. to Bryher, August 17, 1952.
110. H.D. to Bryher, October 14, 1949.
111. H.D. to Bryher, December 8, 1948.
112. Sylvia Beach to Bryher, September 11, 1950.
113. Sylvia Beach to Bryher, October 16, 1949.
114. Sylvia Beach to Bryher, October 31, 1948. Matte Robinson notes Santa Claus as Proteus in *Helen* is "emblematic of gender fluidity." Matte Robinson, *The Astral H.D.: Occult and Religious Sources for H.D's Poetry and Prose* (London: Bloomsbury, 2016), 141.
115. Bryher to H.D., May 5, 1948.
116. Bryher to H.D., February 17, 1951.
117. Bryher to H.D., December 29, 1950.

Chapter 22

1. Bryher to H.D., September 26, 1949.
2. Pearson to Bryher, March 27, 1948.
3. Charles Berryman, a graduate student at Yale in the mid-1960s, offered this phrase. See Michael Holzman, "The Ideological Origins of American Studies at Yale," *American Studies* 40, no. 2 (Summer 1991): 75.
4. H.D. to Bryher, April 13, 1950.
5. Bryher to H.D., April 11, 1950.
6. H.D. to Aldington, October 1, 1950, in *RAHDLY,* 160.
7. Columbia University holds John Schaffner's archival papers of approximately 101 feet. Gifted by Timothy Schaffner.
8. J. V. Schaffner, "The Redheaded Pine Sawfly" (Washington, DC: U.S. Department of Agriculture, 1939), 191; four pages with illustrations.
9. H.D. to Bryher, April 17, 1950.
10. Pearson to H.D., June 24, 1950.
11. H.D. to Perdita, June 22, 1950.
12. H.D. to Perdita, July 14, 1950.
13. H.D. to Bryher, July 17, 1950.
14. H.D. to Bryher, July 19, 1950.
15. Bryher to H.D., September 29, 1950.
16. H.D. to Bryher, October 26, 1950.
17. Bryher to Pearson, Decmber 7, 1950.
18. H.D. to Jordan, January 16, 1951.
19. Bryher to Pearson, January 21, 1951.
20. Bryher to Pearson, December 3, 1950.
21. Bryher to Pearson July 12, 1950.
22. Bryher to Pearson, December 7, 1950.
23. H.D. to Aldington, April 24, 1951, in *RAHDLY*, 169.
24. H.D. to Pearson, May 3, 1951, in *BHP*, 103.
25. Bryher to Pearson, March 3, 1951.
26. H.D. to Bryher, June 2, 1951.
27. H.D. to Bryher, June 7, 1951.

28. H.D. to Bryher, July 2, 1951.
29. H.D. to Bryher, June 3, 1951.
30. Herring to H.D., July 7, 1951.
31. Bryher to Pearson, April 21, 1951.
32. H.D. to Bryher, June 2, 1951.
33. H.D. to Bryher, July 18, 1951.
34. H.D., *Mirror*, 27.
35. Bryher, *Fourteenth*, 160.
36. Marianne Moore, "In Harald's Service," *New York Times Book Review,* April 27, 1952, 4.
37. Bryher, *Fourteenth*, 41, 223.
38. Walter Schmideberg to Bryher, April 12, 1950.
39. Bryher to Pearson, August 7, 1951.
40. Bryher to Pearson, July 26, 1950.
41. Bryher to Pearson, September 8, 1951.
42. H.D. to Bryher, July 24, 1951.
43. Bryher to H.D., July 1951.
44. H.D. to Bryher, August 11, 1951.
45. Bryher to Pearson, August 13, 1951.
46. Bryher to Pearson, October 4, 1951.
47. Bryher to Pearson, October 8, 1951.
48. Bryher to Pearson, October 10, 1951.
49. Melitta Schmideberg to Bryher, January 2, 1952.
50. "Parapsychology FAQ," *British Journal of Psychology,* February 28, 2008, online.
51. Susan Stanford Friedman, *Psyche Reborn* (Bloomington: Indiana University Press, 1981), 280. The "En-Soph" resembles the Gnostic belief in "Infinite Being," an "incomprehensible principle."
52. H.D., *Angels*, 77.
53. Ambelain, *Practical Kabbalah* (1951),7. Online: http://www.markfoster.net/rn/texts/practicalkabbalah-part1.pdf
54. H.D. to Bryher, February 8, 1952.
55. H.D. to Bryher, February 6, 1952.
56. H.D. to Bryher, February 9, 1952.
57. H.D. to Bryher, April 24, 1952.
58. H.D. to Bryher, June 5, 1952
59. H.D. to Bryher, June 26, 1952.
60. H.D. to Bryher, July 7, 1952.
61. H.D. to Bryher, August 24, 1952.
62. H.D. to Bryher, July 18, 1952.
63. H.D. to Bryher, September 20, 1952.
64. H.D., *Sword*, 171.
65. Bethany Hughes, *Helen of Troy: Goddess, Princess, Whore* (New York: Knopf, 2005), 23.
66. Friedman, *Psyche Reborn*, 254, passim.
67. H.D., "Euripides."
68. H.D. to Bryher, September 23, 1952.
69. H.D. to Bryher, October 2, 1953.
70. H.D. to Bryher, September 24, 1952.

71. Pearson to H.D., September 26, 1952.
72. Pearson to H.D., October 2, 1952.
73. Pearson to H.D., September 1, 1952.
74. H.D. to Bryher, September 26, 1952.
75. H.D. sent Hughes a CARE package, that "he might barter for tobacco." H.D. to Bryher, September 25, 1952. She called his notes a "heart-breaking dossier of corrections."
76. H.D. to Bryher, September 28, 1952.
77. H.D. to Bryher, October 2, 1952.
78. H.D. to Bryher, October 3, 1952.
79. H.D. to Bryher October 26, 1952.
80. H.D. to Bryher, October 7, 1952.
81. H.D. to Bryher, October 15, 1952.
82. H.D., *Helen*, 33.
83. H.D. to Bryher, October 10, 1952.
84. H.D. to Bryher, October 14, 1952.
85. H.D. to Bryher, October 8, 1952.
86. H.D. to Bryher, October 14, 1952.
87. H.D. to Bryher, October 15, 1952.
88. Bryher to H.D, October 13, 1952.
89. H.D. to Bryher, October 14, 1952.
90. H.D. to Bryher, October 18, 1952.
91. Bryher to H.D., October 20, 1952
92. H.D. to Bryher, October 20, 1952.
93. H.D., *Helen*, 2, 6, 7–8, 10, 11, 10.
94. H.D. to Bryher, October 11, 1952.
95. Bryher to H.D., October 13, 1952
96. Pearson to H.D., October 2, 1952.
97. H.D., *Helen*, 8.
98. Pearson to H.D., December 22, 1952
99. H.D., *Compassionate*, 99.
100. H.D. to Dobson, January 16, 1953.
101. Bryher to Pearson, January 27, 1953.
102. H.D., *Compassionate*, 104
103. Aldington to H.D., January 7, 1953.
104. H.D. to Aldington, January 30, 1953.
105. Aldington to Bryher, February 12, 1953.
106. Aldington to Bryher, April 5, 1953.
107. H.D. to Bryher, May 8 1953.
108. H.D. to Pearson, May 11, 1953.
109. H.D. to Bryher, May 27, 1953.
110. H.D. to Bryher, May 31, 1953.
111. Aldington to Bryher, June 16, 1953.
112. H.D. to Bryher, June 3, 1953.

Chapter 23

1. H.D., *Mirror*, 35.
2. H.D., *Helen*, 162.
3. Anna Fyta configures *Helen* as a "heterotopia," where space and time, self and other, break down. The epic made Kusnacht feel this way. Anna Fyta, "Ex-centric Narrative," *Journal of Anglophone Literature* 3 (2019): 185–200.
4. H.D., *End*, 11.
5. H.D., *Helen*, 146.
6. I interviewed Ivan Nagel in October 2011 at the American Academy in Berlin; he recalled his lover Heydt and H.D., Schmideberg, and Bryher; Bryher gave him H.D.'s *What Do I Love?*
7. H.D., *Mirror*, 65.
8. H.D. to Bryher, July 15, 1953.
9. H.D., *Helen*, 185.
10. Ashby to H.D, November 17, 1952.
11. H.D., *Compassionate*, 84.
12. H.D., *Mirror*, 22.
13. H.D. to Bryher, July 25, 1954.
14. H.D. to Bryher, August 4, 1954.
15. H.D., *Mirror*, 45.
16. H.D. to Bryher, September 13, 1953.
17. H.D. to Bryher, September 29, 1953.
18. H.D., *Helen*, 138.
19. H.D., *Mirror*, 24.
20. H.D., *Compassionate*, 126.
21. After the phrase Virginia Woolf uses in *Orlando: A Biography* (New York: Houghton Mifflin, 1956) to stage the winter affair between an Elizabethan boy and a boyish woman on a skating tryst, seeing frozen birds beneath the ice. Woolf had approximated "the great frost," the coldest winter in Europe, in 1708–1709. Keeping up with Woolf's work, the pair nonetheless had existed at the margins of Woolf as focal London writer, with a famous father, Sir Leslie Stephen, a prominent chronicler of lives.
22. H.D. to Bryher, January 10, 1954.
23. H.D., *Mirror*, 3.
24. H.D., *Helen*, 177.
25. H.D., *Compassionate*, 135.
26. H.D. to Bryher, September 3, 1953.
27. H.D. to Bryher, September 4, 1953.
28. Bryher, *Roman Wall: A Novel* (New York: Pantheon, 1954), 55.
29. H.D. to Bryher, September 2, 1953.
30. H.D. to Bryher, September 20, 1953.
31. H.D. to Bryher, September 23, 1953.
32. H.D., *Compassionate*, 148.
33. H.D., *Mirror*, 34.
34. H.D., *Helen*, 110.
35. H.D., *Helen*, 154.
36. H.D., *Helen*, 128.

37. H.D., *Compassionate*, 104.
38. H.D., *Compassionate*, 145.
39. Schmideberg to Bryher, January 22, 1954.
40. H.D. to Bryher, January 7, 1954.
41. H.D. to Bryher, January 18, 1954.
42. H.D. to Bryher, February 2, 1954.
43. Dobson to Bryher, February 25, 1954.
44. H.D. to Bryher, January 22, 1954.
45. H.D., *Helen*, 150, 148.
46. H.D. to Bryher, January 25, 1954.
47. H.D. to Bryher, January 18, 1954
48. H.D to Pearson, February 9, 1954, in *BHP* 155.
49. H.D., *Helen*, 155, 160–161, 197, 196.
50. H.D. to Bryher, February 1, 1954.
51. H.D., *Compassionate*, 138.
52. H.D. to Aldington, March 2, 1954.
53. H.D. to Bryher, March 24, 1954.
54. H.D. to Bryher, March 25, 1954.
55. H.D. to Bryher March 31, 1954
56. H.D. to Bryher, May 20, 1933, in Friedman, *AF*.
57. H.D., *Mirror*, 55.
58. H.D., *Mirror*, 69.
59. Dobson, *Mirror*, 615.
60. Bryher, *The Player's Boy* (Ashfield: Paris Press, 2006), 26, 4, 28.
61. Bryher to Pearson, May 2, 1951.
62. H.D. to Bryher, August 3, 1954.
63. H.D. to Bryher, August 5, 1954
64. Schmideberg to Bryher, August 4, 1954.
65. H.D. to Bryher, September 9, 1954.
66. H.D. to Bryher, September 14, 1954.
67. Herring to H.D., October 20, 1954.
68. H.D., *Compassionate*, 149.
69. H.D., *Compassionate*, 127, 122.
70. Bryher to H.D., April 27, 1955.
71. H.D., *Compassionate*, 123.
72. H.D., *Compassionate*, 134.
73. H.D. to Pearson, November 26, 1954.
74. H.D. to Dobson, November 25, 1954.
75. H.D. to Bryher, January 26, 1954.
76. Sylvia Beach to Bryher, October 25, 1954.
77. H.D. to Beach, June 22, 1955.
78. H.D. to Bryher, September 17, 1956.
79. H.D. to Dobson, September 22, 1956.
80. H.D. to Dobson, October 20, 1956.
81. Aldington to Bryher, June 16, 1957.
82. Pearson to H.D., November 21, 1956, in *BHP* 192.

83. H.D. to Pearson, October 23, 1956.
84. Elizabeth Butler, *Fortunes of Faustus: Magic in History* (Cambridge: Cambridge University Press, 1952), 233.
85. H.D., *Vale Ave* (New York: New Directions, 2013), 29.
86. H.D., *Thorn,* 163. "Sagesse" was first printed in *Evergreen Review,* no. 5 (1958).
87. H.D., *Thorn,* 169.
88. The records of Bryher's funding others is staggering, composing hundreds of pages of balance sheets.
89. Dobson, *Mirror,* 624.
90. Beach to Bryher, December 28, 1956.
91. See Erin Carlston, *Double Agent: Espionage, Literature, and Liminal Citizens* (New York: Columbia University Press, 2013).
92. H.D., *Compassionate,* 85.
93. Aldington to Bryher, July 8, 1957.
94. Aldington to H.D., March 21, 1957.
95. H.D., *End to Torment,* 49.
96. H.D. to Dobson, August 18, 1958.
97. H.D. to Dobson, September 16 1958.
98. Bryher to H.D., January 29, 1947.
99. H.D., *Thorn*, 161.
100. Adalaide Morris, *How to Live/What to Do: H.D.'s Cultural Poetics* (Urbana: University of Illinois Press, 2003), 110–111, 130.
101. Aldington to Bryher, June 27, 1957.
102. Bryher to Aldington, July 20, 1957.
103. H.D., *Helen*, 164.
104. H.D., *Thorn,* 165.
105. Henry Abelove, *Deep Gossip* (Minneapolis: University of Minnesota Press, 2005).
106. H.D. to Dobson, September 9, 1959.
107. H.D. to Aldington, September 23, 1959.
108. Harold Doolittle to Bryher, May 9, 1960.
109. H.D., *Thorn*, 174.
110. Robert Duncan, "The Homosexual in Society and Politics," *Outlook*, August 1944, 209–211. The essay was later collected in Robert Duncan, *Selected Prose*, edited by Robert J. Bertholf (New York: New Directions, 1995).
111. Pearson to Bryher, May 27, 1960.
112. Blanche Brunner to Bryher, May 27 1960.
113. Aldington to Bryher, April 12, 1959.
114. H.D., *Thorn*, 190.
115. Beach to Bryher, July 2, 1959.
116. Dobson, *Mirror,* 675.
117. Lawrence Durrell, *Reflections on a Marine Venus: A Companion to the Landscapes of Rhodes* (London: Faber, 1953), 7.
118. H.D. to Dobson, September 9, 1961.
119. Bryher to Dobson, June 6, 1961.
120. H.D., *Hermetic Definition* (New York: New Directions, 1972), 3–4.
121. Bryher to Dobson, September 25, 1961.

122. Bryher to Dobson, October 1, 1961.
123. Mary Renault to Bryher, May 26, 1961.
124. Valentine Schaffner hosted me in July 2009. I explored Bryher's collection of books in a private house devoted to her on the grounds.
125. Austin Briggs to Bryher, June 26, 1970.
126. Perdita Schaffner to Susan Stanford Friedman, April 5, 1980, SSF.
127. Perdita Schaffner to Susan Stanford Friedman, June 5, 1982, SSF.
128. Perdita Schaffner to Susan Stanford Friedman, June 15, 1983, SSF.
129. Bryher, "The Gay Literary Supplement," February 1983, "Clippings," folder 5030.
130. Perdita Schaffner, "They Lived to Write," *New Directions for Women* 18 (July/August 1989), 18–19.

Bibliography

Abelove, Henry. *Deep Gossip*. Minneapolis: University of Minnesota Press, 2003.
Ackroyd, Peter. *T.S. Eliot*. New York: Simon & Schuster, 1984.
Adams, Evangeline. *Astrology: Your Place in the* Sun. New York: Dodd, Mead, 1927.
Aldington, Richard. *Death of a Hero*. London: Hogarth Press, 1984.
Aldington, Richard. *D. H. Lawrence: Portrait of a Genius But...* London: Heineman, 1950.
Aldington, Richard. *Life for Life's Sake: A Book of Reminiscences*. New York: Viking, 1941.
Ambelain, Robert. *Practical Kabbalah*. (1951). http://www.markfoster.net/rn/texts/practical-kabbalah-part1.pdf
Arendt, Hannah. *Men in Dark Times*. New York: Harcourt, 1955.
Baedeker, Karl. *Greece Handbook for Travelers*. Leipzig: Karl Baedeker, 1909.
Baker, J. I. "A Spy's World." *Inside the World of Spies*. Life Magazine, August 8, 2017.
Beach, Sylvia. "Inturned." *PMLA* 124, no. 3 (2009): 940–945.
Beach, Sylvia. *Shakespeare & Company*. New York: Harcourt, 1959.
Belford, Barbara. *Violet: The Story of the Irrepressible Violet Hunt and Her Circle of Lovers and Friends—Ford Madox Ford, H. G. Wells, Somerset Maugham, and Henry James*. New York: Simon & Schuster, 1990.
Benjamin, Walter. *Berlin Childhood around 1900*. Translated by Howard Eiland. Cambridge, MA: Harvard University Press, 2006.
Benjamin, Walter. *Illuminations*. Edited by Hannah Arendt. New York: Schocken Books, 1969.
Benjamin, Walter. *Selected Writings*. Vol. 3, *1936–1938*. Translated by Michael W. Jennings. Edited by Howard Eiland. Cambridge, MA: Harvard University Press, 2002.
Bennett, Jane. *Vibrant Matter: A Political Ecology of Things*. Durham, NC: Duke University Press, 2010.
Benstock, Shari. *Women of the Left Bank: Paris 1900–1940*. Austin: University of Texas Press, 1986.
Beresford, Philip, and William D. Rubinstein, eds. *The Richest of the Rich: The Wealthiest 250 People in Britain Since 1066*. Petersfield: Harriman House, 2011.
Bergner, Daniel. "The Struggles of Rejecting the Gender Binary." *New York Times*, June 4, 2019. https://www.nytimes.com/2019/06/04/magazine/gender-nonbinary.html.
Bernstein, Barton J. "The Atomic Bombings Reconsidered." *Foreign Affairs* 74, no. 1 (1995): 135–152.
Bowen, Elizabeth. *Heat of the Day*. New York: Knopf, 1948.
Bowen, Elizabeth. *The Mulberry Tree: Writings of Elizabeth Bowen*. Edited by Hermione Lee. New York: Harcourt Brace, 1986.
Bryher. *Amy Lowell: A Critical Appreciation*. London: Eyre and Spottiswoode, 1918.
Bryher. *Arrow Music*. London: J. & E. Bumpus, 1922.
Bryher. *Beowulf*. Introduction by Susan McCabe. New York: Pantheon, 1956; Tucson, AZ: Schaffner Press, 2020.
Bryher. *Civilians*. Riant Chateau: Pool Press, 1927.
Bryher. *The Coin of Carthage*. New York: Harcourt Brace, 1963.
Bryher. *The Days of Mars: A Memoir, 1940–1946*. New York: Harcourt Brace, 1971.
Bryher. *Film Problems of Soviet Russia*. Territet: Pool, 1929.
Bryher. *The Fourteenth of October*. New York: Pantheon, 1952.
Bryher. *The Heart to Artemis: A Writer's Memoirs*. New York: Harcourt Brace, 1962.

Bryher. *Manchester. Life and Letters To-Day* 13 (December 1935): 80–112; 15 (Spring 1946): 94–114; 15 (Summer 1936): 74–98.
Bryher. "My Introduction to America," *Life and Letters To-Day* 26 (September 1940): 237–239.
Bryher, "A Note on Beaumont and Fletcher." *Life and Letters* 36 (January 1943): 5-9.
Bryher. *The Player's Boy*. Introduction by Patrick Gregory. Ashfield: Paris Press, 2006.
Bryher. *The Region of Lutany*. London: Chapman & Hall, 1914.
Bryher. *Roman Wall: A Novel*. New York: Pantheon, 1954.
Bryher. *Ruan*. New York: Pantheon, 1960.
Bryher. *South*. Paris: Three Mountain Press, 1921.
Bryher. *Two Novels (Development* and *Two Selves)*. Introduction by Joanne Winning. Madison: University of Wisconsin Press, 2000.
Bryher. *Visa for Avalon*. Introduction by Susan McCabe. Ashfield: Paris Press, 2004.
Bryher. *West*. London: Jonathan Cape, 1925.
Bryher, "The War from Three Angles," *Close Up* 1, no. 1 (July 1927).
Bryher, "Westfront 1918," *Close Up* 7, no. 2 (August 1930).
Bryher, "What Shall You Do in the War?" *Close Up* 10, no. 2 (June 1933).
Budge, E. A. *The Egyptian Book of the Dead*. 1899; New York: Penguin, 2008.
Burke, Carolyn. "'Getting Spliced': Modernism and Sexual Difference." *American Quarterly* 39, no. 1 (1987): 98–121.
Burton, Jean. *Hey-Day of a Wizard*. NewYork: Knopf, 1944.
Butler, Elizabeth. *Fortunes of Faust: Magic in History*. Cambridge: Cambridge University Press, 1952.
Carew, Dorothea. *Many Years Many Girls: The History of a School, 1862–1942*. London: Browne & Nolan, 1967.
Carlston, Erin. *Double Agents: Espionage, Literature, and Liminal Citizens*. New York: Colombia University Press, 2013.
Carr, Helen. *The Verse Revolutionaries: Ezra Pound, H.D. and the Imagists*. London: Jonathan Cape, 2009.
Carroll, Tim. "The Lost Tycoon," *Sunday Times*, October 22, 2006.
Casement, Patrick. *Further Learning from the Patient: The Analytic Space and Process*. London: Routledge, 1990.
Castle, Terry. *The Apparitional Lesbian: Female Sexuality and Modern Culture*. New York: Columbia University Press, 1993.
Chisholm, Dianne. *H.D.'s Freudian Poetics: Psychoanalysis in Translation*. Ithaca, NY: Cornell University Press, 1992.
Chynoweth, John. *Tudor Cornwall*. Stroud: Tempus, 2002.
Christodoulides, Nepji J. "Reflections on H.D.'s *Majic Mirror*." *H.D.'s Web Supplemental Newsletter* 2, no. 1 (Summer 2008).
Coats, Jason M. "H.D. and the Hermetic Impulse." *South Atlantic Review* 77, nos. 1–2 (2012): 79–98.
Collard, Ian. *Ellerman Lines: Remembering a Great Shipping Company*. Stroud: History Press, 2014.
Collecott, Diana. "Bryher's Two Selves as Lesbian Romance." In *Romance Revisited*, edited by Lynne Pearce and Jackie Stacey. New York: New York University Press, 1995.
Collecott, Diana. *H.D. and Sapphic Modernism*. Cambridge: Cambridge University Press, 1999.
Collins, H. P. *Modern Poetry*. London: Jonathan Cape, 1925.
Cope, Karen. *Passionate Collaborations: Learning to Live with Gertrude Stein*. Victoria, B.C.: ELS Editions, 2005.
Cournos, John. *Autobiography*. New York: G. P. Putnam's Sons, 1935.
Debo, Annette. *The American H.D.* Iowa City: University of Iowa Press, 2012.

Debo, Annette. "Norman Holmes Pearson, Canon-Maker." *Modernism/Modernity* 23, no. 2 (April 2016): 443–462.
De Boer, Esther A. *Mary Magdalene: Beyond the Myth*. Norcross: Trinity Press International, 1997.
De Rougemont, Denis. *Love in the Western World*. Princeton, NJ: Princeton University Press, 1983.
Dell'Amore, Christine. "Dung Beetles Navigate via the Milky Way," January 24, 2013, blog. nationalgeographic.org.
Detloff, Madelyn. *The Persistence of Modernism: Loss and Mourning in the Twentieth Century*. Cambridge: Cambridge University Press, 2009.
DiPace Fritz, Angela. *Thought and Vision: A Critical Reading of H.D.'s Poetry*. Washington, DC: Catholic University of America Press, 1988.
Doan, Laura. *Fashioning Sapphism: The Origins of a Modern English Lesbian Culture*. New York: Columbia University Press, 2001.
Donald, James. *Some of These Days: Black Stars, Jazz Aesthetics, and Modernist Culture*. New York: Oxford University Press, 2015.
Donald, James, Anne Friedberg, and Laura Marcus, eds. *Close Up, 1927–1933: Cinema and Modernism*. Princeton, NJ: Princeton University Press, 1998.
Doolittle, C. L. *A Treatise on Practical Astronomy as Applied to Geodesy and Navigation*. 4th rev. ed. New York: John Wiley and Sons, 1893.
Doolittle, C.L. "An Address Delivered for the Alumni Association," Lehigh University, June 17, 1885.
Dowding, Hugh. *Many Mansions*. Guildford, UK: White Crow Press, 2013.
Dreyfuss, Robert. *Devil's Game*. New York: Henry Holt, 2005.
Duberman, Martin. *Paul Robeson*. New York: Knopf, 1988.
Duncan, Robert. *The H.D. Book*. Berkeley: University of California Press, 2011.
Duncan, Robert. *Selected Prose*. Edited by Robert J. Bertholf. New York: New Directions, 1995.
Durrell, Lawrence. *Reflections on Marine Venus: A Companion to the Landscapes of Rhodes*. London: Faber, 1953.
Easwaran, Eknath, trans. *The Upanishads*. Blue Mountain Meditation Center. Tomales, CA: Nilgiri Press, 2007.
Edmunds, Susan. *Out of Line: History, Psychoanalysis, and Montage in H.D.'s Long Poems*. Stanford, CA: Stanford University Press, 1994.
Edwards, Amelia B. *A Thousand Miles Up the Nile*. London: G. Routledge & Sons, 1877.
Eisenstein, Sergei. *Film Form: Essays in Film Theory*. Translated and edited by Jay Leyda. New York: Harcourt, Brace, 1949.
Eisner, Robert. *Travelers to an Antique Land: The History and Literature of Travel to* Greece. Ann Arbor: University of Michigan Press, 1991.
Eliade, Mircea. *The Two and the One*. Chicago: University of Chicago Press, 1979.
Eliot, T.S. "Classics in English," *Poetry 9, no. 2* (November 1916): 101–104.
Eliot, T. S. *Four Quartets*. New York and London: Harcourt Brace Jovanovich, 1971.
Eliot, T. S. *The Complete Poems and Plays: 1909–1950*. New York: Harcourt and Brace, 1962.
Eliot, T.S. *The Complete Prose of T.S. Eliot*. Volume 1 1905–1918. Edited by Jewel Spears Brooker and Ronald Schuchard. Baltimore: Johns Hopkins University Press, 2021.
Eliot, T. S. *The Letters of T. S. Eliot*. Vol. 1, *1898–1922*. Edited by Valerie Eliot and Hugh Haughton. New Haven, CT: Yale University Press, 2009.
Eliot, T.S. "Tradition and the Individual Talent" (1919), in *Sacred Wood*. London: Faber & Faber, 1997.
Eliot, T. S. *Selected Prose of T. S. Eliot*. Edited by Frank Kermode. New York: Harcourt Brace, 1975.
Eliot. T. S. *The Use of Poetry and the Use of Criticism*. London: Faber & Faber, 1933.

Ellerman, John, Jr. *The Families and Genera of Living Rodents*. London: Printed by order of the Trustees of the British Museum, 1940.
Ellis, David. *The Cambridge Biography of D. H. Lawrence: Dying Game 1922–1930*. Cambridge: Cambridge University Press, 1997.
Ellis, Havelock. *Studies in the Psychology of Sex*. Philadelphia, PA: F. A. Davis, 1913.
Ellis, Havelock. "Sexo-Aesthetic Inversion." *Alienist and Neurologist* 24 (1913): 156–167
Euripides. *The Hippolytus*. Translated by Rex Warner. London: Bodley Head, Fitch, 1949.
Euripides. *Medea and Other Plays*. Translated by James Morwood. Oxford: Oxford University Press, 2008.
Evans-Wentz, W. Y. *The Tibetan Book of the Dead*. Foreword by John Woodroffe. Oxford: Oxford University Press, 1936.
Farnell, Lewis Richard. *The Cult of the Greek States*. 5 vols. Oxford: Oxford University Press, 1896–1909.
Feigel, Lara. *The Love-Charm of Bombs: Restless Lives in the Second World War*. London: Bloomsbury Press, 2013.
Fenton, Ben. "Was This the Richest and Most Secretive Tycoon Ever?," *Daily Telegraph*, May 22, 2006.
Flammarion, Cammile. *Death and its Mystery: Proofs of the Existence of the Soul*. New York: Century Company, 1921.
Flaubert, Gustave. *Flaubert in Egypt: A Sensibility on Tour*. Edited and translated by Francis Steegmuller. London: Penguin, 1979.
Fogelman, Aaron Spencer. *Jesus Is Female: Moravians and Radical Religion in Early America*. Philadelphia: University of Pennsylvania Press, 2007.
Fontenrose, Joseph. *Python: A Study of Delphic Myth and Its Origins*. Berkeley: University of California Press, 1959.
Foster, R. F. *W. B. Yeats: A Life*. Oxford: Oxford University Press, 1998.
Frazer, James George. *The Golden Bough*. Edited by Robert Fraser. Oxford: Oxford University Press, 1994.
Freud, Anna. *The Ego and the Mechanisms of Defense*. London: Routledge, 2018.
Freud, Sigmund. *The Standard Edition of the Complete Psychological Works of Sigmund Freud*. Translated and edited by James Strachey. 24 vols. London: Hogarth Press, 1953–1974.
Friedman, Susan Stanford. *Analyzing Freud: Letters of H.D., Bryher and Their Circle*. New York: New Directions, 2002.
Friedman, Susan Stanford. *Penelope's Web: Gender Modernity, H.D.'s Fiction*. Cambridge: Cambridge University Press, 1991.
Friedman, Susan Stanford. *Psyche Reborn*. Bloomington: Indiana University Press, 1981.
Friedman, Susan Stanford. "Who Buried H.D.? A Poet, Her Critics and Her Place in 'The Literary Tradition.'" *College English* 36, no. 7 (1975): 801–814.
Fromm, Gloria G. *Dorothy Richardson: A Biography*. Urbana: University of Illinois Press, 1977.
Frost, Ginger S. *Living in Sin*. Manchester: Manchester University Press, 2008.
Fuechtner, Veronika. *Berlin Psychoanalytic: Psychoanalysis and Culture in Weimar Republic Germany and Beyond*. Berkeley: University of California Press, 2011.
Fyta, Anna. "Ex-centric Narrative." *Journal of Anglophone Literature* 3, (2019): 185–200.
Gaskell, Elizabeth. *Ruth*. Edited by Alan Shelston. Oxford: Oxford University Press, 1985.
Gilbert, Martin. *Churchill and the Jews: A Lifelong Friendship*. New York: Henry Holt, 2007.
Gilbert, Martin. *A History of the Twentieth Century*. Vol. 2, *1933–1951*. New York: Avon Books, 1998.
Gill, Anton. *Art Lover: A Biography of Peggy Guggenheim*. New York: Harper Collins, 2002.
Glendinning, Victoria. *Edith Sitwell: A Unicorn among Lions*. New York: Knopf, 1981.
Goodenough, R. Erwin. *By Light, Light: The Mystic Gospel of Hellenistic Judaism*. New Haven, CT: Yale University Press, 1935.

Gordon, Lois. *Nancy Cunard: Heiress, Muse, Political Idealist*. New York: Columbia University Press, 2007.
Gordon, Lyndall. *T. S. Eliot: An Imperfect Life*. New York: Norton, 1998.
Gourmont, Remy de. *The Natural Philosophy of Love*. Translated by Ezra Pound. Greenville, SC: Antipodes Press, 2017.
Greene, Richard. *Edith Sitwell: Avant Garde Poet, English Genius*. New York: Virago Press, 2011.
Gregg, Frances. "The Apartment." In Arthur Kreymborg's *Second American Caravan*. New York: Macaulay Press, 1928.
Gregg, Frances. "The Apartment." In Arthur Kreymborg's *Second American Caravan*, 1928.
Gregg, Frances. *The Mystic Leeway*. Edited by Oliver Marlow Wilkinson. Ottawa: Carleton University Press, 1995.
Gregory, Eileen. *H.D. and Hellenism*. Cambridge: Cambridge University Press, 1997.
Gregory, Eileen. "Virginity and Erotic Liminality: H.D's 'Hippolytus Temporizes.'" *Contemporary Literature* 31, no. 2 (1990): 133–160.
Grosskurth, Phyllis. *Havelock Ellis: A Biography*. New York: New York University Press, 1985.
Grosskurth, Phyllis. *Melanie Klein: Her World and Her Work*. New York: Knopf, 1986.
Guest, Barbara. *Herself Defined: The Poet H.D. and Her World*. New York: Doubleday, 1984.
Hall, Donald. *Their Ancient Glittering Eyes: Remembering Poets and More Poets*. New York: Ticknor & Fields, 1992.
Hannyngton, Harold. Review of *Street Songs* by Edith Sitwell. *TLS*, February 7, 1942.
Hardy, Thomas. *Two on a Tower*. Edited by Suleiman M. Ahmad. Oxford: Oxford University Press, 1993.
H.D. *Asphodel*. Edited by Robert Spoo. Durham, NC: Duke University Press, 1992.
H.D. *Bid Me to Live*. Edited by Caroline Zilboorg. Gainesville: University Press of Florida, 2011.
H.D. "*Borderline*: A Pool Film with Paul Robeson." In *Cinema and Modernism*, edited by Donald, Friedberg, and Marcus, 221–238.
H.D. *By Avon River*. New York: Macmillan, 1949.
H.D. *Collected Poems, 1912–1944*. Edited by Louis Martz. New York: New Directions, 1982.
H.D. *End to Torment: A Memoir of Ezra Pound*. New York: New Directions, 1979.
H.D., "Excerpts from a record by Agnes Angelica Seidel Howard written for her son," in "Genealogical Notes," box 48, folder 1221.
H.D. *The Gift*. Edited by Jane Augustine. Gainesville: University Press of Florida, 1998.
H.D. "H.D. by Delia Alton." Edited by Morris. *Iowa Review* 16, no. 3 (1981): 180–221.
H.D. *The Hedgehog*. New York: New Directions, 1988.
H.D. *Hedylus*. Redding Ridge: Black Swan Books, 1980.
H.D. *Helen in Egypt*. New York: New Directions, 1961.
Heliodora and Other Poems. London: Jonathan Cape, 1924.
H.D. *Hermetic Definition*. New York: New Directions, 1972.
H.D. *HERmione*. New York: New Directions, 1981.
H.D. *Hippolytus Temporizes and Ion*. New York: New Directions, 2003.
H.D. *Hirslanden Notebooks: An Annotated Scholarly Edition*. Edited by Matte Robinson and Demetres P. Tryphonopoulos. Victoria: ELS Editions, 2015.
H.D. *Ion*. New York: New Directions, 2003.
H.D. *Kora and Ka*. New York: New Directions, 1996.
H.D. (Hilda Doolittle). "A Letter from England." *Bryn Mawr Alumnae Bulletin* 21, no. 7 (July 1941).
H.D. *Magic Mirror, Compassionate Friendship, Thorn Ticket: A Tribute to Erich Heydt*. Edited by Nephie J. Christodoulides. Victoria: ELS Editions, 2012.
H.D. (as Delia Alton). *Majic Ring*. Edited by Demetres P. Tryphonopoulos. Gainesville: University Press of Florida, 2009.
H.D. *The Mystery*. Edited by Jane Augustine. Gainesville: University Press of Florida, 2009.

H.D. *Narthex and Other Stories*. Edited by Michael Boughn. Toronto: Book Thug, 2011.
H.D. *Nights*. New York: New Directions, 1986.
H.D. *Notes on Thought and Vision*. San Francisco: City Lights, 1982.
H.D. *Paint It Today*. Edited by Cassandra Laity. New York: New York University Press, 1992.
H.D. *Palimpsest*. Edited by Harry T. Moore. Carbondale: Southern Illinois University Press, 1968.
H.D. *Pilate's Wife*. New York: New Directions, 2000.
H.D. *Red Roses for Bronze*. New York: Houghton Mifflin, 1931.
H.D. *Selected Poems*. New York: Grove, 1957.
H.D. (as Delia Alton). *The Sword Went Out to Sea (Synthesis of a Dream)*. Edited by Cynthia Hogue and Julie Vandivere. Gainesville: University Press of Florida, 2007.
H.D. *Tribute to Freud*. New York: New Directions, 1974.
H.D. *Tribute to Freud*. Introduction by Adam Phillips. New York: New Directions, 2012.
H.D. *Trilogy*. New York: New Directions, 1973.
H.D. *Vale Ave*. New York: New Directions, 2013.
H.D. *The Walls Do Not Fall*. Oxford: Oxford University Press, 1944.
H.D. (as Delia Alton). *White Rose and the Red*. Edited by Alison Halsall. Gainesville: University Press of Florida, 2009.
H.D. *Within the Walls and What Do I Love*. Edited by Annette Debo. Gainesville: University Press of Florida, 2014.
Halberstam, Judith. *Female Masculinity* Durham, NC: Duke University, 1998.
Hammer, Langdon. *James Merrill: Life and Art*. New York: Knopf, 2015.
Hanscombe, Gillian, and Virginia L. Smyers. *Writing for Their Lives: The Modernist Women 1910–1940*. London: Women's Press, 1987.
Henty, G. A. *Beric the Briton: A Story of the Roman Invasion*. New York: Blackie and Son, 1893.
Herodotus. *The Histories*. Translated by Aubrey De Selincourt. London: Penguin, 1954.
Herring, Robert, editor in chief. *Life and Letters To-Day: An International Monthly of Living Literature* 8–65 (1935–1950).
Hillman, Brenda. *Loose Sugar*. Middletown, CT: Wesleyan University Press, 1997.
Hollenberg, Donna Krolik. *Between History and Poetry: The Letters of H.D. and Norman Holmes Pearson*. Iowa City: University of Iowa Press, 1997.
Holzman, Michael. *James Jesus Angleton, the CIA, and the Craft of Counterintelligence*. Amherst: University of Massachusetts Press, 2008.
Michael Holzman, "The Ideological Origins of American Studies at Yale." *American Studies* 40, no. 2 (1991): 71–99.
Horner, Avril. *Daphne du Maurier: Writing, Identity, and the Gothic Imagination*. New York: St. Martin's Press, 1998.
Howe, Susan. *My Emily Dickinson*. Berkeley, CA: North Atlantic Books, 1985.
Hughes, Bettany. *Helen of Troy: Goddess, Princess, Whore*. New York: Knopf, 2005.
Hulme, T.E. "Romanticism and Classicism" (1911). In *Speculations*, edited by Herbert Read New York: Harcourt, 1934.
Hunt, Violet. *I Have This To Say: The Story of My Flurried Years*. New York: Boni and Liveright, 1926.
Hunt, Violet. *The Wife of Rossetti*. New York: E. P. Dutton, 1932.
Jackson, Zakiyyah Iman. *Becoming Human: Matter and Meaning in an Antiblack World*. New York: New York University Press, 2020.
Johnston, Devin. *Precipitations: Contemporary American Poetry as Occult Practice*. Middletown, CT: Wesleyan University Press, 2002.
Jones, Ernst. *The Life and Work of Sigmund Freud*. 3 vols. New York: Basic Books, 1960.
Joyce, Elisabeth W. "The Collage of 'Marriage': Marianne Moore's Formal and Cultural Critique." *Mosaic* 26, no. 4 (1993): 103–118.

Keats, John. *Selected Letters of John Keats*. Edited by Grant F. Scott. Rev. ed. Cambridge, MA: Harvard University Press, 2002.
Kenner, Hugh. *The Invisible Poet: T. S. Eliot*. New York: McDowell, Obolensky, 1959.
Kenner, Hugh. *The Pound Era*. Berkeley: University of California Press, 1971.
Kerényi, Carl. *Eleusis: Archetypal Image of Mother and Daughter*. Translated by Ralph Mannheim. Princeton, NJ: Princeton University Press, 1991.
Knight, G. Wilson. *The Mutual Flame: On Shakespeare's Sonnets and "The Phoenix and the Turtle."* London: Methuen, 1955.
Kolocotroni, Vassiliki. "Still Life: Modernism's Turn to Greece." *Journal of Modern Literature* 35, no. 2 (2012): 1–24.
Kostenbaum, Wayne. *Double Talk: The Erotics of Male Literary Collaboration*. New York: Routledge, 1989.
Krishnamurti, Jiddu. *Notebooks*. Brambean: Krishnamurti Foundation Trust, 2003.
Laity, Cassandra. *H.D. and the Victorian Fin de Siècle: Gender, Modernism, and Decadence*. Cambridge: Cambridge University Press, 1996.
Lawrence, D. H. *Aaron's Rod*. New York: Viking, 1963.
Lawrence, D. H. *The Letters of D. H. Lawrence*. Vol. 3, *October 1916–June 1921*. Edited by James T. Boulton and Andrew Robertson. Cambridge: Cambridge University Press, 1985.
Leavell, Linda. *Holding on Upside Down: The Life and Work of Marianne Moore*. New York: Farrar, Straus & Giroux, 2013.
Levering, Joseph Mortimer. *A History of Bethlehem, Pennsylvanian, 1741–1892*. 1903.
Lewis, John E. *The Autobiography: 2,000 Years of the Capital's History by Those Who Saw It Happen*. London: Constable & Robinson, 1988.
Love, Heather. *Feeling Backward: Loss and the Politics of Queer History*. Cambridge, MA: Harvard University Press, 2007.
Love, Heather. "Modernism at Night." *PMLA* 124, no. 3 (May 2009): 744.
Lowell, Amy, ed. *Some Imagist Poets*, 1916.
Lowell, Amy. *Tendencies in Modern American Poetry*. New York: Macmillan, 1917.
MacCarthy, Fiona. *William Morris: A Life of Our Time*. New York: Knopf, 1995.
Mackail, J. W. *The Greek Anthology*. London: Longmans, Green, 1890.
Maddox, Brenda. *Freud's Wizard: Ernest Jones and the Transformation of Psychoanalysis*. Cambridge, MA: Da Capo Press, 2007.
Majumbar, Robin, and Allen McLaurin, eds. *Virginia Woolf: The Critical Heritage*. London: Routledge, 1975.
Manchester, William. *The Last Lion: Winston Spencer Churchill, Defender of the Realm, 1940–1965*. New York: Bantam, 2013.
Mandel, Charlotte. "Magical Lenses: Poet's Vision beyond the Naked Eye." In *H.D.: Woman and Poet*, edited by M. King. Orono, ME: National Poetry Foundation, 1986.
Marcus, Laura. *The Tenth Muse: Writing about Cinema in the Modernist Period*. Oxford: Oxford University Press, 2007.
Marek, E. Jayne. *Women Editing Modernism: Little Magazines and Literary History*. Lexington: University Press of Kentucky, 1995.
Martin, Joel, and William J. Birnes. "Who You Gonna Call? Edison's Science of Talking to Ghosts." *Salon*, October 8, 2017. https://www.salon.com/2017/10/08/who-you-gonna-call-edison-and-the-science-of-talking-to-ghosts.
Martin, Joel, and William J. Birnes. *Edison vs. Tesla: The Battle over Their Last Invention* New York: Skyhorse, 2017.
McAlmon, Robert. *Being Geniuses Together, 1920–1930*. Baltimore, MD: Johns Hopkins University Press, 1968.
McAlmon, Robert. *Distinguished Air (Grim Fairy Tales)*. Paris: Three Mountain Press, 1925.

McAlmon, Robert. "Post-Adolesence." In *A Selection of Short Fiction*, edited by Edward N. S. Lorusso. Albuquerque: University of New Mexico Press, 1991.

McGuire, William. *Poetry's Catbird Seat: The Consultantship in Poetry in the English Language at the Library of Congress*. Washington, DC: Library of Congress, 1988.

McIntosh P., Elizabeth. *Sisterhood of Spies: The Women of the OSS*. New York: Dell/Random House, 1998.

McKinstry, Leo. "Revealed: the bizarre life of the RAF's Battle of Britain supremo." *Daily Mail*, November 21, 2007.

Macpherson, Kenneth. "As Is." (On Borderline). *Close Up* 7, no. 1 (July 1930).

Macpherson, Kenneth. "As Is." (On *Borderline*). *Close Up* 7, no. 5 (November 1930).

Meredith, George. *Modern Love and Poems of the English Roadside, with Poems and Ballads*. Edited by Rebecca N. Mitchell and Criscillia Benford. New Haven, CT: Yale University Press, 2012.

Mertz, Barbara. *Temples, Tombs and Hieroglyphs: A Popular History of Ancient Egypt*. New York: Dodd, Mead, 1964.

Modern, Klara. *My Dearest Family: An Austrian Refugee's Letters from London to America, 1938–1945*. Edited by Richard Deveson. Privately printed, 2017.

Monnier, Adrienne. *The Very Rich Hours of Adrienne Monnier*. Translated by Richard McDougall. New York: Simon and Schuster, 1977.

Moody, A. David. *Ezra Pound: Poet—A Portrait of the Man and His Work*. Vols. 1–3. Oxford: Oxford University Press, 2007–2015.

Moore, Marianne. *Adversity and Grace: Marianne Moore, 1936–1941*. Edited by Heather Cass White. Victoria: ELS Editions, 2012.

Moore, Marianne. *The Complete Poems of Marianne Moore*. New York: Penguin, 1981.

Moore, Marianne. *The Complete Prose of Marianne Moore*. Edited by Patricia C. Willis. New York: Viking, 1986.

Moore, Marianne. *The Selected Letters of Marianne Moore*. Edited by Bonnie Costello, Celeste Goodridge, and Cristanne Miller. New York: Penguin Books, 1997.

Morris, Adelaide. *How to Live/What to Do: H.D.'s Cultural Poetics*. Urbana: University of Illinois Press, 2003.

Morris, Adelaide. "The Concept of Projection: H.D.'s Visionary Powers." In *Signets: Reading H.D.*, edited by Susan Stanford Friedman and Rachel Blau DuPlessis. Madison: University of Wisconsin Press, 1990.

Morris, Adelaide. "Signaling: Feminism, Politics, and Mysticism in H.D.'s War *Trilogy*." *Sagetrieb* 9, no. 3 (1990): 121–133.

Murray, Gilbert. *Euripides and His Age*. New York: Henry Holt, 1913.

Murtagh, William J. *Moravian Architecture and Town Planning: Bethlehem and Other Eighteenth-Century Settlements*. Philadelphia: University of Pennsylvania Press, 1996.

North, Michael. *Reading 1922: A Return to the Scene of Modernism*. Oxford: Oxford University Press, 1999.

Pagels, Elaine. *The Gnostic Gospels*. New York: Random House, 1979.

Parslow, Rosemary. *The Isles of Scilly*. New York: Collins, 2010.

Pater, Walter. *The Renaissance: Studies in Art and Poetry*. Edited by Donald L. Hill. Berkeley: University of California Press, 1980.

Paternotte, David, "Disentangling and Locating the Anti-Gender Campaigns in Europe." *Politics and Governance* 6, *no.* 3 (2018): 6–19.

Patmore, Brigit. *My Friends When Young: The Memoirs of Brigit Patmore*. London: Heinemann, 1968.

Payne, Kenneth, and Ulick Brown. *Ellermans in South Africa 1892–1992: The Story of a British Shipping Company's 100 Year Involvement in Trade with South Africa*. Cape Town: Mills Litto, 1992.

Petro, Patrice. *Aftershocks of the New: Feminism and Film History.* New Brunswick, NJ: Rutgers University Press, 2002.
Pondrom, Cyrena. "Marianne Moore and H.D.: Female Community and Poetic Achievement." In *MM: Woman and Poet*, edited by Patricia Willis. Orono, ME: National Poetry Foundation, 1990.
Pound, Ezra. *The Literary Essays of Ezra Pound.* Introduction by T. S. Eliot. New York: New Directions, 1954.
Pound, Ezra. *Selected Poems of Ezra Pound.* New York: New Directions, 1957.
Pound, Ezra. *Selected Prose: 1909–1965.* New York: New Directions, 1973.
Pound, Ezra. *The Spirit of Romance.* New York: New Directions, 1952.
Pound, Ezra, and Ernest Fenollosa. *The Chinese Character as a Medium for Poetry.* San Francisco: City Lights, 1964.
Post, Robert M. "'To Read as a Poet': Major Performances of Edith Sitwell." *Text and Performance Quarterly* 11 (1991): 123–140.
Pressfield, Steven. *Turning Pro: Tap Your Inner Power and Create Your Life's Work.* New York: Black Irish Entertainment, 2012.
Qwiazda, Piotr. *James Merrill and W. H. Auden: Homosexuality and Poetic Influence.* New York: Macmillan, 2007.
Rabaté, Jean-Michel. *The Ghosts of Modernity.* Gainesville: University Press of Florida, 2009.
Rainey, Lawrence. *Institutions of Modernism: Literary Elites and the Public Sphere.* New Haven, CT: Yale University Press, 1999.
Rayor, Diane. *Medea: A New Translation.* Cambridge: Cambridge University Press, 2013.
Rayor, Diane. *Sappho: A New Translation of the Complete Works.* Cambridge: Cambridge University Press, 2014.
Richardson, "The Film Gone Male," *Close Up* 9, no.1 (March 1932): 36–38.
Richardson, Dorothy. *Pilgrimage.* Vols. 1–4. New York: Knopf, 1967.
Riley, Noel. *Sylvia Beach and the Lost Generation: A History of Literary Paris in the Twenties and Thirties.* New York: Norton, 1985.
Roazen, Paul. *Oedipus in Britain: Edward Glover and the Struggle over Klein.* New York: Other Press, 2001.
Robinson, C. E. *Hellas: A Short History of Ancient Greece.* New York: Pantheon, 1948.
Robinson, Matte. *The Astral H.D.: Occult and Religious Sources for H.D.'s Poetry and Prose.* London: Bloomsbury, 2016.
Rubenstein, William D. *Men of Property: The Very Wealthy in Britain Since the Industrial Revolution.* NJ: Rutgers University Press, 1981.
Rubenstein, William D. *The Richest of the Rich.* Hampshire: Great Britain, 2007.
Sachs, Hanns. *Sigmund Freud: Master and Friend.* Cambridge, MA: Harvard University Press, 1944.
Salamon, Gayle. *Assuming a Body: Transgender and Rhetorics of Materiality.* New York: Columbia University Press, 2010.
Schafer, Roy. "Transference and the Conditions for Loving." In *Essential Papers on Transference.* edited by Aaron H. Esman. New York: New York University Press, 1990.
Schaffner, J.V. "The Redheaded Pine Sawfly." Washington, DC: U.S. Department of Agriculture, (1939).
Schaffner, Perdita, "The Egyptian Cat," afterword in H.D.'s *Hedylus*: 142-146.
Schaffner, Perdita. "Running." *Iowa Review* 16, no. 3 (1986): 7–13.
Schaffner, Perdita. "They Lived to Write." *New Directions for Women* 18, no. 4 (July/August 1989): 18–19.
Schmidt, Michael. *Lives of the Poets.* New York: Knopf, 1999.
Schulze, Robin, ed. *Becoming Marianne Moore: The Early Poems, 1907–1924.* Berkeley: University of California Press, 2002.

Scott, Bonnie Kime, ed. *The Gender of Modernism: A Critical Anthology*. Bloomington: Indiana University Press, 1990.
Secor, Robert, and Marie Secor. *The Return of the Good Soldier: Ford Madox Ford and Violet Hunt's 1917 Diary*. Victoria: ELS Editions, 1983.
Segal, Charles. "Simaetha and the Iynx (Theocritus, Idyll II)." *Quaderni Urbinati di Cultura Classica* 15 (1973): 32–43.
Shakespeare, William. *The Tempest*. Edited by Northrop Frye. London: Pelican, 1959.
Sharpe, Ella Freeman. *Collected Papers on Psycho Analysis*. London: Hogarth Press, 1950.
Silverstein, Louis. "H.D. Chronology, Part One (1605–1914)." Accessed August 19, 2018. http://www.imagists.org/hd/hdchron1.html.
Silverstein, Louis. "H.D. Chronology, Part Two (1915–March 1919)." Accessed August 19, 2018. http://www.imagists.org/hd/hdchron2.html.
Sinclair, May. *A Defence of Idealism: Some Questions and Conclusions*. London: Macmillan, 1917.
Sitwell, Edith. *Collected Poems*. New York: Overlook Press, 2006.
Sitwell, Osbert. Review of *Walls Do Not Fall* by H.D. *The Observer*, May 28, 1944.
Smoller, Sanford J. *Adrift among Geniuses: Robert McAlmon, Writer and Publisher of the Twenties*. University Park: Penn State University Press, 1974.
Smyers, Virginia L., and Gilllian Hanscombe. *Writing for Their Lives: The Modernist Women 1910–40*. London: Women's Press, 1981.
Souhami, Diana. *The Trials of Radclyffe Hall*. New York: Doubleday, 1999.
Spoo, Robert. "'Authentic Sisters': H.D. and Margaret Cravens." *H.D. Newsletter* 3, no. 1 (1990): 35–43.
Stauffer, Andrew. "The Germ." In *The Cambridge Companion to the Pre-Raphaelites*, edited by Elizabeth Prettejohn. Cambridge: Cambridge University, 2012.
Steindorff, George. *Egypt*. Photographed by George Hoyningen Huene. New York: George Grady Press, 1943.
Stevens, Wallace. *Letters of Wallace Stevens*. Edited by Holly Stevens. Berkeley: University of California Press, 1996.
Stone, Christopher. *Do Trees Have Standing?* Oxford: Oxford University Press, 2010.
Strachey, James. "Some Unconscious Factors in Reading." *International Journal of Psychoanalysis* 11 (1930): 322–331.
Taylor, Georgina. *H.D. and the Public Sphere of Modernist Women Writers 1913–1946*. Oxford: Oxford University Press, 2001.
Taylor, James. *Ellermans: A Wealth of Shipping*. : Wilton House Gentry, 1976.
Tinker, Carol, and Silvia Dobson. "A Friendship Traced: H.D. Letters to Silvia Dobson." *Conjunctions*, no. 2 (Spring 1982): 112–157.
Tucker, R.H. "Charles Leander Doolittle." *Astronomical Society of the Pacific*, March 20, 1919, 103–104.
Toklas, Alice B. *Staying on Alone: Letters of Alice B. Toklas*. New York: Liveright, 1973.
Underhill, Evelyn. *Mysticism: A Study in the Nature and Development of Man's Spiritual Consciousness*. 1911; Meridian, 1974.
Vetter, Laura: *A Curious Peril: H.D.'s Late Modernist Prose*. Gainesville: University Press of Florida, 2017.
Vetter, Laura. "Representing 'A Sort of Composite Person': Autobiography, Sexuality, and Collaborative Authorship in H.D.'s Prose and Scrapbook." *Genre* 36, no. 1 (2003): 107–129.
Wallace, Emily. "Hilda Doolittle at Friends' Central School in 1905." *H.D. Newsletter* 1, no. 1 (1987): 17–28.
Weiss, Andrea. *In the Shadow of* The Magic Mountain: *The Erika and Klaus Mann Story*. Chicago: University of Chicago Press, 2008.
Weiss, Andrea. *Paris Was a Woman: Portraits from the Left Bank*. San Francisco: Harper San Francisco, 1995.

West, Rebecca. *Return of the Soldier*. London: Penguin, 1998.
Weston, Jessie L. *From Ritual to Romance*. New York: Doubleday Anchor Books, 1957.
Weston, Jessie L. *The Legend of Sir Gawain*. London: David Nutt, 1897.
Wilkinson, Oliver Marlow, ed. *The Letters of John Cowper Powys to Frances Gregg*. London: Cecil Woolf, 1994.
Williams, William Carlos. *The Autobiography of William Carlos Williams*. New York: New Directions, 1967.
Williams, William Carlos. In *The Selected Letters*, edited by John C. Thirlwall. New York: New Directions, 1985.
Willis, Patricia. "A Modernist Epithalamium: Marianne Moore's Formal and Cultural Critique." *Paideuma* 32 (2003): 265–297.
Wilson, A. N. *The Decline of Britain in the World: After the Victorians*. New York: Picador, 2005.
Wilson, Colin. *The Occult: A History*. New York: Vintage, 1973.
Wilson, Leigh. *Modernism and Magic: Experiments with Spiritualism, Theosophy and the Occult*. Edinburgh: Edinburgh University Press, 2012.
Winks, Robin W. *Cloak and Gown: Scholars in the Secret War, 1939-61*. London: Harvill Press, 1987.
Winning, Joanne. *The Pilgrimage of Dorothy Richardson*. Madison: University of Wisconsin Press, 2000.
Winnicott, D.W. "Fear of Breadown." (1963?) *Psycho-Analytic Explorations: Donald Winnicott*. Edited by Clare Winnicott, Shepherd, and Davis (Cambridge, MA: Harvard University Press, 1989).
"Wiretapping, Surveillance, and Detectives." *Life*, August 18, 2017.
Wolle, Francis. *Fresh-Water Algae of the United States; (Exclusive of the Diatomacae) Complimental to Desmids of the United States with 2300 Illustrations*. Vols. 1 and 2. Bethlehem, PA: Comenius Press, 1887.
Wolle, Francis. "A Moravian Village." Boulder, CO: Empire Reproduction and Printing Co., 1972.
Woolf, Virginia. *The Essays of Virginia Woolf: Vol. II (1912–1918)*. Edited by Andrew McNeillie. London: Hogarth Press, 1987.
World Alliance for Combating Anti-Semitism, *J'Accuse* (London: Salomon House, 1933).
Wyss, Johann David. *Swiss Family Robinson*. Edited by John Seylee. New York: Penguin, 2007.
Yeats, W. B. *The Collected Works of W. B. Yeats*. Vol. 3, *Autobiographies*. Edited by William H O'Donnell and Douglas N. Archibald. New York: Scribners, 1999.
Yeats, W. B. *The Collected Works of W. B. Yeats*. Vol. 1, *The Poems*. New York: Scribners, 1997.
Yeats, W. B. *A Vision (1925)*. New York: Scribner, 2008.
Zilboorg, Caroline. *Richard Aldington and H.D.: The Early Years in Letters*. Bloomington: Indiana University Press, 1992.
Zilboorg, Caroline. *Richard Aldington and H.D.: The Later Years in Letters*. Manchester: Manchester University Press, 1995.
Zweig, Stefan. *Mental Healers: Mesmer, Eddy, Freud*. New York: Garden City Publishing, 1931.

Index

For the benefit of digital users, indexed terms that span two pages (e.g., 52–53) may, on occasion, appear on only one of those pages.

Abbot, Berenice, 118
Abelove, Henry, 307–8
Abraham, Karl, 168
Achilles, 71, 289, 291, 292–93, 298, 300
Acropolis, 92, 93
Acts of John, 223, 346n.4
Adams, Evangeline, 314n.32
Adorno, Theodor, 213
Adriatic, SS, 102
"Advent" (H.D.), 16
"Adventure" (Bryher), 72
Adventures of Prince Achmed, 155
Afro-American cinema, 145
Ahlers, Anny, 163, 164, 172
Aiken, Conrad, 171
Aldington, Catherine ("Catha"), 280, 294, 306, 307
Aldington, Richard
    on Bryher's *Development*, 72
    Death of a Hero by, 205
    Dobson, S., and, 204–5
    Ellerman, J. R., on, 70
    H.D., Perdita and, 75–76, 126
    H.D. and, 4, 5, 56, 57–58, 59–60, 61, 62, 63, 64f, 66, 67, 70, 75, 83–84, 94, 126–27, 128, 199–200, 204–5, 224, 272–73, 283, 291, 294–95, 300, 301, 306, 308
    H.D. and Bryher and, 3, 67–69, 70, 71–72, 75–76, 77, 84–85, 198, 273, 276, 304, 307–8
    on H.D.'s *The Sword Went Out to Sea*, 272–73
    "In the Tube" by, 59
    on Lawrence, T. E., 306
    Lowell and, 59–60
    Patmore, B., and, 56, 68, 126, 199
    Patmore, N., and, 199, 205, 306
    Poet's Translation Series of, 56, 60
    on Pound, E., 70
    Reverie: A Little Book of Poems for H.D. by, 67
    "Syracuse" by, 69
    "To Atthis" by, 57–58
    The Viking Book of Poetry of the English-Speaking World edited by, 224
    Wolle, H. E., and, 57
    in World War I, 61, 62, 66, 67–68
    Yorke and, 63, 66, 77, 199–200
Alexandria, 125, 126, 304

Algonquian, 18, 27
Alice in Wonderland (Carroll, L.), 117, 202
Allegra (Origo), 289
Alt, Franz, 10, 204, 207
Alt, James, 10, 207
Ambelain, Robert, 286
American Civil War, 20, 22–23, 274–75, 276
American Revolutionary War, 19
Amy Lowell: A Critical Appreciation (Bryher), 3, 64–65
ancient Greeks, Trojans and, 72–73
"Ancient Wisdom Speaks to the Mountain" (H.D.), 235
Anderson, Judith, 187
"Angel in the House, The" (Patmore, C.), 56
Angleton, James J., 237
Annie Get Your Gun, 271
antiblackness, 148, 152
Antipater, 56–57
anti-Semitism, 29, 62, 148, 167
anti-slavery, 276
Anything Goes, 187
"Apartment, The" (Gregg, F. J.), 136
Aphrodite, 79, 93, 127, 135–36, 164, 303
Apollo, 47–48, 57–58, 72, 81–82, 85–86, 93, 94–95, 98, 167–68, 189–90
apophenia, 98
Aquarian Age, 223, 307
Arendt, Hannah, 214–15
Arrow Music (Bryher), 78–79, 107, 109
Art Deco, 132, 201–2
Artemis, 13, 43, 45, 46–47, 72, 83, 93, 108–9, 114–15, 135–36, 164, 167–68, 185, 189–90
Arthur (king), 13–14, 73, 125, 243
Arthur, Gavin, 146–47
Ash, Louisa, 184, 222, 228, 266, 300
Ashby, Elizabeth, 250–51, 252, 265–66, 287, 297
Ashe of Rings (Butts), 119
Asphodel (H.D.), 49, 50, 75, 320n.31, 329n.2
astrology and astrologers, 7, 9–10, 32, 165, 168, 173–74, 175, 185, 230–31, 250–51, 297, 304–5
astronomy and astronomers, 12, 22–23, 27, 47–48, 92, 98, 165, 221, 232–33, 296

As You Like It (Shakespeare), 250
Athena Promachos, 93
Athene, 96, 97–98, 160–62, 189–90, 191–92
Athens, Greece, 89, 92–93, 94
Atlee, Clement, 250
atom bomb, 253–54, 255, 260, 272, 276–77, 279, 281, 307
Auden, W. H., 14, 308
Audley, 73, 75, 83–84, 101, 114, 130, 132, 140, 169, 171, 182, 213
Austria, 9–10, 168–69, 176, 203
avant-garde, 111, 131, 152

Bacchae, The (Euripides), 66
Baedeker, Fritz, 89–90, 95–96
Baldwin, T. W., 236
Balzac, Honore de, 52
Banfield, Doris, 3, 53–54, 62, 63–64, 67–68, 75, 224–25, 285–86, 289, 302, 303–4
Barnard, Sheila, 176
Barnes, Djuna, 118, 119, 123
Barney, Natalie, 205
Barra, 226
Barsis, Olga, 164
Battle of Britain, 214, 225, 306
Battleship Potemkin, The, 134
Baudelaire, Charles, 12, 213, 287
Beach, Sylvia, 118, 201
 American Embassy exhibition of, 309
 Bryher and, 117–18, 119–20, 123, 200, 205, 212, 215, 244, 280, 299, 303–4, 306, 308, 311*f*, 311
 on Bryher's *Beowulf*, 274
 Herring and, 274, 280
 in internment camp, 243
 Monnier and, 10, 117–18, 123, 193, 194–95, 215, 243, 244, 249, 267, 274–75, 303–4
 at Shakespeare & Co., 117–18, 311
Beaumont, Francis, 236
"Before the Battle" (H.D.), 215
Belgium, 59, 214
Bellagio, 278
Bellario, in *The Merchant of Venice*, 53, 236
Benét, William Rose, 201–2
Benjamin, Walter, 314n.39, 341n.15
 on Baudelaire, 12, 213
 Beach on, 212
 Berlin Childhood around 1900 by, 202, 204
 Bryher and, 134–35, 196, 197–98, 202, 204, 205–6, 207, 211, 212–13, 214–15, 343n.2
 "Eduard Fuchs, Collector and Historian" by, 197–98
 Freund photographing, 205
 "Work of Art in the Age of Mechanical Reproduction" by, 196
Bennett, Jane, 83

Beowulf (Bryher), 213, 220, 233, 236, 241, 264, 268, 274–75, 283, 304
Bergner, Elisabeth, 155–56, 174
 Bryher and, 145, 155, 162, 168–69, 170, 171–72, 187, 194
 in *Escape Me Never*, 171, 186, 187
 in *Fraulein Else*, 145
 Herring and, 168
 in *The Old Maid*, 187–88
 Perdita and, 172, 186, 187–88, 194–95
 in *The Rise of Catherine the Great*, 168
Bergson, Henri, 13, 226–27
Berlin, 118, 119, 133–34, 135–36, 138–39, 154–55, 156–57, 159, 203
Berlin Childhood around 1900 (Benjamin), 202, 204
Berlin Institute, 177
Bethlehem, Pennsylvania, 3, 16–17, 18–19, 20, 22–23, 26, 27, 99, 101, 148–49, 180, 201–2, 227–28, 232–33, 283
Bethlehem Seminary, 46
Bethlehem Steel, 16, 59–60
Beyond the Pleasure Principle (Freud, S.), 177
Bhaduri, Arthur, 246–47, 266, 267
 Dowding and, 238, 239, 240, 248–49
 H.D. and, 227, 228, 241, 248–49, 256, 299
 H.D. and Bryher, séances and, 233–34, 238–39, 240–41, 251
 H.D. and Bryher and, 228, 229–30
Bhaduri, May, 233–34
Bible, 94, 158, 230
Bid Me to Live (H.D.), 294, 301, 308, 309, 327n.19
Big Parade, The, 134–35
biocentric racism, 148
Birmingham, 29–30, 32
Birmingham Museums and Art Gallery, 51
bisexuality, 7, 102, 162, 182, 194, 339n.80
Bishop, Elizabeth, 186, 201
Blake, William, 8
Blakeston, Oswell, 132–33
"Blauer Schmetterling" (Hesse), 271
"Blue Lights" (H.D.), 221
Blunden, Edmund, 235
Boccaccio, Giovanni, 80–81
bodily and sexual dysphoria, of Bryher, 11–12, 155
Body and Soul, 145, 149–50
"Body's Guest, The" (H.D.), 267–68
Boer Wars, 31, 35
Bohemian civil war, 17–18
"Bombardment, The" (Lowell), 63
Bonaparte, Marie, 164, 178, 197, 203, 205
Book of John, 94
Book of Matthew, 94, 230
Borderline
 Berlin screening, 155
 Bryher in, 147*f*, 147–48

censorship of, 152
first screening, 152
H.D. and, 146–47, 148, 150, 151*f*, 152, 154–55, 172, 191, 233–34
Lewin in, 146–47, 164
Macpherson filming, 146–47, 148, 152–53
Pabst on, 152
program for, 156*f*
on race and gender, 147–48, 149–50
Robeson, E., in, 145, 146–47, 149, 150*f*, 151*f*
Robeson, P., in, 7, 145, 147, 148, 149*f*, 149–50, 150*f*, 152, 156*f*
as silent film, 152
"Borderline Pamphlet" (H.D.), 150
Bosigran Castle, 3, 5, 66–67, 158, 266, 278
Boss, Medard, 296
Boston, 186–87
Botticelli, Sandro, 91, 278
Bottomley, George, 235
Bowen, Elizabeth, 213, 214, 218, 221–22, 223, 226, 277
Brandywine, 19
Brashear, John, 27
Brecht, Bertolt, 204, 205–6
British Museum, 4–5, 49–50, 51, 56–57, 93, 156
Brooks, Louise, 138
Brueghel, Pieter, 290
Brunner, Blanche, 271, 308
Brunner, Rudolph, 309
Brunner, Theodore, 261–63, 264, 265–66, 267, 271, 286, 296, 297, 298, 299, 304
Bryher
"Adventure" by, 72
on America, 101, 109
Amy Lowell: A Critical Appreciation by, 3, 64–65
Arrow Music by, 78–79, 107, 109
with Athena haircut, photomontage of, 141*f*
Banfield and, 3, 53–54, 62, 63–64, 67–68, 75, 224–25, 285–86, 289, 303–4
Beach and, 117–18, 119–20, 123, 200, 205, 212, 215, 244, 280, 299, 303–4, 306, 308, 311*f*, 311
Benjamin and, 134–35, 196, 197–98, 202, 204, 205–6, 207, 211, 212–13, 214–15, 343n.2
Beowulf by, 213, 220, 233, 236, 241, 264, 268, 274–75, 283, 304
Bergner and, 145, 155, 162, 168–69, 170, 171–72, 187, 194
in Berlin, 155, 157, 159, 203
birth, 3
bodily and sexual dysphoria of, 11–12, 155
in *Borderline*, 147*f*, 147–48
Bowen and, 218, 222, 226
on Chamberlain, 206
childhood of, 29, 33–40, 53–54

on cinema, 134–35, 157, 158
Civilians by, 132–33
Coin of Carthage by, 310, 335n.17
Colors of Vaud by, 310
in Cornwall, 67–68, 69, 75, 103, 104*f*, 194–95, 224–25, 228, 237, 251–52, 253, 254, 266–67
on cross-dressing, 63–64, 111, 168
Development by, 62, 63–64, 67–68, 69, 71, 72, 76–77, 80–81, 82, 83, 99–100, 106–7, 219–20
Dobson, S., and, 53, 218–19, 309
dreams of, 162, 198, 226, 251
in Egypt, 35–38, 37*f*
eighteen-year-old, 54*f*
on Elizabethans, 38, 63, 68, 168, 236, 250–51, 266–67
Ellerman, John Jr., and, 53, 63–64, 65*f*
Ellerman, J. R., and, 29, 30*f*, 30, 33–34, 34*f*, 35, 38, 39*f*, 39–40, 53, 62, 63–65, 84–85, 99–100, 111–12, 129, 138, 159, 251
Ellerman, J. R., and, will and estate of, 170
Ellis and, 71, 74–75, 76–77, 161, 164
"Eos" by, 80–81
on fascism, 157, 158–59
Feilberg and, 205, 207–8
Film Problems of Soviet Russia by, 138
in Florence, 278
The Fourteenth of October by, 237, 251, 276–77, 278, 279, 280, 282, 283, 284, 285, 287–89, 290–91, 310
French Resistance and, 215
Freud, A., and, 171, 178, 193, 197, 203, 211–12
Freud, M., and, 203
Freud, S., and, 113, 158, 163, 164, 168–69, 182, 211–12
Freund photograph of, 205, 206*f*
Friedman and, 101
as "Gareth," 13–14, 98–99, 136, 239–40, 274
Gate to the Sea by, 310
against gender conformity, 5
Gide and, 215
"The Girl-Page in Elizabethan Literature" by, 68, 74–75, 109, 168, 267
Glover, H., and, 32–33, 39*f*, 40, 53–55, 130, 168, 207–8, 211–12
on H.D.'s *Sea Garden*, 3
The Heart to Artemis by, 33, 310, 314n.27
"Hellenics" by, 93–94
Hemingway and, 118–19
on Henty, 35
Herring and, 169–70, 177, 178, 207, 211–12, 214, 216, 218, 220, 221, 261, 280
at IIPR, 226–27
"In Syria" by, 79
at IPA, 157, 177, 178, 196–97, 205
Irwin and, 217–18, 271

Bryher (*Cont.*)
"I Said" by, 77–78
January Tale by, 310
Jones and, 178
at Kenwin, 161–62, 165, 167, 173, 175, 176, 194, 202–3, 205, 211, 212, 213, 216–17, 266, 267, 300, 310
Kocher and, 217
Larsen and, 199
Life and Letters Today and, 185, 196–97, 201, 202, 219, 230–31, 236
in London, 274
Lowell and, 63–65, 67–68, 82, 83–84, 86, 95, 96, 103
at Lowndes, 220, 226–27, 250–51, 268, 287
Mackenzies and, 226
Macpherson, Herring and, 146*f*, 146
Macpherson, Perdita and, 137, 185, 187, 188, 198–99
Macpherson and, 130, 131*f*, 132, 137, 138, 145, 153, 158, 162, 175, 185, 186, 216–18, 271, 285
Manchester by, 171–72, 185, 186
McAlmon and, 104–5, 106–7, 110–12, 114, 115–19, 124, 127, 277
Modern, K., and, 215–16
modernism of, 39–40
Moore, M., and, 101–2, 103, 106–7, 109–11, 112–13, 120, 170, 187, 193, 201–2, 219, 271
on Morris, W., 272–73
in Mullion Cove, 83, 84*f*
on Nazis, 157, 185–86, 203, 217–18, 251, 284
in New York, 201–2, 207, 271, 287
nonbinary gender of, 53
"A Note on Beaumont and Fletcher" by, 236
on parapsychology, 286
parents of, 33–34, 53, 71, 107–8, 130, 281
in Paris, 35, 36*f*, 114–15, 116–17, 123–24, 128, 193
Paris 1900 by, 196, 202, 204
passport photograph, 1920, 90*f*
Patmore, B., and, 77, 127
Pearson, N. H., and, 201–2, 205, 207–8, 218, 222, 260, 266–67, 277, 278, 281, 282, 283, 285, 310
Perdita and, 9, 86, 127, 132, 137, 139, 164–65, 181, 185, 186–88, 192–93, 194–95, 196, 198–99, 207–8, 212, 214, 228, 237, 249, 270, 273, 289, 310
Pickford and, 107–8
The Player's Boy by, 236, 291, 301, 310
"Pool" by, 109
Pound, E., and, 127, 259, 276, 310
psychoanalysis and, 101, 134, 140–42, 145, 152, 154–55, 158, 162, 168–69, 175, 177, 197, 200, 203
at Queenswood, 53–55, 135, 185, 196–97
on queer men, 10

queerness and, 71, 127–28
Ramuz and, 214
refugee work of, 162, 163, 168–69, 174, 185–86, 188, 198–99, 201, 203–4, 205–6, 207, 211, 216–17
Region of Lutany by, 59, 95–96
Reiniger and, 155, 188, 194, 197, 203
"Rejection" by, 64–65
republished lost works, 7
Richardson and, 115–16, 124, 129, 185
Robesons and, 145–46
Roman Wall by, 285, 287–89, 291, 298, 310
Ruan by, 309–10
Sachs, H., and, 134, 139, 145, 154–55, 157, 158, 163, 164, 168, 171, 175, 179–80, 186–87, 203–4, 260, 271
on Sands, 236
Schmideberg, M., and, 212, 285, 286
Schmideberg, W., and, 174–75, 180, 196–97, 198, 201–2, 203, 205, 212, 270, 280, 284–85, 297, 299, 301, 302
on sex changes and gender reassignment, 6
on Shakespeare, 236, 249–50
Sitwell, E., and, 219–20, 221
Sitwell, O., and, 220, 221, 243
"South" by, 89
Stein and, 118–19, 123, 201–2, 207–8
synesthesia and photographic memory of, 38, 64–65
"To Eros" by, 79
as transgendered, 281, 310–11
Two Selves by, 71, 96, 114, 123
Visa for Avalon by, 354n.30
visions of, 200, 250, 251
"Wakefulness" by, 64–65
"Waste" by, 64–65
West by, 102–3, 106, 107, 109, 112–13, 127, 136
"What Shall You Do in the War?" by, 159, 222
Bryn Mawr, 43–44, 101, 139, 198–99, 256, 259
Bryn Mawr Alumnae Magazine, 224
Buddha, 227
Budge, E. A., 121
Bullingham Mansions, Kensington, 83–84, 101
Burne-Jones, Edward, 273
Burt, Dan, 155–56, 176
Burton, Jean, 275–76
Butler, E. M., 298, 304
Butlin, Mary, 29–30
Butts, Mary, 119, 123–24
By Avon River (H.D.), 266, 267–68, 270–71, 276, 278, 279, 294
Byron, Lord George Gordon, 262, 289
Byron and Goethe (Butler), 304

Caesar, 247
Cairo, 36–38, 58, 121–23, 248

California, 105–9, 307
Cambridge, 218–19, 221
Cammerhof, John Christopher Fredrick, 19, 25–27
Cane (Toomer), 133
Capri, 15, 57, 116–17, 142, 200, 286, 303
Carew, Dorothea Petrie, 54–55
Carmel, California, 107–9, 108*f*, 141*f*, 142
Carnevali, Emanuel, 119
Carroll, Dennis, 260–63, 264, 265–66
Carroll, Lewis, 117, 202, 226–27
Carter, Howard, 121
Cassandra, 14, 202–3
Castor and Pollux, 301
Celtic, SS, 112
Chaboseau, Jean, 296–97
Chadwick, Mary, 135, 140–42, 154–56, 158
Chamberlain, Neville, 206, 207, 219
Champs-Elysées, 35
Chanel, Coco, 3
Chaplin, Charlie, 194, 300
Charcot, Jean-Martin, 247
Charlotte Bronte and Her Circle (Shorter, C.), 64–65
Chaucer, Geoffrey, 218–19
Chevalier, Maurice, 188
Cheverton, Una, 173
"Choruses from Iphigeneia in Aulis" (Euripides, trans. H.D.), 60
Christianity, 56
Christodoulides, Nephi J., 352n.25
Chudleigh, Lillie J., 53
Churchill, Winston, 214, 216, 223, 226, 250
cinema, 8, 97–98
  Afro-American, 145
  avant-garde, 131, 152
  Bryher on, 134–35, 157, 158
  Close Up on, 132–34, 135, 137–38, 145, 154, 155, 157, 158
  experimental, 149–50, 157
  H.D. and Bryher on, 125, 132–33, 137–38, 149–50, 152
  Hollywood, 138
  Palimpsest and, 125
  psychoanalysis and, 134–35, 152
  silent, 152
  the unconscious and, 134–35
  World War I and, 62
"Cinema and the Classics, The: Beauty" (H.D.), 133
"Cinema and the Classics: Restraint" (H.D.), 134
Civilians (Bryher), 132–33
Civil War, US, 20, 22–23, 274–75, 276
Claimont, Claire, 289
Claribel, in Shakespeare's *The Tempest*, 252–53, 256, 259, 263, 266
Clerk's Press, 61, 67
"Cliff Temple, The" (H.D.), 60–61
Clinton, Hilary, 313n.21

Clio, 38–39
Close Up (film journal), 132–34, 135, 137–38, 145, 154, 155, 157, 158
Cloud of Unknowing, 223
Clytemnestra, 291–92
Cocteau, Jean, 123
Coin of Carthage (Bryher), 310, 335n.17
Cold War, 6, 290, 306
Colette, 155
Collected Poems, 1912-1944 (H.D.), 7
Collected Poetry (H.D.), 127
Collier's, 281–82
Collins, H. P., 127
Collins, Wilkie, 274–75
Colors of Vaud (Bryher), 310
Compassionate Friendship (H.D.), 314n.27
"Conflict in Theosophy, The" (van der Leeuw), 178–79
Conquest of Illusion (van der Leeuw), 178–79
Conrad, Klaus, 98
Constantine, Murray (Katharine Burdekin), 185
Contact, 104–5, 106–7, 111, 119–20
Contact Press, 119, 123
Cordell, Henry, 236
Corfu, 95–97, 98–100, 101, 102, 137–38, 162–63, 164, 167–68, 178, 226–27, 237, 239, 246–47, 301
Corinth, 94–95
Cornwall, 3–4, 53–54
  Bryher in, 67–68, 69, 75, 103, 104*f*, 194–95, 224–25, 228, 237, 251–52, 253, 254, 266–67
  H.D. and Bryher in, 78–79, 82, 83, 84*f*, 85*f*, 100, 179–80, 184, 244, 287–89, 309–10
  H.D. in, 66–67, 69, 184, 188, 189, 225
  Lawrences in, 62–63, 66
  Mullion Cove, 78, 82, 83, 84*f*, 100, 184
  Perdita in, 188, 195, 204, 234–35
  Trenoweth Farm in, 179–80, 182, 184, 188, 224–25, 228, 234–35, 254, 266–67, 285
Cournos, John, 57, 63, 83–84, 86, 325n.73
Coventry, bombing of, 219
Covici, Pascal, 283
Coward, Noel, 187–88
Crashaw, Richard, 222
Crete, 91, 222
Crimean War, 274–75
cross-dressing, 44–45, 63–64, 74, 111, 168, 186
Crowley, Alistair, 136
Cunard, Nancy, 118–19, 123, 124, 137, 159, 196
Curie, Marie, 13, 44
Curie, Pierre, 13
Cymbeline (Shakespeare), 35
Czinner, Paul, 162

"Dancer, The" (H.D.), 248
Daniels, Jimmie, 154, 198–99

Dans L'Ombre Des Cathedrales (Ambelain), 286
Dante Alighieri, 8, 278
  Eliot on, 98
  H.D. and, 271, 274–75, 278
  Inferno by, 43
  Paradiso by, 278
  Vita Nuova by, 44
Darantiére, Maurice, 123
Dark Victory, 205
Davis, Bette, 205
D-Day, 243, 244
Dead Priestess Speaks, A (H.D.), 171
Death and Its Mystery (Flammarion), 92, 232–33
death drive and death instinct, 177, 180
Death of a Hero (Aldington, R.), 205
Debo, Annette, 201, 344n.54
Debussy, Claude, 50
Defense of Idealism, A (Sinclair), 321n.4
Defense of the Realm Act of 1914, 62–63
Dekker, Thomas, 68
Delphi, 70, 73, 94–95, 96–97, 98
Delphic Charioteer, 81–82, 97–98, 142
Demeter, 45, 94, 179–80, 235
Description of Greece (Pausanias), 90
Desmids of the United States (Wolle, Francis), 20
Development (Bryher), 62, 63–64, 67–68, 69, 71, 72, 76–77, 80–81, 82, 83, 99–100, 106–7, 219–20
Dial, 102, 111, 120
Diatomoceae of North America (Wolle, Francis), 20
Dietrich, Marlene, 160
Dionysus, 93–94
Dobson, Ethne, 224–25
Dobson, Mollie, 194–95, 228
Dobson, Nanny, 228
Dobson, Silvia, 175, 180, 194–95, 197, 221, 224–25, 235, 243, 266–67, 294–95
  Aldington, R., and, 204–5
  on astrology, 173–74
  astrology charts of, 32, 230–31
  Barnard and, 176
  Bryher and, 53, 218–19, 309
  H.D. and, 173–74, 175–76, 178–79, 182–83, 184–85, 192, 200, 204, 212–13, 221, 230–31, 242, 244–45, 246, 249, 251–52, 259–60, 261–62, 266–67, 270, 303, 304, 309
  H.D. and Bryher and, 173–74, 175, 179, 234–35, 256, 259–60, 307, 308–9
  "Mirror to a Star" by, 320n.55
  Perdita and, 184, 194–95, 202
  psychoanalysis and, 174, 180
  Schmideberg, W., and, 175, 178
"Dock Rats" (Moore, M.), 107
Doctor Faustus (Mann, T.), 285
Dollfuss, Engelbert, 176
Donne, John, 221–22

Doolittle, Abraham, 21–22
Doolittle, Alfred, 21
Doolittle, Alvin, 22–23
Doolittle, Celia, 21
Doolittle, Charles, 21, 22–23
Doolittle, Charles Leander, 17, 20–21, 22–23
  death of, 73, 156–57
  H.D. and, 23, 27, 28, 73, 154–55, 156–57
  at telescope, 24*f*
  A Treatise on Practical Astronomy as Applied to Geodesy and Navigation, 23
  at University of Pennsylvania, 25–26, 27
Doolittle, Eric, 21, 24–25, 296
Doolittle, Gilbert M., 4, 21, 22*f*, 43, 70, 96–97
Doolittle, Harold, 21, 22*f*, 194, 212, 276, 308
Doolittle, Hilda. *See* H.D.
Doolittle, Thomas, 21–22
Douglas, Norman, 116–17, 123, 162, 215, 286
Dowding, Hugh, 8, 255, 260, 302, 305–6
  Bhaduri and, 238, 239, 240, 248–49
  Churchill and, 216
  God's Magic by, 268–69
  H.D. and, 226, 237, 238–40, 241, 254–55, 268–69, 271–72, 302, 307
  H.D. and Bryher and, 248–49, 259, 268–69
  in IIPR, 226–27
  Many Mansions by, 227
  as RAF commander, 214
  Raleigh and, 268
  on Spiritual Movement, 226
"Dowding System, the," 214
Doyle, Arthur Conan, 12–13
Dramatic Literature of the Reign of Queen Elizabeth (Hazlitt), 53
dreaming, poetry and, 98
"Dreams and Occultism" (Freud, S.), 163
Dreyfus affair, 35
Du Barry, The, 163
Duchess of Malfi, The (Webster), 249–50
Dulac, Germaine, 155
Duncan, Isadora, 119
Duncan, Robert, 8, 296, 307, 308
Dunkirk, 214–15, 224, 243
DuPlessis, Rachel Blau, 8
Durrell, Lawrence, 309
Dyer, Edward, 304–5
Dyer, Elizabeth, 304–6

Ealing, 73
"East Coker" (Eliot), 223, 224
Eckington, 220, 221, 222, 224–25, 244, 255
Edinburgh, 53
Edison, Thomas A., 13–14
"Eduard Fuchs, Collector and Historian" (Benjamin), 197–98
Edwardian era, 6, 40

Edwards, Amelia B., 121–22
Edward VIII (king), 196
Egoist, The, 58, 59, 60–61, 63, 101
Egoist Press, 103, 112
Egypt, 9–10
  Bryher in, 35–38, 37*f*
  Cairo, 36–38, 58, 121–23, 248
  Greece and, 122, 125, 127, 129, 156, 290
  H.D. and Bryher and, 121–23, 308–9
  Helen of Troy in, 289
  McAlmon in, 126
  Ptolemy in, 23
Egyptian Book of the Dead, The, 121
Egyptian Sufis, 37–38
Egyptology, 4, 58, 121, 241
Einstein, Albert, 10, 13, 128, 159, 178–79, 238, 253
Eisenstein, Sergei, 132–33, 134, 138, 152
Eitingon, Max, 177
Eleusis, 94
Elgin (lord), 93
Eliot, T. S., 8–9, 12–13, 106–7, 112, 308–9
  Angleton on, 237
  on dreaming and poetry, 98
  "East Coker" by, 223, 224
  at *The Egoist*, 63
  Four Quartets by, 253–54, 276
  at Free French fundraiser, 235
  H.D. and, 60, 118–19, 121, 223, 224, 230, 252, 273, 276
  McAlmon and, 118–19
  mythic method of, 13
  Pearson, N. H., on, 252
  Symons and, 74
  "Tradition and the Individual Talent" by, 60
  The Waste Land by, 276
  "What the Thunder Said" by, 235
Elizabethan Age and Elizabethans, 3–4, 7–8, 38, 63, 68, 72, 83–84, 168, 219, 234, 236, 239–40, 250–51, 266–67, 268, 359n.21
Elizabeth I (queen), 21, 218–19
Elizabeth II (queen), 287, 294–95
Ellerman, Annie Winifred. *See* Bryher
Ellerman, Johann, 29–30
Ellerman, John Jr., 138, 145, 201, 211–12, 287
  birth of, 53
  Bryher and, 53, 63–64, 65*f*, 170
  inheritance and marriage announcement of, 170
  on Malverns, 128, 135
  McAlmon and, 116
  Sola and, 170
  Why Do They Like It? by, 128
Ellerman, John Reeves, 3, 9, 53, 313n.1
  on Aldington, R., 70
  alpine journal of, 30–31
  on America, 101
  anti-Semitism toward, 62

in Birmingham, 29–30
Bryher and, 29, 30*f*, 30, 33–34, 34*f*, 35, 38, 39*f*, 39–40, 53, 62, 63–65, 84–85, 99–100, 111–12, 129, 138, 159, 251
  death of, 169–70, 178, 196
  Glover, H., and, 32–33, 53, 169–70
  H.D., Perdita and, 75–76
  Jewish origins of, 29
  at Kenwin, 157–58, 167
  McAlmon and, 116, 119
  media shares owned by, 62
  obituaries, 31, 32
  Quilter and, 31
  séances of H.D. and Bryher and, 234, 238
  in shipping industry, 31–32, 35, 91
  will and estate, 170
Ellington, Duke, 187
Ellis, Havelock, 12
  Bryher and, 71, 74–75, 76–77, 161, 164
  on cross-dressing, 74
  H.D. and, 85–86, 158, 185
  H.D. and Bryher and, 71, 74, 76–77, 84–85, 89, 91, 92, 94, 99–100, 169–70
  on H.D.'s *Notes on Thought and Vision*, 80
  McAlmon and, 117
  on polysexuality, 76–77
  on psychoanalysis, 74–75
  "A Revelation" by, 85–86
  Sex in Relation to Society by, 76–77
  on sexo-asethetic inversion, 74–75, 85–86
  on sexuality, 74
  Studies in the Psychology of Sex by, 74–75
  Symons and, 74–75
empire, 3, 170, 252
Empire State Building, 187, 198–99
Enabling Act of 1933, 158–59
End of This Day's Business, The (Constantine), 185
End to Torment (H.D.), 306–7
Enoch Arden (Tennyson), 78
En-Soph, 286, 357n.51
Eos, 79, 80–81
"Eos" (Bryher), 80–81
"Epigram" (H.D.), 58
Erechtheus, 93, 189–90
Eros, 80–81, 137–38
"Eros" (H.D.), 72
Escape Me Never, 171, 186, 187
Euripides, 194
  The Bacchae by, 66
  H.D. on, 93–94, 101, 135–36, 191, 223
  on Helen of Troy, 289
  Hippolytus by, adaptation by H. D., 135–36
  Ion by, 4, 9
  Ion by, translation by H. D., 93, 187, 188–93, 194, 196, 201, 303
  Iphigenia in Aulis, 43, 60, 291–92

Euripides and His Age (Murray), 191
Eurydice, 8, 62–63
"Eurydice" (H.D.), 62–63, 66, 86
Eustis, Constance, 101–2
"Evadne" (H.D.), 72
Evans, Arthur, 98, 163–64
experimental cinema, 149–50, 157

Fairbanks, Douglas, 107–8
Farnell, Lewis Richard, 98
Farrand, Martha Cloyes, 22–23
Fascists and Fascism, 6, 17–18, 157, 158–59, 162, 167, 185–86, 194–95, 202, 215, 306–7
Feigenbaum, Dorian, 178
Feilberg, Sergei, 205, 207–8
"Femininity" (Freud, S.), 157
feminism and feminists, 7, 51, 58, 80
Fenichel, Otto, 203
Ferenczi, Sándor, 177
Fibonacci sequences, 230
Film Problems of Soviet Russia (Bryher), 138
Finland, 212, 214
Fire of Creation, The (van der Leeuw), 178–79
Firth, Mary, 68
"Fish, The" (Moore, M.), 101
Fitzgerald, F. Scott, 226
Flammarion, Camille, 13, 92, 232–33
Flaubert, Gustave, 36–37
Fletcher, John, 59, 236
Flint, F. S., 59
Florence, 278
Floride, La, 48–49
Flowering of the Rod, The (H.D.), 26, 248–49, 256, 262
flu pandemic, 1918, 73, 324n.18
Foothills, 137, 138
"Four Marys, The" (Scottish ballad), 19–20
Fournier, Maidi, 203
Four Quartets (Eliot), 253–54, 276
Fourteenth of October, The (Bryher), 237, 251, 276–77, 278, 279, 280, 282, 283, 284, 285, 287–89, 290–91, 310
"Fragment 113" (H.D.), 121, 201
France, 9–10, 35, 202, 212, 213–15, 216, 217–18, 247
Francis of Assisi (saint), 17–18
Franco, Francisco, 194–95, 198–99, 217–18
Frankenstein (Shelley, M.), 13
Fraulein Else, 145
Frazer, James G., 43, 62, 158
Free French fundraiser, 235–36
French Resistance, 215
Freshwater Algae of the United States (Wollfe, F.), 20
Freud, Anna, 164, 165, 171, 178, 193, 197, 203, 205
Freud, Ernst, 237, 255
Freud, Martin, 203, 205

Freud, Sigmund, 16
 arrest of, 203
 Beyond the Pleasure Principle by, 177
 Bryher and, 113, 158, 163, 164, 168–69, 182, 211–12
 Charcot and, 247
 "Dreams and Occultism" by, 163
 "Femininity" by, 157
 H.D. and, 8, 11, 99, 158, 160–64, 165–67, 168–69, 172, 175, 177–78, 180, 181, 182, 205, 207, 246–48, 301
 H.D. and Bryher, 8, 11, 160–65, 166, 167, 168–69, 182, 211–12, 246–47, 248, 266–67, 284
 on H.D.'s *Ion*, 192–93
 H.D.'s *Tribute to Freud* on, 246–47
 Herring on, 175
 Hesse and, 277, 278–79
 in London, 205
 Moore, M., on, 113
 on Moses, 197
 Perdita and, 165
 "Psychogenesis of a Case of Homosexuality in a Woman" by, 117
 Sachs, H., and, 134, 168–69, 197
 on Schmideberg, W., 180
 van der Leeuw and, 178–79
Freund, Gisele, 205, 206f
Freytag, Else Von, 118
Friedberg, Anne, 132–33
Friedenshuetten (Habitations of Peace), 18–19
Friedman, Susan Stanford, 7, 8, 9, 101, 286, 310
Friends' Central School, 43, 44f, 198–99
Fromm, Erich, 177
From Ritual to Romance (Weston), 160
Fry, Robert, 219
Furness, C. J., 287
Fyta, Anna, 359n.3

Garbo, Greta, 125, 133–34, 149, 175, 184–85, 273
"Garden" (H.D.), 59
Gareth, 13–14, 98–99, 136
Gaskell, Elizabeth, 53
Gate to the Sea (Bryher), 310
Gaunt Island (Macpherson), 132–33
Gawain, 13–14
Gay Literary Supplement, 310
gay marriage, 6, 313n.21
Gay Pride, 6
gender designations and vocabulary, 10
gender fluidity, 6, 356n.114
genderqueer, 6
gender reassignment, 6
George V (king), 32
George VI (king), 196, 286–87
Gettysburg, battle of, 20
"Ghost, The" (H.D.), 222

Gibraltar, 92
Gide, André, 186, 196, 215
Gift, The (H.D.), 17, 232–33, 242, 274, 308
"Girl-Page in Elizabethan Literature, The" (Bryher), 68, 74–75, 109, 168, 267
Glendinning, Victoria, 220
Gloucestershire, 250–51
Glover, Edward, 178, 212, 280, 284
Glover, George, 32, 318n.17
Glover, Hannah, 29, 53, 112, 318n.15, 318nn.17–18
    Bryher and, 32–33, 39f, 40, 53–55, 130, 168, 207–8, 211, 212
    death of, 211–12
    Ellerman, J. R., and, 32–33, 53, 169–70
    funeral for, 211–12
    H.D. and, 132, 186, 211
    Herring and, 135
    McAlmon and, 116, 118, 169
    Perdita and, 194, 211–12, 214–15
    séances of H.D. and Bryher and, 238
Glover, Mary, 32
Gnadenhuetten (Habitations of Grace), 18–19
gnosis, 12–13, 17–18, 223, 293
Gnostic Gospels (Pagels), 346n.4
Gnostics, 12–13, 17–18, 26, 241, 272
gnostic texts
    Acts of John, 223
    Gospel of Mary Magdalene, 58, 241, 248
    Gospel of Philip, 248
    Secret Book of John, 58
God's Magic (Dowding, H.), 268–69
Godwin, William, 120
Goethe, Johann Wolfgang von, 298, 304
Golden Bough, The (Frazer), 43, 62
"Golden Wings" (Morrs, W.), 272–73
"Good Frend" (H.D.), 249–50, 252–53, 263
Good Housekeeping, 281–82
Gorgon, 98
Gospel of Mary Magdalene, 58, 241, 248
Gospel of Philip, 248
Gourmont, Remy de, 80–81, 320n.50
Graham, Sheila, 281–82
Gray, Cecil, 4, 66, 67–68, 69, 77, 126, 182–83, 190, 194–95, 199–200
Great Depression, 31
Great London Fire, 1666, 21, 221, 236
Great War, the. *See* World War I
Greece
    Athens, 89, 92–93, 94
    Corfu, 95–97, 98–100, 101, 102, 137–38, 162–63, 164, 167–68, 178, 226–27, 237, 239, 246–47, 301
    Delphi, 70, 73, 94–95, 96–97, 98
    Egypt and, 122, 125, 127, 129, 156, 290
    H.D. and Bryher and, 7–8, 9–10, 11, 89–91, 92–99, 101, 161, 162–63, 182, 192

Greek Anthology, The, 57
Greek mythological and historical figures
    Achilles, 71, 289, 291, 292–93, 298, 300
    Aphrodite, 79, 93, 127, 135–36, 164, 303
    Apollo, 47–48, 57–58, 72, 81–82, 85–86, 93, 94–95, 98, 167–68, 189–90
    Artemis, 13, 43, 45, 46–47, 72, 83, 93, 108–9, 114–15, 135–36, 164, 167–68, 185, 189–90
    Athene, 96, 160–62, 189–90, 191–92
    Cassandra, 14, 202–3
    Castor and Pollux, 301
    Clio, 38–39
    Clytemnestra, 291–92
    Demeter, 45, 94, 179–80, 235
    Dionysus, 93–94
    Eos, 79, 80–81
    Erechtheus, 93, 189–90
    Eros, 80–81, 137–38
    Eurydice, 8, 62–63
    Gorgon, 98
    Helen of Troy, 27, 125, 289, 291–92, 298, 300, 303 (*See also Helen in Egypt* (H.D.))
    Helios, 94–95, 102, 128, 189–90, 191–92, 254
    Hercules, 38–39, 91, 309
    Hermes, 56–57, 60, 228–29
    Hippolyta and Hippolytus, 89, 135–36
    Hyacinthus, 47–48, 85–86
    Ion, 187, 191–92
    Kreousa, 189–91
    Meleager, 56–57, 124–25
    Niké, 93, 97–98
    Odysseus, 96, 134
    Orpheus, 8, 62–63
    Paris, 27, 297, 298, 299, 300, 303
    Persephone, 45
    Perseus, 97–98
    Poseidon, 96
    Theseus, 89, 135–36, 299, 300
    Thetis, 71, 78–79, 292–93, 300
    Zeus, 236, 290, 292
Greek mythology
    Gregg, F. J., on, 47–48
    Pound, E., on, 45
Greek religions, 156, 163–64
Greenslet, Ferris, 185
Greenwich Village, 46, 47f, 103, 109–10
Gregg, Frances Josepha, 4, 5
    "The Apartment" by, 136
    birth and childhood, 45–46
    as feminist, 51
    H.D. and, 43, 46–51, 52, 56, 57–58, 136, 139, 152, 153, 174, 179, 180–81, 182, 184, 188–89, 199
    H.D. and Bryher and, 136, 180–81, 303
    Macpherson and, 127–28, 130, 136, 139
    The Mystic Leeway by, 319n.10

Gregg, Frances Josepha (*Cont.*)
  "Perché" by, 51–52
  Pound and, 48–49, 51, 52
  on Rossetti, 51
  Wilkinson and, 51–52, 127
Gregg, Julia, 45–46, 48–49, 50–51
Gregg, Oliver, 45, 181
Gregory, Eileen, 125, 190
Gregory, Horace, 283, 306
Grynszpan, Herschel, 207
Guest, Barbara, 7, 29, 310, 352n.25
Guggenheim, Peggy, 230–31
Guide to Greece (Baedeker), 89–90, 95–96
Guillén, Jorge, 308
Guthrie, Tyrone, 188
Gutscher, Dori, 307–8

Halifax (lord), 215–16
Hall, Radclyffe, 139
Halley's comet, 47–48
Hamburg, 29–30
Hamilton College, 43, 310
Hannibal, 161, 164, 247
Hanns Sachs Training Fund, 182
Hanscombe, Gillian, 310–11
Hardy, Thomas, 23
Harlem, 187, 198–99
Harriman, Marie, 187
Harrison, Jane, 58
Hasty Bunch, A (McAlmon), 119, 123
Hawthorne, Nathaniel, 191, 276, 278, 281
Haydon, Ann, 318n.17
Hazlitt, William, 53
H.D. *See also* H.D. and Bryher
  abortion of, 138–39, 140–42, 145
  Aldington, R., and, 3, 4, 5, 56, 57–58, 59–60, 61, 62, 63, 64f, 66, 67, 75, 83–84, 94, 126–27, 128, 199–200, 204–5, 224, 272–73, 283, 291, 294–95, 300, 301, 306, 308
  Aldington, R., Perdita and, 75–76, 126, 199–200
  Ambelain and, 286
  Ashby and, 250–51, 252, 266, 287
  with beads and amulet, 1920, 95f
  Bergner and, 172
  Bhaduri, A., and, 227, 228, 248–49, 256, 299
  birth, 3, 21, 23
  bisexuality of, 7
  Borderline and, 146–47, 148, 150, 151f, 152, 154–55, 172, 191, 233–34
  Bowen and, 213, 214, 223
  Brashear and, 27
  breakdown, 259–61, 268–69
  Brunner, T., and, 261–63, 265–66, 267
  Bryn Mawr and, 43–44, 101, 256, 259
  Burt and, 155–56
  in Carmel, 108f, 108–9
  Carroll, D., and, 260–63, 264, 265–66
  Chadwick and, 154–56, 158
  childhood of, 16–17, 28
  on Churchill, 214
  on Constantine, 185
  in Cornwall, 66–67, 69, 184, 188, 189, 225
  Dante and, 271, 274–75, 278
  on death instinct, 177
  death of, 309, 310
  as "Delia Alton," 114–15, 234, 255, 270–71, 272, 279, 308
  Dobson, N., and, 228
  Dobson, S., and, 173, 175–76, 178–79, 182–83, 184–85, 192, 200, 204, 212–13, 221, 230–31, 242, 244–45, 246, 249, 251–52, 259–60, 261–62, 266–67, 270, 303, 304, 309
  Dobson, S., Rodeck and, 173–74, 230–31
  Doolittle, C. L., and, 23, 27, 28, 73, 154–55, 156–57
  Doolittle, E., and, 24–25
  Dowding and, 226, 237, 238–40, 241, 248–49, 254–55, 268–69, 271–72, 302, 307
  dreams of, 161, 162, 163, 165–66, 167–68, 171, 180, 181, 191–92, 241, 302
  Edwards and, 121–22
  on Einstein, 10, 238
  Eliot and, 60, 118–19, 121, 223, 224, 230, 252, 273, 276
  Ellis and, 85–86, 185
  on Euripides, 93–94, 101, 135–36, 223
  family photo with brothers, 22f
  on "The Four Marys," 20
  at Free French fundraiser, 235–36
  Freud, S., and, 8, 11, 99, 158, 160–64, 165–67, 168–69, 172, 175, 177–78, 180, 181, 182, 205, 207, 246–48, 301
  at Friends' Central School, 43, 44f
  as genderqueer, 6
  Glover, H., and, 132, 186, 211
  Gray and, 4, 66, 67–68, 69
  Gregg, F. J., and, 43, 46–51, 52, 56, 57–58, 136, 139, 152, 153, 174, 179, 180–81, 182, 184, 188–89, 199
  on Helen of Troy, 27
  Henderson and, 184–85, 188–89
  Herr and, 46, 224
  Herring and, 243, 245, 252, 260, 266–67, 276–77, 283, 285
  Hesse and, 271, 277
  Heydt and, 296–300, 301–2, 303, 304–6, 307–9
  at Hirslanden Clinique Cecil, 293–94
  in IIPR, 227
  Imagism and, 56, 57, 59, 100, 102
  on James, H., 273

Jordan and, 223, 227, 228, 282–83
at Kenwin, 156–57, 158, 171, 174, 176, 182, 184, 185, 189, 192, 197, 199–200, 203, 206, 207–8, 250, 266–67
at Kusnacht Nervenklinik, 261–68, 270–71, 281, 293–95, 296–301, 302, 303–8, 309
at La Paix, 281, 294–95
in Lausanne, 275–76, 277, 293–94
Lawrence, D. H., and, 62–63, 64f, 77
Lowell and, 59, 60–61, 63, 64, 67, 82
at Lowndes, 184–85, 186, 212–13, 214–15, 218, 221–22, 233, 237, 250–51, 254, 255, 260
in Lugano, 271–72, 274, 277–78, 279, 283, 284, 285, 287, 289, 292, 301–2
Macpherson and, 138–39, 140–42, 145, 152, 154–56, 182, 188–89, 196–97
on Magdalene, 248–49
male persona of, 182
Man Ray photograph of, 119–20, 309, 311f, 311
mediumship of, 148, 201, 234, 241, 270–71
meningitis diagnosis, 259–60
Modern, K., and, 215–16
modernism of, 17–18
Moore, M., and, 61, 101–2, 103, 112, 120, 217, 235–36
on Moravian Church and Moravians, 16–19
on Morris, W., 227–28, 270, 275, 276–77, 280
mysticism of, 12–13
on Native Americans, 148–49
on Nazism, as death drive, 180
"100 years of electricity" stamps, 287, 288f
in Paris, 124
Patmore, B., and, 56, 126
Pearson, N. H., and, 201, 227, 228–29, 232, 235–36, 241, 242, 243, 244, 252, 254, 256, 259, 265, 275, 276–77, 279, 291, 293–94, 306–7, 308–9
Pearson, N. H., *Helen in Egypt* and, 289–91, 293, 303
Pearson, S., and, 245, 249–50, 252
Perdita, Aldington, R., and, 75–76, 126, 199–200
Perdita and, 75–76, 76f, 82, 122, 137, 156, 164–65, 201–2, 212–13, 227, 261, 262, 265–66, 281–82, 287–89, 290, 291
Plank and, 132, 137, 188–89, 228
Pound, E., and, 4–5, 8, 43–45, 48–51, 52, 56–58, 59, 63, 75, 102, 132–33, 139–40, 272–73, 275, 276, 296
pregnancies and childbirth, 4, 5, 59–60, 67–68, 70, 71, 73, 75, 79, 138–39
psychic abilities and psychic experiences of, 11, 13, 80, 156, 227, 232–33
psychic mythopoetic method of, 13
psychoanalysis and, 140–42, 154–57, 158, 191–92, 246–47, 248, 270–71

on Robeson, P., 149
at Roten Kreuz Spiral, 309
Sachs, H., and, 156–57, 158, 160–61, 260
on Sappho, 93–94, 124, 125, 126, 223
Schimideberg, W., and, 260, 261, 262, 263, 265, 282–83, 299
"Shakespeare" poems of, 249–50, 252–53, 259, 263, 266
on Siddal, 274–75
Sitwells and, 222, 223
Snively and, 43, 57, 71
in Stratford, 249–51, 252, 255, 259, 263, 266–67
in Upper Darby, 27–28
in Vienna, 160–61, 162
on vision of artist, 60
visions of, 73, 79–80, 96–99, 260, 298, 299
Wolle, E., and, 20, 25–26, 27, 28, 232–33, 259–60
Wolle, Francis, and, 17, 20, 80
Wolle, H. E., and, 25, 27, 40, 130, 240–41
at Woodhall, 228
on Woolf, suicide of, 221, 222
World War I story of, 206
H.D., drama by
"Choruses from Iphigeneia in Aulis" translation, 60
Hippolytus Temporizes, 93, 135–36, 201
Ion translation, 187, 188–93, 194, 196, 201, 303
Iphigenia, 61
H.D., film writing by
"Borderline Pamphlet," 150
"Cinema and the Classics: Beauty," 133
"Cinema and the Classics: Restraint," 134
H.D., poetry by
"Ancient Wisdom Speaks to the Mountain," 235
"The Cliff Temple," 60–61
Collected Poems, 1912-1944, 7
Collected Poetry, 127
"The Dancer," 248
A Dead Priestess Speaks, 171
"Epigram," 58
"Eros," 72
"Eurydice," 62–63, 66, 86
"Evadne," 72
"Fragment 113," 121, 201
"Good Frend," 249–50, 252–53, 263
"Helen," 125
Helen in Egypt, 7, 286, 289–91, 292–94, 296, 297, 298–99, 301–2, 303, 306, 308–10, 311, 356n.114, 359n.3
Heliodora and Other Poems, 3, 121, 124–25
"Helios and Athene," 94, 102
"The Helmsman," 61
"Hermes of the Ways," 56–57, 58
Hermetic Definition, 9, 309
"Hyacinth," 47–48, 124

H.D., poetry by (*Cont.*)
  Hymen, 71–72, 112, 120–21
  "Islands," 86
  "Leda," 72
  "The Master," 160–61
  "May, 1943," 238
  "Mid-Day," 59, 297
  "Moonrise," 59
  "Odyssey," 96
  "Oread," 9
  "Phaedra Rebukes Hippolyta," 102
  "Phaedra Remembers Crete," 102
  "Pool," 59
  "Priapus," 58
  "Projector," 137–38
  "Pygmalion," 62–63
  "R.A.F.," 225–26, 298
  "Red Roses to Bronze," 149
  Sea Garden, 3, 8, 60–61, 63–64, 78–79, 92, 98
  "Sea God," 61
  "Sea Rose," 59
  Selected Poems, 308
  "The Shrine," 3–4
  "Simaetha," 72
  "Sitalkas," 57–58
  "Storm," 59
  "Thetis," 71, 78–79, 300
  "The Tribute," 61
  Trilogy, 7, 224, 226, 228, 232–33, 242, 247, 248–49, 253–54, 264, 274, 286, 302
    The Flowering of the Rod, 26, 248–49, 256, 262
    Tribute to the Angels, 236, 241–43, 252
    The Walls Do Not Fall, 224, 226–27, 228–30, 239, 241, 243, 248, 263
  "We Two," 124, 309–10
  What Do I Love?, 359n.6
  "Wind Sleepers," 59
H.D., prose and criticism by
  "Advent," 16
  Asphodel, 49, 50, 75, 320n.31, 329n.2
  "Before the Battle," 215
  Bid Me to Live, 294, 301, 308, 309, 327n.19
  "Blue Lights," 221
  "The Body's Guest," 267–68
  By Avon River, 266, 267–68, 270–71, 276, 278, 279, 294
  Compassionate Friendship, 314n.27
  End to Torment, 306–7
  "The Ghost" by, 222
  The Gift, 17, 232–33, 242, 274, 308
  The Hedgehog, 179, 198
  HERmione, 139–40
  Kora and Ka, 175, 179
  "Letter from England," 224
  Madrigal, 66, 277, 294, 301
  Magic Mirror, 314n.27
  Majic Ring, 232–33, 234, 237, 239–40, 277, 301
  Mire Mare, 175
  The Mystery, 280
  "Narthex," 130, 136, 303
  Nights, 155–56, 175–76, 177–79, 182–83, 337n.23
  Notes on Thought and Vision, 79–82, 98, 179
  Paint It Today, 5, 52, 69, 83, 85–86, 108–9, 112, 114–15, 123, 198, 311
  Palimpsest, 122–23, 126, 128, 158, 286
  Pilate's Wife, 12, 128, 185, 270–71, 300–1
  Sagesse, 305–6
  "Secret Name," 122–23
  The Sword Went Out to Sea, 271–73, 274, 276–77, 279, 283, 284, 290–91, 307
  Thorn Thicket, 307, 308–9
  Tribute to Freud, 7, 232–33, 246–47, 260–61, 304
  The Usual Star, 175, 179
  Vale Ave, 304–5, 308
  The White Rose and the Red, 270–71, 273, 274–75, 276–77, 278, 279, 284
  "The Wise Sappho," 82
  "Writing on the Wall," 246–47, 260, 284
H.D. and Bryher
  Aldington, R., and, 3, 67–69, 70, 71–72, 75–76, 77, 84–85, 198, 273, 276, 304, 307–8
  on Aquarian Age, 307
  astrology and, 7
  on atom bomb, 254, 279
  on *The Battleship Potemkin*, 138
  Benjamin and, 197–98
  Bergner and, 168, 172
  Bhaduri, A., and, 228, 229–30, 233–34, 238–39, 240–41, 251
  Brunner, T., and, 261, 262
  on Bryher's male identification, 162
  Bryher's *Two Selves* and, 71, 96, 123
  Bryher's *West* and, 102–3
  Butts and, 123–24
  in California, 105–9
  childbirths and publications, sequence of, 291
  on childhood memories, of H.D., 17
  on cinema, 125, 132–33, 137–38, 149–50, 152, 158
  in Cornwall, 78–79, 82, 83, 84f, 85f, 100, 179–80, 244, 287–89, 309–10
  Cournos and, 83–84
  Dobson, S., and, 173–74, 175, 179, 234–35, 256, 259–60, 307, 308–9
  Douglas and, 116–17
  Dowding and, 248–49, 259, 268–69
  dreams, 72
  Egypt and, 121–23, 308–9

Ellis and, 71, 74–75, 76–77, 84–85, 89, 91, 92, 94, 99–100, 169–70
embodied minds of, 23
European refugees aided by, 10
in flu pandemic of 1918, 73
Freud, S., and, 8, 11, 160–65, 166, 167, 168–69, 182, 211–12, 246–47, 248, 266–67, 284
on George VI, death of, 287
Greece and, 7–8, 9–10, 11, 89–90, 92–99, 101, 161, 162–63, 164, 178, 182, 192
Gregg, F. J., and, 136, 180–81, 303
Guest on, 7
H.D.'s *By Avon River* and, 270–71
H.D.'s *The Gift* and, 232–33, 308
H.D.'s *Helen in Egypt* and, 289–91, 292, 303
H.D.'s *Heliodora* and, 124–25
H.D.'s *HERmione* and, 139–40
H.D.'s *Hymen* and, 71–72
H.D.'s *Ion* translation and, 189–90, 191–93, 194, 196
H.D.'s *Notes on Thought and Vision* and, 79–82, 98
H.D.'s *Paint It Today* and, 83, 114–15, 123
H.D.'s *Palimpsest* and, 126
H.D.'s *Sea Garden* and, 63–64
H.D.'s *The Sword Went Out to Sea* and, 274
H.D.'s *Tribute to the Angels* and, 242
H.D.'s *Walls Do Not Fall* and, 228–29
Henderson and, 185
Herring and, 153–54, 204, 216, 221–22, 234–35, 243, 249–50, 252, 255, 260
Hesse and, 270, 278–79
Heydt and, 296–97
on invisibility, 9
Joan of Arc and, 49
on *The Joyless Street*, 125
Kusnacht Nervenklinik and, 261–68, 299, 300–1, 302
letters between, 9–10
in London, 77–78, 80–81, 114–15, 127, 138, 153, 218–19, 241
as lovers, 14, 114–15
Lowell and, 67–68, 69, 77–78, 82, 102
Lowndes-Kenwin bilocation, 250
in Lugano, 272
Macpherson and, 127–28, 130–34, 135–39, 140–42, 145, 146, 149–50, 153–55, 158, 160, 161, 164–65, 169–70, 175, 177, 180, 182, 185, 216–17, 268
on "madness," 11–12
McAlmon and, 110–12, 115–16, 117, 119, 123, 124, 128, 177
mediumistic practice of, 9
meeting, 3–5, 67–68, 69, 251, 309–10
modernism of, 310–11
the Modern sisters as family, 204
Moore, M., and, 103–5, 106–7, 108–9, 110–11, 113, 114–15, 117, 179, 202, 216, 217–18, 283
mothers of, 40
in New York, 102, 103, 109–10, 198, 201, 304
nicknames and private language, 9–10, 13–14, 179–80
as nonbinary, 6, 10–12, 14, 182–83
on obscenity trial, of Hall, 139
on the occult, 12
ocean voyages and psychic voyages of, 14–15
Pearson, N. H., and, 206–7, 235–36, 241, 266–67, 273, 276, 278, 280, 285, 299–300, 304, 305*f*
Perdita and, 9–10, 75–76, 79–80, 96, 101, 102, 105–6, 106*f*, 108–9, 116–17, 128, 140, 156–57, 158, 161, 167, 169, 181, 184, 186, 188, 189–90, 194, 198, 199–200, 212–13, 224–25, 241, 259, 264, 265, 271, 279, 283, 285, 287–89, 291, 294–95, 304, 310–11
post-Imagist work of H.D. and, 7
Pound, E., and, 83–84, 170
on psychic abilities, 11, 13
psychic experiences and explorations of, 39–40, 232–33
on psychosis, 11–12
queerness and, 5–6, 7–8
Rodeck and, 91–92, 97–98, 100, 102, 128, 145, 157–58, 164, 181
Sachs, H., and, 154, 260
Schaffner, J. V. and, 282, 285
Schaffner, V., and, 282, 284, 285
Schmideberg, W., and, 174–75, 194, 198, 218, 224–25, 234, 264, 265, 284, 302
scrapbook images, 1919-1920, 81*f*
scrapbook photomontage, 141*f*
séance notes of, 233–34, 237, 259, 263, 348n.7
séances of, 8, 13–14, 232–34, 235, 236, 238–41, 244, 251, 255, 271–72, 275
Smyth and, 165
on spiritualism, 12–13
Stein and, 119–20
on true romance, 70
as unseen activists, 5
on U.S., 197–98
in Vienna, 160, 161
visions and psychic experiences of, 7–8, 11, 79–80, 91–92, 96–100, 102, 137–38, 162–63, 164, 181, 226, 246–47, 301
war neurosis and, 7–8
"whole machine" metaphor, for relationship of, 13–14, 239
Wolle, H. E., and, 105–6, 117, 121, 122–23
on World War I, 69, 103
World War II and, 213–15, 216–19, 224, 232, 235–36, 237, 243–44, 250, 254, 259, 260, 276

H.D. studies, 7, 8, 9
Heartt, Gertrude, 45–46
Heart to Artemis, The (Bryher), 33, 310, 314n.27
Heat of the Day (Bowen), 221–22
Hedgehog, The (H.D.), 179, 198
"Helen" (H.D.), 125
Helen in Egypt (H.D.), 7, 286, 289–91, 292–94, 296, 297, 298–99, 301–2, 303, 306, 308–10, 311, 356n.114, 359n.3
Helen of Troy, 27, 125, 289, 291–92, 298, 300, 303
Heliodora and Other Poems (H.D.), 3, 121, 124–25
Helios, 94–95, 102, 128, 189–90, 191–92, 254
"Helios and Athene" (H.D.), 94, 102
"Hellenics" (Bryher), 93–94
"Helmsman, The" (H.D.), 61
Hemingway, Ernest, 118–19
Hemmings, John, 236
Henderson, Cole, 154, 157, 179, 184–85, 188–89, 227–28, 233, 244, 250–51, 260, 268, 285
Henderson, Gerald, 227–28, 233, 236, 244, 260
Henselmann, Herman, 145, 155
Henty, G. A., 35
Hepburn, Katharine, 194–95
Hercules, 38–39, 91, 309
hermaphrodites, 119, 182, 230
Hermes, 56–57, 60, 228–29
"Hermes of the Ways" (H.D.), 56–57, 58
Hermetic Definition (H.D.), 9, 309
hermeticism, 7, 10–11, 56–57
HERmione (H.D.), 139–40
Herodotus, 125
Herr, Mary, 46, 198–99, 201–2, 224, 283
Herrenhuters, 280
Herrick, Robert, 294, 327n.19
Herring, Robert, 10, 133, 135, 145, 147–48, 259
  on Ambelain, 286
  on atom bomb, 254
  Beach and, 274, 280
  Bergner and, 168
  Bryher and, 169–70, 177, 178, 201, 207, 211–12, 214, 216, 218, 220, 221, 261, 280
  on fascist rally, 158–59
  on Freud, S., 175
  H.D. and, 243, 245, 252, 260, 266–67, 276–77, 283, 285
  H.D. and Bryher and, 153–54, 204, 216, 221–22, 234–35, 243, 249–50, 252, 255, 260
  Heydt and, 299
  at *Life and Letters Today*, 185, 186, 188, 201, 212, 219, 260
  in London, 212, 213, 216
  Macpherson and, 146f, 146, 152–53, 180, 185
  Perdita and, 195, 221, 273
  on psychoanalysis, 212
  on Schmideberg, W., 302
  Sitwell, E., and, 222
  Sitwell, O., and, 219–20, 221–22
Herrnhaag, 19
Herrnhut, 18, 133–34
Herself Defined (Guest), 7, 352n.25
Hesse, Hermann, 270, 271, 277, 278–79
Hey Day of the Wizard (Burton), 275–76
Heydt, Erich, 296–300, 301–2, 303, 304–6, 307–9, 341n.15, 359n.6
Hilda's Book (Pound, E.), 44
Hilton, James, 256
Hindenburg, Paul von, 158–59
Hipparchia, 126
Hippolyta, 89, 135–36
Hippolytus, 89, 135–36
Hippolytus Temporizes (H.D.), 93, 135–36, 201
Hiroshima, 253–54
Hirschfeld, Magnus, 118
Hirslanden Clinique Cecil, 293–94
History of the Peloponnesian War (Thucydides), 69
Hitler, Adolf, 157, 158–59, 175, 176, 188–89, 196, 203, 205, 206, 211, 214–15, 216, 249–50, 251–52
Hogarth Press, 218
Hohe Warte, 167
Holland, 214
Holman Hunt, William, 51, 274–75
Home, Daniel, 275–76
Homer, 297
homophobia, 5, 6, 83–84
"Homosexual in Society and Politics, The" (Duncan, R.), 308
homosexuality, 6, 120, 137, 157, 180, 284, 296, 306
Horner, David, 219, 220, 222
Horney, Karen, 177
Hotel Angleterre et Belle Venise, in Corfu, 95–97
Hotel de la Grande Bretagne, 92
Hotel Regina, in Vienna, 160–61
Hughes, Langston, 132–33
Hughes, Randolph, 290, 358n.75
Hull, C., 157
Hull, Dorothy ("Quex"), 157, 158, 161, 171
Hull, England, 29–30
Hulme, T. E., 9
Hungerford, 119
Hunt, Violet, 56, 227–28, 233
  The Wife of Rossetti by, 156, 270–71, 273, 274–75
Hurried Man (Carnevali), 119
Hus, John, 17–18
"Hyacinth" (H.D.), 47–48, 124
Hyacinthus, 47–48, 85–86
Hymen (H.D.), 71–72, 112, 120–21

"Hymn to the Name and Honour of the Admirable Saint Teresa, A" (Crashaw), 222
Hynes, Samuel, 62

"I, John" (H.D.), 247
IIPR. *See* International Institute for Psychic Research
Île de France, SS, 201–2
Imagism and Imagists, 4–5, 7, 8, 9, 56–57, 59, 61, 72, 100, 102, 190, 281–82
Imagistes, Des (Pound, E.), 57–58, 59
imperialism, 35, 62
Impressions That Remained (Smyth), 165
"In a Garden" (Lowell), 63
Indiana, 20, 21, 22–23, 43
"In Exile" (Bryher), 79
Inferno (Dante), 43
Institutions of Modernism (Rainey), 8, 314n.39
International H.D. Society, The, 7
International Institute for Psychic Research (IIPR), 226–27
International Psychoanalytical Journal, 101
International Psychoanalytic Congress (IPA), 157, 177, 178, 196–97, 205, 278
"In the Tube" (Aldington, R.), 59
Ion, 187, 191–92
Ion (Euripides), 4, 9
  H.D. translation, 187, 188–93, 194, 196, 201, 303
IPA. *See* International Psychoanalytic Congress
Iphigenia (H.D.), 61
Iphigenia in Aulis (Euripides), 43, 60, 291–92
Iroquois, 18–19
Irwin, Grace, 217–18, 266, 268, 271
"I Said" (Bryher), 77–78
Isis, 4, 13, 121, 126, 127, 164, 228–29, 286, 291–92, 293
"Islands" (H.D.), 86
Italy, 9–10, 57–58, 99–100, 200, 215, 278
Itea, 94–95
"Itylus" (Swinburne), 46

J'Accuse! (Salomon), 167
Jackson, Zakiyyah Iman, 148
James, Henry, 226, 273, 276
James, Peggy, 101–2
James, William, 101–2
January Tale (Bryher), 310
Japan, 239, 250, 253, 254
  Hiroshima and Nagasaki, 253–54
Jekels, Ludwig, 177, 200, 207
J. Ellerman and Company, 31
Jesuits, 17–18, 174–75
Jesus Christ, 16, 18–19, 26, 70, 94, 128, 223, 242, 248–49, 270–71
Joan of Arc, 49, 67, 125

John (apostle), 242
John of the Cross (saint), 223, 227
Johns, Edith, 53
Jones, Ernest, 157, 178, 203
Jordan, Viola Baxter, 43, 52, 179, 223, 227, 228, 282–83, 314n.32
Joyce, James, 111, 118, 128, 311
Joyless Street, The, 125, 133–34

Kafka, Franz, 186, 205–6
Kaspar, 248–49
Keats, John, 46–47
Kenner, Hugh, 9, 59
Kensington, 74, 83–84, 101
Kenwin, 157–58, 166, 182–83, 188, 261, 279, 297
  Beach at, 200
  Bergner at, 155–56, 162, 168
  Bryher and Macpherson on, 145
  Bryher at, 161–62, 165, 167, 173, 175, 176, 194, 202–3, 205, 211, 212, 213, 216–17, 266, 267, 300, 310
  Daniels at, 154
  Douglas at, 162
  Ellerman, J. R., at, 157–58, 167
  H.D. at, 156–57, 158, 171, 174, 176, 182, 184, 185, 189, 192, 197, 199–200, 203, 206, 207–8, 211, 250, 266–67
  Perdita at, 177, 197, 203, 204
  queers at, 157
  Sachs, H., at, 168–69
  Schaffner, V., at, 285
  Schaffners at, 285
  Schmidebergs at, 285
  Stein and Wilder at, 189
Kern, Jerome, 198–99
Kidnapped (Stevenson), 34–35
Klein, Melanie, 174–75, 178
Knight, G. Wilson, 251–52
Knossos, 98
Koch, Carl, 155
Kocher, Mousieur, 217
Kolonos, 94
Kom Ombo, 38
Kora and Ka (H.D.), 175, 179
Koubokva, Zdeněk, 6
Krafft-Ebing, Richard von, 74
Kreousa, 189–91
Krishnamurti, 178–79
Kristallnacht, 207
Kusnacht Nervenklinik, 260, 261–68, 270–71, 293–95, 296–301, 302, 303–8, 309, 359n.3

Lacan, Jacques, 198
Lady Ellerman. *See* Glover, Hannah
Lake Geneva, 145

Lamb, Charles and Mary, 35
Lang, Fritz, 134
La Paix, 281, 294–95
Larsen, Nella, 199
Lausanne, 202, 212, 261, 266–68, 271, 275–76, 277, 278, 279, 285, 292, 293–94, 299
Lawrence, D. H., 59–60, 62–63, 64f, 66, 67, 77, 78, 314n.28
Lawrence, Frieda, 62–63, 66
Lawrence, T. E., 306
"Leda" (H.D.), 72
Le Havre, 49
Lehigh University, 22–23
Lennon, John, 6
Lesbia Brandon (Swinburne), 290
lesbians and lesbianism, 71, 74–75, 101–2, 157, 161, 168, 171, 174, 186, 310
"Letter from England" (H.D.), 224
Levering, Joseph Mortimer, 19
Lewin, Blanche, 146–47, 164–65
Life and Letters Today, 188–89, 194–95, 271
　Bryher and, 185, 196–97, 201, 202, 219, 230–31, 236
　H.D.'s "Good Frend" in, 249–50
　H.D.'s *Tribute to Freud* serialized in, 232–33
　H.D.'s *Walls Do Not Fall* excerpt in, 229–30
　H.D.'s "Writing on the Wall" in, 246–47, 260
　Herring at, 185, 186, 188, 201, 212, 219, 260
　Pearson in, 252
Life of William Morris, The (Mackail), 272–73
Lillie, Bea, 187
Lisle, Leconte de, 189
Litchfield, Staffordshire, 63
Little Review, 320n.50
Lives of the Poets (Schmidt), 8
Lombroso, Cesare, 13
London, 3, 8, 10, 12–13, 14–15, 17, 19
　air raids and bombings, 212–13, 216, 217, 218–19, 221, 222, 232, 233, 235–36, 243
　Bloomsbury, 29
　Bryher and McAlmon in, 117–18
　Bryher in, 274
　Ellerman, J. R., in, 31
　Freud, S., and family in, 205
　Great London Fire, 1666, 21, 221, 236
　H.D. and Bryher in, 77–78, 80–81, 114–15, 127, 138, 153, 218–19, 241
　H.D. and Pound, E., in, 56–57
　Henderson, C., on, 268
　Herring in, 212, 213, 216
　Mayfair, 4–5, 53, 59, 83–84, 168
　V-bomb attacks on, 243
　Victoria, 52
London Library, 236
London Theatre Studio, The, 188

Long, John, 179–80
Longfellow, Henry Wadsworth, 43
Los Alamos Laboratory, 253
Los Angeles, 109
Lost Horizon (Hilton), 256
Louvre, 49–50
Love, Heather, 5–6
Low, Barbara, 117, 132–33, 178
Lowell, Amy, 3, 69, 82, 83–84, 86, 92, 99–100, 102
　Aldington and, 59–60
　"The Bombardment" by, 63
　Bryher and, 63–65, 67–68, 82, 83–84, 86, 95, 96, 103
　H.D. and, 59, 60–61, 63, 64, 67, 82
　H.D. and Bryher and, 67–68, 69, 77–78, 82, 102
　"In a Garden" by, 63
　Men, Women and Ghosts by, 63
　Pound, E., and, 59
　Russell and, 63
　Some Imagist Poets, 1916 by, 61
　Some Imagist Poets I by, 59
　Tendencies in Modern American Poets by, 64
Lowndes, 244, 274
　Bryher at, 220, 226–27, 250–51, 268, 287
　H.D. at, 184–85, 186, 212–13, 214–15, 218, 221–22, 233, 237, 250–51, 254, 255, 260
　Morris table at, 227–28
　Pearson, N. H., at, 241
Lowndes Group, 234
Loy, Mina, 118, 119–20
Lucerne, 177
Lugano, Switzerland, 266, 270, 271–72, 274, 276, 277–78, 279, 283, 284, 285, 287, 289, 292, 301–2
Lunar Baedeker (Loy), 119–20
Lusitania, 4, 59–60, 301
Luxembourg Gardens, 56
Lykabettos, 94
Lyons, Islay, 285, 286, 293–94, 299, 302, 303, 307–8

MacIntyre, Carlyle, 104–5
Mackail, J. W., 56, 272–73
Mackenzie, Compton, 226
Mackenzie, Faith, 226
Macpherson, Kenneth, 10
　Borderline filmed by, 146–47, 148, 152, 153
　Bryher, Herring and, 146f, 146
　Bryher, Perdita and, 137, 185, 187, 188, 198–99
　Bryher and, 130, 131f, 132, 137, 138, 145, 153, 158, 162, 175, 185, 186, 216–18, 271, 285
　Douglas and, 286
　Ellerman, J. R., and, 170
　on Ellerman, John Jr., 170
　Gaunt Island by, 132–33

Gregg, F. J., and, 127–28, 130, 136, 139
  H.D. and, 138–39, 140–42, 145, 152, 154–56, 182, 188–89, 196–97
  H.D. and Bryher and, 127–28, 130–34, 135–39, 140–42, 145, 146, 149–50, 153–55, 158, 160, 161, 164–65, 169–70, 175, 177, 180, 182, 185, 216–17, 268
  Herring and, 146f, 146, 152–53, 180, 185
  Monkey's Moon by, 145
  in New York, 186, 201, 212, 230–31, 268
  Perdita and, 130, 132, 137, 156, 185, 187, 188, 198–99, 201
  psychoanalysis and, 140–42, 152, 154, 175
  queerness of, 128, 132
  Robeson, P., and, 148, 186
  Schmideberg, W., and, 175, 178, 180, 185
  Slocum and, 153–54
  Wing Beat animation by, 133
Madame Herf, 298, 302
Madrigal (H.D.), 66, 277, 294
  as *Bid Me to Live*, 294, 301, 308, 309, 327n.19
Maedchen in Uniform, 155, 188
Magdalene, Mary, 58, 241–42, 248–49, 270–71, 346n.4
Magic Mirror (H.D.), 314n.27
Magic Mountain, The (Mann, T.), 264
Maison des Amis des Livres, La, 117–18
Majic Ring (H.D.), 232–33, 234, 237, 239–40, 277, 301
Making of Americans, The (Stein), 119–20
Malory, Thomas, 13–14
Malvant, Helene, 274
Malverns, 128, 135
Manchester (Bryher), 171–72, 185, 186
Manchester Gallery, 51
Manikin, 120
"Man-Moth" (Bishop), 186
Mann, Heinrich, 168, 205
Mann, Thomas, 264, 285
Man Ray, 119–20, 123, 309, 311f, 311
Many Mansions (Dowding, H.), 227
Many Years Many Girls (Carew), 54–55
Marble Faun, The (Hawthorne), 278
Marconi, Guglielmo, 81–82
Mare, Walter de la, 235
Marienbad, 196–98, 200
Marlowe, Christopher, 237
"Marriage" (Moore, M.), 120, 125
Marshall Plan, 300
Martz, Louis, 7
Marx Brothers, 194–95, 224
Marxists, 158–59
Mary (princess), 32
Masefield, John, 235
Masons, 12–13

Massacre at Wounded Knee, 27
"Master, The" (H.D.), 160–61
mathematics, 22–23, 43, 139–40, 204, 221, 230
Mauss, Marcel, 10, 307
"May, 1943" (H.D.), 238
Mayfair, London, 4–5, 53, 59, 83–84, 168
McAlmon, Robert
  Bryher and, 104–5, 106–7, 110–12, 114, 115–19, 124, 127, 277
  on Bryher's *Development*, 106–7
  in Egypt, 126
  Ellerman, John Jr., and, 116
  Ellerman, J. R., and, 116, 119, 170
  Glover, H., and, 116, 118, 169
  A Hasty Bunch by, 119, 123
  H.D. and Bryher and, 110–12, 115–16, 117, 123, 124, 128, 177
  Macpherson and, 128
  Moore, M., and, 104–5, 112, 120
  against psychoanalysis, 117
  on Stein, 119–20
  Village by, 123
  Williams and, 104–5, 106–7, 124
mediumistic poetics, 15
mediumistic practice, of H.D. and Bryher, 9
mediums
  Home, 275–76
  Pythia, 94–95
  Rossetti and, 275
  séances and, 233
mediumship, of H.D., 148, 201, 234, 241, 270–71
Meleager, 56–57, 124–25
Men, Women and Ghosts (Lowell), 63
Menninger, Karl A., 178
Mercanton, Jacques, 202
Merchant of Venice, The (Shakespeare), 53, 236, 266
Merman, Ethel, 187
Mesmer, Franz Anton, 13
Methodist Church, 238
Micheaux, Oscar, 145
"Mid-Day" (H.D.), 59, 297
Middleton, John, 73, 80–81
Middleton, Thomas, 68
Midsummer Night's Dream, A (Shakespeare), 140
Milford, Connecticut, 18–19
Millais, John Everett, 51, 274–75
Minerva Hotel, in Lugano, Switzerland, 271, 272, 276
Minoans, 98, 163–64
Mire Mare (H.D.), 175
Miriam (fictional character), in *Pilgrimage*, 33, 129
"Mirror to a Star" (Dobson, S.), 320n.55
Modern, Alice, 10, 157, 161–62, 168, 197, 203, 204, 215–16
Modern, Ernst, 202

Modern, Klara, 10, 161–62, 167, 203, 215–16
modernism, 5, 17–18, 39–40, 52, 212, 242, 276, 310–11
Modern Poetry, 127
Modern Times, 194
Mohicans, 18–19, 27
Monkey's Moon, 145
Monnier, Adrienne, 10, 117–18, 123, 193, 194–95, 196, 212–13, 215, 217, 243, 244, 249, 267, 274–75, 286, 303–4
Monroe, Harriett, 57, 64–65
Monrovia, California, 109
Montaigne, Michel de, 80–81
Monte Carlo, 153, 158, 175
Montreux, 125, 215–16
Moody, A. David, 52
"Moonrise" (H.D.), 59
Moore, John Warner, 101–2, 110–11
Moore, Marianne, 9, 10, 105f, 204
    Bishop and, 186
    Bryher and, 101–2, 103, 106–7, 109–11, 112–13, 120, 170, 187, 193, 201–2, 219, 271
    on Bryher's *Development*, 106
    on Bryher's *West*, 112–13
    "Dock Rats" by, 107
    "The Fish" by, 101
    on Freud, S., 113
    H.D. and, 61, 101–2, 103, 112, 120, 217, 235–36
    H.D. and Bryher and, 103–5, 106–7, 108–9, 110–11, 113, 114–15, 117, 179, 202, 216, 217–18, 283
    on *Maedchen in Uniform*, 155
    "Marriage" by, 120, 125
    McAlmon and, 104–5, 112, 120
    Pangolin and Other Poems by, 193
    "Pangolin" by, 203
    Pound, E., and, 102
Moore, Mary Warner, 101–2, 103–5, 108–9, 111, 271
Moravian Church, 16, 17–18, 198–99
Moravianism, 280
Moravians, 16–19, 20, 232–33, 238, 242
    in Freiberg, 161
    Freud, S., and, 246–47
    Friedenshuetten of, 18–19
    Gnadenhuetten of, 18–19
    Native Americans and, 26–27, 148–49
    Wesley and, 238
    Wunden Eiland of, 18–19, 26
More, Thomas, 19
Morgan, John Pierpont, 31
Morris, Adelaide, 92, 228, 361n.100
Morris, William, 51, 227–28, 233, 250–51, 270, 272–73, 275, 276–77, 279, 280, 354n.30

Morris table, 227–28, 233, 237, 238–39, 240–41, 251, 255, 272, 274
Morse, Samuel Finley Breese, 50
Moses, 161, 197, 227
Mosley, Oswald, 158–59
Mount Parnassus, 94–95
Mozart, Wolfgang Amadeus, 156–57, 296, 298
Mullion Cove, Cornwall, 78, 82, 83, 84f, 100, 184
Murnau, F. W., 134
Murray, Gilbert, 156, 191, 291–92
Museum of Modern Art, 137
Mussolini, Benito, 200
"My Communications with Non-Occupied France, June–September 1940" report (Bryher), 215
Mystery, The (H.D.), 280
mystical experiences, of H.D., 227. *See also* mediumistic practice, of H.D. and Bryher
Mysticism (Underhill), 223
mysticism and mystics, 12–13, 27, 56, 321n.4
Mystic Leeway, The (Gregg, F.), 319n.10

Nagasaki, 253–54
Nagel, Ivan, 296, 297, 300, 303, 341n.15, 359n.6
Napoleon, 14, 34–35, 175, 306
Napoleon III, 276
"Narthex" (H.D.), 130, 136, 303
Native Americans, 26–27, 148–49, 239
Natural Philosophy of Love, The (Gourmont), 320n.50
Nazis and Nazism, 14, 219, 245, 259, 297
    American racism and, 152, 159
    Austrian, 168–69, 176
    book burnings, 168
    Bryher on, 157, 185–86, 203, 217–18, 251, 284
    concentration camps, 159, 215–16
    death drive and, 180
    France and, 215, 217–18
    Hitler, 157, 158–59, 175, 176, 188–89, 196, 203, 205, 206, 211, 214–15, 216, 249–50, 251–52
    Holland and Belgium invasions, 214
    Jewish psychoanalysts and, 177
    Kristallnacht, 207
    Luftwaffe, 214, 236
    Nazi Party, 158–59, 201
    Nazi Youth, 176
    Normans and, 251
    Pearson, N. H., on, 201
    in power, March 1933, 158–59
    Simpson as sympathizer with, 196
    Soviets against, 282
    U.S. neutrality toward, 188–89
    in Vienna, 160, 163
Nephtys, 291–92
Neubablesberg Studio, 134

New Age, 57
New English Review, 223
New Freewoman, 57–58
New Haven, Connecticut, 21–22, 252, 304, 309
Newnham College, Cambridge, 58
New Orleans, 45
New Poor Law of 1834, 53
News from Nowhere (Morris, W.), 272–73
New York
    Bryher and Perdita in, 186, 187, 198–99, 289
    Bryher in, 201–2, 207, 271, 287
    Empire State Building, 187, 198–99
    Greenwich Village, 46, 47*f*, 103, 109–10
    Harlem, 187, 198–99
    H.D. and Bryher in, 102, 103, 109–10, 198, 201, 304
    Macpherson in, 186, 201, 212, 230–31, 268
    Perdita in, 281–82
Nightingale, Florence, 154–55
Nights (H.D.), 155–56, 175–76, 177–79, 182–83, 337n.23
Niké, 93, 97–98
Nile River, 38, 98, 122
Nisky Hill Cemetery, 17, 25, 27, 148–49, 201–2, 215
Nitschmann, David, 18
Noguchi, Isamu, 187
nonbinary gender
    in Balzac's *Seraphita*, 52
    Bhaduri, A., Osiris and, 241
    of Bryher, 53
    Freud, S., on, 166
    of H.D. and Bryher, 6, 10–12, 14, 182–83
    in H.D.'s *Ion*, 191–92
    of Jesus Christ, 223
nonbiological gender, 68
Norcross, Mary, 101–2
Normandie, SS, 198, 201
North American Review, 68
Norway, 214
"Note on Beaumont and Fletcher, A" (Bryher), 236
Notes on Thought and Vision (H.D.), 79–82, 98, 179

obscenity trial, over Hall's *Well of Loneliness*, 139
occult, the, 12, 13, 155–56
Odle, Alan, 331n.63
Odysseus, 96, 134
"Odyssey" (H.D.), 96
Oedipus, 178, 192–93, 201
Oedipus Rex (Sophocles), 192–93
Old Maid, The, 187–88
Old Witchcraft Act, 227
Olive and the Sword, The (Knight), 251–52
Olivier, Laurence, 273
Ontario, Indiana, 21

Oppenheimer, J. Robert, 253
Orange, A. R., 57
"Oread" (H.D.), 9
Organization and Personnel of the Shakespearean Company, The (Baldwin), 236
Orient Express, 130, 174, 212, 213–14
Origo, Iris, 289
Orlando (Woolf), 359n.21
Orpheus, 8, 62–63
Osiris, 4, 121, 228–29, 241
Oxford, 51–52, 238, 243, 275
Oxford Anthology of American Literature, The (Benét and Pearson, N. H.), 201–2
Oxford University Press, 224, 241, 262

Pabst, G. W., 152, 157, 162, 203
    The Joyless Street, 125, 133–34
    Pandora's Box, 138
Pagels, Elaine, 17–18, 242, 346n.4
Pahlen, Anna von, 19, 26
Paint It Today (H.D.), 5, 52, 69, 83, 85–86, 108–9, 112, 114–15, 123, 198, 311
Pakistan, 15, 299–300
Paleokastritsa, 96
Palimpsest (H.D.), 122–23, 125, 126, 128, 158, 286
Pan, 45
Pandora's Box, 138
"Pangolin" (Moore, M.), 203
Pangolin and Other Poems (Moore, M.), 193
Paradiso (Dante), 278
parapsychology, 286
Paris (mythological), 27, 297, 298, 299, 300, 303
Paris, France, 49–50, 117–20
    Benjamin and, 204
    Bryher in, 35, 36*f*, 114–15, 116–17, 123–24, 128, 193
    H.D. in, 124
    liberation of, 244, 249
Paris 1900 (Bryher), 196, 202, 204
Paris Exhibition, 1889, 74
Paris World Exhibition, 1900, 35, 36*f*
Parson, Frank, *The Psychology of Dress* by, 112–13
parthenogenesis, 79, 168
Parthenon Frieze, 93
Pascal, Blaise, 230
Pater, Walter, 58
Patmore, Brigit, 56, 59–60, 68, 71, 77, 78, 123, 126, 199
Patmore, Coventry, 56
Patmore, John Deighton, 56
Patmore, Netta, 199, 205, 306
Patton, George S., 244
Pausanias, 90
Paxnous (chief), 19, 26
Pearl Harbor, 226

Pearson, Norman Holmes, 230–31, 245, 297, 304, 306
   Bryher and, 201–2, 205, 207–8, 218, 222, 260, 266–67, 277, 278, 281, 282, 283, 285, 310
   Bryn Mawr and, 256
   Friedman and, 7
   on Hawthorne, 278, 281
   H.D. and, 201, 227, 228–29, 232, 235–36, 241, 242, 243, 244, 252, 254, 256, 259, 265, 275, 276–77, 279, 291, 293–94, 306–7, 308–9
   H.D. and Bryher and, 206–7, 235–36, 241, 266–67, 273, 276, 278, 280, 285, 299–300, 304, 305*f*
   H.D.'s *Helen in Egypt* and, 289–91, 293, 303
   in London, throughout V-bomb attacks, 1944, 243
   at Lowndes, 241
   on Nazi Party, 201
   The Oxford Anthology of American Literature, edited by Benét and, 201–2
   Perdita and, 221, 234, 282
   on Pound, E., 306–7
   on Soviets, 281, 282
   Wolff, K., and, 283
Pearson, Susan, 245, 249–50, 252
Pelleka, 96
Penn, John, 18
"Perché" (Gregg, F. J.), 51–52
Perdita
   Angleton and, 237
   Bergner and, 172, 186, 187–88
   birth of, 75
   at boarding school, 135, 139, 140
   Bryher, Macpherson and, 137, 185, 187, 188, 198–99
   Bryher and, 9, 86, 127, 132, 137, 139, 164–65, 181, 186–88, 192–93, 194–95, 196, 207–8, 212, 214, 228, 237, 249, 270, 273, 289, 310
   on Bryher's *Manchester*, 185
   Chadwick and, 140
   childbirths, 1951-1960, 291
   in Cornwall, 188, 195, 204, 234–35
   Dobson, S., and, 184, 194–95, 202
   Douglas and, 117
   Freud, S., and, 165
   Friedman and, 310
   Glover, H., and, 194, 211–12, 214–15
   Gregg, O., and, 181
   H.D., Aldington, R., and, 75–76, 126, 199–200
   on H.D., in *Nights* introduction, 337n.23
   H.D. and, 75–76, 76*f*, 82, 122, 137, 156, 164–65, 201–2, 212–13, 227, 261, 262, 265–66, 281–82, 287–89, 290, 291
   H.D. and Bryher and, 9–10, 75–76, 79–80, 96, 101, 102, 105–6, 106*f*, 108–9, 116–17, 128, 140, 156–57, 158, 161, 167, 169, 181, 184, 186, 188, 189–90, 194, 198, 199–200, 212–13, 224–25, 241, 259, 264, 265, 271, 279, 283, 285, 287–89, 291, 294–95, 304, 310–11
   H.D.'s *The Hedgehog* and, 198
   H.D.'s *Ion* translation and, 187, 189–90, 191–92
   Herring and, 195, 221, 273
   at Kenwin, 177, 197, 203, 204
   The London Theatre Studio, 188
   Macpherson and, 130, 132, 137, 156, 201
   Modern, A., as tutor for, 10, 157, 168
   Modern, K., on, 215–16
   naming, 75
   in New York, 281–82
   Patmore, B., and, 78
   Pearson, N. H., and, 221, 234, 282
   psychoanalysis of, 140
   Rodeck and, 165
   Schaffner, E. B., and, 304
   Schaffner, J. V., and, 281–82, 285, 287–89, 310
   Schaffner, N., and, 293–94
   Schaffner, V., and, 282, 283, 284, 285
   on the Seine, 249
   on Simpson, 196
   Wolle, H. E., and, 114, 115*f*
Perse, Saint-John, 308
Persephone, 45
Perseus, 97, 98, 152
Phaedra, 135–36
"Phaedra Rebukes Hippolyta" (H.D.), 102
"Phaedra Remembers Crete" (H.D.), 102
Phaedrus (Plato), 93, 180
Phidias, 93
Philadelphia, 27, 45–46, 49, 51–52, 165, 198–99
Philadelphia Art School, 46
Piccadilly Club, 56
Pickford, Mary, 107–8
Pilate's Wife (H.D.), 12, 128, 185, 270–71, 300–1
Pilgrimage (Richardson), 33, 124, 129
Pillars of Hercules, 38–39, 91, 309
Piraeus, 93, 95
Pisan Cantos (Pound, E.), 273
Plank, George, 77, 132, 137, 179–80, 186, 188–89, 191–92, 193, 203, 211, 214, 224, 228, 234
Plato, 66, 70, 93, 125, 180
Player's Boy, The (Bryher), 236, 291, 301, 310
Poe, Edgar Allan, 226
Poems of Meleager, 56–57
Poetry (magazine), 57, 58, 59, 93–94
Point Pleasant, 43
Poland, Hitler invading, 211
polysexuality, 76–77, 311
Pompeii, 57, 160–61, 176, 228
Pontikonisi, 96
"Pool" (Bryher), 109

"Pool" (H.D.), 59
Pool Group, the, 145, 148. *See also* Borderline
   Close Up film journal of, 132–34, 135, 137–38,
      145, 154, 155, 157, 158
   Foothills by, 137, 138
   queer forms of, 135
   Wing Beat by, 132–34, 136
Pool Publications, 128
Pope, Alexander, 219–20
Porter, Cole, 187
Poseidon, 96
postmodern, the, 6
Pound, Ezra, 8, 57
   Aldington, R., on, 70
   Bryher and, 127, 259, 276, 310
   on Greek mythology, 45
   Gregg, F. J., and, 48–49, 51, 52
   H.D., Aldington and, 57–58, 59
   H.D. and, 4–5, 8, 43–45, 48–51, 52, 56–57, 59,
      63, 75, 102, 132–33, 139–40, 272–73, 275,
      276, 296
   H.D. and Bryher and, 83–84, 170
   Hilda's Book by, 44
   on Imagism, 59
   Des Imagistes, 57–58, 59
   Lowell and, 59
   Moore, M., and, 102
   Pisan Cantos by, 273
   "Psychology and Troubadours" by, 45
   Rossetti and, 275, 276
   The Spirit of Romance by, 271, 276
   treason indictment, 259, 273, 276, 306–7
   on women, 52
Pound, Homer, 43
Pound, Thaddeus, 43
Powys, John Cowper, 51–52, 127, 277
Practical Kabbalah (Ambelain), 286
Prague, 156–57, 185–86, 205–6
Pre-Raphaelite Brotherhood, 59, 273–75
"Priapus" (H.D.), 58
"Projector" (H.D.), 137–38
Prolegomena to the Study of Greek Religion
   (Harrison), 58
Psyche Reborn (Friedman), 310
psychic abilities and psychic experiences, of H.D.
   and Bryher, 11, 13, 80, 156, 227, 232–33,
   250, 251
psychical, the, 9–10
psychic mythopoetic method, 13
psychoanalysis, 8, 9–10, 14–15. *See also* Freud,
   Sigmund
   Bryher and, 101, 134, 140–42, 145, 152, 154–55,
      158, 162, 168–69, 175, 177, 197, 200, 203
   cinema and, 134–35, 152
   Dobson, S., and, 174, 180

Ellis on, 74–75
H.D. and, 140–42, 154–57, 158, 191–92, 246–47,
   248, 270–71
Herring on, 212
Macpherson and, 140–42, 152, 154, 175
McAlmon against, 117
of Perdita, 140
Richardson on, 160
Rodeck against, 157–58
Sachs, H., on, 134
psychoanalysts, 10, 175, 177, 203
"Psychogenesis of a Case of Homosexuality in a
   Woman" (Freud, S.), 117
"Psychology and Troubadours" (Pound, E.), 45
Psychology of Dress, The (Parson), 112–13
Psychopathis Sexualis (Krafft-Ebing), 74
Ptolemy, 7, 23
Pudovkin, Vsevolod, 134
Puritans, 21–22, 33, 89
"Pygmalion" (H.D.), 62–63
Pyrlaeus, John Christopher, 18, 25–26
Pythagoras, 38, 56–57
Pythia, 94–95, 97–98, 139, 190, 326n.42

Quakers, 18, 77, 132, 165, 198–99, 207, 239, 259
Queenswood, 53–55, 135, 185, 196–97
queer community, war community as, 229
queer men, 10
queerness, 5–6, 12
   Bryher and, 71, 127–28
   in Cold War era, 306
   genderqueer, 6
   of H.D., 166
   of Heydt, 296
   of Macpherson, 128, 132
   of Pool Group, 135
queers
   Auden on, 14
   in *Borderline*, 148
   Douglas and, 116–17
   Duncan, R., on literary history for, 308
   at Kenwin, 157
   Schmideberg, W., treating, 185
queer women, 49
Quilter, William Cuthbert, 31

Rabelais, François, 80–81
racism, 35, 146–47, 148, 149, 159, 164
RAF, 214, 219, 239–40
"R.A.F" (H.D.), 225–26, 298
Rainey, Lawrence, 8, 314n.39
Raleigh, Walter, 252, 268, 301, 304–6
Ramuz, Charles Ferdinand, 214
Rank, Otto, 177
The Rape of the Lock (Pope), 219–20

Rauch, Christian Henry, 18–19
"Red Roses to Bronze" (H.D.), 149
Red Tapeworm (Mackenzie, C.), 226
Reeves, Anne Elizabeth, 29–30
Reeves, Timothy, 29–30
Reflections on a Marine Venus (Durrell), 309
Region of Lutany (Bryher), 59, 95–96
Regnier, Henri de, 80–81
Reich, Annie, 212, 218
Reich, Wilhelm, 177
Reiniger, Lotte, 155, 188, 194, 197, 203
"Rejection" (Bryher), 64–65
Renatus, Christian "Christel," 19, 27
Renault, Mary, 309–10
Renishaw, 219–20, 221–22, 223
Renoir, Jean, 196
Reugg, Max, 310
"Revelation, A" (Ellis), 85–86
Revere, Paul, 236
Reverie: A Little Book of Poems for H.D. (Aldington, R.), 67
Revolutionary War, US, 19
Riant Chateau, in Territet, Switzerland, 114–15, 123, 124, 145, 155–56
Richardson, Dorothy, 10, 127, 132–33, 279, 331n.63
   Bryher and, 115–16, 124, 129, 185
   Pilgrimage by, 33, 124
   on psychoanalysis, 160
   on silent film, 152
Richmond, Bruce, 70
Rise of Catherine the Great, The, 168
Roaring Girl, The (Dekker and Middleton, T.), 68
Robeson, Eslanda, 146, 187
   in *Borderline*, 145, 146–47, 149, 150*f*, 151*f*
Robeson, Paul, 146, 152, 186
   in *Body and Soul*, 145, 149–50
   in *Borderline*, 7, 145, 147, 148, 149*f*, 149–50, 150*f*, 152, 156*f*
   Macpherson and, 148, 186
Robinson, Janice, 314n.28
Robinson, Matte, 356n.114
Rodeck, Peter
   excavation research of, 91
   H.D., Dobson, S., and, 173–74, 230–31
   H.D. and Bryher and, 91–92, 97–98, 100, 102, 128, 145, 157–58, 164, 181
   H.D. on ordination of, 178
   Perdita and, 165
   against psychoanalysis, 157–58
Rogers, Ginger, 187, 194–95
Roman Wall (Bryher), 285, 287–89, 291, 298, 310
Rome, 57, 285, 287, 302
Roosevelt, Franklin D., 226, 249–50, 253
Rosetta, SS, 122

Rossetti, Gabriel Charles Dante, 51, 270–71, 273, 274–75, 276
Roten Kreuz Spiral, 309
Rouen, 49
Ruan (Bryher), 309–10
Rubenstein, William D., 313n.1, 318n.17
Rudhyar, F. D., 325n.54
Rukeyser, Muriel, 186, 194–95
Rummel, Walter Morse, 50, 182–83
Ruskin, John, 4, 275
Russell, Ada, 63
Ruth (Gaskell), 53

Sachs, Hanns, 134–35, 138
   American Imago journal of, 197
   Bryher and, 134, 139, 145, 154–55, 157, 158, 163, 164, 168, 171, 175, 179–80, 186–87, 203–4, 260, 271
   on Bryher's *Manchester*, 185
   death of, 271
   on Ellerman, John Jr., 170
   Freud, A., and, 178
   Freud, S., and, 134, 168–69, 197
   H.D. and, 156–57, 158, 160–61, 260
Sachs, Max, 204
Sachs, Olga, 204
Sackville-West, Vita, 53, 139, 235
Sagan, Leontine, 155
Sagesse (H.D.), 305–6
Salomon, S. M., 167
Sand, George, 60–61
Sands, James, 236, 301
Santa Barbara, 105–6, 107
Sappho, 8, 44, 57–58, 82, 93–94, 124, 125, 126, 223, 289
Sarton, May, 186, 221
Schaffner, Elizabeth Bryher, 291, 304
Schaffner, John Valentine, 281–82, 285, 287–89, 310
Schaffner, Nicholas, 291, 293–94, 313n.17
Schaffner, Perdita Macpherson. *See* Perdita
Schaffner, Timothy, 291
Schaffner, Valentine, 282, 283, 284, 285, 287–89, 291
Schmideberg, Melitta, 174–75, 196–97, 205, 212, 224–25, 278, 279, 285, 286, 300, 307–8
Schmideberg, Walter, 10, 207, 278
   Bryher and, 174–75, 180, 196–97, 198, 201–2, 203, 205, 212, 270, 280, 284–85, 297, 299, 301, 302
   death of, 302
   Dobson, S., and, 175, 178
   Freud, S., on, 180
   Glover, E., on, 284
   H.D. and, 260, 261, 262, 263, 265, 282–83, 299

H.D. and Bryher and, 174–75, 194, 198, 218, 224–25, 234, 264, 265, 284, 302
Henderson and, 184–85
at Kusnacht Nervenklinik, 299–301
Macpherson and, 175, 178, 180, 185
in World War I, 174–75
Schmidt, Michael, 8
science, 23, 28, 48–49, 50, 135, 148, 240, 253–54
art and, H.D. on, 44
astrology and, 7
modern, H.D. on, 128
new physics, Einstein and, 10
special theory of relativity, 13
spiritualism and, 12
Scillies, 3, 7–8, 48–49, 53–54, 67, 74, 80, 83, 86, 224–25, 237, 285, 289, 294–95, 309–10
Scottsboro Boys, the, 159
Sea Garden (H.D.), 3, 8, 60–61, 63–64, 78–79, 92, 98
"Sea God" (H.D.), 61
séances, of H.D. and Bryher, 8, 13–14, 244, 271–72, 275
Beaumont and, 236
Bhaduri, A., at, 233–34, 238–39, 240–41, 251
Dowding and, 238–40
Ellerman, J. R., and, 234, 238
H.D.'s *Majic Ring* and, 232–33, 237, 239–40, 301
Morris table in, 233, 237, 238–39, 240–41, 255
notes on, 233–34, 237, 259, 263, 348n.7
possessions of H.D. during, 239
Sitwell, O., and, 235
Wesley and, 238
"Sea Rose" (H.D.), 59
Seashell and the Clergyman, 155
Second American Caravan, 136
Second Boer War, 35
Secret Book of John, 58, 241–42
"Secret Name" (H.D.), 122–23
Sedgwick, Eve Kosofsky, 130
Seidel, Christian, 16, 17, 25–26
Selected Poems (H.D.), 308
Select Epigrams from the Greek Anthology (Mackail), 56
Seraphita (Balzac), 52
sex changes and gender reassignment, 6
Sex in Relation to Society (Ellis), 76–77
sexo-asethetic inversion, 74–75, 85–86
Shakespear, Dorothy and Olivia, 44–45
Shakespeare, William, 4, 32, 118, 215, 218–19, 252, 254, 268
As You Like It by, 250
Bryher on, 236, 249–50
Cymbeline by, 35
H.D.'s "Shakespeare" poems, 249–50, 252–53, 259, 263, 266

Knight on, 251–52
The Merchant of Venice by, 53, 236, 266
A Midsummer Night's Dream by, 140
The Tempest by, 251–53, 256, 259, 263, 266
The Winter's Tale, 75, 243
Shakespeare & Co., 117–18, 311
Shaw, Harriet Weaver, 58
Shawnee, 19, 26, 27
Sheffield, 220
Shelley, Mary, 13, 289
Shelley, Percy Bysshe, 275
Shephard's Hotel, Cairo, 121–23
Sherwood Forest, 222
shipping industry, 29–30, 31–32, 35, 53, 64–65, 91, 118–19, 169, 240
Shorter, Clement, 64–65, 69, 70, 82
Shorter, Doris, 70, 77
"Shrine, The" (H.D.), 3–4
Shubert, Franz, 187–88
Siddal, Elizabeth, 156, 270–71, 273, 274–75
Sidney, Philip, 268
"Simaetha" (H.D.), 72
Simpson, Wallis, 196
Sinclair, May, 50, 56, 59–60, 123, 271, 273, 321n.4
Single Brothers' Festival, 1748, 19
Sinister Street (Mackenzie, C.), 226
Sir John. *See* Ellerman, John Reeves
"Sitalkas" (H.D.), 57–58
Sitwell, Edith, 10, 215, 219–20, 221, 222, 223, 224, 235, 238, 254, 260
Sitwell, Osbert, 10, 219–20, 221–22, 223, 235, 243, 248, 260
Sitwell Arms, 219
Sloane, 127, 131–32, 137–38, 153, 154, 157–58, 163, 171, 275–76
Slocum, Toni, 153–54
Smyers, Virginia L., 310–11
Smyth, Ethyl, 165
Snively, Margaret, 43, 57, 71
sociogeny, 148
Sola, Esther de, 170
Some Imagist Poets, 1916 (Lowell), 61
Some Imagist Poets I (Lowell), 59
Sophocles, 57, 93–94, 192–93
"South" (Bryher), 89
South Wind (Douglas), 116–17
Soviets, 281, 282
Spanish Civil War, 194–95, 217–18, 236
special theory of relativity, 13
Spender, Stephen, 226
Sphere, 64–65
Spirit of Romance, The (Pound, E.), 271, 276
spirit phone, 13–14
spiritualism, 12–13, 226–27, 228, 274–76, 293
Spoo, Robert, 320n.31

Spring & All (Williams), 119
Stalin, Joseph, 214–15
Stein, Gertrude, 14
   Bryher and, 118–19, 123, 201–2, 207–8
   H.D. and Bryher and, 119–20
   The Making of Americans by, 119–20
   Toklas and, 217–18, 306
   Wilder and, 189
Sterne, Laurence, 80–81
Stesichorus, 289
Stevens, Wallace, 106–7
Stevenson, Robert Louis, 34–35, 287
St. Faith's Nursing Home, 73, 75
Stieglitz, Alfred, 207
"Still Falls the Rain" (Sitwell, E.), 224
St. Ives, 3, 66–67
Stone, Christopher, 325n.54
Stonehenge, 66–67
Stonewall, 6
"Storm" (H.D.), 59
St. Ouen, France, 49
Strachey, Alix and James, 177
Stratford, 249–51, 252, 255, 259, 263, 266–67
Strauss, Richard, 156–57
Studies in the Psychology of Sex (Ellis), 74–75
Sulis, 78–79
Sweden, 207
Swedenborg, Emanuel, 275–76
Swinburne, Algernon Charles, 5, 44, 46, 275, 290, 293
Swiss Family Robinson (Wyss), 34–35
Sword Went Out to Sea, The (H.D.), 271–73, 274, 276–77, 279, 283, 284, 290–91, 307
Symbolist Movement in Literature, The (Symons), 74
Symons, Arthur, 74–75
syncretism, 12–13, 223, 229, 293
"Syracuse" (Aldington, R.), 69

Taglicht, Edith, 205–6
Tales from Shakespeare (Lamb, C., and Lamb, M.), 35
Tamburlaine (Marlowe), 237
Tanglewood Tales (Hawthorne), 191
tarot, 43, 163
Tarot, Le (Chaboseau), 296–97
telekinesis, 275–76
telepathy, 8, 50, 133, 135, 136, 161, 163, 286, 291–92
Tempest, The (Shakespeare), 251–53, 256, 259, 263, 266
Temple of Athena, 93
Ten Days, 138
Tendencies in Modern American Poets (Lowell), 64

Tennyson, Alfred Lord, 78, 158
Teresa of Avila (saint), 17–18, 220, 222, 223
Territet, Switzerland, 114–15, 117, 123–24, 135, 138, 140, 142, 145, 146, 155–56
Thayer, Scofield, 102, 111, 120
Theatre of Dionysus, 93–94
Theocritus, 57, 69
Theosophy, 168, 178–79
Theseus, 89, 135–36, 299, 300
Thetis, 71, 78–79, 292–93, 300
"Thetis" (H.D.), 71, 78–79, 300
Thompson, Virgil, 202
Thorn Thicket (H.D.), 307, 308–9
Thoth, 60, 121, 228–29
thought transference, 46–47, 163, 236
Thouless, Robert, 286
Thousand Miles Up the Nile, A (Edwards), 121–22
Three Stories and Ten Poems (Hemingway), 119
Thucydides, *History of the Peloponnesian War* by, 69
Tibetan Book of the Dead, 264
Times Literary Supplement, 70
"To Atthis" (Aldington), 57–58
"To Eros" (Bryher), 79
Toklas, Alice B., 119–20, 123, 217–18, 281–82, 306
Tomb of Erechtheus, 93
Toomer, Jean, *Cane* by, 133
Townshend, Petrie ("Theo"), 185, 186, 196–97
"Tradition and the Individual Talent" (Eliot), 60
transgender, 200, 281, 310–11
trans identities, 6
transphobia, 5
transsexuality, 11–12
transvestite, 44–45
Treasure Island (Stevenson), 34–35
Treatise on Practical Astronomy as Applied to Geodesy and Navigation, A (Doolittle, C. L.), 23
Tregarthen's Hotel, 78
Tregonning, 224–25
Trenoweth Farm, in Cornwall, 179–80, 182, 184, 188, 224–25, 228, 234–35, 254, 266–67, 285
"Tribute, The" (H.D.), 61
Tribute to Freud (H.D.), 7, 232–33, 246–47, 260–61, 304
Tribute to the Angels (H.D.), 236, 241–43, 252
Trilogy (H.D.), 7, 226, 228, 232–33, 242, 248–49, 253–54, 264, 274, 286, 302
   The Flowering of the Rod, 26, 248–49, 256, 262
   "I, John" of, 247
   Tribute to the Angels, 236, 241–43, 252
   The Walls Do Not Fall, 224, 226–27, 228–30, 239, 241, 243, 248, 263
Trojans, 72–73

Trojan War, 251, 289, 290, 297
Truman, Harry, 253–54
Tryphonopoulos, Demetres P., 348n.7
Tschoop (chief), 18–19
Tutankhamun, 121, 122
Two on a Tower (Hardy), 23
Two Selves (Bryher), 71, 96, 114, 123

Ulrich, Karl, 297
Ulysses (Joyce), 118
unconscious, the, 9–10, 134–35, 154–55, 160, 161, 165, 173, 194, 198, 201–2, 211–12, 216–17, 251, 254
Underhill, Evelyn, *Mysticism* by, 223
University of Pennsylvania, 25–26, 27, 43
Upanishads, 121, 330n.43
Upper Darby, Pennsylvania, 25–26, 27–28
Urzidil, Johannes, 205–6
Usual Star, The (H.D.), 175, 179

Vale Ave (H.D.), 304–5, 308
van der Leeuw, Johannes Jacobus, 167, 178–79
Vechten, Carl Van, 207
V-E Day, 250, 260
Venice, 136, 174
Victoria (queen), 33–34
Victoria, London, 52
Victorian era and Victorians, 6, 11–12, 33, 40, 43, 52, 56, 75, 83, 85–86, 121, 166, 184, 191, 200, 270–71, 273, 274, 277, 306
Vidor, King, 134–35
Vienna, 9–10, 14, 156–57, 159, 160–61, 162, 163, 175, 179, 180, 185–86, 204
Vienna State Opera, 163
Viking Book of Poetry of the English-Speaking World, The (Aldington, R.), 224
Village (McAlmon), 123
Visa for Avalon (Bryher), 354n.30
visionary poets, 8
Vita Nuova (Dante), 44
V-J Day, 254
Volkart, Elsie, 171, 192, 194, 196, 217, 261, 267–68, 285, 287, 289
Voyage to Windward (Furness), 287

Wabash College, 43, 44–45
"Wakefulness" (Bryher), 64–65
wall of Euryalus, 38–39
Walls Do Not Fall, The (H.D.), 224, 226–27, 228–30, 239, 241, 243, 248, 263
Waluga, Joan Leader, 302, 303
war trauma and war neurosis, 7–8, 212, 246, 301, 310
Washington, George, 19

"Waste" (Bryher), 64–65
Waste Land, The (Eliot), 276
Watson, James Sibley, 111
Weaver Shaw, Harriet, 58, 63, 103
Webster, John, 249–50
Weiss, George Augustus, 19–20
Weiss, Jedediah, 19–20
Weiss, Mary Stables, 19–20
Well of Loneliness (Hall), 139
Wenders, Wim, 248
Werfel, Franz, 205–6
Wescott, Glenway, 120
Wesley, John, 238
West (Bryher), 102–3, 106, 107, 109, 112–13, 127, 136
West, Mae, 178
Weston, Jessie L., 160
"We Two" (H.D.), 124, 309–10
What Do I Love? (H.D.), 359n.6
"What Shall You Do in the War?" (Bryher), 159, 222
"What the Thunder Said" (Eliot), 235
Wheeler, Monroe, 120
Whitechapel Gallery, 279
White Rose and the Red, The (H.D.), 270–71, 273, 274–75, 276–77, 278, 279, 284
Whitman, Walt, 74, 226, 308
"Who Buried H.D.?" (Friedman), 7
"whole machine" metaphor, for relationship of H.D. and Bryher, 13–14, 239
Why Do They Like It? (Ellerman, John Jr.), 128
Wiesner, Berthold P., 286
Wife of Rossetti, The (Hunt), 156, 270–71, 273, 274–75
Wilde, Oscar, 5–6, 51–52
Wilder, Thornton, 189
Wilkinson, Louis, 51–52, 127, 194–95
Williams, William Carlos, 43, 104–5, 106–7, 119, 123, 124, 132–33
"Wind Sleepers" (H.D.), 59
Windsor, Eve, 313n.21
Windsor Forest (Pope), 219–20
Wing Beat, 132–34, 136
Wings of Desire, 248
Winnicott, D. W., 177–78
Winsor, Rita, 274
Winter's Tale, The (Shakespeare), 75, 243
"Wise Sappho, The" (H.D.), 82
Wolff, Helen, 283
Wolff, Kurt, 283
Wolle, Elizabeth Caroline Weiss Seidel ("Mamalie"), 16, 17, 18–20, 25–27
  H.D. and, 20, 25–26, 27, 28, 232–33, 259–60
Wolle, Francis ("Papalie"), 16, 17, 20, 21f, 23, 25
  H.D. and, 17, 20, 80

Wolle, Fred, 46
Wolle, Helen Euginia, 9–10, 16, 17, 20, 21*f*, 28, 48–49
    Aldington, R., and, 57
    death of, 130
    H.D. and, 25, 27, 40, 130, 240–41
    H.D. and Bryher and, 105–6, 117, 121, 122–23
    in Italy, 57
    Perdita and, 114, 115*f*
Wollstonecraft, Mary, 120
Woman in White, The (Collins, W.), 274–75
Women's World Games, 1934, 6
Wood, Thelma, 119, 123
Woodhall, 202, 228, 244, 245
Woolf, Virginia, 62, 132–33, 139, 205, 218, 219, 221, 222, 359n.21
"Work of Art in the Age of Mechanical Reproduction" (Benjamin), 196
World War I, 4, 5, 7–8, 11–12, 59–60, 63–64, 70, 73, 89, 132–33, 158–59, 201–2, 206, 247, 248, 277, 301, 327n.19
    Aldington, R., in, 61, 62, 66, 67–68
    cinema and, 62
    H.D. and Bryher on, 69, 103
    Pound, E., and, 276
    RAF and, 214
    Schmideberg, W., in, 174–75
World War II, 7, 8, 10, 11, 17, 114–15, 132, 247, 281–82, 296, 309. *See also Trilogy* (H.D.)
    air raids and bombings, of London during, 212–13, 216, 217, 218–19, 221, 222, 232, 233, 235–36, 243
    Battle of Britain, 214, 225, 306
    D-Day, 243, 244
    Dunkirk, 214–15, 224, 243
    George VI during, 286
    H.D. against English neutrality, 224
    H.D. and Bryher and, 213–15, 216–19, 224, 232, 235–36, 237, 243–44, 250, 254, 259, 260, 276
    Hiroshima and Nagasaki bombings, 253–54
    liberation of Paris, 244, 247, 249
    Marshall Plan, 300
    Pearl Harbor, 226
    Spiritual Movement and, 226
    V-E Day, 250, 260
    V-J Day, 254
Wren, Christopher, 221
Writing for Their Lives (Hanscombe and Smyers), 310–11
"Writing on the Wall" (H.D.), 246–47, 260, 284
Wulf (Bryher). *See Fourteenth of October, The* (Bryher)
Wunden Eiland (Island of Wounds), 18–19, 26
Wynter, Sylvia, 148
Wyss, Johann David, 34–35

Yale University, Sterling Library, 304, 305*f*
Yeats, W. B., 8, 12–13, 44–45, 56, 74, 111, 192–93, 298
Yong, Ed, 324n.18
Yorke, Dorothy ("Arabella"), 63, 66, 77, 199–200
Young Ladies' Seminary, 16
Ypres, 59

Zaturenska, Marya, 283
Zeisberger, David, 18
Zennor, 3
Zeus, 236, 290, 292
Zinzendorf, Nikolaus Ludwig von, 18–19, 25–26, 27, 29, 280
Zurich, 145, 160, 212, 261, 266, 267–68, 270, 296, 302, 303–4, 309